EUROPEAN HUMAN RIGHTS AN1

This book examines the potential impact of human rights in the way the law interacts with families. Traditionally family law has been dominated by consequentialist/utilitarian themes. The most notable example of these occurs in the law relating to children and the employment of the 'welfare principle'. This requires the court to focus on the welfare of the child as the paramount consideration. Hitherto the courts and, to a certain extent, family law academics, have firmly rejected the use of the language of rights, preferring the discretion and child-centred focus of welfare. However, the incorporation of the European Convention on Human Rights via the Human Rights Act now requires family law to deal more clearly with the competing rights that family members can hold. In addition, it is clear that, to date, the courts have largely ignored or minimised the different demands that the HRA imposes on the judiciary and, in particular, judicial reasoning. This book challenges that view and suggests ways in which the family courts may improve their reasoning in this field. No longer can cases be dealt with on the basis of a simple utilitarian calculation of what is in the best interests of the child and other family members—greater transparency is required.

The book clarifies the different rights that family members can hold and, in particular, identifies ways in which it may be possible to deal with the clash of rights between family members that will inevitably occur. Whether this requires an abandonment of the utilitarian nature of family law, or a reworking of it, is a theme that runs throughout the book.

Library

British Library of Political
and Economic Science

**Please return this item by the
date/ time shown below**

If another user requests this item, we will contact
you with an amended date for return.

Fines are charged for overdue items.

Renew via the Library catalogue at www.library.lse.ac.uk
or Tel: 020 7955 7229 (10am–5pm Monday–Friday)

Thank you

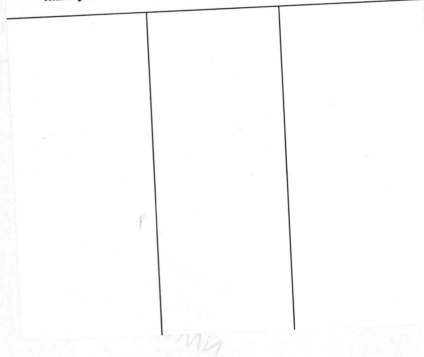

European Human Rights and Family Law

Shazia Choudhry and Jonathan Herring

·HART·
PUBLISHING
OXFORD AND PORTLAND, OREGON
2010

Published in the United Kingdom by Hart Publishing Ltd
16C Worcester Place, Oxford, OX1 2JW
Telephone: +44 (0)1865 517530
Fax: +44 (0)1865 510710
E-mail: mail@hartpub.co.uk
Website: http://www.hartpub.co.uk

Published in North America (US and Canada) by
Hart Publishing
c/o International Specialized Book Services
920 NE 58th Avenue, Suite 300
Portland, OR 97213-3786
USA
Tel: +1 503 287 3093 or toll-free: (1) 800 944 6190
Fax: +1 503 280 8832
E-mail: orders@isbs.com
Website: http://www.isbs.com

British Library Cataloguing in Publication Data
Data Available

ISBN: 978-1-84113-175-7

Typeset by Compuscript Ltd, Shannon
Printed and bound in Great Britain by
TJ International Ltd, Padstow

FOREWORD

The present Conservative Party leader, David Cameron, has more than once said that, if elected, a Conservative government would repeal the Human Rights Act 1998 and replace it with a British 'Bill of Rights' which would set out what would presumably be his government's view of people's responsibilities and rights.[1] The Brown government has taken a more measured stance, and, in an extraordinarily thoughtful document, has proposed retaining the Act, but supplementing it with a new 'Bill of Rights and Responsibilities'.[2] It may be significant that the Chapter on 'Responsibilities' precedes that on 'Rights'. The future of the Human Rights Act, and perhaps even of human rights as a juridical reality in the United Kingdom, may therefore seem to be somewhat uncertain. To produce a book at this time which analyses family law through the perspective of the Human Rights Act might therefore seem a bold move. But it can go a long way towards dispelling the kinds of myths and misunderstandings which build up an impetus of derision about 'rights', especially 'human rights'.

And this is important. Why? We must not forget that the idea of individual rights in its modern form emerged during the 18th-century Enlightenment as part of the movement to restrict the absolutist powers of the *ancien régime*. It culminated most visibly in the American Declaration of Independence and the French Declaration of the Rights of Man, but was a driving feature in Condorcet's *Reflections on black slavery* (1781) and his *On the admission of women to the rights of citizenship* (1790), in Gouges' *The rights of women* (1791), in Wollstonecraft's *A vindication of the rights of women* (1792) and in Paine's *Rights of man* (1791). As the government's Consultation Document rightly observes, claims such as these were about limitations on power.[3] Bentham, however, de-bunked the idea of rights, or at least of 'natural' rights, probably as a reaction against their apparent contribution to the excesses of the French Revolution, and rights discourse became muted in the political conservatism of the 19th century (apart from a brief resurgence in mid-century), the great anti-slavery and franchise reforms being effected more through appeals to religious conscience or enlightened self-interest, and revolutionary socialism based more on claims about historical inevitably, than by claims about individual rights.[4]

Women had to wait over a century before the rights asserted for them in the 1790s were realised, although JS Mill, who wrote (in 1863) 'if (a person) has what we consider a sufficient claim, on whatever account, to have something guaranteed to him by society, we say that he has a right to it',[5] readily referred to the 'rights' women had, or should have, in

---

[1] www.dailymail.co.uk/news/article-1092716/Cameron-calls-UK-Bill-Rights-Straw-reveals-plans-overhaul-Human-Rights-Act.html.
[2] Ministry of Justice, *Rights and Responsibilities: Developing our Constitutional Framework* (2009), 10 (referred to here as 'Consultation Document').
[3] Consultation Document, para 3.2.
[4] The word 'rights' does not even appear in the main text of the Communist Manifesto.
[5] JS Mill, *Utilitarianism* (1863) ch 5.

his *The Subjection of Women* (1869). But the concept of individual rights struggled in the oppressive political climate of the first half of the 20th century.[6] After the Second World War, the resurgence of rights discourse was more a strategy to try to protect individuals against any reversion to excessive centralisation of power than, as in earlier times, a means for re-distributing power. This perhaps explains the perception in the Consultation Document that modern human rights instruments seek stability in times of uncertainty. Nevertheless, appeals to individual rights remain significant aspects of recent and current movements to promote empowerment of various groups, such as married women, fathers, gay people and children.[7]

Of course, the nature and source of 'rights' remains problematic. My own view is that they are no more than instances where 'background' moral values are socially recognised as applying to specific circumstances in such a way that it is held that there is a social responsibility to bring about certain 'end-states' which are desired by their beneficiaries, or reasonably thought would be so desired. Casting these situations in terms of 'rights' implies an equal entitlement to the said 'end-state' for all persons in a similar position. Whether such social recognition of these entitlements exists can of course be heavily contested and that is why it is important that there should be trusted social institutions to resolve the contests. Social recognition need not necessarily mean simple 'majority opinion'. Indeed, it should not, because many rights would be worthless if they could be swept aside on the basis of public sentiment, as indeed the French Revolution and many other political events have demonstrated. Exactly how these rights are given institutional protection is a matter of constitutional governance, and varying solutions are possible, some more robust than others. The United Kingdom 'solution', embodied in the Human Rights Act, has a number of virtues. It locates the 'background' principles which sustain the rights in the European Convention of Human Rights and Fundamental Freedoms, and provides a process for their reasoned application to specific situations through forensic argument and judicial decision. It retains an ultimate check over the process by Parliament, although this in turn could be inhibited by conditions of membership of the Council of Europe. Obviously other models are possible.

But two features of any model seem to be particularly important. One is that individual rights should be capable of being legally enforced, even against the government. Rights are very different from responsibilities in this respect. For while it is undoubtedly true that many duties must be subject to legal enforcement (the duty to respect individual rights being an obvious case), there is a strong reason for holding that the performance of general responsibilities to one's community are often (but not always) better underwritten by appeals to altruistic behaviour (such as community spirit) than legal coercion, whereas rights can *only* be effectively protected by institutional mechanisms, like the law.[8] The reason is that when states proclaim duties they think their citizens owe to their communities, and follow this up with force (or other coercive measures), the ambit of individual liberty narrows and can be seriously threatened. It is therefore comforting that the Consultation

---

[6] See FA Hayek, *The Road to Serfdom* (1944), throughout, and especially pp 63–5.
[7] See John Eekelaar, *Family Law and Personal Life* (2007) ch 6.
[8] *Ibid*, ch 7.

Document strongly hints that any statement of responsibilities that 'we all owe as members of UK society' would not necessarily take the form of legally enforceable duties.[9]

Another feature of the model is that the nature and application of rights should be subjected to continual reasoned debate and evaluation. It is inevitable that this may become complex and difficult. But, as said earlier, the application of even agreed principles to concrete situations can be highly contested. That is the nature of individual rights, and it is naïve to expect otherwise. That is why the analysis of family law in the context of human rights provided in this book is so very important.

John Eekelaar
August 2009

---

[9] Consultation Document, p 9.

ACKNOWLEDGEMENTS

Although the authors have worked together on all the chapters, Shazia Choudhry was primarily responsible for Chapters 1, 2, 4, 5 and 9, while Jonathan Herring was primarily responsible for Chapters 3, 6, 7, 8 and 10.

We are very grateful to John Eekelaar, not only for writing a foreword to this book, but also for being a tremendous support to both in our careers. We are also very grateful to the team at Hart for all help in the preparation of this book.

We have both enjoyed the support and assistance of family and friends, particular thanks being due to both our partners, Ignazio and Kirsten, for their help and support throughout the process. Thanks are also due to Shazia's parents-in-law Silvia and Rino Pompeo who provided her, on many occasions, with the ideal surroundings in Italy in which to work on the book. Finally, Shazia would like to give special thanks to her mother, Irshad, to whom her part of this book is dedicated.

Colleagues are also due thanks. Jonathan Herring is particularly grateful to Michelle Madden Dempsey, Sandra Fredman, Stephen Gilmore, Rebecca Probert, George P Smith II and Julie Wallbank. Shazia Choudhry is particularly grateful to Gavin Phillipson, Julie Wallbank, Lizzie Barmes, Mario Mendez, Eric Heinze and Helen Fenwick. Finally, thanks are also due to the British Academy, whose award of a small grant enabled Shazia to take up a visiting scholarship at the European University Institute in Florence, Italy, where additional research was completed for the book.

CONTENTS

ABBREVIATIONS

AI	artificial insemination
AID	artificial insemination by donor
AITCA	Asylum and Immigration (Treatment of Claimants, etc) Act 2004
ARTs	assisted reproductive technologies
BDRA	Births and Deaths Registration Act 1953
CA	Children Act 1989
CA 2004	Children Act 2004
COA	certificate of approval
CPA	Civil Partnership Act 2004
CRC	United Nations Convention on the Rights of the Child
CSA	Child Support Agency
ECHR	European Convention on Human Rights
ECJ	European Court of Justice
ECtHR	European Court of Human Rights
ESC	European Social Charter
FLA	Family Law Act 1996
FLRA	Family Law Reform Act 1969
GRA	Gender Recognition Act 2004
GRC	gender recognition certificate
HFE Act	Human Fertilisation and Embryology Act 1990
HFE Act 2008	Human Fertilisation and Embryology Act 2008
HFEA	Human Fertilisation and Embryology Authority
HRA	Human Rights Act 1998
ICCPR	International Covenant on Civil and Political Rights
ICESCR	International Covenant on Economic, Social and Cultural Rights
IDIs	Immigration Directorate instructions
IPA	individual placing agreement
JCHR	Joint Committee on Human Rights
LCF	Leonard Cheshire Foundation
MCA	Matrimonial Causes Act 1973
NAA	National Assistance Act 1948
OAPA	Offences Against the Person Act 1861
PCC	Parochial Church Council
PTA	Prevention of Terrorism Act 2005
SDA	Sex Discrimination Act 1975
VAA	Voluntary adoption agency

TABLE OF CASES

European Court of Justice

Israel

South Africa

United Kingdom

United States of America

TABLE OF LEGISLATION

Statutory Instruments

United States of America

TABLE OF CONVENTIONS, TREATIES, ETC

1

The European Convention on Human Rights and Family Law

The impact of the European Convention on Human Rights (ECHR) on family law has undoubtedly been significant. The most relevant article is, of course, Article 8, which directly protects the right to family life and the impact of this Article can most obviously be seen in the law relating to disputes concerning children both in terms of legal process and decision making. However, as we shall see throughout this study, a number of other articles, in addition to Article 8, have had a significant effect in other areas of family law, including, for example, the development of the law relating to corporal punishment, the recognition of transgender rights and the rights of prisoners to access fertility treatments in order to create a family. A detailed analysis of these articles will take place as and when relevant throughout the following chapters. However, it is necessary to outline the basic structure of the main articles that have had the most impact upon family law in order to fully understand how certain principles and concepts employed by the European Court of Human Rights (ECtHR), such as proportionality and the margin of appreciation, which will also be examined in detail in this chapter, affect their operation.

An Introduction to the General Structure of the Convention Articles

Not all the Convention rights are formulated in the same way. There are two types of Convention rights: unqualified rights, some of which are 'non-derogable', and qualified rights. Of those rights that are most relevant to family law the following fall within the unqualified category: the right to life (Article 2); the right to protection from torture, inhuman and degrading treatment and punishment (Article 3), the right to liberty and security (Article 5), the right to a fair trial (Article 6), the right to marry (Article 12), the right to an effective remedy (Article 13) and the prohibition of discrimination in Article 14. Qualified rights that are most relevant to family law include the right to respect for private and family life (Article 8), religion and belief (Article 9), freedom of expression (Article 10), the right to peaceful enjoyment of property (Protocol 1, Article 1) and to some extent the right to education (Protocol 1, Article 2). The main articles of relevance to this chapter will be set out in brief.

Article 2

Article 2 provides:

1. Everyone's right to life shall be protected by law. No one shall be deprived of his life intentionally save in the execution of a sentence of a court following his conviction of a crime for which this penalty is provided by law.
2. Deprivation of life shall not be regarded as inflicted in contravention of this article when it results from the use of force which is no more than absolutely necessary:
   (a) in defence of any person from unlawful violence;
   (b) in order to effect a lawful arrest or to prevent escape of a person lawfully detained;
   (c) in action lawfully taken for the purpose of quelling a riot or insurrection.

Article 2 is therefore an unqualified and 'non-derogable' right: it may not be denied even in time of war or other public emergency threatening the life of the nation.[1] However, it is not entirely absolute, as its terms not only preserve the death penalty[2] but also permit the use of force. Nonetheless, it is clear that it ranks as one of the most fundamental provisions in the Convention and a large amount of case law has been developed from its provisions. This case law has established that Article 2 contains two fundamental elements which are reflected in its two paragraphs: a general obligation to protect the right to life 'by law', and a prohibition of deprivation of life, delimited by a list of exceptions. Although this is similar to the structure of Articles 8–11 of the Convention there are some differences.[3] First, additional weight is given to the right by virtue of the fact that the right itself must be 'protected by law' as opposed to being merely 'provided for'. Second, while States are not generally required to incorporate the Convention into their domestic law, as far as the right to life is concerned, they must still at the very minimum have laws in place which protect that right to an extent and in a manner that substantively reflect the Convention standards of Article 2.[4] The concept of 'law' as required by the Convention in turn means that the relevant rules must be accessible, and reasonably precise and foreseeable in their application.[5] Third, as far as the second paragraph is concerned, Article 2 allows for exceptions to the right to life only when this is 'absolutely necessary' for one of the aims set out in sub-paragraphs (2)(a)–(c) as opposed to, under Articles 8–11, being simply 'necessary in a democratic society' for the 'legitimate aims' listed in them. Finally, the Court has held that Article 2 imposes a 'positive obligation' on States to investigate deaths that may have occurred in violation of this Article.[6]

---

[1] Although 'deaths resulting from lawful acts of war' do not constitute violations of the right to life: see Art 15(2).

[2] Despite this the HRA has given effect to Arts 1 and 2 of Protocol No 6 to the Convention, which provide for the complete abolition of the death penalty except in respect of acts committed in time of war or 'imminent threat of war'.

[3] D Korff, 'The Right to Life—A Guide to the Implementation of Article 2 of the ECHR', *Human Rights Handbook No 8* (Strasbourg, Council of Europe, November 2006) 7.

[4] Cf the discussion of domestic law in *McCann and Others v the United Kingdom* [1996] 21 EHRR 97, paras 151–5.

[5] *Sunday Times v the United Kingdom (I)* (1979) 2 EHRR 245, para 49.

[6] *McCann* (n 4) para 161.

Article 3

Article 3 provides:

No one shall be subject to torture or to inhuman or degrading treatment or punishment.

Article 3 thus prohibits, in absolute terms, torture or inhuman or degrading treatment or punishment. It is therefore an unqualified and non-derogable right. No provision is made for exceptions and no derogation from it is permissible, even in time of war or other national emergency.[7] The Court has referred to the need for the alleged 'ill-treatment' to attain a minimum level of severity[8] if it is to fall within the scope of Article 3. The Court has also made it clear that the assessment of treatment is relative and will depend upon all the circumstances of the case. Factors that have been taken into account by the Court have included the nature and context of the treatment; its duration; its physical and mental effects; and, in some cases, the sex, age and state of health of the victim.[9] Thus, just because a form of conduct is not degrading treatment for one person does not mean that it cannot be so for another. The Court, which views the ECHR as a living instrument,[10] has also stated that it will be possible to reclassify its definition of ill-treatment in light of developments in policy of the Member States.[11]

Article 3 imposes primarily a negative obligation on States: to refrain from inflicting serious harm on persons within their jurisdiction. Most cases involving Article 3 have thus involved State agents or public authorities inflicting treatment on individuals.[12] However, the Court has been developing a certain level of flexibility in addressing the application of Article 3 within the 'private context'[13] which will be examined in detail in this chapter and others where relevant.

Article 8

Article 8 provides:

1. Everyone has the right to respect for his private and family life, his home and his correspondence.
2. There shall be no interference by a public authority with the exercise of this right except such as is in accordance with the law and is necessary in a democratic society in the interests of national security, public safety or the economic well-being of the country, for the prevention of disorder or crime, for the protection of health or morals, or for the protection of the rights and freedoms of others.

---

[7] *Chahal v the United Kingdom* [1997] 23 EHRR para 79.

[8] *Ireland v United Kingdom* [1979] 2 EHRR 25 para 162; *Tyrer v United Kingdom* [1979–80] 2 EHRR 1 para 30 and *A v United Kingdom* [1999] 27 EHRR 61 para 20.

[9] See among other authorities *Costello-Roberts v United Kingdom* [1995] 19 EHRR 112.

[10] *Tyrer v United Kingdom* (n 8) para 31.

[11] In *Selmouni v France* [2000] 29 EHRR 403, for example, the Court stated that it had: 'previously examined cases in which it concluded that there had been treatment which could only be described as torture ... However, having regard to the fact that the Convention is a "living instrument which must be interpreted in the light of present-day conditions" ... the Court considers that certain acts which were classified in the past as "inhuman and degrading treatment" as opposed to "torture" could be classified differently in future. It takes the view that the increasingly high standard being required in the area of the protection of human rights and fundamental liberties correspondingly and inevitably requires greater firmness in assessing breaches of the fundamental values of democratic societies.'

[12] Cases have ranged from prison and detention: *Ireland v United Kingdom* (n 8) and corporal punishment: *Tyrer* (n 8) para 31.

[13] *D v the United Kingdom* [1997] 24 EHRR 423 para 49.

Article 8 is thus a qualified right: the rights contained in the first paragraph may be justifiably interfered with on the basis of the limitations set out in the second. The article has four components: privacy, family life, home and correspondence. As a result a wide array of case law has emanated from its provisions and there have been, as we shall see in subsequent chapters, significant developments in respect of the notion of private and family life. In addition, as Ovey and White[14] note, since each right is reinforced by its context, the grouping together of these four rights within the same article further strengthens the protection given by it. The requirement to provide 'respect' for private and family life, home and correspondence has reinforced the development of positive obligations under the Article because it requires Member States to take positive action rather than to simply refrain from interfering with the rights protected. Positive obligations upon Member States may also arise with respect to protecting an individual against interferences by another individual. These issues will be explored further in the section on positive obligations below and in subsequent chapters where relevant.

Article 12

Article 12 provides:

> Men and women of marriageable age have the right to marry and to found a family, according to the national laws governing the exercise of this right.

Article 12 thus guarantees the right to marry and found a family; however, unlike Article 8, it is not a qualified Article by virtue of the absence of a set of limitations of the kind set out in Article 8(2). Equally, although it is regarded as an unqualified right, some limitations upon the right can be found in the very terms of the Article, that is, the right is limited to men and women of marriageable age *and* in accordance to the national laws governing the exercise of the right. This is not to say that the right can be interfered with by *any* national law no matter how reasonable. The Court has held on a number of occasions that any limitations set by national laws must not restrict or reduce the right in such a way or to such an extent that the very essence of the right is impaired.[15]

Article 14

Article 14 provides:

> The enjoyment of the rights and freedoms set forth in [the] Convention shall be secured without discrimination on any ground such as sex, race, colour, language, religion, political or other opinion, national or social origin, association with a national minority, property, birth or other status.

Article 14 thus represents a general prohibition against discrimination in relation to the rights guaranteed by the Convention, a principle so fundamental that it has an unqualified status. That is not to say, however, that it is without limitations. The right under

---

[14] C Ovey and R White, *Jacob and White: The European Convention on Human Rights* 4th edn (Oxford, Oxford University Press, 2006) 241–2.
[15] *Rees v the United Kingdom* (1987) 9 EHRR 56 para 50; *F v Switzerland* (1988) 10 EHRR 411 para 32.

Article 14 is not a freestanding one; the ECtHR has held that it has effect solely in relation to the 'rights and freedoms' safeguarded by those provisions. Thus, Article 14 will only be engaged if the facts of the case fall within the ambit of one or more of the other Convention rights.[16] In addition, the Court has repeatedly held that a difference in treatment will only be held to be discriminatory if it does not have an objective and reasonable justification, that is, if it does not pursue a legitimate aim or if there is no reasonable relationship of proportionality between the means employed and the aim sought to be realised.[17]

The Role of the Margin of Appreciation and Proportionality

Although the doctrine of proportionality is, in reality, pervasive throughout the whole Convention,[18] it is only with the qualified rights that interference has been specifically provided for, in the conditions laid down in the second paragraph of those rights. As a result, the ECtHR has developed a standard formula in its case law that is followed in cases concerning these 'qualified' rights. Thus, a violation of these Articles will be found unless the interference alleged:

— is 'in accordance with the law'; *and*
— is done to secure a legitimate aim set out in paragraph 2 of the relevant Article, for example for the prevention of crime, or for the protection of public order or health; *and*
— is necessary in a democratic society. In reality this is broken down into two factors that must be satisfied: the interference must fulfil a 'pressing social need', *and* be 'proportionate to the legitimate aim pursued'.

In addition, when assessing whether or not a 'pressing social need' exists the State is generally allowed a certain amount of discretion, the so called 'margin of appreciation'. The important doctrines of proportionality and margin of appreciation will be discussed in full detail below.

General Principles, Doctrines and Aids to Interpretation used by the ECtHR

A number of principles have emerged from the ECtHR's approach towards the interpretation of the Convention in addition to the general principles of international law[19] that apply to the interpretation of treaties.[20] First, that the doctrine of precedent in the Court

---

[16] *Petrovic v Austria* (2001) 33 EHRR 307 para 22.

[17] See *Petrovic* (n 16) para 30; *Fretté v France* [2004] 38 EHRR 438 para 34; and WK Wright, 'The Tide in Favour of Equality: Same Sex Marriage in Canada and England and Wales' (2006) *International Journal of Law, Policy and the Family* 249 for a detailed analysis of Art 14 in relation to same-sex marriage.

[18] It is clear that in practice a balancing exercise will be conducted in relation to almost all of the Convention rights. This point will be illustrated when discussing the non-qualified rights in subsequent chapters but note the excellent summary of how the ECtHR has done this in J Rivers, 'Proportionality and Variable Intensity of Review' (2006) 65 (1) *CLJ* 174, 182–4.

[19] The ECtHR stated in *Golder v UK* (1979–80) 1 EHRR 524 para 29 that these principles should guide the Court when interpreting the Convention. See also Jacobs and White, *European Convention on Human Rights* (n 14) 27–9 for a discussion of those principles.

[20] An account of the actual procedure of an application to the ECtHR will not be outlined here but for a good up-to-date outline see R Stone, *Textbook on Civil Liberties and Human Rights* 5th edn (Oxford, Oxford University Press, 2004) 14–18.

does not operate in the way in which *stare decisis* operates in common law jurisdictions and thus it is not the case that the ECtHR will follow its earlier decisions or reasoning. It is, however, clear that the Court values consistency and reasonable predictability[21] and has thus commented that 'it is in the interests of legal certainty, foreseeability and equality before the law that it should not depart, without good reason, from precedents laid down in previous cases'.[22] Second, the ECtHR adopts a purposive and dynamic approach to the interpretation of its provisions in order to ensure as effective and practical effect of the Convention rights as possible.[23] This ensures the maintenance of the third characteristic of the Convention: that it is meant to be a 'living instrument'. It must therefore be interpreted in the light of the development in social and political attitudes and cannot be confined to the circumstances that existed at the time of its inception.[24] This is no more apparent than in the field of family law. In the 50 plus years since ratification, substantial changes have occurred in the form and definition of 'the family' and the ECtHR has been able to take account of those changes precisely because of the Convention's evolutive nature.[25] At the same time, however, it should be noted that this method of interpretation does not allow the reading of new rights into the Convention that were not included at the out-set.[26] Finally, it should also be noted that the ECHR not only establishes 'vertical' duties between the State and the individual by imposing obligations upon the State to protect the individual against arbitrary interferences by it,[27] but it is also clear that these may include an obligation upon the State to protect a private individual's Convention rights against infringement by other private individuals. In *Hokkannen v Finland*,[28] for example, the grandparents of a child had refused to comply with court orders that had granted the father custody. The ECtHR held that the obligation for the national authorities to take action to facilitate a reunion with his child applied equally to private arrangements. Thus the Convention has a certain amount of 'horizontal effect' by imposing upon the State an obligation to regulate disputes between private individuals.[29] This particular effect of the Convention was greeted with a significant amount of debate and controversy during the passage of the Human Rights Act 1998 (HRA) and the issues it has raised for English law will be fully explored in the next chapter.

---

[21] This is illustrated by Art 30, which allows a Chamber to relinquish a case to the Grand Chamber of the Court 'where the resolution of a question before the Chamber might have a result inconsistent with a judgment previously delivered by the Court'. For a general overview of the principles applied by the Court see D Feldman, *Civil Liberties and Human Rights in England and Wales* 2nd edn (Oxford, Oxford University Press, 2002) 50–58 and Jacobs and White, *European Convention on Human Rights* (n 14) ch 3.

[22] *Goodwin and I v UK* (2002) 35 EHRR 447, 74.

[23] *Loizidou v Turkey* [1996] 20 EHRR 99 para 72. See also J Merrills, *The Development of International Law by the European Court of Human Rights* (Manchester, Manchester University Press, 1988) ch 5.

[24] Eg *Tyrer v United Kingdom* (n 8) para 31.

[25] For example, an unmarried couple can constitute a family: *X, Y and Z v the United Kingdom* Application No 21830/93 (1997) 24 EHRR 143; homosexuality cannot be used as a basis to deny residence to a father: *Salgueiro Da Silva Mouta v Portugal* Application No 33290/96 (2001) 31 EHRR 1055 and a transsexual now has the right to marry in the UK: *Goodwin* (n 22).

[26] So, for example, it was not possible to read into Art 12 (the right to marry and found a family) a right to divorce: see *Johnston v Ireland*, (1986) 9 EHRR 203 para 53.

[27] *Marckx v Belgium* [1979] 2 EHRR 330 para 31.

[28] *Ibid*.

[29] Reinforced by s6 of the HRA, which provides that it is unlawful for a court, as a public authority, to act in a way which is incompatible with a Convention right. See also *Douglas v Hello! Ltd* [2001] 2 All ER 289.

In terms of the Convention, however, the three most important aids to interpretation of it are, undoubtedly, the doctrines of positive obligations, the margin of appreciation and proportionality. These will now be examined in detail.

The Doctrine of Positive Obligations

As can be seen from the brief description of the main Articles that affect family law above, not all the rights protected under the Convention are framed in negative terms—that the State must *refrain* from interfering with those rights. It is clear from both the text of the Convention and the Strasbourg jurisprudence that some of the rights may in fact impose positive obligations upon States to protect their citizens from infringement of those rights. Starmer[30] has argued that the theoretical basis for such obligations arises from three principles within the Convention. First, the requirement under Article 1 that states should secure Convention rights to all persons within their jurisdiction. Second, the general principle that Convention rights must be practical and effective and, finally, the principle, under Article 13, that effective domestic remedy should be provided for arguable breaches of Convention rights. Feldman[31] expands upon this theoretical basis with a thorough account of instances where positive obligations have been expressly imposed by the text of the Convention. However, as he puts it:[32]

> [A] more extensive and less clearly defined set of positive obligations are those which the Commission and Court implied by interpreting the text of the Convention in the light of its underlying values and purposes.

Feldman also considers that the development of such obligations is firmly rooted within the dynamic interpretation of the Convention in the light of changing social and moral assumptions concerning the nature of the rights it protects and, if correct, this would seem to be of significant potential benefit to the field of family law, which is particularly susceptible to changing social and moral assumptions.[33] The doctrine was first referred to in *X and Y v Netherlands*[34] in relation to Article 8 and was further developed with respect to the right to life under Article 2 in both *McCann and Others v United Kingdom*[35] and *Osman v United Kingdom*.[36] Within the family law context the ECtHR has been particularly dynamic in its interpretation of the Convention, demonstrating the real potential of the doctrine.

---

[30] K Starmer, *European Human Rights Law* (London, Legal Action Group, 1999) ch 5.

[31] They can be found in Arts 14, 13, 2(1), 5(1), (2)–(5), 6(1) and 12: D Feldman, *Civil Liberties and Human Rights in England and Wales* 2nd edn (Oxford, Oxford University Press, 2002) 53.

[32] *Ibid.*

[33] *Ibid.*

[34] Where the applicants complained that Dutch law had failed to provide protection under the criminal law for the mentally disabled who had been sexually assaulted. The Court held that breaches of this nature required the protection of the criminal law and that States were obliged to take positive actions to protect people from arbitrary State interference. These extended to protecting individuals from the actions of other individuals. As a result, a breach of the applicants' Art 8 rights had occurred.

[35] *McCann and Others v United Kingdom* (n 4).

[36] In relation to the positive obligation to protect life, the Court held that States were obliged 'not only to refrain from the intentional and unlawful taking of life, but also to take appropriate steps to safeguard the lives of those within its jurisdiction'. This requires States to 'secure the right to life by putting in place effective criminal law provisions to deter the commission of offences against the person backed up by law-enforcement machinery for the prevention, suppression and sanctioning of breaches of such provisions'. In addition, States may be obliged, 'in certain well-defined circumstances', to take proactive, 'preventative operational measures' to protect individuals whose lives are under threat from the criminal activities of another.

The Court has, for example, recognised that the state can be under positive obligations to protect one individual from having their rights under Article 3 infringed by another individual.[37] A positive obligation on the State to provide protection against inhuman or degrading treatment from another individual has thus been found to arise in a number of cases. In *A v the United Kingdom*[38] a child applicant successfully complained that the government had failed to protect him from degrading treatment carried out towards him by his stepfather. The stepfather had caned him on a number of occasions causing him significant bruising but had not been held criminally liable for his actions[39] due to his successful use of the defence of reasonable parental chastisement. The Court reasoned that Article 3 required States to not only protect individuals from treatment which breached Article 3 administered by private individuals, but also that:

> Children and other vulnerable individuals, in particular, are entitled to State protection, in the form of effective deterrence, against such serious breaches of personal integrity.[40]

The Court thus concluded that, by allowing a defence of reasonable parental chastisement to a charge of assault on a child, English criminal law did not provide adequate protection to the applicant against treatment or punishment contrary to Article 3. A violation of Article 3 had therefore occurred.[41]

In *Z and Others v the United Kingdom*[42] the Court went further when it extended the nature and extent of positive obligations under Article 3 to English *civil* law. The case concerned four sibling child applicants who alleged that the local authority had failed to take adequate protective measures in respect of the severe neglect and abuse which they were suffering at the hands of their parents, contrary to Articles 3 and 8. Moreover, they had no access to a court, contrary to Article 6, or to an effective remedy, contrary to Article 13, in respect of this failure. It was argued that these alleged breaches were due to the House of Lords having held that,[43] as a matter of principle, local authorities could not be sued for negligence or for breach of statutory duty in respect of the discharge of their functions concerning the welfare of children. Their domestic action against the local authority for damages for negligence and/or breach of statutory duty had, therefore, been struck out as revealing no cause of action.[44]

---

[37] In *E v the United Kingdom* (2003) 36 EHRR 31 the Court held: 'Article 3 enshrines one of the most fundamental values of a democratic society ... The obligation on all contracting parties under Article 1 of the ECHR ... taken in conjunction with Article 3, requires States to take measures designed to ensure that individuals within their jurisdiction are not subjected to torture or inhuman or degrading treatment, *including such ill-treatment administered by private individuals*' (emphasis added). For a useful analysis of the positive obligation on States under the ECHR see A Mowbray, *The Development of Positive Obligations under the European Convention on Human Rights by the European Court of Human Rights* (Oxford, Hart Publishing, 2003).

[38] *A v the United Kingdom* [1999] 27 EHRR 611.

[39] Of assault occasioning actual bodily harm pursuant to s47 of the Offences Against the Person Act 1861.

[40] *A* (n 38) para 22. Reference was also made to the United Nations Convention on the Rights of the Child, Arts 19 and 37.

[41] The Court did not think it was necessary to examine the applicant's claim that he had also suffered a breach of his right to respect for private life under Art 8 having found a violation of Art 3.

[42] *Z and Others v the United Kingdom* [2002] 34 EHRR 3.

[43] Reported as *X and Others v Bedfordshire County Council* [1995] 3 All ER 352.

[44] This decision became the leading authority in the UK in this area. However, it was distinguished by the House of Lords in two significant judgments concerning the extent of liability of local authorities in childcare matters. In *W and Others v Essex County Council* [1998] 3 All ER 111, foster parents who brought a claim for damages for negligence against a local authority who placed a known suspected sexual abuser within their home had their appeal against the striking out of their action upheld by the House of Lords in relation to the sexual abuse

The Court found a breach of Article 3, as it was clear that the neglect and abuse suffered by the children reached the threshold of inhuman and degrading treatment.[45] In addition, the Court reiterated that Article 3 imposed an obligation on States to take measures designed to ensure that individuals within their jurisdiction were not subjected to such treatment, including that administered by private individuals.[46] These measures, the Court stated, should provide effective protection:

> [I]n particular, of children and other vulnerable persons and include reasonable steps to prevent ill-treatment *of which the authorities had or ought to have had knowledge.*[47] (emphasis added)

This reasoning was later applied in *E v United Kingdom*,[48] a case concerning four sibling applicants who had been sexually abused by their stepfather over a long period of time despite the involvement of social services and their knowledge of the considerable risk their father posed to the children. The Court found that the pattern of lack of investigation, communication and co-operation by the relevant authorities, taken together, amounted to a breach of Article 3. In its judgment the Court reiterated the principle that States should provide effective protection in relation to children and vulnerable adults, particularly where the authorities had or ought to have had knowledge of abuse.[49]

There has also been a considerable development of the positive obligations concerning the protection of family life between a parent and child. It is well established in the Court's case law that the mutual enjoyment by parent and child of each other's company constitutes a fundamental element of family life, and domestic measures hindering such enjoyment can amount to an interference with the right protected by Article 8 of the Convention.[50] Thus, there may be, in addition, positive obligations inherent in effective 'respect' for private or family life.[51] These obligations may involve 'the adoption of measures designed to secure respect for family life in relations between private individuals, including both the provision of a regulatory framework of adjudication and enforcement to protect individual rights'.[52] As a result, the right of parents, in appropriate circumstances, to have measures taken to reunite them with their children has also been included within the positive obligations upon the State. Thus, where the existence of a family tie has been established, the State must, in principle, act in a manner calculated to enable that tie to be

---

and psychiatric illness suffered by their three children and inflicted by the foster child. In *Barrett v London Borough of Enfield* [1999] 3 WLR 79, the plaintiff, who had been in care most of his life, claimed that the local authority had negligently failed to safeguard his welfare causing deep-seated psychiatric problems. Here, the House of Lords held that the judgment in *X and Others and Bedfordshire CC* did not, in this case, prevent a claim of negligence being brought against a local authority by a child formerly in its care.

[45] *Z and Others* (n 42) para 74: 'In their home to what the consultant child psychiatrist who examined them referred as horrific experiences … The Criminal Injuries and Compensation Board had also found that the children had been subject to appalling neglect over an extended period and suffered physical and psychological injury directly attributable to a crime of violence.'

[46] *A* (n 38) para 22.

[47] *Z and Others* (n 42) para 73.

[48] *E* (n 37).

[49] *Ibid*, para 88. *Z v UK* applied. See also *Stubbings v UK* [1997] 23 EHRR 213 para 64.

[50] See, amongst others, *Johansen v Norway* [1997] 23 EHRR 33 para 52.

[51] *X and Y v Netherlands* [1986] 8 EHRR 235.

[52] *Glaser v the United Kingdom* Application No 32346/96 (2001) 33 EHRR 119 para 63 and *Bajrami v Albania* Application No 35853/04 (2008) 47 EHRR 22 for a more recent example of the need to ensure that custody orders are enforced.

developed and take measures that will enable a parent and child to be reunited,[53] although it has also been made clear that this does not require the authorities to go beyond what is reasonable.[54] This applies not only to cases dealing with the compulsory taking of children into public care and the implementation of care measures, but also to cases where contact and residence disputes concerning children arise between parents and/or other members of the children's family.[55]

Other examples of where positive obligations have been developed, for the benefit of claimants within the family law context can be found in claims concerning domestic violence,[56] the rights of transsexuals[57] and the rights of minorities to a home.[58] It is, however, important to note that where such obligations are developed they are *not* absolute and are equally subject to the principles applied to negative obligations. Thus, as we have seen in relation to Article 3 above, liability under the positive obligations of this article will only be incurred if certain criteria are met.[59] In respect of positive obligations concerning the reunification of a parent and a child on the breakdown of the parental relationship, it was held in *Kosmopoulou v Greece*[60] that whilst national authorities must do their utmost to facilitate such a reunion, any obligation to apply coercion in this area must be limited. This is due to the need to take into account the interests as well as the rights and freedoms of all concerned and, more particularly, the best interests of the child and his or her rights under Article 8 of the Convention. Where contact with the parent might appear to threaten those interests or interfere with those rights, it is for the national authorities to strike a fair balance between them.[61] The key consideration is, therefore, whether the State has taken all such steps to facilitate contact as can reasonably be demanded in the particular circumstances of each case.[62]

Thus, in the context of *both* the State's positive and negative obligations, regard must also be had to the fair balance which has to be struck between the competing interests of the individual and the community as a whole, including other concerned third parties—the proportionality principle. In both cases the State also enjoys a certain margin of appreciation.[63]

The Margin of Appreciation

The margin of appreciation doctrine is based on the notion that each signatory state is entitled to a certain amount of discretion in resolving the inherent conflicts between

[53] See, amongst others, *Eriksson v Sweden* [1990] 12 EHRR 183 para 71, and *Gnahoré v France* Application No 40031/98 (2002) 34 EHRR 38 para 51.
[54] *Mihailova v Bulgaria* (Application No 35978/02) 12 January 2006 and *RK and Another v United Kingdom* [2008] All ER 143.
[55] *Hokkanen v Finland* [1995] 19 EHRR 159 para 55.
[56] *Kontrova v Slovakia* Application No 7510/04 [2007] ECHR 31 May 2007.
[57] *Goodwin* (n 22).
[58] *Connors v United Kingdom* [2005] 40 EHRR 9.
[59] The treatment concerned comes within the definition established under Art 3; the State ought to have or had knowledge that such treatment was occurring and that the State failed to take reasonably available measures that could have mitigated the resulting harm. See J Rogers, 'Applying the Doctrine of Positive Obligations in the European Convention on Human Rights to Domestic Substantive Criminal Law in Domestic Proceedings' [2003] *Crim LR* 690 emphasises that it will need to be shown that the criminal law provides an effective deterrent.
[60] *Kosmopoulou v Greece* [2004] 1 FLR 800 para 45.
[61] *Ignaccolo-Zenide v Romania* Application No 31679/96 ECHR 25 January 2000 para 94.
[62] *Hokkanen v Finland* (n 55) para 58.
[63] See *Z and others* (n 42) para 41.

individual rights and national interests or between competing individual rights. However, the doctrine will not be applicable to the question of the *scope* of the individual rights. Put simply, the Court considers that in some cases domestic authorities are better placed than the ECtHR to make these difficult decisions. As a result the Court will defer to the views of the domestic authorities in these circumstances. In addition, the doctrine represents an attempt to strike a balance between national and uniform European views of human rights. As Bernhardt states:[64]

> The margin of appreciation gives the flexibility needed to avoid damaging confrontations between the Court and Contracting States over their respective spheres of authority and enables the Court to balance the sovereignty of Contracting Parties with their obligations under the Convention.

Although the margin of appreciation was referred to in earlier ECtHR jurisprudence,[65] the most decisive explanation of the doctrine was set out by the ECtHR in the *Handyside v UK*[66] case. The Court stated:[67]

> In particular, it is not possible to find in the domestic law of the various Contracting States a uniform European conception of morals. The view taken by their respective laws of the requirements of morals varies from time to time and from place to place … By reason of their direct and continuous contact with the vital forces of their countries, State authorities are in principle in a better position than the international judge to give an opinion on the exact content of these requirements as well as on the 'necessity' of a 'restriction' or 'penalty' intended to meet them … Nevertheless, Article 10 paragraph 2 does not give the Contracting States an unlimited power of appreciation. The domestic margin of appreciation thus goes hand in hand with a European supervision. Such supervision concerns both the aim of the measure challenged and its 'necessity'; it covers not only the basic legislation but also the decision applying it, even one given by an independent court.

The judgment was decisive not only because it set out the 'prototype of margin analysis' with respect to the limitation clauses of Articles 8–11 and Article 2 of Protocol No 4 but it also extended the application of the doctrine to all contexts where a fair balance is to be struck between the right of an individual and the interests of society as a whole.[68] As a result the doctrine is applicable to all Convention rights except those that are non-derogable.[69]

Initially, the purpose of the doctrine was to respond to the concerns of national governments that international policies could jeopardise their national security.[70] However, as

---

[64] R Bernhardt, 'The Convention and Domestic Law' in R St J Macdonald, F Matscher and H Petzold (eds), *The European System for the Protection of Human Rights* (Dordrecht, Martinus Nijhoff, 1993) 123.

[65] The first reference being in *Greece v UK* (Cyprus Case) Application No 176/56 (1956) 25 ILR 168.

[66] *Handyside v UK* (1976) 1 EHRR 737.

[67] *Ibid*, para 48. In finding that the fact that a book that had been sold without restriction in other European countries did not mean that the restrictions imposed on its publication in the UK involved a breach of the publisher's freedom of expression.

[68] Y Arai-Takahashi, *The Margin of Appreciation Doctrine and the Principle of Proportionality* (Antwerp, Intersentia, 2002) 5–8.

[69] Y Arai-Takahashi, *The Margin of Appreciation* (n 68) 8. These rights are the right to life (Art 2), prohibition of torture (Art 3), prohibition of slavery and forced labour (Art 4) and freedom from ex post facto laws (Art 7).

[70] This explained the initial application of the doctrine in the context of derogations from treaty obligations due to self-proclaimed states of national emergency. See on this F Ni Aolain, 'The Emergence of Diversity: Differences in Human Rights Jurisprudence' (1995) 19 *Fordham International Law Journal* 112.

Benvenisiti has pointed out,[71] this rationale has since been expanded to allow each signatory state a wide discretion to select policies that would regulate other potentially harmful activities, such as incitement to violence[72] or racist speech[73] and has further been extended to a variety of issues from the restriction of choice of names for children and[74] the allocation and management of national resources,[75] to the regulation of free speech.[76] Thus, the extension of the doctrine to areas devoid of security considerations reflects, 'an altogether different philosophy, one which is based on notions of subsidiarity and democracy and which significantly defers to the wishes of each society to maintain its unique values and address its particular needs'.[77]

However, the dangers of utilising the margin of appreciation have also been highlighted, in particular, that exercising the margin of appreciation in favour of national institutions in certain conflicts between 'majorities and minorities' may, in fact, exacerbate the existing power differential against the interests of those politically powerless minorities.[78] In addition, critics have argued that the application of the doctrine is, in itself, inconsistent with the idea that individuals hold human rights against the principal subjects of public international law, the States themselves.[79] Further, it has been contended that the judicial self-restraint the doctrine allows serves as an 'abdication' by the Strasbourg institutions of their responsibilities of enforcement under Article 19.[80] In the main, however, criticism has built up and centred upon the unpredictability, incoherency and lack of uniformity in the application of the doctrine by the ECtHR in its case law[81] and the failure to indicate what 'principles or standards' determine the scope of the margin of appreciation.[82] The extent of the resultant lack of faith in the integrity of the doctrine was recently summed up by one author who concluded that the margin of appreciation was merely a label which serves to obscure the true basis upon which the court exercises its real judgement as to whether an intervention is necessary.[83] Thus, critics argue, the concept is meaningless unless the real question of precisely *how* the court reaches its decision on whether to accord a margin of appreciation is answered. As a result a number of authors have tried to make sense of its application by offering some explanation as to its true meaning within the reasoning

[71] E Benvenisiti, 'Margin of Appreciation, Consensus and Universal Standards' (1999) 31 *New York University International Law and Politics* 843.
[72] *Zana v Turkey* (1999) 27 EHRR 667.
[73] *Jersild v Denmark* (1995) 19 EHRR 1.
[74] *GMB and KM v Switzerland* Application No 36797/97 ECHR 12 September 2001.
[75] *James v United Kingdom* Application No 10622/83 ECHR (1986) 8 EHRR 123.
[76] *Handyside* (n 66).
[77] R Bernhardt, 'The Convention and Domestic Law' (n 64) 846.
[78] *Ibid*, 847. It is argued that no margin is called for when the political rights of members of minority groups of members of minority groups are curtailed, eg restrictions on speech or association, but that a wide margin may be appropriate with respect to policies that affect the general population equally, eg restrictions on hate speech.
[79] Y Arai-Takahashi, *The Margin of Appreciation* (n 68) 231.
[80] P Mahoney, 'Judicial Activism and Judicial Self Restraint in the European Court of Human Rights: Two Sides of the Same Coin' (1990) 11 *Human Rights Law Journal* 57.
[81] R St J MacDonald, 'The Margin of Appreciation' in R St J Macdonald, F Matxcher and H Petzold (eds), *European Protection of Human Rights* (n 64) 85.
[82] H Bosma, *Freedom of Expression in England and under the ECHR: In Search of a Common Ground: A Foundation for the Application of the Human Rights Act 1998 in English Law* (Antwerp, Intersentia, 2000) as cited in HM Fenwick and G Phillipson, *Media Freedom under the Human Rights Act* (Oxford, Oxford University Press, 2008).
[83] R Singh *et al*, 'Is There A Role for the "Margin of Appreciation" in national law after the Human Rights Act?' [1999] 1 *European Human Rights Law Review* 4.

process of the ECtHR. Some explanations have focused on theoretical underpinnings,[84] and some have attempted to map out how the margin has been applied by the ECtHR in both chronological[85] and Article specific[86] terms. Others[87] have analysed the case law and attempted to list the factors, in general terms, which will affect the width of the margin that is accorded. It is this method that is probably the most useful way in which to specifically assess its application within the family law context.

The Textual Provisions of the Convention Rights

It has been said that the more precise the terms of the provision, the less scope there is for interpretation of them and for granting a wide margin of appreciation.[88] Conversely, the less precise the terms of the provision are, the higher the scope for a wide margin of appreciation.[89] In the family law context we have also seen that both maxims can be used at the same time with regard to different elements of the process. In *Johnston v Ireland*,[90] the applicants alleged that because of the impossibility under Irish law of obtaining dissolution of the first applicant's marriage and of his resultant inability to marry the second applicant[91] they were both victims of breaches of Articles 12 and 8 of the Convention. Article 12 states that 'men and women of marriageable age have the right to marry and to found a family, according to the national laws governing the exercise of this right'. In its judgment the Court sought to ascertain the ordinary meaning to be given to the terms of this provision in the light of its object and purpose as revealed by the *travaux préparatoires*[92] and looked to the written response provided by the Rapporteur of the Committee on Legal and Administrative Questions for the Consultative Assembly at the time of the drafting of the Article. As a result the Court found:

> That the ordinary meaning of the words 'right to marry' is clear, in the sense that they cover the formation of marital relationships but not their dissolution. Furthermore, these words are found in a context that includes an express reference to 'national laws'; even if, as the applicants would have it, the prohibition on divorce is to be seen as a restriction on capacity to marry, the Court does not consider that, in a society adhering to the principle of monogamy, such a restriction can be regarded as injuring the substance of the right guaranteed by Article 12.[93]

---

[84] G Letsas, 'Two Concepts of the Margin of Appreciation' (2006) 26 (4) *OJLS* 705. He offers an analysis of how the different uses of the doctrine by the ECtHR can be justified within the wider principles of moral and political philosophy.

[85] HC Yourow, *The Margin of Appreciation Doctrine in the Dynamics of European Human Rights Jurisprudence* (The Hague, Kluwer Academic Publishers, 1996).

[86] Y Arai-Takahashi, *The Margin of Appreciation* (n 68).

[87] These general factors are summarised by HM Fenwick and G Phillipson, *Media Freedom* (n 82) but have been variously identified by a number of authors in the field. See, eg, R St J Macdonald, 'The Margin of Appreciation' in R St J Macdonald, F Matxcher and H Petzold (eds), *European Protection of Human Rights* (n 64); F Jacobs and R White, *The European Convention on Human Rights*, 4th edn (Oxford, Oxford University Press, 2006); D Feldman, *Civil Liberties and Human Rights* (2nd edn) (Oxford, Oxford University Press, 2002).

[88] T O'Donnell, 'The Margin of Appreciation Doctrine: Standards in the Jurisprudence of the European Court of Human Rights' (1982) 4 *Human Rights Quarterly* 474 at 496.

[89] J Schokkenbroek, 'The Basis, Nature and Application of the Margin of Appreciation Doctrine in the Case Law of the European Court of Human Rights' (1998) 19 *Human Rights Law Journal* 30 at 36.

[90] *Johnston v Ireland* (n 26).

[91] His partner of over 16 years with whom he was cohabiting and with whom he had a child.

[92] The preparatory work of the Convention, which is invoked as a guide to the general intentions of the signatories. However, it is generally regarded as being of limited use not least because of the fact that the Convention is regarded as a living instrument.

[93] *Johnston v Ireland* (n 26) para 52.

Furthermore, the Court also rejected the use of an evolutive interpretation arguing that they could not 'derive from these instruments a right that was not included therein at the outset. This is particularly so here, where the omission was deliberate.'[94]

Interestingly, the Court did not refer to the margin of appreciation at all in its assessment of Article 12,[95] presumably because none was granted, so it was not necessary to consider the point. However, a *wide* margin of appreciation was accorded in determining the steps to be taken to ensure compliance with the Convention in relation to the positive obligations imposed by Article 8. Nonetheless:

> It is true that, on this question, Article 8 … with its reference to the somewhat vague notion of 'respect' for family life, might appear to lend itself more readily to an evolutive interpretation than does Article 12. Nevertheless, the Convention must be read as a whole *and the Court does not consider that a right to divorce, which it has found to be excluded from Article 12 … can, with consistency, be derived from Article 8 a provision of more general purpose and scope.*[96] (emphasis added)

This illustrates an important point concerning the reliance by the Court upon textual provisions where a number of Articles are in play. If the preciseness of one provision (Article 12) does not allow for a right this will, as a matter of consistency, exclude the possibility of finding the same right in a more general provision (Article 8). Although the Court acted in accordance to both maxims and applied the appropriate standards of review,[97] the outcome of the Article 12 claim, in effect, prejudged the outcome of that made under Article 8.

Subsequently, in *F v Switzerland*,[98] the preciseness of the textual provisions of Article 12 were relied upon again in somewhat reversed circumstances to result in the opposite outcome. The applicant in this case had married four times since 1963. However, during the applicant's third set of divorce proceedings the Swiss Civil Court imposed a three-year prohibition on his remarriage due to the fact that, in its opinion, the applicant's unacceptable attitude rendered him solely responsible for the breakdown of the marriage. The applicant claimed that the prohibition violated Article 12 of the Convention. No claim was made under Article 8. The Swiss Government sought to rely on the Court's earlier judgment in *Johnston* that no right to remarry could be recognised given that the exercise of it necessarily depended on another right—the right to divorce—which did not flow from the Convention. This time, however, the Court found that:

> Article 12 secures the fundamental right of a man and a woman to marry and to found a family … It is 'subject to the national laws of the Contracting States', but 'the limitations thereby introduced must not restrict or reduce the right in such a way or to such an extent that the very essence of the right is impaired,[99]

and:

> Furthermore, and above all, F's situation is quite distinct from Mr Johnston's, since what was at issue in the case of the latter was the right of a man who was still married to have his marriage

---

[94]   *Ibid*, para 53.
[95]   Neither did the Commission.
[96]   *Johnston v Ireland* (n 26) para 57.
[97]   The former resulted in little or no margin and thus a higher intensity of review and the latter resulted in a wide margin and thus a lower intensity of review.
[98]   *F v Switzerland* Application No 11329/85 (1988) 10 EHRR 411.
[99]   *Ibid*, para 32.

dissolved. If national legislation allows divorce, which is not a requirement of the Convention, Article 12 secures for divorced persons the right to remarry without unreasonable restrictions.[100]

Here, in accordance with the first maxim, the Court used the precise terms of the provisions of Article 12 to, impliedly, refuse to accord any margin to the State. However, the outcome was the complete opposite to *Johnston*. Both cases do, however, illustrate an important feature of the margin of appreciation. As Arai-Takahashi notes:[101]

> What is critical for an appraisal of 'margin cases' is not the *result* of review, that is, whether or not the examination has led to a finding of a breach, but the *process* of evaluating the merits, namely, whether the Convention bodies have *deferred* to the appreciation of the national authorities. In other words have they refrained from direct, objective and full-scale appreciation of the merits of the impugned State's conduct in the light of the Convention?

The Existence of any Common Ground Between Different European States

It is apparent that where there is little or no consensus amongst Contracting States on the rights in question and where the decision of the Court concerns the balancing of those rights against social interests, a wide margin of appreciation will be accorded to the State.[102] Moreover, the extent of the positive obligations upon the State in relation to those rights will also be narrowed. This particular factor is best examined by using, as a case study, the transgender cases that have come before the ECtHR.[103] In the first consideration of a transgendered person's claim for official recognition[104] under Article 8 and Article 12 (the right to marry) the ECtHR referred to the lack of a European-wide consensus[105] on the issues as not only the reason for granting a wide margin of appreciation to the UK but also to narrowly interpret the positive obligations placed upon it[106] to ensure an effective respect for the applicant's private life. This interpretation was relied on in each of the three subsequent cases[107] concerning the rights of transsexuals brought before the ECtHR against the UK and it was not until 2002 that the view of the Court changed. In *Goodwin v United Kingdom*[108] and *I v United Kingdom*[109] the ECtHR finally ruled in favour of two transsexual applicants, finding that a breach of both Article 8 and Article 12 had occurred. In doing so, the reasoning relied upon, again, the question of whether there was

---

[100] *Ibid*, para 38.

[101] Y Arai-Takahashi, *The Margin of Appreciation* (n 68) 16.

[102] *Evans v UK* Application No 6339/05 (2006) 43 EHRR 21, paras 77–82.

[103] For a detailed review of the use of the margin of appreciation in these cases see KA Kavanagh, 'Policing the Margins: Rights Protection and the European Court of Human Rights' [2006] 4 *European Human Rights Law Review* 422.

[104] In relation to birth and marriage: *Rees v United Kingdom* [1987] 9 EHRR 56.

[105] *Ibid*, para 37: 'It would therefore be true to say that there is at present little common ground between the Contracting States in this area and that, generally speaking, the law appears to be in a transitional stage. Accordingly, this is an area in which the Contracting Parties enjoy a wide margin of appreciation.'

[106] *Ibid*, para 44: 'In order to overcome these difficulties there would have to be detailed legislation as to the effects of the change in various contexts and as to the circumstances in which secrecy should yield to the public interest. Having regard to the wide margin of appreciation to be afforded to the State in this area and to the relevance of protecting the interests of others in striking the requisite balance, the positive obligations arising from Article 8 cannot be held to extend that far.'

[107] *Cossey v the United Kingdom* (1990) 13 EHRR 622 paras 38–40; *Sheffield and Horsham v the United Kingdom* (1998) 27 EHRR 163 paras 57–61; *X, Y and Z* (n 25) paras 44, 52 in relation to parental rights and transsexuality.

[108] *Goodwin* (n 22) paras 84–6.

[109] *Ibid*, paras 64–5.

a consensus on the issue, except this time the criteria needed for establishing a consensus was changed. Thus, on this occasion, it was the recognition of an *international trend in favour* of an increased social acceptance of transsexuals and of the legal recognition of the new sexual identity of post-operative transsexuals that persuaded the court that less importance should be attached to the lack of evidence of a common European approach to the resolution of the legal and practical problems posed by the legal recognition of post-operative transsexuals.[110] The transsexual cases thus illustrate two important points: first, that the use of the European consensus principle can be highly selective. This has, as a result, attracted considerable criticism on both pragmatic[111] and principled[112] grounds, not least because it illustrates the Court's willingness to *disregard* clear evidence of a consensus, if necessary, if the desired result is that of a wide margin of appreciation. If we look at *Sheffield and Horsham v the UK*,[113] decided prior to *Goodwin* and *I*, the ECtHR seemingly disregarded evidence adduced by Liberty,[114] which, if anything, *made* the case for a European wide consensus surrounding the official recognition of transsexuals. This was done on the fairly tenuous ground that the evidence did not demonstrate a common European approach as to *how* to address the repercussions that the legal recognition of a change of sex may entail for other areas of law such as marriage, filiation, privacy or data protection. However, by the time that *Goodwin*[115] and *I*[116] were heard, despite the fact that no further statistical evidence of a European consensus could be provided by Liberty,[117] it was Liberty's evidence[118] on a continuing *international* trend towards legal recognition of transsexuals that seemed to render previous concerns as to the wider repercussions of official recognition in the *European* signatory states suddenly irrelevant. This illustrates the second point: the Court is now willing to use practices in non-European states to justify a departure from a previous use of the *European* consensus standard. Quite why the practices of Australia and New Zealand as non-contracting parties suddenly became relevant to the ECtHR's reasoning is something that the Court did not specifically address.

[110]   It was this lack of evidence of a common European approach to the resolution of the legal and practical problems posed by the legal recognition of post-operative gender status that the Court had previously relied on in the earlier case of *Sheffield and Horsham* (n 107) in order to accord a wide margin of appreciation to the UK in not finding a breach of either Articles 8 or 12.

[111]   TH Jones, 'The Devaluation of Human Rights under the European Convention' [1997] *PL* 430, 440–1 has discussed how the Court has no particular methodology in assessing whether there is or is not a common European standard in a particular area.

[112]   As discussed by HM Fenwick and G Phillipson, *Media Freedom* (n 82) 50–2 these criticisms centre on the fact 'that the ECtHR rather than setting the standards for Europe, follows them.'

[113]   *Sheffield and Horsham* (n 107).

[114]   In its 1998 study, it had found that over the previous decade there had been an unmistakable trend in the Member States of the Council of Europe towards giving full legal recognition to gender reassignment. In particular, it noted that out of 37 countries analysed only four (including the United Kingdom) did not permit a change to be made to a person's birth certificate in one form or another to reflect the reassigned sex of that person. In cases where gender reassignment was legal and publicly funded, only the United Kingdom and Ireland did not give full legal recognition to the new gender identity.

[115]   *Goodwin* (n 22).

[116]   *I v UK* [2002] 3 FCR 613.

[117]   In its follow-up study submitted on 17 January 2002, Liberty noted that there had not been a statistical increase in States giving full legal recognition of gender reassignment within Europe: *Sheffield and Horsham* (n 107) para 55.

[118]   For example, there had been statutory recognition of gender reassignment in Singapore, and a similar pattern of recognition in Canada, South Africa, Israel, Australia, New Zealand and all except two of the States of the United States of America: *Sheffield and Horsham* (n 107) paras 55–6.

Whether this was merely a cynical use of international evidence to achieve a particular aim in a very particular circumstance or the emergence of an *international* consensus standard is something that remains to be seen.

The Legitimate Aim for Interference Advanced by the State

The non-absolute Articles is where the State will identify, and place into context, the particular aim which is being achieved in interfering with those rights. The legitimacy of the aim is, however, almost always satisfied and very rarely questioned by the ECtHR. The question for consideration is thus if there is more weight attached to some legitimate aims over others. It is fair to say that within the context of family law and particularly with reference to Article 8, the application of which occurs in many different contexts and areas,[119] it is difficult to discern any real 'rules' as to *how* significant a particular legitimate aim is, particularly where those aims concern the application of positive obligations. It is thus difficult to generalise about the Court's likely attitude towards certain legitimate aims when they are being advanced by the State as grounds for interference with a right. However, it is clear that certain 'aims' are seen as being particularly meritorious of a wider margin of appreciation. This point is well illustrated by the issue of immigration control and family life. Throughout the 1980s and 1990, Strasbourg consistently gave a wide margin of appreciation to States in controlling the entry of non-nationals into their territory on the basis that the legitimate aim being relied upon was a State's right to control immigration as a matter of public safety and for the prevention of disorder and crime. This was the case even where it could be demonstrated that there would be a substantial negative impact upon the family lives of those involved if the State got its way. As a result, a rather onerous burden was placed upon the family members of those seeking entry to demonstrate that there were real medical or financial obstacles, to the establishment of family life elsewhere. In *Kamara v the United Kingdom*[120] the applicant suffered from an intestinal disorder and epilepsy and produced a specialist report to demonstrate that there was no appropriate treatment in Sierra Leone, the country to which her husband was being deported. The Commission rejected the allegation that the deportation would be in breach of the applicant's right to enjoy family life with her husband on the basis that the illness was long standing and her husband's deportation order had been made before the spouses had married. The application was therefore declared to be inadmissible. Further, even where an applicant could demonstrate that the decision to remove or refuse entry to a family member of a person settled lawfully would constitute an interference with their family life was still no guarantee that a breach of Article 8 would be found. An apparent willingness to grant a wide margin of appreciation in such cases meant that the decision to remove or refuse entry could still be regarded as a proportionate response, notwithstanding the impact this may have on family life. The legitimate aim of the State to prevent disorder has been particularly relevant in such cases. Thus, the knowledge of the precarious nature of a spouse's immigration status has been

---

[119] For example, taking children into care, adoption, marriage, divorce, private life and the home. It is also suggested that the impact of other international treaties and conventions has also brought in added considerations to the application of Art 8, eg the CRC.

[120] *Kamara v the United Kingdom* Application No 24831/94 ECHR 31 August 1994. See also *Sorabjee v the United Kingdom* Application No 23938/93 [1996] EHRLR 216 where the Commission said there were no insurmountable obstacles to the mother (illegally resident in the UK) and three-year-old child moving to Kenya as the child was of an 'adaptable age'.

held against applicants[121] and considerations of public order such as when an applicant had committed criminal offences, have been regarded as sufficient reasons to expel even where this resulted in applicants being separated from their spouses and children.[122]

However, a change in attitude came about in 2001, when in *Boultif v Switzerland*,[123] the ECtHR took the opportunity to set out the guidelines that were to be considered in cases where the main obstacle to expulsion was that it would result in difficulties for spouses to stay together and, in particular, for one of them and/or the children to live in the other's country of origin:

> The Court will consider the nature and seriousness of the offence committed by the applicant; the duration of the applicant's stay in the country from which he is going to be expelled; the time which has elapsed since the commission of the offence and the applicant's conduct during that period; the nationalities of the various persons concerned; the applicant's family situation, such as the length of the marriage; other factors revealing whether the couple lead a real and genuine family life; whether the spouse knew about the offence at the time when he or she entered into a family relationship; and whether there are children in the marriage and, if so, their age. Not least, the Court will also consider the seriousness of the difficulties which the spouse would be likely to encounter in the applicant's country of origin, although the mere fact that a person might face certain difficulties in accompanying her or his spouse cannot in itself preclude expulsion.[124]

Although broad, these criteria were relevant to the issue of *proportionality* and not to the margin of appreciation. The *margin* remained wide but the factors relevant to the proportionality test were specified to find, this time, that a breach of Article 8 *had* occurred in expecting a Swiss citizen to relocate to Algeria to follow her partner once he had been expelled from the country. The *Boultif*[125] criteria were later applied to find that a breach of Article 8 had occurred in refusing to extend the resident permit of a Turkish long-time resident of the Netherlands, who had at one time been separated from his wife, on the grounds that he had a conviction for drug offences[126] and, further, in finding a breach of Article 8 had occurred in refusing to grant entry to the Eritrean son of an asylum seeker who had herself been granted Dutch citizenship.[127] However, it is also clear that the demonstration of an adverse impact upon family life will still not be capable of automatically overriding State considerations of public order and immigration control. This is because it was the test for proportionality that was changed in *Boultif*[128] and not the width of the margin. Thus, in *Aoulmi v France*[129] the ECtHR found that no breach of Article 8 had occurred in deporting an Algerian national suffering from Hepatitis C, who had lived in France for nearly 40 years despite his having six siblings, all born in France and with French nationality, and a 16-year-old child, on the basis that he had a conviction and served a sentence for supplying heroin. Further, in *Uner v Netherlands*[130] the ECtHR found no breach of Article 8 had occurred in withdrawing a Turkish national's permanent residence permit

---

[121]   *M v United Kingdom* Application No 16382/90 ECHR 7 September 1990.
[122]   *Bouchelkia v France* [1998] 25 EHRR 686; *Uner v Netherlands* [2006] 3 FCR 340.
[123]   *Boultif v Switzerland* [2001] 33 EHRR 50.
[124]   *Boultif* (n 123) para 48.
[125]   *Ibid.*
[126]   *Sezen v Netherlands* [2006] 1 FCR 241.
[127]   *Tuquabo-Tekle v Netherlands* [2006] 1 FLR 798.
[128]   *Boultif* (n 123).
[129]   *Aoulmi v France* Application No 50278/99 (2008) 46 EHRR 1.
[130]   *Uner v Netherlands* (n 122).

on the basis that he had a conviction and had served a sentence for manslaughter despite the fact that he had a spouse and two children aged six and one and a half who were Dutch nationals and resident in the Netherlands.[131] In all the aforementioned cases the legitimate aim of immigration control was not questioned, as would be expected, but the differing outcomes were due to the sensitivity of the cases and driven by considerations of proportionality rather than by the nature of the aim itself. A number of cases since that decision have employed the same approach.[132] We can conclude, therefore, that it is more likely that a wide margin of appreciation will be accorded to the legitimate aims of public safety and the prevention of disorder and crime within the context of immigration control even where family life is adversely affected; however, the proportionality tests may well differ on a case-by-case basis.[133] It is also submitted that the potential exists for another closely linked legitimate aim to be viewed as requiring a particularly wide margin of appreciation and hence a less strict test of proportionality: national security. As yet the ECtHR has not specifically considered the effect of a deportation upon the family life of persons charged, convicted or connected with offences related to terrorism.[134] However, we have seen that, where a State in connection with Article 8, in contexts other than family law, has advanced the legitimate aim of 'interests of national security' this has tended to result in a wider margin of appreciation being accorded.[135] It may be less likely, therefore, that a proposed deportation pursuant to the aims of national security will be held to be in breach of Article 8. These cases must, however, be distinguished from cases where the deportation of an individual may put him/her at risk of Article 3 type treatment in the home State. The Court has recently reaffirmed its judgment in *Chahal v United Kingdom*,[136] that it applies rigorous criteria and exercises close scrutiny when assessing the existence of a real risk of ill-treatment to that individual regardless of the legitimate aim of national security being advanced by a Member State.[137] The margin of appreciation accorded in such cases will thus be narrow.

The Seriousness of the Interference

'The more serious the interference with Convention rights the more closely the decision will be scrutinised.'[138] The ECtHR has recently reaffirmed this point particularly in relation to Article 8:

> A number of factors must be taken into account when determining the breadth of the margin of appreciation to be enjoyed by the State in any case under Article 8. Where a particularly important facet of an individual's existence or identity is at stake, the margin allowed to the State will be restricted.[139]

---

[131] See also *Konstatinov v the Netherlands* Application No 16351/03 ECHR 26 April 2007.

[132] Eg *Grant v United Kingdom* Application No 10606/07 [2009] ECHR 26; *Onur v United Kingdom* Application No 27319/07 [2009] All ER 161.

[133] For a recent case see *Chair and JB v Germany* Application No 69735/01 ECHR 6/12/2007.

[134] Although Art 8 has been raised in such cases the Court has not felt it necessary to consider it separately: *Saadi v Italy* Application No 37201/06 [2008] INLR 621.

[135] *Klass v Germany* [1979–80] 2 EHRR 214 and *Leander v Sweden* [1987] 9 EHRR 433. See also HM Fenwick and G Phillipson, *Media Freedom* (n 82) 53–4 for a discussion on the relevance of national security as a legitimate aim within the context of free speech before the ECtHR.

[136] *Chahal v United Kingdom* (1997) 23 EHRR 413.

[137] *Saadi* (n 134).

[138] HM Fenwick and G Phillipson, *Media Freedom* (n 82) 56.

[139] *Evans* (n 102) para 77.

Thus, in *Z v Finland*[140] the Court emphasised the fundamental importance of protecting the confidentiality of medical data in order to protect personal privacy and found that the disclosure of medical records without the applicant's consent in the course of criminal proceedings against her spouse breached Article 8. However, in the family law context it is clear that the ECtHR has not been consistent in this regard. We have seen with regard to the transgender cases discussed earlier that the Court did not consider the arguably equal intrusion into the privacy of the applicants with respect to their sexual identity as serious enough to warrant the application of a narrower margin of appreciation for over two decades. It may also be thought that little could be more serious than the removal of a child from her parents by the State and that, as such, a narrow margin of appreciation and thus a higher intensity of review would be applied in such cases. The application of the margin of appreciation in such cases is, however, not so straightforward. The ECtHR has accorded a wide margin of appreciation with respect to the *decision* to commence care or adoption proceedings on the grounds that it is not appropriate or realistic to substitute the judgment of a national authority with a decision reached with the benefit of hindsight and without direct contact with the parties involved:

> The Court will have regard to the fact that perceptions as to the appropriateness of intervention by public authorities in the care of children vary from one Contracting State to another, depending on such factors as traditions relating to the role of the family and to State intervention in family affairs and the availability of resources for public measures in this particular area ... Moreover, it must be borne in mind that the national authorities have the benefit of direct contact with all the persons concerned often at the very stage when care measures are being envisaged or immediately after their implementation. It follows from these considerations that the Court's task is not to substitute itself for the domestic authorities in the exercise of their responsibilities for the regulation of the public care of children and the rights of parents whose children have been taken into care, but rather to review under the Convention the decisions taken by those authorities in the exercise of their power of appreciation.[141]

However, in terms of the *process* involved in making the decision to remove the ECtHR appears willing 'to apply the proportionality yardstick against the exercise of national discretion':[142]

> The Court further reiterates that, whilst Article 8 contains no explicit procedural requirements, the decision-making process involved in measures of interference must be fair and such as to afford due respect to the interests safeguarded by that Article.[143]

Thus, what the Court must determine is:

> Whether, having regard to the particular circumstances of the case and notably the serious nature of the decisions to be taken, the parents have been involved in the decision-making process, seen as a whole, to a degree sufficient to provide them with the requisite protection of their interests.

---

[140]   *Z v Finland* (1998) 25 EHRR 371.

[141]   *Johansen v Norway* (n 50) 64.

[142]   Y Arai-Takahashi, *The Margin of Appreciation* (n 68) 65. The author notes, however, that it is not consistently applied in this way.

[143]   *P, C and S v United Kingdom* Application No 56547/00 ECHR 16 August 2002, para 119. Although the Court found that a substantive breach of Art 8 had occurred in relation to the *decision* of the national courts to take S into care or to free her for adoption, they nevertheless found that there had been a violation of Art 8 in respect of the applicants P and C as regards the removal of S at birth and in respect of all the applicants as regards the subsequent procedures concerning the applications for care and freeing for adoption orders.

If they have not, there will have been a failure to respect their family life and the interference resulting from the decision will not be capable of being regarded as 'necessary' within the meaning of Article 8.[144]

The reference to the wide margin of appreciation in cases involving the removal of children thus belies the actual standard of review. The decision to remove may be subject to a wide margin but the reality is that the decision-making process in coming to that decision will be subject to some scrutiny.[145] It is therefore not possible to make any causal connection between the width of the margin and the strictness of the proportionality test here. In the private law context this approach is, to a certain extent, mirrored. A wider margin of appreciation is frequently granted with regard to decisions to grant residence or custody[146] but the ECtHR will often choose to apply a stricter test of scrutiny in relation to decisions regarding contact. This is mainly due to the fact that the Court is extremely aware that restrictions on or refusal to allow contact will, effectively, severely limit the enjoyment of and, in some cases, extinguish family life:

> The Court has recognised that the authorities enjoy a wide margin of appreciation, in particular when deciding on custody. However, a stricter scrutiny is called for as regards any further limitations, such as restrictions placed by those authorities on parental rights of access, and as regards any legal safeguards designed to secure an effective protection of the right of parents and children to respect for their family life. Such further limitations entail the danger that the family relations between a young child and one or both parents would be effectively curtailed.[147]

As a result the breakdown of the matrimonial or other relationship between a child's parents will not automatically extinguish family life and will not deprive those parents of the right to remain in contact with the child. Furthermore it will not deprive the *child* of the right to remain in contact with her parents and/or siblings.[148] In addition, the Court has further incorporated its concern regarding the continuance of family life in such circumstances into the interpretation of the positive obligations inherent in effective 'respect' for family life. These obligations, as discussed above, have thus been interpreted to include the provision of a regulatory framework of adjudicatory and enforcement machinery protecting individuals' rights and the implementation, where appropriate, of specific steps.[149] In the family law context this has meant the Court has found against a State[150] where it did not adequately facilitate contact between a non-resident parent and his child and where sufficient investigation was not pursued in relation to the deterioration of the relationship between a child and his father.[151] It has also found against a State where the relevant domestic law had prevented the administrative decisions placing her children in care from being reviewed by a court.[152]

---

[144] *W v the United Kingdom* (1988) 10 EHRR 29, paras 62, 64; see also *Saviny v Ukraine* Application No 39948/06 ECHR 18 December 2008 for a recent example of the Court finding a breach of Art 8 where children had been taken into care because the judicial process had been found to be lacking.

[145] Y Arai-Takahashi, *The Margin of Appreciation* (n 68) 65.

[146] Eg *Ismailova v Russia* Application No 37614/02 ECHR 29 November 2007.

[147] *Suss v Germany* [2005] 3 FCR 666 para 87.

[148] *Olsson No 1 v Sweden* (1989) 11 EHRR 259.

[149] *Glaser* (n 52).

[150] *Kosmopoulou* (n 60).

[151] *Elsholz v Germany* (2002) 34 EHRR 58.

[152] *Berecova v Slovakia* Application No 74400/01 ECHR 24 April 2007.

Having addressed the general factors, we may now consider whether it is possible to identify any other factors that are particularly relevant to the application of the margin of appreciation in the family law context. Although this specific question has not been addressed in detail within the existing literature it is submitted that two further factors may be of particular relevance.

The Likelihood of Substantial Public Resource Implications

An examination of ECtHR jurisprudence in this area reveals that in spheres involving the application of social or economic policies, the margin of appreciation that will normally be accorded is a wide one.[153] However, most of the cases that involve a consideration of the impact upon public resources, within the family law context, have concerned the 'right to a home' under Article 8 although, as detailed above, these considerations have also come into play when the Court has deferred to the sovereign right of a State to control immigration and thus the equitable distribution of its resources. The development of positive obligations binding on states in this area has therefore not been as extensive as in the case of the right to respect for family life. The interpretation of positive obligations by the ECtHR has, it would seem, tended to centre on the ability to *enjoy* a home and, therefore, upon the issue of respect rather than the *provision* of a home.[154] Indeed the Court has made it abundantly clear that any attempt to interpret this aspect of Article 8(1) in order to impose an obligation to provide a home will be resoundingly rejected. This is presumably due to the fact that to do so would convert this aspect of Article 8 into a socio-economic right. In *Chapman v United Kingdom*, the Court stated:[155]

> It is important to recall that Article 8 does not in terms give a right to be provided with a home. Nor does any of the jurisprudence of the Court acknowledge such a right ... Whether the State provides funds to enable everyone to have a home is a matter for political not judicial decision.

Further, in a number of cases involving Article 1 of Protocol No 1[156] the Court has also stated that in spheres such as housing, which play a central role in the welfare and

---

[153] Thus, in the planning context the Court has found that: 'In so far as the exercise of discretion involving a multitude of local factors is inherent in the choice and implementation of planning policies, the national authorities in principle enjoy a wide margin of appreciation.' *Buckley v the United Kingdom* Application No 20348/92 23 EHRR 191 para 75.

[154] For a general summary of the positive obligations imposed by the Court in this area see A Mowbray, *The Development of Positive Obligations under the European Convention on Human Rights by the European Court of Human Rights* (Oxford, Hart, 2004) ch 6, 181–6. This aspect of Art 8(1) has, thus, been interpreted to impose an obligation upon Member States not to cause, or allow others to create, environmental pollution of such an extent that it may interfere with the right to respect for the home: *Powell and Rayner v UK* (1990) 12 EHRR 355; *Lopez Ostra v Spain* (1994) 20 EHRR 277; *Hatton v United Kingdom* (2003) 37 EHRR 28; *Fadeyeva v Russia* Application No 55723/00 ECHR 9 June 2005; *Guerra v Italy* (1998) 26 EHRR 357 and A Mowbray, '*Guerra and Others v Italy*: The Right to Environmental Information under the European Convention on Human Rights' (1998) 6 (3) *Environmental Liability* 81 and to ensure that the right to respect for the home is not applied in a discriminatory manner: *Larkos v Cyprus* (1999) 30 EHRR 597.

[155] *Chapman v United Kingdom* [2001] 33 EHRR 399 at 427–8 para 99 and *O'Rourke v United Kingdom* Application No 39022/97 ECHR 26 June 2001, 5. Unless the failure to provide assistance would raise an issue in relation to the private life of an individual: see also *Marzari v Italy* (1999) 28 EHRR 175 (CD) 179–80 where, despite being recognised as severely disabled, the applicant had been allocated an apartment which he considered to be inadequate to his needs. He refused to pay rent for it and had been subsequently evicted. The Court found that his eviction from his apartment interfered with his rights under Art 8(1).

[156] Which provides for the peaceful enjoyment of posessions.

economic policies of modern societies, it will respect the legislature's judgment as to what is in the general interest unless that judgment is manifestly without reasonable foundation.[157] However, the Court has also pointed out that where general social and economic policy considerations have arisen in the context of Article 8, the scope of the margin of appreciation will depend upon the context of the case, with particular significance attaching to the extent of the intrusion into the personal sphere of the applicant.[158] In determining whether the respondent State has, when fixing the regulatory framework, remained within its margin of appreciation, the procedural safeguards available to the individual will be especially material and in particular, the Court must examine whether the decision-making process leading to measures of interference was fair and such as to afford due respect to the interests safeguarded to by Article 8.[159] These principles have become particularly relevant for those individuals who are to be deprived of their home. In *Connors v United Kingdom*,[160] the Court chose to narrow the margin of appreciation applied to the UK with respect to a case concerning the eviction of a family from two plots that they occupied on a gypsy site in pursuance of the council's unconditional right to terminate a licence.[161] The issue before the Court was, therefore, whether the interference with the applicants' Article 8 rights, caused by the eviction, was justified under Article 8(2). The Court noted:[162]

> Where general social and economic policy considerations have arisen in the context of Article 8 itself, the scope of the margin of appreciation depends on the context of the case, with particular significance attaching to the extent of the intrusion into the personal sphere of the applicant [emphasis added].

The particularly vulnerable position of gypsies and the perceived need to facilitate the gypsy way of life was referred to extensively by the Court in its reasoning[163] and, as a result, the Court found:[164]

> The serious interference with the applicant's rights under Article 8 requires, in the Court's opinion, particularly weighty reasons of public interest by way of justification and the margin of appreciation to be afforded to the national authorities must be regarded as correspondingly narrowed. The Court would also observe that this case is not concerned with matters of general planning or economic policy but with the much narrower issue of the policy of procedural protection for a particular category of persons. The present case may also be distinguished from the *Chapman* case … in which there was a wide margin of appreciation.

The Court thus narrowed the margin and correspondingly increased the intensity of the proportionality appraisal, finding, as a result, that there had been a violation of Article 8 of the Convention. The issue was re-addressed by the ECtHR following a domestic attempt to restrict the effect of the *Connors*[165] decision to cases concerning the travelling

---

[157] *Mellacher and Others v Austria* (1990) 12 EHRR 391 para 45; *Immobiliare Saffi v Italy* (2000) 30 EHRR 756 para 49.

[158] *Connors* (n 58) para 82.

[159] *Ibid.*

[160] *Ibid.*

[161] *Ibid.* Under the Caravan Sites Act 1968 a local authority is given an unconditional right to terminate a licence on 28 days' notice (by court order only) and without any need to demonstrate cause.

[162] *Ibid*, para 82.

[163] *Ibid*, paras 84–95.

[164] *Ibid*, para 86.

[165] *Ibid.*

community[166] and in *McCann v United Kingdom*[167] the Court made it clear that the principles established in *Connors*[168] were not confined to cases concerning the eviction of gypsies:

> The loss of one's home is a most extreme form of interference with the right to respect for the home. Any person at risk of an interference of this magnitude should in principle be able to have the proportionality of the measure determined by an independent tribunal in light of the relevant principles under Article 8 of the Convention, notwithstanding that, under domestic law, his right of occupation has come to an end.[169]

As the procedural safeguards required by Article 8 for the assessment of the proportionality of the interference had not been met, there had therefore been a breach of Article 8. Thus, in cases concerning broad social and economic policy considerations, a wider margin will generally be applied; however, domestic authorities must ensure, in relation to any Article 8 claims, that the individual affected has had an opportunity for an independent assessment of the proportionality of the measure. A narrow margin of appreciation will be applied with regard to such issues. This may, as the authors have argued elsewhere, hold implications for areas other than housing.[170]

Sensitive Moral or Ethical Issues

The margin of appreciation afforded to the State will be wider where a case raises particularly sensitive moral or ethical issues. Where such issues are raised the Court is also much more likely to engage in an examination of whether a consensus exists within Member States as to the relative importance of the interests at stake or as to the best means of protecting it.[171] As a result the two factors have often been considered together and where both are present there is a greater likelihood of a wider margin being accorded.[172] Examples of cases where these factors have been of particular significance have usually concerned the consequences of transsexuality and homosexuality upon the family. In *X, Y and Z v the United Kingdom*[173] the applicant, a female to male transsexual, alleged a violation of Article 8 had occurred in the refusal to allow him to be registered as the father of a child born via artificial insemination and with the help of an anonymous donor. The refusal by the United Kingdom centred on the basis that only a biological man could be regarded as a father for the purposes of registration. In concluding that Article 8 could *not* imply an obligation to formally recognise as the father of a child a person who is not the biological father the Court referred both to the fact that transsexuality raised complex scientific, legal, moral

---

[166] *R (on the application of Kay) v Lambeth* [2004] EWCA 289 (Civ); see ch 9 for a detailed discussion of the domestic case law in this area.

[167] *McCann and others v the United Kingdom* [1995] ECHR 31.

[168] *Connors* (n 58).

[169] *McCann* (n 167) para 50.

[170] Such as domestic violence; authors have thus argued elsewhere that the victims of domestic violence may well come within this category: S Choudhry and J Herring, 'Righting Domestic Violence' (2006) 20 (1) *International Journal of Law, Policy and the Family* 95 and S Choudhry and J Herring, 'Domestic Violence and the Human Rights Act 1998' [2006] 4 *PL* 752.

[171] *X, Y and Z* (n 25).

[172] That is not to say that the ECtHR will always apply a wide margin where the issues involved are of a sensitive moral nature and no European consensus exists, eg *Dudgeon v United Kingdom* Application No 7525/76 (1982) 4 EHRR 149, where no margin of appreciation was applied to find that legislation criminalising consensual sexual acts between adult men in Northern Ireland was in breach of Art 8.

[173] *X, Y and Z* (n 25).

and social issues but also that there was no generally shared approach among Contracting States on how to deal with them. In *Fretté v France*[174] the Court constantly referred to the 'delicacy' of the issue as well as the lack of consensus amongst Member States in dealing with the rights of homosexuals to adopt.[175] As a result, a wide margin of appreciation was accorded to the issue of whether a violation of Articles 8 and 14 had occurred in the refusal by France to allow the applicant to adopt on the basis of his sexual orientation alone. This approach has now been extended, more recently, to the question of how the use of medical and scientific advances should be governed. In *Evans v the United Kingdom*[176] the ECtHR had to consider the difficult issue of whether the applicant's Article 2, 8 and 14 rights had been breached by Schedule 3 of the Human Fertilisation and Embryology Act 1990, which allowed her former partner to withdraw his consent to the storage and use by her of embryos originally created jointly by them for the purposes of conception. The applicant, who had suffered from ovarian cancer, had had to have her ovaries removed shortly after the extraction of the eggs. As a result, these embryos represented the only opportunity for the applicant to conceive a child to whom she would be genetically related. The ECtHR took the opportunity to set out a number of factors that they considered to be of particular relevance to the breadth of the margin of appreciation to be enjoyed by a State in a case concerning Article 8, some of which have already been detailed above.[177] However, it was the very nature of the issues that the case presented and the fact that there was a lack of consensus amongst Member States upon how to deal with them that they specifically referred to as the basis for granting a wide margin.

> In conclusion, therefore, since the use of IVF treatment gives rise to sensitive moral and ethical issues against a background of fast-moving medical and scientific developments, and since the questions raised by the case touch on areas where there is no clear common ground amongst the Member States, the Court considers that the margin of appreciation to be afforded to the respondent State must be a wide one.[178]

As a result the Court found that there had been no violation of Article 8 in the case.

In summary, it would appear that in the family law context and, particularly in relation to Article 8, that *some* of the general rules concerning the factors that are said to influence the width of the margin will have the same effect in family law. Thus, we have seen that, in general, the more precise the provision the lesser the width of the margin, the more connected the claim is to issues of national sovereignty, such as in immigration, and the more moral or ethical considerations that are involved, the wider the margin. However, within all the other remaining factors the application of the general rules has either been inconsistent, as in the 'European consensus' factor in relation to the transsexual cases, or has been applied in completely the opposite way, due in large part to the factual context of the case. Thus, in cases involving substantial resource implications, in terms of

---

[174] *Fretté v France* (2004) 38 EHRR 438. But see *EB v France* (2008) 47 EHRR 21 where a breach was found.

[175] Although when the court was prepared to reverse its stance with regard to the policy in France such references were noticeably absent: *EB v France* Application No 43546/02 (2008) 47 EHRR 21.

[176] *Evans* (n 102).

[177] *Evans* (n 102) para 77: 'Where a particularly important facet of an individual's existence or identity is at stake, the issue of consensus within the Member States of the Council of Europe, where the case raises sensitive moral or ethical issues and if the State is required to strike a balance between competing private and public interests or Convention rights'.

[178] *Evans* (n 102) para 81.

housing provision for vulnerable groups, a narrower margin was applied; however, in cases concerning the serious decision to terminate or reduce contact between a parent and child a wider margin has been applied.[179] This inconsistency of approach is not so unpredictable, however, when we consider the variety of situations to which the ECHR can be applied in the family law context and that one of the purposes of the doctrine has been to take into account particular cultural and social conditions within individual States. Family law represents one of the most often used vehicles for, at least, the legislative realisation of such conditions within any one State and thus it is not surprising that it is an area where the margin of appreciation may be applied more inconsistently than others. Family law is thus, also, illustrative of the attempt to achieve another purpose of the doctrine. That is to realise a Europe-wide system of human rights protection and the 'uniform standard' of human rights, a process that must, in addition, be a gradual one by necessity.[180] In this sense, it is the factual context of the case that is probably the most relevant consideration when determining the Court's application of the above factors and thus the width of the margin.

The Relationship Between the Margin of Appreciation and Proportionality

Margin of Appreciation

There is a general consensus in the literature upon the fact that a roughly inverse relationship exists between the two doctrines. Thus the wider the margin, the less strict is the standard of review. This has been certainly been evidenced in the family law context in the discussion above. However, if this is correct, the question of which principle is applied first by the Court, and thus which doctrine influences the other, becomes a crucial one. Whilst some may have given up on trying to fathom the ECtHR's approach to the matter due to the inconsistencies that are apparent, others have tried to present a reasoned description of the relationship between the two doctrines. Phillipson and Fenwick[181] have argued that, within the context of Article 10 of the Convention and freedom of expression, 'it is a significant feature of Convention case law that, in determining this key issue of proportionality, the standard of review varies markedly; in justifying applying such a varying standard, the Court often refers to what is known as the margin of appreciation doctrine'. They go on to argue that the 'doctrine allows the Court to defer, to a greater or lesser extent, to the views of the relevant national authorities, both that it was *necessary* to interfere with freedom of expression to protect another interest (for example, the protection of morals), and as regards the choice of *means* to afford that protection (such as criminal prosecutions, injunctions, awards of damages etc)'.[182]

---

[179] Where the margin was narrowed in these cases was on the decision-making procedures that were followed.

[180] R St J MacDonald, 'The Margin of Appreciation' in R St J Macdonald, F Matxcher and H Petzold (eds), *European Protection of Human Rights* (n 64) 123.

[181] HM Fenwick and G Phillipson, *Media Freedom* (n 82) 48.

[182] *Ibid*, 49.

Thus, the argument goes, the intensity of the review by the Court (the width of the margin of appreciation accorded by it) is directly influenced by the type of speech that it is dealing with. It is only once the intensity of the review has been decided, in their view, that the Court, in the majority of cases, *then* chooses the proportionality test it wishes to use to achieve the aim. If the review is to be intense the strictest form of the proportionality test may be utilised: the State will have to show that the infringing measures were the least restrictive possible in the circumstances. If it is to be less intense, the least restrictive proportionality test may be employed: the State will merely have to show that it has struck a fair balance between the right that has been infringed and the societal interests justifying the infringement.

According to the case law to be examined in this chapter, we suggest that this analysis could readily be applied to the field of family law. We have seen that it is the factual context of a case that will heavily influence the way in which the factors that affect the width of the margin will be applied. It is equally plausible that, in the majority of cases, once the court has decided how rigorously it wishes to review a decision, that is, whether to apply a margin of appreciation, the Court then chooses the most appropriate proportionality test. Thus where a wide margin is accorded, such as in the transsexual cases prior to *Goodwin*,[183] cases concerning the decision to take a child into care or award custody, cases concerning the provision of a home, and cases concerning the effects of homosexuality and transsexuality upon family law, the least restrictive test of proportionality has been applied—the 'fair balance' test. Where a narrow margin is accorded, such as in cases concerning restrictions upon the right to marry, cases concerning the decision-making procedures involved in terminating or reducing contact between a parent and a child, the ability to sue a local authority for negligence in relation to its care of children and providing a home for vulnerable groups, a stricter proportionality test—the 'sufficiency test'—has been applied. There is, however, one exception to the applicability of this analysis and that is where, as Takahashi[184] puts it, the Court employs a rhetorical use of the margin of appreciation. In other words, that despite stating that a wide margin of appreciation is being accorded, the Court nevertheless conducts a close review of the merits of the case. A good example of where this has occurred in the family law context can be seen in the immigration and family life cases. Commencing with *Boultif v Switzerland*,[185] the Court reversed the approach that had been followed in all cases prior to this decision. Up until this case the predominant approach of the ECtHR was one in which a wide margin would be accorded and the standard of scrutiny low. However, the Court in *Boultif*[186] took the opportunity to set out a number of guiding principles, which had to be looked at in all such cases in the future. Thus, the intensity of review was in reality increased without, seemingly, disturbing the width of the margin. To talk of the 'wide margin of appreciation' in such cases is, thus, to do so in a purely rhetorical manner. It can only be presumed that this lack of transparency concerning the real width of the margin accorded is due in large part to the conflict its previous reasoning in such cases was causing with the Court's own policies concerning the

---

[183] *Goodwin* (n 22).
[184] Y Arai-Takahashi, *The Margin of Appreciation* (n 68) 18.
[185] *Boultif* (n 123).
[186] Ibid.

preservation of family life and the crucial importance of the best interests of the child and the sovereign rights of the State.

Proportionality

As one author has recently put it, 'the doctrine of proportionality in the wide sense is the name given to the set of tests used to establish whether a limitation of rights is justifiable. Proportionate limitations of rights are justifiable; disproportionate ones are not.'[187] However, the use of the doctrine is not confined to the ECtHR. Clayton[188] has recently provided a comparative analysis of proportionality with reference to its use by EC law, and by courts in South Africa,[189] Canada[190] and New Zealand and suggests, as a result, an international standard of proportionality:[191]

> A number of threads can be drawn together. There is universal acknowledgment that the court is exercising a review function and is not substituting its own judgment for that of the original decision-maker. However, the decision in question is to be subject to an intense standard of review. The necessity of the interference is closely scrutinised and a public authority must usually show it has used the least restrictive means available to it to accomplish its objective.

Does this approach differ from that of Strasbourg? As noted above, with respect to the qualified Articles the ECtHR has developed a standard formula in its case law that is followed in cases concerning these 'qualified' rights. This worth repeating here: a violation of these Articles will be found unless the interference alleged:

— is 'in accordance with the law'; *and*
— is done to secure a legitimate aim set out in the relevant Article, for example for the prevention of crime, or for the protection of public order or health; *and*
— is necessary in a democratic society. In reality this is broken down into two factors that must be satisfied: the interference must fulfil a 'pressing social need', *and* be 'proportionate to the legitimate aim pursued'.

In assessing whether or not a 'pressing social need' exists, the State is generally allowed a margin of appreciation but this is tempered somewhat by the fact that the State must also ensure that the reasons justifying the interference are both relevant and sufficient.[192] In practice, the 'relevance' element can almost always be satisfied by reference to the criteria required to establish a legitimate aim. The 'sufficiency' element is, however, more complicated and is dependent upon a number of factors, such as the nature and effects of the measures and the harm they may cause to the individual, which are closely linked to the exercise of the proportionality principle. Thus, any proportionality assessment cannot take place unless sufficient reasons justifying the measure at issue are adduced. In addition, as noted earlier, the doctrine of the margin of appreciation will also come into play at the

---

[187] J Rivers, 'Proportionality and Variable Intensity of Review' (2006) 65 (1) *CLJ* 174.
[188] R Clayton, 'Regaining a Sense of Proportion: the HRA and the Proportionality Principle' [2001] EHLRR 512.
[189] The leading decision on proportionality in South Africa is generally regarded to be *S v Makwanyane* [1995] 3 SA 391.
[190] As set out by the Canadian Supreme Court in *R v Oakes* [1986] 1 SCR 103, 137–8.
[191] R Clayton, 'Regaining a Sense of Proportion' (n 188).
[192] *Silver and Others v UK* 5 EHRR 347 para 97.

final stage of the above assessment.[193] For it is when the Court makes its assessment of whether a pressing social need exists that both the *scope* of the margin to be accorded to the State is decided and the appraisal of whether the measures at issue are *proportionate* is taken. It is not difficult to see, therefore, why links between the two doctrines have been made. Whilst authors may disagree about in which order the two doctrines influence each other[194] it is fairly clear that a roughly inverse relationship exists between the two. Thus as Arai-Takahashi[195] puts it, 'it is possible to consider the application of the proportionality principle as the other side of the margin of appreciation. The more intense the standard of proportionality becomes, the narrower the margin allowed to national authorities.' In this sense, the proportionality principle should serve as a check or break upon the margin of appreciation.

Having identified how the proportionality principle should operate, how does it *actually* operate in practice? Although it is now well accepted that the ECtHR employs different types of proportionality 'tests', little or no examination of these tests specific to family law has taken place in the existing literature. However, a number of scholars have sought to elucidate upon the tests in addition to the factors that may influence the Court's decision as to which it will apply in general terms. Clayton[196] commences his analysis by observing that the ECtHR has 'not identified a consistent or uniform set of principles when considering the doctrine of proportionality'.

However, it is generally agreed that there are three main types of proportionality test utilised by the ECtHR. The first and strictest of the three tests has been referred to by a number of authors albeit in slightly different forms. Arai-Takahashi,[197] Craig[198] and Harris *et al*[199] all identify a further test, which have in common the requirement upon the Court to answer the following question: is the disputed measure the least onerous/restrictive/intrusive that could be adopted in the circumstances? It should also be noted that, as

---

[193] The principle of proportionality will also apply in the following situations: where the Court assesses whether a State is entitled to derogate from the ECHR in a time of war or public emergency under Art 15; where the ECHR expressly allows a public authority to restrict Convention rights, eg under Art 5(3), under Art 12 or Art 1 of Protocol 1; where the doctrine of inherent limitations applies; where proportionality has defined the limits of positive obligations under the Convention; and where there is a finding of discrimination contrary to Art 14 because there is no reasonable relationship between the means employed and the aim to be realised. As noted by R Clayton, 'Regaining a Sense of Proportion' (n 188).

[194] HM Fenwick and G Phillipson, *Media Freedom* (n 82) argue that, in relation to Art 10, the proportionality test used will dictate the width of the margin.

[195] Y Arai-Takahashi, *The Margin of Appreciation* (n 68) 14.

[196] R Clayton, 'Regaining a Sense of Proportion' (n 188).

[197] Y Arai-Takahashi, *The Margin of Appreciation* (n 68) 88.

[198] P Craig, *Administrative Law* 4th edn (London, Sweet & Maxwell, 1999) 590. His second formulation involves asking the question: is the challenged act suitable and necessary for the achievement of its objective, and one that does not impose excessive burdens on the individual? This, he notes, is the most commonly used version of the test and requires the Court to ask three questions: whether the measure was necessary to achieve the desired objective, whether it was suitable for this end, and whether it none the less imposed excessive burdens on the individual. He terms this second version, 'proportionality stricto sensu' (in a strict sense) and further comments that 'it is important to realise that the tests can be applied more or less intensively'. This point relates, of course, to the margin of appreciation, the application of which has been discussed above. Note also that his analysis of proportionality is not limited to the ECHR.

[199] D Harris, M O'Boyle, E Bates and C Buckley (Harris, O'Boyle and Warbrick), *Law of the European Convention on Human Rights* 2nd edn (Oxford, Oxford University Press, 2009) identify three different uses of the proportionality test. First, a measure is disproportionate if it is not necessary. Second, the interference proposed is not proportionate if a less intrusive means of serving the legitimate aim exists but was not pursued. Third, a measure is not proportionate where the object of the interference cannot be achieved by the interference.

discussed at the beginning of this analysis, it is this version of the test that corresponds to the type of proportionality test used by other international courts. According to Craig,[200] this version is reserved for those cases where the disputed measure is in conflict with a fundamental right and is thus the most onerous test to satisfy. What is of some significance, therefore, is the fact that the Court has, on a number of occasions, applied this version of the test in relation to Article 8 claims outside the family law arena,[201] but, as of yet, has failed to apply the test inside it. As a result there are no examples that can be cited from the jurisprudence of the ECtHR in this regard. This is not the case, however, with the Commission, which as Arai-Takahashi[202] notes, *has* applied this version of the test with respect to family law cases, albeit on two occasions. First, in *Rasmussen v Denmark*,[203] an application which concerned time limits for paternity proceedings imposed upon husbands but not wives, the Commission suggested the Danish 'doctrine of acknowledgement' would have attained the same purpose as the time limiting legislation but with less harm to the interests of the putative father.[204] Secondly, in *Sheffield and Horsham v UK*[205] the Commission not only employed a stricter standard of review by employing, for the first time, the evolutive method of interpretation in relation to cases concerning the rights of transsexuals, but also implicitly employed the least restrictive alternative test in suggesting that rather than denying a change in the birth register outright some other way could be found to recognise the applicant's gender re-assignment:[206]

> The inability of the applicant to obtain legal recognition of her gender re-assignment derives from the principle in domestic law, established in the case of *Corbett v Corbett*, that sex is fixed immutably by conventional biological considerations as existing at the time of birth. It would appear that domestic law could, by whatever means it found appropriate, provide for transsexuals to be given prospective legal recognition of their gender re-assignment, without necessarily destroying the historical nature of the birth register as a record of the facts as perceived at that time.

Unfortunately for both claimants, the Court declined to follow the Commission's reasoning and, thus, the application of the least restrictive alternative test in both cases.

The second type of test used by the ECtHR represents a les stringent form of proportionality than that found in the 'least restrictive' test discussed above. For Clayton, however, the test represents the 'stricter formulation'[207] and the first of the two types of test that he considers are utilised by the ECtHR. He illustrates his term with reference to the *Sunday Times v United Kingdom*[208] case in which the Court set out the 'stricter'

---

[200] Whose analysis of proportionality is not limited to the ECtHR: P Craig, *Administrative Law* (n 198).

[201] Eg, in relation to the restrictions on prisoners' correspondence: (1993) *Campbell v UK* 15 EHRR 137 paras 52–3 and discriminatory treatment of homosexuals; see also *Lustig-Prean and Beckett v United Kingdom* (1999) 29 EHRR 548 para 95 and *Smith and Grady v the United Kingdom* Application Nos 33985/96 and 33986/96 (1999) 29 EHRR 493 para 102.

[202] Y Arai-Takahashi, *The Margin of Appreciation* (n 68) 88–9.

[203] *Rasmussen v Denmark* Application No 8777/79 (1985) 7 EHRR 371.

[204] *Rasmussen* (n 203) para 87.

[205] *Sheffield and Horsham* (n 107).

[206] *Ibid*, para 51.

[207] The stricter formulation, he argues, has been judged to be more appropriate where fundamental rights are at stake such as freedom of expression or intimate aspects of family life: R Clayton, 'Regaining a Sense of Proportion' (n 188). However, see a critique of this element of his analysis in HM Fenwick and G Phillipson, *Media Freedom* (n 82) 76.

[208] *Sunday Times* (n 5).

three-fold test: whether the interference complained of corresponded to a 'pressing social need'; whether it was 'proportionate to the legitimate aim pursued'; and whether the reasons given by the national authority to justify it were 'relevant and sufficient'. This formulation corresponds closely to Arai-Takahashi's 'sufficiency test'[209] where the Court will ask whether there exist both relevant and sufficient reasons justifying the interference at issue. According to Arai-Takahashi, assertion of this particular test in relation to Article 8 has led to three crucial steps.[210] First, a more scrupulous examination of the merits, second, the imposition of a higher evidentiary standard on Member States and, finally, the possibility of the reversal of the burden of proof which will require national authorities to adduce sufficiently convincing reasons for their obstructive actions. In sum, both authors argue that the 'stricter' or 'sufficiency' test represents a more stringent standard of review reserved for cases where fundamental rights are at stake and where the measures proposed are particularly restrictive.

In the family law context this analysis has proved correct; the 'sufficiency' standard has been utilised in cases where the proposed measures may have an irreversible effect upon family ties and, thus, the Court has applied this intense standard of review in a number of cases involving children being taken into care or adopted. Moreover, when applied, the standard will, seemingly, only be satisfied if the measures are regarded by the Court as being in the best interests of the children.[211] For example, in *Eski v Austria*,[212] a father's claim that the adoption of his child without his consent had breached his Article 8 rights was *not* upheld, despite the application of the sufficiency test, on the basis that the measure was regarded by the Court as being in the best interests of the child. Where the measures are not so regarded, the 'sufficiency' standard may not be met. In *Olssen v Sweden*[213] Mr and Mrs Olsson alleged, amongst other matters, that the care decision and the subsequent placement of their children constituted a breach of their Article 8 rights. The Court commenced its proportionality assessment with the following statement:[214]

> [I]n exercising its supervisory jurisdiction, the Court cannot confine itself to considering the impugned decisions in isolation, but must look at them in the light of the case as a whole; it must determine whether the reasons adduced to justify the interferences at issue are 'relevant and sufficient'.

The application of this stricter standard of review resulted in the Court finding that the measures taken in implementation of the care decision[215] were not supported by 'sufficient' reasons justifying them as proportionate to the legitimate aim pursued., Notwithstanding the domestic authorities' margin of appreciation, they were therefore not necessary in a

---

[209] Y Arai-Takahashi, *The Margin of Appreciation* (n 68) 87. He argues that the assertion of this test leads to the following: a more scrupulous examination of the merits, a higher evidentiary standard and the possibility of the reversal of the burden of proof.

[210] Y Arai-Takahashi, *The Margin of Appreciation* (n 68) 87–8.

[211] *Olsson No 1* (n 148) para 72: 'However, it is an interference of a very serious order to split up a family. Such a step must be supported by sufficiently sound and weighty considerations in the interests of the child.' See also *Johansen* (n 50) para 64.

[212] *Eski v Austria* [2007] 1 FLR 1650.

[213] *Olsson No 1* (n 148).

[214] *Ibid*, para 68.

[215] This standard of review also resulted in the Court finding against the applicants on the questions of the taking of the children into care and the refusal to terminate care.

democratic society. The 'sufficiency' standard applied in *Olssen* was later followed in *Johansen v Norway*[216] in which Ms Johansen complained that there had been a violation of her right to respect for family life on account of the order to take her daughter into public care, the subsequent deprivation of her parental rights and the termination of access to her daughter. The Court stated:[217]

> [T]he Court recognises that the authorities enjoy a wide margin of appreciation in assessing the necessity of taking a child into care. However, a stricter scrutiny is called for both of any further limitations, such as restrictions placed by those authorities on parental rights and access, and of any legal safeguards designed to secure an effective protection of the right of parents and children to respect for their family life. Such further limitations entail the danger that the family relations between the parents and a young child are effectively curtailed.

Having applied the 'sufficiency' standard against this background the Court found that a breach of the applicant's Article 8 rights had occurred in so far as the authorities had decided to deprive her of access and parental rights in respect of her daughter.[218] The Court has since adopted the 'sufficiency' standard of review in a number of subsequent care and adoption cases[219] as well as in private law cases involving custody.[220]

The third and final type of proportionality test used by the ECtHR represents the least strict standard of proportionality and is termed by Clayton[221] as the 'looser formulation'. Here, the Court asks whether there is a reasonable relationship between the interference and the legitimate aim pursued or a fair balance between the general and individual interests at stake. This formulation, he argues, is judged to be more appropriate for rights that are not regarded as so fundamental, such as property rights.[222] This is probably the most often used test of proportionality within the general family law context, often termed the 'fair balance test'. However, the greater use of it within family law cases that come before the ECtHR is not, it is submitted, due to the fact the rights concerned are not so fundamental. Few could argue, for example, that the right to marry[223] or to procreate[224] are not matters of fundamental importance. Yet, in both these examples, the ECtHR has chosen to apply the least strict standard of review that is available. As discussed above, in a number of cases involving transsexuals,[225] spanning more than two decades, the Court chose to apply the 'fair balance' test and repeatedly deferred to national decision making

---

[216] *Johansen* (n 50) para 64.

[217] *Ibid.*

[218] However, the Court found against her on her other claims concerning the conduct of the authorities.

[219] See *Kutzner v Germany* (2002) 35 EHRR 653 para 65; *Bronda v Italy* (2001) 33 EHRR 4 para 59; *Gnahoré v France* Application No 40031/98 (2002) 34 EHRR 38 para 54; *K and T v Finland* Application No 25702/94 (2000) 31 EHRR 18 para 154 and *Eski* (n 212) where the application of the sufficiency test resulted in the father's claim in relation to the adoption of his child without his consent *not* being upheld.

[220] See amongst others *C v Finland* (2008) 46 EHRR 24 para 52 where the applicant successfully complained that the Supreme Court wrongly overturned the judgments of two lower courts which had awarded him custody of his children. However, his claims that he was not given adequate contact with his children during the proceedings or any order for contact made after the proceedings were not upheld.

[221] R Clayton, 'Regaining a Sense of Proportion' (n 188).

[222] Eg *James v United Kingdom* (n 75); *Agosi v United Kingdom* (1986) 9 EHRR 1.

[223] Eg *Johnston* (n 26), *Rees* (n 15) and *F* (n 15).

[224] *Evans* (n 102) and *Dickson v UK* (2008) 46 EHRR 41.

[225] Eg *Cossey* (n 107), *Rees* (n 15) and *Sheffield and Horsham* (n 107), although note that in the latter case the Court refused to follow the Commission's change of approach to the standard of review by failing to apply a more intense standard of review.

with regard to claims concerning the changing of the birth register and the right to marry. The 'fair balance' test was also subsequently applied to the question of whether to grant parental rights to a transsexual *de facto* father of a child conceived by artificial insemination by donor.[226] It was only in 2002 that the Court finally departed from precedent and employed the evolutive method of interpretation as a means to undertake a more intense proportionality appraisal,[227] finding that such matters no longer fell within the State's margin of appreciation.[228]

With respect to the right to procreate, we have also seen that in the *Evans*[229] case the Court declined to apply a more strict standard of review in relation to the question whether the applicant should be allowed to use her fertilised embryos after the lawful withdrawal of consent by the sperm donor (her former partner), opting instead to apply a wide margin of appreciation and, thus, to apply the least onerous standard of review:[230] The Court stated:

> The Court accepts that it would have been possible for Parliament to regulate the situation differently. However, as the Chamber observed, the central question under Article 8 is not whether different rules might have been adopted by the legislature, but whether, in striking the balance at the point at which it did, Parliament exceeded the margin of appreciation afforded to it under that Article.

> The Grand Chamber considers that, given the lack of European consensus on this point, the fact that the domestic rules were clear and brought to the attention of the applicant and that they struck a fair balance between the competing interests, there has been no violation of Article 8 of the Convention.

In summary, we can conclude that it is highly likely that within the family law context, the most often-used proportionality test will be the least onerous—the 'fair balance test'. Further, the application of a more onerous standard of review—the 'sufficiency test'—is seemingly dependent upon the current policy considerations of the Court. Of particular note is the fact that the most onerous standard of review—the 'least restrictive alternative'—is yet to be applied by the court within the family law context and this has been the case even when the Commission has considered it to be appropriate.[231] This is of even more significance when we recall that this version of the test and, thus, the highest standard of review, also represents the form of proportionality test applied by other international courts. The ECtHR has thus, within the context of family law, *never* applied a test that is as rigorous as that of most of its international counterparts and, furthermore, even when it has applied the stricter 'sufficiency test' it will still generally be significantly less rigorous. There are two main reasons for this state of affairs. The first reason is provided by Phillipson and Fenwick in their analysis of Article 10 and relates to the apparent

---

[226] *X, Y and Z* (n 25) para 44.

[227] *Goodwin* (n 22) para 88: '[The Court] is not convinced therefore that the need to uphold rigidly the integrity of the historic basis of the birth registration system takes on the same importance in the current climate as it did in 1986.'

[228] *Ibid*, para 93: 'The Court finds that the respondent Government can no longer claim that the matter falls within their margin of appreciation, save as regards the appropriate means of achieving recognition of the right protected under the Convention.'

[229] *Evans* (n 102).

[230] *Ibid*, paras 91–2.

[231] *Rasmussen* (n 203) and *Sheffield and Horsham* (n 107).

unwillingness of the ECtHR to utilise the 'least restrictive alternative' test within the context of freedom of expression:[232]

> [T]he Strasbourg Court is an international court, policing adherence to an international treaty, often entered into by States without popular endorsement, and required to adjudicate upon claims arising from a bewildering variety of societies and legal systems. It is not surprising that it uses at times a much more restrained form of review than a national Constitutional court.

The second reason, it is argued, is due in large part to the application of the margin of appreciation. As detailed above, due to the variety of social and cultural considerations both within and between individual signatories to the Convention concerning family law, the nature of the cases are such that the State will usually be accorded a wide margin of appreciation. The accordance of a wide margin will, in turn, result in the Court applying the lowest standard of review, the 'fair balance test' and the deference to the national appreciation of the matter. However, as we have seen, this will only be the case if the measures concerned do not relate to an area of family law which the Court views as requiring a particularly strict standard of review. Thus, it is those measures which hold particularly serious consequences, such as the severance of family ties and where an overall European consensus on the matter cannot be ignored, that have been held[233] to merit such treatment.

---

[232]   HM Fenwick and G Phillipson, *Media Freedom* (n 82) ch 2, 93.

[233]   For example, Strasbourg's willingness to apply a strict standard of review on matters concerning differential treatment against illegitimate children. See amongst others *Marckx v Belgium* [1979] 2 EHRR 330 para 41 and *Johnston* (n 26) para 40.

2

The Human Rights Act: Scheme, Principles and Implementation

The United Kingdom played a major part in drafting the ECHR and was among the first group of countries to sign the Convention. It was also the first country to ratify it[1] and in 1966 the United Kingdom enabled individuals to bring a case directly against the Government to Strasbourg. However, at the time of ratification it was felt that it was not necessary to write the Convention itself into British law, or to introduce any new laws in the United Kingdom in order to be sure of being able to comply with the Convention.[2] This view prevailed until 1997[3] and at this time all but two of the signatories to the Convention, bar the United Kingdom, had incorporated it into their domestic law.[4] The case for incorporation was based on two grounds. First, it was noted that by not fully incorporating the Convention, access to the rights contained in the Convention were, in practice, costly and difficult to pursue. The Government's introduction to the Bill noted that 'it takes on average five years to get an action into the European Court of Human Rights once all domestic remedies have been exhausted; and it costs an average of £30,000 only after a considerable length of time and at considerable expense'.[5] Second, the number of cases in which the European Commission and Court had found that there had been violations of the Convention rights in the United Kingdom[6] indicated, in the Government's view, that the approach which the United Kingdom has so far adopted towards the Convention had not sufficiently reflected its importance.[7]

The time had come, therefore, 'to enable people to enforce their Convention rights against the State in the British courts',[8] and the aim was even clearer, 'to bring those rights home'.[9] Significantly, the future role of the UK judiciary was also seen as being a major motivation towards incorporation. Noting the high reputation of the UK judiciary the Government stated that:[10]

It will also mean that the rights will be brought much more fully into the jurisprudence of the courts throughout the United Kingdom, and their interpretation will thus be far more subtly and

---

[1] In March 1951.

[2] It was felt that the rights and freedoms which the Convention guarantees were already, in substance, fully protected in British law.

[3] When the Labour Government presented the Human Rights Bill to Parliament. 'Rights Brought Home: The Human Rights Bill' 1997 CM 3872.

[4] Ireland, which had its own Bill of Rights, and Norway, which was in the process of incorporation.

[5] Secretary of State for the Home Department, Introduction to 'Rights Brought Home: The Human Rights Bill' 1997 CM 3872, ch 2, para 1.14.

[6] The number of Court judgments given against the United Kingdom, at 38, is second only to Italy (at 85).

[7] SSHD, 'Rights Brought Home' (n 5) ch 2, para 1.16.

[8] *Ibid*, ch 2, para 1.18.

[9] *Ibid*, ch 2, para 1.19.

[10] *Ibid*, ch 2, para 1.14.

powerfully woven into our law. And there will be another distinct benefit. British judges will be enabled to make a distinctively British contribution to the development of the jurisprudence of human rights in Europe.

Two further aims of the Government in the passage of the Bill have also since been identified,[11] 'to improve awareness of human rights issues throughout our society'[12] and 'to enable individuals to use the UK courts to prevent and remedy the misuse of public power'.[13] It should be noted, however, that although the HRA is based on the Convention it does not fully 'incorporate' the Convention in full. The rights that are given effect under the HRA are listed in section 1 and set out in Schedule 1.[14]

In the run-up to the implementation of the HRA Sir Stephen Sedley[15] noted that a number of issues remained unresolved. The issues in the list that have most exercised academics within the field of human rights have undoubtedly been the doctrine of 'horizontal effect',[16] the domestic impact of positive obligations upon the State, the issue of judicial deference[17] and its relationship to the margin of appreciation doctrine[18] and who or what constitutes a 'public authority' under section 6 of the HRA.[19] All four of these issues, in addition to the discussion[20] surrounding the exact scope of the interpretative duty contained in

---

[11] F Klug and K Starmer, 'Standing Back From the HRA: How Effective is it Five Years On?' [2005] 4 *PL* 716.

[12] Lord Irvine, 'A Culture of Awareness of Human Rights Will Develop' [1997] 582 Hansard, HL, col 1228.

[13] Jack Straw MP and Paul Boateng MP, 'Bringing Rights Home: Labour's Plans to Incorporate the ECHR into UK Law' (Labour Party Consultation Document, 1996) 8, the text of which is published in [1997] *European Human Rights Law Review* 71.

[14] These are: Arts 2–12, 14 and 16–18 of the Convention, Arts 1–3 of the First Protocol and Arts 1 and 2 of the Sixth Protocol.

[15] K Starmers, *European Human Rights Law: the Human Rights Act and the European Convention on Human Rights* (London, Legal Action Group, 1999) Introductory chapter. These were: the relation between the supranational and domestic margins of appreciation; the status of commercial speech under Art 10; the relevance of the Convention to environmental protection; the horizontal applicability of rights; the positive obligations of States; the role of the courts themselves as public authorities; improperly obtained evidence; equality as a free-standing right and the impact of Art 8 on immigration and asylum and on child protection.

[16] The obligation upon the state to protect a private individual's Convention rights against infringement by other private individuals. For an overview of the general debate on 'horizontal effect' see G Phillipson, 'The Human Rights Act, the Common Law and "Horizontal Effect": a Bang or a Whimper?' (1999) 62 (6) *MLR* 824; G Phillipson, 'Clarity Postponed: Horizontal Effect After *Campbell* and *Re S*' in H Fenwick, G Phillipson and R Masterman, *Judicial Reasoning under the Human Rights Act* (Cambridge, Cambridge University Press, 2007) 143.

[17] Akin to the margin of appreciation doctrine but will come into play at the domestic level and to which courts will defer when reviewing the decisions of other public authorities. For a comprehensive discussion, see RA Edwards, 'Judicial Deference under the Human Rights Act' (2002) 65 (6) *MLR* 859. See also *R (Pro Life Alliance) v BBC* [2004] 1 AC 185.

[18] The degree of recognition by the ECtHR of the fact that states are better placed to make the primary judgment as to the needs of the parties involved and the appropriate balance to be struck between them.

[19] See generally D Oliver, 'The Frontiers of the State: Public Authorities and Public Functions Under the HRA' [2000] *PL* 476; M McDermont, 'The Elusive Nature of the "Public Function": *Poplar Housing and Regeneration Community Association Ltd v Donoghue*' (2003) 66 (1) *MLR* 113; J Morgan 'The Alchemist's Search for the Philosopher's Stone: the Status of Registered Social Landlords under the Human Rights Act' (2003) 66 (5) *MLR* 700; P Cane, 'Church, state and human rights: are parish councils public authorities?' (2004) 120 *LQR* 41.

[20] A Kavanagh, 'Unlocking the Human Rights Act: The "Radical" Approach to Section 2(1) Revisited' [2005] 3 *European Human Rights Law Review* 259; D Rose and C Weir, 'Interpretation and Incompatibility: Striking the Balance' in J Jowell and J Cooper (eds), *Delivering Rights* (Oxford, Hart Publishing, 2003); D Nichol, 'Statutory Interpretation and Human Rights After *Anderson*' [2004] *PL* 273; A Kavanagh, 'Statutory Interpretation and Human Rights After *Anderson*: A More Contextual Approach' [2004] *PL* 537; C Gearty, 'Revisiting Section 3(1) of the Human Rights Act' [2003] 119 *LQR* 551 and C Gearty, 'Reconciling Parliamentary Democracy and Human Rights' [2002] 118 *LQR* 248.

section 3(1) of the HRA, continue to be subject to some debate post-implementation and hold particular relevance to family law. The applicability of the horizontal effect doctrine to family law has long been recognised by the ECtHR[21] in respect of positive obligations and should thus provide a good opportunity for its application to family law legislation post-incorporation of the HRA. The scope of the margin of appreciation doctrine and the related issue of judicial deference[22] will vary depending on the Convention rights in play[23] and thus, as discussed in Chapter 1, will be wider when the Convention is applied to questions concerning domestic social policy, particularly in relation to Article 8—the right to respect for the home, private and family life. Legislation on these areas is therefore ripe for interpretation under section 3(1). Finally, the issue of the meaning of a public authority under the HRA should be of particular relevance to the public law elements of family law in terms of the contracting out of children and adult services to private care homes or charities by local authorities.[24]

One would assume, therefore, that the impact of the HRA upon family law would have been quite significant. However, to date, there have been just two declarations of incompatibility[25] in cases concerning family law despite evidence of the significant impact that HRA arguments can have in such cases.[26] Further, many areas of family law have remained largely unaffected by the HRA. These include the removal of children into care and adoption, the maintenance of the 'welfare principle'[27] and the continuance of legislative schemes which maintain differences in treatment between cohabitants and married couples with regard to protection from violence (Family Law Act 1996) and the division of property (Matrimonial Causes Act 1973). If we contrast this with the impact of the HRA generally we can see these statistics in further context. As the Lord Chancellor's 'Review of the Implementation of the HRA' of July 2006 notes:[28]

> No overall statistics are available but the comprehensive *Casetrack* database of appellate cases shows 552 cases under the 'human rights' classification over this period, being approximately 2% of the total number of cases determined by these courts. The highest density of HRA cases is in the House of Lords, concentrating as it does on new issues of principle. The HRA has been substantively considered in about one-third of the 354 cases which the House decided in this period and could be said to have substantially affected the result in about one-tenth of those cases.

We will now turn to an examination of the main areas of debate concerning the implementation of the HRA and their relevance to family law, now and in the future.

---

[21] Eg *Hokkanen v Finland* (1994) 19 EHRR 139.

[22] For a comprehensive discussion, see RA Edwards, 'Judicial Deference' (n 17).

[23] *Johansen v Norway* (1996) 23 EHRR 33, 64.

[24] *R (On the Application of Heather and Others) v Leonard Cheshire Foundation and Another* [2002] 2 All ER 936.

[25] On restricting the rights of those subject to immigration control to enter into a civil marriage: *R (Baiai) v Home Secretary* [2006] EWHC 1111 and provisions preventing a transsexual from marrying: *Bellinger v Bellinger* [2003] 2 AC 467.

[26] On the existence and scope of the courts' inherent jurisdiction to restrain publicity in cases relating to children: *Re S* [2005] 1 AC 593 and the rejection of the Court of Appeal's starring of care plans under s3 of the HRA: *Re S (Minors) (Care Order: Implementation of Case Plan)* [2002] AC 291.

[27] Contained in s1 of the CA. According to that section the child's welfare is the paramount consideration whenever the court is asked to determine the upbringing of a child or the administration of a child's property or the application of any income arising from it.

[28] Department of Constitutional Affairs, 'Review of the Implementation of the HRA' (DCA, 2006) 10.

Section 2: Taking Strasbourg Jurisprudence into Account

Section 2 provides:

> A court or tribunal determining a question which has arisen in connection with a Convention right *must take into account* any:
>
> (a) judgment, decision, declaration or advisory opinion of the European Court of Human Rights ...[29]
>
> whenever made or given, so far as, in the opinion of the court or tribunal, it is relevant to the proceedings in which that question has arisen (emphasis added).

Principles

This section raises a number of points, not least the question of how far the courts should take ECtHR jurisprudence into account. In addition, although the section imposes a duty upon on the courts to consider such jurisprudence the lack of a *stare decisis* system within the Strasbourg jurisprudence has made it difficult to determine how exactly domestic courts should determine which cases and principles of the ECtHR have been established enough to follow.[30] Despite these difficulties a number of principles concerning the application of section 2 have been established. First, in the absence of special circumstances, any 'clear and constant' jurisprudence of the ECtHR should be followed.[31] Dicta in a number of cases have given the following as examples of what may constitute special circumstances: where ECtHR reasoning is 'unpersuasive',[32] where the ECtHR has misunderstood an aspect of English law[33] or where the result of the jurisprudence would 'compel a conclusion fundamentally at odds with the distribution of powers under the British constitution'.[34] Second, the duty to take into account Strasbourg jurisprudence does not require the case law of the ECtHR to be followed in the ordinary common law sense. To do so would not only be inappropriate (given the lack of precedent within the ECtHR system) but also highly undesirable, given the need to ensure that the 'living instrument' nature of the Convention is respected and applied. Thus, the courts will rely primarily on the *principles* that have emerged from Convention case law, the relevance of which can be determined by evidence of a clear and constant line of reasoning:

> It is the duty of this court, while considering the interpretation of the Convention, to have regard to the decisions in the European Court of Human Rights ... These decisions, however, are not to be

[29] And also: (b) opinion of the Commission given in a report adopted under Article 31 of the Convention, (c) decision of the Commission in connection with Article 26 or 27(2) of the Convention, or (d) decision of the Committee of Ministers taken under Article 46 of the Convention.

[30] R Masterman, generally in 'Section 2(1) of the HRA 1998: Binding Domestic Courts to Strasbourg' (2004) *PL* 725 and 'The Status of Strasbourg Jurisprudence in Domestic Law' in H Fenwick, G Phillipson and R Masterman, *Judicial Reasoning After the HRA* (n 16).

[31] *Alconbury Developments Ltd v Secretary of State for the Environment Transport and Regions* [2001] UKHL 23. Lord Slynn stated: 'Although the Human Rights Act 1998 does not provide that a national court is bound by these decisions [of the ECtHR] it is obliged to take account of them so far as they are relevant. In the absence of some special circumstances it seems to me that the court should follow any clear and constant jurisprudence of the European Court of Human Rights. If it does not do so there is at least a possibility that the case will go to that court which is likely in the ordinary case to follow its own constant jurisprudence.'

[32] *R v Spear* [2002] 1 AC 734 para 12 (Lord Bingham).

[33] *R v Lyons* [2003] 1 AC 976 para 46 (Lord Hoffman).

[34] *Alconbury Developments Ltd v Secretary of State for the Environment Transport and Regions* [2001] UKHL 23 para 76 (Lord Hoffman).

treated in the same way as precedents in our own law. Insofar as principles can be extracted from these decisions, those are the principles which will have to be applied.[35]

The ability to draw on principles rather than simply applying precedent has also raised the related question of whether section 2 allows domestic courts to give a more generous interpretation to the scope of a Convention right than that given by Strasbourg. Although the predominant view amongst the judiciary currently appears to be that it does not, there is nonetheless some evidence of disagreement on the point which can be seen from a significant number of dicta either supporting the maximisation of human rights protection or, conversely going against it.[36] The origins of this debate, as Masterman[37] has argued, may be traced back to differing conceptions of the judicial role under the HRA and the resultant constitutional implications for the separation of powers doctrine which, although extremely interesting, are beyond the scope of this discussion. What is certainly clear, and beyond judicial dispute, is that domestic courts are not able to provide *less* protection than that which has been afforded by Strasbourg. Thus as Lord Bingham put it in *R (on the Application of Ullah) v Special Adjudicator*:[38]

> [I]t follows that a national court subject to a duty such as that imposed by s 2 should not without strong reason dilute or weaken the effect of the Strasbourg case law. It is indeed unlawful under s 6 of the HRA for a public authority, including a court, to act in a way which is incompatible with a Convention right. It is of course open to Member States to provide for rights more generous than those guaranteed by the Convention, but such provision should not be the product of interpretation of the Convention by national courts, since the meaning of the Convention should be uniform throughout the States party to it. The duty of national courts is to keep pace with the Strasbourg jurisprudence as it evolves over time: no more, but certainly no less.

If domestic courts are unable to either fall behind Strasbourg or go beyond it then the effect of this so-called 'mirror principle'[39] will, as Masterman[40] predicted, be to rewrite section 2 so as to bind domestic courts to Strasbourg, save where the so-called 'special circumstances' apply. There are a number of disadvantages to such an approach. Apart from the fact that it precludes UK courts going further than Strasbourg and developing their own indigenous human rights jurisprudence, as will be discussed below, there are also problems in following the Strasbourg Court's approach because, as Clayton[41] suggests, it does not develop its principles in the 'careful analytical style of the common law'.[42] Further, the fact that Strasbourg jurisprudence takes precedence over any other comparative jurisprudence[43] may mean that UK courts will be unable to take into account the 'valuable insights from the reasoning of Commonwealth judges deciding issues under different human rights instruments'.[44]

---

[35] *Clancy v Caird* (2000) SLT 546 para 3 (Lord Sutherland). See also *R (on the application of Al-Hasan v Sec of State for the Home Department* [2002] 1 WLR 545, 566 (Lord Woolf); *Runa Begum v Tower Hamlet LBC* [2002] 2 All ER 668 para 17 (Laws LJ) and *R (on the application of Prolife Alliance) v BBC* [2002] 2 All ER 756 para 33–4 (Laws LJ).

[36] R Masterman, 'The Status of Strasbourg Jurisprudence' (n 30) for an excellent summary.

[37] *Ibid.*

[38] *R (on the Application of Ullah) v Special Adjudicator* [2004] UKHL 26 para 20.

[39] As termed by J Lewis, 'The European Ceiling on Human Rights' [2007] 4 *PL* 720.

[40] R Masterman, 'Section 2(1) of the Human Rights Act 1998' (n 30) 726.

[41] R Clayton, 'The Human Rights Act Six Years On: Where Are We Now?' [2007] *European Human Rights Law Review* 11, 18.

[42] *Ibid.*

[43] *Ibid.*

[44] *Sheldrake v DPP* [2004] UKHL 43 para 33 (Lord Bingham).

Judicial justifications for adopting the 'mirror' principle have varied. First, the need for the Convention to be uniformly understood by all Member States,[45] secondly the fact that Strasbourg has a 'deeper appreciation of the true ambit and reach'[46] of the relevant Convention rights and thirdly, the doctrine of comity: where Strasbourg is to re-examine a line of cases 'it would seem somewhat presumptuous for us, in effect, to pre-empt the decision'.[47] However, these justifications are in turn open to question. As Lewis[48] has pointed out, any departure by a domestic court from the Strasbourg interpretation of an Article would only have a bearing on the municipal right contained in the HRA; the Convention right would remain untouched. Further, using the doctrine of comity and Strasbourg's greater appreciation of Convention rights as a justification for interpreting the Convention uniformly blurs the distinction between the domestic interpretation of the rights. This is because the two concepts perform different functions: the doctrine of the margin of appreciation concerns the *application* of a Convention right and the 'mirror principle' concerns its *interpretation*. Their co-existence thus 'hinges upon there being a clear cut distinction'[49] between the two. This, therefore further defeats the very aim of the HRA, which was to bring these rights home.[50]

Application

Although the principles set out in *Ullah*[51] have largely been followed it is also clear that the courts have not felt themselves bound by them. There have been a number of cases where Strasbourg has not been followed and either the 'special circumstances' being cited by the courts have not been particularly convincing[52] or there has simply been no real explanation or justification given. A recent illustration of this approach is the recent House of Lords decision in *R (on the application of Animal Defenders International) v Secretary of State for Culture, Media and Sport*[53] where their Lordships sidestepped fairly clear Strasbourg authority which went against their finding that the statutory ban on 'political' advertising on UK radio and television was compatible with the right to freedom of expression under Article 10 of the ECHR. This was despite the fact that this was an area in which the ECtHR had granted a limited margin of appreciation to Member States and concerned legislation where the Minister concerned had made a statement under section 19(1)(b) of the HRA to the effect that she was *unable* to make a statement of Convention compatibility. There have also been a number of instances where the courts have attracted significant criticism for

---

[45] *Kay v Lambeth LBC* [2006] UKHL 10 para 44 (Lord Bingham); *Anderson R (on the application of Anderson) v Secretary of State for the Home Department* [2002] UKHL 46 para 89 (Buxton LJ).

[46] *Anderson* (n 45) para 65.

[47] *Ibid*, para 66. That is not to say that there is no academic support for such a stance. Aileen Kavanagh is largely in agreement: A Kavanagh, *Constitutional Review under the UK Human Rights Act* (Cambridge, Cambridge University Press, 2009) 153.

[48] J Lewis, 'The European Ceiling on Human Rights' [2007] 4 *PL* 720.

[49] *Ibid*, 738.

[50] *Ibid*, 738.

[51] *Ullah* (n 38).

[52] See the discussion in ch 9, pp 387–94 concerning the line of case law on the applicability of Strasbourg principles to the question of the right to respect for the home under Art 8 and domestic housing law.

[53] *R (on the application of Animal Defenders International) v Secretary of State for Culture, Media and Sport* [2008] UKHL 15. On this see also T Lewis and P Cumper, 'Balancing Freedom of Political Expression Against Equality of Political Opportunity: The Courts and the UK's Broadcasting Ban on Political Advertising' [2009] 1 *PL* 89.

employing a highly selective reading of Strasbourg jurisprudence[54] in order to achieve the desired result. This has been particularly evident in the family law field. Thus, as Loveland argues, in *Ghaidan v Mendoza*,[55] the Court of Appeal demonstrated that it was not engaging in a properly reasoned discussion and evaluation of the pertinent Strasbourg authorities when it chose to ignore a clear line of Strasbourg jurisprudence which went *against* the recognition of same-sex partnerships to find that the gay applicant could be regarded as the former spouse of the deceased tenant in order to succeed to his statutory tenancy. This interpretation of the law was later to be upheld by the House of Lords.[56] However, in direct contrast, in its later decision of *M v Secretary of State for Work and Pensions*,[57] the House chose to adhere to the very same Strasbourg jurisprudence that the Court of Appeal resisted in *Ghaidan*,[58] this time to find against the applicant. The case concerned the compatibility of child support regulations which, unlike in the case of heterosexual parents, did not allow the pooling of the absent parent's income and outgoings with those of his or her new same-sex partner. The claim was primarily based upon Article 14 but relied upon the claim being brought within Article 8 or Protocol No 1 Article 1.[59] In terms of Article 8 the key question was whether a same-sex couple could constitute a 'family'. The House of Lords held that they could not. With only Lady Hale dissenting, both Lord Bingham and Lord Mance were clear in their opinion that the relationship between M and her female partner did not qualify as 'family life' under the case law of the European Court and Commission. However, in considering the same question, it was Lord Nicholls who illustrated some of the difficulties surrounding the application of the mirror principle under section 2 outlined above. In conceding that the decisions in *Fitzpatrick v Sterling Housing Association*[60] and *Ghaidan*[61] pointed 'irresistibly' to the conclusion that under the law of this country 'a same sex couple are as much capable of constituting a 'family' as a heterosexual couple'[62] he nevertheless went on to find that the context within which this question arose was in relation to Article 8 of the ECHR. This was due to the fact that the concept of family life in Article 8 is an 'autonomous' Convention concept having the same meaning in all Contracting States, which he considered 'does not embrace same sex partners'.[63] As a result:

[T]he House will not depart from a decision of the ECtHR on the interpretation of an article in the Convention save for good reason. It goes without saying that it would be highly undesirable

---

[54] Eg the Court of Appeal's decision in *Ghaidan v Mendoza* [2004] 2 AC 557 and the House of Lords' decision in *Qazi v London Borough of Harrow* [2003] UKHL 43. See Ian Loveland's excellent account of how both courts in these two cases failed to follow a clear line of Strasbourg jurisprudence in I Loveland, 'Making It Up as They Go Along? The Court of Appeal on Same-Sex Spouses and Succession Rights on Tenancies' [2003] 2 *PL* 223 and I Loveland, 'The Impact of the Human Rights Act on Security of Tenure in Public Housing' [2004] 3 *PL* 594.

[55] *Ghaidan* (n 54).

[56] *Ghaidan* [2004] UKHL 30.

[57] *M v Secretary of State for Work and Pensions* [2006] UKHL 11.

[58] *Ghaidan* (n 54) (AC).

[59] Art 1 protects the right to property and states: 'Every natural or legal person is entitled to the peaceful enjoyment of his possessions. No one shall be deprived of his possessions except in the public interest and subject to the conditions provided for by law and by the general principles of international law. The preceding provisions shall not, however, in any way impair the right of a State to enforce such laws as it deems necessary to control the use of property in accordance with the general interest or to secure the payment of taxes or other contributions or penalties.' See ch 9 for a detailed discussion of the principles established under this provision by Strasbourg.

[60] *Fitzpatrick v Sterling Housing Association* [2001] 1 AC 21.

[61] *Ghaidan* (n 56) (HL).

[62] *M* (n 57) para 23.

[63] *Ibid*, para 24.

for the courts of this country, when giving effect to Convention rights, to be out of step with the Strasbourg interpretation of the relevant Convention article.[64]

The discrepancy with *Ghaidan*[65] could, as Lewis[66] has argued, be explained by the fact that that case turned on the respect for a home element, where Strasbourg jurisprudence had not placed any obstacles for a surviving same-sex spouse succeeding to a tenancy of a flat, as opposed to the private and family life element in *M*, where Strasbourg jurisprudence against the inclusion of a same-sex couple within the definition of a 'family' was in existence. Nevertheless these cases demonstrate one of the disadvantages of a strict adherence to the mirror principle, namely that a same-sex couple will have to wait until a clear line of principle with regard to family life has developed in their favour at Strasbourg rather than waiting for a UK court to have the courage to develop its own take on this aspect of Article 8.

That is not to say that the courts have always been unwilling to go further than Strasbourg. In the recent decision of *Re P (A Child) (Adoption; Unmarried Couples)*[67] the appellants, P and F, an unmarried heterosexual couple, appealed against a decision rejecting them as prospective adoptive parents. P and F had been living together for more than 10 years and wished to adopt a 10-year-old child of whom P was the natural mother. P and F submitted that Article 14 of the Adoption (Northern Ireland) Order 1987, which restricted the eligibility to be considered as adoptive parents to married couples or single people, contravened their rights to respect for family life under Article 8 taken in conjunction with Article 14 of the Convention. The case raised a number of issues, not least the rather complicated point of the constitutional position of Northern Ireland and whether the courts ought to defer to the legislature in cases such as this, which concern sensitive issues of social policy. This aspect of the case will be discussed in relation to the consideration of judicial deference in general; however, the case was also extremely significant for their Lordships' treatment of the relevant Strasbourg jurisprudence concerning both Article 14 and Article 8. On the question of whether not being married was a 'status' within the meaning of Article 14,[68] their Lordships were unanimous. It was, they said, clear that being married was a status and therefore it must follow that not being married was also a status within the meaning of Article 14. The question was therefore whether unequal treatment between unmarried and married couples could be justified. Their Lordships then turned to an examination of any relevant Strasbourg case law in order to abide by their duty to take it into account under section 2 of the HRA. Noting that no case had yet reached Strasbourg on the issue of discrimination that the case raised, their Lordships went on to consider analogous cases concerning discrimination against

---

[64] *Ibid*, para 29.

[65] *Ghaidan* (n 56) (HL).

[66] J Lewis, 'The European Ceiling' (n 48) 736.

[67] *Re P (A Child) (Adoption; Unmarried Couples)* [2008] UKHL 38.

[68] Art 14 of the ECHR provides that the 'enjoyment of the rights and freedoms set forth in this Convention shall be secured without discrimination on any ground such as sex, race, colour, language, religion, political or other opinion, national or social origin, association with a national minority, property, birth or other *status*' (emphasis added). When assessing what may come within 'other status' the Court has reiterated that Art 14 'is not concerned with all difference of treatment but only with differences having as their basis or reason a personal characteristic by which persons or group of persons are distinguishable from each other': *Jones v UK* Application No 42639/04 ECHR 13 December 2005. See also ch 4 pp 4–5 for a discussion of the main principles that must be followed with respect to this Article.

homosexuals in adoption. Although the decision in *Fretté v France*[69] had, by a narrow majority, not found a prohibition against homosexuals adopting a child to be a breach of Article 14, the later, more recent, decision in *EB v France*[70] which concerned an application to adopt by a single homosexual woman had, their Lordships said, effectively overruled the decision by taking the opposite view in finding that, this time, a breach of Article 14 had occurred. This decision therefore pointed strongly in favour of the view that discrimination on the grounds of marital status in this area of the law generally requires strong justification.[71] Further, their Lordships said that the question of what would happen if Strasbourg were to revert to its position in *Fretté*[72] should make no difference to the duty of the courts under section 2 of the HRA.[73] This was because the limitations imposed on the courts' ability to go further than Strasbourg with regard to the meaning and scope of a Convention right in *Ullah*[74] were not, according to Lord Hoffman, made in the context of a case in which the Strasbourg Court has declared a question to be within the national margin of appreciation.[75] Where such a situation arose the question thus became one 'for the national authorities to decide for themselves and it follows that different Member States may well give different answers'.[76] Further, Convention rights within the meaning of the HRA were domestic and not international rights and in the interpretation of those domestic rights the UK courts had to take into account the decisions of the European Court but were not bound by such decisions.[77] Their Lordships thus concluded that in a case where Strasbourg had deliberately declined to lay down an interpretation for all Contracting States, by holding that the issue was within the margin of appreciation, it was for the courts in the UK to interpret Article 8 and Article 14 of the Convention and to apply the division between the decision-making powers of courts and Parliament in a way which appeared appropriate for the UK.[78] It followed that the House of Lords was free to give what it considered to be a principled and rational interpretation to the concept of discrimination on grounds of marital status.[79] The House of Lords therefore declared that, notwithstanding Article 14 of the 1987 Order, P and F were entitled to apply to adopt the child; it was unlawful for the Family Division of the High Court of Justice in Northern Ireland to reject P and F as prospective parents on the ground only that they were not married. The decision has therefore not only equalised the position for unmarried adopters in Northern Ireland with the rest of England and Wales but it has also created a further exception to the 'no more but no less' rule in *Ullah*.[80] Domestic courts are thus, it would seem, now free to interpret municipal human rights law as protecting interests where Strasbourg has left it within the States' margin of appreciation. In addition, as Feldman

[69] *Fretté v France* (2004) 38 EHRR 438.
[70] *EB v France* (2008) 47 EHRR 21.
[71] *Re P* (n 67) paras 20–6 (Lord Hoffman), paras 50–6 (Lord Hope) and paras 136–43 (Lord Mance). However, note that Baroness Hale did not think it was by any means clear that this would be the case, para 115.
[72] *Fretté* (n 69).
[73] *Re P* (n 67) para 30 (Lord Hoffman).
[74] *Ullah* (n 38).
[75] *Re P* (n 67) para 31 (Lord Hoffman).
[76] *Ibid*, para 31 (Lord Hoffman).
[77] *Ibid*, para 33 (Lord Hoffman).
[78] *Ibid*, para 37 (Lord Hoffman) and paras 128–30 (Lord Mance).
[79] *Ibid*, para 38 (Lord Hoffman).
[80] *Ullah* (n 38).

notes, it is certainly arguable that the same could be said where Strasbourg is yet to rule on an issue.[81]

What has been of most concern, however, about the approach of the family law courts to section 2, has been the failure to incorporate and properly apply the standard Strasbourg methods of rights adjudication when confronted with disputes concerning competing Convention rights, particularly those that are qualified.[82] This has been particularly marked in relation to disputes under the Children Act and the application of the paramountcy principle which, as one of the authors has discussed elsewhere,[83] gives rise to significant compatibility issues with Convention case law. In the majority of cases (although there are some exceptions) Article 8 is either not mentioned, touched upon in an imprecise and superficial manner or, even worse, misunderstood.[84] There is also evidence of a highly selective use of ECtHR jurisprudence[85] in order to avoid issues of incompatibility. We will return to this issue in subsequent chapters when considering the impact of the ECHR and the HRA on the law relating to children.

Section 3: Statutory Interpretation under the HRA

Section 3(1) of the HRA provides that:

> [S]o far as it is possible to do so, primary legislation and subordinate legislation must be read and given effect in a way which is compatible with the Convention rights.[86]

This section is complemented by section 4, which provides that if a Convention-compatible reading of legislation is impossible, then the courts can issue a 'declaration of incompatibility'. However, it should be noted that a declaration of incompatibility does not affect the validity, continuing operation or enforcement of the provision in respect of which it is given. Its effect is simply that it triggers the power to use the 'fast track' procedure to take remedial action to remove the incompatibility under section 10,[87] although this action

---

[81] D Feldman, 'Adoption and Discrimination: What Are Convention Rights?' (2008) 67 (3) *CLJ* 481.

[82] Although see also T Poole, 'The Reformation of English Administrative Law' (2009) 68 (1) *CLJ* 142 at 166 for an argument against this approach within the context of judicial review on the basis that it would lead to a 'formalist and proceduralist jurisprudence'.

[83] S Choudhry, 'The Adoption and Children Act 2002, the Welfare Principle and the HRA 1998—a Missed Opportunity' (2003) 15 (2) *Child and Family Law Quarterly* 119 and S Choudhry and H Fenwick, 'Clashing Rights, the Welfare of the Child and the Human Rights Act 1998' (2005) 25 *OJLS* 453.

[84] *Payne v Payne* [2001] Fam 473 at 487 (Thorpe LJ).

[85] *Re S (A Child)* [2004] WL 62115, paras 15, 27.

[86] Section 3(2) states: 'This section (a) applies to primary legislation and subordinate legislation whenever enacted; (b) does not affect the validity, continuing operation or enforcement of any incompatible primary legislation; and (c) does not affect the validity, continuing operation or enforcement of any incompatible subordinate legislation if (disregarding any possibility of revocation) primary legislation prevents removal of the incompatibility.'

[87] Section 10 of the HRA provides a discretionary power for the relevant Minister to make a remedial order to amend or repeal the infringing legislation. Section 10(2) of the Act provides that this power can only be used where the Minister decides that there is a compelling case for action. A resolution giving effect to such a remedial order must receive the approval of both the House of Commons and the House of Lords. This process can also be used where a Minister takes the view that legislation is incompatible with Convention rights as a result of a decision of the European Court of Human Rights, but only in respect of decisions which the Court has made after s10 came into force.

may only be taken if the relevant minister considers that there are compelling reasons to do so.

The Interpretative Task

It is clear that the terms of section 3(1) provide a strong mandate for the judiciary to reinterpret legislation and even quite radically where required. As a result, section 3(1) has had powerful constitutional implications, not least in terms of the separation of powers doctrine. On the one hand 'constitutionalists' would argue that the HRA has, in effect, vindicated their position—that legal systems are permeated with certain core constitutional values and judges are entrusted, in the main, with the protection of these values. As a result, the judiciary ought to carry out their interpretative obligation under section 3(1) to its maximum effect wherever possible and section 4 should only be used in the last resort.[88] In contrast, critics of the constitutionalist position point to a number of concerns around the nature of the judiciary as a basis for questioning the democratic legitimacy of judicial power and thus any expansion of the judges' interpretative power under the HRA.[89] It is argued, therefore, that the preservation of parliamentary sovereignty should be prioritised by, for example, allowing section 4 of the Act to play a more significant role in determining the limits of interpretative possibility under section 3(1).[90] The question of what constitutes the proper boundaries between legislation and interpretation and how judges ought to approach their duty under section 3(1) is thus of huge constitutional importance. Kavanagh[91] argues that judges must engage in a dual process of evaluation under the HRA. First, judges ought to consider the moral import and meaning of the substantive issues to which the Convention refers—the 'substantive' evaluation; second, they must decide how far they are able to go in terms of achieving a Convention-compatible interpretation—the 'interpretative' evaluation. Further, the interpretative task will require judges not only to apply the existing law but also to develop and improve it.[92] Judicial interpretation will thus always have an applicative *and* a creative aspect. As a result, Parliament must have sanctioned the use of judicial discretion to flesh out the contents of the indeterminate provisions of the HRA in individual cases.[93]

---

[88] G Phillipson, '(Mis) reading Section Three of the Human Rights Act' (2003) 119 *LQR* 183 and M Cohn, 'Judicial Activism in the House of Lords: A Composite Constitutional Approach' [2007] 1 *PL* for an excellent analysis of the constitutionalist position.

[89] A Tomkins, 'In Defence of the Political Constitution' (2002) 22 (1) *OJLS* 157; A Tomkins, *Our Republican Constitution* (Hart Publishing, Oxford, 2005).

[90] C Gearty, 'Reconciling Parliamentary Democracy' (n 20) 250. See also T Campbell, 'Incorporation through Interpretation', in T Campbell, KD Ewing and A Tomkins (eds), *Sceptical Essays on Human Rights* (Oxford, Oxford University Press, 2002) 99–100.

[91] A Kavanagh, 'The Elusive Divide between Interpretation and Legislation under the HRA 1998' (2004) 24 (2) *OJLS* 259.

[92] Referred to by Raz as the 'Janus-like aspect of interpretation'. That is, that interpretation faces both backward, aiming to elucidate the law as it is, and forward, aiming to develop and improve it. J Raz, 'Authority and Interpretation in Constitutional Law' in L Alexander (ed), Constitutionalism: Philosophical Foundations (1998) 177. As discussed by A Kavanagh, 'The Elusive Divide' (n 91).

[93] When doing so, judges must therefore balance two often opposing sets of values: those underlying legal conservatism (authority, continuity and stability) and those underlying legal innovation (just application of the law and legal development) and 'give them appropriate weight in accordance with the circumstances of the case': A Kavanagh, 'The Elusive Divide' (n 91) 268–9.

The role of parliamentary intention is also crucial in the 'process' of statutory interpretation. In addition to the ascendance of the purposive method[94] as the preferred judicial approach to questions of interpretation, the courts will often rely on common law presumptions that Parliament intended to legislate in accordance with certain principles[95] such as the general presumption in favour of individual liberty and the presumption that discretionary powers conferred by statute in absolute terms should be exercised reasonably.[96] In addition to this section 3(1) itself also creates a new presumption of statutory interpretation for post-HRA legislation.[97] Thus, as Clayton and Tomlinson argue:

> the conventional rule [is] that when interpreting a statute, the courts are seeking to determine the 'intention of the legislature' ... Then in all cases in which Convention rights are at play, the effect of section 3 is 'equivalent to requiring the courts to act on a presumption that the intention of the legislature was to enact a provision compatible with Convention rights.[98]

Thus, what judges *do* when interpreting will involve a combination of the following factors: acknowledging the powerful constitutional mandate given to them by virtue of section 3; the need to make, as always, substantive evaluations of the issue in question and the 'new' requirements to make an additional 'interpretative' evaluation of the provision in question; and to apply a presumption of Convention compatibility behind any legislative provision.

Applying Section 3(1)—the Story so Far

In terms of process, post-HRA case law[99] has established that interpretation under section 3(1) is carried out in two stages. At the first stage the courts must establish whether the legislation in question, within its ordinary and natural meaning, has breached any Convention rights.[100] If at this stage it is apparent that an incompatibility with Convention rights exists then the courts will try to establish if it is 'possible', in accordance with section 3(1), to read and give effect to the legislation in a way that is compatible with Convention rights. If this is not possible then a declaration of incompatibility under section 4 must be issued. It is at this point in the process that much of the controversy surrounding section 3(1) has concentrated. At first sight, post-HRA judicial reasoning seemed to suggest that section 3(1) presented a choice between two approaches: the 'radical approach',[101] which views the interpretative obligation as such a strong one that it may

---

[94] This will include the use of the evaluative and applicative factors discussed above. See also J Van Zyl Smit, 'The New Purposive Interpretation of Statues: HRA Section 3 after *Ghaidan v Godin-Mendoza*' (2007) 70 (2) MLR 294, who argues that the HRA has produced a 'heightened degree' of purposive interpretation.

[95] J Bell and G Engle, *Cross on Statutory Interpretation*, 3rd edn (London, Butterworths, 1995) ch 7.

[96] As discussed by A Kavanagh in 'The Role of Parliamentary Intention in Adjudication under the HRA 1998' (2006) 26 (1) *OJLS* 179, 185.

[97] It cannot apply to pre-HRA legislation: see A Kavanagh, *Constitutional Review* (n 47).

[98] R Clayton and H Tomlinson, *The Law of Human Rights* (Oxford, Oxford University Press, 2000) 167. This view has also received judicial support. See also Lord Steyn in *Ghaidan* (n 54) (AC) para 50, as discussed by A Kavanagh in 'The Role of Parliamentary Intention' (n 96) 188.

[99] Eg *Ghaidan* (n 98); *R (Fuller) v Chief Constable of Dorset Constabulary* [2002] 3 WLR 1133; *International Transport Roth GmbH v Secretary of State for the Home Department* [2002] 3 WLR 344; *R v A (No 2)* [2001] UKHL 25; *R v Hasan* [2005] 2 WLR 709.

[100] These stages have been termed the 'natural interpretation' and 'transformative interpretation' stages respectively. See also A Kavanagh, 'The Elusive Divide' (n 91) 274 and C Gearty, 'Reconciling Parliamentary Democracy' (n 20) 252, although the terms 'interpretative' and 'transformative' are Kavanagh's.

[101] Rose and Weir, 'Interpretation and Incompatibility Striking the Balance' (n 20).

involve the 'reading in' of certain words or phrases in order to achieve compatibility, or the 'cautious/deferential' approach,[102] which would bring about as little modification of legislation as possible and would thereby increase the chances of a section 4 declaration being issued. The highly controversial decision of the House of Lords in *R v A*[103] is often quoted as an example of the former. This case concerned the apparent incompatibility presented by section 41 of the Youth Justice and Criminal Evidence Act 1999, which prohibited the admissibility of evidence about a complainant's sexual history with the defendant in proceedings for sexual offences, except with the leave of the court, the circumstances for which were highly circumscribed.[104] The House of Lords held that this provision was so restrictive that it amounted to 'legislative overkill' and moreover was incompatible with the defendant's right to a fair trial under Article 6 of the ECHR. As a result, section 3(1) was relied upon to *read into* section 41 an implied provision that evidence of a complainant's sexual history with the defendant, which was necessary to ensure a fair trial, could not be treated as inadmissible. In effect, this resulted in a return to a greater level of judicial discretion as to whether this type of evidence could be adduced, something that was arguably the exact opposite of what Parliament had intended by passing the Act in the first place. Of particular note were the comments of Lord Steyn, which seemed to support the 'radical approach' to section 3(1): 'A declaration of incompatibility must be avoided unless it is plainly impossible to do so. If a clear limitation on Convention rights is stated in terms, such impossibility will arise.'[105] Thus, in all other cases, the interpretative obligation was such a strong one that it should be applied even in the absence of ambiguity. If necessary, he argued, a 'linguistically strained' construction should be adopted to achieve compatibility.[106] A declaration of compatibility was thereby a last resort.

Conversely, in *Re S and Re W*[107] the House of Lords appeared to demonstrate the 'cautious/deferential approach' to section 3(1). This case concerned the Court of Appeal's earlier decision to 'read into' the Children Act 1989 a 'starred' care plan system under which the courts would be able to monitor the progress of an individual care plan by providing the Children's Guardian and the local authority with the right to apply to the court for further directions if the plan was not administered according to prescribed time limits. Although the need for such judicial monitoring was apparent, it had not been possible due to the fact that any reference to care plans, as such, was entirely absent from the Children Act 1989. However, on appeal, although the House of Lords was sympathetic to the apparent detriment to families caused by unacceptable delays in adhering to care plans,[108] it nevertheless held that the Court of Appeal had gone too far in seeking to amend legislation rather than interpreting it. Thus, section 3(1) could not be used to interpret a provision in a way which departed substantially from a fundamental feature of an Act of

---

[102] *R v Lambert* [2001] UKHL 37 para 81 (Lord Hope), where he remarks that in many cases, it may be sufficient 'simply to say what the effect of the provision is without altering the meaning of the words used'.

[103] *R v A* (n 99).

[104] Section 41(3)(c) permitted a court to give leave only where the sexual behaviour of the complainant to which the evidence related was allegedly so similar to sexual behaviour which took place as part of the alleged event, that the similarity could not be coincidental.

[105] *R v A* (n 99) para 44 (Lord Steyn).

[106] *Ibid*, para 44 (Lord Steyn): 'A declaration of incompatibility must be avoided unless it is plainly impossible to do so. If a clear limitation on Convention rights is stated in terms, such impossibility will arise.'

[107] *Re S and Re W* [2002] UKHL 10.

[108] See also *Re S* [2004] UKHL 47 para 106 (Lord Nicholl's comments).

Parliament.[109] Moreover, Lord Nicholls added that Lord Steyn's observations in *R v A*[110] were not to be read as meaning that a clear limitation on Convention rights in terms was the only circumstance in which an interpretation incompatible with Convention rights might arise.[111]

Subsequent decisions concerning the use of section 3(1) appeared to confuse the complex issue of the scope of the section even further. In *R v Lambert*[112] the House of Lords held that, using section 3(1), it was possible to reinterpret section 28 of the Misuse of Drugs Act 1971[113] to impose an evidential rather than a legal burden of proof on the defendant in order to render it compatible with Article 6 of the Convention. The language of section 28 demonstrated the clear intention of Parliament to impose a legal burden of proof on the defendant[114] in that, 'the matter in question must be taken as proved against the accused unless he satisfies the jury on a balance of probabilities to the contrary'.[115] To impose an evidential burden of proof on the defendant would be different: 'the matter must be taken as proved against the accused unless there is sufficient evidence to raise an issue on the matter but, if there is sufficient evidence, then the prosecution have the burden of satisfying the jury as to the matter beyond reasonable doubt in the ordinary way'.[116] In the event, their Lordships chose the latter option and the words 'to prove' were reinterpreted to mean 'to give sufficient evidence'.[117] However, in *Anderson*,[118] a case concerning the incompatibility of the Home Secretary's role in settling the punitive term of imprisonment for mandatory life sentences with Article 6 of the ECHR, the House of Lords preferred to issue a declaration of incompatibility rather than take the 'illegitimate' step of using section 3(1) to read into section 29 of the Crime (Sentences) Act 1997 a new rule that the Home Secretary may not fix a tariff which exceeds the recommendation of the trial judge and the Lord Chief Justice. Here Lord Steyn shifted from his position in *R v A*[119] somewhat when he stated that 's 3(1) is not available where the suggested interpretation is contrary to express statutory words *or* is by implication necessarily contradicted by the statute'.[120] In *Bellinger v Bellinger*[121] the House of Lords declined to utilise section 3(1) to interpret the words 'male' and 'female' in section 11(c) of the Matrimonial Causes Act 1973 to include a transgender female which would have enabled her to marry despite the fact that this would have been relatively easy to achieve on a linguistic and legal basis. A declaration of incompatibility was, again,

---

[109] *Re S* (n 108) para 40 (Lord Nicholls' comments).

[110] *R v A* (n 99).

[111] *Re S and Re W* (n 107) para 40.

[112] *R v Lambert* (n 102).

[113] Section 28(2) provides that it 'shall be a defence for the accused to prove that he neither knew of nor suspected nor had reason to suspect the existence of some fact alleged by the prosecution which it is necessary for the prosecution to prove if he is to be convicted of the offence charged'.

[114] To establish the defences set out under s28(3) the onus was on the defendant to bring himself within s28 and prove, on the balance of probabilities, that he did not know that the bag contained a controlled drug.

[115] *R v Lambert* (n 102) para 37 (Lord Steyn).

[116] *Ibid*, para 37 (Lord Steyn).

[117] *Ibid*, para 42.

[118] *Anderson* (n 45).

[119] *R v A* (n 99).

[120] *Anderson* (n 45) para 59. As A Kavanagh explains, 'necessary implications' are those 'which are so integral to a legislative provision or series of provisions, that they could bear no other meaning'. Thus, any reinterpretation of the relevant section which could eradicate the Home Secretary's decision-making power (as set out above) would have gone against the necessary implications of the section because the basic tenor of it was that the Home Secretary was not obliged to accept the recommendations of the judiciary as to tariff: A Kavanagh, 'The Elusive Divide' (n 91) 277.

[121] *Bellinger* (n 25).

preferred. However, in *Ghaidan*,[122] now regarded as the leading case on the issue, the House of Lords found it possible to read the words 'living together as his or her wife or husband' in paragraph 2(2) of Schedule 1 to the Rent Act 1977 to include same-sex couples in order for them to be able to succeed to a statutory tenancy on the death of their partner, thereby equalising their position with cohabiting heterosexual couples. The first step, under the two-stage approach to section 3(1), was to establish whether paragraph 2(2) violated Convention rights. Their Lordships were unanimous in answering this in the affirmative; it was clear that same-sex cohabitants were treated differently from heterosexual cohabitants in a manner which discriminated towards same-sex couples and, therefore, Mr Mendoza's Convention rights.[123] The second step was whether this discrimination could be remedied by section 3(1). In doing so their Lordships had to confront the fact that paragraph 2(2) contained gen-der-specific terms, 'husband *and* wife', which, in addition, had clearly never been intended by Parliament to cover same-sex couples.[124] By a four to one majority their Lordships held that these two issues did not preclude a Convention-compatible reinterpretation of the legisla-tion under section 3(1). Lord Nicholls made it clear that the language of the statute would not be determinative of the scope of the application of section 3(1) because to do so would 'make the application of section 3 something of a semantic lottery'.[125] Furthermore:

> Section 3 enables language to be interpreted restrictively or expansively. But section 3 goes further than this. It is also apt to require a court to *read in* words which *change the meaning of the enacted legislation*, so as to make it Convention-compliant. In other words, the intention of Parliament in enacting section 3 was that, to an extent bounded only by what is 'possible', a court can modify the meaning, and hence the effect, of primary and secondary legislation[126] [emphasis added].

Arguably the reinterpretation that occurred in *Ghaidan*[127] was a much more 'linguistically strained' exercise than that refused by the House of Lords in *Bellinger*.[128] Nevertheless it was in *Ghaidan*[129] that the House of Lords provided the most thorough examination, to date, of the relationship between section 3(1) and section 4 respectively and, more impor-tantly, a discussion as to the kind of factors which would determine the limits of judicial intervention under section 3 of the HRA. These factors will now be considered in the section below.

The Factors Behind the Application of Section 3(1)

The focus of the academic debate prior to and post *Ghaidan*[130] demonstrated the dif-ficulty in attempting to discern a particular pattern of judicial interpretation of the duty

---

[122] *Ghaidan* (n 56) (HL).
[123] *Ibid*, para 24 (Lord Nicholls); para 55 (Lord Millett); para 128 (Lord Rodger); para 143 (Baroness Hale). Lord Steyn supported the reasoning of the majority.
[124] This was in fact the basis upon which the House of Lords had rejected the application of the same para-graph to a same-sex couple in *Fitzpatrick v Sterling Housing Association Ltd* [2001] AC 27. Their Lordships chose instead to hold that, for the purposes of the Rent Act 1977, the definition of '*family*' included a same-sex partner of a deceased tenant.
[125] *Ghaidan* (n 56) (HL) para 31 (Lord Nicholls).
[126] *Ibid*, para 32 (Lord Nicholls).
[127] *Ibid*.
[128] *Bellinger* (n 25).
[129] *Ghaidan* (n 56).
[130] *Ibid*.

contained in section 3(1) and the extent of deference that was being accorded to the legislature.[131] Early commentaries asserted that there was a clear pattern in the approach of the courts. Nichol[132] argued that the House of Lords has adopted a generally restrictive use of s3, preferring instead to utilise s4 declarations of incompatibility.[133] Gearty[134] argued that the courts had demonstrated that a reading of legislation under section 3(1) should not depart substantially from a fundamental feature of an Act of Parliament,[135] apparently vindicating his more cautious approach to section 3(1) reinterpretations. However, it is Kavanagh[136] who has provided the most developed and sustained analysis of the current judicial approach (and its apparent contradictions) to section 3(1). Her view is that any assertion that the House of Lords is taking one approach in particular is yet to be proven. Instead, she considers that the approach taken by the House of Lords is a contextual one and dependent upon a number of factors. Indeed this approach would have a further advantage: 'the need to take sides between those who argue that section 3 should be used all or nearly all the time and those who argue that section 4 should be used more often, is obviated.'[137]

The factors are varied, and can be applied in combination. As discussed above, what will be of *primary* concern to the judiciary is the desire not to cross the boundary between interpretation and legislation.[138] Kavanagh provides the following summary of the position on this aspect of section 3(1):[139]

> Contradicting the express words of the provision or re-writing them so that they state the opposite of what they originally stated involves legislation. Changing its implied meaning, and adopting a meaning which is different from its 'ordinary and natural meaning' is part of the interpretative task under section 3. This latter activity may include narrowing down the ordinary meaning, or changing/extending it through additional words or phrases. The meaning can be contracted or enlarged (thus necessarily changing the effect of the legislation) but it cannot contradict the express wording of the section. If an incompatibility with the Convention is not contained in the express terms of the legislation, but is rather inherent in its necessary implications, then it may be impossible to use section 3 to eradicate this incompatibility.

[131]   A Kavanagh, 'Unlocking the Human Rights Act' (n 20); D Rose and C Weir, 'Interpretation and Incompatibility' (n 20); D Nichol, 'Statutory Interpretation and Human Rights After *Anderson*' (n 20); A Kavanagh, 'After *Anderson*: A More Contextual Approach' (n 20); C Gearty, 'Revisiting Section 3(1)' (n 20); and C Gearty, 'Reconciling Parliamentary Democracy' (n 20).

[132]   D Nichol, 'Statutory Interpretation and Human Rights after *Anderson*' (n 20).

[133]   *Ibid.*

[134]   C Gearty, 'Reconciling Parliamentary Democracy and Human Rights' (n 20).

[135]   Which, it is argued, gives weight to his earlier argument that various limits ought to be set upon s3(1) 'by reference to how far interpretation of what was "possible" in any given case could go without substantially impairing the continuing operation or enforcement of the provision under scrutiny': C Gearty, 'Revisiting Section 3(1)' (n 20).

[136]   A Kavanagh, 'After *Anderson*: A More Contextual Approach' (n 20). See also A Kavanagh, 'Judicial Reasoning after *Ghaidan v Mendoza*' in H Fenwick, G Phillipson and R Masterman, *Judicial Reasoning Under the HRA* (n 16). See also, more generally, A Kavanagh, *Constitutional Review under the HRA* (n 97). However, note G Phillipson *et al* in their critique of Kavanagh's argument which is that Kavanagh effectively argues that s3 should be reinterpreted to mean that the courts must interpret statutes compatibly, not where it is 'possible' to do so, but where they think it *appropriate*, all things considered: H Fenwick, G Phillipson and R Masterman, *Judicial Reasoning Under the HRA* (n 16).

[137]   A Kavanagh, 'Judicial Reasoning after *Ghaidan v Mendoza*' (n 135) 134.

[138]   As referred to by H Fenwick, G Phillipson and R Masterman, *Judicial Reasoning Under the HRA* (n 16).

[139]   A Kavanagh, 'The Elusive Divide' (n 91) 279.

Thus, although the courts may be prepared to 'read words into' statutes, as in *R v A*,[140] they will not do so, as the decision in *Re S and Re W*[141] indicates, 'as a way of radically reforming a whole statute or writing a quasi-legislative code granting new powers and setting out new procedures to replace that statute'.[142] This factor clearly heavily influenced the House of Lords in its refusal to allow section 3(1) to be used to introduce a new system of care plan monitoring in *Re S and Re W*[143] and to allow for the marriage of transsexuals in *Bellinger*[144] under the Matrimonial Causes Act 1973. It was also one of the reasons why the court felt able to come to the opposite conclusion in *R v A*[145]—the decision here did not require the setting up of whole procedures or mechanisms to implement it, the problem could easily be remedied by the amendment of one particular subsection of the statute. Similarly, in *Anderson*,[146] although it might have been linguistically possible to have read the Secretary of State's role out of the legislation, the House of Lords referred to the recent acknowledgment by the Home Secretary[147] of the need for a review of some of the administrative arrangements relating to the review and release of mandatory life prisoners as a reason for why the matter could not simply be disposed of by altering one section of the Act.

The second factor influencing the operation of section 3(1)[148] is the need to ensure that any section 3(1) interpretation should not be inconsistent with either the 'fundamental features' of the Act or its 'underlying concept or purpose'. Thus in *Ghaidan*[149] the court examined the basic features of the relationship which qualified for a statutory tenancy under the Rent Act 1977: the sharing of a life and making a home together, in order to establish that same-sex couples also shared these features.[150] As Lord Rodger noted, there was 'no principle underlying the Act as a whole'[151] that would conflict with a section 3(1) interpretation that would include same-sex couples and, moreover, it would not 'contradict any cardinal principle of the Rent Act'.[152] This factor was later applied in *Secretary of State for the Home Department v MB and AF*[153] which concerned MB, a British national of Kuwaiti origin, who was placed under a control order, on suspicion that he had been seeking to fly to Iraq to fight coalition forces there. He was twice stopped by police from flying to Syria and Yemen. The case concerned a challenge to the rules of procedure governing hearings challenging the imposition of Control Orders under the Prevention of

---

[140] *R v A* (n 99).
[141] *Re S and Re W* (n 107). 'The Court of Appeal had read into the Children Act 1989 a range of new powers and procedures by which courts could supervise and monitor the implementation of care orders by local authorities, so as to protect children against violations of their rights under Article 8 ECHR': A Kavanagh, 'After *Anderson*: A More Contextual Approach' (n 20) 538. This decision was reversed unanimously by the House of Lords.
[142] A Kavanagh, 'After *Anderson*: A More Contextual Approach' (n 20) 540.
[143] *Re S and Re W* (n 107).
[144] *Bellinger* (n 25).
[145] *R v A* (n 99).
[146] *Anderson* (n 45). The House of Lords instead issued a declaration of incompatibility on the ground that a power conferred on the Home Secretary by s29 of the Crime (Sentences) Act 1997 to control the release of mandatory life sentence prisoners was inconsistent with the right to have sentence imposed by 'an independent and impartial tribunal': Art 6 ECHR.
[147] Hansard evidence given in response and in relation to how he was going to give effect to a recent ECtHR decision which had found that the power exercised by him under s29 violated Art 6.
[148] A Kavanagh, 'Judicial Reasoning after *Ghaidan v Mendoza*' (n 135) 119–21.
[149] *Ghaidan* (n 56) (HL).
[150] *Ibid*, para 35 (Lord Nicholls).
[151] *Ibid*, para 28, as discussed in A Kavanagh, 'Judicial Reasoning after *Ghaidan v Mendoza*' (n 135) 121.
[152] A Kavanagh, 'Judicial Reasoning after *Ghaidan v Mendoza*' (n 135) 128.
[153] *Secretary of State for the Home Department v MB and AF* [2007] UKHL 46.

Terrorism Act 2005 (PTA). The issue to be decided was whether the procedures provided for by s 3 of the PTA are compatible with Article 6 of the Convention in circumstances where they have resulted in the case made against AF being in its essence entirely undisclosed to him and in no specific allegation of terrorism-related activity being contained in open material. In determining this question the court was also asked to consider whether the provision of special advocates under the PTA, which was meant to serve as a procedural safeguard where such 'closed material' had been used, was sufficient enough to comply with the need for procedural justice under Article 6. Their Lordships held that although the use of special advocates could enhance the level of procedural justice available to a controlled person, this would not guarantee that every control order hearing would comply with Article 6. Rather than issue a declaration of incompatibility, the court chose to 'read down' the relevant terms of the PTA so that they could only take effect 'except where to do so would be incompatible with the right of the controlled person to a fair trial'. In this way, as Kavanagh[154] has observed, the court tried to ensure that two of the main objectives of the PTA were preserved: the Secretary of State's right not to disclose sensitive information if it was contrary to the public interest, while simultaneously ensuring that Article 6 could be complied with in each individual case.

The third relevant factor is the role played by the terms of the legislative provision being interpreted. In *Ghaidan*,[155] the House of Lords were at pains to point out that in considering whether it would be possible to achieve a Convention-compatible meaning under section 3(1), courts should not focus unduly on a close textual analysis of the provision in question. Lord Nicholls stated that the application of section 3(1) should not 'depend critically on the particular forms of words adopted by the Parliamentary draftsman. That would make the application of section 3 somewhat of a semantic lottery.'[156] Thus, if the language of the statute contradicted the 'concept expressed in that language'[157] it was possible for the courts to read in words to enacted legislation in order to make it Convention-compliant. However, as Kavanagh reminds us, the need for some textual analysis has not been entirely removed:

> [W]hilst it is certainly right to say that s 3(1) does not depend on linguistic possibilities alone, we should not be driven to the opposite extreme of denying that the express terms of the statute under scrutiny therefore have no role to play in determining whether a s 3(1) interpretation is appropriate in the context of a particular case.[158]

Thus, in *Anderson*[159] the House of Lords (in addition to other factors) also relied upon the express terms of the statute in coming to the conclusion that it was not possible to re-interpret the 'clear provisions of section 29'[160] so as to remove the Home Secretary's power to determine the length of the tariff period. Further, in *Ghaidan*,[161] the House of Lords noted that had section 2(2) of Schedule 1 to the Rent Act 1977 been confined to the husband and wife

---

[154] A Kavanagh, 'Judging the Judges under the HRA: Deference, Disillusionment and the "War on Terror"' [2009] 1 *PL* 287.

[155] *Ghaidan* (n 56) (HL).

[156] *Ibid*, para 31 (Lord Nicholls).

[157] *Ibid*, para 31 (Lord Nicholls).

[158] A Kavanagh, 'Judicial Reasoning after *Ghaidan v Mendoza*' (n 135) 123.

[159] *Anderson* (n 45).

[160] *Ibid*, para 80 (Lord Hutton).

[161] *Ghaidan* (n 56) (HL).

of the original tenant as opposed to a person 'living together as his or her wife or husband' it would not have been possible to achieve a section 3(1) reinterpretation of the section.[162] The text of the statute continues to play a role post-*Ghaidan*.[163] In *R (Wilkinson) v Inland Revenue Commissioners*[164] the House of Lords rejected a claim by a widower who argued that he should receive a tax allowance that had only been granted to widows under section 262(1) of the Income and Corporation Taxes Act 1998 on the basis that that the term 'widow' could not be reinterpreted so as to include the words 'widower' under section 3 of the HRA. Lord Hoffman was of the clear view that reading section 262 in the context of the statute as a whole, it could be seen that whilst Parliament had used gender-neutral terms in other sections in the Act, it had specifically confined the application of section 262 to widows alone.[165]

Kavanagh's final factor to consider is the remedial nature of section 3(1) itself. In other words, it is the duty of the court to 'strive to do justice for the individual litigant and apply the law fairly and equitably in the context of each case'.[166] This may be of particular relevance when the court is faced between a choice to produce a section 3(1) reinterpretation or a section 4 declaration of incompatibility. It is the application of this factor, Kavanagh argues, that explains the difference in approach between *Ghaidan*[167] and *Bellinger*.[168] Both cases could have been resolved by a relatively easy linguistic adjustment, yet the House of Lords chose only to do so in *Ghaidan*.[169] The reasons for doing so were, she argues, precisely because of the court's awareness of its remedial duty under section 3(1). Had the court chosen to issue a section 4 declaration in *Ghaidan*[170] the applicant could not have succeeded to a statutory tenancy and, moreover, could not have relied upon the Civil Partnership Bill (proceeding through Parliament at the time) as his partner had died. In contrast, in *Bellinger*,[171] where a section 4 declaration was issued, the applicant could be sure that she would be able to get married at some point in the future due to the fact that the Government had confirmed that impending legislation (the Gender Recognition Act 2004) would enable her to do so.

Fenwick and Phillipson[172] add further to this list of factors the subject matter of the statute. Thus, in areas that are considered by the courts as being within their 'own constitutional responsibility',[173] such as aspects of the criminal or civil justice system, they are more likely to take a robust line. This therefore explains the 'activist' uses of section 3(1) in both *R v A*[174] and *R v Offen*.[175] The opposite is true in areas that the courts have not traditionally regarded as being within their constitutional responsibility, such as social policy—*Bellinger*[176] and resource allocation—*Re S*.[177]

---

[162] *Ibid*, para 128 (Lord Rodger).
[163] *Ibid*.
[164] *R (Wilkinson) v Inland Revenue Commissioners* [2006] All ER 529.
[165] *Ibid*, para 15.
[166] A Kavanagh, 'Judicial Reasoning after *Ghaidan v Mendoza*' (n 135) 128–9.
[167] *Ghaidan* (n 56).
[168] *Bellinger* (n 25).
[169] *Ghaidan* (n 56).
[170] *Ibid*.
[171] *Bellinger* (n 25).
[172] H Fenwick and G Phillipson, *Media Freedom under the HRA* (Oxford, Oxford University Press, 2006) 162.
[173] H Fenwick and G Phillipson, *Media Freedom* (n 172).
[174] *R v Offen* [2001] 1 WLR 254.
[175] *Ibid*: the case concerned the 'reading down' of provisions governing mandatory sentences for repeat offenders.
[176] *Bellinger* (n 25).
[177] *Re S* (n 107).

It is now relatively clear that the above factors and the leading case in this area, *Ghaidan*,[178] have continued to be followed by the courts when considering their duty under section 3(1) of the HRA. In sum, as Kavanagh[179] concludes, section 3(1) now operates as a strong presumption of statutory interpretation, 'not easily displaced by express enactment to the contrary'[180] and in doing so there is no denying that section 3(1) gives the courts considerable powers 'to modify the effect of primary legislation and depart from legislative intent where necessary'.[181]

Section 6—The Meaning of Public Authorities

Section 6 of the HRA contains a number of elements which are crucial to an understanding of the level of human rights protection provided for in the HRA. Subsection 1 commences the section by stating that 'it is unlawful for a *public authority* to act in a way that is incompatible with a Convention right'. In doing so, the subsection ensures that the responsibility of the State is engaged for any breaches of the Convention rights committed by public authorities towards private citizens, the so-called 'vertical effect' of the Convention. It should also be noted that State obligations under the Convention are not only framed in negative terms and, as such, section 6(1) will also, by implication, include the duty to ensure compliance with the positive obligations[182] that have been developed by the ECtHR with respect to Convention rights. Section 6(1) is, however, made subject to section 6(2), which states that a public authority does not act unlawfully if 'as a result of provisions contained in primary legislation it could not have acted differently, or if in the case of provisions contained in or made under primary legislation which cannot be read or given effect in a way compatible with the Convention rights, it was acting in accordance with those provisions'. This section thus provides a defence based on primary legislation for those public authorities who may be acting in breach of Convention rights, thereby building upon the other existing provisions in ss 2, 3 and 4 of the HRA, discussed above, in terms of maintaining the necessary constitutional respect for parliamentary sovereignty.[183] It is of some significance that a 'public authority' is not specifically defined anywhere in the Act; however, subsection 3 goes on to state that the definition includes 'a court or tribunal' and 'any person certain of whose functions are functions of a public nature' will be regarded as such. Further, subsection 5 states that 'in relation to a particular act, a person is not a public authority by virtue only of subsection (3)(b) if the nature of the act is private'. Post-HRA case law has demonstrated that the exact definition of a public authority is crucial for defining the exact parameters and reach of the protection afforded by the HRA as it is only those bodies or individuals that are included within the definition of a public authority that will be subject to direct liability under the Act.[184] As we will see from the discussion

---

[178] *Ghaidan* (n 56).
[179] A Kavanagh, *Constitutional Review* (n 47) 108–9.
[180] *Ibid*, 114.
[181] *Ibid*, 114.
[182] See ch 7 pp 248–51 concerning the nature of positive obligations under the ECHR in general.
[183] E Palmer, *Judicial Review, Socio-Economic Rights and the HRA* (Oxford, Hart Publishing, 2009) 138–9.
[184] Although, as will be discussed later on in the chapter, there may be the opportunity to come within the horizontal effect of the Act, this is clearly a weaker foundation for a potential claim.

below this may have significant relevance for local authorities who are increasingly 'contracting out' their social services and housing functions in relation to families in need and children in care to private and/or charitable bodies.

To begin with, it is apparent from the terms of section 6 that two types of public authority have been provided for.[185] First, it includes the 'core' public authorities which under section 6(3)(a) would include government departments, local authorities, immigration officers, prison officers, NHS hospitals, and the police.[186] This type of public authority is obliged to act in accordance with Convention rights in relation to *all* its activities, be they public or private in nature. In addition, such bodies are not able to enforce any Convention rights of their own as, according to Article 34 of the Convention, only individuals and 'non-governmental organisations' can bring such a claim.[187] Second, there is the 'functional'[188] type of public authority, which, under section 6(3)(b), exercises some public *and* some private functions. This type of public authority is only required to comply with Convention rights when it is exercising a 'function of a public nature' and not when it is doing something where the nature of the act is private. Examples of bodies that the courts have regarded as having such functions have been a housing association[189] and a farmers' market.[190] If such a body has breached Convention rights, a claim is only possible under the HRA if the act or decision complained about is pursuant to one of its public functions. Thus, where the act performed concerns regulatory or safety functions then it is likely to be regarded as falling within section 6(3)(b).[191] Consequently and most importantly, those bodies or individuals who perform no public functions at all will fall outside the direct effect of the Act altogether.[192]

In summary, therefore, when approaching the question of whether a particular body falls within section 6 the first question to be determined is whether it is a 'core' public authority. If the answer is 'yes' it must act compatibly with relevant Convention rights in all activities, including the decision in question. If the answer is 'no' and it is not a 'core' public authority, then two further questions must be asked: first, does the body have *some* public functions; second, does the particular act in question fall within the type of functions identified by the case law as being determinative of a 'functional' public authority? Only if the answer to both questions is 'yes' will the body be bound by the Convention rights. It is, however, the definition of a 'functional' public authority which will be of more relevance to family law rather than the definition of a 'core', it being obvious that government departments and local authorities will be included in the latter definition. As a result this section of

---

[185] R Clayton and H Tomlinson, *The Law of Human Rights* (n 98) para 5.08.

[186] Given as examples by the JCHR, 'The Meaning of Public Authority under the HRA 1998', Seventh Report of Session 2003–04, 39 HC 382, 5 and the Department of Constitutional Affairs, 'Guide to the HRA' (DCA, 2006) 8, found at www.dca.gov.uk/peoples-rights/human-rights/pdf/act-studyguide.pdf.

[187] This is because under ss7(1) and 7(7) HRA to be eligible to bring a claim under the HRA a person must be a 'victim' for the purposes of Art 35 ECHR: *Holy Monasteries v Greece* [1995] 20 EHRR 1; *Hautaniemi v Sweden* Application No 24019/94 22 EHRR CD 155.

[188] Also referred to as 'hybrid' but this has been regarded as misleading: D Oliver, 'Functions of a Public Nature under the HRA' [2004] 2 *PL* 329, and unhelpful: JCHR, 'The Meaning of Public Authority' (n 186) 5 and in the DCA's 'Guide to the HRA' (n 186) 6.

[189] *Poplar Housing and Regeneration Community Association Ltd v Donoghue* [2001] EWCA 595 (Civ).

[190] *R v Hampshire Farmers Market ex parte Beer* [2003] EWCA 1056 (Civ).

[191] For example, a company which had the power to exclude the claimant from holding a stall at the local farmers' market was found to be a public authority: *ibid*.

[192] Though the law governing such bodies may be influenced indirectly via the 'horizontal effect' doctrine.

the chapter will explore the courts' approach to defining a 'functional' public authority in more detail.

'Core' Public Authorities

The question of how a 'core' public authority is to be determined was answered by the House of Lords in *Aston Cantlow and Wilmcote with Billesley Parochial Church Council v Wallbank*.[193] The facts concerned the serving of a notice of repair of a chancel upon lay rectors by the Parochial Church Council (PCC) and whether that action constituted a breach of their rights under Article 1 of the First Protocol. In doing so, the House of Lords had to first determine whether the PCC was a public authority for the purposes of section 6(1) of the HRA. A number of factors were held to be relevant in deciding that the PCC could *not* be regarded as a public authority within the meaning of section 6(1). In determining whether a body is a 'core' public authority, the court held that it should always be borne in mind that if that body is regarded as such it will consequently become incapable of enjoying Convention rights under Article 34 of the Convention and section 7 of the HRA:

> [T]his feature throws some light on how the expression 'public authority' should be understood and applied. It must always be relevant to consider whether Parliament can have been intended that the body in question should have no Convention rights.[194]

It was this feature which effectively decided that the PCC could not be regarded as a 'core' public authority; Lord Nicholls felt it would be 'extraordinary' if the PCC would be unable to complain of infringements of their right of freedom of thought, conscience and religion.[195]

The Meaning of a 'Functional' Public Authority under s6(3)(b)—the Case Law

The starting point of the Joint Committee on Human Rights' first report on the meaning of public authority under the HRA[196] was to refer to the international human rights obligations that the Act was supposed to 'bring home'. First, there is the principle that the State cannot evade its responsibility to safeguard Convention rights by delegation to private bodies or individuals. This principle is well established in both Strasbourg jurisprudence[197] and under other international human rights instruments such as the International Covenant on Civil and Political Rights (ICCPR).[198] Second it is a central principle of ECHR law—the doctrine of positive obligations—that the State must in certain circumstances take active steps to protect individual rights against interference by others. Third, the right to non-discrimination in the enjoyment of Convention rights, protected by Article 14, will be highly relevant. It is against this background that the Joint Committee on Human Rights (JCHR) Report went on to examine whether or not the current interpretation of the

---

[193] *Aston Cantlow and Wilmcote with Billesley Parochial Church Council v Wallbank* [2003] UKHL 37.

[194] *Aston Cantlow* (n 193) para 8 (Lord Nicholls).

[195] *Aston Cantlow* (n 193) para 15 (Lord Nicholls). However, see H Quane, 'The Strasbourg Jurisprudence and the Meaning of a "Public Authority" under the HRA' (2006) 1 *PL* 106 for the argument that the ECtHR would make the same distinction between 'core' and 'functional' public authorities concerning Art 34.

[196] JCHR, 'The Meaning of Public Authority' (n 186) 8.

[197] *Van der Musselle v Belgium* [1983] 6 EHRR 163; *Costello Roberts v UK* [1995] 19 EHRR 112; *X and Y v the Netherlands* [1986] 8 EHRR 235 and *Z v UK* [2002] 34 EHRR 3.

[198] Eg comments of the UN Human Rights Committee on the fourth report of the UK, 27 July 1995, CCPR/C/79Add. 55.

meaning of a public authority was in compliance with these obligations. It is also against this background that much of the controversy surrounding the definition of a public authority has been discussed in the academic literature, particularly when we consider that various ministerial statements[199] during the debates on the Human Rights Bill indicated a clear intention to maximise the application of the 'public function' test under section 6(3)(b) in accordance with these principles. Indeed, as the JCHR notes:

> There was a deliberate and considered decision to reject a more prescriptive approach and list those bodies subject to responsibilities under the Act. Such an approach was recognised as potentially limiting the access to remedy of the citizen in ways which might be incompatible with Article 13.[200]

However, in a series of high-profile decisions the judiciary has failed to adopt a maximalist approach to the definition of a public authority which has, in turn, attracted a significant level of criticism for reducing the reach and protection from that originally intended by the legislature.

The first case to seriously consider the question of what constitutes a functional public authority was *Poplar Housing and Regeneration Community v Donoghue*,[201] in which the defendant sought to argue that a possession order that had been obtained against her by Poplar Housing, a housing association, constituted a breach of her right to family life under the HRA. The additional question of whether Poplar Housing was exercising a public function under section 6(3)(b) of the HRA in providing her with social housing was therefore integral to her claim. The Court of Appeal took the opportunity to set down the general principle that 'the fact that a body performs an activity which otherwise a public body would be under a duty to perform cannot mean that such performance is necessarily a public function'.[202] The court considered that three factors were relevant to the question of whether or not a body could be viewed as a functional public authority: the existence of statutory authority for what is being done; the extent of control over the function exercised by another body which is a public authority and the closeness of the relationship which exists between the private body and the delegating public authority. In *Poplar*, it was the third factor that was of most importance: Poplar Housing was created by Tower Hamlets Borough Council to take a transfer of local authority housing stock; five of its board members were also members of Tower Hamlets and Poplar was also subject to the guidance of Tower Hamlets as to the manner in which it acted towards the defendant. As a result the court found that Poplar was so closely assimilated to the activities of the local authority that it was performing public and not private functions. It was also made clear, however, that in a borderline case such as this it was a question of fact and degree. It may be possible therefore that other functions discharged by Poplar and other such housing associations would not be regarded as such.

This reasoning was subsequently followed by the Court of Appeal again in *Heather and Ward v Leonard Cheshire Foundation (A Charity) & Another*[203] in which two long-stay

---

[199] Eg HC Deb, 16 February 1998, col 773 (Home Secretary); HC Deb, 17 June 1998, cols 409–10, 433 (Home Secretary), HL Deb, 24 November 1997, cols 800, 811 (Lord Chancellor).

[200] The obligation to ensure an effective remedy for breaches of Convention rights under Art 13 of the Convention was not included in the HRA for the reason that the Act as a whole was to provide such remedies.

[201] *Poplar* (n 189).

[202] *Ibid*, para 58.

[203] *Heather and Ward v Leonard Cheshire Foundation (A Charity) & Another* [2002] EWCA Civ 366.

residents at a care home sought to challenge the decision by the Leonard Cheshire Foundation (LCF) to close the home and to relocate the residents into community-based units. The home was run by LCF, which was a private charitable organisation, but the residents' places were funded by their local authority under the National Assistance Act 1948 (NAA) as amended. The residents argued that in making the decision to close the home the LCF had exercised functions of a public nature within the meaning of section 6(3)(b) and breached their right to respect for the home under Article 8. After a detailed examination of previous case law on the matter Lord Woolf came to the following conclusion:

> If this were a situation where a local authority could *divest* itself of its Article 8 obligations by contracting out to a voluntary sector provider its obligations under section 21 of the NAA, then there would be a responsibility on the court to approach the interpretation of section 6(3)(b) in a way which ensures, so far as this is a possible that the rights under Article 8 of persons in the position of the appellants are protected. This is not, however, the situation.[204]

He then went on to set out a number of reasons for this conclusion. First, the local authority remained under an obligation to the appellants under section 21 of the NAA[205] to arrange their residential accommodation *and* under Article 8, regardless of the fact that it had used its powers under section 26 of the NAA to enable LCF to provide these services as a third party. Second, the appellants retained their contractual rights against LCF in any event. Third, had the arrangements with LCF been entered into after the HRA came into force, it was also possible, he argued, for a resident to require the local authority to enter into a contract with its provider which fully protected the residents human rights as an additional form of protection.[206]

Ultimately, Lord Woolf considered that these aforementioned matters 'could be put aside' in this case because he considered that the role that LCF was performing 'manifestly' did not involve the performance of public functions. This was because there was no material distinction between the services the care home provided for residents funded by the local authority, and those it provided to residents funded privately. In addition, although LCF was performing functions delegated *under* statutory authority by the local authority, it was not *itself* exercising statutory powers. As a result, LCF was held to be insufficiently 'enmeshed' in the activities of the local authority in the way in which Poplar Housing had been.

These two decisions, unsurprisingly, attracted significant criticism from commentators for adopting an unduly restrictive approach to the meaning of the words 'functions of a public nature' under section 6(3)(b) and therefore denying those who were most in need the protection of the HRA.[207] The Court of Appeal, it was argued, had effectively

---

[204] *Leonard Cheshire* (n 203) (Lord Woolf) para 33.

[205] Section 21(a) NAA concerns the duty of local authorities to provide accommodation. The most relevant part provides: 'Subject to and in accordance with the provisions of this Part of this Act, a local authority may with the approval of the Secretary of State, and to such extent as he may direct shall, make arrangements for providing: (a) residential accommodation for persons aged eighteen or over who by reason of age, illness, disability or any other circumstances are in need of care and attention which is not otherwise available to them'.

[206] However, this was not applicable in this case as the arrangements had been entered into prior to the HRA coming into force.

[207] See amongst others: E Palmer, 'Should Public Health be a Private Concern? Developing a Public Service Paradigm in English Law' (2002) *OJLS* 663; P Craig, 'Contracting Out: The HRA and the Scope of Judicial Review' (2002) 118 *LQR* 551; M Sunkin, 'Pushing Forward the Frontiers of Human Rights Protection: The Meaning of Public Authority under the HRA' (2004) *PL* 643. However, there are those who have argued on ideological grounds

limited the protection of the HRA to some of the most vulnerable in society by rejecting an approach which focused on the nature of the functions discharged by the body in question[208] and adopted instead an 'institutional-relational approach',[209] which focused on the nature of the body providing the service and the closeness of its relationships with core public authorities. This restrictive approach was attributed to a normative climate in which there is a 'vein of orthodox common law thinking that is resistant to the imposition of statutory obligations upon private persons and which prefers obligations to be mediated through the common law'.[210] It was argued that judges displaying this resistance did so because they saw that allowing the imposition of such obligations on the private sector as highly undesirable due to the fact that it would 'roll forward the frontiers of the state and roll back the frontiers of civil society'.[211] Further, it was thought that the fear and cost of litigation that would arise from such liability could also result in the private sector being forced to withdraw from some areas of provision, thereby, ultimately, adversely affecting the interests of the very disadvantaged the HRA sought to protect.[212] Criticism of this mode of thinking has not, however, been restricted to academic quarters: both the Audit Commission[213] and the Joint Committee on Human Rights[214] severely criticised the Court of Appeal's approach for creating gaps in the protection afforded by the HRA towards vulnerable people dependent upon the private sector for their basic day-to-day needs. The problem, as the JCHR put it, is:

> [N]ot just a theoretical legal problem. The development of the case law has significant and imme-diate practical implication. In an environment where many services previously delivered by public authorities are being privatized or contracted out to private suppliers, the law is out of step with reality. The implications of the narrow interpretation of the meaning of public authority are particularly acute for a range of particularly vulnerable people in society, including elderly people in private care homes, people in housing associations accommodation and children outside the maintained education sector, or in receipt of children's services provided by private or voluntary sector bodies.[215]

However, shortly after these two Court of Appeal decisions, some evidence emerged that suggested that the House of Lords may have differed in its approach to section 6(3)(b). Having first established that the Parish Council could not be regarded as a 'core' public

---

that the over-regulation of private power by a too generous interpretation of s6(3)(b) would affect the availability of services for the vulnerable. See D Oliver, 'The Frontiers of the State' (n 19) and D Oliver, 'Functions of a Public Nature' (n 188).

[208] The 'functional approach'.

[209] J Landau, 'Functional Public Authorities after YL' [2007] 4 *PL* 630. He defines the institutional-relational approach as one that focuses on the nature of the person and the closeness of its relationships with pure public authorities.

[210] M Sunkin, 'Pushing Forward the Frontiers' (n 207) 650.

[211] D Oliver, 'The Frontiers of the State' (n 19) and D Oliver, 'Functions of a Public Nature' (n 188) for an overview of this position on s6(3)(b). Professor Oliver's articles were quoted in the *Leonard Cheshire* (n 203) judgment.

[212] D Oliver, 'The Frontiers of the State' (n 19) and D Oliver, 'Functions of a Public Nature' (n 188) for an overview of this position on s6(3)(b).

[213] '[M]ost private organisations that contract with public bodies to provide services do not constitute public bodies for the purposes of the HRA, despite the public nature of the work in which they engage': Audit Commission, 'Human Rights: Improving Public Services Delivery' September 2003 pp 11–12.

[214] JCHR, 'The Meaning of Public Authority under the HRA' (n 186).

[215] *Ibid*, para 44.

authority in *Aston Cantlow*,[216] their Lordships moved on to the question of whether it could be regarded as a functional public authority. In determining if a function is public for the purposes of section 6(3)(b) there could be, Lord Nicholls said, no single universal test of application.[217] Factors which could be taken into account included the extent to which in carrying out the relevant function the body is publicly funded, or is exercising statutory powers, or is taking the place of central government or local authorities, or is providing a public service.[218] The PCC was neither publicly funded nor had anything to do with either central or local government. Any statutory powers it had were not exercisable against the general public. The argument that the PCC, in enforcing a statutory obligation to repair the chancel of a parish church, was performing a public function was therefore rejected. By enforcing its statutory powers in this case, the PCC was merely acting as a private party enforcing a civil liability—the act was one of a private nature. Thus in determining whether a body was a functional public authority, the House of Lords stressed that it was the *nature* of the function being performed that should determine the issue, thereby implicitly rejecting the institutional or relational approach: 'It is the *function* that the person is performing that is determinative of the question whether it is, for the purposes of the case, a "hybrid" public authority.'[219]

Further:

> Giving a generously wide scope to the expression 'public function' in section 6(3)(b) will further the statutory aim of promoting the observance of human rights values without depriving the bodies in question of the ability themselves to rely on Convention rights when necessary.[220]

Thus, as the JCHR notes,[221] the House of Lords adopted a relatively narrow test for 'pure' public authorities but balanced it against a correspondingly 'broad and functional approach' to public authority responsibility under the HRA. However, as they also noted, this approach was not subsequently to find favour in the lower courts.[222] *R v Hampshire Farmers Market ex parte Beer*[223] concerned proceedings brought under judicial review and the HRA by a farmer who had been excluded from participation in the farmers' market. The market had initially been established by Hampshire County Council, which had then set up a private company, HMFL, to run it. However, the Court of Appeal chose to restrict the 'broad and functional' approach of *Aston Cantlow*[224] and noted that neither *Poplar*[225] nor *Leonard Cheshire*[226] had been overruled or expressly disapproved by the House of Lords.[227] The court thus went on to apply an approach in which institutional factors[228]

---

[216] *Aston Cantlow* (n 193).
[217] *Ibid*, para 12 (Lord Nicholls).
[218] *Ibid*, para 12 (Lord Nicholls).
[219] *Ibid*, para 41 (Lord Hope).
[220] *Ibid*, para 11 (Lord Nicholls).
[221] JCHR, 'The Meaning of Public Authority' (n 186) para 26.
[222] JCHR, 'The Meaning of Public Authority' (n 186) 26: 'In the relatively few decided cases, the courts have, in their application of section 6, taken as their starting point the amenability to judicial review of a body discharging a function, and have looked to the identity of the body, and its links with the State, as well as to the nature of the function performed.'
[223] *Beer* (n 190).
[224] *Aston Cantlow* (n 193).
[225] *Poplar* (189).
[226] *Leonard Cheshire* (n 203).
[227] *Hampshire* (n 190) 15.
[228] *Ibid*, para 30.

played an important part: the fact that HMFL owed its existence to the County Council, that it performed functions that had formerly been discharged by the Council and that HMFL had been assisted in its work by the County Council. There was also a 'functional' reason—the power to control the right of access to a public market had a 'public element or flavour'. As a result, Hampshire Farmers Market was deemed to be a functional public authority under section 6(3)(b). In addition, the court held that the company was amenable to both judicial review and proceedings brought under the HRA unless the Strasbourg case law required otherwise.

Thus, at this stage in the case law, a private body was only likely to be considered a 'functional public authority' if either its structures and work were closely linked with the delegating or contracting out state body, or it was exercising powers of a public nature directly assigned to it by statute, or it was exercising coercive powers devolved from the State.[229] As a result, the JCHR concluded that the development in the case law had led to a 'serious gap' in the protection which the HRA was intended to offer and would be likely to lead to a deprivation of avenues of redress for individuals whose Convention rights had been breached.[230]

As a possible answer to these concerns, the JCHR put forward an alternative approach[231] which Sunkin has since referred to as a 'government or state programme test'.[232] Under this test, functional public authorities would be identified without reference to the nature of the organisation itself. The key test for 'public function' would be whether the relevant 'function' is one for which the government has assumed responsibility in the public interest.[233] As an example a distinction was drawn between the discharge of health services which in itself is not a public function and the doing of the work as part of a 'government programme' of health care, which is. Further, under this approach, whether an organisation performs those functions under direct statutory authority, or under contract, should not lead to a distinction in the application of the HRA. This was because a private body operating to discharge a government programme is just as likely as the State to exercise a degree of power and control over the realisation of an individual's Convention rights which, had it not been so delegated, would be exercised directly by the State. Under this test it is arguable, therefore, that a private care home which is providing accommodation for a young person on behalf of the local authority could be performing a function of a public nature because it is providing residential accommodation as part of the programme of care established by the State and set out in the Children Act 1989 towards that person. Where the home is providing accommodation for a young person on a solely private basis and for which government has not assumed any public responsibility it will therefore not be exercising any such function because it is not being provided as part of any such programme of care.

Shortly after this the JCHR reported again on the issue, noting that although there had been a number of significant developments[234] since their last report 'as the law stands,

---

[229] As noted by the JCHR, 'The Meaning of Public Authority' (n 186) 40.

[230] *Ibid*, para 40.

[231] *Ibid*, paras 46–7.

[232] See M Sunkin, 'Pushing Forward the Frontiers' (n 207) for an analysis of the test.

[233] JCHR, 'The Meaning of Public Authority' (n 186).

[234] *Ibid*. The most significant developments had been that the government had accepted the previous report's recommendations and indicated a readiness to intervene in any case at a Court of Appeal level in which the meaning of a public authority was at issue. In addition, the Office of the Deputy Prime Minister published guidance to local authorities on contracting for services in light of the HRA. However, this guidance was heavily criticised

the only guidance that can be given on the important issue of whether a body should be considered a functional public authority for the purposes of the HRA is to seek further 'specialist legal advice'.[235] They were unable to consider the two cases that had been decided on the issue since their last report as they were the subject of appeal to the House of Lords. They concluded, therefore: 'We consider that this represents a serious failure to achieve the aspiration of a human rights culture in which Convention rights are secured for individuals without the need for formal legal proceedings or the involvement of legal advisers.'[236]

However, in a somewhat surprising decision the House of Lords declined to incorporate the suggestions of the JCHR[237] and others who were critical of the test adopted in *Leonard Cheshire*[238] when it delivered its judgment in the subsequent decision of *YL v Birmingham City Council and Others*.[239] Here, the applicant, YL, was aged 84 and suffering from Alzheimer's disease. Pursuant to its duty to provide accommodation to her under section 21 of the NAA[240] the local authority contracted with Southern Cross Healthcare Ltd (SC) to look after her in one of their private care homes. The obligation by SC to observe the Convention rights of residents was an express term of this contract and was also incorporated into the agreement between SC and YL. In addition, YL's fees were almost entirely paid by the local authority and the local NHS Primary Trust.[241] In accordance with the required notice period in the contract, SC subsequently sought to terminate the contract and remove YL from the home. In an action seeking declarations that her removal would breach her rights under certain Articles of the European Convention, the High Court and the Court of Appeal decided as a preliminary issue that SC was not exercising a public function within section 6(3)(b) of the HRA, following the Court of Appeal's previous decisions in the area. On appeal, the House of Lords also held, by a narrow majority, Lord Bingham of Cornhill and Lady Hale of Richmond dissenting, that SC could not be regarded as exercising a public function within the terms of section 6(3)(b) of the HRA. The majority relied on a number of factors in coming to this decision. First, they drew a distinction between *arranging* accommodation, under section 21 of the NAA, which was a non-delegable duty of a local authority, and *providing* care and accommodation, which was a service that could also be performed by either a voluntary organisation or a profit-making company under a bilateral or trilateral contractual arrangement between the local authority, the provider and/or the service user.[242] The position would be different,

---

in their report for being badly written, difficult to follow and for not having had any significant positive impact on the protection of human rights.

[235] *Ibid*, para 27.

[236] *Ibid*, para 27.

[237] *YL v Birmingham City Council and Others* [2007] UKHL 27, paras 89–90 (Lord Mance): via a rejection of the *Pepper v Hart* rule to HRA matters.

[238] *Leonard Cheshire* (n 203).

[239] *YL* (n 237): for a commentary on the case and its general impact on this area see A Williams, '*YL v Birmingham City Council*: Contracting Out and "Functions of a Public Nature"' (2008) 4 *European Human Rights Law Review* 524.

[240] *YL* (n 237) para 14: summarised by Lord Bingham as containing the duty to provide 'residential accommodation plus care and attention for those who, by reason of age, illness, disability or any other circumstances are in need of care and attention which is not otherwise available to them'.

[241] *Ibid*: if the person may also need health care under the National Health Service Act 1977, the local authority must invite the relevant health body to assist in the assessment. A large slice of the social security budget was transferred to local authorities to enable them to meet these new responsibilities. See also paras 49–52: Baroness Hale's summary of the development of the statutory framework.

[242] *Ibid*, para 115 (Lord Mance).

Lord Scott argued,[243] if the managers of privately owned care homes enjoyed special statutory powers entitling them to restrain, discipline or confine residents in some way but that was not the case here. Lord Mance[244] pointed to a number of institutional factors that went against treating SC as carrying out a function of a public nature: providing care and accommodation was not an inherently governmental function and its commercial motivation meant that SC acted as a 'private, profit-earning company'. Second, by paying the fees of those who were assisted under the NAA the local authority was merely paying for a service carried out by the care home. It did not amount to public subsidy and thus was not 'public funding' in the ordinary sense. Furthermore, YL continued 'to enjoy Convention rights in respect of the provision of care and accommodation provided under section 21 of the 1948 Act against Birmingham'[245] which, would in turn, put the onus on the authority to take any steps open to it to protect the resident's human rights.[246] Finally, and above all, the contractual source of the arrangement seems to have been the decisive factor in the majority speeches.[247] The essentially contractual source of SC's activities, it was said, differentiated them from any function of a public nature. The issue fell, therefore, 'to be tested by reference to YL's rights and SC's obligations under the agreement between them; by reference, that is to say, to private law'.[248] There were two issues, however, on which all five judges agreed. First, there was no single test of universal application to determine when functions of a public nature were discharged by non-governmental bodies;[249] second, they expressly disapproved of using a close historical and organisation relationship between the local authority and the private body as a decisive factor in favour of the application of section 6(3)(b).[250] In contrast, Lord Bingham, in his dissenting opinion, felt that although no universal test could be applied to the question of whether a body was performing a function of a public nature, the combined effect of a number of factors[251] led him to consider that it was the ultimate responsibility of the State to ensure that those described in section 21 of the NAA[252] 'are accommodated and looked after through the agency of the

---

[243] *Ibid*, para 28 (Lord Scott). This was presumably a reference to the decision in *R(A) v Partnerships in Care Ltd* [2002] EWHC 529, in which the court held that s6(3)(b) covered the functions of a mental nursing home in which the claimant, who had a severe personality disorder, was compulsorily detained pursuant to the Mental Health Act 1983.

[244] *Ibid*, para 116 (Lord Mance).

[245] *Ibid*, para 149 (Lord Neureberger).

[246] *Ibid*, paras 27 and 29 (Lord Scott), para 149 (Lord Neureberger). Lord Mance did concede that 'at least, in some circumstances, those rights could be of somewhat less value in practice than if they existed against the proprietor'.

[247] *Ibid*, paras 116 and 120 (Lord Mance), para 34 (Lord Scott).

[248] *Ibid*, para 34 (Lord Scott). As a result, it has been argued that the general reluctance to allow public law rights to interfere with private contractual arrangements will always act as an override even where the nature of the function has some public element. Furthermore, this has generally been a feature of judicial review cases: S Palmer, 'Public, Private and the HRA 1998: An Ideological Divide' (2007) 66(3) *CLJ* 559.

[249] *YL* (n 237) para 5 (Lord Bingham), para 65 (Baroness Hale).

[250] *Ibid*, para 61 (Baroness Hale) and the majority opinion at para 105 (Lord Mance).

[251] *Ibid*, paras 6–11. These were: the nature of the function; the role and responsibility of the State in relation to the subject matter in question; the nature and extent of any relevant statutory power or duty; the extent to which the State monitors this duty; whether the function in question is one for which, whether directly or indirectly, and whether as a matter of course or as a last resort, the State is by one means or another willing to pay and the extent of the risk, if any, that improper performance of the function might violate an individual's Convention right.

[252] Section 21 describes these people as those who 'by reason of age, illness, disability or any other circumstances are in need of care and attention which is not otherwise available to them'.

state and at its expense if no other source of accommodation and care and no other source of funding is available'.[253] For Baroness Hale, also dissenting, it was simply 'artificial and legalistic to draw a distinction between meeting those needs and the task of assessing and arranging them, when the state has assumed responsibility for seeing that both are done'.[254] What was key to both dissenting opinions was the vulnerable nature of the individuals affected:

> Despite the intensive regulation to which care homes are subject, it is not unknown that senile and helpless residents of such homes are subjected to treatment which may threaten their survival, may amount to inhumane treatment, may deprive them unjustifiably of their liberty and may seriously and unnecessarily infringe their personal autonomy and family relationships. These risks would have been well understood by Parliament when it passed the 1998 Act. If, as may be confidently asserted, Parliament intended the Act to offer substantial protection of the important values expressed in the articles of the Convention given domestic effect by the 1998 Act, it can scarcely have supposed that residents of privately run care homes, placed in such homes pursuant to sections 21 and 26 of the 1948 Act, would be unprotected.[255]

In a subsequent report on the human rights of older people in healthcare the JCHR took the opportunity to express its disappointment at the decision and agreement with the minority position in the judgment.[256] Shortly after the *YL*[257] decision Government Ministers expressed their agreement with the JCHR's position that the current state of the law was unsatisfactory, particularly for elderly care home residents, and promised to amend the HRA to ensure that all independent providers of publicly funded care homes were bound by the HRA.[258] The JCHR, however, maintained its preference for the scope of the HRA to be clarified by means of a separate Act dealing solely with the general issue of the meaning of 'public authority'. This, it said, would have the benefit of dealing with the problem of scope across the board rather than on a piecemeal sectoral basis, ensuring that the law in this area would be consistent throughout the UK; and bring much needed clarity to a complex area of law.[259] The Government's answer was to pass a separate piece of legislation to deal with the matter. Section 145 of the Health and Social Care Act 2008 provides as follows:

> (1) A person ('P') who provides accommodation, together with nursing or personal care, in a care home for an individual under arrangements made with P under the relevant statutory provisions is to be taken for the purposes of subsection (3)(b) of section 6 of the Human Rights Act 1998 (c. 42) (acts of public authorities) to be exercising a function of a public nature in doing so.

[253] *YL* (n 237) para 15 (Lord Bingham).
[254] *Ibid*, para 66 (Baroness Hale).
[255] *Ibid*, para 19 (Lord Bingham), para 67 (Baroness Hale).
[256] JCHR, 'The Human Rights of Older People in Healthcare' (Eighteenth Report of Session 2006–07) 159.
[257] *YL* (n 237).
[258] Ben Bradshaw MP said during the Committee stage of the Health and Social Care Bill, 'I am happy to repeat the assurance that the Government have made it clear that they are committed to amending the Human Rights Act to ensure that all independent providers of publicly funded care homes are covered by it.' PBC Deb, 15 Jan 2008, c 200. In addition, Vera Baird, the then Parliamentary Under-Secretary of State at the Ministry of Justice, had previously stated that if the House of Lords did not overturn the Court of Appeal's narrow interpretation of 'public authority' in the forthcoming *YL* decision, it was the Government's intention to fill the gap in the protection offered by the HRA. HC Deb, 15 June 2007, c 1045.
[259] JCHR, 'Health and Social Care Bill' (Eighth Report of Session 2007–08) 1.12.

The provision is limited to the residential care home sector and effectively reversed the decision of the House of Lords in *YL*[260] in that it provides that human rights protection travels with a service user who is placed in an independent care home by a local authority. This is because in order for the section to apply in England and Wales, a service user must be placed in residential accommodation under Part III of the NAA.[261] Although this is good news for those residents in this position, section 145 does not affect the human rights obligations of other independent care providers in other sectors contracted to local authorities, they will continue to fall outside the HRA by virtue of the reasoning in *YL*.[262] In this way, the legislation has failed to take the opportunity to, as the JCHR had requested, clarify this complex area of law and ensure that service users in *all* sectors are provided with the same level of protection under the HRA.[263] It remains the case, therefore that, save for those service users who can come within section 145 of the Health and Social Care Act 2008, where public services are being delivered under private contractual arrangements they will be regulated solely by the private law of contract and will remain outside the reach of the HRA. There is seemingly only one real exception allowed for by *YL* and that is if the body in question is exercising special statutory powers of a coercive nature; this may indicate that the function being performed is a public one regardless of whether it is exercised under a private contractual arrangement.[264]

Contracting out Services—the Significance for the Family and Family Law

The current interpretation of a 'functional' public authority to family law is therefore very significant, particularly when we consider the increasingly high level of reliance on the private sector in certain areas of service provisions with regard to housing and social care. For example, in evidence to the JCHR,[265] Shelter reported that nearly 50 per cent of social housing is now out of local housing authority control, and suggested that this figure was likely to increase. In addition, the Department of Health[266] reported that the independent sector provided 92 per cent of care homes and 64 per cent of contact hours of home care. For children's services the position was, as they noted, quite complex. Voluntary organisations provide a range of services for children at a local level. For example, 15 per cent of children in foster placements (excluding those with relatives or friends) are in placements arranged by an independent agency, with the remaining 85 per cent in placements provided by the Council. However, these figures are an average as there will be wide variations by area. Voluntary adoption agencies (VAAs) also make a significant contribution to the adoption service, playing an important supporting role alongside local authorities in assessing prospective adopters. Statistics prepared by the Consortium of VAAs showed

---

[260] *YL* (n 237).
[261] Section 145(2)(a) of the Health and Social Care Act 2008.
[262] *YL* (n 237).
[263] JCHR report, 'The Meaning of Public Authority' (n 186) para 139.
[264] J Landau, 'Functional Public Authorities' (n 209) and S Palmer, 'Public, Private and the HRA' (n 248).
[265] JCHR report, 'The Meaning of Public Authority' (n 186) 5, and DCA, 'Guide to the HRA' (n 186) 20.
[266] JCHR report, 'The Meaning of Public Authority' (n 186) Memorandum of Evidence 2.

that, in 2001–02, 604 children were placed for adoption with adopters approved by their member agencies. This accounts for around 20 per cent of 'looked-after children' likely to have been placed for adoption during the year. The involvement of the private sector in such provision is clearly anticipated by social services legislation[267] and, in the case of children, section 17 of the Children Act 1989 provides that local authorities may make arrangements with others to provide services on their behalf. Local authorities are therefore able to purchase children's services from the public, private and voluntary sectors. This has led to a wide variety of contracting arrangements for services, such as special school placements, residential care placements and foster care placements. The Department for Children, Schools and Families, working with the Department of Health, has supported the development of standardised contracts that can be used by all local authorities when purchasing placements in the private and voluntary sector. The aim of these contracts, according to the 'Every Child Matters: Change For Children' website is 'to minimise duplication; share good practice; simplify transactions for both commissioners and suppliers; and ensure a fair and transparent market'.[268] At the time of writing,[269] three national contracts have been published: for the placement of children in independent special schools; for the placement of children in residential homes and for foster care placements. As a result, local authorities are not only currently placing children in children's homes run by voluntary organisations or private bodies but are actively being encouraged to do so as part of government policy.[270] Furthermore, in evidence to the JCHR, the Children's Alliance for England[271] gave evidence that in addition to adopting and fostering services, the private sector is also involved in the provision of health care, of escort services and tracking schemes for juvenile offenders, for example, Rebound ECD, a subsidiary of Group 4 Falck, is responsible for the running of secure training centres. Thus, children are in constant contact with the private sector and, furthermore, have no choice in the matter. The situation was summed up by the following statement from the JCHR: 'We have not found an area of state provision for children in which the private sector is not involved'.[272]

It is apparent, therefore, that an increasing number of local authority functions concerning families and their children are being 'contracted out' to private service providers. It is also clear that this has arisen as a deliberate policy shift towards an economy of mixed provision of such services from public, private and voluntary sources. Although this shift in policy has raised objections of an ideological nature, this is not the place to discuss them. However, it is clear that this shift in policy has occurred without consideration of the difficulties that such mixed provision will raise within the legal system and in particular, the issue it will raise between the application of public or private law. For the moment, this issue has been resolved in favour of private law and it is clear from the current state of the case law, discussed above, that services delivered under contractual arrangements with

---

[267] Part 3 of the National Assistance Act 1948 (see s26 NAA) is the obvious example for adults. But s29 NAA, s45 of the Health Services and Public Health Act 1968, and Sch 8 to the National Health Service Act 1977, also refer to local authorities 'making arrangements' as respects certain matters.

[268] The Department for Children, Schools and Families at www.everychildmatters.gov.uk.

[269] June 2009.

[270] See, eg, the 'Joint Planning and Commissioning Process' at www.everychildmatters.gov.uk/strategy/planningandcommissioning/about/.

[271] JCHR, 'The Meaning of Public Authority' (n 186) Written Evidence No 17 'Memorandum of Evidence from the Children's Alliance'.

[272] *Ibid.*

private or voluntary sector providers are highly likely to fall outside the ambit of section 6 of the HRA, the exception being provision where statutory powers of discipline, restraint and control are transferred.[273] As a result, service users will have to rely on the private law of contract as a means of protecting their rights under such arrangements. We turn therefore to consider the effectiveness of such provision.

In *Leonard Cheshire*,[274] Lord Woolf suggested that it may be possible for a resident of a private care home to require the local authority who was responsible for the cost of his stay to enter into a contract with the private service provider whereby the latter undertakes to fully protect the residents' Convention rights. In this way, he argued, not only could the local authority rely on the contract to protect residents' Convention rights but so may the resident as the person for whose benefit the contract was made. The National Framework Contract for the Placement of Children in Children's Homes certainly seems to make substantial provision for the protection of children placed.[275] It commences with the provision for 'individual placing agreements (IPAs)' to be made with respect to each child placed, which are in turn subject to the terms of the contract.[276] Further, providers must be registered, licensed or approved in accordance with, and must 'comply with, the provisions of the Children's Homes Regulations 2001, the National Minimum Standards for Children's Homes 2002 and all relevant current and future Acts of Parliament, amendment or re-enactment of any Act, Statutory Regulation and other such laws and statutory guidance relevant to the provision of the service'.[277] Most important of all: 'the Provider will at all times in its performance of the Services and its treatment of Children have regards to, and abide by, the principles of the Human Rights Act 1998, the European Convention on Human Rights and the provisions of the Children Act 1989.'[278]

Reference should also be made to the extent of the liability of a core public authority in relation to functions that it chooses to contract out. One argument[279] is that the public authority itself remains liable under the HRA for any breach of Convention rights that results. Thus, in the case of a local authority, the very act of contracting out one of its functions to a service provider is in itself an exercise of a function for which it remains accountable. This was certainly the view held by the majority in *YL*[280]—it formed the basis of the argument that the human rights of the residents in that case were already well protected and did not additionally require the care home to be made liable under the HRA. The argument essentially relies upon Strasbourg jurisprudence to the effect that a

---

[273] This may certainly be the case with regard to secure accommodation centres and institutions that are concerned with youth offenders.

[274] *Leonard Cheshire* (n 203) para 34.

[275] The National Contract for the Placement of Children in Foster Care also has similar provisions: www.dcsf.gov.uk/everychildmatters/resources-and-practice/IG00316/.

[276] www.everychildmatters.gov.uk/_files/571B2A988D31861A2CC6D2D148CE6009.pdf at 2.2.

[277] www.everychildmatters.gov.uk/_files/571B2A988D31861A2CC6D2D148CE6009.pdf at 3.1, noting also that 'where a placement is made outside of England the Provider must be registered, licensed or approved in accordance with the equivalent legislation, regulations and standards relevant for Wales, Scotland or Northern Ireland'.

[278] www.everychildmatters.gov.uk/_files/571B2A988D31861A2CC6D2D148CE6009.pdf at 3.6. Note also that other provisions are made with respect to children's rights eg the requirement for the Provider to have a clear policy on children's rights and to provide training and guidance on such policy to its staff.

[279] Relied on by the Department of Health and the Deputy Prime Minister, although the Secretary of State for Constitutional Affairs took a more cautious view: JCHR, 'The Meaning of Public Authority' (n 186) 27–8.

[280] *YL* (n 237).

State cannot absolve itself of its Convention obligations by delegating the fulfilment of its obligations to private bodies or individuals.[281] This accountability may thus be further entrenched by entering into a contract with the private service provider to fully protect the Convention rights of the service user as suggested by Lord Woolf and evidenced by the National Framework Contract for the Placement of Children detailed above. The problem is that it seems that the use of such contractual terms may not be so widespread; the Audit Commission[282] found in 2003 that 61 per cent of local government, health and criminal justice bodies have taken no action to ensure that their contractors comply with the HRA. Even if this is no longer the case and the use of such contracts is now widespread, there are still significant concerns regarding the effectiveness of the private contract as a means of protecting the interests, if not the rights, of vulnerable individuals First, there is strong opposition to the view that a local authority that contracts out its services will remain liable in domestic law for any breach of Convention rights by the contracted to body. As the JCHR[283] noted in its first report into the meaning of a public authority, a contracting-out body would be liable for the actions of the contracted-to body in breach of Convention rights only where it could be shown that the public body had a positive obligation to protect rights in the circumstances at issue. A positive obligation to take reasonable steps to prevent a breach exists only where a public authority knows, or ought to know, of a real and immediate risk to the Convention rights of a particular individual or group.[284] Thus, when a local authority has taken reasonable steps to ensure that services are contracted out to organisations that it is reasonably sure will not breach Convention rights, the obligation has been satisfied. In these circumstances, it is argued, there is no reason why the contracting public body would be liable under the HRA for a breach of Convention rights by a contracted-to service provider. What are these reasonable steps? Certainly, making provision, as the National Framework Contract has, for compliance with regulatory frameworks, for spot checks, training and for compliance with legislation concerning the rights of children would seem to fit the bill. However, it is clear from the numerous public inquiries into the unfortunately frequent failures of the child protection system that these are by no means a guarantee of the protection of the rights of children. Viewed from this perspective it is difficult to justify why such children, already made vulnerable by the experiences that have led them into State care, have had the enforcement of their Convention rights made even harder. This is arguably worse than the position of the elderly and the infirm when we consider that children placed in children's homes are there precisely because the system has failed them once already.

Second, the protection of Convention rights through contracts between the public body and the private service provider may raise difficulties of consistency. The terms of such contracts can vary between different local authority areas and, as has been noted by the JCHR, although standard contractual terms devised centrally may mitigate this effect, the reality is that such contracts will be subject to individual negotiation which will, in turn, be dependent upon a number of factors: the willingness of contractors to accept human rights obligations, local financial constraints, the availability of potential contractors in

---

[281] *Ibid.*
[282] Audit Commission, *Human Rights: Improving Public Service Delivery* (September 2003) para 24.
[283] JCHR, 'The Meaning of Public Authority' (n 186) 28–9.
[284] *X and Others v Bedfordshire County Council* [1995] 3 All ER 352.

any given area and where contractual terms are being negotiated between private service providers and individual service users. This raises significant concerns regarding the potential inequality of bargaining power.

Third, a clear potential for inconsistency with regard to enforceability is also apparent when we consider that this will be dependent upon how informed service users are about their contractual rights and whether or not such terms are actually enforceable by users who are not themselves parties to the contract.[285] Research by the Office of Fair Trading[286] found that only about one third of elderly care home residents surveyed were aware of being signatory to a contract, and over two thirds either did not know or could not remember what sort of areas were covered by their agreement with the home. No such research has been conducted in relation to children but it would not be such a huge leap of imagination to conclude that the likelihood of a child, even if *Gillick* competent, either knowing or being aware of the implications of such contractual terms will be very low and will be dependent upon others being willing and able to act on their behalf. It may be the case that children would be just as unaware of their human rights if they were placed in a state-run facility; however, the point is that 'looked-after children' or those acting on their behalf ought to be made aware of the available remedies, and any differences in them. Fourth, the question remains as to what can be practically achieved in terms of enforceability where no such issues exist, that is, where the service provider is not contesting the human rights provision in the contract. For example, if a young person is to be removed from a children's home by a private service provider (under the NFC either party may terminate the IPA by giving seven days' written notice) little can be achieved of practical benefit by seeking to rely on the provisions purporting to protect the Convention rights of the young person. The local authority cannot, where the contractual terms have been complied with, force the provider to take the young person back. In contrast, under section 8(1) of the HRA the court may grant such relief or remedy, or make such order, within its powers as it considers just and appropriate. There is also authority to suggest that the remedy ought to be effective.[287] In any event, the remedies under the HRA are not just limited to damages due to the fact that a wide degree of judicial discretion is allowed for. To a child or young person who is likely to have suffered a significant level of abuse or lack of care and for whom the stability of a placement is therefore crucial, this is no small matter. Finally, as the JCHR noted itself, the development of a human rights culture within the private sector which is dependent upon either litigation or the threat of litigation is hardly the best way in which such a culture could be fostered. A more positive and clear way would be by express and direct obligations under section 6 of the HRA. For now, however, it remains to be seen whether the narrow majority in *YL* will be overturned.

Horizontal Effect

On the face of it section 6(1) lays the obligation to act compatibly with Convention rights solely upon public authorities and not, therefore, upon private bodies or individuals.

---

[285] E Palmer, 'Residential Care: Rights of the Elderly and the Third Party Contracts Act' (2000) 22 *Journal Social Welfare and Family Law* 461 and P Craig, 'Contracting Out' (n 207).

[286] JCHR, 'The Meaning of Public Authority' (n 186) para 123.

[287] D Feldman, 'Remedies for Violations of Convention Rights under the HRA' [1998] *European Human Rights Law Review* 691 and generally, M Amos, *Human Rights Law* (Oxford, Hart Publishing, 2006) ch 6.

This appears to be further confirmed by sections 7 and 8, which deal with proceedings and remedies only in relation to actions against public authorities. However, pre- and post-incorporation of the HRA there was a great deal of discussion concerning the horizontal effect of the Act and particularly whether it was direct, indirect, and whether it was in a strong or weak form.[288] A measure will have direct effect if it imposes direct duties upon a private body to abide by its provisions and it makes any breaches of those duties directly actionable by the aggrieved party. Where it is clear that the rights in question were *not* intended to be directly binding upon a private body and they are therefore not directly actionable, the courts have sometimes applied a form of *indirect* horizontal effect which may be relied upon to influence the interpretation and application of pre-existing law. Suffice to say, the issue has been largely settled and it is now reasonably clear that the Act has created a limited form of *indirect* horizontal effect to the Convention rights; the possibility of direct horizontal effect appears to have been judicially ruled out. The indirect horizontal effect of the Act occurs as a result of three of the provisions contained in it. First, under section 6(3) courts and tribunals are regarded as public authorities themselves and thus the concomitant obligation under section 6(1) to act in a manner that is compatible with Convention rights will apply to their interpretative function concerning both statute[289] *and* common law. Further, other bodies who fall within the definition of a public authority under section 6(3)(b) will also be under the same obligation towards private individuals. Second, under section 3 the courts have a duty in 'so far as is possible to do so' to interpret legislation in a manner which is compatible with Convention rights. This duty will apply in all cases and will include those involving private individuals or public bodies.[290] Third, as noted above, section 2(1) requires courts to 'have regard' to Strasbourg jurisprudence when 'determining a question which has arisen in connection with a Convention right'. This provision enables at the least an, albeit weak, form of indirect horizontal effect because courts must, as a minimum, take into account the Convention rights in interpreting and applying the common law.[291]

However, the debate concerning the extent of the 'horizontal effect' of the Act has, in the main, focused upon the effect that section 6 has had on the interpretation of certain areas of the common law and thus the doctrine has been of most significance to fields outside of family law.[292] However, given that much of family law is now the subject of legislation it would seem that the doctrine's fullest effect has been felt in relation to the impact of a combination of section 6(3) and section 3.[293] For example, in a classic section 8 application

---

[288] For an overview of the general debate on 'horizontal effect' see M Hunt, 'The "Horizontal Effect" of the Human Rights Act' (1998) 3 *PL* 423; W Wade, 'Horizons of Horizontality' (2000) 116 *LQR* 217; R Buxton, 'The Human Rights Act and Private Law' (2000)116 *LQR* 48; A Lester and D Pannick, 'The Impact of the Human Rights Act on Private Law: The Knight's Move' (2000) 116 *LQR* 380; J Beatson and S Grosz: 'Horizontality: A Footnote' (2000) 116 *LQR* 385; G Phillipson, 'A Bang or a Whimper?' (n 16); G Phillipson, 'Clarity Postponed' (n 16); J Morgan, 'Questioning the True Effect of the HRA' (2002) 22 (2) *Legal Studies* 159; see also his 'Privacy, Confidence and Horizontal Effect: "Hello" Trouble' (2003) 62 (2) *CLJ* 444; D Beyleveld and SD Pattinson, 'Horizontality Applicability and Horizontal Effect' (2002) 118 *LQR* 623.

[289] This is in addition to the duty imposed by s3(1) discussed above, which requires courts to read and give effect to primary and secondary legislation in a manner compatible with Convention rights, so far as it is possible to do so. This will apply regardless of whether the statute concerns obligations upon a private or a public body.

[290] *Ghaidan* (n 54).

[291] H Fenwick and G Phillipson, *Media Freedom* (n 172) ch 3.

[292] It has had the most significance in developing a law of privacy; in the family law context see *Re S* (n 108).

[293] However, there are some areas of common law that remain, for example, the law relating to cohabitants and property. The full effect of the horizontal effect doctrine will be discussed in the chapter dealing with this issue.

for contact between a parent and child under the Children Act, the dispute is clearly between two private individuals and thus neither party could be considered a public authority in order to trigger the vertical effect of the Act. However, once the application comes before the court it will, as a public authority under section 6(3), be under a duty to ensure that *it* acts in a manner that is compatible with all the parties' Convention rights under s6 (1) *and* that under section 3, as far as possible, the Children Act must be interpreted in a manner that is compatible with the parties' Convention rights. In addition, the court is also under a duty to 'have regard' to Strasbourg jurisprudence under section 2 when determining the question of the Article 8 rights in the case. In this way both parents, and the child, as private individuals will obtain the benefit of the HRA, horizontally.

Hence, to return to the question of what or whom is termed a public authority under section 6, it is apparent from the discussion above that some form of limited human rights protection for victims of breaches of human rights by those bodies deemed to fall outside of the definition of a public authority will arise from the indirect horizontal effect of the Act. This will be in addition to the general protection afforded by the criminal law and private law actions in tort and contract. However, there is one important limitation: any applications that rely upon the indirect horizontal effect of the HRA cannot be freestanding and will depend upon there being an existing cause of action in order to be able to put the matter before the court. Thus, in the case of a child who is being accommodated by a private care home and who wishes to bring a claim that her human rights have been breached by the private service provider, she cannot simply present herself at court arguing that a breach of, say, her Article 8 rights have occurred. She must make these claims in the context of an existing cause of action against the private service providers. In reality this will mean that there will need to be a clear basis to argue that a breach of contract has occurred. As can be seen from the discussion above concerning contracting out there are significant reasons to doubt that this would be straightforward or effective. It is noteworthy that in *YL*,[294] the act of SC that gave rise to the litigation, the service of a notice terminating the agreement under which she was entitled to remain in the care home, although not the subject of the appeal to the House of Lords, appears to have been valid according to the law of contract. (Fortunately, for YL, by the time the matter was brought to the House of Lords, SC had withdrawn the request to remove her from the home.) As a result, the application of indirect horizontal effect may therefore be of little practical benefit against private service providers.[295]

Proportionality, Judicial Review and Deference

As noted in earlier in this chapter, the doctrine of proportionality relates to the set of tests used to establish whether a limitation of rights is justifiable. The use of the doctrine is not confined to the ECtHR and can be found in use all over the world, most notably at the

---

[294] *YL* (n 237).
[295] K Marcus, 'What is Public Power: The Court's Approach to the Public Authority Definition Under the HRA' in J Jowell and J Cooper, *Delivering Rights* (n 20).

European Court of Justice (ECJ) and in commonwealth jurisdictions such as South Africa, Canada and Australia.[296]

The ECtHR has developed a standard formula with which to approach alleged interferences with the qualified Convention rights and the same procedure, to a large degree, is followed at the domestic level. Once it has been decided that the Convention right is engaged, the next step is to determine whether the interference can be justified by the State concerned. This question will be decided by reference to three factors:

— Is the interference 'in accordance with the law'?
— Is the interference done to secure one of the legitimate aims in the Article?
— Is the interference necessary in a democratic society?

Proportionality comes into the equation at the final stage of this formula; whether the alleged interference is necessary in a democratic society. The interference must fulfil a 'pressing social need', and be 'proportionate to the legitimate aim pursued'. We have also seen that application of the related doctrine of the margin of appreciation will also take place at this stage. For it is when the ECtHR makes its assessment of whether a pressing social need exists that both the *scope* of the margin to be accorded to the State is decided and the appraisal of whether the measures at issue are *proportionate* is taken. Both doctrines are heavily intertwined and a general consensus has formed in the literature that a roughly inverse relationship exists between the two. Thus, the wider the margin, the less strict is the standard of review.

We have also seen that the ECtHR generally applies three forms of the proportionality test, which vary in intensity.[297] The strictest version, 'the least restrictive means' test, requires the court to answer the following question: is the disputed measure the least onerous/restrictive/intrusive that could be adopted in the circumstances? This corresponds to the test adopted by other international jurisdictions. However, it has rarely been applied by the ECtHR and never in the family law context. The second type of test used is the 'sufficiency test', where the Court will ask whether there exist both relevant and sufficient reasons justifying the interference at issue. This represents a more stringent standard of review reserved for cases where fundamental rights are at stake and where the measures proposed are particularly restrictive. The third and final type of test used is the 'fair balance test', where the Court asks whether there is a reasonable relationship between the interference and the legitimate aim pursued or a fair balance between the general and individual interests at stake. This represents the least strict standard of review. It was argued, in Chapter 1, that this version of the test was most likely to be applied in family law cases due to the impact of the often wide margin of appreciation granted in such cases.

Proportionality, Judicial Review and Deference—The Domestic Experience

The impact of the proportionality principle on the doctrine of judicial review has been both controversial and significant. The necessity to take it into account arises once a claim is made that a public authority has breached the human rights of the claimant in its decision. This issue is of particular significance when we consider the variety of areas of

---

[296] See pp 40–41.
[297] See also ch 1 pp 17–24 for a more detailed description of these tests.

family life that can be impacted upon by the decisions of various public authorities, such as local authorities in their educational, housing and childcare functions and in relation to other 'governmental' bodies such as immigration and welfare benefit tribunals. We will now turn to a consideration of how the courts have developed the doctrine of judicial review to accommodate the proportionality principle demanded by the HRA.

Judicial Review and the Concept of Proportionality

As noted throughout this Chapter, the passage of the HRA led to a number of different demands being placed upon the judiciary to which they were previously unaccustomed and posed significant challenges to the constitutional structure of the UK. The doctrine of separation of powers, whilst informal, nevertheless allowed the development of a strong tradition of judicial independence which was, in turn, dependent upon the maintenance of an apolitical judiciary which was respectful of the sovereignty of Parliament. A combination of reliance upon this respect for parliamentary sovereignty and the ultra vires doctrine seemingly went on to form the foundations of an orthodox version of judicial review:[298] the so-called '*Wednesbury* principles'.[299] This version of administrative review envisaged that little or no role would be played by the judiciary in the formulation of policy and thus the courts were confined to checking the legality, as opposed to the merits, of executive actions.[300] The courts were therefore confined to a limited supervisory role. Over time, the *Wednesbury* principles were developed in such a way that a decision of a public body would only be considered unlawful if it fell into the three 'heads' of review: illegality, procedural impropriety or irrationality. Not only did this strictly limit the opportunities to challenge the merits of a decision but it also resulted in a very low intensity of review. The emergence of a theory of 'common law constitutionalism' over the last two decades, however, helped to facilitate an alternative 'rights-based' explanation of the basis of judicial review.[301] Writers from this perspective argued that the underlying purpose of judicial review was, in fact, to promote individual rights[302] and the role of the courts was, therefore, to give effect to the fundamental constitutional rights embodied in international and domestic common law.[303] A decision of a public body, according to this argument, would only be unlawful if it unjustifiably violated the claimant's rights.[304] This version of administrative review

[298] Although, as Ellie Palmer notes in her excellent summary of the constitutional foundations of judicial review, this was somewhat of a fiction: E Palmer, *Judicial Review, Socio-Economic Rights and the HRA* (n 183) 152. This is also referred to as the 'classic English model of judicial review—see C Harlow, 'A Special Relationship? American Influences on Judicial Review in England' in I Loveland (ed), *A Special Relationship? American Influences on Public Law in the UK* (Oxford, Oxford University Press, 1995).

[299] *Associated Provincial Picture Houses Ltd v Wednesbury Corporation* [1948] 1 KB 223.

[300] C Forsyth and M Elliot, 'The Legitimacy of Judicial Review' [2003] 1 *PL* 266; HR Wade and CF Forsyth, *Administrative Law* 8th edn (Oxford, Oxford University Press, 2000) 35–7 and Lord Irvine of Lairg QC, 'Judges and Decision Makers: The Theory and Practice of *Wednesbury* Review' [1996] *PL* 59.

[301] TRS Allan, 'Dworkin and Dicey: The Rule of Law as Integrity' (1988) 8 *OJLS* 266; J Goldsworthy 'Homogenising Constitutions' (2003) *OJLS* 483.

[302] TRS Allan, 'The Constitutional Foundations of Judicial Review: Conceptual Conundrum or Interpretative Inquiry? (2002) 61 *CLJ* 87.

[303] P Craig, *Administrative Law* 3rd edn (London, Sweet & Maxwell, 1994) and Sir John Laws, 'Is the High Court Guardian of Fundamental Constitutional Rights?' (1993) *PL* 59.

[304] For a critique of these rights-based theories of the constitution see T Poole, 'Legitimacy, Rights and Judicial Review' (2005) 25 (4) *OJLS* 697.

therefore required the courts to enter into an evaluative exercise when reviewing administrative decisions.

The obvious tension between these two models of judicial review—orthodox (supervisory) and rights based (evaluative)—were apparent in the case law prior to the incorporation of the ECHR and thus, as Palmer[305] notes, despite the emergence of proportionality as a separate ground for the review of executive action with regard to EU law[306] there was considerable evidence of significant resistance to the use of proportionality outside of this particular context.[307] As a result, although significant developments of the *Wednesbury* review principles subsequently took place, such as the development of 'anxious scrutiny'[308] and the increasing use of the principle of illegality with regard to the protection of fundamental rights,[309] resistance to the use of proportionality as a separate head of review in cases where fundamental rights were at stake continued.[310] The main reason seemingly was the judicial fear that to do so would require the courts to engage in reviewing the merits of policy issues which, seemingly, could not be countenanced.[311]

However, two significant events subsequently occurred which effectively brought this resistance to an end. First, there came the decision of the ECtHR in *Smith and Grady v United Kingdom*[312] in which the Court unanimously held that investigations conducted by the Ministry of Defence in pursuance of its policy to exclude homosexuals from the armed forces constituted a breach of their Article 8 rights. Significantly, the Court also expressly criticised the use of the 'anxious scrutiny' form of the *Wednesbury* principles that had been employed by the domestic courts in reviewing the policy, stating that it 'effectively excluded any consideration by the domestic courts of the question of whether the interference with the applicants' rights answered a pressing social need or was proportionate'.[313] Second, there came the incorporation of the HRA and the subsequent decision of the House of Lords in *R v Secretary of State for the Home Department, ex parte Daly*,[314] which largely settled the debate concerning the appropriate standard of review in human rights cases. Here, the House of Lords affirmed the decision of the ECtHR in *Smith and Grady*[315] and specifically rejected the use of 'anxious scrutiny' as an appropriate method of

---

[305]   E Palmer, *Judicial Review, Socio-Economic Rights and the HRA* (n 183) 158–61.

[306]   Necessitated by the UK's entry into the EU in 1972.

[307]   On the basis that to do so would 'wholly transform the methodology of public law adjudication': Simon Brown LJ in *R v Ministry of Defence, ex parte Smith* [1996] QB 517 at 541. See also *Brind v Secretary of State for the Home Department* [1991] 1 All ER 720 and generally, E Palmer, *Judicial Review, Socio-Economic Rights and the HRA* (n 183) 156–62.

[308]   Which requires that in a case involving fundamental rights at stake only a strong objective justification of the interference will be sufficient. Applied in *Smith* (n 307). See also *R v Lord Saville ex parte A* [1999] 4 All ER 860.

[309]   The principle of legality holds that in construing legislation or other sources of public power, there is a strong presumption against unjustified restrictions upon the rule of law or fundamental rights. For examples see: *R v Secretary of State for the Home Office, ex parte Simms* [1999] 3 WLR 328; *R v Secretary of State for Social Security, ex parte Joint Council for the Welfare of Immigrants (JCW)* [1996] 4 All ER 385 and *R v Secretary of State for the Home Department ex parte Leech* [1994] QB 198.

[310]   P Craig, *Administrative Law* (n 303) 561–3 and J Jowell, 'Beyond the Rule of Law: Towards Constitutional Review' (2000) *PL* 671.

[311]   E Palmer, *Judicial Review, Socio-Economic Rights and the HRA* (n 183) 159.

[312]   *Smith and Grady v United Kingdom* [1999] 29 EHRR 493.

[313]   *Ibid*, para 138.

[314]   *R v Secretary of State for the Home Department, ex parte Daly* [2001] UKHL 26.

[315]   *Smith and Grady* (n 312).

review for cases concerning the HRA.[316] After specifically approving of a number of academic opinions concerning the difference between the traditional grounds of review and the proportionality approach[317] Lord Steyn made the following observations. The starting point in such cases, he said, was that there was an overlap between the traditional grounds of review and proportionality; however, the intensity of review was somewhat greater under the proportionality approach. He went on to point out three concrete, albeit non-exhaustive, differences between the two approaches:

> First, the doctrine of proportionality may require the reviewing court to assess the balance which the decision maker has struck, not merely whether it is within the range of rational or reasonable decisions. Secondly, the proportionality test may go further than the traditional grounds of review inasmuch as it may require attention to be directed to the relative weight accorded to interests and considerations. Thirdly, even the heightened scrutiny test developed in *R v Ministry of Defence, ex P Smith* is not necessarily appropriate to the protection of human rights … The differences in approach between the traditional grounds of review and the proportionality approach may therefore sometimes yield different results. It is therefore important that cases involving Convention rights must be analysed in the correct way.[318]

Importantly, he also made the point that this did not mean that there had been a shift to merits review—the roles of the judiciary and the executive, he said, remained fundamentally distinct.[319] Moreover, the intensity of the review would depend upon the subject matter in hand: 'in law context is everything.'[320] The contours of the proportionality principle were, he said, as set out by the Privy Council in *De Freitas v Permanent Secretary of Ministry of Agriculture, Fisheries, Lands and Housing*.[321] Thus in determining whether a limitation (by an act, rule or decision) is arbitrary or excessive the court should ask itself:

> [W]hether: (i) the legislative objective is sufficiently important to justify limiting a fundamental right; (ii) the measures designed to meet the legislative objective are rationally connected to it; and (iii) the means used to impair the right or freedom are no more than is necessary to accomplish the objective.[322]

The *De Freitas*[323] test appears, therefore, to have been confirmed as the correct approach to judicial review in all human rights cases for the present bar one important omission highlighted in a recent House of Lords decision. In the recent case of *Huang (FC) v Secretary of State for the Home Department*[324] the House of Lords took the opportunity to confirm

---

[316] The House of Lords specifically rejected the use of this approach by the Court of Appeal in an immigration case: *R (on the Application of Mahmood) v Secretary of State for the Home Department* [2001] 1 WLR 840.

[317] J Jowell, 'Beyond the Rule of Law' (n 310); P Craig, *Administrative Law* (n 303) 561–3 and D Feldman, 'Proportionality and the HRA 1998' in E Ellis (ed), *The Principle of Proportionality in the Laws of Europe* (Oxford, Hart Publishing, 1999) 117, 127.

[318] *Daly* (n 314) paras 27–8 (Lord Steyn).

[319] Here Lord Steyn specifically approved of Professor Jowell's approach that in performing the balancing exercise, courts have a secondary responsibility to 'ensure that the decision-maker has acted in accordance with the requirements of legality': J Jowell, 'Beyond the Rule of Law' (n 310) 681.

[320] *Daly* (n 314) para 28 (Lord Steyn).

[321] *De Freitas v Permanent Secretary of Ministry of Agriculture, Fisheries, Lands and Housing* [1999] 1 AC 69.

[322] Lord Steyn is quoting the words of Lord Clyde in *De Freitas* (n 321) 80. However, in *Huang (FC) v Secretary of State for the Home Department* [2007] UKHL 11 para 19, the House of Lords added to this formulation the following overriding requirement: the need to strike a balance between the rights of the individual and the interests of the community.

[323] *De Freitas* (n 321).

[324] *Huang* (n 322).

that the *De Freitas*[325] formulation of proportionality was also subject to the overriding requirement for the 'need to balance the interests of society with those of individuals and groups.'[326] In the subsequent case of *E (A Child) v Chief Constable of Ulster*[327] the House of Lords reaffirmed the point that had been made in *Huang*,[328] stating that it was clear that neither the *Smith*[329] nor the *Wednesbury*[330] test was sufficient to determine an issue of proportionality under the Convention.[331] A domestic proportionality test that *ought* to be used for domestic cases involving human rights has thus been set out. What is of most significance is that the test represents the adoption of a more rigorous form of proportionality than that which is most often used by Strasbourg in cases concerning family law: the 'fair balance' test.[332] The problem is that the domestic courts do not always refer to or set out the proportionality test they are using when deciding cases that involve human rights. This is particularly true of the family bench which has, as the author has noted previously, maintained a certain resistance to a rights-based approach.[333] The type of proportionality test or level of scrutiny that the courts have employed must, in such cases, be discerned by implication alone. What can make this task easier, however, is where the courts have discussed *the amount of deference* they will accord to the legislature. This is because, just as at Strasbourg, the doctrines of deference and proportionality are strongly linked; a roughly inverse relationship exists between the two. Thus, where the domestic courts have accorded a high degree of deference to the legislature they have also applied a correspondingly less strict standard of review, often the 'fair balance' test. An examination of how the courts have approached this question will therefore be crucial to determining what type of proportionality tests, if any, have been applied at the domestic level in family law. This issue will be addressed in the next section.

Deference, Discretionary Areas of Judgment and the Margin of Appreciation

The remark made by Lord Steyn in *Daly*[334] concerning the importance of the role played by context within the administrative review of decisions under the HRA is also significant for its demonstration of the potential route by which the domestic version of the margin of appreciation doctrine could impact upon decisions taken at the domestic level. This is because, as we have seen in the discussion of the doctrine in Chapter 1, a number of factors related to the *context* of the case have been highly relevant to the width of the margin

---

[325] *De Freitas* (n 321).
[326] *Huang* (n 322) 19.
[327] *E (A Child) v Chief Constable of Ulster* [2008] UKHL 66.
[328] *Huang* (n 322).
[329] *Smith* (n 307).
[330] *Wednesbury* (n 299).
[331] *Ulster* (n 327) paras 52–4 (Lord Carswell).
[332] See also ch 6 p 236.
[333] S Choudhry, 'The Adoption and Children Act 2002' (n 83) and S Choudhry and H Fenwick, 'Clashing Rights' (n 83).
[334] *Daly* (n 314).

accorded to the State at the Convention level.[335] Thus, it is fairly clear that where the legitimate aim being advanced by the individual State concerns public safety and the prevention of disorder and crime within the context of immigration control, a wider margin of appreciation will be accorded to the State even where family life is adversely affected, although the proportionality tests used will differ on a case-by-case basis. Further, in cases concerning social and economic policy considerations, a wider margin will generally be applied to the individual State *unless* the applicant can establish that he/she comes within a category deserving of procedural protection. Finally, the margin of appreciation afforded to the individual States will also be wider where a case raises particularly sensitive moral or ethical issues.

In the academic discussion that took place concerning the applicability of the margin of appreciation doctrine in the domestic context prior to the passage of the HRA, a general consensus emerged that the doctrine as applied by the ECtHR could not be utilised at the domestic level.[336] This was primarily because the ECtHR was an international court supervising a wide variety of jurisdictions which, in turn, represented an equally wide level of cultural diversity. However, a domestic equivalent of the doctrine, 'a discretionary area of judgment' or 'judicial deference', which addressed the relationship between the judiciary and the other branches of government soon emerged.[337] This was, in sum, the view that in some instances the court should defer to the greater expertise and/or democratic credentials of the government when deciding upon the proportionality of the measure in question. The first significant judicial recognition of the doctrine is said to have taken place in *R v DPP ex parte Kebiline*[338] in which Lord Hope stated that 'in some circumstances it will be appropriate for the courts 'to recognize that there is an area of judgment within which the judiciary will defer, on democratic grounds, to the considered opinion of the elected body or person'.[339] He then went on to specify these circumstances as where the issues involved questions of social and economic policy, where the rights involved were not of great constitutional importance, and where the courts were not especially well placed to assess the need for protection. In addition, he considered that discretion was more likely to be applicable in relation to the qualified rather than the unqualified Articles because that was where the Convention itself had recognised the need for a balance to be struck. This formulation of the doctrine was subsequently relied upon, as Palmer notes,[340] in a number of decisions to deny Convention claims in areas as diverse as national security, immigration, public order and the allocation of public resources. The ease in which certain areas were regarded as outside the competence of the courts on the basis of deference was

---

[335] See also ch 1, pp 10–26.

[336] Laws LJ, 'The Limitations of Human Rights' (1999) *PL* 254 at 258; D Feldman, 'The Human Rights Act and Constitutional Principles' [1999] 19 (2) *Legal Studies* 165 at 192; D Pannick, 'Principles of Interpretation of Convention rights under the Human Rights Act and the Discretionary Area of Judgement' (1998) *PL* 545; M Hunt, R Singh and M Demetriou, 'Is there a Role for the "Margin of Appreciation" in National Law after the Human Rights Act?' (1999) 1 *European Human Rights Law Review* 15 especially at 17. An early recognition of this can be seen in *Brown v Stott (Procurator Fiscal)* [2001] 2 WLR 817.

[337] D Pannick, 'Principles of Interpretation' (n 336); M Hunt, R Singh and M Demetriou, 'Current Topic: Is there a Role for the Margin of Appreciation in National Law after the HRA?' (1999) *European Human Rights Law Review* 15; A Lester and D Pannick (eds), *Human Rights Law and Practice* (1999) para 3.26 as approved in *R v DPP ex parte Kebiline* [2000] 2 AC 326 and *Brown v Stott* (n 336).

[338] *Kebiline* (n 337).

[339] *Ibid*, 381 (Lord Hope).

[340] E Palmer, *Judicial Review, Socio-Economic Rights and the HRA* (n 183) 170–1.

greeted with some alarm by a number of constitutional lawyers. Allan[341] recently argued forcefully that invoking a doctrine of judicial deference 'effectively places administrative discretion beyond the purview of the rule of law' and thus characterised the doctrine as a 'substitute for legal analysis of specific claims of right, entitled to recognition or denial in accordance with their intrinsic merits'. It has also been suggested that the doctrine is largely unnecessary. Phillipson,[342] for example, has argued that the ECHR and HRA system already contains a substantial amount of provision for deference to democratic governance and cultural variation and has identified three layers upon which this occurs. First, the Convention itself, containing both a derogation clause and very broad restriction clauses on a number of the rights (Articles 8–11), already builds in a relatively high degree of compromise with majoritarianism.[343] Second, the case law of the Strasbourg court is often heavily influenced by the margin of appreciation doctrine, which itself affords sometimes heavy deference to the decisions of national authorities. Third, the design of the HRA then builds in a further and decisive layer of deference by permitting a full over-ride of each and every right in the Convention by Parliament, through its preservation of parliamentary sovereignty, allowing Parliament to violate any Convention rights, including unqualified and non-derogable rights and its preclusion of a strike-down power with regard to the courts. Adding a fourth level of deference at the domestic level may thus, he argues, water down an already weakened system of protection of rights.[344] Murray Hunt[345] has instead attempted to mediate a middle ground between the opposing narratives of democratic pedigree and liberal constitutionalism with his concept of 'due deference' under which the courts' non-interference with legislative, executive or administrative decisions 'must be earned by the primary decision maker by openly demonstrating the justifications for the decisions they have reached and by demonstrating the reasons why their decision is worthy of curial respect'.[346]

These diverging views have to a certain extent been reflected within the judiciary. In *International Transport Roth GmbH v Secretary of State for the Home Department*[347] four groups of lorry drivers and haulage companies sought to challenge the legislative lawfulness of the Home Secretary's fixed penalty scheme which did not allow for degrees of fault but was directed at deterring carriers from bringing illegal immigrants into the UK. The Court of Appeal was asked to consider the proportionality of the measures involved. In direct contrast to Lord Hope in *Kebiline*,[348] Simon Brown LJ, in delivering the majority judgment, considered that despite recognising:

> [T]he wide discretion of the Secretary of State in his task of devising a suitable scheme and a high degree of deference due by the Court to Parliament when it comes to determining its legality … the court's role under the 1998 Act is as the guardian of human rights. It cannot abdicate this responsibility. If ultimately it judges the scheme to be quite simply unfair, then the features that make it so must inevitably breach the Convention.

---

[341] TRS Allan, 'Human Rights and Judicial Review: A Critique of "Due Deference"' (2006) 65(3) *CLJ* 671–2.
[342] G Phillipson, 'Clarity Postponed' (n 16).
[343] C Gearty, *Principles of Human Rights Adjudication* (Oxford, Oxford University Press, 2005) 20–5.
[344] The only exception where domestic courts should exercise a degree of deference is in relation to relative levels of expertise in factual matters. However, such reasoning, he argues, should be approached cautiously.
[345] M Hunt, 'Sovereignty's Blight' (n 345) 339.
[346] *Ibid*, 340. See also generally A Kavanagh, *Constitutional Review* (n 47).
[347] *International Transport Roth GmbH v Secretary of State for the Home Department* [2002] EWCA 158 (Civ).
[348] *Kebiline* (n 337).

As a result Simon Brown LJ had no choice but to find the legislative scheme unfair. In dissent, Laws LJ[349] attempted to draw together the principles that had been developed by the court with regard to the degree of deference that judges ought to pay. Factors that he regarded would be relevant were the fundamental nature of the rights at stake, the degree of democratic accountability of the decision maker, and the expertise of the decision maker weighted against that of the court in any given context. Thus, he found that in the case before him the application of these principles led to the necessity for a higher degree of deference being accorded to the democratic powers: the 'social consequences of illegal immigrants' lay 'obviously far more within the competence of government than of courts'.[350] This theme, of certain areas being unavailable for judicial review, continued in subsequent case law. In *R (on the Application of ProLife Alliance) v BBC*[351] Lord Hoffman delivered his now well-known speech on the matter in which he stated:

> The principles upon which decision-making powers are allocated are principles of law. The courts are the independent branch of government and the legislature and executive are … the elected branches of government. Independence makes the courts more suited to deciding some kinds of questions and being elected makes the legislature or executive more suited to deciding others … The principle that the independence of the courts is necessary for a proper decision of disputed legal rights or claims of violation of human rights is a legal principle … the principle that majority approval is necessary for a proper decision on policy or allocation of resources is also a legal principle. Likewise, when a court decides that a decision is within the proper competence of the legislature or executive, it is not showing deference. It is deciding the law.[352]

This vision of judicial scrutiny has, unsurprisingly, been the subject of some criticism for implying that the courts have no legal right to intervene in certain matters which engage majority choice[353] or on any occasion where a qualified Convention right was claimed to be defeated by a particular public interest.[354] Instead, the better view, it is submitted, is that suggested by Lord Steyn that if there is to be a degree of domestic deference some degree of deference is legitimate but always 'in the context of a specific issue in a particular case'.[355] Thus cases concerning national security or resource allocation may fall into a category necessitating a higher degree of deference; however, it should not be automatic. Only once the circumstances of the particular case are closely examined and judged to warrant such treatment should the deference occur.[356] It is arguably this vision of a doctrine of deference, rooted in institutional competence rather than respect for democratic credentials, which informed the recent House of Lords decision in *Huang*.[357] The case concerned the proper approach to be taken by an immigration adjudicator when deciding whether or not the Secretary of State's decision to remove an individual from the UK was a disproportionate

---

[349] *Roth GmbH* (n 347) paras 83–7 (Laws LJ).
[350] *Ibid*, paras 83–7 (Laws LJ).
[351] *R (on the Application of ProLife Alliance) v BBC* [2003] UKHL 23.
[352] *ProLife* (n 351) para 76.
[353] J Jowell and J Cooper, 'Introduction' in J Jowell and J Cooper (eds), *Delivering Rights* (n 20).
[354] Lord Steyn, 'The Tangled Story of Deference' [2005] *PL* 346.
[355] *Ibid*, 350.
[356] *Ibid*, 352.
[357] M Amos, 'Separating Human Rights Adjudication From Judicial Review—*Huang v Secretary of State for the Home Dept* and *Kashmiri v Secretary of State for the Home Dept*' (2007) 6 *European Human Rights Law Review* 679.

interference with his Article 8 rights. On the practice of deference the House of Lords was clear, it was:

> [T]he ordinary judicial task of weighing up the competing considerations on each side and according appropriate weight to the judgment of a person with responsibility for a given subject matter and access to special sources of knowledge and advice.[358]

As Amos[359] notes, however, there is no mention of democratic accountability in this formulation. Rather, what now seems to be necessary, if the primary decision maker wishes to have their decision taken into account by a court examining the proportionality of an interference with Convention right, is first, that their expertise is *demonstrated*, second, whether he or she has already used such expertise to carry out an assessment of the proportionality of the interference with Convention rights.

Thus, a less intense standard of review/proportionality and thus a higher level of deference should, according to *Huang*[360] and Lord Steyn above, not simply be decided upon the basis of the subject matter in question but rather a close-up examination of whether such treatment has been demonstrated as appropriate by the decision maker. Thus, as Hunt, has argued, 'proportionality is not so much a "test", or "standard", as a new type of approach to adjudication which subjects the justification for decisions to rigorous scrutiny to determine their legality'.[361]

Deference and Proportionality in the Context of Family Law

The debates concerning deference discussed above have been particularly relevant in a number of areas within the family law context and will be discussed where relevant throughout the following chapters. For example, the earlier assertion that greater deference and a correspondingly lower standard of review should be paid to government bodies concerning resource allocation can be illustrated by court decisions in a number of areas. As a number of authors have noted,[362] the courts have exercised a high level of deference with regard to legislative housing schemes even where the result could cause a serious interference with the Article 8 rights of the applicants. The implications of this line of case law for the victims of domestic violence is discussed in detail in Chapter 9. Concerns regarding the increase in pressure upon already scarce public resources is also evident from the line of cases concerning the clash between the general duty of a local authority to provide a range of suitable services for children in need under section 17 of the Children Act 1989 and the prioritisation-focused housing legislation. These cases and the issues they raise are discussed in Chapter 8. However, there are certain contexts in which the issue has been of particular significance and fall for discussion here.

---

[358]   *Huang* (n 322) para 16.
[359]   M Amos, 'Separating Human Rights Adjudication From Judicial Review' (n 357) 7, 10.
[360]   *Huang* (n 322).
[361]   M Hunt, 'Sovereignty's Blight' (n 345) 342.
[362]   E Palmer, *Judicial Review, Socio-Economic Rights and the HRA* (n 183), S Choudhry and J Herring, 'Domestic Violence and the Human Rights Act 1998' [2006] 4 *PL* 752 and I Loveland, *A Special Relationship?* (n 298).

Adoption

As can be seen in the discussion in Chapter 8 concerning adoption in general, the courts have traditionally demonstrated a high level of deference to individual adoption panels with regard to the decision as to who may adopt a child and indeed whether a child ought to be placed for adoption. This is largely due to the fact that the members of such panels and the individual social workers involved who report to them are more often than not best placed in terms of experience and expertise to make such decisions. This approach, as seen from the discussion in Chapter 5, corresponds with the ECtHR's approach to challenges brought by birth parents with respect to such decisions. However, it is also clear that the domestic courts' role is not simply to rubber-stamp such decisions; rather courts must ensure that the children's *and* the parents' Convention rights have been fully respected within the decision-making process. Of greatest importance is the need to ensure that the decision to adopt represents a proportionate interference with such rights. In this respect the courts should employ a high level of scrutiny when considering the involvement of parents within the *process* leading up to the application for adoption. The general question of which *class* of person ought to be eligible to adopt a child is a different matter. Historically, such matters were left largely to the discretion of individual local authorities; however, it soon became clear that potential adopters were being treated differently according to which local authority they happened to live within.[363] This, in addition to other concerns regarding the effectiveness of adoption policy, led to a programme of Government reform culminating in the Adoption and Children Act 2002.[364] The Act represented a wide-scale reform of adoption law and practice; however, what proved to be particularly controversial during its passage through Parliament was the issue of whether to allow cohabiting couples (including gays and lesbians) to adopt. It was only after a considerable amount of resistance from the House of Lords[365] and the Conservative Party that the sections of the Act which enabled such people to adopt[366] were retained. The main reason was the acceptance of the fact that there was a real need to 'increase the pool of adopters'.[367] In Northern Ireland, however, the position remained unchanged and thus, according to Articles 14 and 15 of the Adoption (Northern Ireland) Order 1987[368] only married couples and single people who are not married or civil partners are eligible to adopt. This is because it is with the Northern Ireland Assembly that the responsibility for any reform in adoption legislation in Northern Ireland will lie.[369] In *Re P (A Child) (Adoption; Unmarried Couples)*,[370]

---

[363] I Dey, 'Adapting Adoption: A Case of Closet Politics' (2005) 19 (3) *International Journal of Law, Policy and the Family* 289.

[364] J Eekelaar, 'Contact and the Adoption Reform' in A Bainham, B Lindley, M Richards and L Trinder (eds), *Children and Their Families. Contact, Rights and Welfare* (Oxford, Hart Publishing, 2003).

[365] It was at the Bill's third reading that a free vote was allowed on the amendment which extended eligibility to unmarried couples, including those of the same sex. It was reversed after a vigorous debate in the House of Lords by a majority against it of 34, but reinstated in the House of Commons and finally agreed to in the House of Lords by a majority in favour of 31: *Hansard*, HL Deb, 5 November 2002, vol 640, cols 569, 621.

[366] Section 50 of the 2002 Act read with s144(4) of that Act, as amended by s79(12) of the Civil Partnership Act 2004, provides that couples who are unmarried as well as a married couple and two people who are civil partners of each other may apply to adopt.

[367] J Lewis, 'Adoption: The Nature of Policy Shifts in England and Wales, 1972–2002' (2004) 18 (2) *International Journal of Law, Policy and the Family* 235.

[368] As amended by s203(4) CPA.

[369] In accordance with s6(1) Northern Ireland Act 1998.

[370] *Re P (A Child) (Adoption; Unmarried Couples)* [2008] UKHL 38.

an appeal was brought in relation to this legislation by an unmarried cohabiting couple who wished to adopt a child, who was the natural child of the female member of the couple. The applicants argued that the provisions of Articles 14 and 15 represented a breach of their Articles 8 and 14 rights. The case, as discussed above, appears to have created a further exception to the 'no more, no less' rule with regard to the duty to take into account relevant Strasbourg jurisprudence. It seems that where the case concerns a matter where Strasbourg has granted a wide margin of appreciation to Member States it is open to the domestic courts to go further than Strasbourg if necessary. By employing this approach their Lordships were thus able to take into account the analogous Strasbourg case law on homosexual adoption in order to hold that unequal treatment between unmarried and married couples with regard to adoption was also unjustifiable under Articles 14 and 8 of the ECHR. The case also necessitated a discussion of the amount of deference, if any, that ought to be accorded to the legislature, in this case the Northern Ireland Assembly, in what was clearly an area of sensitive social policy. The Assembly had not yet passed any similar reforms to the England and Wales Parliament on the issue and, furthermore, any attempt to do so looked unlikely to succeed. Lord Hope noted that, in July 2006, the Minister for Health, Social Services and Public Safety had issued for consultation 'Adopting the Future', a strategy document setting out a proposed new approach to adoption in Northern Ireland. The vast majority of responses 'were concerned with one issue, which was the proposal to extend joint adoption to civil partners and unmarried couples. Of these 95% were opposed to the proposal.'[371] Furthermore, 'A striking feature of these responses [was] the lack of support for this proposal among the political parties in Northern Ireland.'[372]As a result Lord Hope concluded that it could not be taken for granted that a similar measure would be passed by the Assembly. The problem, however, was, as Lord Hope pointed out, this: it would be outside the competence of the Assembly 'to legislate in a way that is incompatible with any of the Convention rights'.[373] As a result, Lord Hope felt that the courts' 'vital' role in adjudicating on issues of compatibility arising from Acts of the Assembly and the exercise of functions by the executive authorities[374] must be acted upon. Referring to his comments in *Kebiline*[375] some years earlier, Lord Hope stated that his initial feeling was that the issue was one of sensitive social policy and should therefore be left to the legislature. However, because the case concerned discrimination in an area of social policy, the constitutional responsibility of the court was engaged.[376] The legislation was therefore appropriate for judicial scrutiny:

> Cases about discrimination in an area of social policy, which is what this case is, will always be appropriate for judicial scrutiny. The constitutional responsibility in this area of our law resides with the courts. The more contentious the issue is, the greater the risk is that some people will be discriminated against in ways that engage their Convention rights. It is for the courts to see that this does not happen. It is with them that the ultimate safeguard against discrimination rests.[377]

---

[371] *Ibid*, para 45 (Lord Hope).
[372] *Ibid*, para 45 (Lord Hope).
[373] Section 6(2)(c) Northern Ireland Act 1998; see *Re P* (n 370) para 46 (Lord Hope).
[374] Section 79 of and Schedule 10 to the 1998 Act.
[375] *Kebiline* (n 337).
[376] This was in line with Lord Walker's comments in *Pro Life*; see *Re P* (n 370) para 48 (Lord Hope).
[377] *Ibid*, para 48 (Lord Hope).

This categorisation of the issue as one of constitutional significance was key to the declaration of the unlawfulness of the Order and harked back to their Lordships' earlier reasoning in *Ghaidan*,[378] which had concerned the rights of a same-sex partner to inherit a statutory tenancy. In terms of proportionality, although the State was entitled to take the view that marriage was a very important institution and that in general it was better for children to be brought up by parents who were married to each other than by those who were not, it was, Lord Hoffman said, irrational to adopt a 'bright line rule' to determine what class of people should adopt children.[379] This was due to the fact that such a rule not only defied everyday experience but also contradicted one of the fundamental principles stated in Article 9 of the 1987 Order that the court was obliged to consider whether adoption 'by particular … persons' would be in the best interests of the child. Although the question of whether unmarried couples should be allowed to adopt was a matter of social policy and one which the court would ordinarily regard as being a matter for Parliament, that did not mean that Parliament was entitled to discriminate in any such case; the discrimination must at least have a rational basis. A failure to marry could not, therefore, 'be rationally elevated to an irrebuttable presumption of unsuitability'.[380] What is noteworthy is that none of the speeches explicitly set out the type of proportionality test that was being employed or indeed made any reference to either *De Freitas*[381] or *Huang*.[382] However, it is clear from the discussion above and the speeches that their Lordships viewed the issue of discrimination in the case as one of fundamental constitutional importance; little deference was therefore accorded to the legislature. Further, it is clear that the measure in question was subjected to a high level of scrutiny by the court. Lord Hoffman, in particular, felt that adopting a 'fair balance' test where the interests of the two individual applicants must be balanced against the interests of the community as a whole would mean that:

> [T]he interests of the particular child, which Article 9 declares to be the most important consideration, have disappeared from sight, sacrificed to a vague and distant utilitarian calculation. That seems to me to be wrong. If, as may turn out to be the case, it would be in the interests of the welfare of this child to be adopted by this couple, I can see no basis for denying the child this advantage in 'the interests of the community as a whole'.[383]

Assisted Conception

The final area in which the debates concerning the proper role, if any, of judicial deference and the application of the principle of proportionality can be illustrated is by two high-profile cases concerning access to assisted conception services. One issue that the courts have been faced with is whether the HRA establishes a general right to fertility treatment within the NHS. In *R (On the Application of Assisted Reproduction and Gynaecology Centre*

---

[378] *Ghaidan* (n 54); although that particular piece of legislation was capable of amendment under s3 due to the fact it concerned primary legislation. That was not possible here as the relevant Order constituted secondary legislation.
[379] *Re P* (n 370) paras 13–20 (Lord Hoffman).
[380] *Ibid*, para 18 (Lord Hoffman).
[381] *De Freitas* (n 321).
[382] *Huang* (n 322).
[383] *Re P* (n 370) para 16 (Lord Hoffman).

and H) v HFEA[384] a clinic sought permission to seek judicial review of a decision by the Human Fertilisation and Embryology Authority (HFEA) not to authorise the implantation of more than three embryos in a particular patient. The HFEA code of practice stipulated that no more than three embryos were to be implanted in a woman in any single fertilisation cycle. The clinic contended that, whilst the general prescription on the numbers of embryos to be transferred was reasonable, it was nevertheless appropriate to authorise a departure from the normal rule in the case of a patient who had undergone eight previous unsuccessful attempts at in vitro fertilisation. At the hearing for judicial review, heard in 2001, Ouseley J accepted that the personal circumstances of the patient and the possible impact of the court's decision on her individual and matrimonial fulfilment warranted 'anxious scrutiny'. However, he was also prepared to assume that, as Articles 8 and 12 of the Convention applied, 'a more intrusive form of judicial intervention' was arguably required.[385] However, in refusing the application he went on to accord a high degree of deference to the authority due to its expertise in the area under review:

> However, wherever the boundaries of judicial review are drawn for these purposes, it remains fundamental to the arguability of the claimant's case that there be features demonstrated which arguably take the decision out of the range of available decisions. Even with a more intrusive approach, the court would be bound to allow substantial room for the application of expert and scientific judgment by the bodies specifically entrusted to provide guidance in these sensitive medical and ethical areas.

A further application was made to the HFEA on the basis of new scientific evidence. The application was again refused but this time, the HFEA advised that it had approached the case on the basis that Articles 8 and 12 of the ECHR applied, and expressed the opinion that any interference with those rights was in accordance with the law, given that the Act required it to determine what constitutes suitable practice and to give appropriate advice. The Authority also specifically considered whether the interference pursued a legitimate aim, and decided that it did, namely the obviation of health risks and costs of multiple pregnancy and multiple births. Finally, in considering proportionality, the Authority reported that it had undertaken a proportionality assessment of the impact of the decision, concluding that the interference with the rights in this particular case was more than necessary to meet the legitimate aim. In the subsequent application for judicial review of this decision Sedley J, although doubting the application of Articles 8 and 12 to the case, considered that they had been addressed 'with care' by the HFEA.[386] He also made it clear that this was an area which required a high degree of deference to the decision maker, stating that 'if there was ever a field in which the important thing was a properly considered decision by an expert body and not a court, it is this'.[387] At the subsequent appeal, the Court of Appeal also dismissed the appeal:

> Our first reason for taking this course is that, in common with the three judges before whom the case has come prior to it reaching this court, we do not regard either decision of the Authority

---

[384] *R (On the Application of Assisted Reproduction and Gynaecology Centre and H) v HFEA* [2002] FL 347.

[385] *Ibid*, para 39. This was the second application for judicial review and Ouseley J's comments were later taken by the Court of Appeal to be a direct reference to Lord Steyn's comments in *Daly* (n 314) concerning the appropriate method of review for cases concerning the HRA.

[386] *Ibid*, para 54.

[387] *Ibid*, para 54.

as being capable of challenge by way of judicial review, and we think it important that any future litigant wishing to challenge a decision of, or advice given by, the Authority should be aware of the limits of the court's ability to intervene in the exercise by the Authority of these powers under the Act.[388]

And:

This is an area of rapidly developing scientific knowledge and debate, in which the Authority, as the licensing body established by Parliament, makes decisions and gives advice. It is not the function of the court to enter the scientific debate, nor is it the function of the court to adjudicate on the merits of the Board's decisions or any advice it gives. Like any public authority, the Board is open to challenge by way of judicial review, but only if it exceeds or abuses the powers and responsibilities given to it by parliament.[389]

Although this case was decided before *Huang*[390] it is likely that a high degree of deference will continue to be accorded to the HFEA in any further such claims. This is because, as indicated in *Huang*,[391] what is key to the question of deference is the demonstration of institutional competence and expertise. As long as the HFEA can demonstrate that it has undertaken a careful assessment of the competing interests it is likely that the courts will view that they are best placed to decide these complex moral and ethical issues.

The second issue that has come before the courts in this area has been the question of how far the State must go in facilitating procreation. This question was considered in two different contexts, albeit linked, by both the domestic court and the ECtHR. In *Evans v Amicus Healthcare Ltd & Others*[392] the appellant, who was infertile, appealed against a decision that she was not entitled to use frozen embryos created by IVF treatment after separating from her male partner, who had withdrawn his consent to the treatment. Both had originally given their written consents to each other's treatment 'together' to include the 'use' and storage of their embryos after she was told that she had pre-cancerous tumours in both ovaries. The couple then attended a clinic, eggs were harvested and fertilised and six embryos were created and put in storage. She then had an operation to remove her ovaries. The relationship subsequently broke up and when J notified the clinic he was withdrawing his consent, the clinic informed the claimant that it was under an obligation to destroy the embryos. Proceedings were commenced in the High Court for an injunction to restore her former partner's consent and also her application for a declaration of incompatibility. This was argued on the basis that her rights under Article 8 and Article 14 of the ECHR had been breached by Sch 3 of the Human Fertilisation and Embryology Act 1990[393] due to the fact that, as the embryos represented the last opportunity she had of having a child that was genetically related to her, it was neither necessary nor proportionate to give the power to the gamete provider, as the HFEA did, to determine the issue unilaterally by withdrawing

---

[388] *Ibid*, para 14.

[389] *Ibid*, para 15.

[390] *Huang* (n 322).

[391] *Ibid*.

[392] *Evans v Amicus Healthcare Ltd & Others* [2004] EWCA 727 (Civ).

[393] Section 4 of Schedule 3 deals with the withdrawal of consent and provides: 4 (1) The terms of any consent under this Schedule may from time to time be varied, and the consent may be withdrawn, by notice given by the person who gave the consent to the person keeping the gametes or embryo to which the consent is relevant. (2) The terms of any consent to the use of any embryo cannot be varied, and such consent cannot be withdrawn, once the embryo has been used—(a) in providing treatment services, or (b) for the purposes of any project of research.

his consent. Wall J rejected the application primarily on the basis that, under the terms of the HFEA, it was clear that the continuing consent of both parties from the commencement of treatment to the point of implantation of the embryo was required. In addition the statute gave either party the right to withdraw their consent. As a result, the fact that the applicant's former partner had only ever consented to undergoing treatment 'together' and had not consented to the applicant using the jointly created embryos alone meant that it was perfectly reasonable for him to exercise his right to do so. The Court of Appeal commenced its analysis of the applicability of Article 8 by agreeing with Wall J's assessment that the refusal of treatment engaged the applicant's private life and represented an interference with it. The court then went on to address whether the limitation of the applicant's right was one which was proportionate and in doing so addressed the specific question of whether a 'bright line' rule, such as that set out in the HFEA in relation to consent, could be justifiable in this case. What was notable was the Court's rejection of the view that because the case concerned an area in which the ECtHR had accorded Member States a wide margin of appreciation, this approach could also simply be adopted by a domestic court:

> We consider propositions of this breadth to be a wrong starting point. The margin of appreciation ... is a tool by which the Strasbourg court gauges the relationship of a state's act to the Convention. It has no direct relevance to the process by which a court adjudicates, within a state, on the compatibility of a measure adopted by the executive or the legislature, for it is only at the end of that process that the state's act crystallises. This is why Lord Hope in *R v DPP, ex parte Kebilene* ... took such care to distinguish the Strasbourg approach from what he characterised domestically as the discretionary area of judgment.

However, the court then went on to indicate that it intended to accord a high degree of deference to the legislature in this case, starting first with a conservative statement on the role of the judiciary:[394]

> Discretion implies a choice between two or more legitimate (and therefore proportionate) courses, and where Parliament has made such a choice the courts have no power of intervention under the Human Rights Act.

The court then went on to note with approval Lord Nicholls comments in *Wilson and others v Secretary of State for Trade and Industry*:[395]

> Assessment of the advantages and disadvantages of the various legislative alternatives is primarily a matter for Parliament. The possible existence of alternative solutions does not in itself render the contested legislation unjustified ... The court will reach a different conclusion from the legislature only when it is apparent that the legislature has attached insufficient importance to a person's Convention right ... The more the legislation concerns matters of broad social policy, the less ready will be a court to intervene.[396]

The court then went on to set out how, in its opinion, the legislative measure in question did, in accordance with the *De Freitas*[397] test, in fact represent the least injurious means of accomplishing the objective, which in this case was the protection of the rights and freedoms of the applicant's former partner.

---

[394] *Evans* (n 392) 63.
[395] *Wilson and others v Secretary of State for Trade and Industry* [2003] UKHL 40.
[396] *Ibid*, para 70.
[397] *De Freitas* (n 321).

The less drastic means contended for here is a rule of law making the withdrawal of Mr Johnston's consent non-conclusive. This would enable Ms Evans to seek a continuance of treatment because of her inability to conceive by any other means. But unless it also gave weight to Mr Johnston's firm wish not to be father to a child borne by Ms Evans, such a rule would diminish the respect owed to his private life in proportion as it enhanced the respect accorded to hers … It would also require a balance to be struck between two entirely incommensurable things.

The court further stated that although the case for a bright line required careful examination, particularly if the outcome was the denial of a Convention right to one party, the fundamental question to consider was whether the proposed interference was proportionate.[398] However, the fact that the legislation may produce a harsh or unreasonable outcome in a particular case was not in itself a reason to regard that legislation as disproportionate. As a result the court concluded that:[399]

The need, as perceived by Parliament, is for bilateral consent to implantation, not simply to the taking and storage of genetic material, and that need cannot be met if one half of the consent is no longer effective. To dilute this requirement in the interests of proportionality, in order to meet Ms Evans' otherwise intractable biological handicap, by making the withdrawal of the man's consent relevant but inconclusive, would create new and even more intractable difficulties of arbitrariness and inconsistency. The sympathy and concern which anyone must feel for Ms Evans is not enough to render the legislative scheme of Sch 3 disproportionate.

When the matter reached the ECtHR in *Evans v United Kingdom*[400] the Court dealt with the matter by first determining the width of the margin of appreciation that would be accorded. The case, they said, raised issues of a morally and ethically delicate nature and it was clear that there was no uniform European approach in the field.[401] The Court concluded, therefore, that a wide margin of appreciation must be extended to the State. In addressing the use of a 'bright line' rule in the domestic legislation the court commented that it did not find that the absolute nature of the law was, in itself, necessarily inconsistent with Article 8:[402]

[T]he absolute nature of the rule served to promote legal certainty and to avoid the problems of arbitrariness and inconsistency inherent in weighing, on a case by case basis, what the Court of Appeal described as 'entirely incommensurable' interests. In the Court's view, these general interests pursued by the legislation are legitimate and consistent with Article 8.[403]

In coming to this conclusion it was clear that the Court had been influenced by the fact that the potential problems that might arise from scientific progress in this area had been considered on a number of occasions by Parliament and on a public consultation basis. In particular, the Court noted that the issue of consent was specifically addressed as early as 1984 by the Warnock report[404] and in subsequent Government papers prior to the passage of the Human Fertilisation and Embryology Act 1990 (HFE Act), although this had all occurred prior to the passage of the HRA. In terms of the balance struck between the

---

[398] *Evans* (n 392) para 69 (Thorpe LJ).
[399] *Ibid*, para 69 (Thorpe LJ).
[400] *Ibid*.
[401] *Ibid*, paras 78–81.
[402] *Pretty v UK* (2002) 35 EHRR 1 and *Odièvre v France* (2004) 38 EHRR 43.
[403] *Evans* (n 392) para 89.
[404] Human Fertilisation and Embryology, Warnock Report HC Deb, 23 November 1984, vol 68, cols 528–44.

conflicting Article 8 rights of the parties involved, the central question was not whether different rules might have been adopted by the legislature, but whether in striking the balance as it had, Parliament had exceeded the margin of appreciation afforded to it.[405] Given that there was no European consensus on the matter and that the applicant had been made aware of the clear rules regarding consent before treatment, the Court concluded that a fair balance had been struck between the competing interests. There had accordingly been no violation of Article 8 of the Convention. This analysis of the use of a bright line rule in such cases which concerned areas of moral and social policy was later relied upon by Charles J in *L v Human Fertilisation and Embryology Authority and Secretary of State for Health*[406] when he held that the HFE Act's absolute requirement of effective consent for use of continued storage and use of sperm was not incompatible with the right to private and family life under Article 8.

In contrast, in *Dickson v Premier Prison Service Ltd*,[407] which concerned the Secretary of State's policy with regard to the provision of artificial insemination facilities to serving prisoners, the Court of Appeal felt no need to refer to any discretionary area of judgment despite the fact that the case concerned not only matters of broad social policy but also national security. The policy essentially provided that requests for facilities for artificial insemination by prisoners were considered on individual merit and would only be granted in exceptional circumstances and in doing so a number of general considerations were taken into account.[408] Rather than engage in any assessment as to what degree of deference should be shown to the Secretary of State, the court preferred instead to come to its own conclusion on the compatibility of the Secretary of State's policy with the ECHR. Here the applicants, a married couple, sought permission to appeal against a decision refusing judicial review of the Secretary of State's refusal, pursuant to the above policy under which such requests were considered, to authorise artificial insemination of the wife by the husband, a prisoner serving a life sentence. The wife, a benefit claimant, was 45 years old and the husband's release on licence would not occur at the earliest until she was 51. The reasons given by the Secretary of State for refusal were as follows: (1) the fact that Mrs Dickson would be 51 at the earliest possible date for Mr Dickson's release left her with a very small likelihood of being able to conceive naturally; (2) the fact that their relationship had yet to be tested in the normal environment of daily life, making it difficult to assess whether it would continue after Mr Dickson's release; (3) the seeming insufficiency of resources to provide independently for the material welfare of any child who might be conceived; (4) the seeming paucity of any supportive network for mother and child and the fact that

---

[405]   *Evans* (n 392) para 91.
[406]   *L v Human Fertilisation and Embryology Authority and Secretary of State for Health* [2008] EWHC 2149.
[407]   *Dickson v Premier Prison Service Ltd* [2004] EWCA 1477 (Civ).
[408]   These were: 'whether the provision of AI facilities is the only means by which conception is likely to occur; whether the prisoner's expected day of release is neither so near that delay would not be excessive nor so distant that he/she would unable to assume the responsibilities of a parent; whether both parties want the procedure and the medical authorities both inside and outside the prison are satisfied that the couple are medically fit to proceed with AI; whether the couple were in a well established and stable relationship prior to imprisonment which is likely to subsist after the prisoner's release; whether there is any evidence to suggest that the couple's domestic circumstances and the arrangements for the welfare of the child are satisfactory, including the length of time for which the child might expect to be without a father or mother; whether having regard to the prisoner's history, antecedents and other relevant factors there is evidence to suggest that it would not be in the public interest to provide artificial insemination facilities in a particular case.' Set out in the letter to the applicants refusing their application.

the child would not have the presence of a father for an important part of his or her own childhood; and (5) notwithstanding Mr Dickson's good and constructive prison record, the nature and circumstances of the murder for which he was serving the life sentence meant, in the Secretary of State's words, that:

> [T]here would be legitimate public concern that the punitive and deterrent elements of [his] sentence of imprisonment were being circumvented if [he] were allowed to father a child through artificial insemination while in prison.[409]

The applicants therefore submitted that the policy of the Secretary of State not to allow artificial insemination other than in exceptional circumstances was irrational and contravened their rights under Article 8 of the ECHR. However, this claim was unanimously rejected by the Court of Appeal. Auld LJ relied in principle upon the conclusion of Lord Phillips in a judgment of the Court in *R (on the application of Mellor) v Secretary of State for the Home Department)*[410] where the policy had been similarly challenged but had been found to be compatible with Article 8 after an appraisal of Strasbourg case law on a prisoner's right to conjugal visits:[411]

> The fact that there is no jurisprudence bearing directly on the issue suggests that it has not to date been considered that fundamental human rights include the right of a prisoner to inseminate his wife by artificial means. I have concluded that they do not.[412]

And:

> It does not follow from this that it will always be justifiable to prevent a prisoner from inseminating his wife artificially, or indeed naturally. The interference with fundamental human rights which is permitted by Article 8(2) involves an exercise in proportionality. Exceptional circumstances may require the normal consequences of imprisonment to yield, because the effect of its interference with a particular human right is disproportionate.[413]

The reliance on *Mellor*[414] was, however, problematic for two reasons. First, the court in *Mellor*[415] had considered a policy that was, as counsel for the applicants argued, pre-Convention. Second, the court's consideration of it had been based on the *Wednesbury*[416] irrationality principles, which, since *De Freitas*,[417] should no longer have been applied. However, this did not seem to concern Auld LJ, who, relying on Lord Phillips' assessment of compatibility with Convention rights, and without any reference or application of the *De Freitas*[418] test of proportionality, found that neither the policy nor the decision of the Secretary of State contravened Article 8 of the ECHR.[419]

---

[409] *Dickson* (n 407) para 7 (Auld LJ).
[410] *R (on the application of Mellor) v Secretary of State for the Home Department)* [2002] QB 13.
[411] In *Mellor* the life prisoner was aged 29 at the time of the application. His wife would have been aged 28 at the date of his earliest possible release. They were both refused artificial insemination facilities because it was considered that there was nothing exceptional about their case.
[412] *Mellor* (n 410) 44 (Phillips LJ).
[413] *Ibid*, para 45 (Phillips LJ).
[414] *Ibid*.
[415] *Ibid*.
[416] *Wednesbury* (n 299).
[417] *De Freitas* (n 321).
[418] *Ibid*.
[419] *Dickson* (n 407) para 23 (Auld LJ).

Mr Dickson then took his case before the ECtHR in *Dickson*[420] where, this time, notwithstanding the fact that there was no consensus within the Member States on the issue and that the case raised 'complex issues and choices of social strategy',[421] the Court declined to accord a wide margin of appreciation in this case. Although a wide margin could be applied to the question of whether or not a State made provision for conjugal visits the Court considered that the policy of the Secretary of State in relation to the provision of artificial insemination to prisoners:

> [E]ffectively excluded any real weighing up of the competing individual and public interests, and prevented the required assessment of the proportionality of a restriction, in any individual case.[422]

In particular, the Court considered that the policy placed 'an inordinately high "exceptionality" burden'[423] on the applicants. The effect of the policy was further exacerbated by the fact that it was not embodied in primary legislation and thus neither the competing interests nor the proportionality issues had ever been assessed by Parliament. The absence of proper assessment therefore fell outside any acceptable margin of appreciation. It followed therefore that there had been a breach of Article 8. The Government has since remedied the violation in *Dickson*[424] by amending the policy, under which the Secretary of State will continue to make decisions based on the individual merits of each case on the basis that:

> Only the Secretary of State has the necessary breadth of knowledge relating to the prisoner and the establishment in which they are located, which is relevant to making decisions that impact on particular prisoners and their partners.[425]

This is despite the fact that the JCHR had recently queried[426] why it was felt that the Secretary of State was the most appropriate person to take these decisions, as, in other cases involving access to fertility treatment and the assessment of a child's welfare, decisions about access are taken by a licensed provider of fertility services, subject to the oversight of the HFEA. The JCHR further noted that the Grand Chamber in *Dickson*[427] had commented upon the fact that the policy had never been considered by Parliament, observing that the presentation of the new Human Fertilisation and Embryology Bill could have presented an opportunity to do so. The JCHR clearly felt this was more appropriate given the remarks made by the ECtHR about the fact that a weighing of the competing interests involved in the policy had not been considered by Parliament.

These two cases establish the importance of demonstrating, especially where the Court is being asked to deal with competing Convention rights, that an adequate proportionality assessment has taken place of the competing private and public interests involved. What is also clear is that the domestic courts cannot simply transpose the margin of appreciation into domestic law, nor can they simply decide that the measure in question does not

---

[420] *Dickson* (2008) 46 EHRR 41.
[421] *Ibid*, para 78.
[422] *Ibid*, para 82.
[423] *Ibid*, para 82.
[424] *Ibid*.
[425] Ministry of Justice, 'Responding to Human Rights Judgments: Government Response to the Joint Committee on Human Rights' (January 2009) (Thirty-first Report of Session 2007–08) Cm 7524, 9.
[426] HL, HC and JCHR, 'Monitoring the Government's Responses to Human Rights Judgments: Annual Report 2008, Thirty-first Report of Session 2007–08; HL Paper 173, HC 1078 paras 40–43.
[427] *Dickson* (n 420) (ECHR).

require a proper application of proportionality simply because it appears to be compatible with Strasbourg jurisprudence. Finally, in cases which do involve areas of ethical and social policy the ECtHR is more likely to accord a wide margin of appreciation to the State where there has been a detailed examination by either the legislature or the judiciary of the nature of the competing interests involved.

Proportionality and the Clash of Rights within Disputes Concerning Private Individuals

As at the Convention level, proportionality will be of relevance with regard to all actions concerning the qualified Articles. Similarly, at the domestic level, the court will also be required, in line with its duty under section 6, to make an assessment as to whether the alleged interference by the individual comes within the range of proportionality when assessing the actions of private individuals towards one another which fall within the horizontal effect of the Act. However, the process is far from easy, as when answering the proportionality question the court will also be required to resolve the clash of individual rights. This is unlike the more normal position in which the court is asked to assess the proportionality of an alleged interference by the State in the rights of a private individual. It should also be borne in mind that during the process of ascertaining and balancing the different rights in a family law application, the interests of any children will carry particular weight. The ECtHR, when approaching any question concerning Article 8, starts from the stance that wherever family life is found to be in existence, each of the family members will be entitled independently to respect for their family life. It does not regard the child's interests in this respect as paramount, that is, as displacing considerations of other members' rights.[428] Each family member's right to respect for family life[429] is accorded equal weight before a decision is made as to what extent, if at all, the rights of all the family members are in conflict. The Court will then consider whether any interference with the rights of family members is justified as 'necessary' under Article 8(2); it is only at this point that the welfare of the child becomes relevant[430] and will not inevitably result in the child's interests prevailing.[431]

---

[428] For a recent example where paramountcy was not applied see *Hansen v Turkey* [2004] 1 FLR 142, para 98. The Court has, however, recently used the word 'paramount' in relation to children's interests in *Zawadka v Poland* Application No 48542/99 67 but diluted this term by referring again, in the same paragraph, to the need to take into account 'more particularly' the best interests of the child. It does not seem, therefore, that the Court used 'paramount' in the same sense as in the CA.

[429] Private life is not usually considered separately, although in some circumstances this might be a significant possibility.

[430] Although the welfare of the child will, to some extent, be relevant when the Court considers its right to family life at the first stage under Art 8(1) it will not be considered in relation to the Art 8(1) rights of the other parties.

[431] This is contrary to the current domestic judicial interpretation of Art 8. See: S Choudhry and H Fenwick, 'Taking Fathers' Rights Seriously' (2005) 25(3) *OJLS* 453; H Fenwick, 'Clashing Rights' (n 83), which attacks the effect of the principle in the case of clashes between media freedom and the privacy of the child; S Choudhry, 'The Adoption and Children Act 2002' (n 83); H Fenwick, D Bonner and S Harris-Short, 'Judicial Approaches to the HRA' [2003] 52 *International and Comparative Law Quarterly* 549 at 572–84 esp. 582–4.

It is also clear that although the ECtHR is prepared to concede a margin of appreciation to the national authorities in private family law cases where clashes between the Article 8 rights of the child and the parent occur, it is not as wide as in certain 'clash of rights' instances in other contexts:[432] the Court is prepared to be fairly interventionist where the right of one party to family life would be almost entirely abrogated by the restriction in question.[433] However, Strasbourg clearly accords special importance to the best interests of the child: where a significant conflict between the claims of another party and those interests arises, it will tend to allow the child's interests to determine the outcome. This Court has recently demonstrated a greater willingness to give special consideration to children's rights,[434] which in turn has been attributed to the growing influence upon the Strasbourg jurisprudence[435] of the United Nations Convention on the Rights of the Child (the CRC).[436] More significantly, in succeeding judgments,[437] the Court has reaffirmed the established position whereby the varying Convention rights of the parties concerned are considered by starting from a basis of presumptive equality.[438] In other words, within the margin of appreciation of the Member State, a fair balance must be struck between the Article 8 rights of the child and those of the parent, albeit attaching particular importance to the former, thereby ruling out the use of a presumption that precludes that balancing exercise.

It is thus apparent from the Strasbourg jurisprudence that an individual right cannot figure merely as an exception to another individual right and, in addition, that it cannot be entirely abrogated without an application of the paragraph 2 tests. Instead, the 'parallel analysis'[439] approach must be utilised: both rights must be considered as exceptions to the other, by applying all the tests within paragraph 2 of Article 8. Unlike Strasbourg, which adjudicates between an individual and the State, the Family Division court will have both parties as family members before it and both will claim that their rights as individuals are equally in issue. As a result the domestic courts will need to deal explicitly with the question of clashing rights. Of significant note is the requirement to attach particular importance to the best interests of the child when carrying out the balancing exercise concerning Article 8. This should, as the author has argued elsewhere,[440] provide a powerful justification to

---

[432] *Otto-Preminger Institut v Austria* (1994) 19 EHRR 34; *Tammer v Estonia* (2003) 37 EHRR 43.

[433] *Johansen v Norway* (1997) 23 EHRR 134.

[434] The ECHR itself contains few explicit references to children and their rights, which is generally believed to be due to the era of its inception.

[435] U Kilkelly, 'The Best of Both Worlds for Children's Rights? Interpreting the European Convention on Human Rights in light of the UN Convention on the Rights of the Child' (2001) 23 *Human Rights Quarterly* 308 and M Woolf, 'Coming of Age? The Principle of the Best Interests of the Child' (2003) 2 *European Human Rights Law Review* 205 for an overview of how the principle has been interpreted by the European Court of Human Rights and the UK courts within the context of the UN Convention on the Rights of the Child 1989.

[436] The UK has ratified the CRC and is therefore bound under international law to comply with its requirements. It is still, however, not part of UK law.

[437] *Görgülü v Germany* App no 74969/01 (2004) para 43 and *Hoppe v Germany* (2004) 38 EHRR 15, para 44.

[438] Thus, in *Hansen* (n 428) the Court found 'the rights and freedoms of all concerned must be taken into account, and more particularly the best interests of the child and his or her rights under Article 8 of the Convention. Where contacts with the parent might appear to threaten those interests or interfere with those rights, it is for the national authorities to strike a *fair balance* between them' (emphasis added).

[439] This was argued for by G Phillipson and H Fenwick, 'Breach of Confidence as a Privacy Remedy in the Human Rights Act Era' (2000) 63 (5) *MLR* 660, 686–87 and G Phillipson, 'Transforming Breach of Confidence? Towards a Common Law Right of Privacy under the Human Rights Act' (2003) 66 (5) *MLR* 726, 749–58. H Rogers and H Tomlinson, 'Privacy and Expression: Convention Rights and Interim Injunctions' [2003] *European Human Rights Law Review* 38 at 41 (Privacy—Special Issue) coined the term 'parallel analysis'.

[440] S Choudhry and H Fenwick, 'Clashing Rights' (n 83).

reinterpret any existing domestic requirements to hold such interests as paramount[441] but will also, if necessary, introduce a relatively higher consideration towards the interests of children where no such requirement currently exists.

Not all family law claims will, however, involve the paramountcy principle and, even where it is applicable, the question of how the clash of rights between private individuals and what impact they will have upon the proportionality question still needs to be addressed. Although the academic and judicial debate concerning horizontal effect has largely centred on the legal basis of these claims[442] there has been some evidence of the acceptance of the application of the parallel analysis as a means of resolving disputes concerning the clash of Article 8 and Article 10. We will now turn to a detailed examination of this instance as a means to then extrapolate the correct approach to other clashes of rights.

The Clash of Articles 8 and 10 rights—Welfare v Media Freedom

The parallel exercise of proportionality has most clearly found judicial favour in the context of apparent conflicts between Articles 8 and 10. In the seminal case of *Re S*[443] the Court of Appeal had to deliberate on its ability to restrain the publication of the identity of a defendant and her victim in a murder trial to protect the privacy of her son who was the subject of care proceedings. The victim was S's brother and there was psychiatric evidence to the effect that S, as an already vulnerable child, would suffer greater trauma and be at greater risk of later mental illness if he was subjected to bullying and teasing at school once the identity of his mother became known. In the lower court, Hedley J had decided that he could make a restraining order under the inherent jurisdiction of the High Court but that he should not do so. However, the Court of Appeal found, unanimously, that in seeking to weigh up Articles 8 and 10 against each other in an instance in which, while the child's welfare was engaged, the paramountcy principle did not apply. In addition, it was found, in a highly significant break with the previous line of authority, that they must be considered as independent elements, on the basis, following *Douglas v Hello!*[444] and *A v B plc*,[445] that one does not have pre-eminence over the other.[446] Lady Justice Hale, who gave the leading judgment, relied on Lord Woolf's dicta in *A v B*[447] to the effect that '[the court must] attach proper weight to the important rights which both Articles are designed to protect. Each Article is qualified expressly in a way which allows the interests under the other Article to be taken into account.' In the lower court it had been assumed that press freedom would be afforded primacy and that the Article 8 rights of the child would figure merely as exceptions under Article 10(2). It was accepted that this was clearly the wrong approach. Lady Justice Hale then went on to consider the proportionality of the proposed interference with freedom of expression.

---

[441] In proceedings brought under the CA by virtue of s1 and the so-called 'paramountcy principle'.

[442] See articles on the debate surrounding 'horizontal effect' at n 288.

[443] *Re S* (n 108).

[444] *Douglas v Hello!* [2001] QB 967, 1005, para 24.

[445] *A v B plc* [2003] 3 WLR 542, para 6.

[446] Despite s12(4) HRA: 4) The court must have particular regard to the importance of the Convention right to freedom of expression and, where the proceedings relate to material which the respondent claims, or which appears to the court, to be journalistic, literary or artistic material (or to conduct connected with such material), to a) the extent to which—i) the material has, or is about to, become available to the public; or ii) it is, or would be, in the public interest for the material to be published; b) any relevant privacy code.

[447] *A v B* (n 445).

She had to consider under Article 10(2) what restriction, if any, was needed to meet the legitimate aim of protecting the rights of the child. If prohibiting publication of the family name and photographs was needed, the court had to consider how great an impact that would in fact have upon the freedom protected by Article 10, taking into account the greater public interest in knowing the names of persons convicted of serious crime than of those who are merely suspected or charged. She then went on to consider the matter from the perspective of the child's Article 8 rights, media freedom figuring this time as an exception to them under Article 8(2). In considering the proportionality of the proposed interference with the right of the child to respect for his private and family life, the judge had to take account of the magnitude of the interference proposed. Lady Justice Hale came to the conclusion that since the first instance judge had not considered each Article independently, and so had not conducted the difficult balancing exercise required by the Convention, the appeal should be allowed, in order that the exercise could be properly carried out by the first instance Family Division court. The two judges in the majority, however, disagreed, finding that although the balancing exercise outlined by Lady Justice Hale should have been carried out, the result reached at first instance—that the restraining order should be discharged—would have been reached even if it had been properly carried out. They considered that the first instance judge had not carried out the exercise correctly, but had had factors relevant to the question of proportionality under Article 8 sufficiently in mind.

Nevertheless, there was clear agreement as to the correct approach to be taken towards the proportionality exercise in cases concerning the clashing of rights. Lord Steyn helpfully summarised the approach into four key principles, which he said 'clearly emerge[d] from the speeches given in *Campbell*: first, neither article has as such precedence over the other. Secondly, where the values under the two articles are in conflict, an intense focus on the comparative importance of the specific rights being claimed in the individual case is necessary. Thirdly, the justifications for interfering with or restricting each right must be taken into account. Finally, the proportionality test must be applied to each.'[448] This approach has subsequently been applied and followed in a number of cases.[449]

The Clash of Individual Article 8 Rights—the Children Act as a Case Study

Since *Re S*[450] took as its starting point the presumptive equality of Articles 8 and 10, relying on paragraph 2 of each Article in order to resolve the conflict between them, it is an extremely significant decision. However, as the author has argued elsewhere,[451] a departure from *Re S* is necessary in the sense that this approach should also be adopted in an instance in which the paramountcy principle *does* apply, necessitating, as indicated, the reconfiguration of that principle as one of pre-eminency. Outside the domain of child welfare the

---

[448] *Re S* (n 108) para 17.
[449] Eg *Re LM (A Child) (Reporting Restrictions: Coroner's Inquest)* [2007] EWHC 1902 (Fam); *BBC v Rochdale MBC* [2005] EWHC 2862; *Crawford v Crown Prosecution Service* [2008] EWHC 854 (Admin); *Re East Sussex County Council* [2009] EWHC 935 (Fam); *Re Attorney General's Reference (No. 3 of 1999)* [2009] UKHL 34.
[450] *Re S* (n 108).
[451] S Choudhry and H Fenwick, 'Clashing Rights' (n 83).

presumptive equality approach is becoming dominant.[452] If this is the case it must follow that this approach should be adopted to clashes between differing Article 8 rights to family life. In other words, a parent's Article 8 right cannot figure merely as an exception to the child's right. Still less can it be almost entirely abrogated—as the paramountcy principle currently demands—without a full application of the paragraph 2 tests. Following this argument, the *Re S* approach, while demonstrating up to a point a sensitive understanding of the Convention values, is revealed to be logically flawed since it advocates presumptive equality for two of the qualified Convention rights (Articles 8 and 10) but abandons its own underlying premises as soon as the paramountcy principle comes into play. Thus, in a significant development of the *Re S* model, the rights of all parties should be considered in turn, the rights of others figuring in each instance as exceptions to the Article 8(1) right in question, applying all the tests within Article 8(2) in each instance. Each analysis would therefore parallel the other ones.

In conducting this parallel exercise it should be made clear that it might be possible in exceptional instances at the extremes to resolve the matter within or largely within paragraph 1 of Article 8. For example, a claim for contact by a physically or sexually abusive parent can readily be excluded from the ambit of the guarantees under Article 8(1) since such a parent cannot expect that his or her family life should be respected. A claim for contact by an emotionally abusive parent might be viewed as engaging the parent's right to respect for family life and therefore as requiring justification under paragraph 2 for its denial, but it could be viewed as a form of family life that only marginally deserves to fall within that term and therefore as very readily justifiable. The family relationship claimed might be viewed as so remote or tenuous that the applicant's Article 8 right to family life could not be viewed as engaged. Alternatively, in respect of a potentially very close relationship—that of mother and child—the adult might be viewed as having in effect waived her Article 8 rights where she had, for example, never seen the child since birth.

Thus in most instances it is now necessary for the Family Division to consider the solutions in family proceedings from the perspectives of parent(s) and child under Article 8; so doing requires the courts to conduct the parallel analysis in proportionality. The Court should consider the parent's right to respect for his or her private and family life as creating an exception to the right to respect for private and family life of the child, under Article 8(2). The parent's right should prevail only where the tests of necessity and proportionality are satisfied. Equally, the Article 8(1) rights of the child should be considered as an exception to those of the parent, again demanding that the same tests are satisfied.

Thus it is important to examine the underlying principles at stake in any particular instance. For example, in a contact dispute it might be found that there was in fact a coincidence between the interests of the father and those of the child in terms of furthering the benefits and value of the family life of both—that is, the child might benefit in the long term from a greater degree of contact in terms of mental health and general development. Such contact might in turn foster a long-term relationship between the two, whereas the limitation of access might mean that eventually the relationship became almost non-existent. This argument could be put forward even where the mother as resident parent

---

[452] This was argued for by G Phillipson and H Fenwick, 'Breach of Confidence as a Privacy Remedy' (n 439) at 686–7. See also: G Phillipson, 'Transforming breach of confidence?' (n 439) at 749–58; H Rogers and H Tomlinson, 'Privacy and Expression' (n 439).

was opposed to greater contact where her opposition was founded merely on personal dislike rather than on concerns for the welfare of the child during contact visits. Equally, in instances in which the mother as resident parent and the child had been and still were at risk from physical or emotional abuse restrictions on or complete denial of the non-resident parent's access could be justified from the perspectives of both the mother's and the child's Article 8 rights to respect for private and family life—viewing those rights as exceptions to the father's right under Article 8(1). In such instances, as mentioned above, a right to respect for family life would not readily encompass the provision of a forum in which such abuse could occur since that would amount to a negation of the interests Article 8 is supposed to protect. Thus, interference with the father's Article 8(1) rights would be readily justified. Generally, where there is in fact an underlying harmony between the two apparently competing rights the seemingly difficult exercise in proportionality may in fact quite readily yield an obvious solution. Nevertheless, there is value in looking at the question of harmony in a nuanced fashion on a case-by-case basis.[453]

Conclusion

This Chapter has not sought to present or argue for a particular interpretation of the HRA. It has instead sought to fully set out the relevant debates concerning the interpretation of the most significant sections of the Act and, in doing so, has highlighted the implications for family law. These implications will be fully explored in the subsequent chapters with regard to the subject areas covered. The chapter has also set out how the doctrines of judicial deference and proportionality mirror to a large extent the relationship between the margin of appreciation and proportionality at Strasbourg, discussed in Chapter 1. However, a significant difference between the domestic approach and Strasbourg lies in the domestic version of the proportionality tests with regard to cases involving human rights. The domestic interpretation of the appropriate standard of review in such cases is much stricter than that employed by Strasbourg in family law cases. Nonetheless, the full application of this more stringent standard of review is impeded by the fact that, in some contexts within family law, the courts have accorded a strong degree of deference to the legislature and thereby lowered the standard of scrutiny with regard to the proportionality of the measures in question. However, where the courts consider the issue to concern matters of constitutional or fundamental importance, this is less likely to occur. Furthermore, the courts have proved a willingness to go further than Strasbourg in such cases if it is felt necessary. Finally, the most important aim of this chapter has been to demonstrate the *potential* of the HRA, not only for the family law litigant but also for family law in general. The continuing resistance by those in the field to the employment of such an approach may thus represent a serious impediment to the aim of the Act: to bring these rights home.

---

[453] In *Re L (A Child) (Contact: Domestic Violence)* [2001] Fam 260, the Court of Appeal found that a small degree of domestic violence would *not* result in an automatic denial of contact. See S Choudhry and H Fenwick, 'Clashing Rights' (n 83) for an illustration of the application of the parallel analysis and the proportionality principle to a contact dispute in detail and S Choudhry and J Herring, 'Domestic Violence and the Human Rights Act 1998' [2006] 4 *PL* 752.

3

Human Rights in Family Law

Introduction

The language of rights and human rights has become commonplace not only in academic discourse but also among the general public.[1] Why, even teenagers have been known to mention them! But talk of rights and human rights is often undertaken without a proper understanding of what these terms mean. This has meant that extravagant and inappropriate claims can be made for rights without an appreciation of the complexies of the terminology and the real difficulties with 'rights talk'. It also leads to ill-informed and misleading criticisms of rights being made. Indeed, there is a perception cultivated by some politicians that 'human rights' are getting out of hand. David Cameron has even called for the repeal of the HRA.[2] The then Lord Chancellor, Lord Falconer, following a case which the government lost, said the government needed to act urgently 'to stop the Human Rights Act becoming corrupted to produce perverse results. We need to take steps now to ensure that lawyers and public authorities do not misuse human rights or feel intimidated into focusing on the rights of the offender to the detriment of the public.'[3] As such comments demonstrate, there is a concern that politicians will use absurd rights claims to discredit the notion of rights themselves. In 2009 the Ministry of Justice produced a document[4] which sought consultation on whether there is a need for a UK Bill of Rights, in part because 'responsibilities have not been given the same prominence as rights in our constitutional architecture'.[5]

Much has been written on the jurisprudential basis of the nature of rights. It is not the aim of this Chapter to contribute to that. However, before seeing how an approach based on human rights can be used to tackle those questions which trouble family lawyers it is necessary to have a clear view on what rights are. This Chapter will be in three parts. First, the issues surrounding the definitions and forms of human rights will be discussed. Second, the benefits of adopting a human rights approach will be outlined. Third, the

---

[1] The leading works on rights include the following: R Dworkin, *Taking Rights Seriously* (Cambridge, MA, Harvard University Press, 1977); H Hart, *Legal Rights* (Oxford, Oxford University Press, 1982); J Waldron, *Theories of Rights* (New York, Oxford University Press, 1984); J Raz, *The Morality of Freedom* (Oxford, Oxford University Press, 1986); C Wellman, *The Proliferation of Rights: Moral Progress or Empty Rhetoric?* (Boulder, CO, Westview Press, 1999); A Halpin, *Rights and Law: Analysis and Theory* (Oxford, Hart Publishing, 1997); M Kramer, N Simmonds and H Steiner, *A Debate over Rights* (Oxford, Oxford University Press, 2000); P Eleftheriadis, *Legal Rights* (Oxford, Oxford University Press, 2008).

[2] BBC News Online, 'Cameron "could scrap" Rights Act', 25 June 2006.

[3] C Dyer, 'Lord Chancellor Defends Britain's Commitment to Human Rights', *The Guardian* 17 May 2006.

[4] Ministry of Justice, *Rights and Responsibilities: Developing our Constitutional Framework* (London, Ministry of Justice, 2009).

[5] *Ibid*, 8.

difficulties in utilising human rights in the context of family law will be discussed. As explained in Chapter 1, in our view following the HRA judges have no alternative but to use human rights analysis in considering family law cases under English law. To debate whether or not human rights approaches are useful is therefore a rather sterile exercise. However, an awareness of the potential benefits and disadvantages of the use of rights in the family law context will be essential if rights are to be used effectively.

Rights: Definitions and Understandings

Lord Steyn, writing extra-judicially, has written:

> A constitutional democracy must protect fundamental rights. It is morally right that the state, and all who act on its behalf in a broad functional sense, should respect the fundamental rights of individuals. Without such a moral compass the state is bound to treat individuals arbitrarily and unjustly.[6]

Such an approach puts human rights at the heart of a properly functioning democracy and is essential for the protection of individual freedom.[7] Most commentators agree that rights are important and accept that in some sense they protect individuals from the power of the State. But beyond that there is little agreement over how they work.

What is a Right?

The claim that A has a right to X is a strong one. It is not just saying that it would be nice if A had X, but rather that A has an entitlement to X. It would be good if we could be given freshly squeezed grapefruit juice for breakfast. Indeed that would be good *for us*. However, we could not claim a right to our favourite beverage first thing in the morning. The claim of a right to X therefore requires a stronger argument than that it would benefit the individual to receive X. The claim to entitlement indicates either that society has recognised that it is especially important that A receives X (be that important to A or to society more widely) or that there is some special reason why A should receive X, rather than other people. Hence we have a right to life: life being important to us and human life being something valued in society. A person may also have a right under contract law to a piece of property. This right is not necessarily based on the argument that the piece of property is especially significant, but rather that the individual has a good claim to it. Herbert Hart distinguishes general and special rights.[8] Special rights he sees as flowing from acts done to or by an individual. This would include contractual claims or rights to compensation. General rights, which he sees as including human rights, are given to all people and include, for example, a right to free speech.

---

[6] Lord Steyn, quoted in H Brayne and H Carr, *Law for Social Workers* 10th edn (Oxford, Oxford University Press, 2008) 75.

[7] For Dworkin, *Taking Rights Seriously*, it is equality which is at the heart of human rights.

[8] H Hart, 'Bentham on Legal Rights', in H Hart (ed), *Essays on Bentham* (Oxford, Oxford University Press, 1982).

Next, a distinction should be drawn between legal rights and moral rights. A straight-forward point is that legal systems do not necessarily protect by legal means all the rights that they could. There may, therefore, be cases where morally a person has a right to X, but that moral right is unprotected in the law and so does not exist as a legal right. A child may have a moral claim to be loved by her parents. But such a right could not be effectively protected by the law. Indeed some recognised human rights are not ideally legislated, but are better promoted through other means, including public discussion, appraisal and advocacy.[9] Amartya Sen has argued that rights should not be seen as primarily legal things:

> Human rights can be seen as primarily ethical demands. They are not principally 'legal,' 'proto-legal' or 'ideal-legal' commands. Even though human rights can, and often do, inspire legislation, this is a further fact, rather than a constitutive characteristic of human rights.[10]

Even where rights are recognised in law, it should not be forgotten that they can have an impact well beyond the courtroom. They can affect the way policies are developed by public bodies and how consumers of public services understand their relationship to the State.[11]

The link between a moral and a legal right is far more complex than may at first appear. Legal rights have their origins in moral claims. Tom Campbell defines rights as 'legitimate expectations, arising from the adoption of authoritative rules and the institutions that support them, that identify the interests to be protected and furthered by the acts and forbearances of others'.[12] Further, the fact that morally a person should have a right, some believe, can influence a judge, where s/he is free to do so, to develop the law to give legal protection for that right. If this is accepted, the fact that there is moral right can exert some pull on the development of the law. Indeed, so much so that the moral right becomes legally recognised.

When it is said that A has a right to X that indicates that the law has recognised that there is a good reason why A should be entitled to X. Waldron has written:

> A can be said to have a right (in a moral theory or a legal system) whenever the protection or advancement of some interest of his is recognized (by the theory or the system) as a reason for imposing duties or obligations on others (whether duties and obligations are actually imposed or not).[13]

His explanation requires therefore an identification of the interest of the individual which is protected by the right and an assessment that the interest is sufficient to generate a right. Identification of the interest underpinning the right can be important when a court is seeking to determine the limits of the right, or to balance competing rights. This can be significant when a court is seeking to resolve cases involving clashes between different rights.[14]

---

[9] A Sen, 'Elements of a Theory of Human Rights' (2004) 3 *Philosophy & Public Affairs* 314.

[10] *Ibid*, 314, 315.

[11] S Sceats, S Hosali and J Candler, *The Human Rights Act—Changing Lives* (British Institute of Human Rights, 2008).

[12] See T Campbell, *Rights: A Critical Introduction* (London, Routledge, 2006) 204.

[13] Waldron, *Theories of Rights* (n 1) 10.

[14] See further, ch 2.

Hohfeld and Rights

A significant contribution to the understanding of rights has come from Wesley Hohfeld.[15] He claimed, correctly, that the use of the word right is ambiguous and in fact the term can be used to mean a variety of different concepts. His suggestion was that greater clarity would follow if we separate out the following four meanings of rights.

1. A claim right. If A has a claim right to X against B then B has a duty to ensure A receives X. So under a contract A may have a claim right to receive £1,000 from B; and B will therefore be under a duty to give A £1,000. In Hohfeld's model, A could not point to a right if s/he could not point to someone who has a corresponding duty.
2. A liberty. The crucial difference between a claim right and a liberty is that a liberty does not involve the imposition of a duty. A parent may have a liberty to raise her or his child on a vegetarian diet. Such a liberty does not impose a duty on anyone. It does, however, mean that no one has the right to prevent the parent so raising the child. In other words it is an injunction preventing people acting in a particular way in interfering in how a person wishes to act. Not only does the liberty not require the existence of a duty on someone else, in fact the liberty does not require anything of others. The liberty a parent has to raise a child on a vegetarian diet does not require the state or anyone else to ensure that sufficient amounts of vegetarian food are available to that parent. In other words a liberty does not require anything of anyone else except that they leave someone else free to act as they wish.
3. A power. This is the ability to alter legal rights or duties. A common example is the right to create a will and thereby alter how property would otherwise be distributed on your death in accordance with the intestacy rules. Again there is no corresponding duty that is attached to a power.
4. An immunity. An immunity is not being under a liability to have your legal situation altered by the act of another.

For our purposes in this book it is the division between a claim right and a liberty which is of significance. The extent to which 'the right to respect for family life' in Article 8 of the ECHR generates positive obligations is an issue which will be referred to throughout the book. One aspect of Hohfeld's analysis which requires more discussion is the link between a right and a duty.

Rights and Duties

One of the controversial aspects of Hohfeld's analysis is that rights must be connected with duties. Indeed, under his approach part of the definition of a right is that there is attached to it a corresponding duty. If we cannot identify who owes the duty to ensure we have clean air, we cannot claim a right to clean air. However, that is by no means uncontroversial.

---

[15] W Hohfeld, 'Fundamental Legal Conceptions as Applied in Judicial Reasoning' (1917) *Yale Law Journal* 710.

As quoted earlier, Waldron believes that a right can exist if there is a reason for imposing a duty exists even if the duty has not yet imposed. Similarly, John Eekelaar has written that rights are:

> a complex amalgam compromising a claim of entitlement to an end-state necessary to protect an interest and an implication that the interest possess sufficient weight to impose a duty to activate the means contemplated to achieve the necessary protection.[16]

It seems that for both Waldron and Eekelaar it is not necessary to have identified the duty for the right to be claimed. For example, society may agree that a child with special needs has a right to appropriate educational provision, even if there is on-going debate over who should provide that education. Of course, in terms of legal rights that is problematic. To say to a person they have a legal right, but it is unclear against whom they can enforce that right, makes the right of limited legal value.

Others who reject Hohfeld's approach argue that rather than duties being an essential element of the definition of a right, duties should flow from rights. We should first decide who has a right and then decide on whom the duty should lie. If there is no obvious candidate for a duty we should try harder to find someone. Joseph Raz writes 'Rights themselves are grounds for holding others to be duty bound to protect or promote certain interests of the right-holder'.[17] In other words a duty is not part of the definition of a right, but is the consequence of a finding that someone has the right.[18] The inability to find a corresponding duty to match the alleged right should not cause us to conclude that the right does not exist but rather require that the law determine where the duty should lie.

What is interesting about the way the jurisprudence under the ECtHR has developed is that the obligation to ensure a breach of rights does not occur can fall on the state as well as the individual. So, a child who has been abused by her parents will have had her human rights interfered with by her parents. But, under the ECHR the state has an obligation to ensure that children do not suffer torture or inhuman or degrading treatment and so the state may have interfered in the child's rights too by failing to put in place mechanisms to protect her. This kind of reasoning may assist in cases where the absence of a duty may otherwise be a problem. If the state has failed to impose a duty upon a third party to protect a citizen's rights, that may itself amount to infringement of the citizen's rights by the state.

There is certainly a danger that without emphasising the corresponding duties that correlate with rights, that inappropriately extravagant claims may be made on behalf of rights. Speaking about children's rights in the UN Convention on the Rights of the Child, Baroness Warnock writes:

> If we look at the words of the convention, we find that children must be brought up in their families; that they must not work; that they must be educated, and educated in a particular way, 'to understand human rights', that they must have the opportunity to play and to exercise their imagination in the arts and in free speech. All this is doubtless excellent; but we ought to be clear that the Convention is putting forward an ideal of childhood such as is generally enjoyed by children in liberal Western societies, which are prosperous, and where childhood can therefore be prolonged … it is straining the concept of right to suggest that for every child whose childhood is

---

[16] J Eekelaar, *Family Law and Personal Life* (Oxford, Oxford University Press, 2008) 135.
[17] Raz, *The Morality of Freedom* (n 1) 44.
[18] *Ibid*, 167.

not like this there is a possible breach of duty on someone's part or on the part of that society in which the child grows up.[19]

Will v Interest Theory

A major theoretical issue concerning rights is between those who adopt the 'will theory' and those who adopt the 'interest theory' of rights. Inevitably there are also those who seek to adopt some form of intermediary position between these two. The dispute is between those who see the essence of rights being the protection of the choice of an individual ('the will theory') and those who see rights as being about the protection of interests ('the interest theory').

Under the will theory my rights can only be infringed if the action done is against my wishes. If I consent to what is being done then there is no interference in my rights; but under the interest theory my rights may still be being interfered with even if I consent to the action. Choice theorists tend to emphasise the role that rights play in protecting a person's autonomy and self-fulfilment. Interest theorists might agree that autonomy is an important interest, but argue that there are other interests that require protection. It might, therefore be argued that there is an interest in dignity and you cannot exercise your rights in a way which infringes your right to basic dignity.

Although much of the debate over the theories is conducted at a high theoretical level,[20] in fact the debate raises some important practical issues. Two examples of relevance for family lawyers will be considered. First, under the choice theory rights cannot be held by those unable to exercise a choice. This means that there are difficulties in saying that young children have rights, if they are unable to choose.[21] The interest theory would have no such difficulties.[22] Issues can also arise in relation to domestic violence in a case where the victim does not want legal intervention to protect her from abuse. Under the interest theory her rights may still require protection even though she does not want the intervention; under the choice theory her rights could not be used to justify intervention.

Supporters of the interest theory reject the view that rights can only be violated if there is no consent. After all, even if a person does consent they cannot be lawfully entered into slavery or agree to be paid lower than the minimum wage. Likewise children and mentally incompetent adults are widely regarded as having rights, even though they may lack the capacity to exercise a choice.[23] Choice theorists, however, see no problem with the argument that young children do not have rights. They tend to argue that they are protected by duties of humanity or other moral or legal requirements which can exist even in the absence of rights.[24] Alternatively it can be argued that in the case of a person unable to

---

[19] M Warnock, *An Intelligent Person's Guide to Ethics* (London, Gerald Duckworth & Co, 2006) 94.

[20] W Lucy, 'Controversy about Children's Rights' in D Freestone, *Children and the Law* (Hull, Hull University Press, 1990).

[21] Although under the choice theory it would be possible to argue that children's rights can be used in such a case to protect their ability to choose when they are older.

[22] N MacCormick, 'Children's Rights: A Test-Case for Theories of Rights' (1976) 32 *Archiv fur Rechts-und Sozialphilosophie* 305.

[23] *Ibid*.

[24] Hart, *Legal Rights* (n 1).

make a choice then someone else can exercise their rights (by making the choice) on their behalf. In the case of children their rights can be exercise on their behalf by the parents (or perhaps the state).

Choice theorists warn that there are dangers with the interest theory.[25] John Eekelaar warns against treating someone against their autonomous will in the name of protecting their rights. As he explains, 'powerful social actors could proclaim what they deem to be in the interests of others, establish institutional mechanisms for promoting or protecting those interests, and claim to be protecting the rights of those others, whether or not the others approved or even knew that their interests were being constructed in that way'.[26]

Rights and Utilitarianism

Perhaps the best way to understand rights is to distinguish them from a utilitarian approach. Under a straightforward utilitarian approach, when faced with a decision one should weigh up the benefits and disadvantages of the alternative options and select that which has the most benefits. As Samuel Scheffler puts it for utilitarians:

> The right act in any given situation is the one that will produce the best overall outcome, as judged from an impersonal standpoint, which gives equal weight to the interests of everyone. States of affairs are ranked from best to worst from an impersonal standpoint and an action is right if and only if it will produce the highest ranked state of affairs that the agent can produce.[27]

Utilitarianism has obvious attractions as an approach: it is simple to understand and probably reflects how we make most of our day-to-day decisions. When deciding which flavour ice cream to choose, rarely do people ask more than 'which flavour will I enjoy the most?'

A rights-based approach, however, argues that adopting a utilitarian approach can produce unacceptable results. For example, if a doctor had four patients each of whom urgently needed a different organ transplant, without which they would die, the doctor might argue (on the basis of a utilitarian analysis) that it would be appropriate to kill a nurse and use his organs to save the four patients. After all, by so doing the doctor has produced the greater good: saving four lives, with the loss of just one. Such an example leads rights-based approach advocates to argue that we should not accept that harm can be done to one person in order to improve the lot of another. To be willing to harm someone against their wishes in order to promote other people's welfare is to use someone as a means to someone else's end.[28]

Ronald Dworkin has written of rights as a 'trump'. Even though a certain course of action might produce the greater good, if it involves infringing a right then it is impermissible. It should be noted, then, that a rights-based approach is not fundamentally antagonistic to a utilitarian approach. It can accept that many decisions can be reached on the basis of a

---

[25] J Eekelaar, 'Invoking Human Rights' in T Endicott, J Getzler and E Peel (eds), *Properties of Law: Essays in Honour of Jim Harris* (Oxford, Oxford University Press, 2006) 336.

[26] J Eekelaar, *Family Law and Personal Life* (Oxford, Oxford University Press, 2007) 136.

[27] S Scheffler, *Utilitarianism and Its Critics* (New York, Oxford University Press, 1988) 1.

[28] That would be to infringe the Kantian Imperative: I Kant (translated by J Ellington), *Grounding for the Metaphysics of Morals* 3rd edn (London, Hackett, 1885, 1993).

utilitarian approach, but not where it involves the infringement of a right. Rights, so understood, operate as a break on utilitarianism, rather than an alternative to it.

One particular issue concerning utilitarianism which can lead to injustice is what
Dworkin has described as the problem of 'external preference'. Let us say that in a society
there is a small minority ethnic group which is hated by the majority. It might be shown
that if the government were to persecute the ethnic minority group, by say, removing their
property, this would produce a great deal of happiness to the majority group. Indeed the
happiness created for the majority might outweigh the misery suffered by the minority.
Could that justify the persecution? Surely not. Rights ensure that minorities are not mal-
treated in the name of making the majority happy. As Alon Harel puts it: 'Rights are ...
associated with individuals and their special worth; they protect the individual against the
consequences of uninhibited pursuit of collective or social goods.'[29]

Although utilitarianism and rights-based approaches are often regarded as opposites, in
fact it possible to support a version of rights from a utilitarian perspective. This would be
done by adopting 'rule utilitarianism'. That would be to argue that a society could adopt a
general rule if it could be shown that following that rule will promote general happiness,
even though it might be accepted that on some occasions a particular breach of the rule will
not generate increased happiness. A popular example is a sign saying 'do not walk on the
grass'.[30] Although for a particular individual on a particular day they could say that walking
across the grass would create more benefit than loss (being able to cross the grass means
they will be able to make an important meeting on time; and that just them walking on
the grass might not unduly harm it) we might say that if we add up the losses to everyone
caused by abiding by the rule and the gain of having the rule we should keep it. Perhaps a
good example is free speech. It is not difficult to think of examples where on a particular
occasion the words used by a person cause more harm than good and so we might say
just considering the one event that a utilitarian would justify making that speech illegal.
However, a rule utilitarian might argue that, looking at the benefits and disadvantages
generally of allowing free speech, the benefits will triumph. Rights, therefore, can be justified for a rule utilitarian if existence of the rights, generally, creates greater benefits than
disadvantages. These 'utilitarian' arguments in favour of rights do not convince everyone.
Nigel Simmonds[31] points out that they do not explain the 'stability' of rights. He points
out that there might be times of war or national emergency when the 'rule' of, for example,
free speech, does not increase general utility. So, the utilitarian basis of rights then becomes
unstable. Indeed, he argues, therefore, that using 'rule utilitarianism' as the basis for rights
leads to rights being vulnerable at times when they are most needed. This leaves open the
question of the basis of rights, if they do not lie in utilitarianism. That is a question which
will be considered later, although it is a common view that no entirely satisfactory answer
has been provided to it.[32]

So, rights then can be regarded as a form of break on utilitarianism. Where an act will
involve the interference of a right it is insufficient simply to show that the act will do more

---

[29] A Harel, 'Theories of Rights' in M Golding and W Edmundson (eds), *Philosophy of Law and Legal Theory*
(Oxford, Blackwell, 2004) 191.

[30] See K Greenawalt, *Conflicts of Law and Morality* (Oxford, Oxford University Press, 1987) 105.

[31] N Simmonds, *Central Issues in Jurisprudence* (London, Sweet & Maxwell, 2008) 143.

[32] J Raz, 'Human Rights without Foundations' (March 2007). Oxford Legal Studies Research Paper No 14/2007.
Available at SSRN: http://ssrn.com/abstract=999874.

good than harm. Where there is a breach of a right a serious and important harm is being done to an individual and that cannot be justified simply by the proof that the act will benefit others.

Absolute v Conditional Rights

Many rights supporters emphasise the distinction between an absolute right and a conditional right. An absolute right is a right that can never be justifiably interfered with. It appears that the right to protection from torture in Article 3 of the ECHR is an example of this. However much good one may believe will come from the torture it is never justifiable. This is by contrast with a conditional right where an interference can be justified if there is a sufficiently good reason to do so. The right to respect for one's family and private life in Article 8(1) of the ECHR is of this kind. Article 8(2) sets out the circumstances in which the right can be interfered with. Where there is a conditional right it is not sufficient to simply show that there would be more good than harm in interfering with the right. If that was so, the approach would not differ from utilitarianism in a meaningful way. Instead, what needs to be shown is not just that there is a good reason for interfering with the right, but that there is a good enough reason for interfering with the right. In Article 8(2), for example, it is said that the competing interest must be such as to make the interference 'necessary' for one of the legitimate aims. There are two particular aspects of the word 'necessary' in this context.

First, the reason provided for justifying the interference must be sufficiently strong. If a father has a right to have contact with his children after family separation this right could be interfered with if it was shown that there would be serious harm to the child as a result of the contact. However, if it was the case that contact was thought to harm the child only very slightly then that may not be a sufficiently weighty consideration to justify an interference with the father's right.

Second, the word 'necessary' indicates that it needs to be shown that there is no alternative way to protect the interest apart from interfering in the right. This is reflected in the notion of proportionality. A local authority may be able to show that a child is suffering significant harm at the hands of her parents and argue that this justifies removing the child from the parents which would be an interference in the Article 8 rights of the family members. However, to justify such an interference it must be shown that no alternative course of action (for example, providing the parents with social work assistance) will adequately protect the child. The significance of these aspects of necessity will be considered further at various points throughout this book.

The Limits of Rights

It is important to appreciate that rights analysis does not purport to provide an overarching theory of ethical decision making. Rights analysis will not assist if you are deciding which flavour of yoghurt to buy. Nor does it provide an answer to the many other ethics dilemmas day-to-day life throws up. As already indicated rights only become relevant when a right of an individual is threatened. Where no rights are involved then rights talk has nothing to say about the appropriate course of action. This means that there are many aspects of family life about which a rights-based approach would have little to say.

Another important point to make is that it may be wrong to enforce one's rights.[33] You may as a landlord have a right to evict a tenant who has missed an instalment of rent, but if the tenant is suffering terminal illness and is close to death, that may not be the right thing to do. Rights might inform you what you are permitted to do, they do not tell you what you ought to do.

All these points, then, emphasise that rights talk is only part of the moral picture. There are other important moral values and interests which are not captured within the context of rights. A failure to appreciate this can lead to extravagant claims being made for rights and attempts to force into rights claims that are inappropriate. Michael Freeman summarises this well:

> We do not have a human right to everything that is good, or to everything that we need. We may need to be loved, and it may be good to be loved, but we do not have a human right to be loved, because no one has a duty to love us. The relations among rights and other moral values is complex, therefore, even if it is true that human rights are especially important values.[34]

What Is a Human Right?

It is, somewhat embarrassingly, difficult to define a human right.[35] Indeed it has been claimed that human rights do not exist and those who believe in human rights are like those who believe in unicorns.[36] Such a view may, however, as Michael Freeman has pointed out, be to confuse the nature of rights. 'Rights are ... not mysterious things that have the puzzling quality of not existing, but just claims or entitlements that derive from moral and/or legal rules.'[37] Understood as claims or entitlements, they can hardly not exist, he argues.

Even accepting Freeman's point, there is still left open the question of what is a *human* right. One view may be that human rights are no more than the rights that a human can claim, as opposed to rights that anyone or anything else can claim. That would suggest that rights are linked to those values we see as significant to humanity.[38] The International Bill of Human Rights refers to 'the inherent dignity of all members of the human family' which is regarded as the source of human rights.[39] However, to say that a human right is any right a human can claim may be to produce too wide a definition. A right to enforce a contract is a right humans can claim, but most people would not classify that as a human right. To many, a human right is a particularly important kind of right.[40] Jayakumar Nayar has suggested that central to the notion of human rights are basic human needs, 'those components, qualitatively articulated, which are identified as the universally relevant constituents of what is understood as "human life", irrespective of the rich diversity of humanity, which

---

[33] J Jarvis Thomson, *The Realm of Rights* (Cambridge, Harvard University Press, 1992).

[34] M Freeman, *Human Rights* (Bristol, Polity Press, 2002) 63.

[35] A Williams, 'Human Rights and Law: Between Sufferance and Insufferability' (2007) 123 *LQR* 133.

[36] A MacIntyre, *After Virtue* (London, Duckworth, 1981) 67.

[37] Freeman, *Human Rights* (n 34) 6.

[38] M Perry, *The Idea of Human Rights* (New York, Oxford University Press, 1998) 47 describes human rights as 'what one is due as a human being'.

[39] J Griffin, *On Human Rights* (Oxford, Oxford University Press, 2008) 8–9 sees them reflecting a person's standing as a person. See also J Mahoney, 'Liberalism and the Moral Basis For Human Rights' (2008) 27 *Law and Philosophy* 151.

[40] J Donnelly, *The Concept of Human Rights* (London, Croom Helm, 1985) 1.

when satisfied within specifics social contexts give meaning to a distinctly human life.'[41] He suggests that:

> Everyone has the human rights not to be deprived of, and the human duty not to deprive others of: their means of sustenance; their physical and mental integrity; their means of shelter; their means of cultural identify; their means of self-expression; their means of education; their means of association; and their means of work.[42]

However, it does not necessarily follow that because something is of value to a person they have a right to it.[43] As already mentioned a person may value being loved, but that does not mean they have a right to be loved. Michael Freeman talking of human rights suggests:

> they are rights of exceptional importance, designed to protect morally valid an fundamental human interests, in particular against the abuse of political power. They carry special weight against other claims, and can be violated only for especial strong reasons.

As John Eekelaar points out, one of the consequences of seeing rights as reflecting fundamental human interests is that rights should not necessarily be regarded as individualistic in nature and should be available to everyone. Indeed, they reflect the communality of humanity. As he says, 'if we make a claim to an entitlement by reference to our status as human beings, we are committed to believing that it holds for all other human beings.'[44] That does not mean that human rights cannot be given to a class of people. The right to vote may only be given to citizens of a country. Rights against racial discrimination could plausibly be made available to a group which was the victim of historic prejudice, but not to another group who suffered no disadvantage.[45]

As already noted, human rights are often said to play a crucial role in protecting individuals from exploitation from a corrupt government. Such a view could emphasise the negative nature of human rights: they are about inhibiting the state's power, rather than a positive claim to assistance from the state. Cass Sunstein[46] has argued that this is right and proper. He states that constitutionally protected rights should be of these negative kinds and not require society to provide food, shelter, medical care, and so on. Such rights, he suggests can interfere in the development of the market and can be difficult to enforce.[47] Others, however, would want to include positive rights within the notion of human rights.[48] Is it coherent for a state to protect the right to life, but not the right to have access to a minimally decent health care system? Thomas Pogge has written that human rights 'are not supposed to regulate what government officials must do or refrain from doing, but are to govern how all of us together ought to design the basic rules of our common life'.[49]

Several commentators looking at the development of human rights analysis have seen a progression in the kinds of rights claimed. 'First generation' rights were basic civil and

---

[41] R Jayakumar Nayar, 'Not another Theory of Human Rights' in C Gearty and A Tomkins, *Understanding Human Rights* (London, Continuum, 2000).

[42] *Ibid*, 187.

[43] J Raz, 'Human Rights without Foundations' (n 32).

[44] Eekelaar, *Family Law and Personal Life* (n 16) 137.

[45] For further discussion, see J Harris, 'Human Rights and Mythical Beasts' (2004) 120 *LQR* 428.

[46] C Sunstein, 'Against Positive Rights' (1993) 2 *East European Constitutional Review* 35, 36.

[47] *Ibid*, 36.

[48] M Perry, 'The Idea Of Human Rights and the Matter of Rights-Talk' (1994) 28 *Suffolk University Law Review* 587.

[49] T Pogge, *World Poverty and Human Rights* (Bristol, Polity Press, 2002) 24.

political rights: the right to vote; the right to live; 'second generation rights are economic, social and cultural rights (for example, the rights to education, health care) and third generation rights are solidarity rights (for example, rights to a clean environment). The extent to which these second and third generation rights might be enforceable and against whom is a matter of considerable debate.

This Chapter will now consider the benefits and disadvantages of a rights-based approach. As is clear from Chapter 1, this may be regarded as an academic exercise because the court, following the HRA, must utilise rights-based reasoning. However, a proper awareness of the benefits of using rights and the dangers that can result from some rights thinking will ensure that as a rights-based approach to family law is developed it is done in the best possible way.

The Benefits of a Rights-based Approach

To recap on what a rights-based approach would require of a judge in a typical family law case: the judge will be required to consider the possible rights that each individual who may be affected by the decision might claim. Typically this will involve the parents and the child concerned, but it could involve wider relatives or other children. In family law cases, the rights involved will usually be an aspect of the right to respect for the private and family life of the parties, but other rights can be involved. For each individual whose rights are engaged the court must determine whether or not the rights or interests of others justify an interference in their rights. Where there is a clash between the rights of two or more people, the 'ultimate balancing exercise' must be undertaken, as described in Chapter 1. When doing this, special weight will be attached to the rights or interests of children. What are the benefits of dealing with a family law case in this way?

The benefits of a rights-based approach can best be seen when contrasted with the approach taken in family law prior to the HRA: an approach based on the welfare principle. As is well known, the Children Act 1989 opens in s1 with the declaration that the welfare of the child should be the court's paramount consideration when determining any question with respect to the upbringing of a child. This has been interpreted by the courts to mean that only the interests of children need to be taken into account.[50]

By way of a summary, here three reasons why an approach based on human rights is preferable a system which is dominated by the welfare principle:

A Rights-based Approach Produces Better Results

The UK courts to date have taken the view that there is no practical difference between an approach based on human rights and one based on the welfare principle.[51] For example, *in Payne v Payne* Thorpe LJ considered that:

> [the HRA] requires no re-evaluation of the judge's primary task to evaluate and uphold the welfare of the child as the paramount consideration, *despite its inevitable conflict with adult rights.*[52]

---

[50] See chapter 6 for further discussion.
[51] *Payne v Payne* [2001] EWCA Civ 166, paras 35–37 (Thorpe LJ) and para 82 (Butler Sloss LJ).
[52] At 57.

He supported this conclusion on the basis that:

> the jurisprudence of the European Court of Human Rights inevitably recognises the paramountcy principle, albeit not expressed in the language of our domestic statute. In *Johansen v Norway* (1996) 23 EHRR 33, 72, para 78, the court held that: 'the court will attach particular importance to the best interests of the child, which … may override those of the parent'.[53]

It is respectfully suggested that this understanding of the jurisprudence of the ECtHR should not be accepted. As Sonia Harris-Short notes, Thorpe LJ's quotation from *Johansen* is selective.[54] The actual words of the judgment in *Johansen* give a very different impression to the paraphrased quotation given by Thorpe LJ:

> a fair balance has to be struck between the interests of the child in remaining in public care and those of the parent in being reunited with the child. In carrying out this balancing exercise, the court will attach particular importance to the best interests of the child, which, depending on their nature and seriousness, may override those of the parent.[55]

When seen in its context, the approach of the ECtHR is very different from the welfare principle indicated by Thorpe LJ.[56]

There are two key differences between the welfare principle and the approach in *Johansen*. First, the European Court of Human Rights clearly states that it is engaged in a balancing exercise between the interests and rights of the parties. The welfare principle, on the other hand, does not admit such a balancing exercise; indeed the interests of the parents are strictly speaking irrelevant to the decision unless they affect the welfare of the child. Second, the *Johansen* approach implies that under a rights analysis the interests of the child will not always override those of the parent but that this will depend on the 'nature and seriousness' of those interests. Again, this contrasts with the welfare principle, which demands that the welfare of the child prevails over the rights of the parents without regard to its nature and seriousness.

Despite the oft-quoted statement from *Johansen*, the ECtHR has not used consistent language in stating the test to be used when analysing a clash of rights between parents and children. The *Johansen* test is the most commonly used test,[57] although occasionally the Court has appeared to give more weight to the rights of children by stating that they will be of 'crucial importance' within the balancing test.[58] There is, however, one case that appears to give overriding importance to the rights of children. In *Yousef v Netherlands* the ECtHR stated that:

> The Court reiterates that in judicial decisions where the rights under art 8 of parents and those of a child are at stake, the child's rights *must be the paramount consideration*. If any balancing of interests is necessary, the interests of the child *must always prevail*.[59]

---

[53] At 38–9; see also para 82.

[54] S Harris-Short, 'Family Law and the Human Rights Act 1998: Judicial Restraint or Revolution' [2005] *Child and Family Law Quarterly* 329, 355.

[55] *Johansen v Norway* (Application No 17383/90) (1997) 23 EHRR 33, para 78 (emphasis added).

[56] For extensive criticism of the Court of Appeal's approach see, eg, S Choudhry, 'The Adoption and Children Act 2002, the Welfare Principle and the Human Rights Act 1998—A Missed Opportunity' [2003] *Child and Family Law Quarterly* 119; J Herring, 'The Human Rights Act and the Welfare Principle in Family Law—Conflicting or Complementary' [1999] *Child and Family Law Quarterly* 223; S Choudhry and H Fenwick, 'Taking the Rights of Parents and Children Seriously: Confronting the Welfare Principle under the Human Rights Act' (2005) 25 *OJLS* 453.

[57] See, eg, *Elsholz v Germany* (Application No 25735/94) [2000] 2 FLR 486, para 50, *Sahin v Germany; Sommerfeld v Germany* (Applications Nos 30943/96 and 31871/96) [2003] 2 FLR 671, at paras 64 and 66; *Görgülü v Germany* (Application No 74969/01) [2004] 1 FLR 894, para 43.

[58] *Scott v United Kingdom* (Application 24745/97) [2000] 2 FCR 560, at 572; *L v Finland* [2000] 2 FLR 118, para 118.

[59] *Yousef v Netherlands* (Application No 33711/96) [2003] 1 FLR 210, para 73.

On first reading this test appears to be very close to the test advocated by Thorpe LJ in *Payne*, as it seems to suggest that the interests of children will automatically outweigh any competing parental right. A closer reading, however, suggests that the Court did not intend to make such a radical departure from its previous approach. The Court's use of the word 'reiterates' suggests that it did not intend to create a new principle.[60] Indeed, the cases that the court cites in support of this proposition adopt the conventional balancing test.[61] Later cases in the ECtHR have not adopted this test and have returned to the *Johansen* test.[62]

It seems, then, that the welfare approach adopted by the courts does not give adequate consideration to rights protected by the HRA. Although the ECtHR recognises that children's rights should be given additional weight when balanced against the rights of their parents, the children's rights are not automatically overriding, as they are under the welfare principle. While the parent may not use Article 8 to justify serious harm to the rights of the child,[63] the rights of the child do not remove the need to consider the rights of the parent. Indeed, the welfare principle appears to require the court to make an order which would very slightly improve the welfare of the child even though that would cause a huge level of harm to others. A major benefit of the HRA approach is that it avoids a conclusion that it is appropriate to make an order which causes significant harm to adults because to do so will produce a tiny amount of welfare for the child. If a court is faced with the alternative of two orders: one which will be neutral to the child, but cause no notable harm to the parents; and an order which will slightly benefit the child, but cause a huge amount of harm to the parents, then the second order should be made under the welfare approach.[64]

Clarity of Reasoning

Continuing from the point just made, that the welfare principle can justify making an order which significantly harms parents simply to pursue a small benefit to a child: in fact, reading the court reports, rarely has that been done. In practice, the courts have found a range of ways of protecting parents' interests, while purporting to adhere to the welfare principle.[65] The courts have been able to smuggle the interests of parents into the calculation. If this is in fact being done covertly, would it not be better for the courts to be open about what they are doing? A human rights approach enables the court to specifically consider the rights of parents. In particular, it allows a transparent assessment of the interests of each family member without the need for unsupportable assumptions that identify

---

[60] S Choudhry, 'The Adoption and Children Act 2002' (n 56) 119.

[61] *Elsholz v Germany* (Application No 25735/94) [2000] 2 FLR 486; *TP and KM v United Kingdom* (Application No 28945/95) [2001] 2 FLR 549.

[62] See, eg, *Haase v Germany* (Application No 11057/02) [2004] 2 FLR 39, para 93; *Görgülü v Germany* (Application No 74969/01) [2004] 1 FLR 894, at para 43; *Sahin v Germany; Sommerfeld v Germany* (Application Nos 30943/96 and 31871/96) [2003] 2 FLR 671, paras 64 and 66.

[63] See, eg, *Hendriks v Netherlands* (1982) 5 EHRR 23.

[64] It may be that such a conclusion could be avoided with a more sophisticated version of the welfare test; see J Herring, 'The Human Rights Act and the Welfare Principle' (n 56).

[65] J Herring, 'The Welfare Principle and the Rights of Parents' in A Bainham, S Day Sclater and M Richards (eds), *What is a Parent?* (Oxford, Hart Publishing, 1999).

the interests of one parent with the welfare of the child.[66] A court applying a rights-based approach is likely to consider the same factors as a court adopting a welfare approach, but the court will be required to articulate the independent interests at stake in the decision and to justify the weight assigned to them.

The argument here is that even if the courts are right to say in practice whether the welfare principle or a human rights approach is used will not affect the outcome of a case, there still are reasons for preferring a rights-based approach. It will ensure clarity of reasoning. The interests of each party can be considered, rather than these being smuggled into the welfare principle by a variety of devices. Further, it shows greater respect to each individual. A mother who is the primary carer of her child can be regarded as a person who has interests and rights of her own, rather than simply a channel through which benefits or disadvantages to the child can flow. The relocation cases[67] demonstrate the difficulties with not taking a human-rights-based approach. The rights of a mother to freedom of movement are given no explicit weight, her application must be based on an argument that if she is not given leave to take the child out of the jurisdiction, she will be so distressed that this will harm the child. Making an order based on the harm she will cause the child if the order is not made is not only fictitious, it is cruel. As Alison Diduck has written, complaining that the welfare principle:

> denies parents any legitimate expression of their own individual needs or rights … and assumes that their own individual responsibilities are to their children (and thus to safeguarding the post-divorce family). It thus denies adults expression of any ethic of care of self.[68]

A final point is the appearance of fairness. A human rights approach will ensure that each party can see that the case has been looked at from their point of view. Their rights have been considered and where appropriate the judge has explained why their rights must be interfered with. It may therefore be that parties will leave the court with a greater sense that justice has been seen to be done.

Children's Rights

One of the major criticisms of the welfare principle is its failure to pay due respect to the decision-making abilities of children. Promotion of children's rights emanates from a rejection of paternalism: the assumption that adults know what is best for children, leaving children as little more than objects of adults' concerns to be controlled and kept free from harm. In the early days of child liberation extreme claims were made for children having exactly the same rights as adults. In recent times those emphasising children's rights make more moderate claims, such that children should be able to make decisions concerning their lives, unless there is a sufficiently good reason not to.[69]

This will be discussed later in this Chapter. Suffice for now to note that it is easy to exaggerate the difference between adopting an approach towards children based on rights and welfare. One important point is that most leading exponents of children's rights include a

---

[66] See, eg, the complaints in M Hayes, 'Relocation Cases: Is the Court of Appeal Applying the Correct Principles?' [2007] *Child and Family Law Quarterly* 351.

[67] See, further ch 7.

[68] A Diduck, *Law's Families* (London, LexisNexis, 2003) 91.

[69] L Teitelbaum, 'Children's Rights and the Problem of Equal Respect' (2006) 1 *Utah Law Review* 173.

powerful element of paternalism or welfarism within their description of children's rights. For example, John Eekelaar,[70] Michael Freeman[71] and Jane Fortin[72] in their writing have all explained that children's rights should not be used in a way that seriously harms children. This means that in many cases a welfare and rights perspective will produce the same result. A child welfarist could regard allowing children to make decisions for herself as important for a child's well-being. Indeed it would be quite possible for a children's rights advocate to be less willing than a child welfarist to allow children to make decisions for themselves. This would be so where a children's rights advocate emphasised children's rights to protection from harm, the right to a safe environment or the right to discipline and/or where a child welfarist placed much weight on the benefit to children of developing their own personalities through making decisions for themselves and learning from their mistakes.

Despite these similarities there would be some important differences. There is an important theoretical distinction between a rights-based approach and a welfare approach. The distinction focuses on who is the primary decision maker. For a child's rights advocate it will be the child when competent or, where not, someone acting as a proxy for the child; for the welfarist it will be another (the parents or ultimately the court). Nor should the political or symbolic significance of rights approaches be overlooked. Michael Freeman writes:

> To understand why rights are important … it is worth considering a society where rights did not exist. It would be a society in which relationships would approximate to those between a master and his slave. Might would be right. The powerless could make no demands at all. Such a society would be morally impoverished.[73]

Predictability and prejudice

Probably the most common criticism of the welfare principle concerns the fact that its application is unpredictable.[74] It is quite simply impossible for a court to work out what is in the best interests of the child. The prior facts are often unknown and hotly disputed. They have taken place in private and so there are huge evidential difficulties in establishing them. The welfare principle requires the court to predict the possible outcomes for a child. That is extremely difficult, not least because the courts and professionals are required to assess parents at the time of life when they are in emotional turmoil. Even if the outcomes were known and the likelihood of these outcomes were calculable there might still be much uncertainty over which a court would think was in the best interests of the child. There simply is no agreement within society over how best to raise children.

Rights supporters would be foolish to claim that a rights-based approach will introduce complete certainty. It is true that the concept of welfare is so vague that almost any argument could be phrased in terms of welfare, but this is probably true in terms of respect for 'fam-

---

[70] J Eekelaar, 'The Interests of the Child and the Child's Wishes: the Role of Dynamic Self-Determinism' (1994) 8 *International Journal of Law, Policy and the Family* 48.

[71] M Freeman, *The Rights and Wrongs of Children* (London, Francis Pinter, 1983).

[72] J Fortin, *Children's Rights and the Developing Law* 2nd edn (London, Butterworths, 2003).

[73] M Freeman, *The Rights and Wrongs of Children* (n 71).

[74] Eg R Mnookin, 'Child Custody Adjudication' (1975) 39 *Law and Contemporary Problems* 226; J Elster, 'Solomonic Judgments: Against the Best Interests of the Child' (1987) 54 *University of Chicago Law Review* 1.

ily life' in terms of Article 8. To present a rights-based approach as a 'rules'-based approach to be contrasted with the discretionary-based approach of the welfare principle would be misleading. For one thing it would be false to suggest that there is a sharp dichotomy to be drawn between the certainty provided by a rules-based system and the uncertainty produced by a discretionary based-system. Rules tend to produce their own flexibility and discretion develops certain norms that generate a degree of predictability.[75] In any event rights-based approaches, at least in the case of rights which are not conditional, involve an element of balancing: be that balancing between competing rights; or in determining whether there is a sufficient other interest to justify interfering with an individual's rights. Indeed, in our present society with such a wide range of families, styles of parenting, and structures of relationships we need flexible, responsive, albeit indeterminate, legal principles. While principles of certainty are important where people carry out activities in reliance of legal structures (contract law might be an example), this is of less importance in areas of the law such as family law where people do not live their family lives on the basis of what the law is.

Although a rights-based approach may not lead necessarily to more predictable results, it does have advantages over the welfare principle in relation to some of the other concerns that are expressed about the uncertainty inherent within the welfare principle. One specific complaint that is sometimes made is that under the guise of the welfare principle a judge can use her or his own prejudice to determine the case. John Eekelaar[76] has made the point politely:

> The heavily subjective nature of the power granted to the judge means that, so long as he or she does not claim to be applying it as a conclusive rule of law, a judge can consider almost any factor which could possibly have a bearing on a child's welfare and assign to it whatever weight he or she chooses.

Indeed, many have complained that the courts in applying the welfare principle have discriminated against various groups. It has been criticised as a means of reinforcing patriarchal power over women and children;[77] as working in a way that is prejudicial to gay and lesbian parents;[78] as operating against the interests of fathers;[79] or against the interests of minority cultures.[80] A fair objection is not so much that judges improperly impose their own views on people, but rather that the welfare principle is so vague that it leaves a judge with little to go on but her or his own moral values or those of experts. As Justice Southin, a Canadian judge, stated, when determining a child's best interests 'judges are tied by the invisible threads of their own convictions'.[81]

Whether a rights-based approach would be preferable in these regards is open to debate. Any area of law which contains judicial discretion is open to these arguments. However, it is suggested that the discipline required by a rights-based approach requires a clearer

---

[75] C Schneider, 'The Tension between Rules and Discretion in Family Law: A Report and Reflection' (1993) 27 *Family Law Quarterly* 29.

[76] J Eekelaar, *Regulating Divorce* (Oxford, Oxford University Press, 1991) 125.

[77] S Maidment, *Child Custody and Divorce* (London, Croom Helm, 1984).

[78] H Reece, 'The Paramountcy Principle: Consensus or Construct?' (1996) 49 *Current Legal Problems* 267.

[79] P Millar and S Goldenberg, 'Explaining Child Custody Determinations in Canada' (1998) 13 *Canadian Journal of Law and Society* 209.

[80] S Toope, 'Riding the Fences: Courts, Charter Rights and Family Law' (1991) 9 *Canadian Journal of Family Law* 55.

[81] *Rockwell v Rockwell* (1998), 43 R.F.L. (4th) 450 (B.C.C.A.) at 460.

articulation of judicial reasoning than the welfare principle does. Under the welfare principle a judge is making essentially a finding of fact: what order will best promote the welfare of children. The rights-based approach requires more of a judge. The rights of each party must be articulated and sufficient reasons for any infringement must be provided. While that will not prevent the views of an individual judge influencing a decision, it should leave their decision more open to scrutiny than a system based on the welfare principle.

Problems with a Human Rights Approach

In this section the potential disadvantages of using a human rights approach in family law cases will be considered.

Misuse of Rights

A common complaint with human rights is that whatever their merits in theory, in practice rights can work to the disadvantage of women and children.[82] The history of rights is replete with examples of cases where the rights of women are subsumed within the rights of men and the rights of children within the rights of adults.[83] Rights are of use to those who have the power to assert and claim rights. Where power lies disproportionately in society (for example, on men rather than women, and adults rather than children) the enforcement of rights operates unequally.[84] Even worse, it is claimed that the rights of weaker people (for example, children) can be picked up and used to pursue the agenda of stronger people (for example, adults).[85] It is not difficult to find in the English case law examples of parents' rights which have been presented as children's rights; or cases where human rights have been considered but the rights of children are ignored.[86]

This is a real and genuine concern about a rights-based approach. Indeed, throughout this book examples will be given of where alleged 'rights' have been used in inappropriate ways. In the name of rights, horrors have been committed. This, however, is equally true of the welfare principle or indeed any legal principle. It is a fact of life that the law (however it is structured) is open to misuse by the powerful.[87] The simple point that the rich can afford the best lawyer reveals this.

---

[82] K Knop (ed), *Gender and Human Rights* (Oxford, Oxford University Press, 2004); S Palmer, 'Critical Perspectives on Women's Rights' in A Bottomley (ed), *Feminist Perspectives on the Foundational Subjects of Law* (London, Cavendish, 1996) 223.

[83] S Harris-Short, 'Family Law and the Human Rights Act 1998', 331; J Fortin, 'The HRA's Impact on Litigation Involving Children and their Families' [1999] *Child and Family Law Quarterly* 237, 251.

[84] For an example of the mixed benefits of how rights have operated see also K Richman, '(When) Are Rights Wrong? Rights Discourses and Indeterminacy in Gay and Lesbian Parents' Custody Cases' (2005) 30 *Law and Social Inquiry* 137.

[85] M Guggenheim, *What's Wrong with Children's Rights?* (Cambridge, Harvard University Press) 2005. Hence the argument in favour of the welfare principle that it will ensure that the interests of the party who will otherwise be the quietest (the child) are at the forefront of the court's mind: J Herring, 'Farewell Welfare?' (2005) 27 *Journal of Social Welfare and Family Law* 159.

[86] J Fortin, 'Accommodating Children's Rights in a Post Human Rights Act Era' (2006) 69 *Modern Law Review* 299.

[87] R van Krieken, 'The 'Best Interests of the Child' and Parental Separation: on the "civilizing of parents"' (2005) 68 *MLR* 25.

It is suggested, however, that the rights discourse provides better protection from misuse than other forms of reasoning. It should not be forgotten that many of the major legal advances in protecting vulnerable groups have been done in the name of rights. The form of reasoning required by a rights-based approach requires the rights of each party, however weak and otherwise invisible in society, to be taken into account. Any interference in their rights must be justified. No one should believe for a moment that having an effective legal regime for the protection of rights will ensure that people's rights will be protected or that rights are not open to misuse. But a society which recognises the rights of disadvantaged groups is more likely to protect their interests than one that does not.

Further, as Joseph Raz has written:

> No doubt human rights rhetoric is rife with hollow hypocrisy; it is infected by self-serving cynicism and by self-deception, but they do not totally negate the value of the growing acceptance of human rights in the conduct of international relations. The hypocrite and the self-deceived themselves pay homage to the standard they distort by acknowledging through their very hypocritical and deceitful invocation that these are the appropriate standards by which to judge their conduct.[88]

Weakening the Protection of Children

There are those who would argue that in any case involving children the welfare of the child should be the court's only concern and that any departure from that principle is unjustifiable. In particular that it cannot be appropriate to make an order which is not in the child's best interests in order to protect an adult's rights. A weaker version of this argument has been promoted by John Eekelaar[89] and that is that although the interests of adults may justify making an order which does not promote the welfare of the child as much as an alternative order,[90] they can never justify making an order which harms the child, if another order is available which will not harm the child.[91]

It is important to recall the main arguments in favour of preferring the interests of children over those of adults. First, it recognises the value, the importance and the vulnerability of children. Not only are the impacts of a decision likely to be more serious for a child, but also children have fewer resources open to them if a court order causes a loss or hurt than adults do. Children lack the material, psychological, and relational resources that parents have. If children are the most vulnerable, the law should do most to protect them.

Second the emphasis of the welfare of the child can be regarded as necessary given the form of legal proceedings. In legal disputes over children often there is no independent advocate for the child and rarely are children heard.[92] This is exacerbated by the fact that inevitably a child is the person involved with whom a court will have least empathy. Their silent invisibility needs some counterbalance and that to some extent is provided by

---

[88] J Raz, 'Human Rights without Foundations' (n 32) 1–2.

[89] J Eekelaar, 'Beyond the Welfare Principle' [2002] *Child and Family Law Quarterly* 237.

[90] That is, the court can legitimately prefer an order.

[91] Although in fact a case can be made for saying that even when applying the welfare principle the courts find ways of taking the interests of parents into account; see Herring, 'The Welfare Principle and Rights of Parents' (n 65).

[92] A James, A James, and S McNamee, 'Constructing Children's Welfare in Family Proceedings' (2003) 33 *Family Law* 889.

emphasising the interests of children. That is not to say that much else needs to be done to find a way of ensuring that children's voices are not marginalised in family proceedings.[93]

Third, we must not overlook the power of language and the impact that legal phraseology can play. The welfare principle is one of the few legal principles that is correctly stated in the media and probably one of the most accurately understood legal principles among the general public. To cause separating couples to discuss their disagreements over children in terms of what will promote their children's best interests is a significant achievement. Of course parents can still disagree violently over what is or is not in the best interests of a child. But if the welfare principle does anything to focus the minds of the parents on the child's welfare rather than their own 'rights', it has great value.

Fourth, it should be recalled that children are normally blameless in these disputes. As teenagers love to tell us, they did not choose to be born. The children are the ones least responsible for the creation of the problem and least able to walk away from it. Parents, having accepted the responsibilities of parenthood, should not complain if children's interests dominate any court resolution of a dispute between them concerning their children.

To meet the objections that rights-based approaches will diminish the weight attached to the interests of children, a number of points can be made. First, as already indicated, the approach to rights taken by the ECtHR does place especial emphasis on rights. Where there is a clash between the rights of children and adults, the rights of children are given especial priority, although in what way and to what extent is unclear.[94] This means that only rarely will the interests and rights of children not triumph over those of adults. Perhaps only in those cases where it is only very slightly preferable for a child to have order A, rather than order B, but order A would constitute a significant infringement into an adult's rights, but order B would not. In such a case although order A may be made under the welfare principle[95] order B might be made using a human rights analysis. But this is justifiable.

It must be questioned whether it is in a child's best interests to be raised in a way in which the rights of her or his parents are improperly infringed.[96] Surely no child is, nor should be, raised in a family in which the adult's interests count for nothing. Would any of us have wished our parents to have made enormous sacrifices in order to slightly promote our welfare? Children are best raised with an awareness of the rights and interests of others, as part of a family which respects and upholds the rights and interests of others. To make an order which was not the optimum for the child at that time in order to significantly benefit other family members would not be to demean or devalue the child, but to respect the child as part of a community which is seeking to uphold the interests of all its members, even if children are held in a special place. In John Eekelaar's seminal work on children's rights he posits a model which is designed to 'bring a child to the threshold of adulthood with the maximum opportunities to form and pursue life-goals which reflect as closely as possible an autonomous choice'.[97] It might be argued in addition to (or as part of) this goal that the child will have learned respect for others' rights and been able to negotiate and

[93] *Ibid.*
[94] See further the discussion in Chapter 2.
[95] Although see Herring, 'The Welfare Principle and Rights of Parents' (n 65) for a discussion of how parents' interests are 'smuggled in' by the courts when using the welfare principle.
[96] Reece, 'The Paramountcy Principle' (n 78).
[97] J Eekelaar, 'The Interests of the Child and the Child's Wishes: the Role of Dynamic Self-Determinism' (1994) 8 *International Journal of Law, Policy and the Family* 48.

appreciate the need sometimes to sacrifice one's interests, in a fair and appropriate way, for others'. Children must learn how to be effective members of families or communities, asserting their rights where appropriate, but sacrificing where necessary. To some, this approach is an inappropriate attempt to present the rights of parents through 'the prism of the best interests of the child'[98] and that the rights of parents and others should be protected in their own right. They should be considered separately[99] and not simply as a way of promoting the child's welfare.

The Problem of 'Clashing Rights'

A common complaint about rights is that rights approaches all too easily disintegrate into clashes between competing rights, to which there is no solution. This is so particularly if, as has been suggested by some, rights can mean all things to all people[100] and lack any precise meaning. Indeed it might be thought that any difficult case in family law can be presented as a clash of human rights. Simplistic approaches to human rights which provide no indication of how to deal with clashing human rights leave such cases unresolved and quite properly lead people to question the utility of a rights-based approach. However, as outlined in Chapter 7, there are approaches (such as the parallel analysis) which provide a way of dealing with this criticism and indicate a way that competing claims under Article 8 might be weighed against each other. It is not suggested that this approach provides for easy answers. Disputed family law cases are often truly difficult and any approach which did provide a ready answer should be treated with a great deal of suspicion. However, it provides a principled way of weighing up the competing interests and rights of the parties while fully realising the implications of the HRA.

The Individualisation of Rights

A powerful critique of rights is based on the argument that rights are based on an image of individuals living isolated lives, protected by their rights of privacy and autonomy.[101] Rights, it is said, place no weight on the relationships which tie people together. David Archard puts the argument this way:

> The language of rights is represented as part of a more general moral and political discourse which sees society principally as a contractual association of independent, autonomous, self-interested individuals governed by certain rules or principles.[102]

---

[98] E Bonthuys, 'The Best Interest of Children in the South African Constitution' (2006) 20 *International Journal of Law, Policy and the Family* 23, 38.

[99] S Choudhry and H Fenwick, 'Taking the Rights of Parents and Children Seriously' (n 56).

[100] S Scheingold, *The Politics of Rights: Lawyers, Public Policy, and Political Change* (New Haven, CT, Yale University Press, 1974) 5.

[101] Many making these criticisms have been attracted to an ethic of care. See, eg, C Gilligan, 'Moral Orientation and Moral Development' in E Kittay and D Meyers (eds), *Women and Moral Theory* (Totowa, Rowman and Littlefield, 1987); M Friedman, *Liberating Care* (Ithaca, Cornell University Press, 1993); S Sevenhuijsen, *Citizenship and The Ethics of Care* (London, Routledge, 1998); R Groenhout, *Connected Lives: Human Nature and an Ethics of Care* (Totowa, Rowman and Littlefield, 2004); V Held, *The Ethics of Care* (Oxford, Oxford University Press, 2006).

[102] D Archard, *Children, Rights and Childhood* (London, Routledge, 2004) 118.

Annette Baier promotes an ethic of care as an alternative 'to the individualism of the Western tradition, to the fairly entrenched belief in the possibility and desirability of each person pursuing his own good in his own way, constrained only by a minimal formal common good, namely, a working legal apparatus that enforces contracts and protects individuals from undue interference by others'.

The argument that rights fail to place weight on the values attached to relationships can be broken down into a number of points:

1. Rights can all too easily be formulated as claims relating to a specific point in time and fail to take account of the relationship between the parties in the past and in the future.[103] The claims of parties need to be examined in the context of the relationships between the parties and not simply the arguments that might be made at the particular point in time the decision has to made. The fact, for example, that a parent has and will continue to provide 24-hour-a-day care for a disabled child, making enormous personal sacrifices, may be a great significance in a case involving a contact or relocation dispute. Her position may be quite different from a resident parent for whom the sacrifices are less. Describing cases in terms of a right of freedom of movement or a right of contact can lose sight of the history of the care and an understanding of what future obligations the parties must bear. However, it is not impossible for a rights analysis to take a broad time frame. This can be done especially with a more expansive understanding of what 'respect for family life' entails. In this book it will be shown how a broader conception of rights can avoid the dangers of seeing a case as a 'snap shot'.

2. The second aspect of the individualism of the rights claim is that separating out the parents and child's interests may be said to be improper.[104] Mary Ann Glendon has written of the way that rights can create 'hyperindividualism' and 'exceptional solitariness'.[105] She writes:

> the most distinctive features of our American rights dialect ... its penchant for absolute, extravagant formulations, its near-aphasia concerning responsibility, its excessive homage to individual independence and self-sufficiency, and its habitual concentration on the individual and the state at the expense of the intermediate groups of civil society ...[106]

It is not possible to consider one person's interests in isolation from those with whom they are in relationship with.[107] One cannot separate the child's interests as somehow independent from the interests of her carer.[108] To harm the child is to harm her carer and to harm the carer is to harm the child. Further, the values that the law should seek to uphold, especially in the context of the family, are not those usually promoted by human rights analyses such as individual autonomy or freedom of movement, but rather those of

---

[103] M Glendon, *Rights Talk: Impoverishment of American Discourse* (New York, Free Press, 1991) 45–6.

[104] H Lim and J Roche, 'Feminism and Children's Rights, in J Bridgeman and D Monk (eds), *Feminist Perspectives on Child Law* (London, Cavendish, 2000).

[105] M Glendon, *Rights Talk* (n 103) 15.

[106] *Ibid*, 14.

[107] J Nedelsky, 'The Practical Possibilities of Feminist Theory' (1993) 87 *Northwestern University Law Review* 1286, 1295–6.

[108] E Scott and R Scott, 'Parents as Fiduciaries' (1995) 81 *Virginia Law Review* 2401.

nurturing and care. Rights work well for a society full of 'self-interested individuals',[109] but not those whose lives are centred on inter-dependency and nurturing.

Again these concerns are justified; however, they can be met within a human rights framework. After all, the key right in many family law cases is the right to respect for family life: a right which emphasises the importance of relationships. Some commentators have developed visions of relational rights:[110] perhaps the best known are writings on relational autonomy.[111] Although in truth there has been some powerful theoretical work,[112] their proponents are yet to be developed into an approach which would readily translate into judicial guidance. But such approaches would enable courts to seek to develop understandings of rights that respect and uphold relationships. Rights which respect the obligations that flow from a relationship and emphasise the importance of the relationship. Any rights granted would be those needed to enable the relationship to flourish. Such models seek to regard dependency as the norm.[113] Some models emphasise the importance of respecting the views of the person in the closest relationship with the child: the primary carer.[114] These enable the law to promote those values of dependency, mutuality and vulnerability which are such an important part in so very many people's lives.

A rather different response to the argument that rights do not respect relationships is to argue that rights are not inconsistent with relationship. Michael Meyer argues that:

> Individual moral rights provide individuals with a certain secure moral standing. A proper sense of self-worth is not inconsistent with the virtues of friendship. Clearly, habits of self-respect inspired by rights can encourage such virtues among one's friends.[115]

In a similar vein Susan Okin has suggested that:

> however much the members of families care about one another and share common ends, they are still discrete persons with their own particular aims and hopes, which may sometimes conflict. [W]e must see the family as an institution in which justice is a crucial virtue.[116]

This response argues that rights and relationships are not incompatible.[117] In fact, respecting the rights and obligations of each other is an important aspect of a relationship; although it may be that this is only so if rights here are understood in a way which is supportive of the values underpinning relationships of interdependence and mutuality.[118] There is, for example, a tension between respecting the notion of commitment, which is an

---

[109] F Olsen, 'Statutory Rape: A Feminist Critique of Rights Analysis' (1984) 63 *Texas Law Review* 387.

[110] D Meyer, 'The Modest Promise of Children's Relationship Rights' (2003) 11 *William and Mary Bill of Rights Journal* 1117.

[111] J Nedelsky, 'The Practical Possibilities of Feminist Theory' (n 107).

[112] Eg C McKenzie and N Stoljar, *Relational Autonomy* (New York, Oxford University Press, 2000).

[113] MA Fineman, 'What Place for Family Privacy?' (1999) 67 *George Washington Law Review* 1207; S Sevenhuijsen, *Citizenship and Ethics of Care* (n 101).

[114] M Fineman, *The Autonomy Myth* (New York, Free Press, 2004).

[115] M Meyer, 'Rights Between Friends' (1992) 89 *Philosophy* 467, 474–5. See the general discussion in J Murphy, 'Rules, Responsibility and Commitment to Children: The New Language of Morality in Family Law' (1999) 60 *University of Pittsburgh Law Review* 1111.

[116] S Okin, *Justice, Gender and the Family* (New York, Basic Books, 1992) 32.

[117] Also for a view that approaches based on care and those based on rights are not compatible see S Ruddick, *Maternal Thinking: Towards a Politics of Peace* (Boston, Beacon Press, 1996).

[118] M Nussbaum, 'Aristotle, Feminism and Needs for Functioning' (1992) 70 *Texas Law Review* 1019, 1027.

important part of family relationships,[119] within a model of rights which overemphasises the importance of autonomy.[120]

A different response to the argument that rights undermine relationships is that although in intact families the talk of rights have little meaning, when a family breaks down then it is appropriate and necessary to talk in terms of rights. David Archard writes:

> the exercise of rights may be regarded as an indication that certain kinds of relationship, those of natural love and care, have broken down. Rights compel the performance of actions which do not come naturally to those under the correlative duties. The assertion and exercise of rights thus marks the absence or breakdown of relations characterised by mutual dispositions of benevolence.[121]

While it is true that on parental separation the relationship between the parents will change and often the parent–child relationships will too, this does not mean that the values of love, dependency and mutuality are not still there. The rights that have been developed and work effectively between strangers may need to be reworked for those in intimate (or formerly intimate) relations. For example, the weight placed on 'market-valued' rights such as the freedom of movement may be overemphasised, and other rights, such as those recognising the importance of being able to effectively nurture the child, may need to be given more weight.

3. A third aspect of this argument is that rights talk means that 'real experiences' are converted into 'empty abstractions'.[122] As Carol Smart puts it:

> the rights approach takes and translates personal and private matters into legal language. In so doing, it reformulates them into issues relevant to law rather than to the lives of ordinary people. It also positions people in opposition to one another and this can be particularly problematic for children. But the rights-based approach also individualises issues in that it removes and isolates the individual who is claiming rights from their family or social context. This means that, for the duration of the conflict of rights, the individual cannot be part of their family or context and, after the conflict is over, has to find ways of re-entering into those relationships, assuming that they are not removed entirely.[123]

To clump together the claims of all the non-resident parents in these cases under the umbrella claim of a right to respect for family life is to overlook the vastly differing realities behind the claims. Smart and Neale have promoted 'the principle of actuality'; namely that 'decisions would not be made on the basis of abstract notions of child welfare, but in relation to the needs and wishes of actual children'.[124] There is a danger that with rights talk the particular circumstances of an individual's situation are transformed into the language of a particular right and thereby lose their unique features.

There is another aspect of the abstracting nature of rights. Nicola Lacey questions how 'the framework of rights can provide not only a formal articulation of individual entitlements,

---

[119] M Regan, *The Pursuit of Intimacy* (New York, New York University Press, 1993).
[120] For further discussion see J Herring, 'Relational Autonomy and Family Law' in J Wallbank, S Choudhry and J Herring, *Family Gender and Rights* (London, Routledge, 2009).
[121] Archard, *Children, Rights and Childhood*, 120 (n 102).
[122] M Tushnet, 'A Critique of Rights' [1984] *Texas Law Review* 1363, 1364.
[123] C Smart, 'Children and the Transformation of Family Law' in J Dewar and S Parker, *Family Law: Processes, Practices, Pressures* (Oxford, Hart Publishing, 2003) 238–9.
[124] C Smart and B Neale, *Family Fragments* (Bristol, Polity Press, 1999) 195.

but also accommodation of the contextual factors which shape the capacity of differently situated subjects to take up and realise their rights'.[125] She goes on to argue:

> Liberal rights and limits and limits on government power are derived from an a priori idea of the nature of the human being which underplays the extent to which social and political institutions shape individual preferences, attitudes, and dispositions. The screen brought in by an implicit, purportedly gender-neutral image of human nature obscures the assumptions being made about women and about sexual difference which feminism wants to reveal and criticise.[126]

It is, as Lacey emphasises, crucial to ensure not only that individuals have rights in a conceptual sense, but also that these are rights that can be used in practice. Where individuals are not readily able to access their rights then there should be in place a mechanism for ensuring that those rights can be protected. In the context of family law, women,[127] children and those from minority ethnic communities[128] are those who have found it hardest to access rights.

4. It has also been argued that rights downplay or even ignore the importance of responsibilities.[129] Rights fail to place values on issues such as commitment and obligation.[130] Smart and Neale in their sample of separating couples found that while men talked of the issues in terms of rights, women talked in terms of responsibilities and obligations.[131] Hence Sir John Laws has argued:

> the idea of a rights-based society represents an immature stage in the development of a free and just society ... nothing is more important, if we are truly dedicated to freedom and justice, than to see the shortcomings of this fragile pedestal. A society whose values are defined by reference to individual rights is by that very fact already impoverished. Its culture says nothing about individual duty—nothing about virtue. We speak of respect for other people's rights. But, crudely at least, this comes more and more to mean only that we should accept that what someone wants to do, he should be allowed to do. Self-discipline, self-restraint, to say noting of self-sacrifice, are at best regarded as optional extras and at worse (and the worst is too often the reality) as old-fashioned ideas worth nothing but a scoff and a gibe.[132]

Ribbens *et al* have sought to promote an ethic of care as an alternative to a rights-based approach which is about 'responsibilities (what is the fair course of action, who should take fair action, whose needs for fairness should be met) rather than rights (to fairness and to have needs met)'.[133] However, Michael Freeman does not accept that the notions of rights must diminish a commitment to a duty. As he emphasises, just because one has a right to do X does not mean that it is right to do X. This is true, but as regards the court making a decision it is concerned with what a person may do, not what s/he should do.

---

[125] N Lacey, 'Feminist Legal Theory and the Rights of Women' in K Knop (ed), *Gender and Human Rights* (Oxford, Oxford University Press, 2004), 20–1.

[126] *Ibid*, 21.

[127] C Smart, *Feminism and the Power of Law* (London, Routledge, 1989), ch 8.

[128] P Andrews, 'Making Room for Critical Race Theory in International Law' (2000) 45 *Villanova Law Review* 855.

[129] Regan, *The Pursuit of Intimacy* (n 119); Glendon, *Rights Talk* (n 103).

[130] M Regan, 'Law, Marriage and Intimate Commitment' (2001) 9 *Virginia Journal of Social Policy and the Law* 116.

[131] Smart and Neale, *Family Fragments* (n 124).

[132] J Laws, 'The Limitation of Human Rights' [1998] *PL* 254, 255. See also J Laws, 'Beyond Rights' (2003) 23 *OJLS* 265.

[133] J Ribbens McCarthy, R Edwards and V Gillies, *Making Families* (Bristol, Sociology Press, 2002) 142.

There is another point to be made against Laws' views and that is that rights identify not just that a person has breached their obligation, but also who has been wronged. As Nicholas Wolterstorff[134] puts it:

> it is on account of her worth that the other comes into my presence bearing legitimate claims against me as to how I treat her. The rights of the other against me are actions and restraints from action that due respect for her worth requires of me. To fail to treat her as she has a right to my treating her is to demean her, to treat her as if she had less worth than she does. To spy on her for prurient reasons, to insult her, to torture her, to bad-mouth her, is to demean her.

> And to demean her is to wrong her. If I fail to treat her in the way she has a right to my treating her, I am guilty; but she is wronged. My moral condition is that of being guilty; her moral condition is that of having been wronged. The language of duty and guilt enables the battered wife to point to the effect of her spouse's actions on his moral condition; he is now guilty. The language of rights and of being wronged enables her to point to the effect of her spouse's action on her own moral condition; she has been wronged, deprived of her right to better treatment, treated as if she were of little worth. He is not only guilty of having acted out of accord with the moral law; he is guilty of having wronged *her*—perhaps even by trying to make her feel guilty when it is he who is guilty.

Wolterstorff makes an important point here in emphasising what would be lost in a system which emphasised obligations, but not rights.

Alternatives to Rights: Ethics of Care

Many of those rejecting the individualised vision of rights have turned to ethics of care as an alternative.[135] The ethic of care has been particularly developed and found support among feminist thinkers. It promotes a vision of us with mutually interdependent relationships as the norm around which legal and ethical responses should be built. At the heart of this approach is that the activity of caring[136] is undervalued. Caring is a gendered activity. It is seen as 'women's work' and as such is ignored in the 'male gaze'. Care of children and vulnerable adults has an enormous economic value and yet it is not given the respect or recognition that other higher-profile 'economically productive' activities have. All this is convenient to a society in which 'men's' work goes rewarded and valorised, while 'women's' work is invisible and unrecognised. The lack of respect owed to caring has played a significant role in the unequal economic position of women.[137]

An approach which took caring more seriously would place relationships at the heart of its thinking. So rather than the focus of the enquiry being whether it is my right to do X, the question is what is my proper obligation within the context of this relationship.[138]

---

[134] N Wolterstorff, *Justice: Rights and Wrongs* (Princeton, Princeton University Press, 2008) 8–9.

[135] Eg Held, *The Ethics of Care* (n 101).

[136] We are talking here about caring for someone not caring about someone: see J Masson, 'Parenting by Being; Parenting by Doing—In Search of Principles for Founding Families' in J Spencer and A du Bois-Pedain (eds), *Freedom and Responsibility in Reproductive Choice* (Oxford, Hart Publishing, 2006).

[137] C Ungerson, 'Thinking about the Production and Consumption of Long-term Care in Britain: Does Gender Still Matter?' (2000) 29 *Journal of Social Policy* 623.

[138] A Tauber, *Patient Autonomy and the Ethics of Responsibility* (Cambridge, MIT Press, 2005) 25: V Held, *The Ethics of Care* (n 101) 1.

The law presumes an autonomous competent man who can enforce his rights. The reality is that we are ignorant, vulnerable, interdependent individuals, whose strength and reality is not in our autonomy, but our relationships with others.[139]

Carol Gilligan explains,

> The ideal of care is thus an activity of relationships, of seeing and responding to need, taking care of the world by sustaining the web of connection so that no one is left alone.[140]

Our visions of ourselves must be fluid: we cannot easily break down into 'me' and 'you' when in a relationship. To harm a child is to harm her carer; to harm the carer is to harm the child. To claim, as some judges shockingly have done, that a father can be violent towards his child's mother, but be committed to the child, is to separate individuals inappropriately.[141] The values that are promoted within an ethic of care are not isolated autonomy or the pursuance of individualised rights, but rather those of promoting caring, mutuality and interdependence.

Here are the key aspects of the ethic of care:

1. The inevitability of interdependence, not self-sufficiency.

Care is an inevitable part of life.[142] At the very start of life we are in a relationship of dependency, and often we are just as dependant at the end of life. Care is a daily reality for most people. It is true that during the course of life the balance between caring and being cared for may shift. But, caring is the very essence of life.[143] It is part of being human. Without it society would soon collapse. The law must regard relationships as key to its thinking and not ignore them.

2. The value of care

Care ethicists would argue that not only is care an inevitable part of life, but that it is a good part of life. As Robin West puts it:

> Caregiving labor (and its fruits) is the central adventure of a lifetime; it is what gives life its point, provides it with meaning, and returns to those who give it some measure of security and emotional sustenance. For even more of us, whether or not we like it and regardless of how we regard it, caregiving labor, for children and the aged, is the work we will do that creates the relationships, families, and communities within which our lives are made pleasurable and connected to something larger than ourselves.[144]

Caring, then, is a 'major life activity'[145] which benefits not just the person receiving the care, but also the person giving the care and society more widely.[146]

---

[139] C Meyer, 'Cruel Choices: Autonomy and critical care decision-making' (2004) 18 *Bioethics* 104.

[140] C Gilligan, *In a Different Voice: Psychological Theory and Women's Development* (Cambridge: Harvard University Press, 1982) 73.

[141] *Re JS* [2002] 3 FCR 433.

[142] Fineman, *The Autonomy Myth* (n 114) xvii.

[143] F Williams, 'The Presence of Feminism in the Future of Welfare' (2002) 31 *Economy and Society* 502.

[144] R West 'The Right to Care' in E Kittay and E Feder (eds), *The Subject of Care: Feminist Perspectives on Dependency* (Lanham, Rowman & Littlefield, 2002) 89.

[145] A Hubbard, 'The myth of independence and the major life activity of caring' (2004) 8 *Journal of Gender, Race and Justice* 327.

[146] L McClain, 'Care as a Public Value: Linking Responsibility, Resources, and Republicanism' (2001) 76 *Chicago-Kent Law Review* 1673; M Daly, 'Care as a good for Social Policy' (2002) 31 *Journal of Social Policy* 251.

From a feminist perspective there is a danger in seeking to have care valued. The danger is that they might be seen as justifying or encouraging women to undertake unpaid care work. However, care ethics seeks to ensure that value is attached to care so that those who undertake 'love labour'[147] are not disadvantaged. If society were to attach importance and value to care it might become an activity in which both men and women would seek to partake equally.[148]

3. The relational approach of ethics of care

One of the most attractive aspects of an ethic of care approach is that it seeks to move away from an atomistic picture of individuals with rights which compete against each other to a model which emphasises the responsibilities of people towards each other in mutually supporting relations.[149] So rather than the focus of the enquiry being whether it is my right to do X, the question is what is my proper obligation within the context of this relationship.[150] Virginia Held makes the point by contrasting ethics of care and an ethic of justice:

> An ethic of justice focuses on questions of fairness, equality, individual rights, abstract principles, and the consistent application of them. An ethic of care focuses on attentiveness, trust, responsiveness to need, narrative nuance, and cultivating caring relations. Whereas an ethic of justice seeks a fair solution between competing individual interests and rights, an ethic of care sees the interest of carers and cared-for as importantly intertwined rather than as simply competing.[151]

It should be added that Held makes it clear that an ethic of care includes justice:

> There can be care without justice. There has historically been little justice in the family, but care and life have gone on without it. There can be no justice without care, however, for without care no child would survive and there would be no persons to respect.[152]

There is another important aspect of this issue. That is that emphasising interdependence and mutuality means that the division between carer and cared for dissolves. As Michael Fine and Caroline Glendinning argue:

> Recent studies of care suggest that qualities of reciprocal dependence underlie much of what is termed 'care'. Rather than being a unidirectional activity in which an active care-giver does something to a passive and dependent recipient, these accounts suggest that care is best understood as the product or outcome of the relationship between two or more people.

In truth there is often give and take in the 'carer' and 'cared for' relationship. Their relationship is marked by interdependency.[153] The 'cared for' provides the 'carer' with gratitude, love, acknowledgement and emotional support. Indeed often a 'carer' will be 'cared for' in

---

[147] See K Silbaugh, 'Turning Labor into Love: Housework and the Law' (1996) 91 *Northwestern University Law Review* 1.

[148] J Williams, 'From Difference to Dominance to Domesticity; Care as Work, Gender as Tradition' (2001) 76 *Chicago-Kent Law Review* 1441. There would also need to be changes in the employment market to ensure that employed work was a realistic and attractive option for women: T Knijn and C Ungerson, 'Introduction: Care work and Gender in Welfare Regimes' (1997) 32 *Social Politics* 323.

[149] G Clement, *Care, Autonomy and Justice: Feminism and the Ethic of Care* (New York, Westview, 1996) 11.

[150] V Held, *The Ethics of Care* (n 101) 1.

[151] *Ibid*, 15.

[152] *Ibid*, 17.

[153] T Shakespeare, *Help* (Birmingham, Venture, 2000) and T Shakespeare, 'The Social Relations of Care' in G Lewis, S Gewirtz and J Clarke (eds), *Rethinking Social Policy* (London, Sage, 2001).

another relationship. As Diane Gibson has argued, our society is increasingly made up of overlapping networks of dependency.[154]

Clare Ungerson has convincingly argued that it is wrong to see the relationship between 'carer' and 'cared for' as one where the 'carer' has power over the 'cared for'.[155] The 'cared for' might have a range of powers they can exercise. The emotional well-being of the carer can depend on the attitude and response of the 'cared for' person to the carer. The 'cared for' has the power to make the life of the carer unbearable.

Critics of an Ethic of Care

Of course, the concept of an ethic of care is not without its critics. Emily Jackson has recently described the ethic of care as 'an inherently vague concept, which could be used to justify almost any plausible moral argument'.[156] She points out that in relation to euthanasia, ethics of care could be used to support or oppose euthanasia. This is, with respect, a rather unfair criticism. Exactly the same thing could be said about the concept of human rights. Indeed one should be highly sceptical of any broad ethical approach which provides a single answer to a complex issue such as euthanasia. An ethic of care, like the concept of rights, provides ethical tools with which to analyse a situation, but it does not provide the answer. The fact that it can be used to support and oppose euthanasia should be seen as a strength, not a weakness of the concept.

Jackson's argument that the notion of care itself—which is at the heart of the approach— is vague has more merit. This, however, is to overlook the extensive work that ethics of care theorists have done to give greater clarity to the concept of care.[157] Even if it does still lack precision, this is equally true of concepts such as the right to dignity, justice or privacy, which are widely respected and used by lawyers and ethicists.

Another common criticism of an ethic of care relates to a rather unfortunate aspect of its history. The ethic of care rose to prominence with the writing of Carol Gilligan,[158] who sought to distinguish between a 'male' approach to ethical issues, which focused on concepts of justice, and a 'female' approach to ethical issues, which focused on concepts of care. While undoubtedly the 'grandmother' of care ethics (and who would want to speak ill of their grandmother), the 'second generation'[159] of care ethicists have tended to downplay the argument that the ethic of care is a female way of thought.[160] Further, the sharp divide between justice and care is not normally relied upon nowadays. An ethic of care wishes to promote relationships, but only those relationships which are just. As Robin West puts it:

> Relationships of care, untempered by the demands of justice, resulting in the creation of injured, harmed, exhausted, compromised, and self-loathing 'giving selves', rather than in genuinely compassionate and giving individuals, are ubiquitous in this society.[161]

---

[154] D Gibson, *Aged Care: Old Policies, New Solutions* (Melbourne, Cambridge University Press, 2005).

[155] C Ungerson, 'Social Politics and the Commodification of Care' (1997) 4 *Social Policy* 362.

[156] E Jackson, *Medical Law* (Oxford, Oxford University Press, 2006) 22.

[157] Eg Held, *The Ethics of Care* (n 101); D Koehn, *An Ethic of Care* (London, Routledge, 1998).

[158] C Gilligan, *In a Different Voice* (n 140) 1–4, 24–63.

[159] O Hankivsky, *Social Policy and the Ethic of Care* (Vancouver, University of British Columbia Press, 2005) 2.

[160] Repeats of the experiments used by Carol Gilligan in European countries have not found the differing responses to ethical issues tied to sex in the way she did: A Vikan, C Camino and A Biaggio, 'Note on a cross-cultural test of Gilligan's ethic of care' (2005) 34 *Journal of Moral Education* 107.

[161] R West, *Caring for Justice* (New York: New York University Press, 1997) 81.

So arguments that an ethic of care perpetuates assumptions that women are naturally drawn to caring roles,[162] or that it overlooks the potential for abuse within relationships, are usually based on a rather old-fashioned (mis)understanding of what the ethic of care is about.

Ethic of Care and Rights

An approach based on an ethic of care has much to say that is of value. Indeed the authors are sympathetic and supportive of the general flavour of the approach. However, the values and principles underpinning an ethic of care can be used within the context of rights. It has already been mentioned that work has been done to promote relational visions of rights which give proper weight to relationships. Indeed, the right in the ECHR which is the most important right is the right to family life: itself a right which emphasises the importance of rights. Perhaps most significantly following the HRA for lawyers in practice there is little point in supporters of ethic of care principles bemoaning the fact that we have a rights-based approach rather than an ethic-of-care-based approach; rather it is in a practical sense more useful to consider how a rights-based approach can be used to take account of, in so far as is possible, the principles underpinning an ethic of care. In particular, then, we should be wary of uses of rights which promote individualism. We must accept that for many people their rights are interdependent. The protection of one person's rights can involve necessarily the protection of another person's rights. One cannot always easily tease out the rights individually.

It not possible here to undertake a full analysis of an ethic of care. The main point for the purposes of this book is that an ethic of care could be promoted through the tools of rights.[163] It is true it would be necessary to reframe some of the rights and to appreciate them in a more relational way, but a rights analysis is not per se inimical to an approach based on an ethic of care. Indeed there are some particular benefits of an ethic of care seeking to utilise the language of rights, rather than reject it out of hand.

First, in practical terms supporters of an ethic of care are more likely to find their agenda being persuaded if it can be put in terms of a currently used legal framework rather than seeking a complete overhaul of the legal system, an approach which is unlikely to meet with practical success. Second, a rights-based approach emphasises the importance of obligations and responsibilities towards others, something that is a key element in an ethic of care approach. While it is true that notions of autonomy can be seen to be incompatible with notions of responsibility and commitment, nevertheless that should not be so. Third, rights might offer some protection from the concerns that have been raised about an ethic of care, many of which are acknowledged by their supporters. There is a danger that the ethic valorises the practice of care in a way which overlooks the interests and importance of the person being cared for. Also that an ethic of care could be used in a way which fails to protects rights to justice and equality.[164] Michael Freeman has written of the way that rights are a 'resource in structuring and constraining relationships'.[165] The point he is alluding to there is that relationships can be tools of oppression as well as of liberation.

---

[162] Jackson, *Medical Law* (n 156) 22.

[163] Although, arguably, the concerns of an ethic of care could also be pursued though the welfare principle: J Herring, 'The Human Rights Act and the Welfare Principle in Family Law—Conflicting or Complementary?' (1999) 11 *Child and Family Law Quarterly* 223.

[164] T Cockburn, 'Children and the Feminist Ethic of Care' (2005) 12 *Childhood* 71.

[165] M Freeman, 'The Future of Children's Rights' (2000) 14 *Children and Society* 277.

Ethic of care theorists have long struggled to find a way of determining which relationship deserve nurturing and which need challenging.[166] No supporter of an ethic of care would seek to promote abusive relationships. Virginia Held makes it clear that an ethic of care includes justice:

> [t]here can be care without justice: There has historically been little justice in the family, but care and life have gone on without it. There can be no justice without care, however, for without care no child would survive and there would be no persons to respect.[167]

Rights could provide some tools in ensuring that justice can be met within an ethic of care.[168] A final point is that it should not be thought that adopting a rights-based approach means that other values should be set aside.[169] Rights could set a minimum framework of responsibilities onto which could be added further policies designed to promote relationships. The values of care, love and commitment are not necessarily inconsistent with a rights-based approach and could be promoted independently of it.

Children and Rights

As already mentioned, a major difference between a welfare-based approach and one based on rights is the scope it gives to attaching weight to the rights of children. It is important to separate out two questions that arise over the issue of children's rights: should children have all the rights that adults have? Should children be given more rights than those adults have?[170]

Should Children Have the same Rights that Adults Have?

One extreme school of thought has taken the view that children should have the same rights that adults do, including the right to vote, work, and engage in sexual relations.[171] Such a view is often promoted by those who regard society's attitudes towards children as patronising and failing to recognise their status as human beings. John Holt has written of the law's view that the child is 'wholly subservient and dependent … being seen by older people as a mixture of expensive nuisance, slave and super-pet'. Child liberationists are happy to accept that there are concerns that children will be harmed by treating them in the same way as adults, but argue freedom is not given to people because they use it to promote their welfare, but because it is an aspect of humanity. Many adults use their freedom to make decisions which harm themselves or others and are foolish. That they do so is not a reason for denying them their rights. So the fact children might do the same with their freedom is no reason not to grant it.[172]

---

[166] E Kittay and E Feder, *The Subject of Care* (Lanham, Rowman & Littlefield, 2003).

[167] Held, *The Ethics of Care* (n 101) 17.

[168] H Kuhse, P Singer and M Rickar, 'Reconciling impartial morality and a Feminist Ethic of Care' (1998) 32 *The Journal of Value Inquiry* 451.

[169] C Mcglynn, *Families and the European Union* (Cambridge, Cambridge University Press, 2006) 44.

[170] J Herring, 'Children's Rights for Grown-Ups' in S Fredman and S Spencer (eds), *Age as an Equality Issue* (Oxford, Hart, 2003).

[171] Holt, *Escape from Childhood* (New York, Holt Associates, 1996); H Foster and D Freund, 'A Bill of Rights for Children' (1972) 6 *Family Law Quarterly* 343.

[172] R Farson, *Birthrights* (London, Penguin, 1978).

While this argument has some attraction, its practical implications are unacceptable to many. Jane Fortin complains that it fails to appreciate the physical and mental differences between children and adults.[173] Giving children the same rights to sexual freedom as adults is likely to lead to their abuse and oppression, rather than their liberation. But this is too easy a rejection of the child liberationist argument. If we accept that children and adults have the same rights, then children who lack capacity will be protected by, inter alia, the Mental Capacity Act 2005, just as adults who lack capacity are. So, in the same way it is an offence to engage in sexual relations with an adult who lacks the capacity to consent or whose mental disorder impedes their choice,[174] so it would be with children who lack the ability to consent or whose ability to consent is impaired. In other words the child liberationist position is not opposed to protecting children who lack capacity, it is opposed to the assumption that children lack capacity. In short, children should not be discriminated against on the grounds of their age.[175] The law currently does use age as a cut-off to determine when a person may or may not engage in certain activities. This produces some anomalies, for example a 16 year old is deemed mature enough to consent to sexual relations with his or her MP, but not to vote for him or her.[176]

Using age restrictions for determining competence has its advantages. It is certainly the most pragmatic approach. It would simply be unworkable to require a bartender to interview everyone who orders a drink to determine whether they had sufficient understanding to the issues surrounding alcohol to buy a drink. Not only that, it might be regarded as offensive and intrusive for everyone to have their capacity tested whenever they buy anything dangerous from a shop.[177] So there is a trade-off. Age is used as a crude device to determine capacity, but it has the benefit of ease, cost and protection of privacy.

The argument just made assumes that age is used as a shorthand for lack of capacity. However, an argument can be made that the reason why children are not given the same autonomy rights as adults is not just that they are said to lack capacity.

John Eekelaar has developed a sophisticated theory of children's rights, which has garnered much attention and much support. He sets out three kinds of interests that children may be said to have:

1. Basic interests. These are the things that are basic requirements for living: food, clothing, emotional well-being.
2. Developmental interests. Eekelaar explains that 'all children should have an equal opportunity to maximise the resources available to them during their childhood (including their own inherent abilities) so as to minimise the degree to which they could enter adult life affected by avoidable prejudices incurred during childhood'.[178]
3. Autonomy interests. This is the freedom for the child to be able to make decisions about how to live their life.

---

[173] Fortin, *Children's Rights* (n 72) 5.
[174] Sexual Offences Act 2003, ss30–3.
[175] Herring, 'Children's Rights for Grown-Ups' (fn 170).
[176] *Ibid.*
[177] L Teitelbaum, 'Children's rights and the problems of equal respect' (1999) 27 *Hofstra Law Review* 799.
[178] J Eekelaar, 'The importance of thinking that children have rights' (1992) 6 *International Journal of Law, Policy and the Family* 221.

Eekelaar acknowledges that these three interests can clash. Where they do he argues that the autonomy interest should be subordinate to the developmental or basic interests. So, children would be allowed to make decisions for themselves, but not if these were decisions harming one of their basic or developmental interests. The reason for this is that it is necessary to restrict children's autonomy interests during childhood to enable them to have maximum autonomy as they enter adulthood. He explains that the aim of his approach is:

> To bring a child to the threshold of adulthood with the maximum opportunities to form and pursue life-goals which reflect as closely as possible an autonomous choice.[179]

To effect this:

> in making decisions about children's upbringing, care should be taken to avoid imposing inflexible outcomes at an early stage in a child's development which unduly limit the child's capacity to fashion his/her own identity, and the context in which it flourishes best.[180]

This leads him to support what he calls dynamic self-determinism, under which children have a greater say over their lives as they grow up. Autonomy, he claims, needs to be learned and developed. That can happen only through practice. He explains that dynamic self-determinism 'is dynamic because it allows for revision of outcomes in accordance with the child's developing personality, and involves self-determination because of the scope given to the child to determine the outcome. Its operation involves a range of complex practical factors. These include exposure (or at least openness) of the child to a range of influences to enhance the scope of choice, and assessment of the child's competence to bring about these results, especially if these are irreversible.'[181]

Eekelaar seeks to garner support for his argument by suggesting that his approach is how most of us would choose to be raised: that we would be allowed to make some decisions for ourselves, but not to the extent of causing us serious harm, and that we allowed to make an increasingly broad selection of choices. Further, he sees recognising rights for children to be an essential aspect of a free society:

> A society can be imagined whose members consider that autonomous self-determination by children, and indeed by the succeeding adult generation, is deemed to be in no one's interests. But such a society would not be an open society. It is a precondition for an open society that the exercise of autonomy by an agent is assumed to be in that agent's interests, and it is a precondition of believing that people have rights to hold that they have a right to achieve competence and articulate their own self-interest.[182]

This approach has many echoes in Joel Feinberg's claim that children have 'a right to an open future'.[183]

---

[179] J Eekelaar, 'The interests of the child and the child's wishes: the role of dynamic self-determinism' (1994) 8 *International Journal of Law and the Family* 42. See also J Eekelaar, 'Children's Rights: From Battle Cry to Working Principle' in J Pousson-Petit (ed), *Liber Amicorum Marie-Thérèse Meulders-Klein: Droit Comparé Des Personnes Et De La Famille* (Brussels, Bruylant, 1998).

[180] Eekelaar, 'Beyond the Welfare Principle' (n 89).

[181] J Eekelaar, *Family Life and Personal Life* (Oxford, Oxford University Press, 2007) 157.

[182] *Ibid*, 156.

[183] J Feinberg, 'The Child's Right to an Open Future' in W Aiken and H La Follette (eds), *Whose Child? Children's Rights, Parental Authority and State Power* (Totowa, NJ, Rowman and Littlefield, 1980). For further discussion see N Lotz, 'Feinberg, Mills, and the Child's Right to an Open Future' (2006) 37 *Journal of Social Philosophy* 537.

It would be possible to interpret Article 8 of the ECHR in a way which would reflect an approach based on Eekelaar's model. But doing so is not without difficulties. Children can be seen as having rights under Article 8 to respect for their private life. This could be said to include a right to make decisions for themselves, at least where those decisions relate to personal decisions about themselves. This right is not an absolute right and can be justifiably interfered with under paragraph 2 of Article 8. Under Eekelaar's model the argument would be that the child's interest in their basic and developmental interests justify an interference in their autonomy. However, the wording of Article 8(2) setting out the justification for interference in a right to respect for private or family life only includes the rights of 'others'. One response is to bring the protective element within the notion of protecting 'health or morals' but that may not be sufficiently wide to protect the developmental interests Eekelaar wishes to protect. The answer may, therefore, lie in simply interpreting the right to private life for a child to include the right to make decisions, but only of the kind that do not interfere with development or basic interests. Alternatively it may be appropriate to regard the Article 8(1) right to respect for private life as covering both a right to make decisions for oneself and also the right to be protected from harm and to develop. Where, therefore, a child wants to make a decision which will cause her harm, there is a clash between two Article 8 rights of a child.

Eekelaar's approach is highly appealing, although it is not without its difficulties. There are problems with Eekelaar's aim of seeking to keep open a range of options for children. Is it wrong of parents of a child who appears to be unusually gifted in sport or music or is academic to channel the child's time and efforts in that direction, or is that unduly restricting the child's autonomy when they reach adulthood? Should children not be raised with a particular religious or cultural identity for fear of restricting their choices in adulthood? Claudia Mills argues that it impossible for parents to provide their children with an open future:

> the impossibility of an open future is not something to be regretted, but to be accepted, and even embraced. On no reasonable view of parenting do we truly want parents to give their children as many open opportunities as possible—we want the list bounded by morality and law. And even when the list is narrowed to morally and legally acceptable or desirable opportunities, the goal of pursuing all options leads to a life that is superficial and glib, as well as frenetic and exhausting.[184]

Eekelaar accepts that parents should be free to raise children with strong religious or cultural identities and children should be free to develop their own sense of identity as they grow up.[185] He writes of his approach:

> it is not to be implied that children should not be brought up in only one culture, or that parents must make anxious efforts to expose their children to as many religious or cultural influences as possible. There can be nothing wrong, either, if a child is encouraged to develop a particular talent, even if this means less time is devoted to other pursuits; but even here the approach suggests a balance should be maintained. A child may well find life difficult if its talents are developed too exclusively in one direction.[186]

This, it is submitted, must be correct, but it acknowledges that there are other values that need to be weighed into the balance along with enabling a child to have maximum autonomy.

---

[184] C Mills, 'Children's Right to an Open Future' (2003) 23 *Journal of Social Philosophy* 499.
[185] J Eekelaar, 'Children Between Cultures' (2004) 18 *International Journal of Law, Policy and Family* 178.
[186] *Ibid*, 186.

These Eekelaar does not fully explore, nor explain why it is permissible to restrict a child's autonomy in this way. It also raises the question of how the interests of adults and children can be balanced.

A second problem is that it is unclear why Eekelaar's analysis should be restricted to childhood. Its essential appeal to restricting autonomy now, in order to maximise autonomy later, could apply equally to an adult. Yet the law currently allows adults to make decisions which will severely jeopardise their future autonomy, indeed even which will lead to death.

A third problem is that its focus is on autonomy. While it is correct that it is good that a child reaches maturity with a broad range of options for their life and having learned how to exercise autonomy, this is not the only skill we may seek for a child. What about learning to co-operate with others; living in a family or community environment? This may involve the child in not being able to make a decision for him or herself, because that does not fit in with the family life at that point in time. To take a trivial example, if a great-aunt is ill and it is decided the family should visit her, should a 12 year old be able to refuse? Under Eekelaar's model the refusal will not cause an interference with the basic or developmental interests of the child, yet we may feel that this is a situation where the child's views should not be respected, as long as on other occasions in the family life the child's views are followed.

Michael Freeman's approach to children's rights has also attracted much attention and shares many of the features of Eekelaar's. He promotes a fourfold classification of rights:[187]

1. A right to welfare: this would include a right to adequate nutrition; housing and medical care.
2. A right to protection: this would protect children from neglect and exploitation.
3. A right to be treated as adults: this would require a justification for any age-based classifications.
4. Rights against parents: these would be independence from parental control.

Michael Freemen acknowledges the tension between protecting a child's current autonomy and their future autonomy. He argues: 'We have to treat them as persons entitled to equal concern and respect and entitled to have both their present autonomy recognised and their capacity for future autonomy safeguarded.'[188]

Freeman justifies his approach on this basis:

The question we should ask ourselves is: what sort of action or conduct would we wish, as children, to be shielded against on the assumption that we would want to mature to a rationally autonomous adulthood and be capable of deciding on our own system of ends as free and rational beings? We would, I believe, choose principles that would enable children to mature to independent adulthood.

This model presupposes a vision of 'independent adulthood' as an ideal. This may be regarded by some as being based on false picture of what is an ideal or practical adulthood. It shows recognition of the relationships, obligations and caring dependencies which make up the reality of life for most people.[189]

[187] Freeman, *The Rights and Wrongs of Children* (n 71) 40–54.
[188] M Freeman, 'Taking children's rights more seriously' (1992) 6 *International Journal of Law, Policy and the Family* 52.
[189] See further J Herring, 'Relational Autonomy and Family Law' (n 120).

Protectionist Models of Rights

There are some models of children's rights which appear to be difficult to distinguish from a welfarist approach.[190] Hence James Dwyer argues that the primary right of a child is a right to have their welfare promoted.[191] Jane Fortin is adamant that children's rights should never be used in a way which harms them. She argues:

> Neither adults nor children have a 'right' to be treated in a way that fundamentally harms them. The rights contained in the European Convention are formulations, albeit sometimes in awkward phraseology, of aspects of the good life, not the bad and should be interpreted in a way that enhances a person's life. Admittedly, a person may suffer a deficit in well-being if his or her rights are displaced by those of another, but no concept of rights can prevent such an occurrence nor can the courts always balance the rights of one person against another in an ideal fashion. Developing this notion, and adopting an interest theory of rights as a basis for the proposition that children are rights holders, it follows that a child's welfare cannot be inconsistent with his rights. Consequently any evidence which a court would traditionally consider when assessing how to accommodate a child's welfare must be accommodated within arguments about his rights. In other words, there cannot be two categories of evidence, one relating to the child's rights and another relating to his welfare.[192]

Fortin's approach sees less conflict between a rights-based approach and a welfare approach than other commentators. Indeed in the quotation she insists that welfare cannot be inconsistent with rights. Notably this is an approach she sees as true for adults as for children. Her approach, in so far as it differs from Eekelaar's approach, does so due to a difference in understanding rights generally, rather than a point specific to children's rights. Given her reluctance to allow adults the right to cause themselves fundamental harms, she faces less difficulty in allowing children rights than commentators who are willing to allow adults the right to cause themselves fundamental harm. This gives rise to an important issue which is that many of the disputes over children's rights involve, at least in part, a dispute over the nature of rights generally. One's understanding of the nature of rights is likely to impact on whether one believes children should have rights.[193]

Fortin's claim that a rights-based approach involves the court considering the same evidence that is considered when a discussion about rights is undertaken is controversial. Eekelaar is critical of rights based on adults determining what is best for children.[194] Indeed an approach towards children's rights which is based on adults determining what children's interests are is not properly regarded as a rights-based approach at all, he argues. He warns of the lessons of history where we now look back in horror at the things done to children which were, at the time, assumed by adults to be good for children.[195] Further, as Federle claims:

> When we intervene on behalf of children to protect them from others, we implicitly acknowledge their powerlessness, but rather than empowering children through rights, we empower ourselves

---

[190] See the discussion in A Bainham, 'Can we protect children and protect their rights?' [2002] *Family Law* 279.

[191] J Dwyer, *The Relationship Rights of Children* (Cambridge, Cambridge University Press, 2006) 132.

[192] J Fortin, 'Accommodating Children's Rights' (n 86) 311.

[193] See, eg, J Herring, 'Children's Rights for Grown-Ups' (n 170) for an argument that adults' rights should look more like children's rights.

[194] R van Krieken, 'The "Best Interests of the Child" and Parental Separation: On the "Civilising of Parents"' (2005) 68 *MLR* 25.

[195] J Eekelaar, '"The Chief Glory": The Export of Children from the United Kingdom' in N Lowe and G Douglas (eds), *Families across Frontiers* (Nijhoff 1996).

to intervene in their lives … Although it may rely upon the language of nurturance and caring, paternalism nevertheless perpetuate existing structures of power and dominance.[196]

There is, however, a difficulty here. At least in relation to children who lack capacity to make decisions for themselves, there is no real alternative but for an independent assessment of a person's best interests or what they would want if they had capacity. Inevitably that is where decisions can go wrong. It is not obvious that the examples of evacuation that Eekelaar discusses[197] would not have occurred under a rights-based approach. What they do highlight is the care that needs to be taken in determining what is in children's interests.

Arguments against Children's Rights

There are those who oppose the notion of rights altogether and so inevitably oppose the notion of children's rights.[198] Those arguments will not be considered here. Further, there are some supporters of the will theory of rights who argue that this renders support for children's rights problematic. These were discussed above and will not be repeated further.[199] Rather the focus will be on some of the other arguments against the recognition of children's rights.

Protection Concerns

First, there are those who think that the primary obligation of the law should be to protect children, rather than protect their rights. The concern is that the use of rights could undermine the duty to protect, control and discipline children in a way which is essential if they are to become functioning adults. The giving of children's rights will lead to them either being open to exploitation by adults, or making foolish decisions which will harm them in the long run. These points are often bolstered by references to the vulnerability, immaturity and inexperience of children. Sir Thomas Bingham MR in *Re S (A Minor)(Independent Representation)*[200] has stated:

> a child is after all a child. The reason why the law is particularly solicitous in protecting the interests of children is that they are liable to be vulnerable and impressionable, lacking the maturity to weight the longer term against the shorter, lacking the insight to know how they will react and the imagination to know how others will react in certain situations, lacking the experience to match the probable against the possible.

As seen above, the strength of such objections depends on the approach to rights that is adopted. Some children's rights advocates, such as Fortin, regard the protection of children from harm as a central aspect of rights. So, although those who wish to emphasise the protection of children may have reason to oppose some forms of rights approaches, they do not have cause to reject the notion of children's rights out of hand. Indeed, with the

---

[196] K Federle, 'Rights flow Downhill'(1994) 2 *International Journal of Children's Rights* 343, 365.

[197] J Eekelaar, "The Chief Glory" (n 195).

[198] See, eg, the discussion in E Kingdom, *What's Wrong with Rights? Problems for Feminist Politics of Law* (Edinburgh, Edinburgh University Press, 1991).

[199] See also T Cambpell, 'The rights of the minor: as person, as child, as juvenile, as future adult' (1992) 6 *International Journal of Law, Policy and the Family* 1, 4–5; W Lucy, 'Controversy about Children's Rights' in D Freestone (ed), *Children and the Law* (Hull, Hull University Press, 1990).

[200] [1993] 2 FCR 1.

enforceable obligations which flow from rights of protection a rights-based approach can prove more effective at protecting children than a welfare-based approach.[201]

Rights and Individualism

A rather different concern about rights is that it fails to recognise that children are dependent on their parents or other carers. In the kinds of family settings most children are raised in the language of rights is inappropriate. Family life is marked by give and take, sacrifice and mutual support, rather than individualist concepts of rights. These concerns mirror the broader concerns about the individualised nature of rights.[202] Sometimes these concerns are voiced by conservative commentators concerned about state intervention in family life. For example, Lynette Burrows argues:

> State intervention into family life is feared and loathed by most children more than anything. They are more troubled by the state interfering than they are reassured by the protection offered. Children do not want rights, they want love and protection and the majority of them do not want social workers or anyone else coming into their families and telling their parents they are not behaving properly.

In the academic literature the concerns about the individualist nature of rights have been most loudly voiced by feminist commentators, especially those supportive of relational concepts or rights or ethics of care. These concepts were considered further in Chapter 3. Typical of such writings is Carol Smart, who comments that the ethic of care is preferable to a rights-based approach. She argues that the law on children:

> need not be carried forward on the basis of individual rights in which the child is construed as an autonomous individual consumer of oppositional rule-based entitlement, but more where the child is construed as part of a web of relationships in which outcomes need to be negotiated (not demanded) and where responsibilities are seen to be reciprocal.[203]

This powerful critique of rights is important in any debate on children's rights.[204] The argument is that rights are based on an image of individuals living isolated lives, protected by their rights of privacy and autonomy. Rights, it is said, place no weight on the relationships between children and adults. The complaint can be broken down into a number of points.

The first is that rights claims can be too easily formulated as claims relating to a specific point in time and fail to take account of the relationship between the children and parents in the past and in the future.[205] For example, the claim in a case concerning relocation[206] can be presented as a clash between rights of 'free movement' and 'contact' in a way that fails to locate the dispute in a context of the lengthy relationship between children and parents.

---

[201] See further the discussion in ch 8.

[202] See J Herring, 'Relational Autonomy and Rape' in S Day-Sclater, F Ebtehaj, E Jackson and M Richards, *Regulating Autonomy: Sex, Reproduction and Family* (Oxford, Hart Publishing, 2009).

[203] C Smart, 'Children and the Transformation of Family Law' in J Dewar and S Parker (eds), *Family Law: Processes, Practices, Pressures* (Oxford, Hart Publishing, 2003), 239.

[204] E Kingdom, *What's Wrong with Rights? Problems for Feminist Politics of Law* (Edinburgh, Edinburgh University Press, 1991); H Lim and J Roche, 'Feminism and Children's Rights' in D Monk and J Bridgman, *Feminist Perspectives on Child Law* (London, Cavendish, 2000); E Kiss, 'Alchemy or Fool's Gold? Assessing Feminist Doubts about Rights' in M Shanley and U Narayan (eds), *Reconstructing Political Theory* (Bristol, Polity, 1997).

[205] M King and C Piper, *How the Law Thinks about Children* (London, Gower, 1990) 68.

[206] See ch 6 for a discussion of these cases.

This is a genuine danger, but there is no reason why rights need to work in this myopic way. Indeed the phrase 'right to respect for family life' invites a broader consideration of the family life over time between the parties. Indeed, as mentioned shortly, relational versions of rights enable such a broader analysis to be undertaken within the context of a rights analysis.

Second, there is a danger that the law places people into one of two boxes either competent and right holding; or non-competent and not right-holding. Minow argues:

> The rhetoric of rights dominant in legal discourse poses a choice between persons under the law being treated either as separate, autonomous, and responsible individuals entitled to exercise rights and obliged to bear liabilities for their actions, or else as dependent incompetent, and irresponsible individuals denied rights, removed from liabilities, and subjected to the care and protection of a guardian—or the state.[207]

She argues that neither of these categories is appropriate for children and we need to develop a middle way for granting children some rights, but short of full autonomy rights.[208] Certainly a crude form of autonomy-based rights thinking would fail to capture the complexities that are involved in determining whether a person has capacity and what amounts to an autonomous choice. There is no need, however, for a rights-based approach to rely on a rigid distinction between capacity and incapacity.[209]

A third aspect of the individualism complaint about children's rights is that they involve separating out the parents' and child's interests in a way which may be said to be improper.[210] Mary Ann Glendon has written of the way that rights can create 'hyperindividualism' and 'exceptional solitariness'.[211] It is not possible to consider one person's interests in isolation from those with whom they are in relationship.[212] One cannot separate the child's interests as somehow independent from the interests of her carer.[213] To harm the child is to harm her carer and to harm the carer is to harm the child.

Again, these concerns are justified. However, they can be met within a human rights framework. After all, the key right in many family law cases is the right to respect for family life: a right which emphasises the importance of relationships. Some commentators have developed visions of 'relational rights': perhaps the best known being writings on relational autonomy.[214] Rights and relationships are not incompatible. In fact respecting the rights of each other is an important aspect of a relationship, although it may be that this is only so if rights here are understood in a way which is supportive of the values underpinning relationships of interdependence and mutuality.[215] Indeed one of the authors (Herring) has argued that those who claim that children are too vulnerable and dependent on others

---

[207] M Minnow, 'Rights for the next generation: a feminist approach to children's rights' (1986) 9 *Harvard Women's Journal* 15.

[208] See J Herring, 'Losing It? Losing What? The Law and Dementia' [2009] *Child and Family Law Quarterly* 3 where the same complaint is made concerning those suffering dementia. C Smith, 'Children's Rights: Judicial Ambivalence and Social Resistance' (1997) 11 *International Journal of Law, Policy and the Family* 103.

[209] J Herring, 'Losing It? Losing What? The Law and Dementia' (n 208).

[210] M Glendon, *Rights Talk* (n 103) 15.

[211] *Ibid*, 15.

[212] J Nedelsky, 'The practical possibilities of feminist theory' (n 107).

[213] E Scott and R Scott, 'Parents as Fiduciaries' (1995) 81 *Virginia Law Review* 2401.

[214] See C McKenzie and N Stoljar (eds), *Relational Autonomy* (Oxford University Press, 2000); J Herring, 'Relational Autonomy and Family Law' (n 120).

[215] M Nussbaum, 'Aristotle, Feminism and Needs for Functioning' (1992) 70 *Texas Law Review* 1019, at 1027.

to be given the rights adults have are missing the point. He argues that adults are far less self-sufficient, fully competent adults, concluding 'once co-operative care-giving relationships among vulnerable people (rather than autonomous individuals) are seen as the basis around which rights work, the difficulties with children having the same rights to a large extent fall away'.[216] Hence the writing on 'relational autonomy' which seeks to reconceive the right of autonomy in a way which acknowledges that relations with others play an important part in the way people develop and exercise their autonomy.[217]

Even under a more traditional approach to rights it might be said that children's rights can avoid the complaint of being individualistic. As Andrew Bainham argues:

> the concept of welfare, as interpreted in English case-law, is a highly individualist notion which is inadequate to embrace the multifarious legal and moral claims which children may be thought to have as a matter of social justice. The concentration is wholly on doing what is best for an individual child in an individual set of circumstances and it is often said that each as must turn on its own facts. Rights, on the other hand, although clearly capable of assertion in individual cases, are designed to safeguard the interests of all children as a class.[218]

Similarly in Eekelaar's model of rights he explains:

> In a rights-oriented world, adults are entrusted with developing its new members in such a way that they can exercise their autonomy as fully as possible when competent. This demands, of course, health and intellectual development. It also demands maximizing opportunities for self-determination in establishing relationships and self-identity.[219]

A further aspect of the argument against rights is that they are individualistic and that 'rights talk' means that 'real experiences' are converted into 'empty abstractions'.[220] As Carol Smart puts it: 'the rights approach takes and translates personal and private matters into legal language. In so doing, it reformulates them into issues relevant to law rather than to the lives of ordinary people.'[118] Carol Smart and Bren Neale have promoted 'the principle of actuality'; namely that 'decisions would not be made on the basis of abstract notions of child welfare, but in relation to the needs and wishes of actual children'.[221] This danger must also be appreciated in the use of talk of children's rights. However, this danger is not an inevitable consequence of using rights. An approach which seeks to ascertain the views of a child and and respects the private and family life of this particular child in this particular context, can promote the 'principle of actuality'.[222]

A final aspect of this criticism is that the focus on rights downplays or even ignores the importance of responsibilities.[223] Rights fail to place value on issues such as commitment and obligation.[224] Sir John Laws has argued that a rights-based society which fails to place

---

[216] Herring, 'Children's Rights for Grown-Ups' (n 170), 172.
[217] See J Herring, 'Relational Autonomy and Family Law' (n 120).
[218] Bainham, *Children, The Modern Law*, (Bristol, Jordans, 2005) 100.
[219] J Eekelaar, 'Children's Rights: From Battle Cry to Working Principle' (n 179) 207.
[220] M Tushnet, 'A Critique of Rights' (1984) *Texas Law Review* 1363, at 1364.
[221] C Smart, 'Children and the transformation of family law' (n 123).
[222] L Purdy, 'Why Children Shouldn't Have Equal Rights' (1994) 2 *International Journal of Children's Rights* 223, 227.
[223] M Regan, *The Pursuit of Intimacy* (n 119); K Bartlett, 'Re-Expressing Parenthood' (1988) 98 *Yale Law Journal* 293, at 295; M Glendon, *Rights Talk* (n 103).
[224] M Regan, *The Pursuit of Intimacy* (n 119) esp ch 2.

appropriate weight on duty and self-sacrifice is at an 'immature stage of development'.[225] In assessing this criticism it should be borne in mind that, under a human rights analysis, with rights come responsibilities. It must be accepted that the notion of children's responsibilities is somewhat under-analysed.[226] Nevertheless the proper use of rights will emphasise the importance of the responsibilities that arise from rights.

The concerns about children's rights raised in this section are significant and important. There is no doubt that they highlight justified concerns about the way some rights analysis can ignore the interdependency between people and over-emphasise individualistic concepts of rights over relational ones. There are also powerful concerns about the way rights can lead to an abstraction of the legal and moral issues and fail to see them in the particular context of the individuals concerned. However, rights analysis does not have to work in that way. It is possible to develop forms of rights-based reasoning that do attach weight to relational values and do recognise the particular context of the individuals concerned. As has been argued above, a rights-based approach is not, for example, inconsistent with one based on an ethic of care.

Concerns about Children's Rights in Practice

Another set of concerns about children's rights are not so much at the theoretical level than the practical. Most prominent are concerns that children's rights will be used not to further the interests of children but to the disadvantage of women and children. Rights gain their primary force from enforcement, but there is a fear that children's rights will be used most effectively by those who have power in our society. This will involve men using rights to the disadvantage of children and women.[227] These concerns can find some support in English law where there are concerns that children's rights are only raised if it is convenient for an adult to do so. In *R (On the Application of Williamson) v Secretary of State for Education and Employment* Baroness Hale opened her speech:

> My Lords, this is, and has always been, a case about children, their rights and the rights of their parents and teachers. Yet there has been no one here or in the courts below to speak on behalf of the children … The battle has been fought on ground selected by the adults.[228]

It is not difficult to find examples of children's rights in the family law context which appear to be only given effect to when an adult seeks to enforce that right for their own ends: the right to know one's genetic origins and the right to contact might be two examples.[229] While this is a real danger it should not lead to an abandonment of children's rights. Not least because even though children's rights can be misused to pursue the agenda of others, that is equally true of the notion of children's welfare. Any legal system in its practice is likely to reflect the inequalities of the society it is governing. Indeed a rights-based approach may be slightly better at combating that danger than other approaches.[230]

---

[225] Laws J, 'The limitation of human rights' [1998] *PL* 254, at 255.
[226] See K Hollingsworth, 'Responsibility and Rights: Children and their Parents in the Youth Justice System' (2007) 21 *International Journal of Law, Policy and the Family* 190.
[227] F Olsen, 'Children's Rights: Some Feminist Approaches to the United Nations Conventions on the Rights of the Child' (1992) 6 *International Journal of Law and the Family* 192–220.
[228] *R v Secretary of State for Education and Employment and others ex parte Williamson* [2005] UKHL 15, para 1.
[229] Herring, *Family Law*, ch 8.
[230] M Freeman, 'Why it Remains Important to take Children's Rights Seriously' (2007) 15 *International Journal of Children's Rights* 5.

Responsibilities, not Rights

Onora O'Neill has argued that rather than focusing on rights for children, the law should focus on responsibilities. She argues: 'Those who urge respect for children's rights must address not children but those whose action may affect children; they have reason to prefer the rhetoric of obligations to that of rights, both because its scope is wider and because it addresses the relevant audience more directly.'[231] Further she rejects analogies drawn between campaigns for recognition of children's rights, with those for other oppressed groups:

> where colonial people, or the working classes or religious and racial minorities or women have demanded their rights, they have sought recognition and respect for capacities for rational and independent life and action that are demonstrably there and thwarted by the denial of rights … but the dependence of children is very different from the dependence of oppressed social groups on those who exercise power over them.[232]

Professor O'Neill makes an important point. An approach which were to advocate rights for children but neglected to mention the obligations on adults would indeed be futile. Her objection in some ways is one based on policy or politics, rather than principle. That the messages that need to be imparted about children are best conveyed through the language of obligations than rights. What her approach does not sufficiently recognise is the political, legal and moral power that rights provide. An obligation which is imposed as a result of a right leads to ready enforceability. Given the well-established legal tradition of the law protecting human rights and placing burdens on the state to ensure those rights are protected, there is much to be said in favour of utilising the concept of rights to further protection of children's interests. As Michael Freeman has argued:

> Rights are important because those who lack rights are like slaves, means to the ends of the others, and never sovereigns in their own right. Those who may claim rights, or for whom rights may be claimed, have a necessary pre-condition to the constitution of humanity, of integrity, of individuality of personality.[233]

Conclusions

This Chapter has set out to provide a discussion as to the meaning of rights and the intense jurisprudential debate over the nature of rights. Although these debates can appear abstract and overly technical they have some important implications for issues which concern family lawyers, as we shall see in the subsequent Chapters of this book.

The Chapter has also considered some of the arguments in the debate over the benefits and disadvantages of rights. The debate tends to be polarised with rights enthusiasts not always appreciating the genuine concern raised by opponents; and critics often criticising a particular image of rights, without appreciating the flexibility of rights. One cannot simply

---

[231] O O'Neill, 'Children's rights and children's lives' (1992) 6 *International Journal of Law, Policy and the Family* 24, 39.

[232] *Ibid*, 36.

[233] Freeman, 'Why it Remains Important to take Children's Rights Seriously' (n 230) 56. See also J Roche, 'Children: Rights, Participation and Citizenship' (1999) 6 *Childhood* 475.

says 'approaches based on rights' are good or 'rights-based approaches are bad' because so much depends on how rights are understood and used. As emphasised earlier, under our current legal system the HRA requires the use of rights-based approaches. This book will set out how rights can be used to approach the cases which appear before family courts. Whether their use will be beneficial or not remains to be seen. Rights approaches *can* be used effectively to produce cases which are more clearly reasoned; where the interests of all parties are given proper weight; and in which the relationship between families can be encouraged or flourished. They could equally be used in a way which achieves the opposite of this. It will be the job of lawyers and judges to ensure that rights are put to good use.

4

Marriage

Despite the fact that some doubt has been cast upon its use in this manner,[1] the enduring power and influence of the *Hyde v Hyde*[2] definition of marriage nevertheless continues and, as will be discussed in this Chapter, has, to a large extent, been unaffected by the passage of the HRA. A number of issues have arisen in respect of this area under the HRA, concerning namely the rights of transsexual people to marry, whether same-sex couples should be afforded the right and, generally, under what circumstances it is permissible to restrict the right. Some of these issues have largely been dealt with. In the case of transsexuals, outstanding incompatibilities were rectified as a result of the combined effect of the decisions of the ECtHR and domestic legislation triggered by a domestic decision of incompatibility. In the case of same-sex partnerships, legislation reform appears to have been a direct by-product of the legislation triggered by the HRA with respect to transsexuals and to ensure the continued application of domestic principles such as the opposite-sex requirement in marriage. There have also been significant developments of the law with regard to certain restrictions upon *who* can marry and found a family either because of their status as a prisoner, as an immigrant or as a result of their relationship. These issues and others will be considered in detail throughout the Chapter. To start, the most relevant Article of the ECHR, the right to marry, will be set out along with the general principles that it has established.

Article 12

Article 12 provides that 'Men and women of marriageable age have the right to marry and to found a family, according to the national laws governing the exercise of this right'.

Article 12 thus secures the fundamental right of a man and woman to marry and to found a family; however, the right to divorce cannot be derived from it.[3] The terms of the Article also make it clear that the right is subject to the national laws of the Contracting States. This is not to say, however, that the right will be subject to *any* national law.

---

[1] Rebecca Probert, '*Hyde v Hyde*: Defining or Defending Marriage?' (2007) 19 (3) *Child and Family Law Quarterly* 322.

[2] (1866) LR 1 P&D 130. Lord Penzance's now famous definition was as follows: 'Marriage as understood in Christendom, may ... be defined as the voluntary union for one life of one man and one woman to the exclusion of all others.'

[3] *Johnston v Ireland* (1986) 9 EHRR 203 para 52, where the Court concluded that the *travaux préparatoires* disclosed no intention to include in Art 12 any guarantee of a right to have the ties of marriage dissolved by divorce.

The Court has held on a number of occasions that any limitations set by national laws must not restrict or reduce the right in such a way or to such an extent that the very essence of the right is impaired.[4] The role of national law is therefore to 'govern the exercise of the right'[5] and this will include rules relating to the formalities of marriage, such as notice and licensing, and more substantive rules on matters such as capacity, consanguinity and consent. National law may also introduce prohibitions on the basis that they are necessary to protect the interests of the wider society such as the prohibition of bigamous and polygamous marriages, discussed below. Any such restrictions must, however, be in pursuit of a legitimate aim and must be proportionate; the very essence of the right must be retained. 'National law may not otherwise deprive a person or category of persons of full legal capacity of the right to marry. Nor may it substantially interfere with their exercise of the right.'[6] Thus, in *B v UK*[7] the Court held that where an applicant could only exercise her right to marry her father-in-law if a private Act of Parliament were passed, the impediment placed on such marriages served no useful purpose of public policy. The inconsistency between the stated aims of the incapacity and the waiver applied in some cases not only undermined the rationality and logic of the measure but also served to reduce the significance that the Court would otherwise attach to the legislature's consideration of the matter.[8] Furthermore, the rather cumbersome and expensive vetting process that was provided for did not appear to offer a practically accessible or effective mechanism for individuals to vindicate their rights.[9] A violation of Article 12 had therefore occurred. In addition, the Court has also made it clear that any temporary prohibitions upon the right to marry, even if the legitimate aim being advanced is to protect the institution of marriage, will constitute a breach of the right. In *F v Switzerland*,[10] a three-year prohibition on the applicant's ability to remarry affected the very essence of the right and was therefore held to be disproportionate to the legitimate aim being pursued.

The question to be asked in any claim brought under Article 12 is, therefore, whether the alleged restriction restricts or reduces the right in such a way or to such an extent that the very essence of the right is impaired, so as to be disproportionate to any legitimate aim pursued. Before answering this question, however, the Court, as discussed in Chapter 2, will first determine the extent, if any, of the margin of appreciation that it is to apply. The court has acknowledged that exercising the right to marry will often engage issues of social and legal policy and has indicated that it will be slow to intervene where the reason for introducing the restriction is justified on these grounds. It has also stated that 'given the sensitive moral choices concerned and the importance to be attached in particular to the protection of children and the fostering of secure family environments', it 'must not rush to substitute its own judgment in place of the authorities who are best placed to assess and respond to the needs of society'.[11] The application of these principles by the ECtHR and, where

---

[4] *Rees v the United Kingdom* (1987) 9 EHRR 56 para 50; *F v Switzerland* Application No 11329/85 (1988) 10 EHRR 411 para 32.

[5] *Hamer v UK* (1979) 4 EHRR 139 para 60.

[6] *Ibid*, para 62.

[7] *B v UK* (2005) 42 EHRR 195.

[8] *Ibid*, para 40.

[9] *Ibid*, para 40.

[10] *F* (n 4).

[11] *B and L v UK* (2006) 42 EHRR 11.

relevant, the domestic courts, will now be examined in relation to a number of different areas. Some areas will also consider the application of Articles 8, 9 and 14 where necessary.

Transgender Persons

Section 11(c) of the Matrimonial Causes Act 1973 (MCA) provides that a marriage shall be void on the ground 'that the parties are not respectively male and female'. The words 'male and female' had for a long time after the decision in *Corbett v Corbett*[12] been interpreted as referring to sex, determined by reference to physical indications: chromosomal (males having XY chromosomes and females XX chromosomes), gonadal (the presence or absence of testes and ovaries), and genital (the presence or absence of internal or external sex organs). As a result, the new gender of a transsexual person was not legally recognised and they were not able to validly contract a marriage under English law. Furthermore, despite advances in medical understanding which arguably invalidated the *Corbett*[13] definition and suggestions[14] that the words 'male' and 'female' could be interpreted as referring not to sex but instead to gender, the English courts continued to adopt this position.[15] This caused significant problems for post-operative transsexuals who were still regarded in law as having the sex with which they were registered and resulted in, as the JCHR noted,[16] some rather curious consequences. Thus, prior to the passage of the Gender Recognition Act 2004 (GRA) a male-to-female transsexual remained, for legal purposes, a man, who could marry a woman but not a man, who could draw a pension at 65 but not at 60; and[17] could not claim to have been unlawfully discriminated against on the ground of sex under the Sex Discrimination Act 1975 (SDA) if people treated her less favourably than a man because she appeared to be a woman. In addition, official records may continue to record the person as being of his or her original gender, causing difficulties and embarrassment. Such difficulties arguably engaged Articles 8, 12 and 14 of the ECHR and as a result a number of challenges were taken to the ECtHR in respect of these provisions. However, in a series of cases decided between 1986 and 1998[18] the ECtHR applied a wide margin of appreciation, albeit by a steadily narrowing majority, to find that, although English law relating to transsexuals engaged the right to respect for private life under Article 8 and the right to marry under Article 12, no breach of either of these Articles had occurred because of the lack of a European consensus on the matter.[19] Nevertheless, in each progressive case that came before it, it became clear that the Court recognised that some form of consensus amongst Member States was steadily growing. The Court therefore repeatedly urged the UK to keep the matter under careful review. The only area in which the ECtHR was willing to find a

---

[12] *Corbett v Corbett (April Ashley)* [1970] CLY 808.

[13] *Ibid.*

[14] Eg SM Cretney and J Masson, *Principles of Family Law*, 5th edn (London, Sweet & Maxwell, 1990) 46–8.

[15] *S-T (formerly J) v J* [1998] Fam 103; *Bellinger v Bellinger* [2003] 2 WLR 1174 (HL) (Lord Chancellor intervening).

[16] See the JCHR's report on the Draft Gender Recognition Bill, Nineteenth Report of Session 2002/3 vol 1, p 11, para 9.

[17] Except in relation to employment and vocational training, where Community law has intervened.

[18] *Rees* (n 4); *Cossey v the United Kingdom* (1990) 13 EHRR 622; *Sheffield and Horsham v the United Kingdom* (1998) 27 EHRR 163.

[19] See the discussion of this case law in pp 48–9.

violation was in relation to countries where people were required to carry identity cards and to produce them to officials on request, or as a condition for obtaining access to public benefits. Thus, in *B v France*,[20] owing to the frequent necessity for the applicant to disclose personal information to third parties, the Court found that there had been a violation of the Article 8. Nevertheless, the Court also noted[21] that although there had been a change in attitude to transsexuals, and a greater awareness of the problem of transsexualism, there was still uncertainty about the legitimacy of surgical intervention and extreme complexity of the consequent legal situation. There was still an insufficient level of consensus between the Member States to overrule the *Rees*[22] and *Cossey*[23] judgments.

Nonetheless, the UK found itself increasingly isolated in its continuing refusal to recognise the reassigned sex of a transsexual and by the time of the passage of the HRA in 1998 only Ireland, Andorra and Albania shared its view. However, failing intervention by the ECtHR, the UK courts continued to apply *Corbett*.[24] In *Bellinger v Bellinger*[25] the Court of Appeal dismissed an appeal by B, a transsexual female, against a decision refusing her petition for a declaration that her marriage to a male was valid and subsisting on the basis of the test laid down in *Corbett*. The judgment was, however, noteworthy for its early indication of the court's views on the application of section 3 of the HRA and its reluctance to go further than Strasbourg. Thus, although the court noted with dismay[26] that no steps had been taken or were intended to be taken to review the legislation in this area, it considered that, save the strongly worded dissenting judgment of Thorpe LJ, nonetheless, the recognition of a change in the gender assigned to a person at birth was a matter for Parliament and could not be properly decided by the court. The fate of transsexuals was once again in a state of limbo with, it seemed, little prospect of change. However, it was only one year later, in 2002, in two landmark decisions, that the ECtHR reversed its previous decisions and substantially narrowed the margin of appreciation that it had previously applied.[27] In *Goodwin v UK*[28] and *I v UK*[29] both applicants sought a declaration that their Article 8 and 12 rights had been violated. In *Goodwin*[30] the applicant, a 65-year-old male-to-female transsexual, argued that as a result of the fact that she was still legally regarded as a man it had been necessary for her to continue to pay national insurance contributions until the age of 65 whereas if she had been legally recognised as a woman such liability would have ceased at the age of 60. She had also been obliged to pay the contributions directly in order to avoid a query from her employers and contended that the fact that she retained the same national insurance number had led to a humiliating situation whereby her employers had been able to discover that she had previously been employed by them under a different name as a man. In *I*, a 47-year-old male-to-female transsexual had formerly been employed as a dental nurse but had been unable to gain admittance to a nursing course

---

[20] *B v France* [1992] 2 FLR 249.
[21] *Ibid*, para 48.
[22] *Rees* (n 4).
[23] *Cossey* (n 18).
[24] *Corbett* (n 12).
[25] *Bellinger v Bellinger* [2001] EWCA Civ 1140.
[26] Butler Sloss LJ regarded this as 'a failure to recognise the increasing concerns and changing attitudes across western Europe which have been set out so clearly and strongly in judgments of Members of the European Court at Strasbourg, and which in our view need to be addressed by the UK'.
[27] Based, as discussed, in ch 1 on the finding of a new version of the European consensus standard.
[28] *Goodwin* (2002) 35 EHRR 447.
[29] *I* [2002] 3 FCR 613.
[30] *Goodwin* (n 28).

since she refused to provide her birth certificate. In consequence she had been unemployed since 1988. Both applicants complained that their inability to marry a male partner also breached their Article 12 rights.

In unanimously granting both applications, the ECtHR held that whilst both applicants had undergone gender reassignment surgery and lived as women they were still legally regarded as men, something that had clear implications in the field of pensions and retirement. The ensuing conflict between social reality and legal status placed transsexuals in a position whereby they were potentially subject to feelings of vulnerability, humiliation and anxiety. Further, the Court considered that there was no evidence before the Court to indicate that any third party prejudice would be likely to ensue from changes to the system of birth registration in order to recognise gender reassignment. Nor was it likely that potential problems in the areas of access to records, family law, affiliation, social security and insurance would prove insuperable.[31] Having regard to the fact that the fundamental essence of the Convention was the respect for human dignity and human freedom there had clearly been a breach of Article 8. In a direct response to the domestic decision of *Corbett*,[32] the Court noted that although Article 12 referred to the right of a man and woman to marry, such a right was not restricted to purely biological criteria.[33] It was, they said, artificial to assert that post-operative transsexuals had not been deprived of the right to marry since, although free to marry an individual of the opposite sex to their former gender, they were precluded from marrying the opposite sex to their adopted gender. Accordingly the fundamental essence of the right had been infringed.[34]

A few months after those decisions of the Strasbourg Court, the House of Lords decided the appeal in *Bellinger*[35] where, this time, the applicants also, following the decision in *Goodwin*,[36] sought a declaration under section 4 of the HRA that the provisions of section 11(c) of the MCA were incompatible with ECHR Articles 8 and 12. The Lord Chancellor, intervening, accepted that there was an incompatibility in the light of the recent decisions of the Strasbourg Court, but argued that the House should exercise its discretion against making a declaration of incompatibility because the Government was actively planning legislation to remedy the incompatibility. Their Lordships considered that the words 'male' and 'female' were to be given their ordinary meaning and referred to a person's biological gender as determined at birth so that, for purposes of marriage, a person born with one sex could not later become a person of the opposite sex. They therefore held that it was not possible under English law for a person to marry another person who was of the same gender at birth, even if one of them had undergone gender reassignment surgery. They did, however, issue a declaration that section 11(c) of the MCA represented a continuing obstacle to the ability of the (male-to-female) transsexual petitioner to enter into a valid marriage with a man, and that it was therefore incompatible with her rights under Articles 8 and 12 of the Convention. The judgment, however, received a great deal of attention in the literature in terms of its implications for the applicability of section 3 versus section

---

[31] *Ibid*, paras 89–91.
[32] *Corbett* (n 12).
[33] *Goodwin* (n 28) para 100.
[34] *Ibid*, para 101.
[35] *Bellinger* (n 25).
[36] *Goodwin* (n 28).

4 of the HRA.[37] However, as Kavanagh[38] has argued, although a reinterpretation of the words 'male' and 'female' in section 11(c) would have been relatively easy to achieve on a linguistic and legal basis the House of Lords was clearly influenced, in its preference for a section 4 declaration, by the fact that the Government had confirmed that impending legislation would enable the applicant to marry in due course. The House was also more generally concerned by the complex procedural issues that would ensue in terms of who would qualify for recognition and on what evidential basis.

Shortly afterwards, the GRA was passed which, amongst other matters, did indeed enable transgender people to marry in their newly acquired gender, subject to obtaining a gender recognition certificate. It seemed, therefore, that many of the incompatibility issues raised by the ECHR were largely resolved by the provisions of the Act. However, there were some provisions of the Act which remained controversial. First, the MCA was amended by the insertion into section 12 a new paragraph (h) which added a new ground for when a marriage was voidable, which is that 'the respondent is a person whose gender at the time of the marriage had become the acquired gender under the Gender Recognition Act 2004'.[39] This meant that a person who marries in their acquired gender will be entering a voidable marriage unless they disclose to their spouse before the marriage the fact that they have 'changed' gender.

This requirement might be said to involve an interference with a transgender person's Article 8 and/or Article 12 rights particularly when we consider that there is no general obligation on would-be spouses to disclose information to each other about themselves. However, it may also be argued that the failure to disclose such information is in effect comparable to that of a consent based upon a mistake as to the identity of a person[40] and should therefore form a separate ground for voidability. It is open to question, therefore, whether the imposition of such an obligation upon transgender people only represents a proportionate response to what was presumably the aim of requiring parties to enter into marriage on a free and full consensual basis.[41] A second issue concerns intersex people. Where a person is born with mixed chromosomal, genital and gonadal factors there is no option for such a person to be registered as an intersex person, or later to apply for a gender recognition certificate that they are intersex. The law only permits two options as regards a person's sex: that they may be male or female. It is suggested that an intersex person has a strong claim under Article 8 to be recognised as intersex. Such a right is, after all, simply a claim to have the biological truth recognised.[42]

---

[37] See the discussion in ch 1 at p 49.
[38] A Kavanagh, 'Statutory Interpretation and Human Rights after Anderson: A More Contextual Approach?' [2004] *Public Law* 537.
[39] Those transgender persons who have not obtained a gender recognition certificate are still unable to marry in their acquired gender. The common law authority of *Corbett* will therefore still have application in these cases.
[40] See *Moss v Moss* [1897] 263.
[41] Article 16(2) of the Universal Declaration of Human Rights 1948 states that 'Marriage shall be entered into only with the free and full consent of the intending spouses'.
[42] For further discussion see J Herring and P-L Chau, 'Defining, Assigning and Designing Sex' (2002) 16 *International Journal of Law Policy and the Family* 327; J Herring and P-L Chau, 'Men, Women and People' in A Bainham *et al* (eds), *Sexuality Repositioned: Diversity and the Law* (Oxford, Hart Publishing, 2004).

The final controversy results in large part from the clear intention of the legislature to maintain the common law position of *Hyde v Hyde*[43] and *Corbett*[44] that marriage was only possible between a man and a woman. The effect of the GRA in relation to marriage was therefore simply to provide a procedure by which a person could acquire legal recognition of their new gender which at the same time preserved the legislative status quo which prohibited marriage between same-sex couples. The GRA was therefore drafted to include provisions which required a transgender person who was within a valid existing marriage to either divorce or formally nullify their existing marriage before he/she could obtain a gender recognition certificate (GRC).[45] It was this issue that was brought before the ECtHR in the admissibility decision of *Parry v UK*.[46] Here, the applicants had married in 1960 and had three children. Both held deep religious convictions, the first applicant having been ordained as a church minister in 1970. The first applicant was born male but shortly after 1998 undertook gender reassignment surgery and changed her name by deed poll. She contended that she was in all private and public relationships a woman. The second applicant was her legal wife and had stood by the first applicant, contending that they remained together as a loving and married couple. Following the introduction of the GRA, the first applicant made an application to the Gender Recognition Panel for the issue of a GRC but because she was still married, the Panel could only issue an interim GRC. She was therefore required to annul her marriage before she could obtain a full GRC, a formal recognition of her acquired gender. Neither of the applicants wished to annul their marriage and brought their application directly to the ECtHR, having made no claim in the domestic courts. The complained that the GRA represented an unjustified interference with their rights under Articles 8, 12 and 9 of the Convention because the UK had made the recognition of the first applicant's acquired gender contingent on the dissolution of their marriage.

The Government's argument[47] was that the effects of the provisions of the GRA was not to impair or restrict the very essence of the right to marry and, in fact, were well within the range of 'national laws' that were appropriate in governing its exercise. Thus, it was argued that the applicants were not required to bring to an end their marriage; it was a matter of choice for the second applicant as to whether to obtain a full GRC. Further, both applicants would be free to marry a person of the opposite gender once a full GRC had been issued or enter into a civil partnership as a result of the Civil Partnership Act 2004. The Government also referred to issues which they felt necessitated the application of a wide margin of appreciation on the matter, arguing that as the law of marriage referred to marriage between different sexes it was a sensitive area with profound cultural and religious connotations.[48] It was therefore legitimate for the Government to have regard to social, religious, ethical and cultural views within a society when introducing legislation such as the GRA. In fact it stated that, during the passage of the legislation, it and the legislature had been well aware of the concerns now expressed by the applicants for preservation

---

[43] *Hyde v Hyde* (n 2).
[44] *Corbett* (n 12).
[45] GRA, Sch 2, Part 1.
[46] *Parry v UK* Application No 42971/05. See also *R and F v UK* Application No 35748/05, decided on the same day with very similar facts and the same outcome.
[47] *Ibid*, 8.
[48] *Ibid*.

of existing marriages after a change of gender by one of partners but decided that it was appropriate for a clear 'bright line' rule to be maintained, reserving marriage for couples of different sexes. This was felt to be proportionate due to the fact that the Civil Partnership Act 2004 (CPA) permitted transsexuals to enter into a civil partnership with their former spouse and thus enabled them to enjoy the same financial and other legal benefits associated with marriage.

The ECtHR seemingly agreed and in declaring the application inadmissible noted that the requirement that the applicants annul their marriage was a result of the fact that same-sex marriages were not permitted under UK law. However, in terms of Article 8, the Court held that the effects of the system could not be said to have disproportionately interfered with their rights because it was apparent that the applicants could continue their relationship in its current form and may obtain a legal status akin, if not identical, to marriage, through a civil partnership.[49] With regard to Article 12, the Court observed that the legislature had been fully aware of the fact that there were a small number of transsexuals in subsisting marriages when drafting the GRA but had deliberately made no provision for those marriages to continue in the event that one partner made use of the gender recognition procedure.[50] Noting that same-sex marriage was not permitted in the UK, the Court went on to state that Article 12 of the Convention similarly enshrined the traditional concept of marriage as being between a man and a woman. While it was true, the Court said, that there are a number of Contracting States which have extended marriage to same-sex partners, this right could not be said to flow from an interpretation of Article 12 as laid down by the Convention.[51] The Court concluded, therefore, that the matter fell within the margin of appreciation of the Contracting State as to how to regulate the effects of the change of gender in the context of marriage.

The judgment is interesting for a number of reasons. First, because the Court took the opportunity to reiterate its view that a declaration of incompatibility issued by the domestic courts, under section 4 of the HRA, to the effect that a particular legislative provision infringed the Convention, could not yet be regarded as an effective remedy within the meaning of Article 35. This was essentially because there is no legal obligation on the minister to amend a legislative provision which has been found by a court to be incompatible with the Convention.[52] Second, the judgment is yet another example of the court's approval of the deployment of a 'bright line' rule as being within the margin of appreciation. The Court was seemingly influenced, as in *Evans v UK*,[53] by the fact that the legislature had recently considered the conflicting interests involved when drafting the GRA.[54] Finally, the judgment appears to confirm that, at least at that time (2005), a right to same-sex marriage could be drawn from Article 12. It is this issue that we will turn to next.

---

[49] *Ibid*, 10.

[50] *Ibid*, 12.

[51] *Ibid*.

[52] However, the Court did set out that it was possible that at some future date evidence of a long-standing and established practice of ministers giving effect to the Court's declarations of incompatibility may be sufficient to persuade the Court of the effectiveness of the procedure. At the present time, however, there is insufficient material on which to base such a finding.

[53] *Evans v UK* Application No 6339/05 (2006) 43 EHRR 21.

[54] See discussion in ch 1 concerning the application of bright line rules at the domestic level.

Same-sex Marriage

Although the CPA accorded the majority of the same rights and responsibilities to same-sex couples as those obtained by heterosexual couples upon marriage, it may have arguably failed to accord the most important right of all, and that is the right to marry. A detailed review of the CPA[55] reveals that although the Act allows same-sex couples 'a formal status with virtually identical legal consequences to those of marriage'[56] it nevertheless did so 'with the exception of the form of ceremony and the actual name and status of marriage'.[57] There is clearly some disagreement amongst the same-sex community as to, first, whether this distinction is in actual fact desirable[58] and, second, whether it is indeed worth arguing over when so many other sites of discrimination remain.[59] Examining how claims for same-sex partnership rights are treated is nonetheless necessary, mainly because, as Bamforth has argued, these issues raise important questions of constitutional law concerning the fundamental rights of citizens and the respective powers of courts and legislatures.[60] Bamforth has further argued,[61] in an excellent analysis of the type of methodology that ought to be utilised, that if any claim is to be made for a right to marry, it is imperative that it is based on sound philosophical and constitutional arguments. The point is that any argument which is predicated upon the provisions of the HRA and the ECHR will be impossible to construct without such a foundation. Thus, he argues, it is first necessary to show *why* it is morally permissible in principle for the law to be used to protect such a right and, second, that the right must be shown to fall within the proper constitutional powers of the legislature or the courts in order for it to be constitutionally legitimate.[62] In terms of any claims brought under the HRA the crucial question to determine is whether the recognition of the right to marry falls within the discretionary area of judgment and thus outside the realms of court interpretation.

It is beyond the scope of this chapter to consider in detail the advantages and disadvantages of the different types of philosophical arguments that could be used to argue for the recognition of a right to marriage for same-sex couples. It is accepted nonetheless that the strength and value of these arguments as to the concepts of justice, autonomy and equality can be evidenced in the decisions of the judiciary and the development of a number of constitutional conventions.[63] It is on this basis that the question of why such a claim ought to be protected by the HRA can therefore be answered. What this section will seek to do, however, is to first consider whether a right to same-sex marriage is capable of recognition under the ECHR and the HRA and, if so, set out how this could be achieved.

---

[55] See N Bamforth, 'The benefits of marriage in all but name? Same-sex couples and the Civil Partnership Act 2004' [2007] *Child and Family Law Quarterly* 133 for an excellent review.

[56] *Secretary of State for Work and Pensions v M* [2006] UKHL 11, para 99 (Baroness Hale).

[57] *Wilkinson v Kitzinger* [2006] EWHC 2022 (Fam) para 49 (Sir Mark Potter P).

[58] K McNorrie, 'Marriage is for heterosexuals—may the rest of us be saved from it' [2000] *Child and Family Law Quarterly* 363.

[59] See R Auchmuty, 'What's So Special About Marriage? The Impact of *Wilkinson v Kitzinger*' [2008] *Child and Family Law Quarterly* 475.

[60] See N Bamforth's two excellent articles on the issue, 'The Role of Philosophical and Constitutional Arguments in the Same-Sex Marriage Debate: A Response to John Murphy' [2005] *Child and Family Law Quarterly* 165 and 'Same-Sex Partnerships: Some Comparative Constitutional Lessons' [2007] EHRLR 1, 47–65.

[61] N Bamforth, 'A Response to John Murphy' (n 60), 168.

[62] *Ibid*, 169.

[63] See discussion in ch 1.

The ECHR

A claim to same-sex marriage may engage several articles under the ECHR, namely Articles 8, 12 and 14. Article 14 is set out as follows:

> The enjoyment of the rights and freedoms set forth in [the] Convention shall be secured without discrimination on any ground such as sex, race, colour, language, religion, political or other opinion, national or social origin, association with a national minority, property, birth or other status.

However, the right under Article 14 is not a free-standing one; the ECtHR has held that it has effect solely in relation to the 'rights and freedoms' safeguarded by those provisions. Thus, Article 14 will only be engaged if the facts of the case fall within the ambit of one or more of the other Convention rights.[64] A difference in treatment will only be held to be discriminatory if it does not have an objective and reasonable justification, that is, if it does not pursue a legitimate aim or if there is no reasonable relationship of proportionality between the means employed and the aim sought to be realised.[65] In terms of discrimination based upon the ground of sex, the Court has said that very weighty reasons would have to be put forward before the Court could regard a difference in treatment based exclusively on the ground of sex as compatible with the Convention.[66] In addition, it has also stated that differences based on sexual orientation require particularly serious reasons by way of justification.[67]

The two Articles of most relevance to a claim for same-sex marriage in conjunction with Article 14 are Articles 8 and 12. However, in relation to a claim made in conjunction with Article 8 it is fairly clear that there is not yet enough of a basis to found the claim in relation to the family life aspect of the Article. Although there are a number of cases in which the Court has found that adverse treatment on the basis of an individual's sexual orientation was unjustifiable, this was found in relation to respect for private life rather than family life.[68] In addition, there have been a number of decisions[69] concerning same-sex relationships where the Court has declined to find that the Article 8 right to family life has been engaged.[70] Nonetheless, what is reasonably clear is that where it can be shown that the restrictions concerned impact upon the most intimate part of a person's private life, the

---

[64] *Petrovic v Austria* DR 1998-II 585, para 22.

[65] *Ibid*, 586, para 30 and WK Wright, 'The Tide in Favour of Equality: Same Sex Marriage in Canada and England and Wales' (2006) *International Journal of Law Policy and the Family* 249 for a detailed application of Art 14 to this issue.

[66] *Burghartz v Switzerland*, 22 February 1994, Series A Application No 280-B 29, para 27; *Karlheinz Schmidt v Germany*, 18 July 1994, Series A Application No 291-B 32–3, para 24; *Salgueiro da Silva Mouta v Portugal* Application No 33290/96 ECHR 1999-IX, para 29; *Smith and Grady v the UK* Application Nos 33985/96 and 33986/96 (1999) 29 EHRR 493, para 94; *Fretté v France* Application No 36515/97 ECHR 2002-I §§ 34 and 40; and *SL v Austria* Application No 45330/99 ECHR 2003-I, para 36.

[67] *Smith and Grady* (n 66) para 90 and *SL v Austria* (n 66) para 37.

[68] These cases concerned, for example, the criminal prohibition of consensual, private, same-sex sexual activity: *Dudgeon v UK* Application No 7525/76 (1982) 4 EHRR 149; *Norris v Ireland* Application No 10581/83 (1991) 13 EHRR 186, and prohibitions on same-sex relationships within the military: *ADT v UK* Application No 35765/97 [2000] 2 FLR 697, para 38; *Sutherland v UK* Application No 25186/94 (1997) 24 EHRR 22, para 57.

[69] *Estevez v Spain*, 10 May 2001, Application No 56501/00 (unreported). Even in *Karner v Austria* [2003] 2FLR 623, para 33 note that the Court did not find it necessary to determine the notions of 'private life' or 'family life' because it considered that, in any event, the applicant's complaint related to the manner in which the alleged difference in treatment adversely affected the enjoyment of his right to respect for his home guaranteed under Art 8.

[70] *Smith and Grady v UK* (n 66); *Lustig-Prean and Beckett v UK* (1999) 29 EHRR 548.

Court will apply a narrow margin of appreciation. That is not to say, however, that a claim based on the private life limb of Article 8 will always be a successful one; it may be difficult to establish that the alleged discrimination is unjustified due to the Court's general policy of protection of the traditional family and the child's best interests. Thus, although in *Karner v Austria*[71] the Court found that the narrow interpretation of the relevant Rent Act which had prevented a surviving partner of a same-sex couple from taking over a tenancy was a breach of his Article 8 and Article 14 rights, it also stated that 'the protection of the family in the traditional sense',[72] even in cases concerning differences of treatment based on sexual orientation, may, in appropriate circumstances, be a weighty and legitimate enough reason which would justify a difference in treatment. Further, in *Fretté v France*[73] the court found that the refusal to allow a gay man to adopt a child because of his sexual orientation did not constitute a breach of his right to private life under Article 8 taken in conjunction with Article 14. A wide margin of appreciation was applied due to 'the delicate issues raised in the case' which touched on areas where there was little common ground amongst the Member States. In sum, a combination of a restrictive approach to the establishment of family life between same-sex couples without children and the application of a wide margin of appreciation where any such discrimination is founded on the belief that it is necessary to protect the conventional family form and the interests of children, may make the chances of a successful claim under Article 8 of the ECHR difficult.

In terms of Article 12, the task may be even more difficult and this, as a number of commentators[74] have noted, is largely due to Strasbourg case law which will make it difficult to fit a claim for same-sex marriage within its ambit. This is mainly due to the fact that the ECtHR has made it clear that the right to marriage that is protected by the Article is marriage between two people of the opposite sex.[75] In *Sheffield and Horsham v UK*,[76] the Court stated:

> The right to marry guaranteed by Article 12 refers to the traditional marriage between persons of the opposite biological sex ... Furthermore, Article 12 lays down that the exercise of this right should be subject to the national laws of the Contracting States. The limitations thereby introduced must not restrict or reduce the right in such a way or to such an extent that the very essence of the right is impaired. *However, the legal impediment in the UK on the marriage of persons who are not of the opposite biological sex cannot be said to have an effect of this kind* [emphasis added].

Further, in *Goodwin*[77] the Court noted that that the findings in the cases of *Rees*,[78] *Cossey*[79] and *Sheffield and Horsham*[80] were 'based variously on the reasoning that the right to marry referred to traditional marriage between persons of opposite biological sex'.[81]

---

[71] *Karner* (n 69).
[72] *Ibid*, 41.
[73] *Fretté v France* (2004) 38 EHRR 438.
[74] Eg R Clayton and H Tomlinson, *The Law of Human Rights* (Oxford, Oxford University Press, 2000) para 13.73; Bamforth; and WK Wright.
[75] *Rees* (n 4); *Cossey* (n 18); *Sheffield and Horsham* (n 18).
[76] *Sheffield and Horsham* (n 18) para 66.
[77] *Goodwin* (n 28).
[78] *Rees* (n 4).
[79] *Cossey* (n 18).
[80] *Sheffield and Horsham* (n 18).
[81] *Goodwin* (n 28) para 97.

More recently, in *L v Lithuania*,[82] a case concerning the rights of a transsexual male, the Court appeared to confirm this view of Article 12 when it found that the applicant's complaint under the Article was premature in that, under the domestic law, should he complete full gender-reassignment surgery, his status as a man would be recognised together with the right to marry a woman. The key issue in that case was one of general gender recognition.[83] In addition, as Bamforth has noted, there seem to be few examples of a successful alignment of an Article 12 and an Article 14 claim.[84]

Domestic Law

There have been a number of domestic cases where these questions concerning the ambit of Articles 8, 12 and 14 have been discussed. *Ghaidan v Mendoza*[85] concerned Schedule 1 of the Rent Act 1977, which seemingly restricted the succession of a protected tenancy of property to the surviving partner of an unmarried heterosexual couple who had lived together as husband and wife. A claim was brought by the surviving member of a same-sex couple to succeed to the tenancy of their former flat under the same provision. The House of Lords took the opportunity to review the relevant jurisprudence of the ECtHR, finding that the protection of the traditional family unit, as espoused in *Karner*, could only justify differential treatment in 'certain contexts'.[86] In addition, they reiterated the point that a difference in treatment based upon sexual orientation was generally unacceptable under Article 14 unless there was the existence of a good reason.[87] Nonetheless, any justifications so advanced required 'careful scrutiny'.[88] As a result, the court declined to defer to the legislature on this point, applied an intense level of scrutiny with regard to the proportionality of the measure and found that a breach of both Articles 8 and 14 had occurred.[89] In doing so, however, the court did not discuss whether the claimant's family life had been interfered with or whether it could, in any case, be included within the definition.[90] This question was, however, addressed in *Secretary of State for Work and Pensions v M*,[91] where the applicant argued that the fact that, under the Child Support Act 1991, a parent who lived with a same-sex partner was assessed less generously than a parent who lived with an opposite-sex partner, constituted a breach of Article 14 coupled with the 'family life' limb of Article 8. However, although there was a great deal of discussion as to whether a same-sex couple could come within the ambit of 'family life' under Article 8, it is difficult to extrapolate much from the case given that, as Bamforth has noted, four of the five judgments differed about how the ECtHR had interpreted the same matter.[92] Moreover, as he

---

[82] *L v Lithuania* Application No 27527/03 (2008) 46 EHRR 22.

[83] *Ghaidan v Mendoza* [2004] UKHL 30, para 64.

[84] N Bamforth, 'Same-sex couples' (n 55).

[85] *Ghaidan* (n 83).

[86] *Ibid*, 16.

[87] *Ibid*, 9.

[88] *Ibid*, 136.

[89] The court went on to reinterpret the relevant section of the Act to include same-sex couples under s3 of the HRA. See ch 2 pp 41 for a discussion of this aspect of the case.

[90] N Bamforth, 'Same-sex couples' (n 55).

[91] *Secretary of State for Work and Pensions v M* [2006] UKHL 11; see also R Wintemute, 'Same-sex couples in *Secretary of State for Work and Pensions v M*: identical to *Karner* and *Godin-Mendoza*, yet no discrimination?' [2006] *European Human Rights Law Review* 722.

[92] N Bamforth, 'Same-sex couples' (n 55).

rightly concludes, although a number of the judgments contained hints that the domestic courts may go further than Strasbourg and include same-sex partnerships within the ambit of family life, the fact that the court relied heavily (and possibly erroneously) on the wide margin of appreciation given by the ECtHR in the area could indicate that a domestic court is, in any case, likely to defer to the legislature in any future claim that the marriage/civil partnership distinction in the CPA was a breach of Article 8 and/or Article 14.[93]

The exact question of whether the marriage/civil partnership distinction provided for by the CPA constituted a breach of the HRA was soon to be brought before the court. In *Wilkinson v Kitzinger*[94] a British lesbian couple married in British Colombia, Canada and upon their return to the UK instituted proceedings to have their Canadian marriage recognised as marriage under section 5 of the Family Law Act 1986. The claim was based upon their Articles 8, 12 and 14 rights and they sought, in the event that their claim was unsuccessful, a declaration that section 11(c) of the MCA and Chapter 2 of the CPA were incompatible with the obligations imposed by the same Articles of the ECHR. Aside from the general question of compatibility of UK law the case was also of interest with regard to its implications for private international law. Generally speaking marriages contracted abroad by persons who lack capacity to marry under UK law are not recognised as valid marriages in the UK.[95] Furthermore, the CPA provides that any relationship registered abroad which meets the requirements of a civil partnership under UK law is to be treated as a civil partnership in the UK,[96] regardless, it seems, of whether that relationship was in fact recognised as a marriage in the country where it took place.

In a contentious judgment[97] Sir Mark Potter found that Article 8 was not engaged. Same-sex childless couples could not, in his view, come within the ambit of 'family life';[98] however, sexual orientation clearly did engage aspects of a person's intimate private life. He went on to accept, therefore, that, according to Strasbourg jurisprudence, particularly weighty reasons must exist to justify any restriction on or interference with that right.[99] Further, in his view, following *M*,[100] when considering the engagement of the private life limb of Article 8 the court must consider whether there had been a failure to respect the Article 8 rights of a claimant, implying that if no such failure could be shown, neither could the engagement of 'private life'.[101] He went on to add that when determining this question, the court ought to principally concern itself with 'de facto' practical and intrusive effects upon the private or family life of a claimant rather than 'de jure' theoretical and non-intrusive effects.[102] The state could not, he said, have improperly intruded or interfered with the private life of a same-sex couple by declining to recognise a same-sex partnership as a marriage in legislation whose purpose and thrust was to enhance their rights.[103]

---

[93] N Bamforth, 'Same-sex couples' (n 55).

[94] *Wilkinson v Kitzinger* [2006] EWHC 2022 (Fam).

[95] *Pugh v Pugh* [1951] P 482.

[96] CPA, s215.

[97] R Auchmuty, 'What's So Special About Marriage?' (n 59) for a detailed critique.

[98] *Pugh* (n 95) para 75. He concluded this by relying on *Secretary of State for Work and Pensions v M* as authority: 'In my view it is clear that the House recognised that the Convention concept of family life does not in the present state of Strasbourg law extend to childless same sex couples'. See also paras 71–7.

[99] *Pugh* (n 95) para 69.

[100] *M* (n 91).

[101] *Pugh* (n 95) paras 76–84.

[102] *Ibid*, para 87.

[103] *Ibid*, para 85.

As a result of applying this analysis he thus found that a failure to show respect for the private life of the claimants had not been shown and the claim could not be brought within the ambit of Article 8:

> Withholding of recognition of their married status does not criminalise, threaten, or prevent the observance by, such couples of an intimate, private life in the same way as a married heterosexual couple and indeed provides them, as so far European jurisprudence does not dictate, with all the material legal rights, advantages (and disadvantages) of those enjoyed by married couples. Not only does English law recognise and not interfere with the right of such couples to live in a very close, loving, and monogamous relationship; it accords them also the benefits of marriage in all but name.[104]

By rejecting the claim that Article 8 was engaged the only possibility left open for the claimants was their argument under Article 12 in conjunction with Article 14. However, this was to be rather summarily dismissed, Sir Mark Potter choosing to read the scope of Article 12 in a 'straightforward manner' as being restricted to marriage between two opposite-sex partners. Noting that there was 'a clear line of Strasbourg jurisprudence' that because of a lack of European wide consensus, had accorded a wide margin of appreciation on the matter, he further declined to develop or go further than Strasbourg citing his clearly minimalist view[105] of the purpose of section 2 of the HRA:

> The purpose of s2 is to ensure that the same Convention Rights are enforced under the HRA by the UK courts as would be enforced by the ECtHR in Strasbourg. However, where UK law is clear, it is no part of the purpose of s2 to oblige courts to interpret Convention rights, or to *develop* European jurisprudence, in a manner inconsistent with it.[106]

However, when it came to determining whether the claimants' arguments could be said to fall within the ambit of Article 12 for the purposes of establishing a sufficient basis for the Article 14 claim Sir Mark felt that, here, in contrast to Article 8, the court ought to concern itself with the 'de jure' effects upon the right to marry that were being claimed. As a result he preferred to adopt the 'broader' approach and, rather than consider the core value of Article 12 as concerning only the restrictions placed upon the right of opposite-sex couples to marry he decided to view the core value as concerning the general limitations placed upon the rights of an individual to marry the partner of his/her choice.[107] In this way by:

> Treating the matter on the basis that, although Parliament had no positive obligation under the Convention to take steps to redress the perceived social disadvantages experienced by same-sex partners as compared with married persons, by embarking on legislation designed to alleviate such social disadvantage and passing the measures contained in the CPA which provided for recognition and treatment of a foreign marriage as a civil partnership only, brought the facts of the Petitioner's situation within the ambit of Article 12.

He went on to hold that the difference in treatment was indeed based upon the claimants' sexual orientation but that the legislation served a legitimate aim, which by reference to Strasbourg jurisprudence[108] he deemed to be the protection of the traditional form of the

---

[104] *Ibid*, para 88.
[105] See discussion of s2 of the HRA in ch 2, pp 32–44.
[106] *Pugh* (n 95) para 63.
[107] *Ibid*, para 110.
[108] *Ibid*, para 116, referring to paras 45–7.

family. In addition, regrettable as the adverse effects may have been upon the claimant, he was not persuaded that as a matter of legislative choice and method, the provisions of the CPA represented an unjustifiable exercise in differentiation in the light of its aims.[109] Those aims were, he considered, to encourage monogamy and the procreation of children and their development and nurture in a family unit in which both maternal and paternal influences are available in respect of their nurture and upbringing.[110] This did not mean, however, that English law suggested that single-sex partnerships were inferior but rather that 'as a matter of objective fact and common understanding, as well as under the present definition of marriage in English law, and by recognition in European jurisprudence, they are indeed different'.[111] To the extent that by reason of the distinction under the CPA discriminated against same-sex partners, such discrimination therefore had a legitimate aim, was reasonable and proportionate, and, moreover, fell within the margin of appreciation accorded to Convention States.

There have been a number of criticisms of this decision, one of the main reasons undoubtedly being Sir Mark Potter's reliance upon the apparent inability of a same-sex couple to procreate as the crucial distinguishing feature between a civil partnership and a marriage[112] in finding that any discrimination between the two was legitimate and proportionate. As Bamforth has commented,[113] aside from seemingly ignoring the present-day reality that same-sex couples are indeed able to bring up children, this comment failed to face up to the numerous comments made in *Ghaidan*[114] concerning the lack of significance of procreation to supply a legitimate reason in terms of Article 14 for distinguishing between same-sex and opposite-sex couples. Further, there is also evidence of confusion in the judgment regarding the proper role of the margin of appreciation;[115] presumably Sir Mark meant to refer to his desire to accord a discretionary area of judgment which would be more appropriate given that this was a decision by a domestic court on an area of social policy. The judgment has also been criticised for falling foul of both sociological facts and jurisprudential trends in that, contrary to the comments of Sir Mark, an increasing number of European governments are opening marriage up to gay couples and the prevalence of statistics demonstrating that if marriage exists to encourage monogamy it is surely failing.[116] If we add to this the increasing irrelevance of procreation as a condition of marriage it can be seen that Sir Mark Potter could be accused of invoking a particularly traditional vision of marriage which may no longer bear any real relationship to reality for a large number of people. Nonetheless, on a doctrinal basis, even if Sir Mark had found that the case came within the ambit of Article 8 it is not entirely clear that the judgment of his court or any future court would be any different. The reality is that to hold the CPA as being in breach of either Article 8 or 12 in conjunction with Article 14 will necessitate a domestic court going further than Strasbourg. As evidenced from the discussion in Chapter 2, the

---

[109]   *Ibid*, para 117.
[110]   *Ibid*, para 118.
[111]   *Ibid*, para 121.
[112]   *Ibid*, para 122.
[113]   N Bamforth, 'Same-sex couples' (n 55). Bamforth also makes the point that Sir Mark's analysis of the applicability of Art 8 arising from *M* may not have been correct, as well as others.
[114]   *Ghaidan* (n 83).
[115]   *Ibid*.
[116]   R Auchmuty, 'What's so special about marriage?' (n 59).

likelihood of a court doing so in an area which one would normally expect domestic courts to defer to the legislature[117] is quite slim.

Restrictions upon the Right to Marry

Prisoners

There have been a number of cases brought before the ECtHR over the years concerning the rights of prisoners to both marry and found a family under Article 12. The general principle that has been established in relation to prisoners is that they will, in general, continue to enjoy all the fundamental rights and freedoms guaranteed under the Convention save for the right to liberty, where lawfully imposed detention expressly falls within the scope of Article 5 of the Convention.[118] It is clear from the case law that this will also include the right to marry as established by *Hamer v UK*.[119] Here, both applicants, a man and woman, wished to marry but the man was serving a sentence of imprisonment, his earliest parole date being some 15 months away. In accordance with the practice at that time the Secretary of State refused to permit arrangements to be made that would enable the marriage to take place either in the prison or in an alternative place outside the prison. In finding that a breach of the applicants' Article 12 rights had occurred, the Commission stated that Article 12 was essentially the right to form a legal relationship and to acquire a status. Further, its exercise by prisoners involved no general threat to prison security as the ceremony could take place under the supervision of the prison authorities. Thus:

> In considering whether the imposition of such a delay breached the applicant's right to marry, the Commission does not regard it as relevant that he could not have cohabited with his wife or consummated his marriage whilst serving his sentence. The essence of the right to marry, in the Commission's opinion, is the formation of a legally binding association between a man and a woman. It is for them to decide whether or not they wish to enter such an association in circumstances where they cannot cohabit.[120]

Having held that the right to marry was not incompatible with a prisoner's deprivation of liberty,[121] the Commission considered the extent to which it was legitimate to delay the exercise of that right in the case of a prisoner. They held that any restriction or regulation of the right to marry should not be such as to injure its substance. Any substantial period of delay in permitting the exercise of the right should be seen as an injury to the substance of the right to marry. On the facts of the case the Commission held that delaying the right

---

[117] This is due to the fact that it concerns an area of social policy which has recently been discussed by Parliament.

[118] *Hirst v the UK* (No 2) GC Application No 74025/01 6 October 2005.

[119] *Hamer v UK* Application No 7114/75 [1979] 4 EHRR 139. See also *Draper v the UK* Application No 8186/78 [1980] DR 24, 72.

[120] *Hamer* (n 119) para 71.

[121] This finding addressed an argument of the UK which was more fully dealt with in *Draper* (n 119) at para 62 where the Commission rejected the submission that a restriction on the right of life sentence prisoners was justified because, at least in some categories of offence, the public would be outraged if prisoners were allowed to marry.

for 15 months to the earliest parole date for the applicant was an unjustifiable interference with his Article 12 rights.

Although prisoners have the right to marry under Article 12 they do not, however, hold a corresponding right to consummate it. The Commission has therefore held that imprisonment per se does not unlawfully infringe the right conferred by Article 12 to found a family. In *X v UK*[122] the Commission stated:

> Although the right to found a family is an absolute right in the sense that no restrictions similar to those in paragraph 2 of Article 8 of the Convention are expressly provided for, it does not mean that a person must at all times be given the actual possibility to procreate his descendants. It would seem that the situation of a lawfully convicted person detained in prison in which the applicant finds himself falls under his own responsibility, and that his right to found a family has not otherwise been infringed.[123]

In *X & Y v UK*[124] a married couple detained in the same prison, but in separate confinement, for a period of about two months, complained that they had been deprived of sexual relations during this period and that their Articles 8 and 12 rights had been violated. In terms of Article 8 the Commission found that the interference with the right to respect for family life was justified under Article 8(2) due to legitimate concerns regarding security and good order in the prison. In terms of Article 12, the Commission held that an interference with family life which is justified under Article 8(2) could not at the same time constitute a violation of Article 12.

Some years later another couple tried to challenge prison policy with respect to facilitating the founding of a family under Article 12 by arguing that their circumstances were exceptional due to their religious beliefs. In *ELH and PBH v UK*[125] the applicants were a married couple who were Roman Catholics. The wife was 33 years old and the husband 37. The husband was serving a sentence of imprisonment of 20 years. The wife applied to the Home Secretary for permission for conjugal visits because she wished to have a child by her husband. However, in order to be able to conceive, she required major surgery to her fallopian tubes which would increase her prospect of conceiving, but only for a limited period. Her wish was to have the surgery and to follow this with conjugal visits because their religious beliefs precluded the use of assisted conception. Her application was refused by the prison governor on the ground that there was no statutory provision for such visits. In finding the application inadmissible the submission that the applicants should receive special consideration because, as Roman Catholics, they did not feel able to resort to artificial insemination (AI) was rejected. In fact it was the very availability of assisted conception that influenced the Commission's finding that their rights had not been violated.[126] Whether they would have found interference had the couple been willing to use assisted conception but that possibility had been refused by the prison was not, however, considered.

This very issue came before the domestic court in *R (on the application of Mellor) v Secretary of State for the Home Department*.[127] The applicant in this case was serving a life sentence for murder at the time of the application. The tariff element of his life sentence

---

[122] *X v UK* (1975) 2 DR 105.
[123] *Ibid*, cited in *Mellor v Secretary of State for the Home Department* (2000) HRLR 846 para 25.
[124] *X and Y v UK* (1978) 13 DR 105.
[125] *ELH and PBH v UK* (1997) 91 AD&R 61.
[126] *Ibid*.
[127] *Mellor* (n 123).

was due to expire in 2006, by which time he would have been 35 years old and his wife 31 years old. They had married while he had been in prison. Both he and his wife wished to found a family and he applied to the Secretary of State for the Home Department for permission to have access to facilities for AI on the basis that there were no guarantees that he would be released in 2006 and that his wife may not be able to conceive due to her age at that time. The Secretary of State refused his application on the basis of a policy that stated that the grant of AI for prisoners and their partners would normally be refused unless there were exceptional circumstances to justify otherwise. In this case, two reasons were given: first, that there was no medical need for AI in order for the applicant and his wife to conceive; and second, that there was some concern about the stability of their relationship, given that it did not exist prior to the applicant's imprisonment, and had not been tested under normal circumstances. He then applied for judicial review of the Home Secretary's decision, which was dismissed, and he appealed against that judgment. The Court of Appeal also dismissed his appeal against the Secretary of State's decision by adopting a restrictive interpretation of the relevant Strasbourg jurisprudence, discussed above. In terms of the application of the Convention, the court found that although imprisonment was incompatible with the exercise of conjugal rights and consequently interfered with the right to respect for family life under Article 8 and with the right to found a family under Article 12, this restriction was ordinarily justifiable under the provisions of Article 8(2).[128] It was accepted, nonetheless, that in exceptional circumstances it may be necessary to relax the imposition of detention in order to avoid a disproportionate interference with a human right.[129] However, owing to the fact there was no case which indicated that a prisoner was entitled to assert the right to found a family by the provision of semen for the purpose of artificially inseminating his wife, the court concluded that it did not. The court did, however, leave open the possibility of Article 12 creating this right in 'exceptional circumstances' on the basis that this had been implicit in the ECtHR's reasoning in *ELH and PBH*[130] and was also necessary for the exercise of proportionality under Article 8(2). What would count as exceptional circumstances was not, however, defined. In terms of the application for judicial review, the court rejected that the Secretary of State's decision had been irrational or unlawful on the basis that it was legitimate to have regard to public perception when considering the characteristics of a penal system:

> A policy which accorded to prisoners in general the right to beget children by AI would, I believe, raise difficult ethical questions and give rise to legitimate public concern.[131]

In addition, it was also considered legitimate, if not desirable, that the Secretary of State considers the effect upon the child being brought up in a single-parent family in considering whether or not to grant the application for AI.[132]

The Secretary of State's policy was directly considered by the ECtHR recently in *Dickson v UK*[133] where the first applicant was in prison due to a conviction for murder and was

---

[128] *Ibid*, para 39 (Lord Phillips).
[129] *Ibid*, para 39 (Lord Phillips).
[130] *ELH* (n 125).
[131] *Mellor* (n 123) para 66 (Lord Phillips).
[132] *Ibid*, para 67 (Lord Phillips).
[133] *Dickson v UK* (2008) 46 EHRR 41. See also the discussion of this case with respect to its implications for the role of deference at the domestic level in ch 5 at p 206.

sentenced to life imprisonment with a tariff of 15 years. His earliest expected release date was 2009. He had no children. In 1999 he met the second applicant, while she was also imprisoned, by correspondence through a prison pen-pal network and she had since been released. In 2001 the applicants married. The second applicant already had three children from other relationships. In 2001 the applicants applied for facilities for artificial insemination and relied upon the length of their relationship and the fact that, given that at the first applicant's earliest release date the second applicant would be aged 51, it was unlikely that they would be able to have a child together without the use of AI facilities. The application was rejected by the Secretary of State for very similar reasons to those given in *Mellor*[134] notwithstanding the difference in age between the women involved[135] and was upheld by the Court of Appeal on the basis that it was not able to seek to re-open the validity of the Secretary of State's policy which the court had previously held in *Mellor*[136] to be rational and otherwise lawful.[137] However, the ECtHR preferred to examine the complaint under Article 8, finding it unnecessary to consider the complaint under the 'found a family' limb of Article 12. In doing so, however, the Court took the opportunity to review the decisions of the Court of Appeal in both *Mellor*[138] and *Dickson*[139] finding that, although this was an area which would normally be accorded a wide margin of appreciation, the Secretary of State's policy and the domestic court's consideration of it had effectively excluded any real weighing of the competing individual and public interests, and prevented the required assessment of the proportionality of a restriction, in any individual case.[140] The absence of such an assessment as regards a matter of significant importance for the applicants must, they said, be seen as falling outside any acceptable margin of appreciation so that a fair balance was not struck between the competing public and private interests involved. There had, accordingly, been a violation of Article 8 of the Convention. What this case makes clear is that a blanket ban on the provision of AI for prisoners either under Article 8 or 12 is not permissible under the Convention. If AI is to be refused it must be after a proper weighing-up of the competing interests at stake. This is not to say, however, that the same interests that were cited by the Secretary of State could be regarded as legitimate. In specifically doubting the impact of three of the main reasons given for refusal by the Secretary of State, the ECtHR strongly implied that the policy must be changed. Although the Court accepted that punishment remains one of the aims of imprisonment, it also underlined the

---

[134] *Mellor* (n 123).

[135] The reasons given by the Secretary of State for refusal were as follows: (1) the fact that Mrs Dickson would be 51 at the earliest possible date for Mr Dickson's release left her with a very small likelihood of being able to conceive naturally; (2) the fact that their relationship had yet to be tested in the normal environment of daily life, making it difficult to assess whether it would continue after Mr Dickson's release; (3) the seeming insufficiency of resources to provide independently for the material welfare of any child who might be conceived; (4) the seeming paucity of any supportive network for mother and child and the fact that the child would not have the presence of a father for an important part of his or her own childhood; and (5) notwithstanding Mr Dickson's good and constructive prison record, the nature and circumstances of the murder for which he was serving the life sentence meant, in the Secretary of State's words, that 'there would be legitimate public concern that the punitive and deterrent elements of [his] sentence of imprisonment were being circumvented if [he] were allowed to father a child through AI while in prison'. See also *Kirk Dickson, Lorraine Dickson v Premier Prison Service Ltd, Secretary of State for the Home Department* [2004] EWCA Civ 1477, para 6.

[136] *Mellor* (n 123).

[137] *Kirk Dickson* (n 135) paras 21–6 (Auld LJ).

[138] *Mellor* (n 123).

[139] *Dickson* (n 133).

[140] *Ibid*, para 82.

evolution in European penal policy towards the increasing relative importance of the reha-
bilitative aim of imprisonment, particularly towards the end of a long prison sentence.[141]
To that end, the Court stated that whilst the inability to beget a child might be a consequence of imprisonment, it was not an inevitable one, the grant of AI facilities would not
involve any security issues or impose any significant administrative or financial demands
on the state.[142] The Court was also, it said, prepared to accept as legitimate, for the purposes
of the second paragraph of Article 8, that the authorities, when developing and applying
the policy, should concern themselves, as a matter of principle, with the welfare of any
child. However, that could not go so far as to prevent parents who so wish from attempting
to conceive a child in the circumstances of the case, especially as the second applicant was
at liberty and could have taken care of any child conceived until such time as her husband
was released.[143] The Government has since remedied the violation in *Dickson*[144] by apparently amending the policy[145] to ensure that permission will not be limited to exceptional
circumstances. However, the Secretary of State will still be free to take into account any factors or considerations which he considers relevant. The policy states that each case will be
considered on its merits and no single factor will be weighed more heavily than another.[146]
The Government took the view that:

> The Grand Chamber's judgment does not require primary legislation to be changed: it focused
> on the point that the Secretary of State failed to consider the proportionality of the restric-
> tions against the individual circumstances of the applicant. The remark that Parliament had
> not had an opportunity to weigh arguments of proportionality was incidental to the Court's
> decision.[147]

However, as the JCHR pointed out,[148] the only significant change in policy appears to have
been the removal of the express statement that permission for AI will only be granted in
'exceptional circumstances'. In addition, a number of the considerations listed in the policy
appear to be based directly on public interest arguments which the Grand Chamber considered would be illegitimate or unjustifiable if applied too broadly. It remains to be seen,
therefore, whether the new policy, by removing the need for exceptionality, will be any better in respecting the Articles 8 and 12 rights of prisoners who wish to found a family. The
fact that the JCHR does not 'share the Government's confidence that the minor changes to
existing policy agreed so far will be adequate to eliminate the risk of a further finding of a
breach'[149] does not inspire confidence that it will.

---

[141] *Ibid*, para 75.
[142] *Ibid*, para 74.
[143] *Ibid*, para 76.
[144] *Ibid*.
[145] Thirty-First Report of Session 2007–08; HL Paper No 173 HC 1078, paras 38–9.
[146] *Ibid*. A non-exhaustive list of factors has been provided which includes the following considerations: the
welfare of the child; the wishes, consent and medical fitness of both parties; the reasonableness of any delay, taking into account the prisoner's release date and his ability to assume parental responsibilities; information about
the offending history of the prisoner, including any risk of harm and 'other factors which suggest it would not be
in the public interest' to permit him to access AI facilities; 'whether the prisoner and his partner are in a well-
established and stable relationship which is likely to continue after the prisoner's release'; and whether the provision of AI facilities are the only means by which conception is likely to occur.
[147] See also 'Responding to Human Rights Judgments: The Government Response to the Joint Committee on
Human Rights' Thirty-first Report of Session 2007–08, January 2009, Cm 7524, 9.
[148] Thirty-First Report (n 145) para 39.
[149] *Ibid*, para 43.

Immigration

Although the right of a foreign person to enter or remain in a country is not as such guaranteed by the Convention, the ECtHR has established that immigration controls must be exercised consistently with Convention obligations.[150] The Commission has therefore held that the exclusion of a person from a country where his close relatives reside may raise an issue under Article 8 of the Convention.[151] As a result a series of attempts were made to extend the reach of Article 8 and Article 12 to include a general obligation to respect the choice of residence of a married couple and to accept the non-national spouse for settlement in the state concerned.[152] These claims were, however, rejected usually on the basis of a combination of the reasons given for refusal by the domestic immigration authorities and the fact that the applicant had not shown that there were obstacles to establishing family life in her husband's home country where he or she had already lived for a short period before her marriage. The ECtHR thus clearly established that the right to live in the same country together could not be derived from either Article 8 or Article 12.

The reason for these decisions is undoubtedly because the ECtHR views restrictions imposed by national laws that serve to pursue the legitimate aim of immigration control as generally permissible under Article 12. However, the restrictions must be reasonable. In a number of cases the Court has ruled that a national authority may thus properly impose reasonable conditions upon the right of a third-country national to marry in order to ascertain whether a proposed marriage is one of convenience and, if it is, to prevent it. In *Sanders v France*[153] the applicants, a Turkish man aged 50 and a French woman aged 24, living together in Istanbul, complained of difficulties they encountered at the French consulate general in Istanbul in obtaining a certificate of capacity to marry. To preclude marriages of convenience, French law provided for the issue of a certificate, to be granted on application to State Counsel (in Nantes, in the case of French citizens residing abroad). State Counsel could oppose or postpone a marriage. The applicants' complaint under Article 12 was held to be manifestly ill founded. It was held that substantive rules, the purpose of which was to preclude marriages of convenience between French citizens and aliens, were not a limitation that was contrary to Article 12. The delay, although regrettable, did not impair the very essence of the right to marry. In *Klip and Krüger*[154] the applicants were a Dutch man and a German woman. The formalities which gave rise to the dispute were required by Dutch legislation which was intended to prevent and suppress marriages of convenience. It sought to establish a systematic examination of all marriages involving aliens, and to that end required completion of a standard questionnaire. Where the Aliens Department had a reasonable suspicion that the intended marriage was one of convenience, certain further steps were then required to be taken. The public prosecutor was therefore able to oppose a marriage as contrary to Dutch public order where the primary object of one or both of the future spouses was to obtain entry into the Netherlands. The

---

[150] *Abdulaziz, Cabales and Balkandali v UK* (1985) 7 EHRR 471, para 59.
[151] *Mahfaz v the UK* Application No 20598/92, para 1.
[152] See the following Commission decisions: *S v UK* Application No 12236/86; *Patel v UK* Application No 14069/88; *Babul v UK* Application No 17504/90; *C v UK* Application No 18713/91; *NA v UK* Application No 17229/90; *S v UK* Application No 19788/92; *Mahfaz v the UK* (n 151).
[153] *Sanders v France* (1996) 87 B-DR 160.
[154] *Klip and Krüger* (1997) 91 A-DR 66.

applicants' complaint to the Commission under Article 12 was also rejected as manifestly ill founded. It was accepted that the law could prevent marriages of convenience between Dutch citizens and aliens for immigration purposes. The obligation to submit a statement was therefore not objectionable.

These cases were recently reviewed by the House of Lords when it heard an appeal against a declaration of incompatibility that was issued in respect of the Asylum and Immigration (Treatment of Claimants, etc) Act 2004 (AITCA) in *R (on the application of Baiai and another) v Secretary of State for the Home Department (Nos 1 and 2) (Joint Council for the Welfare of Immigrants and another intervening).*[155] The Act introduced highly controversial provisions to restrict and regulate the ability of persons subject to immigration control to marry and this case was a joint appeal by a number of applicants affected by the provisions. Most of the controversy surrounds section 19 of the Act, which applies to either a marriage which is to be solemnised on the authority of a certificate issued by a superintendent registrar under Part III of the 1949 Act, or a marriage where one or other or both parties is or are subject to immigration control. Section 19 does not therefore apply to Anglican marriages which follow the ecclesiastical preliminaries governed by Part II of the 1949 Act. Subsection (4) defines a person subject to immigration control as someone who is not an EEA national and he or she requires leave to enter or remain in the UK (whether or not such leave has been given) under the Immigration Act 1971. Section 19(3) provides that the superintendent registrar shall not enter in the marriage notice book notice of a marriage covered by the section unless satisfied by the provision of specified evidence of the following three conditions. First, that the party has an entry clearance granted expressly for the purpose of enabling him or her to marry in the UK. Second, that the person has the written permission of the Secretary of State to marry in the UK. Third, that the party falls within a class specified for the purposes of paragraph (c) by regulations made by the Secretary of State.[156] Further, the Immigration (Procedure for Marriage) Regulations 2005 provided that an application for permission to marry to the Secretary of State must be made in writing and a fee of must be paid, which was set at £295 at the time of the appeal. The criteria to be applied by the Secretary of State in granting a 'certificate of approval' (COA) were contained in non-statutory guidance[157]and those who did not qualify under these criteria would normally have their applications refused. The problem was that the criteria for the grant of a COA were wholly concerned with immigration status and did not include any criteria based around the nature of the relationship between the persons to be married.[158] The process did not therefore provide any opportunity for an assessment of the relationship of the persons to be married or of whether any immigration advantage was actually obtained. Persons subject to immigration control in a genuine relationship who did not qualify for a COA were therefore caught by this policy by virtue of their

---

[155] *R (on the Application of Baiai and Another) v Secretary of State for the Home Department (Nos 1 and 2) (Joint Council for the Welfare of Immigrants and Another Intervening)* [2008] UKHL 53.

[156] The only class so specified is persons settled in the UK, as defined in the Immigration Rules, HC 395, para 6.

[157] Contained in the Immigration Directorate Instructions (IDIs) ch 1 s15 Annex NN. A person had to apply for a certificate of approval (COA). In order to qualify for a COA a person had to have valid leave to enter or remain, to have been granted leave for more than six months on this occasion and to have at least three months of leave remaining at the time of the application for a COA. However, a COA could nonetheless be granted where there were compelling and compassionate circumstances.

[158] Even the compassionate circumstances that permitted the grant of a COA to persons whose immigration status was an insufficient basis for qualification were not based on the nature of the relationship.

immigration status. In effect it was not considered problematic that those prohibited by virtue of immigration status formed a class which may or may not have contained those seeking an improper immigration advantage. At the High Court, Silber J[159] concluded that the section 19 regime was disproportionate and constituted a substantial interference with Article 12 rights. In addition, the distinction made between marriages conducted in the Anglican churches and all others rendered the scheme unjustifiably discriminatory under Article 14 of the Convention in conjunction with Article 12. He thus made a declaration of incompatibility with this aspect of the Act. This latter point was accepted by the Secretary of State who stated that she would remove this aspect of the provisions when the matter was appealed.

The Court of Appeal agreed with the lower court's assessment.[160] The government's argument was, essentially, that conditions on the right to marry that served the interests of an effective immigration policy were justifiable, provided that such measures satisfied the requirement of proportionality. In addition, it was also submitted that any such permissible restrictions on the right to marry might lawfully affect marriages which were genuine and not only sham marriages. After reviewing the relevant ECtHR authorities, discussed above, the House of Lords found that although they established that a Member State may take steps to prevent marriages of convenience, 'they gave no support to the proposition that a significant restriction may be placed on all such marriages, or on a sub-class of such marriages, irrespective of whether they are marriages of convenience or genuine marriages and with no procedure to ascertain whether they are the one or the other'.[161] Their Lordships took some time to emphasise the importance of the right and the protection afforded to the right to marry, rejecting any claims that it could be qualified.[162] In terms of the proportionality of the scheme, the court felt that it could only be justified to the extent that it operates to prevent marriages of convenience which, because they are not genuine marriages, do not earn the protection of the right to marry. If the section 19 scheme restricts the right to marry to a greater extent than that, it followed that it is disproportionate.[163] In assessing the scheme the court did not find either the terms of section 19 or the 2005 regulations to be disproportionate, save the level of the fee.[164] The real problem for their Lordships lay with the Immigration Directorate's Instructions, which, without any parliamentary scrutiny, contained conditions, none of which had any relevance to the genuineness of a proposed marriage, which is the only relevant criterion for deciding whether permission should be given to an applicant who is qualified under national law to enter into a valid marriage.

> Thus, subject to the discretionary compassionate exception, the scheme imposes a blanket prohibition on exercise of the right to marry by all in the specified categories, irrespective of whether their proposed marriages are marriages of convenience or whether they are not. This is a disproportionate interference with exercise of the right to marry.[165]

---

[159] *Baiai* [2006] EWHC 823 (Admin) paras 109–50.
[160] *Baiai* [2007] EWCA Civ 478 (Waller, Buxton and Lloyd LJJ).
[161] *Baiai* (n 155) para 23 (Lord Bingham).
[162] *Ibid*, paras 44–6 (Lady Hale).
[163] *Ibid*, para 25.
[164] *Ibid*, para 25, which was regarded at being at such a level that it would impair the essence of the right to marry for a needy applicant. See also para 50 (Lady Hale).
[165] *Ibid*, para 31 (Lord Bingham). See also paras 41–7 (Lady Hale).

The declaration of incompatibility that had been issued at first instance in relation to section 19(3) was thus amended to refer only to section 19(1), which was the basis for the discrimination between civil and Anglican preliminaries to marriage. Any amended scheme will need to be amended[166] to remove the two features that were singled out by the judges. First, that the level of the fee had been set too high, and second, that any categorical exclusion from marriage on the basis of immigration status alone constituted an unjustifiable interference with the right to marry. The new scheme will thus need to provide some method by which it can be reasonably concluded that the proposed marriage is one of convenience. Given that the main reason for not providing for this in the first place was that it would be too expensive and administratively burdensome[167] may lead the Secretary of State to the conclusion that it may be better to drop this aspect of the scheme altogether.

Cultural and Religious Issues

The ECtHR has established a number of principles with respect to restrictions imposed on the form of marriage. First, the obligation to contract a marriage in accordance with forms prescribed by law rather than a particular religious ritual is not a refusal of the right to marry. In *X v Federal Republic of Germany*,[168] the applicant complained that in failing to recognise as a marriage, his having sexual intercourse with a woman after reading out verse 16 of the 22nd chapter of the second book of Moses in the Old Testament, the German authorities had breached his Convention rights. However, the Commission found that in asking the applicant to marry in the prescribed form did not constitute a denial of his right to marry. This principle has also been applied to marriages conducted according to cultural rites. In *Hopic and Hopic-Destanova v the Netherlands*[169] the applicants claimed that the refusal by the domestic authorities to recognise their marriage, conducted according to gypsy rites, as a lawful marriage for the purposes of granting a residence permit, constituted a breach of the applicants' Articles 8 and 12 rights. The applicants had then gone on to marry in a manner which would be recognised by the Dutch authorities; however, the fact that the refusal was based on their prior status was not held to be a breach of either Articles. Implicit in the decision is the view that Dutch law, in not recognising such marriages, did not impair the very essence of their right to marry and a national law which requires the parties to take part in a prescribed marriage ceremony will not be regarded as disproportionate.

A claim made in conjunction with Article 9 is also likely to fail due to the fact that the Court has held that under that Article marriage cannot be considered simply as a form of expression of thought, conscience or religion but is governed by the specific provisions of Article 12. *Janis Khan v the UK*[170] dealt with a direct conflict between the rules of an organised religion, Islam, and the criminal law. Here, a 21-year-old male Muslim took part in an Islamic marriage with a 14½-year-old female Muslim without the permission of her family. The male was subsequently charged and convicted of child abduction and

---

[166] L Pilgram, 'Tackling "Sham marriages": The Rationale, Impact and Limitations of the Home Office's Certificate of Approval Scheme' (2009) 23 (1) *Journal of Immigration Asylum and Nationality Law* 24–40.
[167] *Baiai* (n 155) para 31 (Lord Bingham).
[168] *X v Federal Republic of Germany* Application No 6167/73 18 December 1974.
[169] *Hopic and Hopic-Destanova v the Netherlands* Application No 13158/87 13 August 1987.
[170] *Janis Khan v UK* Application No 11579/85 7 July 1986.

sexual intercourse with a girl under the age of consent and was sentenced to nine months in prison. He claimed that a breach of his Article 9 rights had occurred in that he had been prevented from manifesting his religion through marriage by the Sexual Offences Act 1956 and that, further, the custodial sentence imposed on him by the same Act prevented him from being able to consummate his marriage and found a family under Article 12. In rejecting both claims, the Commission held that the term 'practice' under Article 9 did not cover every act which is motivated by religion or belief. In terms of Article 12 the obligation to respect the legal marriageable age did not constitute a denial of the right to marry, even if the individual's religion permits marriage at a younger age.

It has also been made clear that Article 9 does not oblige the states to ensure that churches within their jurisdiction grant religious freedom to their members and servants. Further, a church is free to enforce uniformity in religious matters, and it is not obliged to accept a pastor as its servant or to allow him to carry out certain duties even if that may result in an interference with a person's Article 12 rights. In *Spetz and Others v Sweden*[171] the applicants consisted of four pastors of a Swedish nonconformist organisation which was part of the Swedish Pentecostal movement and a couple who had recently been married by one of the pastors. By government decision of 12 September 1952, the Pentecostal movement was granted a right to celebrate marriages. Since the Pentecostal movement consisted of several independent congregations which did not have a common administration, a special Marriage Board was set up within the movement to authorise celebrants. Only officials of Pentecostal congregations with specified qualifications were to be authorised and any such authorised officials must, before conducting any marriage ceremonies, have obtained a certificate showing their competence from the County Administrative Board. The application centred on the fact that the licences of the four pastors had been revoked by the Marriage Board because it considered that they had demonstrated, by actively supporting breakaway factions, that they did not consider themselves to be part of the Pentecostal movement. This decision had been upheld by the Swedish government and the Supreme Administrative Court on the basis that they did not have competency to decide the matter, that having being given to the Marriage Board. In terms of the couples who had been married by the four pastors in the interim, the government had indicated that they could apply for a declaration of validity which would be received favourably.[172] The couple before the Commission had chosen not to do so, claiming that the very fact that they had to make an application to have their marriage recognised by the state was a breach of their Articles 8, 9 and 12 rights.[173] Noting that that the right to marry under Article 12 was subject to the national laws governing the exercise of the right, the Commission found that the fact that the couple, by applying to the government, could have had their marriage declared valid meant that there had not been any violation of their right to marry. Further, any alleged violations of their right to found a family under Article 8 were all consequences of the invalid marriage and consequently, the Commission considered that this provision had not been violated either.

The question of whether a polygamous marriage is compatible with the Convention has not, however, been dealt with as an aspect of Article 12 due to the fact that the one case

---

[171]   *Spetz and Others v Sweden* Application No 20402/92 12 October 1994.

[172]   In fact the government had granted all the applications that had been received.

[173]   The four pastors also claimed that their Art 9 rights had been infringed by having their licences to marry revoked by the Marriage Board.

that has been considered concerned an application for the right of entry for a polygamous wife and the claim related to her right to respect for family life.[174] In *Bibi v the UK*[175] the applicant's mother had been denied permission to enter the UK due to the fact that she was the first of two women who had married the applicant's father. Section 2 of the Immigration Act 1988 provided that a woman would not be granted a certificate of entitlement to the right of abode, on the basis of a polygamous marriage, if another woman had already been admitted to the UK as the wife of the same husband. The second wife of the applicant's father had already settled in the UK. The applicant therefore complained of an infringement of her right to respect for family life and alleged that the refusal to allow her mother to enter the UK as her father's wife discriminated on the grounds of sex in that it allowed the husband to choose the wife who shall join him in the UK. The decision is interesting for a number of reasons. First, for the way in which the Commission considered that family life had been established between mother and daughter. The existence of family life is, they said, presupposed from a relationship which has arisen from a lawful and genuine marriage even if, as was the case here, there was no evidence in the case file that the parties to the marriage had lived together for any prolonged period of time. In addition the fact that the applicant had spent the first nine years of her life with her mother all resulted in family life being established between the two. Second, although the refusal to allow entry constituted an interference with the applicant's right to family life, the interference was in accordance with the law which was intended to prevent the formation of polygamous households, the practice of polygamy being deemed unacceptable to the majority of people who live in the UK.[176] Third, a wide margin of appreciation would generally be accorded to a state concerning its immigration policy in establishing an immigration policy on the basis of family ties. A Contracting State cannot be required to give full recognition to polygamous marriages which are in conflict with their own legal order.[177] Finally, noting that the aim of the provision would appear to be 'the preservation of the Christian based monogamous culture dominant in that country'[178] the Commission took the view that the family life circumstances in the present case did not outweigh the legitimate considerations of an immigration policy which rejects polygamy and is designed to maintain the UK's cultural identity in this respect. It is debatable if this particular aim could subsequently be regarded as illegitimate for the purposes of any future claim under either Article 8, 9 or 12 were the cultural and religious map of the UK to significantly change in this regard due to the sensitivity of the area.

The refusal to recognise a polygamous marriage is now well entrenched within UK immigration law,[179] the reasons for which are, as indicated in *Bibi*,[180] related to concerns regarding

---

[174] *Khan v the UK* Application No 19628/92 29 June 1992 did consider this specifically from the point of view of Art 12 with respect to a husband seeking permission to enter for his second wife, however, the claim was deemed inadmissible for reasons concerning the time limit for the submission of the application. The substantive claims under Arts 8 and 12 were not dealt with.

[175] *Bibi v the UK* Application no 19628/92 29 June 1992.

[176] *Ibid*, para 1. The Commission noted that for centuries it has been an offence in the UK, by virtue of the criminal law on bigamy, to contract a marriage with more than one woman at a time on UK territory.

[177] Referring to *Alilouch El Abasse v the Netherlands* Application No 14501/89 6 December 1992, para 1.

[178] *Ibid*.

[179] Indeed, were a person to go through more than one official process of marriage it would render them liable for the criminal offence of bigamy under s57 OAPA.

[180] *Bibi* (n 175).

public policy and the incompatibility of such marriages with the Christian-inspired definition of marriage as being monogamous.[181] The direct question of whether a second wife could obtain a right of abode in the UK, unaddressed in *Bibi*,[182] was subsequently reaffirmed in the negative by the court in *R v Immigration Appeal Tribunal ex p Begum (Hasna)*.[183] Here the court dismissed an application by the first wife of a man who had applied for judicial review of a decision to refuse entry to a second wife. The fact that when another wife was alive and permanently settled in the UK made such refusals mandatory under the immigration rules did not render them ultra vires. In terms of the rights of children born as a result of polyga-mous marriages, the Court of Appeal, shortly after the decision in *Bibi*,[184] appeared to reverse the previously held approach that the Legitimacy Act 1976 permitted such children to acquire citizen status through the father even though such marriages may not have been considered valid under English law.[185] However, the court did so without any reference to either the deci-sion in *Bibi*[186] or the Convention. In *Azad v Entry Clearance Officer Dhaka*[187] the appeal was against a decision of the immigration tribunal which had refused to grant the son of a third wife a certificate of the right of abode. The applicant was entitled to such a certificate if he was a British citizen and he could only be regarded as such if he was a legitimate son of the father who was a British citizen. Section 1(1) of the Legitimacy Act 1976[188] provided that the child of a void marriage would be regarded as legitimate if both or either of the parties to the mar-riage believed it to be valid. The marriages to the second and third wife, although regarded as valid under Bangladeshi law, were regarded as void under UK law due to the fact that the father was domiciled in the UK and the marriage was polygamous. As the father knew that these marriages would be invalid, it was the belief as to the validity of the mother with which the case was concerned. In dismissing the appeal the court held that as there was no material from the third wife as to her belief about the position under English law at all, the question of whether it was a reasonable belief was never reached. The question of whether this obvious interference with the family life of the parties involved was justified did not seem to concern the court, who also failed to consider the basic preliminary question of whether family life had been established between either the husband and his wives, or his children. Although these cases may represent a worrying trend towards a 'highly negative private international law position led primarily by immigration control concerns'[189] and may itself be a breach of the human rights of those separated by such control, it is not apparent that the approach is incompatible with the ECHR. Although the rather complex intersection between immigra-tion law and the right to family life is beyond the scope of this book it is fairly clear, from the discussion concerning how the ECtHR has viewed immigration concerns when deciding

---

[181] For a critical analysis of how successful legislation in this area and others has been at reducing the level of polygamy in the UK see P Shah, 'Attitudes to Polygamy in English Law' (2003) 52 (2) *International & Comparative Law Quarterly* 369–400.

[182] *Bibi* (n 175).

[183] *R v Immigration Appeal Tribunal Ex P Begum (Hasna)* [1995] Imm AR 249, although there had been a number of such cases decided before the ECtHR's decision in *Bibi*—see P Shah, 'Attitudes to Polygamy' (n 181) for more on this.

[184] *Bibi* (n 175).

[185] P Shah, 'Attitudes to Polygamy' (n 181) 395.

[186] *Bibi* (n 175).

[187] *Azad v Entry Clearance Officer Dhaka* [2001] Imm AR 318.

[188] Sub-section (4) created a presumption of legitimacy but it did not apply to the appellant because he was born before s28 of the 1987 Act came into force.

[189] P Shah, 'Attitudes to Polygamy' (n 181) 396.

the width of the margin of appreciation,[190] that such decisions may well be within the state's margin, particularly where family life has not been established between the parent who has the right to remain and the child.

The Role of Marriage in Creating 'Family Life' Under Article 8

Although the right to marry is considered specifically under Article 12 the importance of the institution to the ECtHR is also reflected in its jurisprudence on Article 8. An examination of this jurisprudence reveals that when looking at the question of whether family life has been established the Court will first consider the form of the family and, as such, consider whether it corresponds to what it has referred to as 'a conventional family based unit' which will consist of a heterosexual married couple who may or may not have children. Such families are automatically accorded family life and thus placed at the top of an evidentiary hierarchy where nothing more is required to demonstrate family life. It is also clear that there is no requirement for members of such units to continue to live together[191] or remain married as family life will be in existence by virtue of fulfilling this norm. It is no surprise, therefore, that the Court has been charged with privileging the traditional or 'ideal' family form; however, this is something about which the ECtHR has been unapologetic. The Court has often reiterated that marriage confers a 'special status' upon those who enter into it, something which is quite obviously underscored by the protection of the right to marry as a separate Article within the Convention itself. Thus, in *Shackell v the UK*[192] the Court held that the difference of treatment, for the purposes of the grant of social security benefits, between an unmarried applicant who had a long-term relationship with the deceased, and a widow in the same situation, was justified, marriage remaining an institution that was widely accepted as conferring a particular status on those who entered it. The Court decided in *Shackell*,[193] therefore, that the promotion of marriage by way of the grant of limited benefits for surviving spouses could not be said to exceed the margin of appreciation afforded to the respondent state. Although this provision may in large part be due to marriage being the predominant family form at the time of the drafting of the Convention, the Court has maintained its preference for the institution of marriage as a reflection of the continuing privileging of it by most, if not all, of the Contracting States. In other words, this is an inevitable consequence of the operation of the margin of appreciation by a supranational court.[194] Although problematic, what is often obscured in such discussions is the fact that by privileging marriage in this manner the Court is demonstrating what is arguably the real focus of the court: to ascertain

---

[190] See ch 2, pp 17–19.
[191] *Abdulaziz et al v UK* (1985) 7 EHRR 471.
[192] *Shackell v UK* Application No 45851/99 27 April 2000.
[193] *Ibid.*
[194] However, if we recall the critique of this approach to the doctrine discussed in ch 2 we can see that it can also be argued that it is precisely because the ECtHR is a supranational court that it should be leading the way by setting a more inclusive test.

the *intention* to create family life. The Court has referred to marriage as 'a public and legal undertaking which carries with it a recognisable body of rights and obligations of a contractual nature towards one another and any children' and thus, in purely evidential terms, represents the ultimate evidence of the intention to create family life. Indeed, such is the symbolic power of marriage, it is capable of satisfying the Court even where some doubt exists as to its legal validity; a ceremony of marriage and the belief that it is genuine is seemingly enough.[195] However, while this does nothing towards answering the criticism that the Court continues to privilege marriage over other forms of relationship, one advantage that appears to have emerged from this approach is that other, similar, public and legal undertakings could also be afforded the same treatment. In *Burden v UK*[196] the Grand Chamber had to consider whether the Article 1 of Protocol No 1 and the Article 14 rights of two elderly cohabiting sisters had been breached due to the fact that when one of them died, the survivor would face a significant liability to inheritance tax, which would not be faced by the survivor of a marriage or a civil partnership. Although the sisters did not bring any claims under Article 8 the Grand Chamber considered, in some detail, the status of their relationship in comparison to that of a marriage or a civil partnership. In doing so, they held that the legal consequences of civil partnership under the CPA, which couples expressly and deliberately decided to incur, set these types of relationship apart from other forms of co-habitation.

Rather than the length or the supportive nature of the relationship, what is determinative is the existence of a public undertaking, carrying with it a body of rights and obligations of a contractual nature. Just as there can be no analogy between married and CPA couples on one hand, and heterosexual or homosexual couples who choose to live together but not to become husband and wife or civil partners on the other hand, the absence of such a legally binding agreement between the applicants renders their relationship of co-habitation, despite its long duration, fundamentally different from that of a married or civil partnership couple.

Family life, as with married couples, could also automatically arise in relation to any children either born or adopted within a civil partnership.

With respect to family forms outside either marriage or a civil partnership, it is fair to say that the Court will adopt a somewhat functional test of whether they will constitute family life which, again, demonstrates a certain preoccupation with the intention behind the arrangements. It should also be noted that this functional approach has been facilitated by the Court's recognition of the changes in family form and structure that have occurred over the years, made possible by the evolutive and dynamic nature of the Convention. Thus, an unmarried couple may establish family life if certain factors are present,[197] such as whether the couple live together, the length of their relationship and whether they have demonstrated their commitment to each other by having children together or by any other means.[198] These factors have also been used to extend the concept of family life from unmarried couples who have children to others. Thus, family life was

---

[195] *Abdulaziz* (n 191) para 63.
[196] *Burden v UK* Application No 13378/05 12 December 2006.
[197] *Lebbink v the Netherlands* Application No 45582/99 (2005) 40 EHRR 18.
[198] *Kroon v the Netherlands* Series A No 297 (1995) 19 EHRR 263.

found to be in existence in relation to a transsexual father and his child born as a result of artificial insemination by donor (AID),[199] an uncle and nephew,[200] and a grandparent and grandchild.[201] At the same time, the lack of existence of such factors has been applied to hold *against* the establishment of family life and thus it will not be held in existence by the mere donation of sperm[202] and in relation to stillborn children.[203] The existence or non-existence of 'family life' has thus become, in essence, a question of fact depending upon what the Court has referred to as 'the real existence in practice of close personal ties'[204] and to a certain extent reflects a recognition of the social parent over the genetic. Nonetheless it is clear that when examining whether family life is in existence the Court will first consider whether there is evidence of an intention to create family life by virtue of form before moving to function. A married couple will thus have established family life with each other and with any of their children; any other forms of relationship will, in essence, have to satisfy the 'function' test.

It is important to note, however, that while there may be a privileging of marriage with respect to the engagement of family life under Article 8(1),[205] any difference in treatment towards children which is rooted in family form will fail to satisfy the Article 8(2) test. Both the ECtHR and the Council of Europe[206] have demonstrated their commitment to the equal treatment of children born within and outside marriage which is, in turn, in line with a number of international and regional instruments[207] all of which prohibit discrimination on the grounds of birth. Thus, in *Marckx v Belgium*[208] the ECtHR held that although it was not a requirement of Article 8 that a child or parent be entitled to a share in the estate or for a parent to leave property in a certain way, it would constitute a breach of their Article 8 and Article 14 rights if any such provision discriminated between legitimate and illegitimate children. Thus, once family life has been established, the Court makes no distinction between the legitimate and illegitimate family and prohibits discrimination grounded on birth.

These principles concerning the establishment of family life at the ECtHR will now be examined with regard to the establishment of parenthood in the next Chapter.

---

[199] *X, Y and Z v the United Kingdom* Application No 21830/93 (1997) 24 EHRR 143.

[200] *Boyle v UK* (1994) 19 EHRR 179.

[201] *L v Finland* Application No 25651/94 [2000] 2 FLR 118.

[202] *M v the Netherlands* Application No 16944/90 1993 DR 74, 120.

[203] *Znamenskaya v Russia* Application No 77785/01 (2007) 44 EHRR 15.

[204] *K and T v Finland* Application No 25702/94 (2000) 31 EHRR 18.

[205] The ECtHR has held on a number of occasions and over a variety of contexts that differences in treatment between married and unmarried couples can be justified if there is a rational basis for doing so and a wider margin of appreciation will be accorded—eg *Mc Michael v UK* Application No 16424/90 (1995) 20 EHRR 205 and *Saucedo Gomez v Spain* Application No 33784/94 26 January 1999.

[206] In accordance with the European Convention on the Legal Status of Children Born Out of Wedlock 15 October 1975—see also the Committee of Ministers Policy referred to in *Marckx v Belgium* [1979] 2 EHRR 330.

[207] Art 2 of the UN Convention on the Rights of the Child, Art 2.1 of the International Covenant of Civil and Political Rights and Art 21 of the European Charter of Fundamental Rights.

[208] *Marckx* (n 206) and *Johnston* (n 3).

5

Parenthood and Parental Rights

Intention, Family Life and the Parent

The ECtHR does not discuss concepts such as motherhood or fatherhood but rather approaches the question from the point of view of whether family life has been established under Article 8 and, as argued in Chapter 4, employs a test of intentionality in doing so. The best evidence of the intention to create family life, from the Court's point of view, can be found where the conventional 'public undertaking' forms of relationship such as marriage or civil partnerships are in existence. The Court will then move on to a more functional-based analysis of intentionality in relation to any relationship outside this paradigm. Thus, an unmarried couple may establish family life if certain factors are present[1] such as whether the couple live together, the length of their relationship and whether they have demonstrated their commitment to each other by having children together or by any other means.[2] These factors have also been used to extend the concept of family life from unmarried couples who have children to others. Thus, family life was found to be in existence in relation to a transsexual father and his child born as a result of assisted reproduction using donated sperm,[3] an uncle and nephew,[4] and a grandparent and grandchild.[5] At the same time, the lack of existence of such factors has been applied to hold *against* the establishment of family life and thus it will not be held in existence by the mere donation of sperm[6] and in relation to stillborn children.[7] The existence or non-existence of 'family life' has thus become, in essence, a question of fact depending upon what the Court has referred to as 'the real existence in practice of close personal ties'[8] and to a certain extent reflects a recognition of the social parent over the genetic. Nonetheless it is clear that when examining whether family life is in existence the Court will first consider whether there is evidence of an intention to create family life by virtue of form before moving to function. A married couple will thus have established family life with each other and with any of their children; any other forms of relationship will, in essence, have to satisfy the 'function' test.

The establishment of family life has not been a central aspect of English family law, although following the implementation of the HRA the courts will need to ensure that they comply with their duty under section 6 of the HRA to apply the law in a manner

---

[1] *Lebbink v the Netherlands* Application No 45582/99 (2005) 40 EHRR 18.

[2] *Kroon v the Netherlands* Series A No 297 (1995) 19 EHRR 263.

[3] *X, Y and Z v the United Kingdom* Application No 21830/93 (1997) 24 EHRR 143.

[4] *Boyle v UK* (1994) 19 EHRR 179.

[5] *L v Finland* Application No 25651/94 [2000] 2 FLR 118.

[6] *JRM v the Netherlands* Application No 16944/90 8 February 1993, Commission Decision.

[7] *Znamenskaya v Russia* Application No 77785/01 (2007) 44 EHRR 15, although the mother's relationship with the stillborn child was recognised as part of her right to respect for her private life.

[8] *K and T v Finland* Application No 25702/94 (2000) 31 EHRR 18.

which is compatible with Convention rights. However, it is also clear that the courts do not routinely approach every application of family law in the same way as the ECtHR nor is an analysis of Convention rights undertaken in every case. Quite apart from the fact that there may be incompatibilities between the two approaches, there is also some evidence of a lack of understanding of the demands of the exercise under Article 8 amongst the UK judiciary. A further problem in assessing compatibility between the two systems is that the ECtHR, by its very nature, adjudicates over a variety of different legal systems, which employ a variety of different legal concepts. Under the UK legal system an individual may acquire legal parenthood in a number of different ways and, particularly since the increased use of new technologies in assisted conception, is not something that is dependent upon a genetic link with the child. The extension of legal parenthood to individuals who are not genetically related to a child has been the subject of much discussion in the literature and it is here that Bainham's[9] distinction between *parentage* and *parenthood* may be of particular usefulness in breaking down what exactly is meant by the term 'parent'. Under this analysis parentage is viewed as having a 'one off' character and is essentially concerned with a genetic link. Parenthood, on the other hand, conveys an ongoing status in relation to the child and is closely associated with the responsibility for raising the child.[10] This distinction is important for its ability to help navigate the debates surrounding the value of psychological parenting as compared to the value of the genetic link between a parent and a child. Identifying the values attached to these two concepts thus helps to understand the development of two increasingly powerful, but possibly contradictory movements; for children to be given as full information as possible regarding their genetic origins and for psychological parents to be given equal status to the biological. A further complicating factor in these debates is the concept of 'parental responsibility', which can give an individual all the rights, duties and powers of a parent without being dependent upon the establishment of parentage or parenthood. These concepts and the debates surrounding them will be fully examined against the general principles established by the ECtHR across its relevant case law throughout this Chapter. This section of the Chapter will start with a consideration of the question of parenthood and will move on to consider the question of parental responsibility separately.

Fatherhood

Fathers, 'Close ties' and the ECHR

Fatherhood is not something that the ECHR specifically refers to, although there have been a number of cases where the Court has considered the establishment of the legal tie of fatherhood, discussed below. However, prior to doing so the Court will start with a discussion as to whether or not family life has been established between father and child. Here,

---

[9] A Bainham, 'Parentage, Parenthood and Parental Responsibility' in A Bainham, S Day-Schlater and MPM Richards (eds), *What Is a Parent?* (Oxford, Hart, 2000).

[10] See also S Gilmore, J Herring and R Probert, 'Parental Responsibility: Law, Issues and Themes' in S Gilmore, J Herring and R Probert, *Responsible Parents and Parental Responsibility* (Oxford, Hart, 2009) for a discussion of the differences between the legal position of those with parents with parental responsibility and those without.

the test of intentionality in relation to the establishment of family life differs from that of mothers, in that it is not in any way related to his contribution to the conception and birth of the child or the fact that official registration of legal fatherhood has taken place. Thus, in *Lebbink v the Netherlands*[11] the ECtHR stated:

> The Court does not agree with the applicant that a mere biological kinship, without any further legal or factual elements indicating the existence of a close personal relationship, should be regarded as sufficient to attract the protection of Article 8.

The key factor appears to be whether the 'father' has cohabited with the mother and the child presumably because that will often be the best evidence of the establishment of 'close ties' between father and child. This will be the case even where there may be no biological link between them. In *X, Y and Z v the United Kingdom*[12] X, a transsexual, had undergone gender reassignment surgery and had lived with Y, as her male partner, since 1979. The couple subsequently applied jointly for, and were granted, treatment by AID to allow Y to have a child; nevertheless, X could not be deemed the child's legal father under English law.[13] Although the Court held that a breach of X's Article 8 rights had not occurred in this case[14] it did consider that, because X was involved throughout the process of conception and had acted as Z's father in every respect since the birth, there were sufficient enough 'family ties' to establish family life between them. What the case also reiterates is that whether or not the father has entered into marriage with the mother is irrelevant to the question of family life; at the time of the application, transsexuals could not legally marry under English law. It is *cohabitation as a family unit*, rather than marriage (or presumably any status gained by virtue of surrogacy or adoption) that is placed at the top of the evidential hierarchy in terms of proving the intention to create family life between father and child. This is not to say, however, that family life cannot be evidenced without it. The Court has also consistently reiterated its commitment to the 'potential relationship which may develop between a natural father and a child born out of wedlock'[15] and thus, where there has been no cohabitation, has been willing to find evidence of intentionality by reference to a number of factors which will include the nature of the relationship between the natural parents and the demonstrable interest in and commitment by the natural father to the child both before and after the birth. In *Görgülü v Germany*,[16] the commitment of the father in instituting proceedings for custody of his child who had been placed with foster parents and was later adopted was significant to the finding of family life between him and his biological child, even though there had been limited and supervised contact between them since his birth.[17]

It is noteworthy that where family life has been found without cohabitation as a family unit it has always been in relation to what the Court has termed a 'natural' father. Although

---

[11] *Lebbink* (n 1) para 37.
[12] *X, Y and Z* (n 3).
[13] This has now been rectified by the GRA s12, which states that where an individual has obtained a gender recognition certificate this 'does not affect the status of the person as the father or mother of the child'.
[14] Mainly due to a wide application of the margin of appreciation because of a lack of consensus on the treatment of transsexuals across the Member States at the time.
[15] *Nylund v Finland* Application No 27110/95 (1999-VI) 14.
[16] *Görgülü v Germany* Application No 74969/01 (2004).
[17] See also *Johnston v Ireland* (1986) 9 EHRR 203, where the fact that the mother and father were in a committed relationship at the time of conception was regarded as important. They had later separated, however.

the term has not been expressly defined by the ECtHR we can assume, however, from the cases in which the term has been used, that the Court is referring to a biological father. The ECtHR is yet to be faced with a claim from a non-biological father seeking to establish family life with a child that he has not lived with. That is not to say, however, that it would be impossible for him to do so. The foundations for a claim to family life could be drawn from the ECtHR's comments in *X, Y and Z*[18] where the Court specifically referred to the fact that the applicant had been jointly involved in the process of conception, via the use of AID, as a factor which led to the establishment of family life between himself and his child.[19] Establishing family life does not of course guarantee that a breach of Article 8 will be found. The Court has also indicated that any differences in treatment between non-biological fathers and biological fathers may not necessarily constitute a breach of Articles 8 or 14. Although the applicant was found to have family life with his child, the Court in *X, Y and Z*[20] went on to note that a wide margin of appreciation would be accorded to cases involving the social relationship between a child conceived by AID and the person who performs the role of father. This was due to the lack of existence of a generally shared approach amongst the Member States with regard to the manner in which these relationships should be reflected in law. In *X, Y and Z*[21] this ultimately meant that the inability of the transgender applicant to be legally recognised as his child's father did not amount to a failure to respect his family life.

The court has also, however, made it clear that the mere fact of biological fatherhood will not automatically result in family life being found and where father and child have not lived together the question will be dependent upon the existence of certain factors that have been laid down as discussed above. Consequently, in *JRM v the Netherlands*,[22] it was held that where the applicant had donated sperm to enable a woman to become pregnant through artificial insemination this did not, of itself, give the donor a right to respect for family life with the child.[23] Nor will the mere fact of financially supporting a child.[24] In such cases the Court may, instead, take the view that a close relationship short of family life would fall within the scope of 'private life'.[25] This analysis was applied to a case concerning a deceased father in *Znamenskya v Russia*[26] where the applicant mother complained of the impossibility of having her stillborn's patronymic name and surname amended so as to reflect its biological descent from her late partner. However, due to the fact that the child was stillborn and because its biological father had been separated from the applicant before its birth and died shortly thereafter, the Court considered that the relationship could not fall within 'family life'. This was because 'close, personal ties' could not have been developed between the child and its parents. However, the matter was instead dealt with as

---

[18]   *X, Y and Z* (n 3).
[19]   However, the Court also referred to the fact that he had acted in every respect as the father of the child since its birth.
[20]   *X, Y and Z* (n 3).
[21]   *Ibid.*
[22]   *JRM* (n 6).
[23]   *Ibid*; *G v the Netherlands* (1990) 16 EHRR 38.
[24]   *Haas v the Netherlands* [2004] 1 FCR 147.
[25]   Eg *Wakefield v the United Kingdom* Application No 15817/89, 1 October 1990, Commission decision: Relationship between a prisoner and his fiancée; *X and Y v the United Kingdom*, Application No 9369/81, 3 May 1983, Commission decision: Same-sex relationship; *X v Switzerland*, Application No 8257/78, 10 July 1978, Commission decision: Relationship between a foster mother and the child she had looked after.
[26]   *Znamenskya v Russia* Application No 77785/01 2 June 2005.

an aspect of the applicant's private life and a breach of the applicant's Article 8 rights was subsequently found on this basis.

Establishing Family Life in the UK

In the UK legal fatherhood is established primarily[27] through a biological or genetic link, although the courts have acknowledged, in line with ECtHR jurisprudence, that this, in itself, will be insufficient to create family life between father and child. In *Leeds Teaching Hospital NHS Trust v A*[28] Mrs A's eggs were mixed by mistake with the sperm of Mr B, rather than that of her husband Mr A. It was held that because Mr A had not consented to the treatment of his wife with Mr B's sperm he was therefore not the father under section 28 of the HFE Act: it was Mr B who was deemed to be the legal father of the children. The Court also made it clear that, in accordance with *Lebbink*,[29] discussed above, Mr B could, not, however, have said to have established family life with the children under Article 8. Nonetheless, the significance of this distinction collapses somewhat when we recall that the ability to make an application under section 8 of the Children Act 1989 (CA) in relation to a child, something very pertinent to the question of family life between father and child can be exercised on the basis of legal parenthood alone. A matter that was acknowledged in *Leeds Teaching Hospital*:

> Mr B is the legal father of children born outside a marriage, and he can therefore make a section 8 application by virtue of section 10(4) of the Children Act. It is clearly a case to remain in the High Court. Such an application, if made, would be decided under the provisions of the Children Act, in which the welfare of the children is paramount.[30]

This is arguably further than the ECtHR would have gone; if the Court had found that family life did not exist between Mr B and the twins, that would have been the end of the matter. Mr B would not have been able to argue that an inability to bring a claim under section 8 was a breach of his Article 8 rights if his relationship with the twins did not fall within it. Thus, while UK law may acknowledge that biology alone is insufficient to create family life between father and child it is clearly sufficient to determine the ability to claim *access* to family life by, for example, making a contact application which may or may not be granted depending upon what is deemed to be in the best interests of the child.

The contradiction between denying the father–child relationship on the one hand and facilitating access to, albeit in a limited sense, family life was further evidenced recently in *Re B (Role of Biological Father)*,[31] which involved a dispute between the biological father of a child and a lesbian couple. The father, who was also the brother of one member of the couple, claimed that he had donated his sperm on condition that a real, albeit limited, role had been agreed for him, involving both contact and some role in the major decisions in his life. The couple claimed, in contrast, that the only role agreed for the donor father was a 'rather distant avuncular one'. After the birth of the child the donor father applied for

---

[27] There are two important exceptions to this: adoption and assisted conception, which will be examined later on in the chapter.

[28] *Leeds Teaching Hospital NHS Trust v A* [2004] EWHC 644 (QB).

[29] *Lebbink* (n 1).

[30] *Leeds Teaching Hospital* (n 28) para 51.

[31] *Re B (Role of Biological Father)* [2007] 1 EWHC 1952 (F).

contact and parental responsibility having had two successful supervised contact sessions with the child. The judgment of the High Court, rather unusually, was delivered in open court, owing to the apparent importance of the issues that the case raised, most notably 'the question of the proper place of the biological father in a same-sex family intended to be self-sufficient'. It is even more surprising, therefore, that absolutely no reference to either the HRA or the ECHR was made. Had this been done, the court would have found ample authority from ECHR case law to hold that family life had not been established between the donor father and the child. The Commission's decision in *JRM*[32] would have been particularly relevant as the case also concerned a disagreement between a donor father and a lesbian couple as to the future role to be played by him. However, his claim was simply dismissed as being manifestly ill founded due to the fact that the sperm donation and limited contact was insufficient to establish family life under Article 8. In *Re B*,[33] the outcome was quite different; no order was made in relation to parental responsibility ostensibly to prevent any undermining of the status of the two female partners towards the child. However, an order for direct contact four times a year, plus some indirect contact, was made. Although it was stressed that the contact ordered was not meant to allow the development of a parental relationship because that would threaten the autonomy of the nuclear family, the court felt, nonetheless, that it was in the child's interests to have someone from whom he could satisfy his natural curiosity when he inevitably came to ask questions as to who his biological father was. The motivation for ordering the contact was therefore clearly grounded in the belief that the children should be told the truth about their 'natural parents' which was, in turn, predicated on an acceptance of the importance of the biological tie between parent and child. Again, the court may have gone further than the ECHR would require. Although, as the discussion below will demonstrate, the right of a child to determine his/her paternity must be facilitated by the state, this does not necessarily translate into an obligation to facilitate contact between father and child. That will be dependent upon the establishment of family life. It is of course, depending upon the interpretation of the duty contained in section 2 of the HRA taken; open to a UK court to go further than the ECtHR, however, it would be perhaps pertinent that at least some demonstration of an appreciation of that case law be attempted before doing so.

The Donor Father and Surrogacy

Donor fathers involved in surrogacy may represent the one type of sperm donor where family life could be found to be established under the ECHR. Although the Court is yet to hear such a claim it is possible that, unlike the sperm donors in *Re B*[34] and *JRM*,[35] such a donor may be able to establish family life by virtue of demonstrating the necessary interest and commitment to the child. Although there was some disagreement in both these cases as to what their future role would be in relation to the child, both donors had had some contact. In *JRM*[36] this was deemed not to have established sufficient enough 'close personal ties' to attract the protection of Article 8 and this should equally have been the case in

---

[32] *JRM* (n 6).
[33] *Re B* (n 31).
[34] *Ibid.*
[35] *JRM* (n 6).
[36] *Ibid.*

Re B[37] had Article 8 been raised at all. A donor faced with a surrogacy dispute may find himself in the exact same position;[38] however, his situation could be distinguished from the donors in *Re B*[39] and *JRM*.[40] These two donors knew from the outset that they would not be one of the main carers of the child; in other words, they were facilitating the conception of a child and the creation of a family unit *for another couple*. In a situation of surrogacy, the intention is quite different: here the donor intends to facilitate the conception of a child and the creation of a family unit *for him* and possibly another. This difference in intentionality could make the difference in affording such a donor the protection of Article 8. If family life was found, this may in turn require the facilitation of contact depending upon an appraisal of any conflicting interests of the child and the mother. It should also be added that the same analysis could be applied to a donor mother who has provided her egg for the purposes of surrogacy on the basis that she will be bringing up the child.

Cases involving disputed surrogacy agreements in the UK are thankfully rare; however, they have the advantage of illustrating the different approaches that have been taken by the courts when faced with claims made by the donor father. In *A v C*[41] the father had been living with a woman who was unable to have any more children. Both then agreed to find a surrogate mother, who would be artificially inseminated with the father's sperm. Having both found a woman willing do so she changed her mind during the pregnancy and refused to hand the child over to the father after the birth. Although the father had been having regular contact with the child, he commenced wardship proceedings seeking custody of the child but later, on advice, withdrew the application. Contact between father and child was subsequently granted but the mother's appeal against the order was allowed on the basis that there was no positive reason, apart from the mere fact of paternity, for granting contact.[42] In coming to this conclusion the court was clearly influenced by the conduct of the father and his partner, referring to it as 'wholly distasteful'. The key motivation in refusing to allow contact was, however, to safeguard the best interests of the child:

> The fact that in any given case generation of a child has been achieved by what is described as AID, as compared to natural methods of conception, can have no effect upon the duty of a court to try to afford that child such a life as will best promote the child's welfare.[43]

By contrast, in *Re N(A Child)*,[44] decided after the passage of the CA and the HRA, the appellant mother appealed against a decision transferring residence of her 18-month-old child to the biological father. The child was born as a result of a surrogacy agreement between the mother and the father but had lived with the mother and her family since birth. A key factor in the initial decision was again the conduct of one of the parties. At first instance the judge had found that the mother had deliberately embarked on a path of deception driven by a compulsive desire to bear further children and had no other objective than to obtain insemination by surrogacy with the single purpose of obtaining another child. This, combined with other factors, was enough to override the child's existing attachment

---

[37] *Re B* (n 31).
[38] This would apply equally to same-sex partners who are using a surrogate.
[39] *Re B* (n 31).
[40] *JRM* (n 6).
[41] *A v C* [1985] FLR 445 (CA).
[42] *Ibid*, 457 (Ormrod J).
[43] *Ibid*, 459 (Cumming-Bruce LJ).
[44] *Re N (A Child)* also known as *Re P (A Child)* [2007] EWCA Civ 1053.

to his mother and her family. The decision was confirmed by the Court of Appeal, Thorpe LJ going so far as to, erroneously, state that the donor father was to be treated as the legal father under section 28 of the HFE Act. In fact, as pointed out by Lloyd LJ, it was the husband who had to be treated as the legal father under the Act due to the fact that the insemination was conducted with the consent of M's husband.[45]

As Richard Collier and Sally Sheldon[46] have noted, the decision in *A v C*[47] is a product of its time, made prior to the passage of the HFE Act and therefore demonstrating some preoccupation with the preservation of the nuclear family. They argue that *Re N*,[48] although unusual, could demonstrate how a future disputed surrogacy case would be decided. The fact that the donor father was treated as the legal father of the child in *Leeds Teaching Hospital*[49] combined with the emergence of calls for children to be told the truth about their genetic origins reflect, they argue, a change in the legal landscape which means that the donor father in *A v C*[50] may now have a much stronger claim than he would have had when that case was decided. The landscape has undoubtedly shifted for the reasons that Collier and Sheldon advance, but the additional point that must be made is that even if it had not, the situation could not have remained as it was, after the passage of the HRA. Indeed, we can also add that it was the passage of the HRA that must also have been a significant driver behind these changes in the legal landscape. All this is, of course, something that would perhaps have been obvious to a family bench which was routinely complying with its duties under sections 2 and 6 of the HRA; however, yet again, the judgments in *Re N*[51] are noteworthy for their failure to address the Convention rights of either of the parties. Had it done so, the court may well have found the basis for distinguishing between the donor father in the *Leeds Teaching Hospital*[52] case and the donor father in *Re N*[53] by applying the intentionality analysis set out above. A finding of family life between the donor father and child in *Re N*[54] would arguably not have changed the outcome: the court could still have, after considering the conflicting rights of the mother and the child, gone on to apply the balancing exercise under Article 8(2) in his favour. Furthermore, addressing the HRA would also have provided the Court of Appeal with the opportunity to consider the more interesting question of whether the effect of section 28 of the HFE Act, in not allowing the donor father to be recognised as the legal father of the child, was in fact compatible with his Article 8 rights under section 3 of the HRA. Instead we see the courts, yet again, ignoring the real demands of the HRA and resolutely sticking to the application of the welfare principle *simpliciter*.

Cases Involving AID

Here the person claiming legal fatherhood will not have any biological link with the child. Under section 35 of the HFE Act 2008 the woman's husband will be the father where a

---

[45] *Re N* (n 44) para 19 (Lloyd LJ).
[46] R Collier and S Sheldon, *Fragmenting Fatherhood: A Socio Legal Analysis* (Oxford, Hart, 2008) 90, 91.
[47] *A v C* (n 41).
[48] *Re N* (n 44).
[49] *Leeds Teaching Hospital* (n 28).
[50] *A v C* (n 41).
[51] *Re N* (n 44).
[52] *Leeds Teaching Hospital* (n 28).
[53] *Re N* (n 44).
[54] *Ibid.*

child results from regulated assisted reproductive technologies (ARTs), unless it can be demonstrated that he did not consent to the treatment. An unmarried man will be deemed to be the legal father if he satisfies one of the 'agreed fatherhood conditions' set out in section 37. These conditions are satisfied by the ongoing and written consent of both parties to the man being treated as father of a child resulting from treatment and the woman not having since consented to anyone else being treated as either the child's father or female parent. The Act appears to be employing its own version of a test of intentionality to enter into fatherhood. At the top of the evidential hierarchy is the fact of marriage, which requires no proof of consent and after that comes the requirement of some evidence of active and ongoing consent. It does not, of course, address the question of how family life is established between father and child but it would appear that the scheme is quite different from the test of intentionality that is employed by the ECtHR when it does so. As discussed above, the Court is concerned with whether 'close, personal ties' have developed between father and child and as such it is cohabitation as a family unit rather than marriage that is at the top of the evidential hierarchy in demonstrating the intention to create these ties. If cohabitation is not present then the Court will search for other evidence of an intention to create 'close, personal ties' through other factors such as the nature of the relationship between the natural parents and the demonstrable interest in and commitment by the father to the child. We have seen that this test was satisfied in a case involving AID and a transsexual father partly on the basis that the father in that case had jointly entered into the conception process with the mother and partly on the basis that he had, for all intents and purposes, behaved as the father of the child since its birth. A man involved in the AID process could be said, as Collier and Sheldon[55] have noted, to have demonstrated some level of 'emotional investment' by virtue of facilitating the process of finding a donor which matches as far as possible his characteristics. The fact that such a man who has also fulfilled the agreed fatherhood conditions under the HFE Act sufficient to create a legal tie between him and the resulting child may also serve to demonstrate a close and personal relationship between the two.[56]

'Deceived' Fathers

Could the above analysis be applied to cases where a man has raised a child believing erroneously that the child is his own? It would seem that as he has lived with the child in a family unit he is able to demonstrate the existence of close personal ties sufficient to establish family life between himself and the child under Article 8. How far the state should go in terms of respecting his Article 8 rights is, however, dependent upon the application of the balancing exercise in Article 8(2). It would seem at the very least that such an applicant, unless there are significant reasons as to why it would be against the child's interests, should be granted contact with the child and possibly even residence or parental responsibility. This was in fact what happened in *Re A (Joint Residence: Parental Responsibility)*[57] although, again, without any reference to the HRA and the Convention rights of the parties

---

[55] R Collier and S Sheldon, *Fragmenting Fatherhood* (n 46). See their discussion of *Re R* at 84.

[56] In *Lebbink* (n 1) the Court referred to the absence of 'any further legal or factual elements indicating the existence of a close personal relationship' as a factor in holding that family life had not been created between a biological father and his child.

[57] *Re A (Joint Residence: Parental Responsibility)* [2008] EWCA Civ 867.

involved. Here, the applicant lived with the child and the mother for a period of two years believing that the child was his own. After the relationship broke down and proceedings were commenced by him for parental responsibility, residence and contact it emerged that he was not the biological father of the child. Again, a key factor in the case was the conduct of one of the parties, the court finding that the mother was determined and controlling in her desire to marginalise the man's role in the child's life and that she wanted to relocate to another area of the country to have greater control. A joint residence order was eventually made along with a generous order for contact between the applicant and the child, relocation having been permitted. The mother appealed the joint residence order arguing that the court had failed to give proper weight to the status of either of the child's natural parents. The orders were, however, upheld. Although the man could not be regarded as the child's father either in common parlance or under any statutory definition this did not, in the court's opinion, justify the mother seeking to ignore or belittle the applicant as the 'father figure' in the child's life.

Deceased Fathers

Znamenskya v Russia[58] confirmed that any claims concerning the legal recognition of the fatherhood of a deceased man and a stillborn cannot be considered as an aspect of his family life under the ECHR. Close personal ties could not sufficiently be developed in that case due to the fact that the child was stillborn and that the father had also died. The matter was instead dealt with as an aspect of private life. Where the child is born alive and the father had been fully involved in the conception process either as a result of natural or assisted reproduction it is arguable that the matter could fall within either the father's or the child's family life. Either way, it is clear that a state cannot prevent the registration of his legal fatherhood of the child and, in the UK, after a high-profile challenge[59] to previous legislation which prevented a deceased father being treated as the father of a child born after his death using assisted conception, the Human Fertilisation and Embryology (Deceased Fathers) Act 2003 remedied the position. Such fathers can now be registered as the father of the child, a matter recently confirmed by section 40 of the new HFE Act 2008.

A Father's Right to 'Respect' for Family Life under the ECHR—Establishing Paternity and Legal Fatherhood

There have been a number of decisions of the ECtHR that have addressed claims made by putative fathers with regard to establishing the paternity of a child. The outcome of these cases has turned upon the Court's interpretation of the notion of 'respect' for family life and the positive obligations that have been developed in this regard. The first point to note about these cases is that such claims are *not* dependent upon the existence of family life being found between the applicant and the child. If family life is not found to be in existence the Court will deal with such claims as an aspect of private life. Where family life *is* in

---

[58] *Znamenskya* (n 26).

[59] *Diane Blood* 1 March 2003 (unreported). Human Fertilisation and Embryology (Deceased Fathers) Bill HC 2003 (63). She successfully challenged this provision of the 1990 Act but the basis of her challenge was that her child's human rights were being breached.

existence but the paternity proceedings are aimed at the dissolution of existing family ties between a father and child, the Court has left open the question of whether such proceedings concern the applicant's family life, finding instead that the determination of the legal relationship between them both will, in any event, concern his private life.[60]

Generally speaking, the requirement of respect for family life places both positive and negative obligations on the state.[61] In other words, states must not only ensure that the Article 8 rights of its citizens are not disproportionately interfered with but also must take certain positive actions to promote family life. These positive obligations have been interpreted in a number of ways under Article 8 but, specifically, in this context, have been used to imply a duty upon Member States to take positive measures to not only resolve paternity disputes in an efficient and accurate manner[62] but also, as Bainham has noted,[63] to afford the individual at least one opportunity to bring the claim.

In addition, regard must also be had to the fair balance that has to be struck between the competing interests of the individual and of the community as a whole and in both contexts the state enjoys a certain margin of appreciation. However, the Court has repeatedly reiterated that its task is not to substitute itself for the competent domestic authorities in regulating paternity disputes at the national level, but rather to review under the Convention the decisions that those authorities have taken in the exercise of their power of appreciation. As a result, where a state has failed to adequately apply the balancing exercise the Court has found, in a number of cases, that the Article 8 rights of the individual bringing the paternity claim have been breached.[64] What is of particular note is that in all but *two* of these cases reference was made by the Court to the interests of the child in establishing the truth of paternity.[65] Thus, the claim was recognised as an aspect of the child's rights, rather than the father's. In *Kroon v the Netherlands*[66] a mother and natural father of a child complained that they were unable under the domestic law to obtain recognition of his paternity of the child due to the fact that it was not open to a married woman to deny the paternity of a child born in wedlock to another man. The natural father could only legally recognise the child after the husband's paternity had been successfully denied; however, the husband of the mother was untraceable. The ECtHR considered that sufficient family ties existed between the natural father and his child to create family life between them; however, the two alternatives suggested by the domestic authorities that would have created the legal ties between them were held to be incapable of being regarded as compatible with the notion of 'respect' for family life. This was because the first, step-parent adoption, would have required both parties to marry, and the second, joint custody, would have left the

---

[60] *Shofman v Russia* Application No 74826/01 (2007) 44 EHRR 35 para 30; *Rasmussen v Denmark* Application 8777/79 (1985) 7 EHRR 371 para 33.

[61] See also F Jacobs and R White, *The European Convention on Human Rights* 4th edn (Oxford, Oxford University Press, 2006) 242–5.

[62] See also N Moreham, 'The Right to Respect for Private Life in the European Convention on Human Rights: A Re-examination' [2008] 1 *European Human Rights Law Review* 44.

[63] A Bainham, 'Arguments About Parentage' (2008) 67 *CLJ* 288.

[64] Eg *Znamenskaya* (n 26); *Mizzi v Malta* Application No 26111/02 (2008) 46 EHRR 27; *Paulik v Slovakia* Application No 10699/05 (2008) 46 EHRR 142; *Rozanski v Poland* Application No 55339/00 (2006) 2 FLR 1163; *Tavli v Turkey* Application No 11449/02 (2009) 48 EHRR 11.

[65] Note that *Znamenskaya* (n 26) involved a claim brought by the mother in respect of the right to have the paternity of a stillbirth recorded.

[66] *Kroon* (n 2).

legal ties between the child and the husband intact. Accordingly, a breach of the applicants' Article 8 rights was found to have occurred.

In *Shofman v Russia*[67] what appeared to be particularly relevant was that for some two years after the child's birth the applicant did not suspect that the child was not his and reared him as his own. The fact that the applicant was prevented from disclaiming paternity because he did not discover that he might not be the father until more than a year after he learnt of the registration of the birth was held to be disproportionate to the legitimate aims pursued. A fair balance had not been applied between the general interest of the protection of legal certainty of family relationships and the applicant's right to have the legal presumption of his paternity reviewed in the light of the biological evidence. The overwhelming concern of the Court to avoid a situation in which a legal presumption is allowed to prevail over what the Court has termed the 'biological and social reality' was, therefore, very much, in these two cases, analysed from the point of view of the adults involved. However, this approach does not appear to be one that has been taken in the rest of the cases where a breach of the Article 8 rights of the putative father has been found. What is apparent from these cases is that in finding a breach of Article 8, the Court noted that a good enough case had *not* been made out with respect to the interests of the children involved in order to lead to the denial of the applicants the ability to bring a claim for the determination of paternity. In *Mizzi v Malta*[68] the applicant claimed that he had doubts as to his paternity of his daughter since her birth but had been unable to refute the legal presumption of paternity because she was born during his marriage to her mother. Although he had complied with his maintenance obligations towards his daughter he ensured that he did not establishing any father–daughter relationship with her. He claimed that the daughter contacted him at age 26 (she was 39 at the time of the judgment) and agreed to undertake a blood test. Despite the fact that the results of this test showed that he was not her father, the applicant was prevented from bringing a claim to contest his paternity because according to the domestic law he could only do so within six months of her birth. In finding this restriction of the applicant's right to institute proceedings to be a disproportionate interference with his Article 8 rights, the ECtHR rejected the government's argument that the 'daughter' had always enjoyed the 'social reality' of being the applicant's daughter and it would be detrimental to her to take away her identity and expel her from the applicant's family:[69]

> The potential interest of Y in enjoying the 'social reality' of being the daughter of the applicant cannot outweigh the latter's legitimate right to have at least the opportunity to deny paternity of a child who, according to scientific evidence, was not his own.[70]

In *Rozanski v Poland*[71] the applicant was unable to bring proceedings to determine the paternity of a child that he believed to be his because under domestic law he did not have the consent of the mother and because her new partner had legally recognised the child as his

---

[67] *Shofman* (n 60).
[68] *Mizzi* (n 64).
[69] The daughter provided a statement in which she said she had always used his surname and would like to continue doing so, and disputed the applicant's version of events.
[70] *Mizzi* (n 64) para 112.
[71] *Rozanksi* (n 64).

own. In finding that a breach of his Article 8 rights had occurred, the ECtHR acknowledged that although the domestic authorities:

> Might not have wanted to disturb the legal relationship between the child and his mother's new partner, it is open to criticism that no examination of these interests against the factual background of a particular case has been effected or even considered. Moreover, it was not examined at all whether in the circumstances of the case the examination of the applicant's paternity would harm the child's interests or not.[72]

In *Paulik v Slovakia*[73] the applicant sought a review of the judicial declaration of his paternity in the light of new biological evidence, which was not known to him at the time of the original paternity proceedings, but proved that he was not the father of the child. The court found that the fact that the child was now 40 years old, did not object to the proceedings, had her own family and was not dependent upon the applicant for maintenance[74] meant that the general interest in protecting her rights at this stage had lost much of its importance compared to when she was a child. In *Tavli v Turkey*[75] the applicant also complained that new scientific evidence, which demonstrated that he was not the father of the child born to his former wife, could not be re-examined by the domestic courts. At the time that the ECtHR heard the matter, the child involved was 26 years old. In finding a breach of the applicant's Article 8 rights, the ECtHR found that it was 'not convinced by the Government's argument that the domestic courts have protected the interest of the child and the family, rather than the applicant. In particular, it had not been shown how the interest of the child was protected.'[76] In all three of these cases the clear implication is that the claim could have been denied had it been demonstrated that it would have gone *against* the interests of the children to allow the determination of paternity claim to proceed.

What is clear, therefore, is that the ECtHR's concern for the interests of children and the social and biological reality may be why an absolute right to determine paternity has not been established.[77] This is because a significant factor in decisions where the Court has found that a breach of Article 8 has *not* occurred has been the interests of the children. In *Rasmussen v Denmark*[78] the case involved an applicant who 'had known with certainty, or had had grounds for assuming, that he was not the father from the first day of the child's life but—for reasons unconnected with the law—had taken no steps to contest paternity within the statutory time limit'.[79] His application to bring his claim out of time was subsequently denied by the domestic authorities. The case was unusual in that the applicant brought his claim primarily under Article 14 (in conjunction with Articles 6 and 8) due to the fact that under the domestic law his right to contest his paternity of a child born during the marriage was subject to time limits, whereas his former wife was entitled to institute paternity proceedings at any time. Nonetheless, in rejecting his claim that a breach of any

---

[72]   *Ibid* para 78.
[73]   *Paulik* (n 64).
[74]   *Ibid* para 46.
[75]   *Tavli* (n 64).
[76]   *Ibid* para 34.
[77]   A Bainham, 'Truth Will Out: Paternity in Europe' (2007) 66 *CLJ* 278.
[78]   *Rasmussen* (n 60).
[79]   As discussed in *Shofman* (n 60) para 39. Cases where this was applied were *Rasmussen* (n 60) and *Yildrim v Austria* Application No 34308/96 (1999).

of his Convention rights had occurred[80] the ECtHR stated that the introduction of time limits for the institution of paternity proceedings was justified 'by the desire to ensure legal certainty in family relations *and* to protect the interests of the child'. In *Nylund*[81] the mother of the child discovered that she was pregnant just before her relationship with the applicant broke down. She went on to marry another man one month later. Under the domestic law a legal presumption of the husband's paternity followed because the child was born in wedlock. The applicant, believing he was the father, sought to bring proceedings to establish his paternity of the child, something that was denied by the mother; she maintained that she had already had a relationship with her husband around the time of the child's conception. The domestic courts denied the applicant the ability to bring his claim on the basis that establishing his paternity without the consent of the child's parents would disturb relations in the child's family.[82] The ECtHR found that no breach of the applicant's Article 8 rights had occurred, the case being distinguishable from *Kroon*[83] because there:

> [T]he obstacle to bringing paternity proceedings ran counter to the wishes of those concerned, in the instant case it accords with the wishes of the married couple in whose wedlock the child was born. In fact, the obstacle is a result of their opposition.

Further, in *Kroon*,[84] the Court noted that the legal presumption of paternity did not actually benefit anyone.[85] It was therefore 'justifiable for domestic courts to give greater weight to the interests of the child *and the family in which it lives* than to the interest of an applicant in obtaining determination of a biological fact'[86] (emphasis added). In *Yildrim*[87] the applicant had known that he was not the father of the child born to his wife after they had separated. However, under the domestic law, because he and his wife were still married at the time of the birth, the child was deemed to be their legitimate daughter and was entered in the birth register as such. The applicant argued that he only discovered this presumption operated after the time limit to bring an action to contest the legitimacy of a child born in wedlock had expired. He also claimed that his wife had assured him that the name of the natural father had been entered in the birth register. During domestic proceedings to consider whether the applicant should be allowed to bring his claim it became clear that it may not be possible to determine who the natural father of the child was. As a result the domestic authorities considered that because the applicant's action could result in the finding that the applicant was not the child's father, she risked losing her maintenance claim against him. It was therefore not in the child's interests to allow the claim to proceed. The ECtHR seemingly agreed, finding that 'once the limitation period for the applicant's own claim to contest paternity had expired, greater weight was given to the interests of the child

---

[80] Primarily because the ECtHR found that the reason for this difference in treatment was justified, a wide margin of appreciation having been applied on account of the lack of common ground amongst Member States with regard to the subject matter.

[81] *Nylund* (n 15).

[82] When the case reached the ECtHR the government further argued that the purpose of the provisions of the domestic law along with its legal presumption was to protect a marriage-based family, including the child, from an action for the annulment of the paternity of the husband, brought by any man outside the family.

[83] *Kroon* (n 2).

[84] *Ibid.*

[85] *Ibid*, para 15.

[86] *Ibid*, para 15.

[87] *Yildrim* (n 79).

than to the applicant's interest in disproving his paternity'.[88] The clear assumption in all three cases is that the interests of the child were greater served by *maintaining* the child's link within the married family rather than allowing it to be challenged.

Finally, in the remarkable decision of *Yousef v the Netherlands*[89] the ECtHR felt it necessary to do something which it had never done before and refer to the child's interests as being *paramount* when it found that no breach of the applicant's Article 8 rights had occurred where legal recognition of his fatherhood had been denied. The facts of the case were unusual in that all the parties involved, including the Court itself, acknowledged that the applicant's paternity of the child was not in dispute. In addition, it was also conceded that the applicant had established family life with his child by virtue of having had regular contact with her. The case centred instead on the application of the domestic law, which lay down that a man could only recognise a child born out of wedlock, as was the case here, if the mother of the child had given her prior written permission. This had not been given and, moreover, the mother had expressly stated in her will that she did not wish this to occur after her impending death. The mother had subsequently died and the child had been residing with a member of her mother's family ever since. The Supreme Court of the Netherlands ruled that the mother's refusal of such permission no longer had any effect after her death, even if it had been recorded in her will. However, in deciding whether to grant legal recognition to a father, the Court stated that it should, after the death of a mother who had refused permission, balance the interests of the natural father in having his paternity recognised against the rights of the child protected by Article 8 of the Convention. The main reason for the Supreme Court's subsequent refusal to allow the formal recognition of the applicant's fatherhood centred on the consequences of such a declaration, that is, it would give him the ability to make an application for the child to reside with him. This was also the applicant's stated intention. A change in residence of the child in this manner, however, was felt by the Supreme Court, for a number of reasons,[90] not to be in the child's best interests. Although the ECtHR found that the Article 8 rights of the applicant had been breached in this case, they did not find 'any indication that the domestic courts in striking the balance they did between the rights of the applicant and those of the child, failed to take the applicant's rights sufficiently into account or decided in an arbitrary manner'. The Court also distinguished the case from *Kroon*:[91] 'in that case, no other reason than a formal one was found for denying the father, who lived together with the child, the right to legal recognition of his paternity.' In actual fact, the natural father in *Kroon*[92] had *not* been living with the child but, as with the applicant in *Yousef*,[93] had established family life with the child on the basis of their 'close family ties'. The real reason for distinction could perhaps have been that in *Kroon*,[94] no conflicting interests were presented on behalf of the child but this was not something that the ECtHR referred to in *Yousef*.[95] Most importantly of all, however, the Court seemed to have disregarded what should have been a crucial point in

---

[88] *Ibid*, para 6.
[89] *Yousef v the Netherlands* Application No 33711/96 [2002] 3 FCR 577.
[90] Detailed by the ECtHR as being because he had never taken care of her before, had never indicated previously that he wished to and hadn't established convincingly that he could.
[91] *Kroon* (n 2).
[92] *Ibid*.
[93] *Yousef* (n 89).
[94] *Kroon* (n 2).
[95] *Yousef* (n 89).

its assessment of Article 8(2) and one that was made by the applicant. The legal recognition of the applicant's fatherhood would not in itself have resulted in any change in the child's residence. That, according to Dutch law, could only have resulted from his appointment as the child's guardian, which would require separate proceedings involving an examination of precisely that issue. The reasons given by the Supreme Court for denying his application for legal recognition of his fatherhood could presumably have been utilised to deny any such subsequent claim if that was the concern of the domestic authorities. Moreover, it is striking that at no point in the judgment was the child's interest in obtaining a legal father articulated as a positive matter for her. Nonetheless, the case confirms that the ECtHR may allow for legal presumptions to prevail over biological reality where it assesses the matter as being one in which sufficient conflicting interests of children are in existence.

A Child's Right to Determine Paternity by DNA/Blood Tests and the ECHR

Few applications have been brought by children seeking to determine their paternity before the ECtHR; however, a number of principles can be discerned from these judgments. First, in line with the case law concerning applications by putative fathers discussed below, it has been held that the imposition of statutory time limits upon bringing such claims is not in itself incompatible with Article 8. The key question for the Court to consider in such cases is whether the nature of the time limit in question and/or the manner in which it is applied is compatible with the Convention. Further, in performing the 'balancing of interests test' the Court will take a number of factors into consideration, such as:

> The particular point in time the applicant became aware of the biological reality … and whether or not an alternative means of redress exists in the event the proceedings in question are time-barred. This would include for example the availability of effective domestic remedies to obtain the reopening of the time limit or exceptions to the application of a time limit in situations where a person becomes aware of the biological reality after the time limit has expired.[96]

In *Phinikaradou v Cyprus*[97] the applicant claimed that she did not know who her biological father was until her mother's death in 1997 by which time the domestic statutory time limit within which she could institute proceedings for judicial recognition of paternity had expired. The domestic law made no allowance for children in the applicant's situation who did not acquire knowledge of the material facts pertaining to paternity until after the three-year period had elapsed. The ECtHR thus found that the applicant was deprived of the possibility of obtaining judicial determination of paternity as a result of the rigid application of this time limit even though she was in a situation where she had not had any realistic opportunity to go to court at any earlier stage. Such a radical restriction of the applicant's right to institute proceedings for the judicial determination of paternity was not proportionate to the legitimate aim pursued. In particular, the Court stated that it had not been shown how the general interest in protecting legal certainty of family relationships or the interest of the presumed father and his family outweighed the applicant's right to have *at least one opportunity* to seek judicial determination of paternity.[98]

---

[96] *Phinikaradou v Cyprus* para 54.
[97] *Ibid.*
[98] *Ibid*, para 64.

Second, where the domestic legal system is not able to compel a person to undergo DNA testing and is faced with an individual who is actively avoiding it the court has held that 'a procedural provision of a general character, giving discretionary power to courts to assess evidence, is not in itself a sufficient and adequate means for establishing paternity'.[99] In *Mikulic v Croatia*[100] the applicant had brought judicial proceedings against an individual whom she believed to be her father in order to determine her paternity. No measures existed under domestic law to compel him to comply with the first-instance court's order that DNA tests be carried out. Nor were there any direct provisions governing the consequences of such non-compliance. The courts were free, however, to give judgment according to their own discretion after assessing all the evidence that had been presented. Some three and a half years later, during which time the putative father failed to appear at six appointments for DNA testing, the first-instance court concluded that he was indeed the applicant's father. It based its conclusion on the testimony of the applicant's mother and on the fact that he had been avoiding DNA tests. On appeal, the domestic court found this evidence insufficient for establishing his paternity. For the ECtHR the fact that there had been no means by which the domestic authorities could compel an individual to undertake DNA testing was not in itself incompatible with the positive obligations deriving from Article 8. However, the lack of any procedural measure to compel the alleged father to comply with the court order could only be in conformity with the principle of proportionality if 'it provides alternative means enabling an independent authority to determine the paternity claim speedily'.[101] Furthermore, in determining an application to have paternity established, the courts were required to have regard to the basic principle of the child's interests. The procedure available in this case did not therefore strike a fair balance between the right of the applicant to have her uncertainty as to her personal identity eliminated without unnecessary delay and that of her supposed father not to undergo DNA tests. The Court concluded therefore that the inefficiency of the courts had left the applicant in a state of prolonged uncertainty as to her personal identity and that there had been a subsequent failure to secure to the applicant the 'respect' for her private life under Article 8. What this case seems to imply is that the operation of a legal presumption in favour of paternity, rather than the application of judicial discretion, will almost certainly come within the type of procedural measure that the ECtHR required in terms of compelling an individual to comply with a court order to undertake DNA testing. Where such a presumption does not exist, domestic authorities will need to establish some form of independent authority invested with the power to determine the issue of paternity.

The final point to be made is that in all the cases[102] brought by children with regard to establishing paternity the ECtHR has referred to 'third party interests', the implication being that if they were serious enough they could outweigh the child's right to the establishment of his/her paternity. However, there is clearly a high threshold to reach in order to override the applicant child's right to determine his/her paternity. In *Jaggi v Switzerland*[103]

---

[99] *Mikulic v Croatia* Application No 53176/99 [2002] 1 FCR 720 para 62.

[100] See also *Ebru and Tayfun Engin Çolak v Turkey* Application No 60176/00 (2006) as a further example of a child bringing the claim (the judgment is in French, however).

[101] *Mikulic* (n 99) para 64.

[102] *Ibid*, para 63; *Phinikaradou* (n 96) para 53; *Jaggi v Switzerland* Application No 58757/00 (2008) 47 EHRR 30 paras 38–9.

[103] *Jaggi* (n 102).

the 67-year-old applicant claimed that the refusal of his request for DNA tests to be carried out on the remains of a deceased individual whom he believed to be his father constituted a violation of his Article 8 rights. The ECtHR started by noting that the protection of third persons may preclude their being compelled to make themselves available for medical testing of any kind, including DNA testing.[104] However, in weighing up the different interests at stake, consideration should be given, on the one hand, to the applicant's right to establish his parentage and, on the other hand, to the right of third parties to the inviolability of the deceased's body, the right to respect for the dead, and the public interest in preserving legal certainty.[105] In this case, due to the fact that the deceased's family had not cited any religious or philosophical grounds for opposing the taking of a DNA sample and it was a measure which is relatively unintrusive,[106] the third party interests were not sufficiently serious to override the applicant's right to establish his parentage. A breach of the applicant's Article 8 rights was thus found. What kind of third party interest will be sufficient? An indication was given in *Phinikaradou*[107] when the Court referred to the fact that in addition to the conflict of interest between the party seeking to establish paternity and the party thought to be the father, other interests may come into play, 'such as those of third parties, essentially the presumed father's family'.[108] It is suggested that the most relevant type of third party interest would be the interests of any *children* in the presumed father's family although if it could be demonstrated that any adult relationships could be adversely affected by such a claim they would also have to be taken into account.

Is there any Conflict between a Child's Right to Determine Paternity and that of a Father's?

In all the cases discussed above concerning claims brought by children to determine paternity, the claims were brought once they themselves had reached adulthood. It should also be noted that the Court found that a breach of their Article 8 rights had occurred in all the cases where a claim was made. This, in turn, is due to the clear significance that the ECtHR has attached to the vital interest, protected by the Convention, in receiving the information necessary to uncover the truth about an important aspect of their personal identity.[109] Furthermore, the Court has stated that the right to an identity, which includes the right to know one's parentage, is an integral part of the notion of private life[110] and it is regarded as so important that the Court has gone so far as stating that particularly rigorous scrutiny is called for when weighing up the competing interests.[111] However, it should also be noted that the third party

---

[104] *Ibid*, para 38.

[105] *Ibid*, para 39.

[106] The Court also noted that in any event, the deceased's body will be exhumed when the current lease expires in 2016. The right to rest in peace therefore enjoys only temporary protection. With regard to the deceased's own right to respect for his private life, the Court referred to its position in *Estate of Kresten Filtenborg Mortensen v Denmark* Application No 1338/03 [2006] ECHR paras 41–2, in which it found that the private life of a deceased person from whom a DNA sample was to be taken could not be adversely affected by a request to that effect made after his death.

[107] *Phinikaradou* (n 96).

[108] *Ibid*, para 53.

[109] *Jaggi* (n 102) para 38; *Phinikaradou* (n 96) para 53; *Mikulic* (n 99) para 64.

[110] *Jaggi* (n 102) para 37.

[111] *Ibid*, para 37.

interests of any children of the putative fathers in these cases were not pleaded and one can only speculate as to the impact any such interests may have had on the outcomes.

Do these cases present any difficulty with the principles established by the Court concerning claims brought by natural fathers for the determination of their paternity? We have seen that the interests of children have not always been expressly considered in cases where a breach of the Article 8 rights of the natural father has been upheld. The clear assumption here has been that the interests of the children will coincide with those of the applicant. However, as the discussion above demonstrates, in the cases where the father's application to determine paternity has been denied and a breach of Article 8 has *not* been found it has been done precisely upon the basis of the children's interests. It is clear, therefore, that the Court does not consider that the right to determine paternity is *always* in the interests of the children involved.

Establishing Paternity under UK Law

Leeds Teaching Hospital NHS Trust v A[112] confirmed the position in UK law that a man is the father of a child who is genetically related to him. However, the ability to determine genetic fatherhood as a certainty via DNA testing is a relatively recent phenomenon and, thus, prior to the availability of such methods the law relied on certain legal presumptions of paternity. These presumptions are still of relevance as they will set out the legal position with regard to the fatherhood of a child if these tests have not been carried out.

There are four circumstances in which fatherhood will be presumed. The first is where the *pater est quem nuptiae demonstrant* presumption applies, that is if a married woman gives birth it is presumed that her husband is the father of the child.[113] The presumption will still apply even if the conception took place before the marriage but the birth took place during it and if it is clear[114] that the conception took place during a marriage, even if death or divorce has ended that marriage by the time the birth occurs.[115] The continued relevance of the presumption has, however, unsurprisingly been put in doubt[116] by the availability of DNA testing.

Second, the law presumes that if a man's name appears on the birth certificate of a child, he is the child's father.[117] However, as Bainham[118] has noted, the way that the UK birth

---

[112] *Leeds Teaching Hospital* (n 28).

[113] *Banbury Peerage Case* (1811) 1 Sim & St 153 (HL). The Lord Chancellor's Department (1999) suggested that the *pater est* presumption should be put on a statutory footing. The presumption does not apply in cases of disputed fatherhood under the Child Support Act 1991 s26 or to unmarried cohabitants. It does to parties in a void marriage: Legitimacy Act 1976 s1.

[114] The court will refer to the normal gestation period, although there has been some difficulty in defining this, eg *Preston-Jones v Preston-Jones* [1951] AC 391 (HL).

[115] There will, therefore, as Herring has noted, be conflicting presumptions if the child could have been conceived during a first marriage but is born during the course of the wife's second marriage. It is not clear who the law would regard as the father in such a situation. Herring suggests that the second husband should be regarded as the father, it being more likely that he is the genetic father. He is also the man who would act in the parental role during the child's upbringing. J Herring, *Family Law* 4th edn (Harlow, Longman, 2009) ch 7.

[116] *Re H and A (children)* [2002] 2 FCR 469 (Thorpe LJ) stated that 'as science has hastened on and as more and more children are born out of marriage it seems to me that the paternity of any child is to be established by science and not by legal presumption of inference' (at 479).

[117] Births and Deaths Registration Act 1953 (BDRA) s34(2).

[118] A Bainham, 'What is the Point of Birth Registration?' [2008] *Child and Family Law Quarterly* 449.

registration system operates may, in the case of married couples, actively work against the truth being told where the mother knows that her husband is not the biological father. This is due to the fact that, unlike the unmarried mother, a married mother cannot jointly initially register the birth of the child with a man other than her husband. This will be the case even where that man and/or the husband are in complete agreement on the matter. The only way in which a registrar will agree to register a man other than her husband as the father will be if she provides clear proof of alternative paternity. Although this may be problematic it is unlikely to cause any compatibility issues with the ECHR given that, where a man believes himself to be the father, he has the ability to prove his genetic father-hood by DNA sampling where all the parties are willing to co-operate or by making an application to the court for a declaration of his paternity which may or may not involve DNA testing. This would satisfy the ECtHR's general requirement that fathers are given at least one opportunity to bring a claim for paternity and, either way, if it is proved that he is indeed the father then the husband's name will be removed from the register and his inserted by means of a correction.[119] The UK birth registration system could also, as Bainham[120] demonstrates, be said to operate against the interests of fathers of children born to an unmarried mother. The registration of a father born to an unmarried mother can, at present, only take place if a certain set of circumstances exists. These circumstances are effectively dependent upon the co-operation of the mother as it is her sole right and duty to register the birth. The only circumstance that does not require her co-operation is if he has obtained a declaration of paternity from the court. It should be noted, however, that the government is proposing[121] the establishment of a system of joint registration of births to unmarried mothers where the duty to register will fall to both mother and father subject to certain exemptions to protect the vulnerable.[122] In particular, a man would be able to register himself as the father of a child even where the mother does not wish this.[123] In order to do this, however, her acknowledgment of his fatherhood would be required as well as an assessment of any evidence against his registering. If the acknowledgment is not forthcoming or there is significant evidence against his registration he will have to obtain a declaration of paternity from the courts in order to be registered as the father. Although this does not grant an absolute right to register as a father of a child, it nevertheless goes some way to address some of the concerns that have been raised. It is difficult to see how any remaining differentials between married and unmarried fathers in this respect could fall foul of the ECHR given the application of a wide margin of appreciation in cases where such differentials have been justified on the basis of the child's interests.[124]

Third, in *R v Secretary of State for Social Security, ex p West*[125] it was suggested that a paren-tal responsibility order by consent could be regarded as evidence of paternity by the Child Support Agency. Finally, the court may also infer paternity simply from the facts of the case and evidence adduced regarding the couple's behaviour around the time of conception.

---

[119] BDRA, s29.

[120] A Bainham, 'What is the Point of Birth Registration?' (n 117) 455.

[121] Welfare Reform Bill (2009–10) 32.

[122] For the argument that this list of exemptions should be restrictively applied to further the child's interest, see A Bainham, 'What is the Point of Birth Registration?' (n 117) at 460.

[123] See also J Wallbank, 'Bodies in the Shadows, Joint Birth Registration, Parental Responsibility and Social Class' (2009) 21 (2) *Child and Family Law Quarterly* 1 for a critique of these proposals.

[124] In helping to distinguish between meritorious and non-meritorious fathers—see *McMichael v UK* Application No 16424/90 (1995) 20 EHRR 205.

[125] *R v Secretary of State for Social Security, ex p West* [1999] 1 FLR 1233.

Rebutting the Presumptions under UK Law

These presumptions are, however, capable of rebuttal,[126] and as already discussed with regard to the system of birth registration the most reliable method[127] of doing so is by seeking a court direction for genetic testing under section 20 of the Family Law Reform Act 1969. If a man is shown to be the father of the child through genetic tests then he is legally the father of the child, and if another man was presumed to be the father he is no longer so regarded. The refusal by a man to undergo genetic tests may also lead to a presumption that he is the legal father and will be held to strengthen the presumption of legitimacy.[128]

In deciding whether to order tests, the paramountcy principle does not apply because the child's upbringing is not in question. Instead, the test is as set out by the House of Lords in *S v S; W v Official Solicitor (or W)*:[129] 'the court ought to permit a blood test of a young child to be taken unless satisfied that that would be against the child's interests'.[130] The case law on whether tests should be ordered demonstrates, as Herring[131] has noted, that the courts view the matter as involving two conflicting interests: the child's right to know their genetic origins and the interests of the family unit which may be disrupted and, in turn, cause harm to the child.

The leading case in favour of not ordering tests is *Re F (A Minor) (Blood Test: Parental Rights)*.[132] Here, the mother had conceived the child at a time when she was having sexual relations with both her husband and the applicant. The mother's relationship with the applicant ended before the birth and the child was at all times since then treated as a child of the family by the mother and her husband. The applicant had had no contact with the child but subsequently applied for parental responsibility and contact orders in respect of her, on the basis that he was her natural father, which the mother denied. The mother gave evidence to the effect that the mother's marriage would be harmed and the security of the child's upbringing would be diminished if the blood tests showed the applicant to be the father. On appeal by the father, the Court of Appeal upheld the decision of the lower court; the child's interests lay in the continued stability of the family unit and these concerns outweighed any interests that she may have had in knowing the outcome of the blood tests:

> [W]here a child is conceived and brought up in an existing marriage as a child of the family, and the association of the mother with a man who claims to be the putative father has terminated well before the birth of the child, and such association co-existed with sexual relations with the husband, a court should decline to exercise its discretion to order a blood test for DNA profiling under s20.

---

[126] Section 26 of the Family Law Reform Act 1969 states that the legal presumptions can be rebutted on the balance of probabilities. Moreover, in *S v S; W v Official Solicitor (or W)* [1972] AC 24 it was suggested that the presumptions should be regarded as weak, and could be rebutted with little evidence. Subsequently in *Re Moynihan* [2000] 1 FLR 113 a higher standard of proof was suggested, but the Court of Appeal in *Re H and A (Children)* [2002] 2 FCR 469 preferred *S v S*.

[127] The other way of rebuttal would be to introduce evidence to undermine the logical basis of the presumption by, for examples as Herring suggests, introducing evidence that he was abroad at the time of the alleged conception or that he was impotent.

[128] Section 23(1) of the Family Law Reform Act 1969 states that if a person fails to take a biological test, the court will draw inferences from that refusal as to paternity. See *F v CSA* [1999] 2 FLR 244. See also *Secretary of State for Work and Pensions v Jones* [2003] EWHC 2163 (F).

[129] *S v S* (n 126).

[130] As summarised in *Re F (A Minor) (Blood Test: Parental Rights)* [1993] Fam 314, 318; see also J Fortin, *Children's Rights and the Developing Law* 3rd edn (Cambridge, Cambridge University Press, 2009).

[131] J Herring, *Family Law* (n 114) chs 7 and 8.

[132] *Re F* (n 130), as discussed in J Fortin, *Children's Rights* (n 130).

The child's welfare in this case was therefore regarded as being 'inextricably bound up with the welfare of the family unit of which she forms part'. Although the case did not include a specific examination of the conflicting rights and interests of all the parties concerned, some form of balancing exercise was clearly undertaken by the court. The case was, of course, decided prior to the passage of the HRA but this did not preclude a discussion of the ECHR jurisprudence on the issue, and, rather surprisingly, despite its obvious relevance, it was not discussed by the courts or pleaded by any of the parties. What was discussed, however, was the effect of Article 7 of the CRC, which provides for the child to have 'as far as possible, the right to know and be cared for by his or her parents'. This matter was raised by the applicant on the child's behalf but was rather summarily dismissed by the Court of Appeal, Balcombe LJ noting:[133]

> Whether or not B is included in this definition of a parent within the meaning of this article, it is not in fact possible for E to be cared for by both her parents (if B is such). No family unit exists, or has ever existed, between B and Mrs F, and if B were able to assert his claims to have a share in E's upbringing it would inevitably risk damaging her right to be cared for by her mother.

However, three years later the Court of Appeal appeared to reverse its position on Article 7 of the CRC. In *Re H (A Minor) (Blood Tests: Parental Rights)*[134] the mother gave birth to a son conceived at a time when she was having sexual relations with both her husband, who had had a vasectomy operation five years earlier, and the applicant. A few months before the birth of the child she ended her relationship with the applicant and had subsequently brought the child up with her husband and their two children. The applicant, believing himself to be the natural father of the child, applied for contact and parental responsibility orders in respect of the child and, if paternity was disputed, for DNA tests. The wife, supported by the husband, opposed the applications for contact and parental responsibility orders, and refused to consent to the use of blood testing to establish paternity on the ground that it would be detrimental to the child's welfare. The case was further complicated by the fact that the mother had disclosed to her eldest child that another man was the father of his new brother.[135] At first instance, it was held that it would be better in the interests of the child to order the use of blood tests than not to do so. The mother's appeal against the decision was also dismissed on the basis that 'every child has a right to know the truth unless his welfare clearly justifies the cover-up'.[136] In direct contrast to the court's earlier decision in *Re F*,[137] the basis of the right could now be found in Article 7 of the CRC.[138] Referring to Balcombe LJ's comments in *Re F*[139] above, Ward LJ said:[140]

> That passage concentrates on the child's right to be cared for by his or her parents. I do not read it as refuting what to me seems the clear intent of the article that there are two separate rights, the one to know, and the other to be cared for by, one's parents.

---

[133] *Re F* (n 130) 321.

[134] *Re H (A Minor) (Blood Tests: Parental Rights)* [1996] 3 FCR 201.

[135] She had done this because at that time she had apparently been thinking of ending her marriage and moving the applicant into her home.

[136] *Re H (A Minor) (Blood Tests: Parental Rights)* [1996] 2 FLR 65, 80 (Ward LJ).

[137] *Re F* (n 130).

[138] The importance of ascertaining the truth was emphasised by the Court of Appeal in *Re H and A (Children)* [2002] 1 FLR 1145.

[139] *Re F* (n 130).

[140] *Re H* (n 134) 107.

The fact that the husband had had a vasectomy and the elder child had been told that he may not be the father of the child in question meant, therefore, that it was unrealistic to pretend that the child would not at some point in the future face doubts about his paternity. It was better, therefore, to have the issue resolved now than for the child to find out later.[141] Again, at no point was the ECHR referred to throughout the judgment.

What brought about this shift in the court's approach is quite evident, a growing movement for recognition of the child's right to know their genetic origins heavily influenced by research pertaining to the psychological need for information which enables one to ascertain and preserve one's identity[142] and the negative experiences of adopted children who had had the truth hidden from them.[143] Research demonstrating how crucial a child's knowledge of her background to the formation of a positive self-identity[144] was thus used to argue that the disclosure of such information should override any claims by parents to withhold the truth from their children.[145] The ground was thus ripe for legislative reform following the implementation of the HRA and thus, following the discussion in *Re O and J (Paternity: Blood Tests)*[146] of the possible incompatibility of the Family Law Reform Act 1969 (FLRA) with Article 8, because it did not give a court the power to direct paternity tests where the carer did not consent, came the decision to amend it in order to make this possible. It was unsurprising, therefore, that the first of these cases to specifically discuss the impact of Article 8 was also the first case to be decided after the amendment was passed. In *Re T (A Child) (DNA Tests: Paternity)*,[147] although the correct procedure in terms of addressing Article 8 was not followed,[148] Bodey J nevertheless correctly identified that a balancing of the competing Article 8 rights of all the parties must be undertaken, noting that in doing so the crucial importance of the rights and best interests of the child fell particularly to be considered. He concluded that:[149]

> For the reasons set out above, under the heading 'Domestic law' (which are equally apposite here) I am entirely satisfied that in evaluating and balancing the various rights of the adult parties and of T under Article 8, the weightiest emerges clearly as being that of T, namely that he should have the possibility of knowing, perhaps with certainty, his true roots and identity.

These reasons were, first, that doubts about the child's paternity were already in the public domain, giving rise to a significant risk that the child would be informed about them sooner rather than later. Second, the relationship between the mother and her husband was a stable one and both were already aware of the paternity doubts and, finally, blood tests (depending on how they turned out) might actually determine the applications for

---

[141] This case has been followed in several other cases, eg *Re G (Parentage: Blood Sample)* [1997] 2 FCR 325.

[142] M Freeman, 'The New Birthright? Identity and the Child of the Reproductive Revolution' (1996) 4 *International Journal of Children's Rights* 273 and J Masson and C Harrison, 'Identity: Mapping the Frontiers' in N Lowe and G Douglas (eds), *Families Across Frontiers* (The Hague, Martinus Nijhoff, 2006) 277.

[143] KW Ruyter, 'The Example of Adoption' in D Evans (ed), *Creating the Child: The Ethics, Law and Practice of Assisted Procreation* (The Hague, Martinus Nijhoff, 1996) 177.

[144] J Triselotis, *In Search of Origins: The Experiences of Adopted People* (London, Routledge, 1973).

[145] S Maclean and M Maclean, 'Keeping Secrets in Assisted Reproduction—the Tension Between Donor Anonymity and the Need of the Child for Information' (1996) 8 (3) *Child and Family Law Quarterly* 243.

[146] *Re O and J (Paternity: Blood Tests)* [2000] 1 FLR 418. See also J Wallbank, 'The Role of Rights and Utility in Instituting a Child's Right to Know her Genetic History' (2004) 13 SLS 245 for a discussion of the case.

[147] *Re T (A Child) (DNA Tests: Paternity)* [2001] 2 FLR 1190.

[148] The balancing exercise under Art 8(2) was discussed before the applicability of Art 8. He also failed to consider that the applicant's right to private life would be engaged by the application if his family life could not.

[149] *Re T* (n 147) 1197 (Bodey J).

contact and parental responsibility. All three led him to the conclusion that it would be in the best interests of the child to order that tests take place. Thus, by explicitly undertaking a balancing exercise in relation to the competing rights involved and addressing the proportionality of the measure, the decision in *Re T*[150] represents, to date, the most compatible approach with that of the ECtHR. This is because the approach taken in that case was one which demonstrated *on the facts* how the case could be distinguished from that of *Re F*[151] where, in line with ECHR jurisprudence, not enough reasons existed, from the perspective of the child's best interests, to challenge the protection of the family's right *not* to be told the truth of her origins. Thus, contrary to Ward LJ's statement in *Re H*[152] when discussing *Re F*[153] that 'it is seldom useful in a case which depends on the exercise of judicial discretion to attempt to draw factual similarities between cases'[154] this is, in fact, precisely what the courts are required to do when undertaking the balancing exercise under Article 8 in a manner compatible with that of the ECtHR.

The approach of both *Re F*[155] and *Re T*[156] has subsequently been followed[157] in cases where the particular facts of the case demonstrate that ordering tests may not be in best interests of the child; however, mention of the HRA or the ECHR is notably absent from these cases. In *Re D (Paternity)*[158] what seemed to have particularly influenced the court in refusing the application were the very strong views expressed by the 11-year-old child involved against the tests being undertaken. Nonetheless Hedley J made clear that he was departing from the general approach:[159]

> [T]he general proposition that truth, at the end of the day, is easier to handle than fiction and also it is designed to avoid information coming to a young person's attention in a haphazard, unorganised and indeed sometimes malicious context and a court should not depart from that approach unless the best interests of the child.

Thus, as Fortin[160] has pointed out, current case law suggests that putative fathers will have little difficulty in obtaining directions for genetic testing to take place. Indeed such was the court's commitment to revealing the truth in one case that it granted an injunction to prevent a mother (who was seeking to avoid the carrying out of tests) leaving the country.[161] What is most concerning about such case law, however, is that it is the approach of the court in *Re H*[162] rather than *Re F*[163] or *Re T*[164] that has become entrenched. An approach which, as we have seen, fails to fully consider the balancing exercise under Article 8 and, more importantly, fails to give the same recognition that has been given by the ECtHR to the importance of the stability of the family within which the child is being brought up.

---

[150] *Ibid.*
[151] *Re F* (n 130).
[152] *Re H* (n 134).
[153] *Re F* (n 130).
[154] *Re H* (n 134) 106.
[155] *Re F* (n 130).
[156] *Re T* (n 147).
[157] *Re K (Specific Issue Order)* [1999] 2 FLR 280; *J v C* [2006] EWHC 2837 (F).
[158] *Re D (Paternity)* [2006] EWHC 3545 (F).
[159] *Ibid*, para 22.
[160] J Fortin, *Children's Rights* (n 130) 398.
[161] *Re E (A Minor) (Blood Tests: Parental Responsibilities)* [1993] 3 All ER 596.
[162] *Re H* (n 134).
[163] *Re F* (n 130).
[164] *Re T* (n 147).

This failure was graphically illustrated by another Court of Appeal decision in *Re H and A (Children)*.[165] Here, following an extra-marital affair, the wife gave birth to twins. She informed the man that he was the father, and gave him some contact. However, the husband, who knew nothing of the affair, believed that he was the father of the twins and became their primary carer when the wife went out to work. Following a quarrel with the wife the man brought a paternity action, which the wife successfully concealed from the husband for almost one year. The wife refused consent to a blood test. By the time of the trial the husband had, by accident, become aware of the action, although he was not aware at this stage of the extent of the wife's relationship with the man. The husband gave evidence that he would be very likely to leave the family home if the blood tests established that he was not the father of the twins. As a result the trial judge refused to give the court's consent to a blood test, on the basis in part that there was a risk that the test would damage the twins' family life.[166] In doing so, he sought to distinguish the facts of the case from those of *Re H*[167] and *Re T*:[168]

> The balancing exercise therefore that I have to conduct is to weigh the advantage of scientific truth against uncertainty, to consider the interest that the community has in establishing such certitude on the one hand and on the other hand the possible, and I believe, my finding, probably disastrous disintegrative effects of a finding that Mr B in fact is the father. I bear in mind my impressions in relation to all the other matters. This to my mind is a case very different from that of Re H and Re T that I have mentioned. In Re H the mother's husband had undergone a vasectomy, in Re T the husband suffered a very low sperm count and there was the near certainty that he was infertile. This is a very, very different case and in all the circumstances, conducting that balancing exercise as carefully as I can, I come to the conclusion that the application for tests should be dismissed.[169]

The Court of Appeal, however, allowed the appeal on the basis that the trial judge had erred in not placing enough emphasis on the need for certainty. In doing so, they expressly disapproved of his attempt to undertake the difficult balancing exercise of the two conflicting interests at play: the certainty of knowledge and the stability of the family unit. The issue was one of principle rather than the more nuanced approach of Article 8 to the individual facts of a case:

> I do not consider that that factual distinction begins to displace the points of principle to be drawn from the cases, first that the interests of justice are best served by the ascertainment of the truth and second that the court should be furnished with the best available science and not confined to such unsatisfactory alternatives as presumptions and inferences.

Given that under the ECHR the right to knowledge of one's genetic identity is not absolute and can be displaced by the interests of others the transformation of the right into an adjudicatory principle by the UK courts is difficult to justify by reference to the Convention alone. The situation has been further exacerbated by the fact that the UK courts have employed at best a selective view of ECtHR jurisprudence on the matter and at worst ignored it. One reason for this may be the courts' usage of Article 7 of the CRC.

---

[165] *Re H and A (Children)* [2002] 1 FLR 1145.
[166] It appears that this reference to family life was in the general sense and no reference to Art 8 was made.
[167] *Re H* (n 134).
[168] *Re T* (n 147).
[169] *Re H and A* (n 165) para 16 (Thorpe LJ).

As noted above, this is one convention that has consistently been referred to in most of the cases concerning paternity tests in the UK. Although this is not necessarily a bad thing, the convention has, after all, been ratified by the UK. What is surprising, however, is that this has apparently been done *instead* of referring to a convention that has actually been incorporated into UK law, the ECHR. Doing this becomes even more problematic when we consider that the CRC alone is perhaps not the best convention to refer to when dealing with the conflict of interest that is apparent in an application for DNA testing. As Besson[170] reminds us, Article 7 of the CRC does not settle the issue of which among the child's interests should prevail in case of conflict between the interest to know the truth of her origins and the interest in remaining in her undisturbed existing family unit. Nor does it provide any criteria as to how to balance the child's interests with those of others in case of conflict, such as the mother and her husband or indeed any siblings. There is also some argument that the right contained in Article 7 may be qualified by the need to take into account any conflicting rights stemming from national and other international human rights obligations. It is unlikely, however, as Besson[171] argues, that this situation will be clarified by the Committee of the Rights of the Child due to the fact that there is no mechanism for individual petition under the CRC and there has been no trace in any of the committee's recommendations of principles that could guide the balancing of the right of the child to know and any conflicting interests when that conflict has not been resolved by the national authorities. Although far from perfect, the ECHR and the jurisprudence of the ECtHR appear to be far more capable, as an international human rights instrument, to deal with the conflicts raised by the right to know when compared to the CRC. Although concepts such as the margin of appreciation and its supranational nature prevent the Court from commenting specifically on how individual cases have been resolved, the ECtHR has nonetheless produced a set of guiding principles which can help domestic courts to navigate the resolution of the conflict of interests that are present in such cases. It is of some concern, therefore, that the UK courts have elevated the importance of Article 7 of the CRC over the incorporated convention rights guaranteed by the HRA.

The Removal of Donor Anonymity

In light of the discussion above, mention must be made here of the removal of donor anonymity pursuant to the Human Fertilisation and Embryology Authority (Disclosure of Donor Information) Regulations 2004.[172] As a result, children born from sperm, eggs or embryos donated after April 2005 have the right to know the donor's identity.[173] Aside from debates concerning whether the legislation represents a misguided shift towards the elevation of genetic parenthood or that it has not gone far enough in terms of respecting the child's right to know the truth of her origins by, for example, imposing a corresponding duty upon the parents of such children to tell them how they were conceived, it seems to

---

[170] S Besson, 'Enforcing the Child's Right to Know Her Origins: Contrasting Approaches Under the Convention on the Rights of the Child and the European Court of Human Rights' (2007) 21 *International Journal of Law, Policy and the Family* 137.

[171] *Ibid*, 150.

[172] SI No 1511.

[173] SI No 1511 paras 2, 3.

have been erroneously accepted in the literature that such legislation was required in order to fully comply with the child's right to know the truth of her genetic origins. This may have been partly due to concern expressed by the Committee on the Rights of the Child[174] that children born as a result of assisted fertilisation in the UK do not have the right, as far as possible, to know the identity of their biological parents. The Committee thus recommended that, in light of Articles 3 and 7 of the CRC that the UK state 'undertake all necessary measures to allow all children irrespective of the circumstances of their birth or adoptive children to obtain information on the identity of their parents as far as possible'.[175] Quite how important this aspect of UK law actually was to the Committee is a moot point; its most recent report[176] reviewing the UK's compliance with the CRC is notable for the Committee's failure to specifically refer to the removal of donor anonymity within the UK at all. Nevertheless, as discussed above, it is certainly arguable that compliance with the Committee's recommendations in this regard may well be contrary to the UK's obligations with respect to other international human rights obligations. In addition to concerns that the Committee has failed to consider the possibility of any conflicting interest of both the child and other members of her existing family, it has also been argued[177] that, in any event, Article 7 could be read in conjunction with Article 3 in a manner which would allow the imposition of limits upon the child's right to know in cases where it would be contrary to the child's interests. It should also be added that the words 'as far as possible' are open to interpretation and could further allow for consideration of any conflict with the rights of others.

Although the ECtHR has not faced the question of donor anonymity directly, it has provided some indication of how it would deal with claims concerning the use of new technologies with regard to reproduction and how to balance the conflicting interests of the children and the genetic parent who wishes to remain anonymous. In *X, Y and Z*,[178] considered above, the Court made it clear that a wide margin of appreciation would be accorded to Member States in how they deal with respecting the rights of parties involved in the use of such technologies. Furthermore, from the discussion above it is clear that the right of the child to knowledge of her origins is not an absolute one and must be balanced against any conflicting interests. This was something that was specifically discussed and acknowledged by the UK judiciary before donor anonymity was removed. In *Rose v Secretary of State for Health and Human Embryology Authority*,[179] the applicant, who had been born by artificial insemination, sought judicial review of decisions of the Secretary of State and the HFEA, which refused her requests for access to non-identifying information and, where possible, identifying information in respect of anonymous sperm donors and for the establishment of a voluntary contact register. However, as the government was giving serious consideration to its recently published consultation document on the removal of donor anonymity, certain issues in the litigation were stood over pending ministerial decisions on the appropriate government response. The court was therefore asked

---

[174] Committee on the Rights of the Child, Second Concluding Observations Report on the UK (2002).
[175] *Ibid*, para 32.
[176] Third and Fourth Concluding Observations Reports on the UK (2008).
[177] R Hodgkin and P Newell, *The Implementation Handbook for the Convention on the Rights of the Child* (New York, UNICEF, 2002) ch 7 as discussed by S Besson, *Enforcing the Child's Right to Know* (n 170).
[178] *X, Y and Z* (n 3).
[179] *Rose v Secretary of State for Health and Embryology Authority* (2002) EWHC 1593 (Admin).

specifically to consider the question of whether Article 8 of the ECHR was engaged by the claim.[180] After reviewing the relevant ECHR and domestic jurisprudence, Scott Baker J concluded that Article 8 was engaged both with regard to identifying and non-identifying information, commenting that it was 'entirely understandable that AID children should wish to know about their origins and in particular to learn what they can about their biological father or, in the case of egg donation, their biological mother'.[181] However, he also made the important point that this did not necessarily result in the right to *all* the available information relating to the donor:

> What is wanted is non-identifying information and a voluntary contact register. I do emphasise, lest there be any doubt about it, that the fact that Article 8 is engaged is far from saying that there is a breach of it.[182]

And then:

> The distinction between identifying and non-identifying information is not relevant at the engagement stage of Article 8, but it is likely to become very relevant when one comes to the important balancing exercise of the other considerations in Article 8(2).[183]

The removal of donor anonymity across Member States is by no means in the majority with only Sweden, Norway and the Netherlands having done so. A consensus amongst Member States with respect to the issue has thus far from been established. It is unlikely, therefore, that the ECtHR would require a Member State to implement such legislation in respect of complying with its positive obligations under Article 8 towards the children born of such donors as long as there was some mechanism for ensuring that the domestic authorities can undertake a proper balancing of the conflicting interests involved in any request for such information.[184] Research on the impact of the removal of donor anonymity in those countries where anonymity has been removed is mixed, but recent evidence demonstrates that the Netherlands and Norway have seen a reduction in the number of donors.[185] Few studies are available as to the impact of donor anonymity removal in the UK due to the relatively recent change in policy. However, there is some evidence to suggest that the impact on donor numbers in the UK has been a negative one.[186] In a recent article Turkmendag *et al*[187] have also demonstrated that contrary to what was stated by the government at the time, support for a change in the law was not uniform or fully sought out and was dominated by a rather questionable analogy with adoption. If this is indeed the case this would mean that the number of donors has been reduced to a dangerously low level in pursuance of an erroneous belief that to have left the law as it is would be incompatible with the child's right to know the truth.

---

[180] This is because if it was found that Art 8 was engaged it would be necessary at any adjourned hearing to go on and consider the balancing exercise under Art 8(2) and whether Art 8 has been breached: *ibid*, para 20 (Scott Baker J).

[181] *Ibid*, para 47 (Scott Baker J).

[182] *Ibid*, para 46 (Scott Baker J).

[183] *Ibid*, para 47 (Scott Baker J).

[184] *Odièvre v France* (2004) 38 EHRR 43.

[185] I Turkmendag, R Dingwall and T Murphy, 'The Removal of Donor Anonymity in the UK: The Silence of Claims by Would-be Parents' (2008) 22 *International Journal of Law, Policy and the Family* 283.

[186] According to a recent BBC investigation and current HFEA records of registered donors. See also *ibid*, 296–7.

[187] *Ibid*.

Motherhood

Gestation and the ECHR

The closest the ECtHR has come to referring to the concept of motherhood has been in referring to the 'natural tie' between mother and child, which will, in itself, give rise to family life between them.[188] This should also be the case if the birth comes about via assisted conception—as long as it is the gestational mother who is claiming family life. The key issue is therefore who has given birth, as, once this has occurred, family life will be established even where a child has been given up for adoption shortly after.[189] In contrast, although the ECtHR has not yet been faced by any such claims, non-gestational mothers, so called 'psychological' mothers, should be able to demonstrate their intention to create family life by proving the existence of close and personal ties between themselves and the child as discussed above. As with fathers, close relationships that fall short of establishing 'close ties' will fall under 'private life'.[190] Although this should not in reality create too much difficulty for those who are actively caring for a child, biological motherhood will nonetheless be placed at the top of the evidential hierarchy and remain privileged as a means of demonstrating the intention to create family life.

The Court is, however, yet to specifically consider a claim arising from a woman who may be genetically related to the child but is not the gestational mother. If the woman merely donated her egg in order to assist someone else to give birth and bring up a child it is likely that the Court will regard this as insufficient to establish family life between her and any resulting child. In *JRM v the Netherlands*[191] the Commission viewed sperm donated to facilitate assisted conception for the benefit of a lesbian couple as insufficient to establish family life despite the fact that the sperm donor had had weekly contact with the child for the first eight months of its life. The main reason given for this decision was that the Commission considered the contact to have been limited both in time and intensity. An aggravating factor also appears to have been that he had failed to make any contribution, financial or otherwise, to the child. However, this reasoning seems at odds with the application of the 'close and personal ties' test, which had been established with regard to non-cohabiting fathers. The real reason, it is suggested, for the Commission's reluctance to hold that family life was in existence must be that they preferred the account given by the lesbian couple in which they contended that although they intended the child to 'know' its father it was *never intended* that the sperm donor should actively play that role. These issues should help to settle the question of whether or not family life has been established; however, what has not yet been deliberated upon by the ECtHR is whether the lack of biological link with the child would make any difference in terms of the positive obligations upon the state to facilitate contact or indeed residence between the non-biological parent and child should

---

[188] *Marckx v Belgium* Application No 6833/74 (1979) 58 ILR 561 paras 31–2.
[189] *Kearns v France* Application No 35991/04 [2008] ECHR.
[190] This was the view taken in *Znamenskaya* (n 26), where the Court considered that a complaint from a mother that she was unable to amend her stillborn child's birth certificate to reflect the patronymic name and surname of his late father was a matter concerning her private life. This was because she must have developed a strong bond with the embryo that she had almost brought to full term and that she had also expressed the desire to give him a name and bury him. The establishment of his descent therefore 'undoubtedly affected her private life'.
[191] *JRM* (n 6).

the relationship between the two partners break down. To recall, it is well established in the Court's case law that the mutual enjoyment by parent and child of each other's company constitutes a fundamental element of family life, and domestic measures hindering such enjoyment can amount to an interference with the right protected by Article 8 of the Convention.[192] Thus, there may be, in addition, positive obligations inherent in effective 'respect' for private or family life.[193] It is difficult to see, however, how such a distinction could be justified as once the existence of a family tie has been established, the state must, in principle, act in a manner calculated to enable that tie to be developed and take measures that will enable a parent and child to be reunited.[194] We must also remind ourselves that where such obligations have been developed, they are not absolute. Thus, in the context of reunifying a parent and a child on the breakdown of the parental relationship the Court has made clear the need to take into account the interests as well as the rights and freedoms of all concerned and, more particularly, the best interests of the child and his or her rights under Article 8 of the Convention. Where contact with the parent might appear to threaten those interests or interfere with those rights, it is for the national authorities to strike a fair balance between them.[195] This fair balance will be subject to the principle of proportionality and the margin of appreciation.

The matter will thus turn upon whether the Court would regard any privileging of the biological parent as a legitimate enough reason to interfere with the Article 8(1) rights of the non-biological parent and whether such privileging is a proportionate response. Factors which would be relevant to the width of the margin accorded in such circumstances would undoubtedly be the European consensus factor and the legitimacy of the aim. It is arguable, however, as to how far a state can seek to rely on a wide margin of appreciation in an area where, as in the UK, it has also legislated to facilitate equality in status between non-biological and biological parents; quite apart from the obvious implications such legislative policy will have for the credibility of the argument that a privileging of biology is a legitimate aim.

Anonymous Birth

There is, however, one exception to the centrality of the question of who has given birth when determining family life and that is where a state allows for anonymous birth such as in France.[196] The crucial point to note is that, unlike under English law, the act of giving birth is not enough in itself to confer the legal status of motherhood.[197] Indeed, the French Civil Code approaches the question negatively; providing for *how* legal maternity can be established or annulled rather than expressly providing for *who* should be regarded as the legal mother of the child.[198] Thus, on giving birth, the mother may request that her

---

[192] Eg *Johansen v Norway* (1997) 23 EHRR 33 para 52.

[193] *X and Y v the Netherlands* (1986) 8 EHRR 235.

[194] Eg *Eriksson v Sweden* [1990] 12 EHRR 183 para 71; *Gnahoré v France* Application No 40031/98 (2002) 34 EHRR 38 para 51.

[195] *Ignaccolo-Zenide v Romania* Application No 31679/96 ECHR 25 January 2000 para 94.

[196] Under the 'births by an unidentified person' (*accouchement sous X*) system.

[197] Article 310-1 French Civil Code provides that legal affiliation is established by registration, acknowledgement, apparent status or judicial establishment. See also C Forder and K Saarloos, 'The Establishment of Parenthood—A Story of Successful Convergence?' Maastricht Faculty of Law Working Paper No 2007/1.

[198] *Ibid*, 8.

admission to hospital and identity shall remain secret, which, in turn, will create an estoppel defence to proceedings to establish maternity. There is, therefore, no mother in the legal sense of the word and, moreover, the surest evidence, on the part of the mother, *not* to create family life between herself and the child. The ECtHR's response has therefore been to hold that, where mothers have taken advantage of such a procedure, the natural parental tie and thus family life will not have been formed between mother and child.[199] As a result, where applications have been made by the (now adult) child concerning the identity of the mother, the Court has viewed the birth, and in particular the circumstances in which the child was born, as part of the child's, and subsequently the adult's, *private* life. The intention to create family life thus resurfaces as an important determining factor for the establishment of family life, except here, under the anonymous birth system, giving birth alone will be evidentially insufficient. Mothers under such systems will be required to give birth *and* comply with official procedures concerning the legal establishment of mother-hood[200] and, by doing so, will demonstrate the best evidence of the intention to enter into family life with the child. Choosing to exercise the option of anonymous birth and thereby rejecting the official means by which legal motherhood can be established demonstrates exactly the opposite—a *lack* of intention to create family life with the child, something that in *Odièvre*[201] was further demonstrated by the mother's conduct:

> In the present case, the applicant's mother never went to see the baby at the clinic and appears to have greeted their separation with total indifference … nor is it alleged that she subsequently expressed the least desire to meet her daughter. The Court's task is not to judge that conduct, but merely to take note of it.[202]

It is arguable, however, that by making reference to her conduct in this way, the Court in *Odièvre*[203] left open the possibility that had she formed an attachment with the child by visiting or expressing regret at her removal. This could have demonstrated some evidence of intentionality that could perhaps have overridden her decision to enter into anonymous birth. However, until that is specifically considered by the ECtHR, it is clear that entering into anonymous birth is treated as effective evidence of a lack of intention to create family life between mother and child.

Although anonymous birth is available in only a few of the Member States, the principles that were established in *Odièvre*[204] could, however, have application to situations in Member States that make no such provision. One potential consequence of the significance attached to the legal establishment of motherhood by the ECtHR is in the evidentiary advantage this should give to non-gestational mothers who have nonetheless obtained legal recognition of their status as mothers. Thus, surrogate or adoptive mothers should be able to demonstrate their intention to create and, therefore, the existence of family life with their child by virtue of obtaining the relevant court orders alone.[205]

---

[199] *Odièvre* (n 184).
[200] If by registration, this must take place within three days of the birth.
[201] *Odièvre* (n 184).
[202] *Ibid*, para 3.
[203] *Ibid*.
[204] *Ibid*.
[205] See ch 8, pp 336–9 for a further discussion of anonymous birth in the context of adoption.

Establishing Motherhood in the UK

In the UK, legal motherhood is a rather straightforward matter, the determining factor here being one of gestation rather than genetics.[206] Thus as section 33 of the HFE Act 2008 sets out, it is only the woman who is carrying or has carried a child as a result of the placing in her of an embryo or of sperm and eggs, and no other woman, who is to be treated as the mother of the child. Such is the importance of gestation to the English concept of motherhood that this is the case even where conception takes place as a result of egg donation. Egg donation will not in itself make a woman the parent of a child carried by another woman.[207] However, unlike the ECtHR, no one approach to parenthood can easily be discerned, particularly as English law employs the concept of parental responsibility in addition to that of parenthood which widens the category of people who may act in a parental role towards a child. Both statute and case law thus demonstrate evidence of a number of approaches such as intentionality and function as well as the application of certain legal assumptions and principles all of which serve to produce a somewhat confused picture. There are some reasonably clear conclusions to be drawn, however. One is that, if there is a hierarchy of motherhood, it is clear that it is the gestational mother who is placed at the top, the psychological and the genetic following after. This can be evidenced by examining the application of the law to women who have conceived during a same-sex relationship. Here, in accordance with the HFE Act, the woman who has given birth will be regarded as the 'mother' even where the other partner has contributed the egg. Although the new HFE Act has now made provision for the other partner to be regarded as the 'second legal parent', a clear indication has recently been given by the courts that this legislative vision of equality is yet to be fulfilled; gestation appears to have retained its ability to trump both genetic and psychological motherhood. In *Re G (Children)*[208] the House of Lords were faced with a dispute over residence and contact involving a lesbian couple who had made the conscious decision to have children together and arranged for anonymous donor insemination at a clinic abroad. They had both gone on to bring the children up together until their relationship broke down. Baroness Hale considered the first of two issues of principle that she felt fell for consideration as being the weight that ought to be attached to the fact that one party is both the natural and legal parent of the child and the other is not. She then went on to set out, in a now well-quoted extract, how, in her view, there were three ways in which a person could become a 'natural' parent, these being genetic, gestational and psychological. The difficulty here was that the partner in this case was neither a genetic nor a gestational parent of the two children involved and the dispute had arisen over the gestational mother's clear disobedience of a court order requiring her to remain resident in Leicester in order to facilitate contact between the children and her former partner by her subsequent relocation to Cornwall. After a consideration of the types of 'natural parent' and despite conceding that she had 'behaved very badly', the court ordered a reversal of the Court of Appeal's order, which had transferred residence of

---

[206] By HFE Act 2008 s33 the woman who is carrying or has carried a child as a result of the placing in her of an embryo or of sperm and eggs, and no other woman, is to be treated as the mother of the child.

[207] HFE Act 2008 s47, although parenthood can be conferred by other legal provisions.

[208] *Re G (Children)* [2006] UKHL 43.

the children from the gestational mother to her former partner. Baroness Hale's reasoning was as follows:[209]

> I am driven to the conclusion that the courts below have allowed the unusual context of this case to distract them from principles which are of universal application. First, the fact that CG is the natural mother of these children in every sense of that term, while raising no presumption in her favour, is undoubtedly an important and significant factor in determining what will be best for them now and in the future. Secondly, while it may well be in the best interests of children to change their living arrangements if one of their parents is frustrating their relationship with the other parent who is able to offer them a good and loving home, this is unlikely to be in their best interests while that relationship is in fact being maintained in accordance with the court's order.

While the case has been commented upon a great deal for the obvious significance this judgment has for the status of same-sex parents and their children,[210] there are three points to note in particular for our purposes. First, there is the apparent elevation of the value of genetic fatherhood over genetic motherhood. When discussing the types of natural parent, Baroness Hale discussed the significance of genetic parenthood almost entirely from the point of view of the gametes provider despite the fact that the reasons she specified could equally have applied to egg donors in a same-sex relationship:[211]

> The first is genetic parenthood: the provision of the gametes which produce the child. This can be of deep significance on many levels. For the parent, perhaps particularly for a father, the knowledge that this is 'his' child can bring a very special sense of love for and commitment to that child which will be of great benefit to the child. For the child, he reaps the benefit not only of that love and commitment, but also of knowing his own origins and lineage, which is an important component in finding an individual sense of self as one grows up. The knowledge of that genetic link may also be an important (although certainly not an essential) component in the love and commitment felt by the wider family, perhaps especially grandparents, from which the child has so much to gain.

Second, Baroness Hale provides us with a significant insight into why gestational motherhood is privileged:[212]

> The second is gestational parenthood: the conceiving and bearing of the child. The mother who bears the child is legally the child's mother, whereas the mother who provided the egg is not: 1990 Act, s 27. While this may be partly for reasons of certainty and convenience, it also recognises a deeper truth: that the process of carrying a child and giving him birth (which may well be followed by breast-feeding for some months) brings with it, in the vast majority of cases, a very special relationship between mother and child, a relationship which is different from any other.

It can be seen therefore that this 'deeper truth', which arises by virtue of the period of gestation and birth, is closely related to the concept of the 'natural tie' referred to by the ECtHR discussed earlier. Finally, the judgment is noteworthy for providing a clear definition of

---

[209] *Ibid*, para 44 (Baroness Hale).
[210] See also 'Get over your (legal) "self": a brief history of lesbians, motherhood and the law' (2008) 30 (2) *Journal of Social Welfare and Family Law* 95; J Millbank, 'The limits of functional family: lesbian mother litigation in the era of the eternal biological family' (2008) 22 (2) *International Journal of Law, Policy and the Family* 149 and A Diduck, 'If only we can find the appropriate terms to use, the issue will be solved: law, identity and parenthood' [2007] 19 (4) *Child and Family Law Quarterly* 458.
[211] *Re G* (n 208) para 43 (Baroness Hale).
[212] *Ibid*, para 34 (Baroness Hale).

psychological parenthood, a definition that, again, has similarities with the 'close, personal ties' test of the ECtHR:[213]

> The third is social and psychological parenthood: the relationship which develops through the child demanding and the parent providing for the child's needs, initially at the most basic level of feeding, nurturing, comforting and loving, and later at the more sophisticated level of guiding, socialising, educating and protecting.

However, where the decision parts company with the approach of the ECtHR is in its apparent approval of an approach which, all other things being equal, effectively gives 'the edge' to the biological parent in any residence dispute which involves a non-biological parent. In *Re G*, the respective positions of both parents were rather artificially equalised; the significance of the biological mother's clear flouting of a court order in the recent past was downplayed on the basis that contact since her unauthorised relocation had been complied with.

Had this case been decided in accordance with Article 8—and the judgment is notable for its failure to mention either the HRA or the ECHR—the process of reasoning would have been very different. As discussed in earlier Chapters, the Court would start with establishing whether or not the Article 8 rights of both parents had been engaged. It is clear from the discussion above that both parents here would have been able to establish family life and prima facie, the need for the state to fulfil its positive obligations towards her in ensuring that contact was facilitated. Could the non-biological mother have complained that the House of Lords' decision failed to adequately respect her Article 8 rights by not awarding her residence of the children? As there appears to be a conflict of Article 8 rights in this case, the parallel analysis would need to be employed. The Court should consider the parent's right to respect for his or her private and family life as creating an exception to the right to respect for private and family life of the child, under Article 8(2). The parent's right should prevail only where the tests of necessity and proportionality are satisfied. Equally, the Article 8(1) rights of the child should be considered as an exception to those of the parent, again demanding that the same tests are satisfied.

The key point is that this apparent policy of 'biology is best where possible' as a means of ensuring the best interests of the child would need to be *justified*. As we know, in the case of qualified Articles this question will be decided by reference to three factors: is the interference 'in accordance with the law'? Is the interference done to secure one of the legitimate aims in the Article? Is the interference necessary in a democratic society?

Given that the government has indicated its commitment to the equal treatment of same-sex couples by its recent introduction of the concept of the 'legal second parent' it is difficult to see how these questions, if the case was being decided now, could be answered in the positive. In addition, both partners in this case had shared residence of the children and it is certainly arguable that a change in residence would not necessarily have been *against* their best interests given the circumstances of the case. It is questionable, therefore, whether the courts can continue to employ such distinctions in light of their own section 6 obligations under the HRA and more importantly, whether this constitutes an area in which they ought to defer to the clear intention of the legislature which has been to equalise the position of same-sex parents.[214]

---

[213] *Ibid*, para 35 (Baroness Hale).
[214] If the matter was looked at by the ECtHR, the margin of appreciation would be employed. Here, it is less likely that the court would intervene in the decision as it has made clear that on custody issues a wide margin

Surrogacy and Deceased Mothers

In *Re B*,[215] discussed above, we saw a male donor who was also the uncle of the child seeking a number of section 8 orders. The UK courts are yet to be faced with a similar claim from, say, a female donor who has donated her egg to a male same-sex couple. If this case did arise, it is suggested that the court should employ the same analysis as set out above in relation to *Re B*. That is, family life has not been established between the female donor and the child because of a lack of intention to become a main carer of that child.

The Partner Egg Donor

What would the position be, however, for the female same-sex *partner* who is not giving birth? What is clear, from the discussion in relation to fathers above, is that regardless of whether she has donated the egg the key factor which should fall for consideration in establishing family life between her and any resulting child is the existence of a joint intention of creating a child together with her partner and, more particularly so, where both partners have been involved in actively caring for the child after the birth. Such partners may be able to demonstrate this intention by virtue of complying with the provisions of the new HFE Act 2008 where, under section 42, a woman who is a civil partner of the woman undergoing artificial insemination will be treated as the 'second legal parent' of any resulting child unless it can be demonstrated that the partner did not consent to the treatment. Those women who are not in a civil partnership will have to satisfy the 'agreed female parenthood conditions' set out in section 44 if they wish to be recognised as a second legal parent of the child. These conditions, as with the agreed fatherhood conditions, are dependent upon the ongoing and active consent of the partner. As with male partners who have fulfilled the fatherhood conditions, the fact that the woman has fulfilled the agreed female parenthood conditions under the HFE Act may well be sufficient to create a legal tie between her and the resulting child and may also serve to demonstrate a close and personal relationship between the two.[216]

Deceased Female Parents

The ECtHR has not dealt with any claims arising in relation to a deceased female parent or female civil partner but it is suggested that due to the lack of a European consensus on how such parents are to be treated in this situation it is likely to accord a wide margin of appreciation on the matter. Fortunately, the position in the UK has been settled by section 46 of the HFE Act 2008, which will obviate the need for any such claim to be made on the parents' behalf. This section essentially enables the child born after the death of a deceased female parent or civil partner to be treated as the parent of that child and to be registered as such.

---

will be applied in recognition of the fact that a domestic court is best placed to make such decisions. However, a stricter scrutiny is called for where there are 'any legal safeguards designed to secure an effective protection of the right of parents and children to respect for their family life'. It is certainly arguable that by granting residence to this mother the court was not effectively ensuring her continued custody. See also *Görgülü* (n 16) para 42.

[215] *Re B* (n 31).
[216] In *Lebbink* (n 1) the court referred to the absence of 'any further legal or factual elements indicating the existence of a close personal relationship' as a factor in holding that family life had not been created between a biological father and his child.

The Relationship between Children and their Parents under the ECHR

We can extrapolate a number of principles from those applied to mothers and fathers as outlined above. Children will have family life with their mothers by virtue of the birth relationship, unless their birth was under a system that preserves the anonymity of the mother. They will have family life with their fathers only if they have established close and personal ties with him, the best way being by cohabitation together as a family unit. Where there has been no such cohabitation, if close and personal ties have been established by other means such as regular contact, family life will be established. The requirement for the establishment of close and personal ties should thus facilitate the recognition of family life in relation to all other relationships pertaining to the child such as step-parents, grandparents, uncles and siblings. The advantage of the close-tie approach is also, of course, that it facilitates the recognition of anyone who has acted as psychological parent towards the child.

Parents and Respect for Family Life

Bringing an Application under the Children Act 1989

A parent's ability to bring an application in relation to his child could, of course, in general, engage issues relevant to Article 8. Any examination under the Article would first necessitate an examination of whether family life existed between the potential applicant and the child before deciding upon whether any legislative restrictions upon bringing an application had unjustifiably interfered with his Article 8 rights. The fact that UK law does not restrict the ability to bring an application under Section 8 of the CA to the 'natural' (biological) parent alone, is clearly in line with ECtHR case law. In addition, by enabling any party to a marriage who has treated the child as a 'child of the family' or any person with whom the child has lived for at least three years to apply for a residence or contact order in relation to that child,[217] the CA also effectively allows for those who can establish the intention to create family life to make an application, on the basis of evidence relating to both form *and* function. Those individuals who do not come within these categories may still have the ability to apply for any section 8 orders provided that the leave of the court has been obtained. The question of leave is governed by section 10(9) of the CA where a number of factors are to be considered, the most relevant[218] of which are the nature of the proposed application; the applicant's connection with the child; and any risk there might be of that proposed application disrupting the child's life to such an extent that he would be harmed by it. These factors are clearly significant in their potential for demonstrating both the legitimate aim and the justifications for any interference in the Article 8 rights of the applicant where family life has been established. However, given that it is cohabitation and the existence of 'close, personal ties' with the child which is of most relevance to the ECtHR in establishing family life between a father and child, section 10,

---

[217] Under the CA, s10.

[218] An additional factor is s10(9)(d), where the child is being looked after by a local authority: (i) the authority's plans for the child's future; and (ii) the wishes and feelings of the child's parents.

as it currently stands, could arguably unjustifiably interfere with the Article 8 rights of a non-biological father who is not married to the mother of the child but who has spent less than three years living with them both. This analysis could also be applied to a non-biological mother who is in the same position with respect to a child. In other words, imposing a time limit on cohabitation with the child according to which the necessity to apply for leave is decided could arguably constitute a disproportionate interference with the Article 8 rights of non-biological parents where family life has been established with that child. Why should someone who has spent two years and 11 months living with the child have to make an application for leave to apply when someone who has lived with the child for one further month does not? It is difficult to see the legitimate aim and justification for the imposition of such an arbitrary time limit and this particular provision could be regarded as incompatible with Article 8 as a result. The solution is not one that could be achieved under section 3 of the HRA as it would require legislative amendment, as what is necessary is the removal of the time limited category and the reference to 'any party to a marriage'. In other words, the ability to make an application without leave would be granted as of right to those who have treated the child as a 'child of the family'. This could be evidenced by way of cohabitation or a demonstration of commitment and contact sufficient to establish 'close, personal ties' between the individual and the child. In the event of any disagreement on the matter it would be left to the court to decide, on the facts.

Does 'Respect' Extend to Establishing a Right to Assisted Conception?

This issue is discussed in detail in Chapter 2 as an example of the application of the concepts of deference and proportionality. Suffice to say that discussion makes it clear that if such a right exists it is capable of limitation. In terms of the right to fertility treatment under the NHS[219] this will be because any such claims will involve significant resource implications for the state. It is also clear that the state is not required to facilitate an individual's ability to procreate where this represents a disproportionate interference in the rights of others[220] or where the interference with this right can be justified as being in the interests of national security.[221] However, the ECtHR has recently made it clear that where the right is being interfered with without a demonstration of an adequate assessment of the proportionality of it, it is likely to be held to be a breach of the ECHR.[222]

Parental Rights and Responsibility

Parental Responsibility

The question of parental rights in UK law is a complicated one, covering a number of areas that concern the upbringing of a child such as the naming of the child, its education and its religion. The impact of the ECHR upon parental rights in respect of these issues

---

[219] *R (On the Application of Assisted Reproduction and Gynaecology Centre and H) v HFEA* [2002] Fam Law 347.

[220] *Evans v UK* Application No 6339/05 (2006) 43 EHRR 21.

[221] In terms of not having to provide the right to conjugal visits for prisoners see *R v Secretary of State for the Home Department, ex p Mellor* [2000] 3 FCR 148.

[222] *Dickson v UK* Application No 44362/04 (2007) 44 EHRR 21.

will be dealt with in detail in Chapter 7. What is clear from that discussion is that the ability to exercise such rights is not necessarily dependent upon the existence of parental responsibility. Who obtains parental responsibility has been the subject of much criticism[223] mainly because the CA originally ensured that unmarried fathers could not obtain parental responsibility without, effectively, the consent of the mother or the court. The fact that most fathers were unaware of this undoubtedly added to the pressure for reform.[224] As a result, the CA[225] was amended and now provides that an unmarried father will obtain parental responsibility by jointly registering the birth of the child with the mother. This reform, although welcome, did not resolve the issues that had been raised; the preference for married fathers continues to be reflected in the legislation. The reform has also raised issues from the point of view of the children. One result of the reform was, as Eekelaar[226] has noted, to create three categories of children all of whom have slightly different legal relationships with their parents. First, marital children, second, non-marital children with 'birth certificate fathers' and third, non-marital children whose fathers are not identified on their birth certificates. Fortin[227] has added a fourth group, created by the fact that the amendment to the CA is not retrospective. These children, born before the reforms, and despite their fathers' name being recorded on their birth certificates, will be treated the same as Eekelaar's third group. More reform is afoot: in a recent White Paper[228] the government has proposed a further change in the law, which seeks to establish a norm of joint registration of births to unmarried mothers by requiring justification for a sole registration. This will not, however, equalise the position between married and unmarried fathers completely.[229]

Is the law in this area compatible with the ECHR? The issue has been specifically considered by the ECtHR and it seems that it is, largely due a wide margin of appreciation being accorded on the issue[230] and, as a result, the Court has held that the difference in treatment between married and unmarried fathers with respect to the awarding of parental responsibility automatically to unmarried fathers does not constitute a breach of Articles 8 or 14.[231] In *B v the United Kingdom*,[232] an unmarried father applied for parental responsibility and other orders; however, the mother took the child to Italy. The father then unsuccessfully sought the child's return under the Hague Convention on the Civil Aspects of International Child Abduction 1980, the Court having concluded that the father had no formal rights of custody. The father brought a complaint to the ECtHR on the basis

---

[223] N Lowe, 'The Meaning and Allocation of Parental Responsibility—A Common Lawyer's Perspective' (1997) *International Journal of Law, Policy and the Family* 192; J Eekelaar, 'Rethinking Parental Responsibility' (2001) *Family Law* 271; and R Probert, S Gilmore and J Herring, *Parental Responsibility* (n 10).

[224] See Lord Chancellor's Department (LCD), *Guidelines for Good Practice on Parental Contact in Cases where there is Domestic Violence* prepared by the Children Act Sub-Committee of the Lord Chancellor's Advisory Board on Family Law (2002) and research conducted by R Pickford, 'Unmarried Fathers and the Law' in A Bainham, S Day Schlater and M Richards (eds), *What is a Parent?* (n 9).

[225] CA s4(1)(a) as inserted by the Adoption and Children Act 2002.

[226] J Eekelaar, 'Rethinking Parental Responsibility' (n 223).

[227] J Fortin, *Children's Rights* (n 130) 390.

[228] Department for Work and Pensions and Department for Children, Schools and Families, *Joint Birth Registration: Recording Responsibility* Cm 7293 (TSO, 2008).

[229] A Bainham, 'What is the point of Birth Registration?' (n 117) for a critical review of the effect of these proposals.

[230] *McMichael v UK* (n 123) para 98.

[231] See J Fortin's discussion of the issue in *Children's Rights* (n 130) 390–4.

[232] *B v the United Kingdom* [2000] 1 FLR 1.

that his rights as an unmarried father were not protected in the same way as those of a married father. In declaring the application inadmissible the Court held that in relation to applications brought under the Hague Convention there was an objective and reasonable justification why F, who merely had contact with the child, should not be treated as being on an equal footing with an applicant who had the child in his care. They considered that a father having parental responsibility for a child bore different responsibilities from those of a father having only the right of contact with the child. There had been no discrimination as between married and unmarried fathers. The Court stated:[233]

> It is true that under the Children Act 1989 married fathers have parental responsibility automatically, while unmarried ones need to acquire it in accordance with the provisions of the Act. However, the Court has considered that the relationship between unmarried fathers and their children varies from ignorance and indifference to a close stable relationship indistinguishable from the conventional family-based unit (*McMichael v UK*). For this reason the Court has held that there exists an objective and reasonable justification for the difference in treatment between married and unmarried fathers with regard to the automatic acquisition of parental rights.

Accordingly, the different treatment of the applicant was not in breach of Article 14 of the ECHR. The likelihood of any further challenges being successful, given the reforms in the area since the case was decided, is therefore extremely low.

Parental Rights—The Right to Administer Punishment?

There are a number of rights exercisable by a parent in relation to a child and an assessment of the impact of the ECHR has been considered in relation to disputes concerning children, covered in Chapter 7, and child protection, covered in Chapter 8. However, the extent to which a parent has the right to administer corporal punishment upon a child is one area in which the jurisprudence of the ECtHR has had significant impact upon UK law and has not yet been addressed. The extent of the right will now be examined in detail.

The Development of the Law

As early as 1860, in the seminal case of *R v Hopley*,[234] it was made clear that the right of a parent to administer corporal punishment in the UK was not an unfettered one but, in fact, subject to some regard for proportionality:

> If it [the punishment] be administered for the gratification of passion or rage or if it be immoderate or excessive in its nature or degree, or if it be protracted beyond the child's power of endurance or with an instrument unfit for the purpose and calculated to produce danger to life and limb [then] the punishment is unlawful.[235]

However, despite a number of reforms along the way, a defence of 'reasonable and moderate' punishment remained a defence to any civil or criminal liability of a parent or a teacher *in loco parentis* administering such punishment to a child right up until the 1970s. A series of

---

[233] *Ibid*, para 5.
[234] *R v Hopley* (1860) 2 F & F 202.
[235] *Ibid*, 206 (Cockburn CJ).

challenges at the ECtHR soon changed the situation, however,[236] and corporal punishment was finally banned from all schools in England and Wales in 1998.[237] The right of the parent to administer physical chastisement within the home, however, remained. What is particularly significant is that despite its clear leanings towards the rights of children and the introduction of the concept of parental responsibility the CA had no effect upon the continued availability of the common law defence of 'reasonable chastisement'[238] to parents. Any 'parent' charged with *any* offence under the Offences Against the Person Act 1861 (OAPA) (ranging from s18 wounding with intent to s39 common assault) could therefore utilise the defence with regard to criminal charges brought in relation to the physical punishment of their children, albeit subject to the requirement of reasonableness. However, there was significant evidence to suggest that 'reasonable' was being 'interpreted by juries and the courts to cover a range of behaviour that many people would consider went beyond a 'loving smack'.[239] It was the decisions of the ECtHR and other international pressure that were to pave the way for further reform. For, once it had been decided that a responsible parent ought not to allow corporal punishment of their child at school, sufficient to engage Article 3 type treatment, it was not such a great leap to the next logical conclusion that a responsible parent ought not to administer the same kind of corporal punishment to the same child within the home. In 1995 the UN Committee on the Rights of the Child, after examining the UK's first report under the CRC, expressed concern at the existence of the 'reasonable chastisement' defence and the level of violence against children in the UK and recommended the prohibition of all corporal punishment in the family.[240]

The United Kingdom has, of course, ratified but not incorporated the CRC; nevertheless, its influence is still strong, particularly within the ECtHR. Article 19 of the CRC, for example, in which states are enjoined to take all appropriate measures 'to protect the child from all forms of physical or mental violence, injury or abuse', was specifically referred to by the European Commission in its decision in the case of *A v the United Kingdom*.[241] Here, a nine-year-old child applicant complained that the government had failed to protect him from degrading treatment carried out towards him by his stepfather. The applicant had been beaten with a garden cane on two or more occasions in the course of one week and at least some of the strokes were inflicted directly onto the bare skin causing him significant bruising. The stepfather was subsequently charged with assault occasioning actual bodily harm pursuant to section 47 of the OAPA, but he was not held liable for his

---

[236] *Tyrer v the United Kingdom* (1978–80) 2 EHRR 1; *Campbell and Cossans v the United Kingdom* [1982] 4 EHRR 293; *Maxine and Karen Warwick v the United Kingdom* [1986] DR 60; *Y v the United Kingdom* [1992] Series A No 247; *Costello- Roberts v the United Kingdom* (1995) 19 EHRR 112, which concerned a public school; and *A v UK* (1999) 27 EHRR 61.

[237] Education Act 1996 ss548–549 as inserted by the School Standards and Framework Act 1998 s131.

[238] *Hopley* (n 234) (Cockburn CJ).

[239] See para 99 of the JCHR's report on the UN Convention on the Rights of the Child (Session 2002–03) Tenth Report.

[240] '[T]he Committee is worried about the national legal provisions dealing with reasonable chastisement within the family. The imprecise nature of the expression of reasonable chastisement as contained in these legal provisions may pave the way for it to be interpreted in a subjective and arbitrary manner. Thus, the Committee is concerned that legislative and other measures relating to the physical integrity of children do not appear to be compatible with the provisions and principles of the Convention, including those of its articles 3, 19 and 37' 15 February 1995, CRC/C/15/Add.34 paras 16, 31 and 32.

[241] *A v UK* (n 236).

actions[242] thanks to his successful use of the defence of reasonable parental chastisement. The Commission noted the comments made by the English judge in the criminal proceedings in his summing up to the jury:

> What is it the prosecution must prove? If a man deliberately and unjustifiably hits another and causes some bodily injury, bruising or swelling will do, he is guilty of actual bodily harm. What does unjustifiably mean in the context of this case? It is a perfectly good defence that the alleged assault was merely the correcting of a child by its parent, in this case the stepfather, provided that the correction be moderate in the manner, the instrument and the quantity of it. Or, put another way, reasonable. It is not for the defendant to prove it was lawful correction. It is for the prosecution to prove it was not.[243]

While acknowledging that, unlike the cases concerning corporal punishment administered by a teacher, no direct responsibility could attach to the UK under the Convention for the acts of the applicant's stepfather, the Commission recalled that it had previously held that, even in the absence of any direct responsibility for the acts of a private individual under Article 3 of the Convention, state responsibility may nevertheless be engaged through the obligation imposed by Article 1 of the Convention 'to secure ... the rights and freedoms defined in Section 1 of this Convention'. The ECtHR subsequently followed the reasoning of the Commission when it upheld its decision. The Court considered that the availability of the 'reasonable chastisement' defence to a charge of assault on a child and the fact that the burden of proof was on the prosecution to establish beyond reasonable doubt meant that the assault went beyond the limits of lawful punishment. This had therefore made it possible for the jury to acquit the child's stepfather, despite the fact that the applicant had been subjected to treatment of sufficient severity to fall within the scope of Article 3. The Court found that as UK law had not provided adequate protection to the applicant against treatment or punishment contrary to Article 3, his Article 3 rights had been breached.

The reaction of the UK government, unlike after Costello, was *not*, however, to effect an immediate change in the law. Although the UK government had, during the course of the case, accepted that the law currently failed to provide adequate protection to children and should be amended, it did nothing towards achieving further change other than publishing a consultation document upon the issue[244] and, arguably, passing the HRA. In particular, section 2 of the HRA requires courts, when determining a question which has arisen in connection with a Convention right, to take into account Convention law, which includes the judgments and declarations of the ECtHR, opinions of the European Commission of Human Rights and decisions of the Committee of Ministers of the Council of Europe. Further, section 3 provides that all legislation must, as far as it is possible to do so, be read and given effect in a way that is compatible with the Convention rights. This applies to all legislation whenever enacted.

Regardless of whether the government had intended the HRA to form the catalyst for a change in the law it soon became clear that the courts had decided to comply with their duties under it before it had even come into force. In *R v H (Assault of Child: Reasonable*

---

[242] Of assault occasioning actual bodily harm pursuant to the OAPA s47.

[243] *A v UK* (n 236) para 19.

[244] This ruled out the possibility of an outright ban of corporal punishment by parents. See *Protecting Children, Supporting Parents: A Consultation Document on the Physical Punishment of Children* (Department of Health, 2000) para 1.5.

Chastisement)[245] the Court of Appeal took the opportunity to take into account the decision in *A v the United Kingdom*[246] and, more specifically, the criteria that were referred to by the ECtHR in order to establish whether or not the treatment administered crossed the threshold of entry into Article 3:

> The assessment of this minimum level of severity depends on all the circumstances of the case. Factors such as the nature and context of the punishment, the manner and method of its execution, its duration, and its physical and mental effects and, in some instances, the sex, age and state of health of the victim must all be taken into account.[247]

However, as has been noted by a number of authors,[248] the Court erroneously went further than the ECtHR in seemingly extending the criteria to include the reasons for the punishment. Although questions of motive or reason for parental chastisement could lead to a higher likelihood of conviction if the punishment appeared disproportionate to the 'wrong' being chastised or if they could be regarded as generally unworthy, they could also easily water down the protection afforded by the decision of the ECtHR in *A v UK*[249] by potentially leading to further acquittals from juries sympathetic to the reasons given, even where the threshold of treatment had crossed that of Article 3. More importantly, however, questions of motive are, as far as the ECHR is concerned, irrelevant when considering whether the treatment comes within the ambit of Article 3. What is of most concern under Article 3 are questions that relate directly to the severity of the punishment. The confidence in which the Court of Appeal professed this 'incremental development' of the law as being compatible with Convention case law was seemingly misplaced. This was confirmed by a number of international reports critical of the state of the law, which concluded that even if the development of the common law in this manner was correct it was still not enough to satisfy the obligations created by a number of international treaties and conventions.[250] The government's response to the pressure was, however, to resist amendments[251] which would have introduced a complete ban on the physical chastisement of children and instead to support an amendment which would limit the availability of the reasonable chastisement defence for parents to the offence of common assault alone. This was despite the fact that the JCHR[252] issued a report urging a complete abolition of the defence of 'reasonable chastisement' in order to meet human rights obligations under three international treaties.[253] However, regardless of such objections, the Children Act 2004 (CA 2004) was passed with the amendment intact and contained in section 58 but, significantly, with a commitment that the government would review the practical consequences of the section and seek parents' views

---

[245] *R v H (Assault of Child: Reasonable Chastisement)* [2002] 1 Cr App R7.

[246] *A v UK* (n 236).

[247] The Court referred to para 30 of the judgment in *Tyrer v UK* (n 236).

[248] J Rogers, 'A Criminal Lawyer's Response to Chastisement in the European Court of Human Rights' [2002] *Crim LR* 98; R Smith, 'Hands-Off Parenting? Towards a Reform of the Defence of Reasonable Chastisement in the UK' (2004) 16 (3) *Child and Family Law Quarterly* 261 and H Keating, 'Protecting or Punishing Children: Physical Punishment, Human Rights and English Law Reform' [2006] 26(3) *Legal Studies* 394.

[249] *A v UK* (n 236).

[250] See S Choudhry, 'Parental Responsibility and Corporal Punishment' in S Gilmore, J Herring and R Probert, *Parental Responsibility* (n 10).

[251] For a comprehensive account of the passage of the Bill see H Keating, 'Protecting or Punishing Children: Physical Punishment, Human Rights and English Law Reform' [2006] 26 (3) *Legal Studies* 394.

[252] JCHR, Nineteenth report on the Children's Bill (2003–04 Session) paras 118–77.

[253] The UN Convention on the Rights of the Child, the International Covenant on Economic, Social and Cultural Rights and the European Social Charter.

on smacking two years after its commencement. Of particular note is that the definition of 'parents' within the context of section 58 remained the same, that is, parents and adults acting *in loco parentis*, excluding those expressly prohibited (such as teachers and childminders). Thus there is no requirement that the 'parent' exercising the corporal punishment should hold parental responsibility for the child. Further changes in the practical application of the law came shortly after the passage of the Act when the Crown Prosecution Service amended the charging standard on offences against the person. The standard now states that the vulnerability of the victim, such as being a child assaulted by an adult, should be treated as an aggravating factor when deciding the appropriate charge. Injuries that would normally have led to a charge of common assault are not to be charged as assault occasioning actual bodily harm under section 47 of the OAPA, under which the defence of reasonable punishment will not be available. Furthermore, in January of 2006 the UK's four Children's Commissioners[254] called upon the government and the Scottish Executive to introduce legislation that would ban the defence of reasonable chastisement/punishment throughout the UK.

It has now been two years since section 58 of the CA 2004 has been in force and the government recently published its promised review of the section following a consultation exercise. The report[255] notes at the outset that a substantial majority of the respondents said that section 58 had not improved legal protection for children and that the defence should be removed in its entirety. However, these responses were rather summarily dismissed on the basis that no evidence was offered for these views and that they were simply statements of belief.[256] Some concessions were made: 'much of the evidence gathered suggests that there is a lack of understanding about the law'[257] which referred, it is presumed, to evidence contained in the review that the CPS had in some cases allowed the defence to be raised where it should not have been made available and that a number of agencies said that the legal position on physical punishment is not well understood by parents and made it difficult for practitioners to work with them.[258] In order to rectify this, the government states in the review that the CPS will issue a bulletin to their staff reminding them of section 58 and will ask them to continue to monitor the use of the defence. Ultimately, the review concludes that through the enactment of section 58, the UK has met its international obligations under Article 3 of the ECHR and will retain the current law in its present form in the absence of evidence that it is not working satisfactorily.

In short, despite considerable domestic and international opposition the Government is sticking to its guns on the preservation of the parental right to administer 'reasonable punishment' albeit in much more limited form. Moreover, its conduct since *A v UK*[259] has demonstrated that it is not interested in the philosophical, theoretical or sociological arguments for and against the smacking of children and whether it can ever be in the interests of children. It resists a change in the law in pure doctrinal reliance of the fact that the current state of the law does not represent any problems of incompatibility. The next section will examine, in detail, if this is the case.

---

[254] Letter to Ruth Kelly, Secretary of State for Education, *The Times*, 21 January 2006.
[255] The review of the Children Act 2004 s58 by the DfES can be viewed at www.dfes.gov.uk/publications/section58review/.
[256] *Ibid*, paras 20–6.
[257] *Ibid*, paras 48.
[258] *Ibid*, paras 25–6, 37–8.
[259] *A v UK* (n 236).

Is the Parental Defence of Reasonable Punishment Compatible with the ECHR?

It is of significance that when the government talked of compatibility in its recent review of section 58 it did so in relation to the ECHR alone. As detailed above, the current law on corporal punishment could be said to be in breach of a number of other international conventions that the UK has entered into, these being the CRC,[260] the International Covenant on Economic, Social and Cultural Rights (ICESCR)[261] and the European Social Charter (ESC).[262] Indeed, the JCHR stated as much when it concluded that:

> Although clause 49 achieves a greater degree of compatibility with the UK's obligations under the CRC by restricting the scope of the reasonable chastisement defence, by preserving it as a defence to common assault it does not achieve full compatibility with the UK's obligations under the CRC as interpreted by the UN Committee on the Rights of the Child, or under the ICESCR, as interpreted by the Committee on Economic, Social and Cultural Rights, or under the European Social Charter, as interpreted by the European Committee of Social Rights.[263]

However, none of these instruments, although significant, have been incorporated and thus the UK is under no legal obligation to change its law. It is the ECHR, alone, which is binding upon the UK. So, it is to the ECHR that questions of compatibility must be addressed.

The Applicability of Article 3

Generally speaking, Article 3 imposes primarily a negative obligation on states to refrain from inflicting serious harm on persons within their jurisdiction. Most cases involving Article 3 and the infliction of corporal punishment had, therefore, prior to the decision in *A v UK*,[264] involved state agents or public authorities inflicting treatment on individuals.[265] However, the Court had been developing a certain level of flexibility in addressing the application of Article 3 within the 'private context'[266] and this flexibility was further developed by

---

[260] Articles 19 and 37. Article 19(1) states: 'States Parties shall take all appropriate legislative, administrative, social and educational measures to protect the child from all forms of physical or mental violence, injury or abuse, neglect or negligent treatment, maltreatment or exploitation, including sexual abuse, while in the care of parent(s), legal guardian(s) or any other person who has the care of the child'. Article 37 contains the equivalent of Art 3 ECHR and states: 'States Parties shall ensure that: (a) No child shall be subjected to torture or other cruel, inhuman or degrading treatment or punishment'.

[261] The UN Committee on Economic, Social and Cultural Rights has interpreted the ICESCR as imposing the same obligation to prohibit physical punishment of children in families. Specifically, Art 10.1 states: 'The widest possible protection and assistance should be accorded to the family, which is the natural and fundamental group unit of society, particularly for its establishment and while it is responsible for the care and education of dependent children. Marriage must be entered into with the free consent of the intending spouses.' And Art 10.3 states: 'Special measures of protection and assistance should be taken on behalf of all children and young persons without any discrimination for reasons of parentage or other conditions. Children and young persons should be protected from economic and social exploitation. Their employment in work harmful to their morals or health or dangerous to life or likely to hamper their normal development should be punishable by law. States should also set age limits below which the paid employment of child labour should be prohibited and punishable by law.'

[262] The European Committee of Social Rights, which monitors compliance with the European Social Charter, has also interpreted Art 17 of that instrument as requiring a prohibition of physical punishment of children, in light of the position under the CRC. Article 17 concerns the right of children and young persons to social, legal and economic protection.

[263] JCHR Report (n 252) para 161.

[264] *A v UK* (n 236).

[265] *Tyrer v the United Kingdom* (n 236).

[266] *D v the United Kingdom* (1997) 24 EHRR 423 para 49.

the Court in *A v UK*[267] (detailed above) in recognising that the state can be under positive obligations to protect one individual from having their rights under Article 3 infringed by another individual.[268] It was for this reason that in *A v UK*[269] the Court held that not only was the level of severity of the punishment of the child sufficient to constitute inhuman or degrading treatment, but also that the responsibility of the state was engaged under Article 3 in respect of the acts of private individuals. However, it is also clear that although Article 3 is drafted in absolute terms, the *duties* imposed by these positive obligations are not. It is for this reason that the Commission in *A v UK*[270] was able to state explicitly that corporal punishment of children is not per se a violation of Article 3 of the ECHR:

> The Commission would emphasise that this finding does not mean that Article 3 is to be interpreted as imposing an obligation on States to protect, through their criminal law, against any form of physical rebuke, however mild, by a parent of a child.[271]

Further, in *Z v the United Kingdom*[272] and *E v the United Kingdom*,[273] two cases decided after *A v UK*,[274] the Court set out further guidance as to the nature and extent of positive obligations under Article 3 in relation to claims under English civil law. In its judgments the Court reiterated the principle that states should provide effective protection in relation to children and vulnerable adults, particularly where the authorities had or ought to have had knowledge of abuse.[275]

> The test under Article 3 however does not require it to be shown that 'but for' the failing or omission of the public authority ill-treatment would not have happened. *A failure to take reasonably available measures which could have had a real prospect of altering the outcome or mitigating the harm* is sufficient to engage the responsibility of the State[276] [emphasis added].

Thus, if, the state can show that it has taken all reasonably available measures to provide effective protection against a breach of the Article 3 rights of children then liability for any breach may not, as a result, attach to it. It is here that the new charging standard issued in conjunction with section 58 is of crucial significance for it was argued by the government that its very existence would mean that, in all cases concerning treatment which cross the Article 3 threshold, a more serious offence than common assault would be charged. This reasonable chastisement defence would therefore not be available in relation to such treatment. If this is indeed the case then the JCHR's[277] conclusion may well be correct:

> That the combination of the new clause and the new charging standard may well be considered sufficient to satisfy the UK's obligation to comply with the judgment of the European Court of Human Rights in *A v UK*, because it makes the defence unavailable in relation to treatment or punishment which is contrary to Article 3.

---

[267] *A v UK* (n 236).
[268] For a useful analysis of the positive obligation on states under the ECHR see A Mowbray, *The Development of Positive Obligations under the European Convention on Human Rights by the European Court of Human Rights* (Oxford, Hart, 2004).
[269] *A v UK* (n 236).
[270] *Ibid.*
[271] *Ibid*, 624 para 55.
[272] *Z v the United Kingdom* (2002) 34 EHRR 3.
[273] *E v the United Kingdom* (2003) 36 EHRR 31.
[274] *A v UK* (n 236).
[275] *E v UK* (n 273) para 88. *Z v UK* (n 272) applied. See also *Stubbings v UK* (1997) 23 EHRR 213 para 64.
[276] *E v UK* (n 273) para 99.
[277] JCHR Report (n 263) para 137.

It is certainly arguable, however, that the charging standard may *not* adequately protect children from treatment that crosses the threshold of the degrading elements of Article 3. This is because the focus of the charging standard upon the physical nature of the punishment[278] may mean that in instances where the Article 3 threshold is crossed by virtue of psychological or emotional harm the charging standard does not ensure that a charge higher than common assault will be brought against the defendant. This is despite the fact that it is clearly established within criminal law that psychological illnesses could, under s47 of the OAPA, be included in the term 'actual bodily harm' as long as the harm was a medically defined illness and not a mere emotion, such as fear or panic.[279] If this is the case the section 58 defence could still be available in cases that breach the Article 3 rights of the child.

The government review of section 58 notes that the charging standard has clarified the boundary between what constitutes common assault and what constitutes assault occasioning actual bodily harm and takes into account the particular seriousness of an adult assaulting a child.[280] It also records the fact that the standard may have resulted in the removal of a certain amount of discretion from the police, which has had the added effect of providing *more* protection for children:

> However, it (the charging standard) means that the police sometimes have to record as assault occasioning actual bodily harm a crime which is not perceived as being particularly serious, best dealt with by children's social care rather than the criminal justice system, and which previously would have been recorded as common assault.[281]

However, no information is given with regard to how many cases involving psychological as opposed to physical injury are charged under section 39 or section 47 of the OAPA. It is therefore difficult to assess whether the government's claim that current UK law on the parental defence of reasonable punishment in relation to common assault is, in the absence of a further decision on the matter from the ECtHR, compatible with Article 3 of the ECHR.

The Applicability of Article 8

Thus far questions of compatibility that have arisen before the ECtHR have concerned Article 3 alone, despite the fact that rights under Article 8 may also be claimed: for example, the right to administer physical punishment to one's child as an aspect of family life. However, the ECtHR has expressly declined to consider Article 8 cases in such cases. In *A v UK*[282] the applicant invited the Court to rule also on the merits of his Article 8 complaint, which he argued was necessary in order to provide guidance for the government and

---

[278] The Charging Standard for Offences Against the Person states that where the following aggravating features exist a s47 charge of assault occasioning actual bodily harm should be considered: '[T]he vulnerability of the victim, such as when the victim is elderly, disabled or a child assaulted by an adult (so that where an assault causes any of the injuries referred to in sub-paragraph (vii) above, other than reddening of the skin, the charge will normally be assault occasioning actual bodily harm, although prosecutors must bear in mind that the definition of assault occasioning actual bodily harm requires the injury to be more than transient and trifling).'

[279] *R v Chan-Fook* [1994] 2 All ER 552; *Ireland v Burstow* [1998] AC 147, [1997] 4 All ER 225 (HL).

[280] Review (n 255) para 45.

[281] *Ibid.*

[282] *A v UK* (n 236).

protection for children against all forms of deliberate violence. However, the Court declined to do so, holding that having found a violation of Article 3 it was not necessary to examine whether the inadequacy of legal protection was also in breach of Article 8.[283] This does not, however, preclude future cases finding that Article 8 applies to such cases. We will now turn to an examination of the applicability of Article 8 to the parental right to reasonable chastisement of a child.

Article 8 provides for the right to respect for both privacy (including a person's physical and mental integrity) and family life. The right to private life is a wide-ranging right. Of particular relevance to the corporal punishment context are three points. First, 'the concept of private life covers the physical and moral integrity of the person'.[284] In *X and Y v the Netherlands*[285] the lack of effective protection under the criminal law against sexual assault for a mentally ill woman was said to amount to an infringement of her right to private life. The state, it was said, is required under Article 8 to protect one person's right to private life against unwanted contact or infringements to moral integrity. The state may thus be required to protect a vulnerable person from violence under Article 8.[286] Mental health and stability is said to be part of a person's moral integrity.[287] Second, the ECtHR has stated that Article 8 is concerned with protecting a person's physical and psychological integrity[288] and their right to identity and personal development.[289] Third, the ECHR is increasingly referring to the CRC in the course of its judgments in cases concerning children and their right to physical integrity. In *Sahin v Germany*,[290] for example, the Court recently said 'the human rights of children and the standards to which all governments must aspire in realizing these rights for all children are set out in the Convention on the Rights of the Child'.[291] These three points form the basis, therefore, for the argument that the existence of a parental right to reasonable chastisement, at any level, would in fact breach the child's Article 8 right to personal integrity and private life.[292]

However, Article 8 will also require a consideration of the right to family life. Once the question of whether or not family life is in existence has been established[293] there may be, in addition, positive obligations inherent in effective 'respect' for private or family life.[294] These obligations may involve the adoption of measures designed to secure respect for family life in relations between private individuals, including both the provision of a regulatory

---

[283]   However, one member of the Commission in *A v UK* (n 236) would have preferred to deal with that case under Art 8 rather than Art 3: see Concurring Opinion of Mr EA Alkema (1999) 27 EHRR 611, 628–9.

[284]   *X and Y* (n 193).

[285]   *Ibid.*

[286]   *Costello-Roberts v the United Kingdom* (n 236).

[287]   *Bensaid v the United Kingdom* (2001) 33 EHRR 10.

[288]   *Pretty v UK* (2002) 35 EHRR 1 para 61.

[289]   *Bensaid v the United Kingdom* (1995) 19 EHRR 112 para 45.

[290]   *Sahin v Germany* (2003) 15 BHRC 84.

[291]   *Ibid*, paras 39–41, 64.

[292]   Indeed the JCHR concluded that, 'Although the Court has yet to address the gaps between the ECHR's protection for the rights of children and that provided by the CRC, we think it is likely, given the near-universal acceptance of the standards contained in the CRC, that the Court will begin to close the gaps in protection by interpreting Convention standards in light of the CRC, and that, eventually, the continued availability of the defence of reasonable chastisement may be held to be incompatible with Convention rights'. See the JCHR Report (n 263) para 141.

[293]   The existence or non-existence of 'family life' for the purposes of Art 8 is, thus, essentially, a question of fact depending upon the real existence, in practice, of close personal ties: see *K and T* (n 8) para 150.

[294]   *X and Y* (n 193).

framework of adjudication and enforcement to protect individual rights.[295] Most cases concerning these rights have concerned alleged interference with the right for a parent and a child to enjoy each other's company.[296] However, can a parent claim a right to administer punishment to his/her child as an aspect of their right to family life? This question, as the JCHR noted,[297] has already been answered by the European Commission of Human Rights, in *Seven Individuals v Sweden*.[298] This case concerned a Swedish amendment to criminal law, which equalised the law of assault to adults with children. Parents who claimed that the scope of the criminal law of assault failed to respect their right to respect for private and family life challenged this extension of the law of assault. In rejecting the complaint as manifestly ill founded and therefore inadmissible the Commission found that:

> The fact that no distinction is made between the treatment of children by their parents and the same treatment applied to an adult stranger cannot, in the Commission's opinion, constitute an 'interference' with respect for the applicant's private and family lives since the consequences of an assault are equated in both cases. Nor does the mere fact that legislation, or the state of the law, intervenes to regulate something which pertains to family life constitute a breach of Article 8(1) unless the intervention in question violates the applicants' right to respect for their family life. The Commission finds that the scope of the Swedish law of assault and molestation is a normal measure for the control of violence and that its extension to apply to the ordinary physical chastisement of children by their parents is intended to protect potentially weak and vulnerable members of society.[299]

If we add to this the observation made above, the fact that the ECtHR is increasingly influenced by the CRC, adopted by the UK since the decision, it is not difficult to see why the JCHR thought it likely that 'the Court of Human Rights would today reach the same conclusion in any similar Article 8 challenge to a law which removed the defence of reasonable chastisement'.[300]

However, the question of whether the parental defence of reasonable punishment is incompatible with Article 8 is not, it is submitted, completely answered by the above analysis. It is of particular noteworthiness that the case above is a fairly old admissibility decision of the Commission and concerned a case where parents sought to challenge the *removal* of the right to physically chastise a child brought in by the state and, therefore, as the analysis below will demonstrate, was an entirely different structural argument. At present, the UK government has made it clear that it does not intend to equalise the law regarding assault between adults and, as a result, supports a limited right of parental chastisement. We must therefore consider an alternative use of Article 8, that is a claim brought by a child that his/her right to private life is being breached by the existence of section 58.

Unlike Article 3, Article 8 is not an absolute Article and therefore allows for a balancing exercise for which in particular the second paragraph of Article 8 contains explicit criteria. Further, even in cases where Article 8 implies a positive obligation for the state the second paragraph 'may be of certain relevance'[301] and offers the basis for testing the

---

[295] *Glaser v the United Kingdom* Application No 32346/96 (2001) 33 EHRR 119 para 63.
[296] Eg *Johansen v Norway* (n 192) para 52.
[297] JCHR Report (n 263) paras 173–5.
[298] *Seven Individuals v Sweden* (1982) 29 DR 104.
[299] *Ibid*, para 114.
[300] JCHR Report (n 263) para 174.
[301] *Rees v the United Kingdom* (1987) 9 EHRR 56 para 37.

proportionality of legislation seeking to protect children against abuse. This means that, unlike in Article 3, an assessment of all the conflicting rights will occur within the context of paragraph 2: specifically, in the case of a challenge to current UK law the right of the parent wishing to preserve the right to administer corporal punishment as an aspect of family life and the right of the child not to be subject to a breach of his/her right to privacy and personal integrity. Integral to the 'balancing exercise' will undoubtedly be the type and level of punishment that is being proposed and if we consider that the combination of section 58 and the current charging standard may not be sufficient to breach Article 3 it is not immediately apparent that what amounts to the ability to administer 'common assault' upon a child by a parent will automatically be regarded as disproportionate. But what of the much-quoted influence of the CRC and where exactly does its influence lie in the process? They key area in which arguments based on the provisions of the CRC and other international instruments will operate is in relation to the margin of appreciation (or area of discretion at the national level)—a certain discretion for the state which is indispensable where the state's responsibility, as in the case between a conflict of rights between private individuals, is an indirect one. The margin of appreciation is closely connected to the proportionality exercise and, as discussed in Chapter 2, it is apparent that where there is little or no consensus amongst Contracting States on the rights in question and, where the decision of the Court concerns the balancing of those rights against social interests, a wide margin of appreciation will be accorded to the state[302]—the so-called European consensus standard. Moreover, the extent of the positive obligations upon the state in relation to those rights will also be narrowed. The impact of the doctrine of the margin of appreciation is therefore of real significance in terms of assessing how the ECtHR is likely to interpret any claim founded in Article 8 that section 58 may breach the right to personal integrity. As stated above, where little or no consensus exists amongst Contracting States a wide margin of appreciation will be accorded and it may be thought that the opposite would therefore be true: where such consensus exists, the margin will be narrowed. However, as the transgender cases that have come before the ECtHR[303] demonstrate, this is not always the case. At first sight it would appear that the issue of European consensus was integral to the decision to find a breach of Articles 8 and 12, particularly when this was explicitly referred to by the Court, in a number of cases that found that no breach had occurred[304] under Article 8 (the right to privacy) and Article 12 (the right to marry) and then in finding, finally, that a breach *had* occurred.[305] In the latter cases, it was the recognition of an international trend in favour of an increased social acceptance of transsexuals and of the legal recognition of the new sexual identity of post-operative transsexuals that seemingly persuaded the Court. It may be thought, therefore, that the considerable evidence of a growing European and international consensus on the removal of the parental right to chastise would be decisive

---

[302]   See *Evans v the United Kingdom* (n 220) paras 77–82.

[303]   For a detailed review of the use of the margin of appreciation in these cases see KA Kavanagh, 'Policing the Margins: Rights Protection and the European Court of Human Rights' (2006) 4 EHRLR 422.

[304]   In relation to birth and marriage: *Rees* (n 301) para 37 states: 'It would therefore be true to say that there is at present little common ground between the Contracting States in this area and that, generally speaking, the law appears to be in a transitional stage. Accordingly, this is an area in which the Contracting Parties enjoy a wide margin of appreciation.' See also *Cossey v the United Kingdom* (1990) 13 EHRR 622 paras 38–40; *Sheffield and Horsham v the United Kingdom* (1998) 27 EHRR 163 paras 57–61; *X, Y and Z* (n 3) paras 44, 52 (in relation to parental rights and transsexuality).

[305]   *Goodwin v UK* (2002) 35 EHRR 447 paras 84–86 and *I v UK* [2002] 3 FCR 613.

in narrowing the margin of appreciation accorded, particularly when we consider that more than a third of European countries now afford children equal protection from assault.[306] However, the margin of appreciation, as these cases also demonstrate, does not operate in a straightforward manner. The use of the European consensus principle can be highly selective and illustrates the Court's willingness to *disregard* clear evidence of a consensus, if necessary, if the desired result is that of a wide margin of appreciation. Second, that there might be the beginnings of the emergence of a new *international consensus* standard, more influential than a European consensus standard. These two points mean that the claim that section 58 breaches the Article 8 right of a child to physical integrity is not in any way secure and is therefore highly dependent upon how the ECtHR wishes to proceed. If the Court were minded towards the abolition of the defence to reasonably punish it could easily do so on the apparent existence of a European consensus on the issue in addition to its apparent regard for the vulnerability of children. Equally, however, if the Court were minded towards allowing the UK a wider margin of appreciation on the issue, the apparent European consensus on the issue could easily be circumvented as demonstrated by the transsexual cases. The transsexual example in itself demonstrates how the Court has, in the past, shown a certain willingness to allow the UK to come towards the European consensus on an issue in its own time, it having taken some 15 years for the ECtHR to hold the UK in violation of the rights of transsexuals under Articles 8 and 12.

The analysis above does not, of course, preclude the domestic courts from going further than the ECtHR particularly when we consider that the concept of the margin of appreciation will not operate in the same way. The UK courts could choose to interpret section 58 as being incompatible with the HRA under section 6 of the Act. However, this would require the courts to also choose not to accord due deference to the legislature in the area. An indication of how the courts could view the matter was recently provided by the House of Lords. Although the case concerned the delegation of the right of parental chastisement to a school, it could be seen to indicate that any challenge by a parent to the removal of the section 58 defence may be unsuccessful from the point of view of the child. In *Williamson v Secretary of State for Education and Employment and Others*[307] a group of parents sought to challenge the application of the 1986 ban on the administration of corporal punishment within the voluntary aided school system.[308] In contrast to other cases brought before the courts concerning corporal punishment, the parents in this case *wanted* corporal punishment to be administered to their children whilst in school as an expression of their Christian belief, the aim being 'to help form godly character'. As such, they claimed that the statutory ban was incompatible with their Article 9 rights to freedom of religion and freedom to manifest their religion in practice by delegating the administration of corporal punishment to teachers at these schools. There was also discussion of the proposed punishment[309] and whether the applicants' argument, presumably in reliance

---

[306] Countries where children have equal protection are: Sweden (1979), Finland (1983), Norway (1987), Austria (1989), Cyprus (1994), Denmark (1997), Latvia (1998), Croatia (1999), Bulgaria (2000), Germany (2000), Iceland (2003), Hungary (2004), Romania (2004) and Ukraine (2004), Italy and Portugal (2005).

[307] *Williamson v Secretary of State for Education and Employment and Others* [2005] UKHL 15.

[308] See also ch 7 for a further discussion of this.

[309] *Williamson* (n 307) para 10 (Lord Bingham): '[T]he corporal punishment of boys takes the form of administering a thin, broad flat "paddle" to both buttocks simultaneously in a firm controlled manner. Girls may be strapped upon the hand. The child is then comforted by a member of the staff and encouraged to pray. The child is given time to compose himself before returning to class. There is no question of "beating" in the traditional sense.'

upon *Costello-Roberts v UK*,[310] that it would not contravene Article 3[311] was correct. In a unanimous judgment the applicants' arguments were rejected and the House of Lords had no difficulty in applying the case law of the ECtHR to conclude that, although the Article 9 rights of the claimants were engaged, and were plainly being interfered with by the existence of the ban, such interference was necessary in a democratic society for the protection of the rights and freedoms of others. The state was entitled therefore to limit the practice of corporal punishment in all schools, in line with its positive obligations under Article 3, to protect the rights and freedoms of all children. Prohibiting only such punishment as would violate their rights under Article 3 would bring difficult problems of definition, demarcation and enforcement and would not meet the authoritative international view of what other international instruments required.[312] Even if it could be shown that a particular act of corporal punishment was in the interests of an individual child, it was clear, Baroness Hale said, that a universal or blanket ban may be justified to protect a vulnerable class; it was the vulnerability of the class which provided the rationale for the law in question.[313] What was particularly striking about this case, therefore, was the lack of consideration for the point of view of children:

> This is, and has always been, a case about children, their rights and the rights of their parents and teachers. Yet there has been no one here or in the courts below to speak on behalf of the children. No litigation friend has been appointed to consider the rights of the pupils involved separately from those of the adults. No non-governmental organisation, such as the Children's Rights Alliance, has intervened to argue a case on behalf of children as a whole. The battle has been fought on ground selected by the adults.[314]

Meanwhile, the pressure for removal of the defence has intensified. In October 2008, the United Nations Committee on the Rights of the Child delivered its concluding observations on the UK:[315]

> The Committee is concerned at the failure of the State party to explicitly prohibit all corporal punishment in the home and emphasises its view that the existence of any defence in cases of corporal punishment of children does not comply with the principles and provisions of the Convention, since it would suggest that some forms of corporal punishment are acceptable.

The Committee responsible for monitoring implementation of the CRC thus called on the UK to 'prohibit as a matter of priority all corporal punishment in the family, including through the repeal of all legal defences, in England and Wales, Scotland, and Northern Ireland'.[316] This is the third time that this body has urged the UK to give children equal protection from assault: will it be the last?

---

[310] *Costello-Roberts v UK* (n 236).
[311] *Williamson* (n 307) Note 18 paras 10, 27 (Lord Bingham); paras 77, 80 (Baroness Hale).
[312] Such as the CRC: see *Willliamson* (n 307) para 86 (Baroness Hale).
[313] *Ibid*, para 80.
[314] *Ibid*, para 71.
[315] CRC Concluding Observations Report (2008) CRC/C/GBR/CO/4 para 40.
[316] *Ibid*, para 42.

6

Children's Rights

The issue of children's rights has divided family lawyers for decades.[1] For some they offer hope for respecting children as full human beings, rather than mini-slaves or 'superpets'.[2] For others talk of children's rights is dangerous, risking harm to children in the name of their 'liberation'. Others have talked of a 'deep ambivalence about the concept of children's rights within contemporary legal, political and social thinking'.[3] Nevertheless, few would deny that children have *some* rights.[4] The issue is therefore not so much whether children should have any rights, but rather which rights they should have. The debate about children's rights has largely centred on children's rights of autonomy: the right of children to make decisions for themselves.

Chapter 3 considered some of the theoretical issues that arise concerning children's rights—in particular, the tension between protecting children from harm and allowing children the right to make decisions for themselves. That material will not be repeated here. Instead, this Chapter will consider how an approach based on the ECHR to children's rights might differ from that taken currently in English law. It will not be possible to consider every possible ramification of adopting a child's rights approach; however, four broad issues will be considered: children's autonomy rights in the medical setting; questions of how to balance the interests of parents and children; corporal punishment; and access to the courts.

Children's Rights under the ECHR

It is remarkable how few cases before the ECHR have specifically addressed the issue of children's rights to autonomy.[5] Remarkable, but readily explicable. Few children will have the stamina, money, or time to bring a case to the ECtHR. Where children's rights are brought to the Court's attention this is normally done in a case where an adult is seeking to rely on children's rights to pursue their own agenda.[6] That said, of course, in many cases

---

[1] L Houlgate, *Children's Rights, State Intervention, Custody and Divorce* (London, Edwin Mellen Press, 2005); M Freeman, 'Why it Remains Important to take Children's Rights Seriously' (2007) 15 *International Journal of Children's Rights* 5; D Archard and C Macleod, *The Moral and Political Status of Children* (Oxford, Oxford University Press, 2004); J Fortin, 'Rights brought home for children' (1999) 62 *MLR* 350; J Dwyer, The Relationship Rights of Children (Cambridge University Press, 2006); J Fortin, *Children's Rights and the Developing Law* (2003, Cambridge University Press); M Freeman, *The Moral Status of Children* (Oxford, Oxford University Press, 1997).

[2] J Holt, *Escape from Childhood* (New York, EP Dutton Publishers, 1975).

[3] S Harris-Short and J Miles, *Family Law* (Oxford, Oxford University Press, 2007), 625.

[4] Of course, there are those who deny the existence of rights for anyone and for them there will be no rights for children.

[5] U Kilkelly, *The Child and the European Convention on Human Rights* (Aldershot, Ashgate, 1999).

[6] Baroness Hale, 'Understanding children's rights: theory and practice' (2006) 44 *Family Court Review* 350.

involving the enforcement of an adult's rights a child's rights will be enforced at the same time.[7] Still the lack of detailed consideration has led one leading commentator to complain of the 'pitifully inadequate response thus far by the European institutions to the equally independent rights of children under the Convention'[8] and another to talk of the ECHR's 'relatively poor reputation' in protecting children's rights.[9]

The starting point for a consideration of children's rights under the ECHR is that children have all the same rights under the ECHR that adults do.[10] An argument that, for example, children have no rights under Article 8 will simply not get off the ground. The ECtHR has readily held that children have the right to protection under Articles 3 and 8.[11] Further, there are plenty of cases considering the discrimination against children on the basis of the marital status of their parents.[12] However, there are two major gaps in the protection of children's rights.

First, as discussed in Chapter 3, simply matching the rights of children to adults may mean that children's rights are not adequately protected.[13] Children may require more rights than adults.[14] Rights to education and financial support may be appropriate to children, of a kind not appropriate for adults. Indeed it has been argued that the Convention was clearly designed with adults in mind.[15] Indeed it is interesting to note the recent supportive comments made in the Grand Chamber in *Sahin v Germany* about the CRC:

> The human rights of children and the standards to which all governments must aspire in realising these rights for all children are set out in the Convention on the Rights of the Child.[16]

This could be read as at least implicitly recognising that the ECtHR does not deal with the rights of children in a completely satisfactory way.

One area where children's rights are not seen as necessarily identical to adults is the area of privacy. Children's rights to privacy have been protected under Article 8. In *Murray v Big Pictures (UK) Ltd*[17] proceedings were brought by Joanne Murray (better known as JK Rowling) to protect the privacy of her young son, David. She sought an injunction to prevent further publication of a photograph of David in a street, and from the taking of photographs in similar circumstances. His Article 8 rights played an important part in determining the level of protection to which he was entitled. It was held:

> It seems to us that, subject to the facts of the particular case, the law should indeed protect children from intrusive media attention, at any rate to the extent of holding that a child has a reasonable

---

[7] J Herring, *Family Law* 4th edn (Harlow, Pearson, 2009), 402.

[8] A Bainham, 'Contact as a Fundamental Right' (1995) 54 *CLJ* 255, 258.

[9] U Kilkelly, 'Effective protection of children's rights in family cases: an international perspective' (2002) 12 *International Law and Contemporary Problems* 335, 336 refers to the 'relatively poor reputation' of the ECHR's protection of children's rights.

[10] *Nielsen v Denmark* (1989) 11 EHRR 175.

[11] See, eg, *A v UK (Human Rights: Punishment of Child)* [1998] 2 FLR 959; *Nielsen v Denmark* (1989) 11 EHRR 175, and the wider discussion in ch 7.

[12] *Mazurek v France* [2000] ECHR 34406/97.

[13] J Fortin, 'Accommodating Children's Rights in a Post Human Rights Act Era' (2006) 69 *MLR* 299.

[14] J Herring, 'Children's Rights for Grown-Ups' in S Fredman and S Spencer (eds) *Age as an Equality Issue* (Oxford, Hart, 2003)

[15] G Douglas, 'The Family and the State under the European Convention on Human Rights' (1988) 2 *International Journal of Law and the Family* 76.

[16] *Sahin v Germany* [2003] ECHR 340, para 39.

[17] *Murray v Big Pictures (UK) Ltd* [2008] 2 FLR 599.

expectation that he or she will not be targeted in order to obtain photographs in a public place for publication which the person who took or procured the taking of the photographs knew would be objected to on behalf of the child. That is the context in which the photographs of David were taken.[18]

Second, the ECtHR has been reluctant to recognise that children have rights to autonomy. As seen in Chapter 3 it is the right to autonomy which is a key marker on whether a legal system protects children's rights, as opposed to protecting their interests. The leading case on children's autonomy rights in the ECtHR is *Nielsen v Denmark*,[19] which concerned a 12-year-old boy who had been detained in a psychiatric ward for over five months. There was no evidence that he was suffering from a psychiatric disorder, but his mother had approved his detention. Proceedings were brought on behalf of the boy challenging the detention. His application failed by nine votes to seven. His Article 5 rights were not engaged because the detention was justified by the responsible exercise of the mother's parental rights. The Court explained that:

> family life in the Contracting States encompasses a broad range of parental rights and responsibilities in regard to care and custody of minor children. The care and upbringing of children normally and necessarily require that the parents or an only parent decide where the child must reside and also impose, or authorise others to impose, various restrictions on the child's liberty … Family life in this sense, and especially the rights of parents to exercise parental authority over their children, having due regard to their corresponding parental responsibilities, is recognised and protected by the Convention, in particular by Article 8. Indeed the exercise of parental rights constitutes a fundamental element of family life.[20]

That is a very broad interpretation of the rights of parents.[21] Under it children's rights are virtually entirely subsumed within the rights of parents.

There is precious little other litigation on the autonomy rights of children. In *X v the Netherlands*[22] a 14-year-old runaway failed in a claim that the police had interfered in her rights by being returned home. This fell within the state's margin of appreciation. Hence, in *X v Denmark*[23] parents who complained that the state had failed to return their runaway child to them lost too. It was within the state's margin of appreciation how to respond to such a case.

Where weight is given to the views of children by the ECtHR, this is often expressed as a pragmatic consideration. Hence in *Damnjanovicì v Serbia*[24] the children's resistance to moving from their father back to their mother was seen as justification for the state not enforcing a custody order in the mother's favour. The case was not seen, as it might have been, as a case about children having the right to determine with which parent they should live.

---

[18] Para 57.
[19] *Nielsen v Denmark* (1989) 11 EHRR 175.
[20] Para 61.
[21] R Taylor, 'Reversing the retreat from *Gillick*? R *(Axon) v Secretary of State for Health*' [2007] *Child and Family Law Quarterly* 81.
[22] (1975) 76 D and R 118.
[23] (1978) D and R 81.
[24] (Application no 5222/07), [2009] 1 FLR 339.

Nielsen[25] was relied upon by Sue Axon in her claim in the English courts that a parent had the right to be informed of and involved in discussions between a girl and her doctor over an abortion decision.[26] Silber J read *Nielsen* as a case concerned only with Article 5 and parental decisions over a child's liberty and a place of residence, and so not of application in relation to other kinds of decision. With respect it is hard to see anything in the decision of the ECtHR which justifies such a narrow reading, particularly as the case was primarily argued in relation to a parent's Article 8 rights. Further, if a parent has control over a child's liberty, it would seem that any rights a child has can be rendered effectively meaningless.

Nielsen appears to indicate that respect for a child's family life involves giving legal weight to the decision of her parent. Similarly in *Glass v UK*[27] the failure to consult with his parents was found to be an interference with David Glass's Article 8 rights. These views reflect a controversial understanding of the *Gillick* decision which is that a parental right under Article 8 only exists for the benefit of the child.[28] As a child grows in maturity so the parental right dwindles. Sibler J adopted such a view in *Axon*[29] and held:

> As Lord Scarman explained [in *Gillick*], a parental right yields to the young person's right to make his own decisions when the young person reaches a sufficient understanding and intelligence to be capable of making up his or her own mind in relation to a matter requiring decision, and this autonomy of a young person must undermine any Article 8 rights of a parent to family life.[30]

Silber J's claim that the right to family life itself ends when the child reaches maturity is controversial and seems doubtful. It certainly does not sit with the case law that a parent can consent to treatment for a child even when a child refuses.[31] In any event it means there is no recognition that a parent has a major interest in what happens to a child, even if mature.[32] To take but one example the decision of a 13 year old to take a pregnancy to term is highly likely to impact on the family life of her parents. That is not to say that she should not have the right to make the decision, but to suggest that the parents do have an interest in what is decided, even if their rights are readily overridden by the more significant right of the girl to decide the course of the pregnancy. Of course it will often, even always, be the case that the decision of a mature child will justify an interference in the parent's right, but that is not the same thing as saying that the parent has no right. As Rachel Taylor[33] points out, in *Hokkanen v Finland*,[34] when it was found that the state was not required to enforce contact in a case where a mature 12-year-old child did not want to see her father[35] the ECtHR held that the father's rights were justifiably infringed, rather than saying that he had no rights.

[25] (1989) 11 EHRR 175.
[26] *R (Axon) v Secretary of State for Health* [2006] 2 FCR 131.
[27] [2004] 1 FCR 553.
[28] See further S Gilmore, 'The Limits of Parental Responsibility' in R Probert, S Gilmore and J Herring (eds), *Responsible Parents and Parental Responsibility* (Oxford, Hart, 2009).
[29] *R (Axon) v Secretary of State for Health* [2006] 2 FCR 131.
[30] *Ibid*, at para 130.
[31] Discussed above at p 230.
[32] Of course, children have a major interest in the medical treatment of their parents too: see J Herring, 'Relational Autonomy and Family Law' in J Wallbank, S Choudhry and J Herring (eds), *Rights, Gender and Family Law* (London, Routledge, 2009)
[33] *Ibid*.
[34] [1996] 1 FLR 289.
[35] Although there had been a breach in the earlier failure to enforce the contact orders.

The ECtHR has been far more comfortable with the notion that parents have rights over their children than the English courts have. While under the CA it is responsibilities of parenthood which are emphasised and rights are mentioned merely as an aspect of parental responsibility, under the ECHR the rights of parents are regularly protected.[36] Baroness Hale in *Williamson*[37] has explained why it is important to recognise that parents have rights over their children:

> Children have the right to be properly cared for and brought up so that they can fulfil their potential and play their part in society. Their parents have both the primary responsibility and the primary right to do this. The state steps in to regulate the exercise of that responsibility in the interests of children and society as a whole. But 'the child is not the child of the state' and it is important in a free society that parents should be allowed a large measure of autonomy in the way in which they discharge their parental responsibilities. A free society is premised on the fact that people are different from one another. A free society respects individual differences. 'Only the worst dictatorships try to eradicate those differences': see *El Al Israeli Airlines Ltd v Danielowitz* [1994] Isrl LR 478 at para 14 per Barak J. Often they try to do this by intervening between parent and child. That is one reason why the European Convention for the Protection of Human Rights and Fundamental Freedoms 1950 (as set out in Sch 1 to the Human Rights Act 1998) restricts the power of the state to interfere in family life (Art 8) or to limit the manifestation of religious or other beliefs (Art 9) and requires it to respect the religious or philosophical convictions of parents in the education of their children (First Protocol, Art 2).[38]

The protection of children's rights under the ECHR is, therefore, still something of a work in progress. There is general acceptance that children have the same rights that adults do. However, rarely has the ECtHR enforced the independent rights of children: nearly all the cases have involved parents seeking to enforce the rights of children on their behalf. In particular there is little discussion on the extent to which children have autonomy rights. This reflects the fact that the ECHR was not created with children's rights as a primary issue of concern. In the light of this it is, perhaps, not surprising that the ECtHR has acknowledged the significance of the CRC.

United Nations Convention on the Rights of the Child

The primary focus of this book is on the ECHR, but it will outline briefly the CRC. The CRC has been signed by the UK government but this does not mean that it is enforced directly. There are no legal proceedings in any court or tribunal that could be brought on the basis that a child's CRC rights have been interfered with. This is not to say that the CRC is without legal significance. The UK courts do occasionally refer to the Convention to support a particular interpretation of the law,[39] as does the ECtHR.[40] Although it is

---

[36] Eg *Hokkanen v Finland* [1996] 1 FLR 289.
[37] *R (Williamson) v Secretary of State for Education and Employment* [2005] UKHL 15.
[38] Para 72.
[39] Eg *Re H (Paternity: Blood Tests)* [1996] 2 FLR 65; *Re L, V, M and H* [2000] 2 FLR 334; *Re J (Specific Issue Orders: Child's Religious Upbringing and Circumcision)* [2000] 1 FLR 571; *Mabon v Mabon* [2005] EWCA Civ 634; *Payne v Payne* [2001] EWCA Civ 166; *In re B (Children)* [2008] UKHL 35.
[40] Eg *Saviny v Ukraine* (Application No 39948/06); *V v UK* (Application No 24888/94); *Güveç v Turkey* (Application No 70337/01).

not possible to point to a case where the Convention seems actually to have affected the result reached, it is generally referred to to help justify a conclusion which the court would probably reach in any event.[41] The significance of the CRC may therefore be in political and educational terms rather than legal enforceability,[42] although the impact it can play on local authorities and non-governmental organisations dealing with children should not be overlooked.[43]

The CRC seeks to provide an authoritative statement of the rights of children.[44] The very fact that there is a special convention on the rights of children acknowledges that there is something about children and their rights that cannot simply be assumed to match those of adults. In the preamble to the Convention we find this statement:

> the child, by reason of his physician and mental immaturity, needs special safeguards and care, including appropriate legal protection, before as well as after birth.

The list of rights in the Convention need, however, to be treated with care. First, some of these rights listed should be regarded as aspirations for children, rather than purporting to grant legal rights that can be enforced. Second, many of the rights will depend on the cultural and socio-economic circumstances of the individual country. To take an obvious example, the contents of rights to health care will vary depending where in the world the child is.

This has led to a questioning of whether the Convention is of any value at all.[45] Bainham has emphasised the value of educative and symbolic value of the Convention, even if unenforceable.[46] Critics have also complained that it is a conservative Convention which emphasises the protection of children over their empowerment and replicates rights from existing human rights instruments, rather than developing a child-centred approach to rights.[47]

The Convention applies to all children below the age of 18 'unless, under the law applicable to the child, majority is attained earlier'.[48] The most important rights mentioned include the rights to life[49] and identity; the right to 'be known and be cared for by his or her parents';[50] a right to expression;[51] and rights to protection from abuse or violence.[52]

---

[41] Although see U Kilkelly, '*The Best of Both Worlds for Children's Rights? Interpreting the European Convention on Human Rights in the Light of the UN Convention on the Rights of the Child*' (2001) 23 *Human Rights Quarterly* 308, who argues that the CRC has played a significant role in the development of the ECtHR jurisprudence.

[42] There are also regular reports by the UN Committee on the position of the rights of children in the UK, which may be of political significance. Although see M Freeman, 'The End of the Century of the Child?' (2000) 53 *Current Legal Problems* 505 for criticism of the government's response to them.

[43] J Williams, 'Incorporating children's rights: the divergence in law and policy' (2007) 27 *Legal Studies* 261.

[44] See P Alston, S Parker and J Seymour, *Children, Rights and the Law* (Oxford, Oxford University Press, 1992); L LeBlanc, *The Convention on the Rights of the Child* (Lincoln, University of Nebraska Press, 1995); G van Bueren, *The International Law on the Rights of the Child* (Amsterdam, Kluwer, 1998); Freeman, *The Moral Status of Children* (n 1); D Fottrell (ed), *Revisiting Children's Rights 10 Years of the of the UN Convention on the Rights of the Child* (The Hague, Kluwer, 2000).

[45] D McGoldrick, 'The United Nations Convention on the Rights of the Child' (1991) *International Journal of Law and the Family* 132.

[46] A Bainham, *Children: The Modern Law* (Bristol, Jordans, 2007), 77.

[47] See the discussion in Freeman, *The Moral Status of Children* (n 1) ch 7.

[48] Article 1.

[49] Article 6.

[50] Article 7.

[51] Article 12.

[52] Article 19.

At the heart of the Convention is Article 3(1), which states:

> In all actions concerning children, whether undertaken by public or private social welfare institutions, courts of law, administrative authorities or legislative bodies, the best interests of the child shall be a primary consideration.[53]

As Andrew Bainham has noticed, there are two notable differences from this and the welfare principle in the CA.[54] First, the interests of children are expressed to be primary, rather than paramount. Second, they are only *a* consideration and not *the sole* consideration. Indeed the difference with the welfare principle is more apparent, as stated in Article 3(2):

> State parties undertake to ensure the child such protection and care as is necessary for his or her well-being, taking into account the rights and duties of his or her parents, legal guardians, or other individuals legally responsible for him or her, and, to this end, shall take all appropriate legislative and administrative measures.

Further, there is support for parents' rights under the Convention in Article 5:

> States Parties shall respect the responsibility, rights and duties to parents, or where applicable, the members of the extended family or community as provided for by local custom, legal guardians or other persons legally responsible for the child, to provide, in a manner consistent with the evolving capacities of the child, appropriate direction and guidance in the exercise by the child of the rights recognized in the present Convention.

These provisions indicate the difficulties in finding an appropriate balance between the interests of children and adults; and indeed the difficulties in separating them out. The CRC provides no real guidance in achieving the balance, although is perhaps more open about the fact there is a balance that needs to be struck than either the CA or the ECHR.

Children's Rights under the Children Act 1989

In Chapter 3 the differences between welfare-based and rights-based approaches were discussed. At first sight English law is clearly welfarist. Section 1 of the CA states:

> When a court determines any question with respect to—
>
> (a) the upbringing of a child; or
> (b) the administration of a child's property or the application of any income arising from it,
>
> the child's welfare shall be the court's paramount consideration.

However, to conclude from this provision that English law is welfarist, rather than rights-based, would be to over-simplify the issue.[55]

First, in many cases making an order which will promote the welfare of a child will also protect his or her rights. So an order removing a child from abusive parents can be justified not only as promoting his or her welfare, but also as protecting his or her rights.[56] Indeed

---

[53] Article 3(1).
[54] A Bainham, 'Can we Protect Children and Protect Their Rights?' (2002) 22 *Family Law* 279.
[55] See further the discussion in ch 3.
[56] See ch 7.

it is noticeable that rights supporters do not suggest that there are a large number of cases where a rights-based approach would produce a different result from that reached using a welfare analysis.[57] It would only be borderline cases where there would be a clear difference in outcome.[58]

Second, even under the welfare principle the court will attach weight to the wishes of a child. Indeed section 1(3) of the CA lists factors which a court should take into account when considering what order would best promote the welfare of the child. The very first of these are 'the ascertainable wishes and feelings of the child concerned (considered in the light of his age and understanding)'.[59] However, there are dangers in reading too much into this provision. First, courts do not normally hear the children directly, but rely on reports from court officers. However, there are concerns over the extent to which court reports accurately reflect the views of children.[60] Further, as Alison Diduck has argued, children's wishes are filtered through the welfare discourse:

> a child's wishes and feelings are more likely to be respected if they conform to adult (and universal normative rather than individualised) ideas of welfare and suggests that law here takes the romantic developmentalist view of its child.[61]

Third, the courts have been willing to use rights-based arguments where the welfare principle is seen not to apply.[62] This indicates that the courts acknowledge that there is a difference between a welfare and a rights-based approach. To give just one example in *R (on the application of Begum) v Head teacher and Governors of Denbigh High School*[63] the House of Lords considered a school dress code which prevented Sabina Begum from wearing a jilbab: a coat-like garment she believed she was require to wear by her religion. The case was analysed in HRA terms. It was accepted that she had the right to manifest her religion under Article 9 of the ECHR. A child had just as much a right to do this as an adult. However, it was held that there was no interference with her rights because she was free to go to another school which had dress codes which would have allowed her to wear the jilbab. Even if that had not been so, any breach of her Article 9 rights were justified in order to protect the freedoms of other pupils at the school (particularly girls) who might otherwise feel pressurised into wearing the jilbab against their wishes.

As these points demonstrate, there is certainly scope in the law for the use of ECHR rights and it would be wrong to say there is no protection of rights of children in the law. It also demonstrates the rather selective use of the HRA and the rights-based approach that it mandates. On the other hand there are dangers that academics keen to promote a more rights-based approach to children have over-egged the significance of children's rights in

---

[57] See J Herring and R Taylor, 'Relocating Relocation' [2006] *Child and Family Law Quarterly* 517, arguing that even in the controversial relocation case law a rights-based approach would not produce a different result from that currently reached by the courts using the welfare principle.

[58] S Choudhry and H Fenwick, 'Taking the Rights of Parents and Children Seriously: Confronting the Welfare Principle under the Human Rights Act' (2005) 25 *OJLS* 453.

[59] CA, s1(3)(a).

[60] J Fortin, 'Children's Rights: Substance or Spin' [2006] *Family Law* 757; Baroness Hale, 'The voice of the child' (2007) *International Family Law Journal* 171.

[61] A Diduck, *Law's Families* (London, LexisNexis, 2003) 91.

[62] Eg *Clayton v Clayton* [2006] EWCA Civ 878.

[63] [2006] 1 FCR 613. See also *Re Trinity Mirror Plc and others (A and B (Minors, acting by the Official Solicitor to the Supreme Court) Intervening)* [2008] EWCA Crim 50.

the current law.[64] Indeed it is noticeable that despite the amount of academic attention paid to the notion of children's rights, the concept is rarely mentioned by the judiciary.

That may, however, be about to change. In *Mabon v Mabon* Thorpe LJ in the Court of Appeal stated:

> there is a keener appreciation of the autonomy of the child and the child's consequential right to participate in decision-making processes that fundamentally affect his family life.[65]

And:

> this case provides a timely opportunity to recognise the growing acknowledgement of the autonomy and consequential rights of children, both nationally and internationally.[66]

Certainly, gone are the days when it would be simply assumed that fathers made the best decisions about children's upbringing and that the courts should be very reluctant to interfere in such decisions. That kind of view was well exemplified by *In Re Agar Ellis*:

> this Court holds this principle: that when, by birth, a child is subject to a father, it is for the general interest of families, and for the general interest of children, and really for the interest of the particular infant, that the Court should not, except in very extreme cases, interfere with the discretion of the father, but leave to him the responsibility of exercising that power which nature has given him by the birth of the child.[67]

There is no doubt that the courts will now make assessments of what is in a child's best interests and where necessary that will involve overruling the views of the parents.[68] But that leaves the question of whether this is done in the name of promoting welfare or rights. As already mentioned, the courts have held that by applying the welfare principle they are in effect protecting the rights of parties under the HRA. So, from the courts' perspective in many of the cases where the welfare principle is applied we see the courts protecting children's rights. What we see here is a reflection of the point expanded at page 121 that in many cases whether one applies the welfare principle or a rights-based approach the result reached will be the same, although it was argued at page 122 that this would not always be the same. So it is not possible to tell from most cases whether the courts are indeed taking a welfare or a rights-based approach. That said, it is clear that, as required by the statute, it is the language of welfare that predominates.

The rather precarious position of children's rights in English law is revealed by the fact that the Children's Commissioner has no obligation to promote children's rights. What is required is that he or she promotes an 'awareness of the views and interests of children in England'.[69] This is in contrast with the obligations imposed on children's commissioners in other parts of the UK, and indeed the world, where the promotion of children's rights is seen as a key part of the commissioner's role.[70]

---

[64] S Gilmore, 'The Limits of Parental Responsibility' (n 28).

[65] *Mabon v Mabon* [2005] EWCA Civ 634, applied in *Re C (Abduction: Separate Representation of Children)* [2008] 2 FLR 6.

[66] *Ibid.*

[67] *In Re Agar Ellis* (1883) 24 Ch D 317, 334.

[68] M Brazier, 'An Intractable Dispute: When Parents and Professionals Disagree' (2005) 13 *Medical Law Review* 412.

[69] Children Act 2004, s2(1).

[70] J Fortin, 'Children's Rights: Substance or Spin' [2006] *Family Law* 759.

In seeking to determine whether a legal system does take a rights based approach or a welfare-based approach to children, there are three issues which are particularly revealing. First, there is the extent to which children are permitted to make decisions to pursue a course of action which will cause them harm. Second, the extent to which children's voices are heard in court cases. Third, the extent to which obligations are imposed on the state to protect children's interests. That third issue is addressed particularly in Chapter 7, and as a result this chapter will focus on the first two.

The Recognition of Autonomy Rights in Medical Cases

While 'autonomy issues' tend to be regarded as the touchstone of whether a legal system protects children's rights, it would be easy to overemphasise their significance. A child welfarist can readily accept that children should be able to make decisions for themselves, even causing them some harm. It may, on a broad assessment of welfare, be seen as a useful part of their educational development to learn from their mistakes. Indeed, it would be quite possible for a children's rights advocate to be less willing than a child welfarist to allow children to make decisions for themselves. This would be so where a children's rights advocate emphasised children's rights to protection from harm, the right to a safe environment or the right to discipline and/or where a child welfarist placed much weight on the benefit to children of developing their own personalities through making decisions for themselves and learning from their mistakes. So whether or not children can take harmful decisions is one factor and one factor only in considering whether a legal system takes children's rights seriously.

Cases involving the medical treatment of children have proved particularly revealing on the English courts' approach to autonomy rights. This case law has been well covered elsewhere,[71] and so will only be very briefly summarised here. In essence the current law is that if a child is found to be sufficiently competent to make the decision ('*Gillick* competent') then she is able to consent to receive medical treatment if the doctor has determined that that treatment is in her best interests. However, if a competent child refuses to consent, a parent with parental responsibly or the court can authorise the giving of treatment, thereby rendering it lawful. In determining whether a child is competent a judge will consider whether a child has sufficient maturity to understand the issues involved and make her own decisions.[72] Children suffering anorexia nervosa[73] or other mental disorders[74] have been found to lack capacity.[75] Similarly children raised in strict religious households may be found to lack a sufficiently broad experience of the world to be able to reach their own decisions on an issue.[76]

---

[71] Eg J Fortin, *Children's Rights and the Developing Law* 3rd edn (Cambridge, Cambridge University Press, 2009).

[72] *Re L (Medical Treatment: Gillick Competence)* [1998] 2 FLR 810.

[73] *Re W* [1993] 1 FLR 64.

[74] *Re KWH (minors) (medical treatment)* [1993] 1 FLR 854.

[75] *Re L (Medical Treatment: Gillick Competence)* [1998] 2 FLR 810. For arguments that even young children have capacity to make decisions see P Alderson, K Sutcliffe, K Curtis, 'Young Children's Rights' (2006) 91 *Archives of Disease in Childhood* 300.

[76] *Re E (A Minor) (Wardship: Medical Treatment)* [1992] 2 FCR 219.

Does the law in this area indicate a rights-based approach or not? Certainly the initial *Gillick* decision,[77] which recognised that children could effectively consent to receiving contraception, was seen by some as heralding the advent of a recognition of children's rights.[78] In retrospect the case law, as it has developed, cannot justify such a bold statement.

First, while it is true that the courts appear to acknowledge that children have the right to consent to medical treatment, it has denied them the right to refuse. In effect, the child has the right to say 'yes' or the right to say 'no'. To many rights-based advocates this is simply illogical and many have called for children to have the right to refuse treatment. There is, indeed, something odd about the law saying that if a child is competent to answer a question their answer will be respected only if they say 'yes'. As John Harris argues:

> The idea that a child (or anyone) might competently consent to a treatment but not be competent to refuse it is palpable nonsense, the reasons for which are revealed by a moment's reflection on what a competent consent involves. To give an informed consent you need to understand the nature of the course of action to which you are consenting, which, in medical contexts, will include its probable and possible consequences and side effects and the nature of any alternative measures which might be taken and the consequences of doing nothing.

> So, to understand a proposed treatment well enough to consent to it is to understand the consequences of a refusal. And if the consequences of a refusal are understood well enough to consent to the alternative then the refusal must also be competent.[79]

That implies that what is driving the respect shown to the child's choice is the fact that it is one that is approved of, rather than genuine respect for the child's decision.[80] However, the law is perfectly logical from a welfare perspective. If it is assumed that if the doctor wants to provide a treatment then that treatment will promote the child's welfare, it is not surprising that the law will allow either a competent child or parent to be able to consent. That is the best way to ensure that children receive the medical treatment they need. *Gillick* is, therefore, better seen as a case about restricting parents' rights, preventing a parent from vetoing treatment a child should receive, than a case about children's rights.

Second, it was emphasised even in *Gillick* that a doctor could rely on a child's consent only if the treatment was in the best interests of the child. There is nothing here, then, to suggest that children have the right to make mistakes which is the hallmark of true autonomy. Nevertheless it is easy to make too much of this remark. After all doctors should not give adults medical treatment which is harmful. To do so would probably be negligent and possibly criminal.[81] However, it may be that Lord Fraser was seeking to suggest that the issue was different for adults and children. In relation to adults, a doctor may provide treatment consented to by a patient from within a range of acceptable alternatives. It would not, for example, be in any sense unlawful for a doctor to perform cosmetic surgery on a patient with the patient's consent, even though the doctor may personally be of the opinion that the cosmetic surgery would not improve the patient's appearance or benefit them. However, Lord Fraser may have been suggesting that a child's consent is only effective if the treatment provided to the child is positively in that child's best interests and is the best

---

[77] *Gillick v West Norfolk & Wisbech HA* [1986] AC 112 (HL).
[78] J Eekelaar, 'The Emergence of Children's Rights' (1986) 6 *OJLS* 161.
[79] J Harris, 'Consent and End of Life Decisions' (2003) 29 *Journal of Medical Ethics* 10, 15.
[80] Although see Gilmore, 'The limits of parental responsibility' (n 28).
[81] See further J Herring, *Medical Law and Ethics* 2nd edn (Oxford, Oxford University Press, 2008) ch 3.

available treatment—and that that is a stronger requirement than one that the treatment does not cause the patient clear harm.

Does this analysis lead to the conclusion that the medical cases indicate that children's autonomy rights are not protected? Not necessarily. There are ways in which it might be argued that the law does protect children's rights. First, one way of interpreting the law is that although children's autonomy rights are protected, they are protected to a lesser extent than adults' rights. This would mean that although the weight attached to an adult's autonomy right is sufficient to justify allowing them to die, the weight attached to a child's right is not. Children's autonomy rights may be strong enough to allow them to make other harmful decisions but when it comes to medical decisions involving death or serious harm they are not. Such a view is problematic. If a child who is *Gillick* competent is as mature as an adult, should not her views count the same as an adult's? That might push one towards a second possible justification that we do not believe even a mature child is as competent as an adult. Where the decision involves death or serious harm there are higher standards of capacity than decisions which involve less harm.[82] This assumes that children have lower levels of capacity than adults. It does not provide an adequate response for those cases where the child in question has at least the same degree of understanding as an adult.[83]

The failure to grant competent children the same degree of capacity as adults in this arena indicates that children's autonomy rights are not protected to the same extent as an adult's. The current law on children's autonomy is best explained in terms of children's welfare, but may also be explained in terms of children having autonomy rights, but that they are only weakly protected.

Balancing Children's Rights and Adults' Rights

Jane Fortin has complained of the failure of the English court to address HRA issues in family law cases. She writes:

> By far the most common approach in this area of law is for the judiciary to omit any mention of the European Convention or of the rights of the players involved in the dispute. A second approach is for the family courts to pay lip service to the demands of the HRA by making a very brief passing reference to the rights of the parents and children under Article 8 of the European Convention. But even in these cases there is no attempt to analyse exactly what rights, within Article 8, each might have.[84]

These complaints have much validity. In particular there is a concern that where HRA reasoning is used there is little attempt to fashion the independent rights that children have. She points to the *Axon* case as one which was revealing because it was thought that a mother *might* have a case for requiring a doctor to disclose her daughter's abortion

---

[82] This may either be on the basis that issues with more serious consequences involve more complex issues; or the concept of 'risk-relative capacity' which recommends a sliding scale for capacity, depending on the severity of the issue at hand: See J Herring, 'Losing It? Losing What? The Law and Dementia' [2009] *Child and Family Law Quarterly* 3.

[83] For an argument that equalising the position of adults and children in this area should not necessarily be by both following the adult model, see J Herring, 'Relational Autonomy and Family Law'.

[84] Fortin, 'Accommodating Children's Rights'.

decision or even to be involved in the decision itself.[85] The very fact that such a possibility was entertained by her lawyers, and seriously considered by the court, reveals the failure to take account of the rights of children.

As noted in Chapter 3, a conflict between individuals' rights is almost bound to arise in any difficult family law case. The European Convention itself gives little guidance on how to deal with cases where the interests of children and adults clash. We have, however, now received some guidance from the European Court on this issue. It is clear that when weighing the competing rights of adults and children, children's rights should carry greater weight.

In *Hendriks v Netherlands*[86] it was held:

the Commission has consistently held that, in assessing the question of whether or not the refusal of the right of access to the non-custodial parent was in conformity with Article 9 of the Convention, the interests of the child would predominate.[87]

Later decisions appear to take an even stronger line in favour of children. When considering clashes between parents' and children's rights, children's rights have been said to be of 'crucial importance' (*Scott v UK*[88]) or of 'particular importance' (*Hoppe v Germany*[89]). Such tests appear to leave room for the possibility that parents' interests could trump those of children, where parents' interests are very strong and children's interests weak. The strongest statement was in *Yousef v the Netherlands*,[90] where the Court held that children's interests were 'paramount':

The Court reiterates that in judicial decisions where the rights under Art 8 of parents and those of a child are at stake, the child's rights *must be the paramount consideration*. If any balancing of interests is necessary, the interests of the child *must always prevail*.[91]

On first reading the *Yousef* approach appears to be very close to the welfare principle, as it seems to suggest that the interests of children will automatically outweigh any competing parental right. A closer reading, however, suggests that the Court did not intend to make such a radical departure from its previous approach. As Shazia Choudhry notes, the Court's use of the word 'reiterates' suggests that it did not intend to create a new principle.[92] Indeed, the case law Yousef cites in support of its formula[93] uses the crucial formulation. More recent cases have preferred the *Scott*[94] or *Hoppe*[95] formulation.[96] Even if the *Yousef*

---

[85] *Ibid.*

[86] (1982) 5 D & R 219.

[87] This was accepted as a statement of the correct approach towards the ECHR in *Re L (A Child) (Contact: Domestic Violence)* [2000] 2 FCR 404.

[88] [2000] 2 FCR 560, 572.

[89] [2003] 1 FCR 176, para 49.

[90] [2000] 2 FLR 118, para 118. See also *Marie v Portugal* [2004] 2 FLR 653, para 77 and *Monory v Romania and Hungary*, Application No 71099/01 para 83; *Zawadka v Poland*, Application No 48542/99 para 67.

[91] *Yousef v Netherlands* (Application No 33711/96) [2003] 1 FLR 210, para 73 (emphasis added).

[92] S Choudhry, 'The Adoption and Children Act 2002, the Welfare Principle and the Human Rights Act 1998—A Missed Opportunity' [2003] *Child and Family Law Quarterly* 119.

[93] *Elsholz v Germany* [2000] 3 FCR 385, para 48; *TP and KM v the United Kingdom* [2003] 2 FCR 1, para 70.

[94] *C v Finland* [2006] 2 FCR 195, para 52.

[95] *Hasse v Germany* [2004] 2 FCR 1, para 93; *Suss v Germany* [2005] 3 FCR 55, para 88; *Hunt v Ukraine* (Application No 31111/04), para 54; *Eski v Austria* (Application No 21949/03), para 35.

[96] Although see *Kearns v France* [2008] ECHR 35991/04, para 79, which uses paramount.

formulation is followed it is far from clear that the Court understood paramountcy in the sense it has been interpreted in English law to mean that the interests of children will always trump the interests of adults. The current approach of the European Court can be summarised in this way: where there is a clash between the interests of children and adults, special weight will be attached to the interests of children. This does not mean that the interests of children will always outweigh the interests of adults, but unless the interests are adults are significantly stronger than the interests of children, the weighing will result in protecting the interests of children.

More needs to be said, however, about this. First, how are the respective rights of adults and children to be weighed? How do we know if the rights of an individual are to count greatly or less so? As suggested in Chapter 3 the best way to deal with clashes between rights is to consider the values underpinning those rights. Sometimes in the case of family life it is the value of autonomy, the value to live one's life as one chooses, which is at the heart of the right claimed. So, the question for a court would then be the extent to which the proposed order leads to a blight on the person's opportunity to live out their version of the good life. This was discussed further in Chapter 3. But there are some important points to make here when the interests of children are taken into account.

Jane Fortin[97] has interpreted the ECHR case law to mean that adult rights will be protected unless to do so would be contrary to the best interests of the child. This suggests that any amount of harm to the child will automatically justify an interference in a parental right. This is not to say that she regards the ECHR approach as identical to a welfare principle approach. Under the welfare principle a parent would have no claim to a parental right, whereas under Fortin's approach parents would have rights they could claim, as long as protecting the parents' rights did not involve harming children. Fortin's approach has an appeal. It enables her to emphasise that parents' rights should never be used to pursue a result which harms children. Her approach, however, is hard to reconcile with the wording of Article 8 and with the wording used by the ECtHR, not least because it renders the balancing process under Article 8(2) irrelevant. The ECtHR has always emphasised that any interference with the interests of parents be proportionate and necessary. If any departure from welfare will justify an interference with the rights of parents then the notions of necessity and proportionality appear to have no role to play. Furthermore, the description of children's interests being of 'particular' or 'crucial' importance by the ECtHR seem to leave open the possibility that children's interests could be outweighed by those of adults.

This leads to the crucial question. Why is it that children's interests should be seen as being particularly important as compared to the interests of an adult? An order which is interfering in a child's right to private or family life is likely to be far more of a blight than an identical order on an adult's life. This is because a child is less equipped to deal with setbacks in their interests and life chances. They lack the practical possibilities of remaking life plans and the experience, maturity or even intelligence to develop alternatives. They may also lack the support of friends or family or the emotional maturity to deal with the situation. Consider, for example, a case where a person is going to be moved from a place where they have an established set of friends and community support to a place where they know no one. While this would be disturbing for anyone it is particular serious for a child,

---

[97] J Fortin 'The HRA's Impact on Litigation Involving Children and their Families' [1999] *Child and Family Law Quarterly* 237.

who will be less equipped to find and develop new friends; less experienced to realise that any sense of loneliness and isolation will last for a relatively short time; and less equipped to rely on the support of existing friends.

For another example, let us consider a dispute over a child's surname. Both the child and an adult have strong views. For the sake of argument let us assume that to each of them the issue is equally important and both will feel upset to the same extent if they lose. Yet if the adult loses we might properly expect that he or she will have the intellectual, emotional and social support to see him or her through the disappointment. The child will have far less of these things. Further, the child is liable to suffer far more from embarrassment or bullying from the unwanted surname than an adult would.[98]

This leads us to conclude that generally speaking the interference in the interest of a child will be worse than the same interference in the right of an adult. However, and this is the key question, how does this fit into the reasoning of the ECtHR? Is the Court saying that generally interferences in children's rights will be far worse than the interference for an adult and so should be preferred; or is it saying that even taking on board the vulnerabilities of a child and even if the interference of the interests is similar, there is a reason for preferring the interests of the child over the interests of an adult? This is something that the ECtHR has not specifically addressed and thus we cannot know the answer to the question. However, it raises this question: are children's rights given an elevated status over adults because we believe that children are more vulnerable and less able to deal with breaches of their rights; or because children's rights are inherently more valuable and that even if the impact on their lives will be equal, children deserve a stronger protection of their rights by virtue of them being children? That is a question which the ECtHR is yet to fully explore and yet is central to a proper understanding of the special place that children's interests hold in ECtHR jurisprudence.

Reconciling Welfare and the HRA

Can the welfare principle be reconciled with an approach based on human rights?[99] Lord Justice Thorpe and Dame Elizabeth Butler Sloss, in *Payne*, both defended the welfare principle, finding that it was essentially the same as the approach of the ECtHR. In particular, Lord Justice Thorpe considered that:

> [the HRA] requires no re-evaluation of the judge's primary task to evaluate and uphold the welfare of the child as the paramount consideration, *despite its inevitable conflict with adult rights*.[100]

He supported this conclusion on the basis that:

> the jurisprudence of the European Court of Human Rights inevitably recognises the paramountcy principle, albeit not expressed in the language of our domestic statute. In *Johansen v Norway*

---

[98] See further J Herring, 'The Shaming of Naming' in R Probert, S Gilmore and J Herring (eds), *Responsible Parents and Parental Responsibility* (Oxford, Hart, 2009).

[99] J Eekelaar, 'Beyond the Welfare Principle' [2002] *Child and Family Law Quarterly* 237; H Reece, 'The Paramountcy Principle—Consensus or Construct?' (1996) 49 *Current Legal Problems* 267; N Lowe, 'The House of Lords and the Welfare Principle' in C Bridge (ed), *Family Law Towards the Millennium: Essays for PM Bromley* (London, Butterworths, 1997); J Herring, 'The Human Rights Act and the Welfare Principle in Family Law—Conflicting or Complementary? [1999] *Child and Family Law Quarterly* 237; J Fortin, 'The HRA's Impact' (n 97); A Bainham, 'Can we Protect Children and Protect Their Rights?' (2002) 22 *Family Law* 279.

[100] *Payne v Payne* [2001] EWCA Civ 166.

(1997) 23 EHRR 33, 72, para 78, the court held that: 'the court will attach particular importance to the best interests of the child, which … may override those of the parent'.[101]

Thorpe LJ's comments represent a misunderstanding of both Conventions. As Sonia Harris-Short notes, Thorpe LJ's quotation from *Johansen* is selective.[102] The actual words of the judgment in *Johansen* give a very different impression from the paraphrased quotation given by Thorpe LJ:

> a fair balance has to be struck between the interests of the child in remaining in public care and those of the parent in being reunited with the child. *In carrying out this balancing exercise,* the Court will attach particular importance to the best interests of the child, which, *depending on their nature and seriousness,* may override those of the parent.[103]

In taking this approach the Court of Appeal was following a well-established line of authority. In *Re B (Adoption: Natural Parent)*[104] Lord Nicholls stated:

> The court decides that an adoption order is best for the child in all the circumstances. I do not see how an adoption order made in this way can infringe the child's rights under Article 8. Under Article 8 the adoption order must meet a pressing social need and be a proportionate response to that need: see, for example, *Silver v United Kingdom* (1983) 5 EHRR 347, 376–377, paragraph 97(c). Inherent in both these Convention concepts is a balancing exercise, weighing the advantages and the disadvantages. But this balancing exercise, required by Article 8, does not differ in substance from the like balancing exercise undertaken by a court when deciding whether, in the conventional phraseology of English law, adoption would be in the best interests of the child. The like considerations fall to be taken into account. Although the phraseology is different, the criteria to be applied in deciding whether an adoption order is justified under Article 8(2) lead to the same result as the conventional tests applied by English law. Thus, unless the court misdirected itself in some material respect when balancing the competing factors, its conclusion that an adoption order is in the best interests of the child, even though this would exclude the mother from the child's life, identifies the pressing social need for adoption (the need to safeguard and promote the child's welfare) and represents the court's considered view on proportionality. That is the effect of the judge's decision in the present case. Article 8(2) does not call for more.

Despite the consistent judicial approach[105] there has been near-universal academic disapproval of it.[106] There are two key differences between the welfare principle and the approach in *Johansen*. First, the ECtHR clearly states that it is engaged in a balancing exercise between the interests of the parties. The welfare principle, on the other hand, does not admit such a balancing exercise; indeed the interests of the parents are strictly irrelevant to the decision unless they affect the welfare of the child. Secondly, the *Johansen* approach

---

[101] *Ibid*, paras 38–9; see also para 82.

[102] S Harris-Short, 'Family Law and the Human Rights Act 1998: Judicial Restraint or Revolution' [2005] *Child and Family Law Quarterly* 329, at 355.

[103] *Johansen v Norway* (1997) 23 EHRR 33, para 78 (emphasis added).

[104] [2001] UKHL 70, para 31.

[105] Indeed it has become so widely accepted that it seems rarely to be argued that the welfare principle can be challenged under a human rights approach: certainly that is not an argument the courts have recently addressed.

[106] S Harris-Short, '*Re B (Adoption: Natural Parent)*, Putting the Child at the Heart of Adoption?' [2002] 14 *Child and Family Law Quarterly* 325, 336–8; S Choudhry, 'The Adoption and Children Act 2002' (n 92); J Eekelaar, 'Beyond the welfare principle' (n 99); J Fortin, 'Children's Rights: Are the Courts Now Taking Them More Seriously?' (2004) 15 *Kings College Law Journal* 253; S Choudhry and H Fenwick, 'Taking the Rights of Parents and Children Seriously: Confronting the Welfare Principle under the Human Rights Act' (2005) 25 *OJLS* 453.

implies that the interests of the child will not always override those of the parent but that this will depend on the 'nature and seriousness' of those interests. Again, this contrasts with the welfare principle, which demands that the welfare of the child prevails over the rights of the parents without regard to its nature and seriousness. As Bainham puts it:

> Adults rights to respect for private and family life *must* be respected and must not be interfered with unless the specific justification envisaged by Article 8(2) exist and only then when they are *necessary* and *proportionate* to a legitimate State aim. This is prima facie very much more prescriptive than merely leaving it to a court to decide at large what course of action is in the best interests of a child.[107]

If the welfare approach is incompatible with the HRA, the question remains what should be done. The courts are obliged by statute to apply the principle and such a statutory obligation takes precedence over their role under section 6 of the HRA. Nevertheless, section 3 of the HRA obliges the court to interpret the welfare principle, as far as possible, to be compatible with the parties' Convention rights. As Choudhry and Fenwick point out, one way in which the welfare principle can be interpreted compatibly with Convention rights is to interpret 'paramount' to mean 'most important'.[108] In other words, the interests of the child will be the most important consideration for the court but will not inevitably determine the outcome, particularly where there are weighty countervailing interests. On this interpretation, the welfare principle can be read compatibly with the approach of the ECtHR, to require a 'parallel analysis' balancing exercise between all the rights involved, but with particular importance given to the rights and interests of the child within that analysis.

Children's Rights and Corporal Punishment

The issue of corporal punishment has been one where the impact of the ECHR has been particularly significant.[109] Particularly because it is an area of law where the independent rights of children have been given explicit attention. In Chapter 5 this issue was considered from the point of view of parents' rights. In *A v UK*[110] the ECtHR considered the UK law at the time, which permitted a defence of 'reasonable chastisement' to a charge of assault on a child. The step-father in that case had caused injuries of sufficient severity to fall within the scope of Article 3, but still the jury had acquitted him, accepting the defence of reasonable chastisement. The case was taken in the child's name to the ECtHR, where it was found that the UK law did not provide adequate protection to the applicant against treatment or punishment contrary to Article 3. It was held the beating breached the child's Article 3 rights. In assessing whether it did so the Court said that all the circumstances of the case had to be considered. This included the nature and context of the treatment; its duration; its physical and mental effects; and, in some cases, the sex, age and state of

---

[107] Bainham, *Children: The Modern Law* (n 46), 738.

[108] Choudhry and Fenwick, 'Taking the rights of parents and children seriously' (n 106).

[109] H Keating, 'Protecting or punishing children: physical punishment, human rights and English law reform' (2006) 26 *Legal Studies* 394; S Choudhry, 'Corporal Punishment and Parental Responsibility' in R Probert, S Gilmore and J Herring (eds), *Responsible Parents and Parental Responsibility* (Oxford, Hart, 2009). This section has relied on the second of these articles.

[110] (1999) 27 EHRR 61.

health of the victim.[111] Thus, just because a form of conduct is not degrading treatment for one person does not mean that it cannot be so for another. The ECtHR confirmed that Article 3 imposed primarily a negative obligation on states to refrain from inflicting serious harm on persons within their jurisdiction. However, there were positive aspects of the rights as well. In particular it was the responsibility of the state to protect one citizen from having her Article 3 rights infringed at the hands of another individual. The UK law at the time of *A v UK* failed to ensure the applicant protection of his Article 3 rights at the hand of his father. As a result of the decision the law in the UK was amended through section 58 of the Children Act 2004, which reads:

(1) In relation to any offence specified in subsection (2), battery of a child cannot be justified on the ground that it constituted reasonable punishment.
(2) The offences referred to in subsection (1) are—
    (a) an offence under section 18 or 20 of the Offences against the Person Act 1861 (c. 100) (wounding and causing grievous bodily harm);
    (b) an offence under section 47 of that Act (assault occasioning actual bodily harm);
    (c) an offence under section 1 of the Children and Young Persons Act 1933 (c. 12) (cruelty to persons under 16).
(3) Battery of a child causing actual bodily harm to the child cannot be justified in any civil proceedings on the ground that it constituted reasonable punishment.

In addition, shortly after the passage of the Act the Crown Prosecution Service amended the charging standard on offences against the person, which now states that the vulnerability of the victim, such as being a child assaulted by an adult, should be treated as an aggravating factor when deciding the appropriate charge. Injuries that would normally have led to a charge of common assault will now be charged as assault occasioning actual bodily harm under section 47 of the OAPA under which the defence of reasonable punishment will not be available. A subsequent government review of section 58 notes that the charging standard has clarified the boundary between what constitutes common assault and what constitutes assault occasioning actual bodily harm and takes into account the particular seriousness of an adult assaulting a child.[112] It also records the fact that the standard may have resulted in the removal of a certain amount of discretion from the police which has had the seemingly unintended result of providing *more* protection for children:

> However, it (the charging standard) means that the police sometimes have to record as assault occasioning actual bodily harm a crime which is not perceived as being particularly serious, best dealt with by children's social care rather than the criminal justice system, and which previously would have been recorded as common assault.[113]

As a result, it is certainly arguable that current UK law on the parental defence of reasonable punishment in relation to common assault is, in the absence of a further decision on the matter from the ECtHR, compatible with Article 3 of the ECHR, in that it is unlikely that behaviour which was merely a battery and which caused no actual bodily harm would infringe Article 3. The issue may not be entirely beyond doubt, however. A corporal punishment administered in highly degrading circumstances might reach Article 3 levels,

---

[111] See among other authorities *Costello-Roberts v United Kingdom* [1995] 19 EHRR 112.
[112] Department for Education and Skills, *Review of s58 of the Children Act 2004* (London, DfES, 2008).
[113] *Ibid*, para 45.

even if only a battery occurred. Further, even if the corporal punishment is only a battery which does not reach Article 3 levels, it may still involve a breach of Article 8.[114]

Access to Courts

A clear indication of whether a legal system would take children's rights seriously is the rights of access to children to the courts. If children have rights, but no effective means of bringing their complaints to the courts, then the claim that children's rights are only enforced at the convenience of adults is stronger, in which case the claims are better seen as adult rather than child rights. Indeed, the right of children to be heard in court proceedings does not need to be linked to the view that they have a right to be able to make decisions for themselves.[115]

On the face of the ECHR there appears to be a strong claim for children to have a right to bring cases to court. There is nothing in the wording of Article 6 to suggest that the right of access to the court does not apply to children. Such a claim may be bolstered by reference to Article 12(2) of the CRC, which requires states to provide children with:

> the opportunity to be heard in any judicial and administrative proceedings affecting the child, either directly, or through a representative or an appropriate body, in a manner consistent with the procedural rules of national law.

Indeed the UN Committee on the Rights of the Child complained that the UK had not effectively ensured that children were heard in private law proceedings about children.[116]

The ECtHR has had relatively little to say about the access of children to courts, nor their representation in court hearings, under Article 6.[117] Notably the Court has had more to say about the representation of children in court proceedings as part of the procedural protection of rights under Article 8.[118] In *Elsholz v Germany*;[119] *Sahin v Germany; Sommerfeld v Germany; Hoffman v Germany*[120] it was held that in private law cases concerning children the failure to either hear the child directly in open court or obtain an expert psychological assessment of the child's views would infringe the child's Article 8 rights. However, this approach was reversed by the decision of the Grand Chamber in 2003 in *Sahin v Germany; Sommerfeld v Germany*[121] which held that the earlier decisions had gone too far in saying that hearing the child or receiving an expert report was an essential requirement for Article 8. The court must ensure that the proceedings were fair, but how the child's views

---

[114] See further S Choudhry and J Herring, 'Righting Domestic Violence' (2006) 20 *International Journal of Law, Policy and the Family* 65.

[115] D Archard and M Skivenes, 'Balancing a Child's Best Interests and a Child's Views' (2009) 17 *International Journal of Children's Rights* 1.

[116] UN Committee on the Rights of the Child, *Concluding Observations: United Kingdom and Northern Ireland* (2002), para 29.

[117] See also the European Convention on the Exercise of Children's Rights 1996, which has not been signed by the UK.

[118] Munby J, 'Making Sure the Child is Heard' [2004] *Family Law* 427.

[119] [2002] 2 FLR 486.

[120] [2003] 2 FLR 671.

[121] *Ibid.*

should be considered would depend on the child's age and maturity and an assessment of the specific circumstances of each case.

Children can bring proceedings either through a solicitor or through a next friend (normally one of their parents). To bring proceedings using a solicitor a child normally needs leave,[122] and this has proved problematic. Rarely have the courts given leave. A typical example of the case law is *Re C (A Minor) (Leave to seek Section 8 Order)*,[123] where the court refused to allow a 14 year old who wanted to go on holiday with her friend's family to Bulgaria against her parents' wishes. The issue was regarded as too trivial. If so then most issues relating to autonomy which a child might want to raise in a court will also be too trivial. The courts have also held that if the proceedings are complex or likely to cause emotional harm it will be better for the child not to be involved.

The courts appear to be more wiling to allow children to express their views when they wish to be involved in litigation between their parents. In *Re A (Contact: Separate Representation)*[124] Dame Butler Sloss P stated that the HRA had strengthened the claim for children seeking separate representation. While accepting that it was unusual for a child to have separate representation she held:

> There are cases where they do need to be separately represented and I suspect as a result of the European Convention ... becoming part of domestic law, and the increased view of the English courts, in any event, that the children should be seen and heard in child cases and not always sufficiently seen and heard by the use of a court welfare officer's report, there will be an increased use of guardians in private law cases. Indeed, in the right case I would welcome it. I hope with the introduction of CAFCASS in April of next year ... it will be easier for children to be represented in suitable cases.[125]

In *Mabon v Mabon*[126] the Court of Appeal overturned the decision of a judge that three 'educated, articulate and reasonably mature' boys aged 17, 15 and 13 should not be separately represented in a sharply contested residence and contact dispute. Thorpe LJ held that 'it was simply unthinkable to exclude these young men from knowledge of and participation in legal proceedings that affected them so fundamentally'.[127] He thought children should be involved in litigation if they wished, even if to do so might cause them some harm. He explained that 'the right of freedom of expression and participation outweighs the paternalistic judgement of welfare.'[128] In making these points he made specific reference to the children's rights under Article 8 of the ECHR and Article 12 of the CRC.

Despite the statement in *Mabon* a recent study found that separate representation is rarely ordered by courts. This is largely because the judiciary are aware that CAFCASS simply lacks the resources to represent children in as many cases as may be appropriate. Jane Fortin claims that 'children's rights are systematically downgraded for financial reasons'.[129]

---

[122] Rule 9.2A Family Proceedings Rules 1999, SI 1999/3491. Technically this is not necessary where the solicitor has found the child competent to give instructions, but where the child seeks an order under the CA, s8, which is the most likely section to be used, the application must be brought.

[123] [1996] 1 FCR 461.

[124] [2001] 1 FLR 715.

[125] Paras 21–2.

[126] [2005] 2 FCR 354.

[127] At para 52.

[128] At para 53.

[129] J Fortin, 'Children's Rights: Substance or Spin?' (n 60).

One concern is that increasingly couples are encouraged to engage in dispute resolution rather than taking cases to court. However, there are concerns that when the emphasis is on finding agreement between the parents the views of the child are not heard.[130] Even when cases do get to court there are serious concerns over the effectiveness of court welfare reports in accurately representing the views of children.[131] Indeed in one study in 2005 over a third of court reports did not reach the standards expected of government inspectors.[132] Another report by the government inspectorate found that some reports were recording the author's views of what was in the child's best interests rather than accurately reflecting the child's views.[133] A Cardiff University study found that children felt that their views were not being accurately reported.[134]

Conclusions

A delegation of children appearing before a special UN session on children's rights made this statement:

We are not the sources of problems;
We are the resources that are needed to solve them.
We are not expenses; we are investments.
We are not just young people; we are people and citizens of this world ...
You call us the future, but we are also the present.[135]

As we have seen in this chapter such sentiments have led many to call for a greater recognition of the rights of children. To date the recognition of children's rights to protection in both the ECtHR and the English courts is stronger than that given to their autonomy rights. Indeed it is fair to say that within both the ECtHR and English courts there has been little attention given to the independent rights of children, which are often subsumed within claims to the rights of their parents. This Chapter has explored some of the ways the ECtHR and, through the HRA, English law, could develop an approach more focused on children's rights.

---

[130] HM Inspectorate of Court Administration, *Domestic Violence, Safety and Family Proceedings: Thematic review of the handling of domestic violence issues by the Children and Family Court Advisory and Support Service (CAFCASS) and the administration of family courts in Her Majesty's Courts Service (HMCS)* (London, HM Inspectorate of Court Administration, 2005) para 3.75.

[131] J Fortin, 'Children's Representation Through the Looking Glass' (2007) 37 *Family Law* 500.

[132] HM Inspectorate of Court Administration, *Domestic Violence, Safety and Family Proceedings*, at para 3.41.

[133] HM Inspectorate of Court Administration, *Safeguarding Children in Family Proceedings* (London, HM Inspectorate of Court Administration, 2005) para 2.29.

[134] G Douglas, M Murch, C Miles and L Scanlan, *Final Report for the Department of Constitutional Affairs: Research into the Operation of Rule 9.5 of the Family Proceedings Rules 1991* (London, Department of Constitutional Affairs, 2006), ch 3, esp at para 3.84.

[135] Children delegates to UN special session, quoted in BB Woodhouse, *Hidden in Plain Sight: The Tragedy of Children's Rights from Ben Franklin to Lionel Tate* (Princetown, Princetown University Press, 2008) 29.

7

Private Law Children Cases:
A Rights Perspective

Introduction

This Chapter will consider the relevance of the HRA to disputes between adults concerning children. Any order made under the CA is likely to amount to an interference in the right to respect for family life by a public authority (the court).[1] Certainly whenever a court is deciding a dispute over who a child should live with, or the extent of contact with a non-resident parent, or an issue relating to a child's upbringing, the Article 8 rights of the parties will be involved.[2] As already emphasised, there is an important distinction between analysing the case based on the welfare principle in the CA and an approach based on a human rights analysis.[3] The focus of the welfare principle is on the child alone and the sole question for the court is an assessment of what is in the child's welfare, whereas under a human rights approach the rights of each party need to be considered and an assessment made of whether an interference with those rights is justified. As seen in Chapter 3, the English courts have stated that whatever differences there may be in the form of reasoning used, there is no difference in practice between the approach adopting the welfare principle and an approach taken using human rights.[4] In the earlier discussion, while it was accepted that in many cases a welfare-based approach and a human-rights-based approach would produce the same answer, that would not be true for all cases. Further, it was argued that even if the results are the same, the rights-based analysis would have some benefits over the welfare-based analysis in bringing out the issues more clearly.

This Chapter will consider further how using a human rights approach might lead to changes in the reasoning used by the courts and occasionally the results reached. It will not be possible to discuss every conceivable kind of dispute that might arise between parents. Rather, the focus will be particularly on one of the most controversial issues: contact disputes. It will also look at cases involving religious issues and relocation cases and cases involving wider family members, such as grandparents. These will be used to illustrate the way an approach using the ECHR would deal with the wide range of issues over which parents can dispute.

---

[1] *Re H (Contact Order) (No 2)* [2002] 1 FLR 23.
[2] For a comparative consideration of this issue see H Rhoades and S Boyd, 'Reforming Custody Laws: A Comparative Study' (2004) 18 *International Journal of Law, Policy and the Family* 18.
[3] See chs 1 and 3.
[4] *Re H (children) (contact order) (No 2)* [2001] 3 FCR 385, para 59.

Contact and the ECHR

Establishing the Right to Contact

The approach of the ECHR to contact cases is relatively straightforward.[5] It will be briefly summarised before a more thorough analysis is undertaken. Where a person has a right to respect for family life with a child under Article 8(1) this is taken to include the right to have contact with the child.[6] Similarly where a child has family life with an adult the child has a right to have contact with that adult. As was said in *Kosmopoulou v Greece*:[7]

> the mutual enjoyment by parent and child of each other's company constitutes a fundamental element of family life, even if the relationship between the parents has broken down, and domestic measures hindering such enjoyment amount to an interference with the right protected by Art 8 of the Convention.[8]

Such rights can be interfered with if that can be justified under Article 8(2). Hence, when parents separate on divorce if the child lives with the mother the father has a right to contact the child, but that right can be interfered with if that is necessary in the interests of the child, or for some other reason in Article 8(2). Where there is no sufficient justification for an interference, contact must be permitted and the state must take reasonable steps to enforce that right.

Some of those points will now be considered in more detail. The first point to emphasise is that a person only has a right of contact with a child under Article 8 if they have family life with the child. As seen in Chapter 5 most, but not all, parents have family life with their children.[9] That is not, of course, to say that a person whose relationship with a child does not fall under Article 8 should not have contact under a contact order, but rather that such a claim will not fall under Article 8. It also should be noticed that under Article 8 not only does a parent have a right to contact a child, but a child has a right to contact a parent.[10]

The Court has found that included within the right to family life is the right to contact.[11] Stephen Gilmore has challenged the assumption that a right to respect for family life necessarily includes a right to contact.[12] Respect for family life may involve supporting contact and enabling contact, but does not necessarily require the substantive law to be based on there being a right to contact. That argument has not been addressed by the ECtHR, indeed it has assumed that contact is an inherent part of respect for family life. It will be consider further later.

As already mentioned, the Court may find that under Article 8(2) there is sufficient justification for an interference in a child's or parents' Article 8 rights. Now consideration will be given to what these justifications may be.

---

[5] Art 9(3) of the United Nations Convention on the Rights of the Child declares that:

'States Parties shall respect the right of the child who is separated from one or both parents to maintain personal relations and direct contact with both parents on a regular basis, except if it is contrary to the child's best interest.'

[6] *Hokkanen v Finland* (1994) 19 EHHR 139; *Sahin v Germany* [2003] 2 FLR 671.
[7] [2004] 1 FLR 800.
[8] At para 47.
[9] See further the discussion in ch 4.
[10] *Re D (Intractable Contact Dispute: Publicity)* [2004] 1 FLR 1226, para 26.
[11] *Hokkanen v Finland* (n 6).
[12] S Gilmore, 'Disputing Contact: Challenging some Assumptions'.

The Views of the Child

The opposition of the child to contact can justify not ordering contact under Article 8(2).[13] The ECtHR in *Hokkanen v Finland*[14] did not question the correctness of the final orders of the Finnish courts which, after placing considerable weight on the views of the 12-year-old girl who did not want to have contact with her father, declined to make a contact order. It seems, however, that it would be wrong to assume that where a mature child opposes contact, that automatically justifies an interference in a non-resident parent's right to contact. In *C v Finland*[15] the father's rights to contact with his teenage children were held to be infringed. The children opposed contact and the Finnish Supreme Court had simply followed the views of the children and there was not even an oral hearing.[16] The ECtHR was critical of the decisive weight given to the children's wishes. Doing so had given the children, in effect, 'an unconditional veto power'. The ECtHR concluded:

> The decision was reached in a manner which understandably left the applicant with the impression that L, the mother's partner, had been allowed to manipulate the children and the court system to deprive him unjustifiably of his parental role.[17]

This was held by the ECtHR to infringe the father's rights. While it was accepted that the views of teenage children carried weight, and could justify interfering in the father's right of contact, it was necessary for the national court to consider all the competing interests. All that said, the Court accepted:

> On a practical basis, there may also come a stage where it becomes pointless, if not counter-productive and harmful, to attempt to force a child to conform to a situation which, for whatever reasons, he or she resists.[18]

Nevertheless the message from *C v Finland* is clear: that even where mature children have clear views there needs to be a careful and full consideration of all the evidence and a weighing up of the competing rights. In *Nanning v Germany*[19] a court expert recommended increasing the level of contact between a mother and her 16-year-old daughter, despite the daughter's opposition to doing so. The failure to take steps to enforce the order breached the mother's Article 8 rights. That case reinforces the point that even the views of a mature child will not necessarily determine the issue. However, in the most recent decision of *Kaleta v Poland*[20] it was accepted that as a child matured, her views would determine the nature and extent of contact between her and her father. So, although a court when considering an application for contact must undertake a full consideration of the issues, the views of the child may well, at the end of the day, determine what will happen.

The court will also be alert to the fact that children's expressed views may not be their genuine views. A report from psychologists is required to ensure that the child is truly opposed to contact and not simply representing the views of the resident parent.[21] Even

---

[13] *Hokkanen v Finland* (n 6).
[14] *Ibid.*
[15] [2006] 2 FCR 195, at paras 58 and 59.
[16] *Hansen v Turkey* [2003] 3 FCR 97.
[17] Para 58.
[18] Para 57.
[19] [2007] 2 FCR 543 at paras 26 and 72–7.
[20] [2009] 1 FLR 927.
[21] *Ignaccolo-Zenide v Romania* (2001) 31 EHRR 7.

then the fact a child may have been influenced by a resident parent will not mean their views will discounted. In *Suss v Germany*[22] the Court summarised its conclusion in these terms:

> In these circumstances, the Court finds that the national courts' decisions to suspend the applicant's access to his daughter can be taken to have been made in the child's best interest, which, due to its serious nature, must override the applicant's interests. Even though the Court agrees with the national courts and the applicant that the child's negative attitude towards her father was presumably partly caused by GS's influence, it had nevertheless been the child's firm wish not to see her father which had prevailed. The national courts did not limit in time the prohibition of access, but made it clear that GS was obliged to contribute to a change in F's negative attitude towards her father. They had therefore been aware of their duty to preserve the uniting bonds between father and daughter (see, *mutatis mutandis, Nekvedavicius v Germany* [2003] ECHR 46165/99), and had tried to overcome any obstacles to granting at least a limited access. Consequently, the Court is satisfied that the German courts adduced relevant reasons to justify their decisions refusing access.

The ECtHR case law makes it clear that the views of children will carry considerable weight and can justify not ordering contact. However, in each case a careful consideration should be made of the competing rights and the court should ensure that the expressed views of the child have been reached by the child independently. It should also be remembered that compelling a child to see a parent against the child's wishes is likely to interfere with the child's right to respect for his or her private life under Article 8. While, therefore, the court should consider all the relevant issues even where a child has strong views, it will be rare that the court will force contact on a child.

The Interests of all the Family Members

The court should consider interests of the child, father, mother and wider family in deciding whether any right to contact should be enforced.[23] This indicates that harm to the resident parent, or indeed a wider family member, can be taken into account. The court must take the interests of the resident parent into account and consider the impact that contact would have on them.[24]

One major issue in this regard is how the court should deal with a case where the interests of the child and adults clash. It has been confirmed that in deciding whether or not an interference is justified the best interests of the child are 'crucial'.[25] That terminology leaves us with two crucial questions. The first is in what circumstances will the interests of the adults justify interfering in a child's right to contact. For example, when will harm to the resident parent in allowing contact permit a court to interfere in a child's right of contact. It may be that only a significant level of harm to a resident parent would in itself justify interfering with a child's right to contact. A case indicating that the evidence to justify the breach of the non-resident father's rights must be strong is *Görgülü v Germany*.[26] There a child was placed for adoption by the mother after the mother and father's relationship broke down during the pregnancy. A Mr and Mrs B adopted the child and cared for him from birth. The father sought contact and custody of the child. The national court accepted

---

[22] [2005] ECHR 40324/98, para 91.
[23] *Nuutinen v Finland* [2000] ECHR 32842/96.
[24] *Sahin v Germany* [2003] 2 FLR 671.
[25] Eg *Sahin v Germany* (n 6), para 64. For further discussion see p 247.
[26] [2004] 1 FCR 410.

that the father was in a position to care for the child, but held that the child was well settled with Mr and Mrs B and did not order contact. The ECtHR emphasised that in cases of restricting contact the national authorities had a narrower margin of appreciation and stricter scrutiny was called for any limitation. In this case it was accepted that the child had never lived with the father and further that the child had formed a bond with Mr and Mrs B. Nevertheless, depriving the natural father of his rights required consideration of all the alternatives open to the court and a consideration of the long-term well-being of the child. The consideration by the national courts of the alternatives had been inadequate.

Another, and in a way more significant, question is what if there is a clash between two rights of a child. For example if there is evidence that contact between a father and child will pose a risk to a child's welfare, the child may have a right under Article 8 which protects her interest in contact with her father and also rights under Article 8 which protect her interests in keeping safe. This is an issue on which there is little guidance from the ECtHR. Certainly where there is evidence of significant harm, contact is unlikely to be ordered.[27] But quite how the balance should be struck where the contact will cause some harm is unclear from the current case law. Shortly it will be argued how this might be done.

One final point on cases where the court is considering whether an interference in an Article 8 based right to contact is that there must be no discrimination in contact disputes between mothers and fathers;[28] married fathers and unmarried fathers;[29] or on the grounds of sexual orientation.[30] In *Salgueiro da Silva Mouta v Portugal*[31] the ECtHR accepted that discrimination against same-sex couples or against a gay or lesbian person could amount to discrimination on the basis of sexual orientation. This means that a parent's sexual orientation should not count against them in any contact or custody issue.[32]

Procedural Issues

Part of the protection of the right to respect for family life in a contact case involves there being procedural safeguards for the parties' interests. These procedural requirements are seen as an aspect of respect for a party's family life under Article 8. In *Sahin v Germany*[33] the ECtHR held:

> The Court has recognised that the authorities enjoy a wide margin of appreciation when deciding on custody matters. However, a stricter scrutiny is called for as regards any further limitations, such as restrictions placed by those authorities on parental rights of access, and as regards any legal safeguards designed to secure the effective protection of the right of parents and children to respect for their family life. Such further limitations entail the danger that the family relations between a young child and one or both parents would be effectively curtailed.[34]

---

[27] *Sahin v Germany* (n 6).
[28] *Ibid.*
[29] *Sommerfeld v Germany* (2003) 36 EHRR 565, paras 51 and 55, upheld on this ground by the Grand Chamber [2003] 2 FLR 671, paras 93–4.
[30] *Salgueiro da Silva Mouta v Portugal* [2001] 1 FCR 653, discussed in J Herring, 'Gay Rights Come Quietly' (2002)118 LQR 31.
[31] [2001] 1 FCR 653. However, in *Fretté v France* [2003] 2 FCR 39 it was held to be within a state's margin of appreciation to hold that a bar on same-sex adoption was not permitted.
[32] See further the discussion on same-sex parents and family life in ch 4.
[33] *Sahin v Germany* (n 6).
[34] Para 65.

As this makes clear, the ECtHR, when considering contact cases, while granting states a margin of appreciation when dealing with the substantive issue, will impose stricter requirements on procedural matters. In *Suss v Germany*[35] it was explained:

> In assessing whether those reasons were also sufficient for the purposes of Art 8(2), the Court will notably have to determine whether the decision-making process, seen as a whole, provided the applicant with the requisite protection of his interests. This depends on the particular circumstances of the case. The applicant must notably have been placed in a position enabling him to put forward all arguments in favour of obtaining access to his child.[36]

A refusal of contact should follow an oral hearing,[37] although an appeal against a refusal of contact does not necessarily require an oral hearing.[38] 'Exceptional diligence' is required before an order not allowing contact is made. The Court has also made clear that it is important that 'correct and complete' information about the child's views are gathered.[39] At one point there was a suggestion in the case law that there was a requirement that a child attend court to give evidence before contact could be denied, but this was rejected by the Grand Chamber in *Sahin v Germany*.[40] However, where the child does not attend, there needs to be proper evidence of a child's views, such as an expert report. If the report is inadequate that may lead to an infringement of the parties' rights. In *Sahin*,[41] where a report was presented to the Court, the failure of the expert to have questioned the child about the father led to an infringement of his Article 6 rights. In *Kosmopoulou v Greece*[42] the report had interviewed only one of the parents and the child, which was held to be inadequate and led to a finding of a lack of protection of the mother's Articles 6 and 8 rights.

Parties should be able to cross-examine witnesses and have access to reports which formed the basis of court orders.[43] The ECtHR has said that:

> it is of paramount importance for parents always to be placed in a position enabling them to put forward all arguments in favour of obtaining contact with the child and to have access to all relevant information which was at the disposal of the domestic courts.[44]

Even where the result of the hearing may seem obvious, that does not obviate the need for a proper hearing. In *Kosmopoulou v Greece*[45] a child refused to stay with the non-resident mother. The child was taken to the police station where the mother was seen to kick the child and pull out clumps of hair. Contact with the mother was stopped, but it was found that this was done without a proper hearing and hence her Article 8 rights were infringed.

The ECtHR case law makes it clear that contact should only be denied after a hearing where the Court has been able to assess all the relevant evidence, particularly in relation to the children's views, and each side has been able to present their case effectively.

---

[35] [2005] ECHR 40324/98.
[36] See also *TP and KM v UK* [2001] ECHR 28945/95 at paras 78–83; *Sommerfeld v Germany* [2003] ECHR 31871/96 at paras 68–9; *Jucius and Juciuvienė v Lithuania* [2009] 1 FLR 403 at para 30.
[37] *Elsholz v Germany* [2000] 3 FCR 385.
[38] *Hoppe v Germany* [2003] 1 FCR 176.
[39] *Sahin v Germany* (n 6) para 48.
[40] *Ibid.*
[41] *Ibid.*
[42] [2004] 1 FCR 427.
[43] *Kosmopoulou v Greece* [2004] 1 FCR 427.
[44] *Ibid*, at para 49.
[45] [2004] 1 FCR 427.

Enforcement

Once a right of contact is established, the state is under a positive obligation to take steps to protect a parent's right to have contact with their child. This was expounded on in *Hokkanen v Finland*,[46] where it was held:

> The Court recalls that the obligation of the national authorities to take measures to facilitate reunion is not absolute, since the reunion of a parent with a child who has lived for some time with other persons may not be able to take place immediately and may require preparatory measures being taken to this effect. The nature and extent of such preparation will depend on the circumstances of each case, but the understanding and co-operation of all concerned will always be an important ingredient. Whilst national authorities must do their utmost to facilitate such co-operation, any obligation to apply coercion in this area must be limited since the interests as well as the rights and freedoms of all concerned must be taken into account, and more particularly the best interests of the child and his or her rights under Article 8 of the Convention. Where contacts with the parent might appear to threaten those interests or interfere with those rights, it is for the national authorities to strike a fair balance between them (see the above-mentioned *Olsson v Sweden (No 2)* judgment, pp 35–36, § 90).
>
> What is decisive is whether the national authorities have taken all necessary steps to facilitate reunion as can reasonably be demanded in the special circumstances of each case (*ibid*). The court does not deem it necessary to deal with the applicant's and the Commission's general argument on an obligation under Article 8 to take forcible measures.[47]

The failure to enforce a contact order can give rise to both Article 6 and Article 8 issues. As was explained in *Immobiliare Saffi v Italy*:[48]

> 63 ... the right to a court would be illusory if a contracting state's domestic legal system allowed a final, binding judicial decision to remain inoperative to the detriment of one party. It would be inconceivable that Art 6(1) should describe in detail procedural guarantees afforded to litigants—proceedings that are fair, public and expeditious—without protecting the implementation of judicial decisions; to construe Art 6 as being concerned exclusively with access to a court and the conduct of proceedings would be likely to lead to situations incompatible with the principle of the rule of law which the contracting states undertook to respect when they ratified the Convention. Execution of a judgment given by any court must therefore be regarded as an integral part of the 'trial' for the purposes of Art 6.
>
> 66 ... the right to a court as guaranteed by Art 6 also protects the implementation of final, binding judicial decisions, which, in states that accept the rule of law, cannot remain inoperative to the detriment of one party. Accordingly, the execution of a judicial decision cannot be unduly delayed.[49]

It important to emphasise that while there is a positive obligation to enforce contact orders, the state is only required to take reasonable steps to do this.[50] As well as attempts to coerce the parties to comply, it includes a requirement that the state do its utmost to facilitate co-operation between the parties.[51] Where there is intense conflict between the parents, the courts accept that the extent to which contact can be enforced is limited.[52]

---

[46] [1995] 2 FCR 320.
[47] Para 58.
[48] (1999) 7 BHRC 256, paras 63, 66.
[49] Also see *Hornsby v Greece* (1997) 24 EHRR 250, para 40.
[50] Eg *HN v Poland* [2005] 3 FCR 85.
[51] *Hokkanen v Finland* [1995] 2 FCR 320, para 58; *Ignaccolo-Zenide v Romania* (2001) 31 EHRR 7, para 94; *Nuutinen v Finland* (2000) 34 EHRR 358, para 128; *Glaser v UK* [2000] 3 FCR 193, para 66; *Hansen v Turkey* [2003] 3 FCR 97, para 98; and *Kosmopoulou v Greece* [2004] 1 FCR 427, para 45.
[52] *Kaleta v Poland* [2009] 1 FLR 927.

The obligation requires there to be an 'enforcement machinery' to protect an individual's rights and, where appropriate, that the state take specific steps to enforce the order.[53] The ECtHR, however, has made it clear that this does not necessarily require the imprisonment of the resident parent who has refused to allow contact to take place. Doing that would be likely to infringe the rights to respect for the family life of the child.[54] In some cases if the parent and child have not been in contact for some time preparatory work may be required before contact can take place.[55] That would mean immediate enforcement of contact may not be appropriate. In *Tomic v Serbia* it was stated:[56]

> The nature and extent of such measures shall depend on the circumstances of each case, but the understanding and co-operation of all those concerned are important ingredients.

In *Nuutinen v Finland* it was added:

> In examining whether the non-enforcement of the access arrangements amounted to a lack of respect for the applicant's family life the Court must strike a balance between the various interests involved, namely the interests of the applicant's daughter and her *de facto* family, those of the applicant himself and the general interest in ensuring respect for the rule of law.[57]

The ECtHR has been adamant that the obligation to facilitate is not absolute.[58] In particular any obligation to apply coercion will be limited.[59] 'What is decisive is whether the national authorities have taken all necessary steps to facilitate access as can reasonably be demanded in the special circumstances of each case.'[60] An example of where the court was found to have acted sufficiently was *Nuutinen v Finland*,[61] where the applicant had previously been imprisoned following an assault on the mother while she was pregnant. The court subsequently ordered contact and encouraged the parties to allow contact to take place. However, they did not use coercive measures and this, the applicant alleged, infringed his Article 8 rights. His application failed, but notably it was not the harm done to the mother which justified the limited intervention of the state to enforce contact orders, but the applicant's aggressive and unco-operative behaviour.

Another case which demonstrates the procedural requirements of the ECtHR is *Hansen v Turkey*.[62] The father had been awarded residence but refused to allow the mother to have contact. The court's sole attempts to enforce the order were by means of fines. This the Court found inadequate. Usefully the Court indicted what the state could have done. These included:[63]

1. seeking the advice of social services or the assistance of psychologists or child psychologists to create a better relationship between the parents and to facilitate contact;
2. allowing the children an opportunity to develop a relationship with their mother in a calm environment, so that they could express their feelings;

[53] *Zawadka v Poland* [2006] 1 FCR 371, para 53.
[54] *Re S (a child) (contact)* [2004] EWCA Civ 18, para 15.
[55] *Hansen v Turkey* [2003] 3 FCR 97.
[56] [2007] ECHR 25959/06, para 103.
[57] *Nuutinen v Finland* (2000) 34 EHRR 358, para 129.
[58] *Ibid*, para 128.
[59] *Ibid*, para 128.
[60] *Ibid*, para 128.
[61] *Ibid*.
[62] [2003] 3 FCR 97.
[63] At 103–12.

3. taking steps to locate the children when the father failed to produce them for contact sessions;
4. taking 'realistic' coercive measures against the father, in addition to the fines. The court did not amplify what these might be.

That case can be contrasted with *Glaser v UK*,[64] where there was a protracted contact dispute. At one point the mother and children disappeared and the UK's Official Solicitor was involved. They were found in Scotland and there were lengthy proceedings seeking her return. The father accepted that the UK government had taken steps to enforce the order, but his complaint was that they had shied away from enforcement, either through transferring residence to him or by committing the mother to prison. The ECtHR felt both those would have not have been reasonable. The state had made persistent and reasonable efforts to enforce the order, even though these had not been successful.

To similar effect is *Mihailova v Bulgaria*,[65] where a father snatched the child from the mother in court when the mother was granted residence. Despite repeated orders, the child had not been returned. The ECtHR noted that the courts had made numerous attempts to get the child returned and had imposed sanctions upon the father. These had failed, but that did not, per se, indicate a failure by the state to take reasonable steps.

It should not be forgotten that enforcing contact can work against the interest of the children and if so that may well be a justification for non-enforcement. As already mentioned, imprisoning the resident parent will, for example, inevitably interfere with the child's right to family life. However, the ECtHR has not ruled out using coercion against children. As the Court said in *Ignaccolo-Zenide v Romania*:[66]

> Although coercive measures towards children are far from desirable in such sensitive matters, sanctions should not be ruled out where the parent living with the children acts unlawfully.

Those comments were made in the context of a contact case which had involved the husband illegally abducting the children and repeatedly failing to comply with court orders.

That said, it will be very rare for coercion against children to lead to effective contact and will itself involve an interference in some of the children's rights. Indeed as that case also states, the interests of all those concerned must be taken into account:

> any obligation to apply coercion can only be limited since the interests, rights and freedoms of all concerned must be taken into account, and more particularly the best interests of the child and [his or her] rights under Article 8 of the Convention.[67]

All in all, coercion must involve a fair balance being struck between the interests of the different parties involved. As was explained in *Kosmopoulou v Greece*:

> the national authorities' obligation to take measures to facilitate reunion is not absolute, since the reunion of a parent with children who have lived for some time with the other parent may not be able to take place immediately and may require preparatory measures to be taken. The nature and extent of such preparation will depend on the circumstances of each case, but the understanding and co-operation of all concerned is always an important ingredient. Whilst national authorities must do their utmost to facilitate such co-operation, any obligation to apply coercion in this area

---

[64] [2000] 3 FCR 193.
[65] [2006] 1 FCR 327, paras 92–6.
[66] (2000) 31 EHRR 212, para 106. To similar effect see *Hansen v Turkey* [2003] 3 FCR 97, para 106.
[67] *Ignaccolo-Zenide v Romania* (2001) 31 EHRR 7, para 94.

must be limited since the interests as well as the rights and freedoms of all concerned must be taken into account, and more particularly the best interests of the child and his or her rights under Art 8 of the Convention. Where contact with the parent might appear to threaten those interests or interfere with those rights, it is for the national authorities to strike a fair balance between them.[68]

To similar effect are these comments from *Sylvester v Austria*:[69]

In cases concerning the enforcement of decisions in the realm of family law, the Court has repeatedly found that what is decisive is whether the national authorities have taken all the necessary steps to facilitate execution as can reasonably be demanded in the special circumstances of each case. In examining whether non-enforcement of a court order mounted to a lack of respect for the applicants' family life the court must strike a fair balance between the interests of all persons concerned and the general interest in ensuring respect for the rule of law. In cases of this kind the adequacy of a measure is to be judged by the swiftness of its implementation, as the passage of time can have irremediable consequences for relations between the child and the parent who does not live with him or her.[70]

As can be seen, therefore, although the ECtHR requires states to enforce contact orders there is an acknowledgement that there are limits on what the state can do. Indeed there is a danger that enforcement mechanisms can themselves interfere in the rights of the parties.

Resident Parents who Do not Permit Contact

One troublesome issue is whether the refusal of the resident parent to co-operate is a reason for the state not seeking to enforce a contact order. The ECtHR has accepted that the 'the co-operation and understanding of all concerned'[71] is important if contact is going to take place. Nevertheless the Court has held that a lack of co-operation does not exempt the authorities from taking steps to facilitate co-operation over contact. But facilitation does not necessarily require enforcement.[72] A dramatic example is *Zawadka v Poland*,[73] where a father had a contact order, but had not seen the child. He removed the child by force and kept the child for 16 months. When the child was recovered and returned to the mother his parental rights were removed and the courts refused to assist him in seeking to recover the child. The Court, perhaps surprisingly, found there had been an infringement of his Article 8 rights in the failure to enforce his contact order.[74] The basis of this was that, although this was a case where enforcement was not appropriate, given the mother's feelings about the father, the court had not sought to encourage the parties to co-operate.

The state has a positive duty to enable contact and it is not necessarily a defence for the state to point to the fact that the applicant has failed to take steps to enforce the order.[75]

---

[68] [2004] 1 FCR 427, para 45.

[69] [2003] 2 FCR 128 at 141, paras 59–60.

[70] *Kosmopoulou v Greece* (n 51), para 47; *Glaser v UK* (n 51), para 66. Some of these cases involve Hague Convention applications, rather than straightforward contact dispute cases. Nevertheless the reasoning has been adopted in cases of contact dispute (eg *Hansen v Turkey* (n 51), 111; *Tomic v Serbia* [2007] ECHR 25959/06). So any earlier questioning of whether the Hague Convention cases applied more widely (eg G Douglas, 'Comment' [2003] *Family Law* 639) seems unfounded.

[71] *Zawadka v Poland* (n 53) para 67.

[72] *Kosmopoulou v Greece* (n 51).

[73] [2006] 1 FCR 371.

[74] *Re K (Children: Committal Proceedings)* [2003] 2 FCR 336.

[75] *Ignaccolo-Zenide v Romania* (2001) 31 EHRR 7, para 111.

As it was put in *Sylvester v Austria*[76] an applicant's omission cannot absolve the authorities from their obligations in the matter of execution, since it is they who exercise public authority. That is a rather odd explanation. A better point would be to rely on the child's right of contact and to argue that the fact the parent does not seek contact does not mean that the child should lose her right.

Another factor that the ECtHR will take into account, especially in contact disputes involving child abduction, is the principles of international law. Thus in *Maire v Portugal* it was held:[77]

> The Court considers that the positive obligations that Art 8 of the Convention lays on the Contracting States in the matter of reuniting a parent with his children must be interpreted in the light of the *Hague Convention* (see *Ignaccolo-Zenide v Romania*, at para 95) and the *United Nations Convention on the Rights of the Child 1989*.[78]

The principle of the rule of law is also a relevant factor. In *Sylvester v Austria*[79] the ECtHR said:

> In examining whether non-enforcement of a court order amounted to a lack of respect for the applicants' family life the court must strike a fair balance between the interests of all persons concerned and the general interest in ensuring respect for the rule of law (see *Nuutinen*, at para 129).[80]

Similarly, in *Hansen*, it said:

> The Court, therefore, has to ascertain whether the national authorities took all necessary steps to facilitate execution as could reasonably be demanded in the special circumstances of the case … and whether the national authorities struck a fair balance between the interests of all persons concerned and the general interest in ensuring respect for the rule of law.[81]

By referring here to principles of the rule of law the court must have in mind the importance of ensuring the court orders are complied with. It is, however, difficult to ascertain the weight attached to this by the ECtHR.

Munby J has helpfully summarised the principles that underlie the Strasbourg jurisprudence relating to enforcement of contact and residence orders in *Re D (Intractable Contact Dispute: Publicity)*:[82]

> (i) the mutual enjoyment by parent and child of each other's company is a fundamental element of family life;
> (ii) cases must be dealt with speedily to ensure that they are not determined by effluxion of time;
> (iii) Art 8 includes 'a right for the parent to have measures taken with a view to his or her being reunited with the child and an obligation for the national authorities to take such action and, as part of their obligation to take measures to facilitate contact the courts must do their utmost to facilitate co-operation between parents;
> (iv) the right to a court hearing also protects the implementation of final binding judicial decisions which cannot remain inoperative to the detriment of one party;

---

[76] [2003] 2 FCR 128, para 71.
[77] [2004] 2 FLR 653.
[78] Para 72.
[79] *Sylvester v Austria* [2003] 2 FCR 128.
[80] Para 59.
[81] Para 99.
[82] [2004] 3 FCR 234, para 25.

(v) the positive obligations on a court extend in principle to the taking of coercive measures not merely against the recalcitrant parent but even against the child;

(vi) any obligation to apply coercion can only be limited since the interests, rights and freedoms of all concerned must be taken into account, and more particularly the best interests of the child and [his or her] rights under Article 8 of the Convention.

Delay

The ECtHR is alert to the concern that delay in hearing applications for contact or enforcing orders can mean that enforcement becomes impossible.[83] In *Glaser v UK* [84] the ECtHR held, with admirable clarity: 'It is … essential that custody and contact cases be dealt with speedily.' A delay in hearing the case or enforcing the order could involve a breach of rights under Articles 8 or 6.[85] Even where steps have been taken to enforce contact, it may be that the delay in doing so is such that there is an interference in the rights of the parties.[86] A particular concern for the courts is that delay by the authorities in seeking to enforce contact may render contact practically unrealistic. As it was put in *Sylvester v Austria*:[87] 'the Court reiterates that effective respect for family life requires that future relations between parent and child not be determined by the mere effluxion of time.' This is particularly true in cases of child abduction.[88] The phrase that has been used in the most recent cases is that the state must exercise 'exceptional diligence' in seeking to enforce contact orders. In *Hoppe v Germany*[89] it was held that:

> in cases concerning a person's relationship with his or her child, there is a duty to exercise exceptional diligence in view of the risk that the passage of time may result in a de facto determination of the matter.

When considering the reasonableness of the length of time the proceedings have taken the ECtHR will take into account the complexity of the case and the conduct of the parties and the importance of the issue to the applicant.[90] The state must act positively to enforce orders and cannot blame the applicant's failure to seek to enforce to justify their own inactivity. Indeed in *Pawlik v Poland*[91] it was held that the state had failed to comply with their Article 8 obligations because 'the inaction of the authorities placed on the applicant the burden of having to have constant recourse to a succession of time-consuming and ultimately ineffectual remedies to enforce his rights'.

Sometimes delay can be justified. The Court may accept that where a child is settled with the other parent and there had not been contact for some time, there may be a need to prepare for the contact to take place.[92] Indeed a failure by the non-resident parent to appreciate this may lead to it being justifiable to deny contact.[93] A purposeful delay to lay the ground work for contact may, therefore, be appropriate. Further, the ECtHR has accepted that there

---

[83] *Deak v Romania and United Kingdom* [2008] 2 FLR 994.
[84] [2000] 3 FCR 193, at para 93.
[85] *HN v Poland* [2005] 3 FCR 85, para 73. See also *Pawlik v Poland* [2007] ECHR 11638/02.
[86] *Sylvester v Austria* (n 79).
[87] [2003] 2 FCR 128, para 69.
[88] *Ibid.*
[89] [2003] 1 FCR 176, para 54.
[90] *Nuutinen v Finland* (n 23); *M v Serbia* [2007] 1 FCR 760.
[91] [2007] ECHR 11638/02.
[92] *Sobota-Gajic v Bosnia and Herzegovina* [2007] ECHR 27966/0662; *Nuutinen v Finland* (n 90).
[93] *Mihailova v Bulgaria* [2006] ECHR 35978/02.

may be cases where after an order has been made there has been a change in circumstances which mean the order should not be enforced. However, that change in circumstances must not have been brought about by the state's failure to enforce the order.[94]

Section 1(2) of the CA recognises the potential harm to children of delay:

> In any proceedings in which any question with respect to the upbringing of a child arises, the court shall have regard to the general principle that any delay in determining the question is likely to prejudice the welfare of the child.

The ECHR obligation is wider than this because it applies not only to the courts but to all state authorities. Certainly the HRA now means that especial weight should be attached to avoiding delay in contact cases.[95]

The English Courts' Approach to Contact

It has proved remarkably difficult to state with confidence the current law in relation to applications for a contact order under the CA.[96] The following extracts from some of the leading family law textbooks indicate the diversity of views. If some of the explanations of the law sound a little confused, that may be a reflection of judicial uncertainty:

> As with all issues directly concerning the child's upbringing, the controlling principle in deciding whether or not to make a contact order is the paramountcy of the child's welfare … Bearing this principle in mind, it would be wrong to say that as a matter of law there is a presumption that a parent should be permitted contact. Nevertheless, the de facto position is that the courts are predisposed to maintaining contact with both parents, it being repeatedly said that the court should be slow to deny contact between a child and his or her parents.[97]

> While it is now generally accepted in England that contact with parents is a fundamental right of children, it remains a matter of controversy whether it may also legitimately be regarded as a right of parents. It was suggested earlier that it is perhaps best regarded as a matter of mutual interest and right of both parent and child.[98]

> Some cases have talked of children having a right to contact … However, to talk of a right to contact is a misnomer because section 1(1) of the Children Act 1989 applies to contact applications and so the key question is whether or not the contact will promote the child's welfare.[99]

---

[94] *P v Poland* [2008] ECHR 8677/03.

[95] *Re F (a child: contact)* [2002] All ER (D) 333 (May).

[96] For a sample of the literature see C Willbourne and J Geddes, 'Presumption of Contact—What Presumption?' [1995] *Family Law* 87; C Smart and B Neale, 'Arguments Against Virtue—Must Contact Be Enforced?' [1997] *Family Law* 332; J Wallbank, 'Castigating Mothers: The Judicial Response to "Wilful" Women in Disputes Over Paternal Contact in English Law' (1998) 20 *Journal of Social Welfare and Family Law* 357; F Kaganas and S Day Sclater, 'Contact and Domestic Violence—The Winds of Change' [2000] *Family Law* 630; R Bailey-Harris, 'Contact—Challenging Conventional Wisdom?' [2001] *Child and Family Law Quarterly* 361; S Gilmore, 'Disputing Contact: Challenging Some Assumptions' [2008] *Child and Family Law Quarterly* 285; A Bainham, 'Contact as a Right and Obligation' in A Bainham, B Lindley, M Richards and L Trinder (eds), *Children and Their Families: Contact, Rights and Welfare* (Oxford, Hart, 2003); J Herring, 'Connecting Contact' in A Bainham, B Lindley, M Richards and L Trinder (eds), *Children and Their Families: Contact, Rights and Welfare* (Oxford, Hart, 2003); J Wallbank, '(En)gendering the Fusion of Rights and Responsibilities in the Law of Contact' in J Wallbank, S Choudhry and J Herring (eds), *Rights, Gender and Family Law* (London, Routledge, 2009).

[97] G Douglas and N Lowe, *Bromley's Family Law* (Oxford, Oxford University Press, 2006) 597.

[98] A Bainham, *Children: The Modern Law* (Bristol, Jordans, 2005) 156–7.

[99] J Herring, *Family Law*, 3rd edn (Harlow, Pearson, 2007) 506.

There is no statutory presumption of contact and no duty on the carer to permit it unless there is a court order, but the courts have repeatedly stated that maintaining contact with the non-residential parent is almost always in a child's interests.[100]

There is little doubt that the welfare principle applies to an application for contact under section 8 of the CA.[101] What is in question is whether when considering such an application the courts will find there to be a right or presumption in favour of contact, either by virtue of the judicial interpretation of the Act; as a result of judicial 'common sense'; or by virtue of the HRA.

In a seminal case the Court of Appeal in *Re L (a child) (contact: domestic violence)*[102] held that to talk of a 'right to contact' in English law would be inappropriate.[103] Further, it would be wrong to say that there is a presumption in favour of a non-resident parent being permitted to have contact. Indeed Baroness Hale, albeit writing extra-judicially, has stated that references in the case law supporting a 'presumption of contact'[104] are 'surely *per incuriam*'[105] if they refer to a presumption of law.

Thorpe LJ in *Re L* went on to state that the most that could be said is that it would generally assumed that contact was beneficial to the child. Such an assumption, he suggested,

> perhaps more accurately reflects the base of knowledge and experience from which the court embarks upon its application of the welfare principle in each disputed contact application.[106]

However, the strength of assumption will depend on the strength of the relationship. As Thorpe LJ put it:

> However the general judicial approach may currently be expressed I doubt that sufficient distinction has been made between cases in which contact is sought in order to maintain an existing relationship, to revive a dormant relationship or to create a non-existent relationship. The judicial assumption that to order contact would be to promote welfare should surely wane across that spectrum. I would not assume the benefit with unquestioning confidence where a child has developed over its early years without any knowledge of its father, particularly if over those crucially formative years a psychological attachment to an alternative father has been achieved.

Since the decision in *Re L (a child) (contact: domestic violence)*,[107] the Court of Appeal in *Re C (Child)*[108] has held:

> The guiding principle ... is that the welfare of the child is the paramount consideration of the court. That is the only duty imposed upon the court by s 1 of the Children Act. In many cases

---

[100] J Masson, R Bailey-Harris, and R Probert, *Cretney's Family Law* (Sweet & Maxwell, 2008) 590.

[101] This may be an order for direct or indirect contact: A Perry and B Rainey, 'Supervised, supported and indirect contact orders: Research findings' (2007) 21 *International Journal of Law, Policy and the Family* 21.

[102] [2000] 4 All ER 609.

[103] In *A v L (contact)* [1998] 2 FCR 204 Holman J described contact as 'a fundamental right of a child', but that was not followed by the Court of Appeal, although the phrase was referred to in *Re D (a child) (intractable contact dispute)* [2004] EWHC 727 (Fam), para 26 in a summary of the European aspects of the law.

[104] Connell J in *Re A (Contact: Domestic Violence)* [1998] 2 FLR 171; Neill LJ in *Re M (Contact: Welfare Test)* [1995] 1 FLR 274, 281 may be an example.

[105] She cites *Re A (Contact: Domestic Violence)* [1998] 2 FLR 171.

[106] At 638.

[107] [2000] 4 All ER 609.

[108] Unreported, 29 July 1999, quoted in Gilmore, 'Disputing Contact: Challenging Some Assumptions' (n 96) 289.

that does and will involve the court recognising that it is wrong to deprive the non-residential parent of contact without there being cogent reason for doing so. If it is wished to call that a presumption, then it is there in the practice of the courts. What reasonable contact is is a matter which depends on the facts and circumstances of the individual case, as to which there is a broad discretion.

In those statements, although the word 'presumption' is used, it is clear that the courts are using it not in its formal legal sense but simply as a general observation that in many cases the court will require cogent reasons if there is not to be contact.

Indeed it is noticeable in the judgment of Nicholas Mostyn QC in *Re SC*,[109] where attention was paid to the ECtHR jurisprudence, but even basing an approach on that did not create a presumption in favour of contact, quite:

> Given the terms of the Strasbourg jurisprudence to which I have referred it is almost as if there is a presumption in favour of normal contact and it is for those who say it is inappropriate to prove by clear evidence why this is so.[110]

So, the current position is that the courts do not talk in terms of there being a right of contact nor in terms of there being a presumption in favour of contact, but prefer to talk of there being an assumption that contact is beneficial. Even so there is, as Gilmore notes, some ambiguity over precisely what the assumption is.[111] Is it that generally speaking children benefit from contact; or is it an assumption that in this particular case this child will benefit from contact? If it is the former then it must play only a most limited role in the decision for the judge concerning any particular child. If it is the latter it will play a more significant role, but, as Gilmore claims, it is doubtful there is any evidence to support such an assumption.[112] Indeed the research suggests that it is the quality and nature of contact, rather than contact per se, which are important for the child's welfare. Reading Thorpe LJ's speech as a whole and its emphasis on considering the particular child in question, it seems that the assumption that Thorpe LJ is making is just that generally children do benefit from contact. Indeed his acknowledgment that the strength of the assumption depends on the quality of the relationship between parent and child indicates that. That also seems to be how Wall LJ in *Re Bradford; Re O'Connell*, understood the issue:

> The court starts from the premise that, generally speaking, the application of the welfare test in s 1 of the Children Act 1989 means: (1) that contact with a non-resident parent is in the best interests of children; and (2) that it requires compelling evidence for such contact to be refused.[113]

If this interpretation is right and the statement is a general one about children and parent, rather than a specific assumption about the particular parent and child in the case at hand, then the assumption should play only a minor role in the decision making in the particular case.

---

[109] [2005] EWHC 2205 (Fam).

[110] *Ibid.*

[111] S Gilmore, 'The Assumption that Contact is Beneficial: Challenging the "Secure Foundation"' [2008] *Family Law* 1226.

[112] S Gilmore, 'Contact/Shared Residence and Child Well-being: Research Evidence and its Implications for Legal Decision-Making' (2006) 20 *International Journal of Law, Policy and the Family* 344.

[113] [2006] EWCA Civ 1199, para 70.

That said, it is clear that it is very rare that contact is denied to a non-resident father.[114] The following cases indicate how contact will be ordered by first instance judges even where there appear to be strong reasons against ordering it:

— In *Re J-S (a child) (contact: parental responsibility)*[115] a father had behaved in a deplorable way to the mother: he had been violent to her; made false allegations of violence and neglect to the social services; and sought to persuade the child that he had been abused by the mother's new partner. The father's application for contact was rejected at first instance but the father's appeal was successful. The court's paramount concern had to be the child's welfare, the Court of Appeal emphasised. The child had established attachment to the father and it would be harmful to the child to refuse contact.
— In *Re H (a child) (contact: domestic violence)*,[116] despite serious violence leading to the hospitalisation of the mother the judge at first instance had ordered supervised contact. The decision was overturned on appeal as the judge had not fully considered the factors to be considered in contact cases involving domestic violence listed in *Re L*.[117]
— In *Re U (Children) (Contact with father)*[118] a father sought contact. When he had been 22 (at the time of the hearing he was nearly 40) he was sentenced to four years' imprisonment following an indecent assault on an 11-year-old girl. As this sentence indicates, the assault was 'particularly unpleasant and brutal'. There were complaints of domestic violence by the wife, but it was her discovery of the husband's conviction (which he had kept from her) which seems to have precipitated the breakdown of the marriage. Contact initially was not ordered, especially following evidence of the effect enforced contact would have on the wife. However, a later application in which the father claimed he had attended classes to address his behaviour towards children was dismissed on the paperwork by the judge. The Court of Appeal held this was inappropriate and ordered specialist reports to be prepared to assess the current dangerousness of the father and the impact of contact on the mother and children.
— In *Re M (Children)*[119] even though the father was facing charges of possession of paedophilic literature and was found to have an unhealthy interest in teenage girls, it was held not to be plainly wrong to allow a boy aged 9 and girl aged 6 to live with the father.

More significant than a sample of cases is the fact that the statistics speak for themselves: in 2006, 62,672 contact orders were granted and in only 366 cases did courts refuse an application for a contact order.[120]

---

[114] *Re B (A Minor) (Contact: Stepfather's Opposition)* [1997] 2 FLR 579. It was stated (at 583) that the 'court's general policy is clear: contact between a child and its natural parent is something which should be maintained wherever this is practical'. There is no presumption in favour of contact between a child and step-parent (*Re H (A Minor) (Contact)* [1994] 2 FLR 776 (CA)) nor between a parent and an adult child (*Re D-R (Adult: Contact)* [1999] 1 FLR 1161 (CA)).

[115] [2002] 3 FCR 433.

[116] *Re H (a child) (contact: domestic violence)* [2005] EWCA Civ 1404.

[117] See now *Practice Direction (residence and contact orders: domestic violence and harm)* [2009] 1 FCR 223 which sets down detailed guidance on how the courts should deal with contact cases where there are allegations of domestic violence.

[118] [2004] EWCA Civ 71.

[119] [2008] EWCA Civ 225.

[120] Ministry of Justice, *Judicial and Court Statistics* (London, The Stationery Office, 2008).

The assumption in favour of contact can be self-reinforcing, because it means that a resident parent (typically a mother) who opposes contact will often be seen as selfish and not having her children's interests at heart.[121] This can have the effect of doubling the impact of the assumption: now not only is there an assumption that contact is beneficial, but also there is the fact that the mother is selfish and does not recognise what is best for the child.[122]

Why Have the Courts Avoided the Use of the Language of Rights in Contact Cases?

Although the courts have avoided the language of rights in the contact setting, they have not made it clear why they have done so. Perhaps the first point to make is that in interpreting the welfare principle the courts have generally been wary of introducing rights or presumptions. They have preferred to leave the themselves with an unfettered use of the welfare principle.[123] The desire to avoid use of rights and presumptions and simply to rely on the welfare principle is strong in all areas of application. Contact cases are therefore not unusual in this regard.

Thorpe LJ in *Re L (a child) (contact: domestic violence)*[124] explained why he thought it inappropriate to talk of there being, in English law, either a presumption or assumption in favour of contact:

> There is a danger that the identification of a presumption will inhibit or distort the rigorous search for the welfare solution. There is also the danger that a presumption may be used as an aid to determination when the individual advocate or judge feels either undecided or overwhelmed.[125]

Thorpe LJ wanted there to be a weighing up of the benefits and disadvantages of contact in each case, before a decision was reached over whether or not contact would promote the welfare of the child. He was concerned that use of either a right of contact or even a presumption of contact would detract from a consideration of the benefits or disadvantages of contact in the particular case. It is not clear that this is necessarily so. If one started from the assumption that children and parents had a right of contact with each other under Article 8, there would still need to be a consideration of whether or not there was sufficient justification under Article 8(2) to interfere with that right. That would inevitably involve a consideration of the strength of the right under Article 8(1) and the strength of the arguments that could be used to justify an interference under Article 8(2). While it is true there may be a temptation for a judge to turn to the parent opposing contact and ask 'well, what reasons can you give for interfering with the right' and such an approach meaning that there is not an effective consideration of the both the *benefits* and disadvantages of contact, that is not likely to occur in a case of disputed contact where there will be arguments to be made on

---

[121] H Rhodes, 'The "No Contact Mother": Reconstructions of Motherhood in the Era of the "New Father"' (2002) 16 *International Journal of Law, Policy and the Family* 16.

[122] R Bailey-Harris, J Barron and J Pearce, 'From Utility to Rights? The Presumption of Contact in Practice' (1999) 13 *International Journal of Law, Policy and the Family* 111.

[123] Eg *Dawson v Wearmouth* [1999] AC 308. Although there seem to be certain judicial assumptions (eg that young children should remain with their mothers) which play an important part in the way the welfare principle is used in practice.

[124] [2000] 4 All ER 609.

[125] At 637.

both sides of the case. At best, then, the argument warns of the dangers of a sloppy use of rights; it does not provide an argument that a rights approach will necessarily fail.

There is a second reason for rejecting the use of rights is raised by Thorpe LJ. He highlighted the point that a right requires a corresponding duty:[126] 'The errant or selfish parent cannot be ordered to spend time with his child against his will however much the child may yearn for his company and the mother desire respite.'[127] He could have added that had the right been seen as the right of a parent it would mean that a child could be compelled to see the parent. As he believes that such obligations would never be imposed, this indicates that it would be inaccurate to describe this as a right.

There are a few responses to this argument. One is simply to deny, as some legal philosophers have, that a right must have a correlative duty.[128] That issue need not detain us. First, because few legal philosophers have taken this view. Second, if it is correct and it creates a right of contact with no duty on *anyone* then the right to contact is of limited value and of little practical significance, although it may still have relevance for its symbolic importance.

A second point is that there is a well-acknowledged duty that Thorpe LJ has simply overlooked, namely the duty on the resident parent. In other words the corresponding duty to the right of the non-resident parent to contact lies not on the child, but on the resident parent to permit contact to take place. Similarly the corresponding duty to the child's right of contact is the duty on the resident parent to allow the child to have contact. This can be supported by reference to the wording of section 8 of the CA, which defines a contact order as 'an order requiring the person with whom a child lives, or is to live, to allow the child to visit or stay with the person named in the order, or for that person and the child otherwise to have contact with each other'. That definition indicates that only the resident parent can infringe the order. If this is correct it is then misleading to talk of a 'right to contact' and instead the court should talk of a 'right not to be prevented from seeing a child or parent'.

A third possible response to the no corresponding obligation argument is to respond that the courts should make orders forcing reluctant children to see their parents; and indeed reluctant parents to see their children.[129] The fact that the courts have failed to do so should not be accepted as a reason for not finding a right. Perhaps, however, this gets to the nub of the issue. The reason the courts have not done so is because doing so would seem pointless. Forcing a reluctant parent to see a child is unlikely to benefit the child or the adult. If the order is made on the basis of what is in the welfare of the child, it would seem counter-productive to enforce the order if doing so will harm the child.

Another way of justifying the refusal of the courts to use the language of rights is to argue that a rights-based approach will produce a result no different from a welfare approach. Indeed Dame Butler Sloss sees no difficulty in applying the welfare principle to contact disputes, while also confirming: 'Since the implementation of the Human Rights Act 1998, the court has specifically to take into account the rights of each parent and of the child enshrined in Art 8.'[130] This argument has already been discussed at page 122. Shortly put, the argument is that where contact is found to harm the child it will not be ordered

---

[126] See ch 3 for a further discussion of this issue.
[127] At 638.
[128] See ch 3 for a further discussion of this issue.
[129] A Bainham, 'Contact as a Right and Obligation' (n 96).
[130] See *Re S (a Child) (contact)* [2004] EWCA 18, para 15.

under the welfare principle, and will be sufficient to justify an interference in the non-resident's right to contact. So, the result will be the same under either approach. Similarly where the contact is found to be beneficial to the child the welfare principle will support contact and so too will a rights-based approach . This was criticised at page 122 and we will not repeat those points here, save to emphasise that the HRA *at least* requires the courts to ensure that the approach they are adopting does not interfere with parties' ECHR rights. While, therefore, they are not obliged to operate a rights-based approach as their primary reasoning mechanism, they are required to at least cross-check that the rights of the parties have not been unjustifiably interfered with.

Gilmore's analysis of the significance of Article 8 is helpful. He argues that Article 8 requires the state to respect family life. That is not the same thing as saying there is a right to contact. He argues:

> English law recognises a right to *respect for* the mutual enjoyment by parent and child of each other's company as a fundamental *element* of the right to respect for family life within Article 8 of the ECHR. There must be a lawful justification for interfering with that element of family life. There are several other elements of family life, however, which can also command such respect (such as protection of the welfare or personal safety of individuals to allow them to enjoy family life) and which can constitute a justification for denying contact. There is thus some substantive protection of the parent/child relationship and reasons must be advanced for denying contact. It has been suggested, however, that it is unhelpful to describe this protection as a 'right of contact'.[131]

Gilmore argues that what 'respect for family life' means will vary from case to case. There may be many cases where respect will involve contact, but Gilmore's point is that that will not necessarily be so. This is an important contribution to the debate. However, as we have seen, it is not one that has so far been reflected in the approach taken by the ECtHR, which seems to assume that contact is an inevitable part of respect for family life. Gilmore's approach offers the court a more nuanced consideration of what respect for family life entails. It may be that in the future as the jurisprudence on contact and Article 8 develops, the courts will adopt an approach more in line with Gilmore's, but currently, as we shall see shortly, the ECHR assumes that where there is family life, respect requires there to be contact and the 'work' is done by Article 8(2), which sets out the circumstances in which interference with Article 8(1) is justified.

Despite the apparently clear statement of the English law in the cases discussed above, Andrew Bainham has claimed that 'those who assert that there is no right or presumption of contact are not merely misguided, but are plainly wrong'.[132] As one the country's leading family lawyers, his claim deserves careful analysis.

Bainham is clearly correct in suggesting there is a right of contact between parents and children under the ECHR and indeed the UN Convention on Human Rights. We shall consider that shortly. What is less clear is whether such a right is part of English law. Indeed in light of the clear statements of the Court of Appeal in *Re L* his claims appear very bold, to say the least. However, his view may not be as startling as first appears. We will now consider two ways that it might be claimed that despite the apparently clear statements in the Court of Appeal there is in fact a right of contact.

---

[131] S Gilmore, 'Disputing Contact: Challenging some Assumptions' (n 96).
[132] A Bainham, 'Contact as a Right and Obligation' (n 96) 61.

First is to argue that, although the courts say there is no presumption in favour of contact or a right to contact; the law is in fact structured in such a way that it is. In other words, whatever Thorpe LJ may have said, in practice the courts operate on the assumption that contact should take place; in fact any family lawyer would acknowledge that if one went into court in a case representing a resident parent opposed to contact and were unable to provide one good reason why contact should not be permitted, it would be extremely unlikely that a contact order would not be made. As already mentioned, in practice, it is rare for the courts to refuse to make a contact order—a point powerfully backed up by the statistics. However, Bainham's claim is not simply a statement of empirical observation and he is making a claim about what the law is.

A second argument is that in saying there is no right to contact, the courts are overlooking their obligation under the HRA to give effect to the rights protected in the ECHR and therefore despite judicial comments to the contrary, English courts are required to recognise rights to contact whether they like it or not.[133] This may be what Bainham's real claim is. Such an argument is, however, based on misinterpretation of the HRA. The Act does not require the courts to recognise and give effect to ECHR rights, rather that when interpreting legislation (in this case the CA) the court must ensure it is interpreted in a way which is compatible with the ECHR rights.[134] The courts are, therefore, entitled to say there is no right to contact in English law, as long as if in doing so they ensure that people's ECHR rights are not threatened. This, it might be said, is a rather pedantic point. Bainham may argue that what matters is not the language used, but whether the results of the cases ensure that rights of contact are protected.

In conclusion in this question, it is submitted that the current law on contact is that the court will apply the welfare principle and although it is assumed that contact generally between children and parents is beneficial there is no presumption that this is so, nor does the law explicitly find there to be a right to contact. Nevertheless the courts are required to ensure that parties' ECHR rights are not improperly interfered with in applying this law and in effect the law operates as if rights are protected.

Putting these discussions to one side, we now turn to consider what the law on contact would look like if the courts decided to adopt explicitly an approach based on that taken by the ECtHR.

Application of the ECHR Principles to English Law

How might an approach based on human rights look?[135] A judge following a human rights approach in relation to a contact dispute should consider the case in this way. It would be necessary to consider the Article 8 rights of all the parties, and indeed any other convention right that could be relevant. For each party it would be necessary to consider their rights in turn. First, it would be necessary to consider whether they have a right under Article 8. This would primarily involve ascertaining whether there was family life between the adult

---

[133] R Bailey-Harris, 'Contact—Challenging Conventional Wisdom?' (n 96).
[134] HRA, s3.
[135] See S Choudhry and H Fenwick, 'Taking the Rights of Parents and Children Seriously: Confronting the Welfare Principle under the Human Rights Act' (2005) 25 *OJLS* 453, on which the following discussion relies.

and the child. Second, it would be necessary to determine whether there was a justification under Article 8(2) which justified breaching that right. Such an analysis has been described as a 'parallel' analysis.[136]

This process may resolve the case at hand. For example, it could be that a father and child have a right to contact which is protected under Article 8 and there are insufficient reasons to justify infringing those rights, while there is a sufficient reason for interfering with the mother's right to family and private life that might be caused by ordering contact, namely the interests of the child. In such a case the rights-based analysis would lead to an order for contact. Similarly it could be that there are sufficient reasons to justify any rights of contact and the court will not order contact. However, it would be possible where following that process there would be two competing rights, neither of which could be justifiably infringed. This might arise where, for example, a father has a right of contact with the child and there are insufficient reasons to justify an interference in that, while the mother has a right to respect for her private and family life which will be interfered with by a contact order, and there is insufficient reason to justify any interference in that. In short, that will arise where the interests of the individuals concerned on either side of a case are well matched, or where an individual has two rights which clash (for example, there is conflict between a child's right of contact and a child's right to protection from harm). In such a case it would be necessary to undertake what Choudhry and Fenwick have described as the 'ultimate balancing exercise'.[137] They explain:

> Following this reasoning model, a child's Article 8 right cannot figure merely as an exception to the parent's right, and vice versa. Still less can the parent's right be almost entirely abrogated—as the paramountcy principle currently demands—without a full application of the paragraph 2 tests. Following this argument, in a significant development of the *Re S* model, the rights of all parties should be considered in turn, the rights of others figuring in each instance as exceptions to the Article 8(1) right in question, applying all the tests within Article 8(2) in each instance. Each analysis would therefore *parallel* the other ones. This is clearly in essentials a parallel exercise in proportionality. It may well be a tripartite analysis where, for example, the parents or carers are in conflict and the child's rights require independent consideration, as they normally would do.[138]

The parallel analysis would involve examining the underlying values at stake in any particular claim. It is suggested that in relation to Article 8, the underlying value is that of autonomy: the rights of individuals to pursue the goals in their life. If that is correct then one might ask, as they do, 'which interference will constitute a greater blight on the vision of the good life that each had'.[139] However, it would be wrong to suggest that autonomy values are the only ones at stake in an Article 8 claim. There may be other values, about personal identity, and the significance of family ties and relationships which carry value in themselves, independent of any relevance to autonomy.

It is not suggested for a moment that this ultimate balancing exercise is easy or that it will automatically indicate the correct result in all cases. Indeed much will depend on the weight the decision maker attaches to different values; nevertheless it provides as clear a guidance as can be given, bearing in mind the complexity of the issues involved.[140]

---

[136] *Ibid.*

[137] *Ibid.*

[138] *Ibid*, at 469.

[139] Herring and Taylor, 'Relocating Relocation' [2006] *Child and Family Law Quarterly* 517.

[140] Although see the concerns of J Fortin that this leaves the law approach too vague in J Fortin, 'Accommodating Children's Rights in a Post Human Rights Act Era' (2006) 69 *MLR* 299.

If we were to apply this to a contact dispute the approach might work in this way. As explained, each party's rights would need to be considered separately. In relation to the child, it would be necessary to ask whether making the contact order would show respect for the child's family life.[141] It is suggested that where there is a good established relationship between the parent and child there will be a right to respect for family life and that will prima facie involve the state making a contact order to enable contact to take place.[142] It may be argued that, where there is family life, but contact would pose a risk to the child, therefore, respect for family life would not require a contact order. This raises a difficult issue and that is whether the harm to a child by contact feeds into a finding that respect for family or private life does not require contact and so Article 8(1) is not engaged, or whether the harm comes in as a factor justifying interference in that right under Article 8(2); or indeed whether it has a role to play in both issues. For reasons of clarity there is something to be said for setting up the right of contact by virtue of the family life between the child and non-resident parent, and leaving the harmfulness as a justification for infringing it.[143] The argument against this is threefold.

First, the language of Article 8(2) does not readily give itself to claims that the interests of the individual claiming the right can be taken into account. Indeed it specifically refers to the 'rights and interests of *others*'. Second, there may be objections to a recognition of a right to something which it is known will cause serious harm to the child.[144] Third, as already noted, it is important to appreciate that Article 8 does not itself create a right to contact, but rather a right to respect for family life. The question must be whether respect for family life would indicate promoting or not promoting contact in a particular case. That might turn on what the value of family life is.[145] Defining the true value of family life is a complex task which, at the very least, requires a detailed consideration of a number of philosophical questions which are beyond the scope of this Chapter. However, John Eekelaar has recently provided the following definition: 'the value of having space to develop one's personality and personal interaction free from the external gaze.'[146] He emphasises the importance of intimacy which is necessary so that love can flourish. Others may emphasise families as places where relationships of care and interdependency can flourish.[147] If values such as these are regarded as central to the value of family life, it is clear that respect for them will not require contact automatically. Indeed not ordering contact may be necessary for family life to flourish. That would be where compelling contact would generate or maintain pain, mistrust or abusive relationships. Bren Neale and Jennifer Flowerdew argue for:

> the need to focus rather more on relationships and rather less on contact when considering the quality of young people's family lives. Good contact, it would seem, is not lots of contact but

---

[141] S Choudhry and H Fenwick, 'Taking the Rights of Parents and Children Seriously' (n 135) suggest asking: 'Would the granting of the application interfere with the child's right to respect for his or her family or private life under Article 8(1)?' That seems to be putting it in a negative way, such as would be appropriate for determining whether the order would interfere with the child's rights such as to justify not making the order. That question must be asked, but when determining whether there is a justification for interfering in someone's rights.

[142] *Keegan v Ireland* (1994) 18 EHRR 342; *Johansen v Norway* (1997) 23 EHRR 33, and *Bronda v Italy* Application No 22430/93.

[143] Although see J Herring, 'Respecting Family Life' (2008) 75 *Amicus Curiae* 21 for an argument that a highly abusive family situation does not deserve respect.

[144] J Fortin, 'Accommodating Children's Rights in a Post Human Rights Act Era' (n 140).

[145] See C Smart, *Personal Life* (Bristol, Polity Press, 2007).

[146] M Fineman, *The Autonomy Myth* (New York, New Press, 2004).

[147] J Eekelaar, *Family Life and Personal Life* (Oxford, Oxford University Press, 2007) 84–5.

contact based on a good quality relationship: it should be measured in terms of its quality rather than its quantity. Likewise, poor contact is not diminished contact but contact based on a poor quality relationship.[148]

Emphasising that contact is a means to respecting family life may enable points such as these to be taken into account when determining what respect for family life requires. We can conclude, therefore, that any potential harm to the child should be a factor in determining whether or not the child or parent has a right to contact, rather than being solely a reason for denying contact.[149] What is more complex is when the harm to the child is such that the right cannot be found to arise, or indeed whether the right only arises when the contact is beneficial to the child.

A key question in considering this and indeed in considering how the competing rights and interests can be weighed in a contact case is whether the contact provides a benefit to the child which has intrinsic value.[150] By this we mean to ask whether contact with a parent has value which is not measurable in terms of pleasure or pain. Plainly if contact were shown to provide neither pleasure nor pain for the child would it still promote the child's well-being to engage in contact? It is submitted that it would. There is value in the relationship between parent and child 'in itself'; and not just for the goods that it produces. If that is correct, and it is accepted that this is an issue over which people may disagree and is one which would involve extensive argument, then it seems correct to say that the right arises independently of any welfare issue. In other words, the right arises out of an acceptance of the inherent good of children and parents being in contact. It is not, therefore, necessarily denied by empirical research suggesting that contact does not produce a benefit.

Our claim, therefore, is that there is an intrinsic value in a child maintaining a relationship with parents. That is independent of an assessment of welfare and therefore exists in every contact case. However, we would not place great weight on the intrinsic value. It could readily be outweighed by a finding that contact will harm the child or disrupt other relationships that a child may have.[151] Further, there are other intrinsic values at play too—the value of the family life; the relationship between the child and resident parent; the child's emotional and physical health—which need to be brought into the analysis of what respect for family life entails.

The issue is made even more complex by the fact that harm to the child may also generate claims involving the child's right to respect for her private life. Included within the right to respect for private life is the right to bodily integrity. The right to private life includes the right to 'psychological integrity … a right to personal development, and the right to establish and develop relationships with other human beings and the outside world'.[152] If contact would harm the child, either emotionally, psychologically or physically, then not only would that mean that respect for her family life would entail *not* ordering contact, it might also mean that the child is entitled to protection from contact with that person under Article 8.

---

[148] B Neale and J Flowerdew, 'New Structures, New Agency: The Dynamics of Child–Parent Relationships after Divorce' (2007) 15 *International Journal of Children's Rights* 25.

[149] For the avoidance of doubt, we think it can also operate as a reason to justify interfering in another's right.

[150] For a discussion of what is 'intrinsic value' see M Zimmerman, *The Nature of Intrinsic Value*, (Lanham, Rowman and Littlefield, 2001).

[151] As we shall see shortly, the harm to the child can also be relevant in justifying a parents' right to contact the child.

[152] *Pretty v UK* (2002) 12 BHRC 149, para 61.

If, after consideration of all the issues above, it is concluded that the child's right to respect for family life includes ordering contact, it would then be necessary to turn to Article 8(2). There would be little difficulty in establishing that making or not making a contact order would be 'in accordance with the law', if the order is made under the CA. It would be hard to imagine a contact order not being made or an order being made, but for a legitimate aim (promoting the rights of others). Therefore the central issue will be whether making the order or not making the order would be necessary 'in a democratic society'. This involves weighing up the right of the child with the competing interests of others—in particular whether the proposed order will promote a proportionate response. Shazia Choudhry and Helen Fenwick suggest that these factors become relevant when that is considered:

> Would the proposed increase in contact be highly beneficial to the parent in Article 8 terms while creating only a minor and probably short term detriment to the child? If so, the interference with the child's Article 8 right represented by increasing the level of contact would be justifiable since to do otherwise would be disproportionate to the aim pursued. In seeking to answer the question a number of factors could be taken into account. What would be the benefits, if any, of the contact requested for the child and what would be the impact, if any, on the child's family life in granting the application? What were the reasons for the current level of contact and are they still pertinent? Consideration of this question would invite an examination of the opposing arguments; it would enable the Court to consider at this stage if there was any issue of harm to the child's welfare and to elevate this to the 'crucial importance' test discussed in *Johansen v Norway*. What is the age of the child and her ascertainable wishes and feelings towards contact? Finally, taking the findings gleaned into account, the Court would consider whether there were sufficient compelling reasons to justify an interference in the child's Article 8 rights by granting the non-resident parent's application.[153]

This approach, then, like the welfare approach, considers a wide range of issues relating to children's interests. Unlike the welfare principle there does need to be a weighing up of the interests of the child and the other adults involved and wider societal interests. It requires careful consideration of the importance of contact to the child as a matter of their private or family life. It also allows children's interests to be privileged, for the reasons discussed in Chapter 6. This means that in balancing the non-resident parents' rights with the child's it is extremely unlikely that an order would be made where there was harm or risk of harm to the child. The difficulty is where that level of harm will be. The temptation is to call for a definitive rule: such as 'contact will be ordered unless the harm to the child is significant'. But this must be rejected. It is necessary to look at the importance of contact to the parent and child; and indeed family life in general. Further, it is necessary to consider what levels of contact currently will in fact promote the values of family life. Such questions mean that the issue cannot be resolved in a simple test of how much harm there must be before contact can be ordered. Rather it is necessary to consider the significance of harm to the parties; their past and current relationship. Further, it is necessary to consider the future and the relationships between the parties.

Choudhry and Fenwick suggest the following factors should be considered:

> The Court could in particular consider the degree of contact the non-resident parent is asking for and the impact on his family life of not granting his application or of allowing only a slight increase in contact. Again the reasons for the current level of contact and their continuing

---

[153] S Choudhry and H Fenwick, 'Taking the Rights of Parents and Children Seriously' (n 135).

pertinence in terms of the crucial importance of the child's welfare would be examined. The *benefits* and detriments, long and short term to the child, of increased contact, should be considered. It would be at this point that the harmony between the claims in question could be evaluated. Once these factors had been considered it might become apparent that a modest increase in contact, far from creating detriment in terms of the child's welfare, might be likely to be beneficial in the long term. At the same time, it might be clear that no increase in contact would be severely detrimental in terms of the non-resident parent's family life in the sense that he or she would be likely to begin to feel estranged from the child as it grew older. In such an instance the failure to increase contact would represent a disproportionate interference with the non-resident parent's family and (arguably) private life. Therefore in such an instance sufficient and compelling reasons to justify an interference in the non-resident parent's Article 8 rights by refusing to grant his application would not have been established.

In addition to the rights claimed by the non-resident parent, the rights of the resident parent must be considered too. As will be clear from the above discussion, they may be relevant either on the basis of claims to Article 8 rights, or as a means of justifying an interference in another party's rights. A resident parent may claim that contact will itself involve an interference in her private and family life. That seems a strong claim because where a contact order is in force the resident parent must arrange her family life so that the child is ready for contact with the non-resident parent at the appropriate time. Further, she may need to be available to collect the child at the end of the contact session. Perhaps more significant will be cases where the resident parent fears that the contact sessions will pose a risk to herself or to the child. In such a case to order contact against her wishes will cause significant distress. Where such fears are justified the risk of those harms themselves must also be considered. It may be that some of these fears can be dealt with by having contact supervised or arrangements being made to have the child dropped off with a third party.[154] When considering whether there is a justification for interfering in a non-resident parent's right, the interests of children and resident parent need to be considered. So it may be that although in isolation they do not provide a sufficient justification for the interference, in combination they might.

Would Adopting an ECtHR Approach Make a Difference?

As mentioned in Chapter 3, in most cases the result of a contact case is unlikely to turn on whether a rights-based approach or a welfare-based approach is used. Or, to put the point more precisely, in terms of results what matters far less than whether a rights-based or welfare-based approach is how strongly the law assumes that contact between a parent and child will promote a child's welfare (under a welfare approach) or how strong the right of contact is (under a rights-based approach). One could easily imagine a rights-based approach which was far less protective of the interests of non-resident parents than a welfare approach. Imagine, for example, a welfare-based approach operating in a legal system which assumed that contact between children and parents was always very much in children's welfare; with a rights-based system that accepted a right to contact, but regarded it as a weak right which could be readily overridden if harm to the child could be shown. Despite this, as argued above,[155] even if the results reached using a welfare

---

[154] A Perry and B Rainey, 'Supervised, supported and indirect contact orders: Research findings' (n 101).
[155] See further the discussion in ch 3.

or rights-based approach were similar there would still be a difference in the reasoning process.[156]

It may, therefore, be that in all the heat of the debate over whether or not contact disputes should be based on a rights-based approach or a welfare-based approach the more important question has been lost: how important is contact to a child? To answer that question would require an extensive analysis of the evidence which space prevents us undertaking here. Reference can be made to Stephen Gilmore's summary of his extensive analysis of the work in this area which concludes:

> What the research evidence shows is that children can *under certain conditions* benefit from contact with a non-resident parent. An assumption in decision-making in individual cases cannot follow from the conclusion that children can *under certain conditions* benefit from ongoing contact, because those conditions cannot be assumed in any individual case ... Recent reviews of the research evidence have highlighted a range of factors potentially impacting on the relationship between child well-being and post-separation parenting arrangements. It has been argued that the complexity revealed by the research 'does not advocate a form of legal decision-making which relies on generalisations'. Indeed, given knowledge of the deleterious effects of conflict on child well-being, the adoption of a presumption (or indeed an assumption) in favour of contact seems particularly contraindicated in disputed contact cases, with their profile of high conflict demonstrated in recent research.[157]

Even if, despite the lack of evidence, it is believed that the law should make a general assumption about the benefits of contact, there is still a question about whether the assumption should apply in cases of domestic violence, in which the evidence of risk of harm is overwhelming.[158]

As mentioned above, the impact of the ECtHR is not limited to the substantive decision but also impacts on the procedures used. It was accepted by the Court of Appeal in *Re T (a child: contact)*[159] that English courts would need to ensure that they complied with the procedural requirements of the ECHR. As Thorpe LJ said:

> I reject [counsel's] dismissive submission that the Strasbourg cases add nothing to the domestic jurisprudence. Those cases as they stand suggest that the methods and levels of investigation that our courts have conventionally adopted when trying out issues of alienation may not meet the standards that Arts 6 and 8 ... require. There are policy issues here that the government and the judiciary may need to consider collaboratively.[160]

In particular there are the concerns raised in Chapter 5 about the representation of children or an effective report of their wishes. Further, the emphasis that the ECtHR places on

---

[156] See further J Herring, 'The Human Rights Act and the Welfare Principle in Family Law—Conflicting or Complementary?' [1999] *Child and Family Law Quarterly* 223; J Fortin, 'The HRA's Impact on Litigation Involving Children and their Families' [1999] *Child and Family Law Quarterly* 237; A Bainham, 'Can we Protect Children and Protect Their Rights?' (2002) 22 *Family Law* 279.

[157] S Gilmore, 'Disputing Contact: Challenging some Assumptions' (n 96).

[158] A Buchanan, J Hunt, H Bretherton and V Bream, *Families in Conflict: Perspectives of Children and Parents on the Family Court Welfare Service* (Bristol, Policy Press, 2001); L Trinder, J Connolly, J Kellett and C Notley, *A Profile of Applicants and Respondents in Contact Cases in Essex* (DCA Research Series 1/05) (London, Department of Constitutional Affairs, 2005); A Perry and B Rainey, 'Supervised, Supported and Indirect Contact Orders: Research Findings' (2007) 21 *International Journal of Law, Policy and the Family* 21, at 29; GT Harold and M Murch, 'Inter-parental conflict and children's adaptation to separation and divorce: theory, research and implications for family law, practice and policy' [2005] *Child and Family Law Quarterly* 185.

[159] *Re T (a child: contact)* [2003] 1 FCR 303.

[160] Para 25.

ensuring that delay does not mark the process is a significant one. In *Re D*,[161] Munby J, in a blistering attack on the current way of dealing with contact cases, provides this summary of the father's concerns:

> Seen from a father's perspective, a case such as this exhibits three particularly concerning features:
> i) the appalling delays of the court system, exacerbated by the absence of any meaningful judicial continuity, seemingly endless directions hearings, the lack of any overall timetable, and the failure of the court to adhere to such timetable as has been set;
> ii) the court's failure to get to grips with the mother's (groundless) allegations; and
> iii) the court's failure to get to grips with the mother's defiance of its orders, the court's failure to enforce its own orders.[162]

All of these could form the basis of claims that the father's Article 8 rights have been interfered with. Further, the failure of the courts to adequately respond to and deal with concerns over domestic violence may raise Article 8 issues too.[163]

Feminist Concerns about Rights and Contact

The use of human rights analysis in contact cases is controversial. For some, such as Jane Fortin, there are concerns that the use of the analysis will give greater power to fathers:

> It has been urged elsewhere that it is unjustifiable to use the language of children's rights to mask orders which do more to promote judicial perceptions of father's rights. There is now a risk, however, that implementation of the HRA will accelerate this trend. A father opposing an order reducing his contact to the child will undoubtedly force the court to consider the issue in terms of his own rights—he will cite Convention case-law indicating that the right to enjoy his child's company is a fundamental element of family life. Faced with such arguments, the domestic courts might feel fully justified in openly placing far greater weight than before on the father's own rights. Indeed, only Article 8(2) will prevent fathers' rights always trumping those of their children.[164]

This is a legitimate concern. However, any non-resident father who thinks that a rights-based approach will *necessarily* strengthen his position in a contact dispute may be misguided. Indeed, a rights-based approach requires the court to consider the interests of the resident mother, in a way the welfare principle does not. Indeed, the very fact that the courts will consider the rights of fathers and mother, as well as children, is a benefit. As Choudhry and Fenwick argue:

> The argument for placing disputes over children in a rights-based framework can be situated in the context of broader, ongoing changes in cultural expectations of parenting. The proposed unpacking and reconfiguring of the paramountcy principle in relation to the Article 8 rights of parents would mean that while fathers are likely to find that the importance of their relationship with their child gains greater legal recognition, societal perceptions of fathers may also change. Closer examination of the competing claims of the parties under the parallel analysis may tend to aid in changing cultural constructions of the father and of parenting.[165]

---

[161] [2004] EWHC 727 (Fam).
[162] Para 22.
[163] See the cases discussed at p 257.
[164] J Fortin, 'The HRA's Impact' (n 156).
[165] S Choudhry and H Fenwick, 'Taking the Rights of Parents and Children Seriously' (n 135) 491–2.

The requirement of the courts to consider the rights of the resident mother might open up arguments of the kind promoted by Helen Reece based on women's autonomy:

> These critiques point to the division of labour that still exists within the intact nuclear family, characterised primarily by women taking the main responsibility for childcare, and secondarily by gendered roles in relation to shared childcare, with fathers tending to perform discrete, fun activities (such as taking children to the park) and mothers tending to remain in charge of the more repetitive, continuous and mundane day-to-day care. They argue that the strong assumption of substantial post-separation contact between fathers and children is one mechanism by which the law ensures that parental separation does not fundamentally disrupt this division of labour: instead, the nuclear family is replicated post-separation ... These critiques argue that in essence former spouses are required to continue their joint parenting project despite their separation, but in effect only resident parents are bound by this obligation. Put more strongly, mothers are responsible for maintaining the family unit even after separation, locking them into a perpetual 'marriage' and thereby hampering their self-development. In contrast fathers are provided with a capacity for self-determination which is denied to mothers, as well as the power to constrain the mother's autonomy.[166]

As Reece argues, the current welfare-based approach forces resident mothers into putting their arguments in terms of the welfare of the child. Given the importance that is generally attached to maintaining contact, this means that unless they argue that there has been domestic violence, it is unlikely that they will succeed if they wish to dispute contact. A rights-based approach opens up the opportunity for a resident mother to have her own rights considered.

There is a further issue here. Julie Wallbank has argued:

> Parental attitudes to contact are likely to be influenced by the pattern of care-giving and the responsibilities assumed which existed prior to the relationship breakdown. It is crucial therefore that both the relative investments and types of responsibilities assumed by mothers and fathers are taken into account when considering the level, form and degree of contact.[167]

As she points out, there is a danger that rights discourse (and indeed a welfare one) considers the issue of contact from a snap-shot of time: an examination of the particular rights that can be claimed as the parties stand before the court. While her criticism is certainly valid of the way rights are commonly used in contact cases, these are an inevitable consequence of a rights-based approach. A richer appreciation of what respect for family life might mean, particularly bearing in mind the analysis above, may enable a court to take into account the concerns of Wallbank and other commentators in this regard.

A rather different concern is the way that rights talk leads to enforcement measures being taken against resident parents, normally mothers, rather than non-resident parents, normally fathers. Julie Wallbank has written:

> It is not too difficult to conclude that despite the existence of formal equality in the legislation, in practice it is mothers who will be detrimentally affected and that the enforcement measures are designed to target individual mothers who are identified as failing to achieve the norm of the responsible parent in respect of the facilitation of contact.[168]

---

[166] H Reece, 'UK Women's Groups' Child Contact Campaign: "So Long as it is Safe"' [2006] *Child and Family Law Quarterly* 538.

[167] J Wallbank, '(En)Gendering the Fusion of Rights and Responsibilities in the Law of Contact' (n 96).

[168] J Wallbank, 'Parental Responsibility and the Responsible Parent: Managing the "Problem" of Contact' in R Probert, S Gilmore and J Herring (eds), *Responsible Parents and Parental Responsibility* (Oxford, Hart, 2009).

This concern, too, may to some extent be met by a rights-based approach. Coercive measures against the resident parent involve an interference in the mother's right to respect for private and family life, and probably that of the child. This means that they require careful justification. It must be admitted that the ECtHR has not placed as much weight on the impact of enforcement on the Article 8 rights of the child and resident parent as it might. Given the emphasis placed on enforcement by the ECtHR case law, Wallbank's concerns have legitimacy. However, as just argued, there is scope in a rights-based approach to require a careful consideration of the impact of enforcement on the rights of all the parties. Further, there would be a need to ensure that the impact of enforcement of contact disputes was not effectively discriminating against mothers.

Grandparents and Other Relatives

Family law disputes tend to be between parents and about children, but wider relatives can become involved.[169] They can claim to have family life with children. Siblings appear automatically to have family life with each other.[170] With other relatives the ECtHR appears to focus on the quality of the relationship between the adult and the child. Hence in *Boyle v UK*[171] where the uncle was 'a father figure' to the child there was no difficulty in deciding that he had family life with the child. The courts, it seems, will be particularly willing to accept that grandparents have family life with their grandchildren.[172] In *Marckx v Belgium*[173] the ECtHR confirmed that Article 8 rights were not restricted to parents and children and 'include at least the ties between near relatives, for instance those between grandparents and grandchildren, since such relatives may play a considerable part in family life'.[174] In *L v Finland* the ECtHR stated:

> The Court recalls that the mutual enjoyment by parent and child, as well as by grandparent and child, of each other's company constitutes a fundamental element of family life.[175]

For the tie to exist, there must be a fairly close relationship between the child and grandparent.[176] So, no doubt there would be family life if the child were living with her grandparents[177] or had regular contact with them.[178]

Once it is established that a grandparent, or other relative, has family life with a child, then, of course, the relationship is protected under Article 8. This means that any lack of respect for the right to family life must be justified in accordance with Article 8(2).

---

[169] F Kaganas and C Piper, 'Grandparents and Contact: "Rights v Welfare" Revisited' (2001) 15 *International Journal of Law, Policy and the Family* 205.

[170] *Moustaquim v Belgium* (1991) 13 EHRR 802.

[171] (1994) 19 EHRR 179. See also *Jucius and Juciuvienė v Lithuania* [2009] 1 FLR 403.

[172] See *Re J (Leave to Issue Application for Residence Order)* [2003] 1 FLR 114. For an argument that there should be an acknowledgment of grandparental legal rights see M Ognibene, 'A Constitutional Analysis of Grandparents' (2005) 72 *University of Chicago Law Review* 1473.

[173] 13 June 1979 (Application No 6833/74).

[174] *L v Finland* [2000] 2 FLR 118.

[175] At para 101.

[176] *S and S v United Kingdom* (1984) 40 DR 196; *X, Y and Z v United Kingdom* [1997] 24 EHRR 143, para 52.

[177] *X v Switzerland* (1981) 24 DR 183.

[178] *Price v United Kingdom* (1988) 55 DR 224. See also *Boyle v United Kingdom* (1994) 19 EHRR 179.

Consideration will now be given to the extent to which the legal regulation of the relationships between relatives and child in English law is compatible with the ECHR.

It is perhaps surprising that there is no special legal status that applies to grandparents in English law. They are recognised in section 105 of the CA as being relatives, along with uncles and aunts and siblings. Not that that means much. The significance of being a relative lies in two areas. First, if a relation has lived with the child for three years they can apply for a residence or contact order without leave of the court.[179] If the time spent is less than three years then leave of the court is required. Second, when deciding whether or not to make an adoption order the child's links with the wider family should be considered.[180] So as far as the CA is concerned, apart from the few grandparents who have their grandchildren living with them and grandparents whose grandchildren are being considered for adoption, being a grandparent grants one no special legal rights or responsibilities.

So, in strict legal terms most grandparents are in the same formal legal position in relation to their grandchildren as any other adult in the country. However, the courts are normally willing to find that a child benefits from relationships with grandparents. Further, the benefit of grandparental–grandchild contact is widely accepted in our society as a benefit and this norm is often reflected in negotiated settlements between parents. So even though being a grandparent does not grant one a special legal status, courts seek to promote the interests of the child and will often seek to preserve the grandparent–grandchild link.[181]

There may, therefore, be some HRA challenges to the law on grandparents and these will be considered next.

Disputes over Residence

Where a grandparent or other relative is seeking a residence order[182] as against the parent they will face an uphill task. The court will consider any application by a grandparent based on what will promote the child's welfare.[183] The courts have stated that in deciding a dispute over residence it is strongly presumed that a child is better off with a 'natural parent' than anyone else. This presumption was applied in *Re D (Care: Natural Parent Presumption)*[184] where a father of a child had a history of drug abuse and had had a number of children by different women. The child's grandparents sought a residence order. The application failed with the court preferring the natural parent (that is, the father). Only had he been shown to be clearly unsuitable would the court consider giving residence to the grandparents.

An example of a case where a grandparent did succeed in a residence dispute with a birth parent is *Re H (Residence: Grandparent)*.[185] There the child had been living with grandparents for about six years when the mother sought the return of the child. This time the grandparents were awarded residence because the grandparents had become the 'natural

---

[179] CA, s8.
[180] Adoption and Children Act 2002, s1.
[181] F Kaganas, 'Grandparents' Rights and Grandparents' Campaigns' [2007] *Child and Family Law Quarterly* 17.
[182] CA, s8.
[183] CA, s1.
[184] [1999] 1 FLR 134.
[185] [2000] Fam Law 715.

parents' of the child.[186] The psychological bond between the child and grandparents had come to resemble that between children and parents. These cases suggest that grandparents are only likely to succeed in obtaining a residence order against the wishes of a parent where the parent is clearly posing a risk of harm to the child or where the child has lived with the grandparents for sufficient time so that they become the social parents of the child.

In *CP v AR and another; Re R (a child) (residence order)*[187] the Court of Appeal overturned an order granting residence to grandparents, rather than to parents. It was held that the judge had failed to grapple with 'the fundamental proposition that children have a right to be brought up by their natural parents unless their welfare positively demands the replacement of that right'.[188] The court did not specify the origins of this right, but might well have had in mind Article 8 of the ECHR. However, the Court of Appeal's comments should be read with the decision of the House of Lords in *Re G (Children)*[189] where Baroness Hale, in the context of a residence dispute between a lesbian couple who had raised a child together, stated:

> the fact that CG [one of the women] is the natural mother of these children in every sense of that term, while raising no presumption in her favour, is undoubtedly an important and significant factor in determining what will be best for them now and in the future.[190]

The ECtHR has not given a clear view on whether the 'natural parent' presumption is compatible with the ECHR. Imagine a case where a child has been staying with grandparents for several years, but the parents now seek the return of the child. While family life will no doubt be found involving the child and both the grandparents and the parents it is unclear whether there would be any intrinsic value attached to the parental link.[191] Indeed, given that not all parents automatically have family life and that the existence of family life requires an element of caring for the child, it may be that the ECtHR would not attach weight to the biological link per se in the context of a residence dispute.

Disputes over Contact

More common than residence disputes are cases where a relative seeks a contact order. This is most likely to arise where following a divorce or separation the resident parent refuses to allow the child to see the non-resident parent's parents or other family member. In such a case, if the relative is seeking a contact order they must first obtain the leave of the court to make the application.

Seeking Leave

The precise role and nature of the leave requirement is uncertain. Before the application for contact can be made, a short hearing will be required before a judge. The judge is

---

[186] Contrast *Re N (Residence: Appointment of Solicitor: Placement with Extended Family)* [2001] 1 FLR 1028, where the child had lived with an uncle and aunt for two years following his mother's death, but it was ordered he should return to his father. The first instance judges who had ordered that the child stay with the aunt and uncle were held on appeal to have paid insufficient attention to the fact that the child should be raised within the birth family.

[187] [2009] 2 FCR 203.

[188] Para 126.

[189] [2006] UKHL 46.

[190] Para 44.

[191] *Adam v Germany* [2009] 1 FLR 560.

required when considering whether to grant leave to consider the factors in section 10(9) of the CA:

(a) the nature of the proposed application for the section 8 order;
(b) the applicant's connection with the child
(c) any risk there might be of that proposed application disrupting the child's life to such an extent that he would be harmed by it;
(d) where the child is being looked after by a local authority—
    (i) the authority's plan for the child's future, and
    (ii) the wishes and feelings of the child's parents.

There is little doubt that a grandparent seeking contact with a child with whom they have a good relationship is likely to be granted leave.[192] Clearly the issue could not be said to be a frivolous one. Indeed it has been held that refusal to give leave is a serious issue and reasons must be provided for the refusal.[193] Refusing leave could be seen as potentially violating a party's rights under Articles 6 or 8 of the ECHR.[194] However, leave requirements do not automatically infringe Convention rights. The ECtHR has approved of leave requirements in other contexts as long as they are seen as proportionate and appropriate.[195]

The interpretation given to the leave requirement means that unless there are good reasons, leave will be granted. Perhaps the most common example of where leave is refused is where there is intense animosity between the grandparents and parents.[196] In *Re A (A Minor) (Contact: Leave to Apply)*[197] Douglas Brown J upheld the decision of the magistrates' court not to allow leave to apply for contact, given the 'long-standing, serious disharmony between the parties'. Any order for contact against the wishes of the parents was likely to cause the child more harm than good, he concluded.[198] In *Re A (Section 8 Order: Grandparent Application)*,[199] Butler-Sloss LJ also noted that contact between a grandparent and child may not benefit the child where there was animosity between the grandparent and the parent. However, she emphasised that it should not be thought that, simply because the parents oppose contact, leave should not be granted. Indeed it has been argued that while parents may have a good reason for opposing contact, it will be rare that there will be a good reason for objecting to leave.[200] What, however, the court will be wary of is allowing an application to proceed which will significantly increase the animosity between the parties and as a result harm the child. It seems that the approach taken by the court is likely to be consistent with the ECHR as any interference in the rights of grandparents will be justified due to the potential harm to the child. However, where the relationship between the child and the relative is a strong one, the evidence of harm must be clear.

---

[192] *Re M (Care: Contact: Grandmother's Application for Leave)* [1995] 2 FLR 86, 95; Law Commission Report 172, *Review of Child Law* (London, Law Commission, 1988) para 4.41.
[193] *T v W (Contact: Reasons for Refusing Leave)* [1996] 2 FLR 473.
[194] *Re J (Leave to Issue Application for Residence Order)* [2002] EWCA Civ 1346; discussed in G Douglas, 'Case Commentary—*Re J (Leave To Issue Application For Residence Order)*: Recognising Grandparents' Concern or Controlling Their Interference?' [2003] 15 *Child and Family Law Quarterly* 103.
[195] *Golder v United Kingdom* (1979–80) 1 EHRR 524, and *H v United Kingdom* (1985) 45 DR 281; *Re P (Section 91(14) Guidelines) (Residence and Religious Heritage)* [1999] 2 FLR 573.
[196] *Re M (Minors) (Sexual Abuse: Evidence)* [1993] 1 FLR 822, 825.
[197] [1995] 3 FCR 543.
[198] To similar effect see *Re A (Section 8 Order: Grandparent Application)* [1995] 2 FLR 153, 154.
[199] [1995] 2 FLR 153, 154.
[200] R Nugee, *Relative Values … Missing out on Contact* (London, Grandparents' Association, 2003) 5.

The Substantive Hearing

As with any application concerning the upbringing of children the welfare of the child will be the paramount consideration when a court considers an application by a grandparent for a contact order.[201] In *Re A (Section 8 order: grandparent application)* the Court of Appeal said that there was no presumption in favour of ordering contact between a grandparent and child. However, if it is shown that in the circumstances of the particular case contact between the child and grandparent would be in the interests of the child's welfare, then the court will order contact.[202] Thorpe LJ has commented:

> It is important that trial judges should recognise the greater appreciation that has developed of the value of what grandparents have to offer, particularly to children of disabled parents.[203]

When considering the approach adopted by the courts in relation to grandparental contact it is worth remembering that there is not even a presumption in favour of there being contact between a father and child, although the courts will assume that contact is beneficial.[204] Seen in this light the courts' rejection of a presumption in favour of grandparental contact is less surprising.

Even where it is found that contact will benefit the child, the court may not order contact if it involves forcing unwilling parents to allow contact and that will be a cause of greater harm to the children than denying contact.[205] In *Re S (Contact: Grandparents)*[206] Wall J found the mother's hostility to contact to be unreasonable and found the child would suffer significant harm without contact. However, that case appears to be exceptional. In *Re W (Contact: Application by Grandparent)*[207] Hollis J held that where there was ongoing hostility between the mother and the maternal grandmother, it was a matter of 'common sense' that contact might harm the child. Indeed it is now generally accepted that it will be very unlikely that a court would order contact to a grandparent against the wishes of a parent.[208]

Even if there is no presumption in favour of contact for grandparents Felicity Kaganas has argued that it has become an extra-legal norm that grandparents should see their grandchildren and this has become so generally accepted that it exercises a powerful influence over negotiations settling disputes over families.[209] Indeed, it may be that the establishment of such a norm is more important than any formal legal status, simply because the vast majority of disputes are settled between the parties, than by means of a contested court case.[210] Notably in *Adam v Germany*[211] the ECtHR found the grandparents had a

---

[201]   CA, s1(1).

[202]   *Re M (Care: Contact: Grandmother's Application for Leave)* [1995] 3 FCR 550.

[203]   *Re J (Leave to Issue Application for Residence Order)* [2002] EWCA 1346.

[204]   See the discussion of the law on fathers and contact in J Herring, *Family Law* (Harlow, Pearson, 2009) ch 9.

[205]   *Re F and R (Section 8 Order: Grandparent's Application)* [1995] 1 FLR 524; *Re A (Section 8 Order: Grandparent Application)* [1995] 2 FLR 153; *Re W (Contact: Application by Grandparent)* [1997] 1 FLR 793.

[206]   [1996] 1 FLR 158.

[207]   [1997] 1 FLR 793, 797.

[208]   F Kaganas and C Piper, 'Grandparents and Contact' (n 169). See also C Smart, V May, A Wade and C Furniss, *Residence and Contact Disputes in Court* (London, Department of Constitutional Affairs, 2003). Those authors suggest that courts seemed unlikely to order contact in favour of a grandparent against a parent's wishes. However, they found that, although the court made an order for 'no order' in one case out of the seven in their sample, the rest of the applications were withdrawn and the cases settled (28–29).

[209]   F Kaganas, 'Grandparents' Rights and Grandparents' Campaigns' (n 181).

[210]   N Ferguson, G Douglas, N Lowe, M Murch and M Robinson, *Grandparenting in Divorced Families* (Bristol, Policy Press, 2004), ch 12.

[211]   [2009] 1 FLR 560.

right to contact under Article 8 and interference was not justified by the opposition of the mother.

However, establishing the existence of family life will be only the first hurdle for any human rights claim. Article 8(2) justifies an interference in the rights of grandparents where that is (inter alia) necessary in the interests of others. Kaganas and Piper argue that if the parents object to grandparental contact the case will be seen as involving a clash between the rights of grandparents and parents. They argue in that case that the strong line of cases from the ECtHR on respecting parental authority[212] means that the rights of parents will win out. Harris *et al* agree, suggesting that in such a case the parents' 'right to control the personal relationships … of their children' will win the day.[213] Douglas and Ferguson also support such a line referring to *L v Finland*[214] where the grandparental relationship was held not to have the same quality or significance as the parental one.

Despite the academic support for this view it is not beyond question. First, in the analysis presented above the cases are treated as involving a clash between the rights of parents and grandparents. However, there are the rights of the children to take into account. Indeed the ECtHR has held that the rights of children should be regarded as crucial. It may be argued that children, especially where they have a close relationship with their grandparents, have important rights that the relationship be retained, even if that is against the wishes of their parents.

Second, even if the case is seen as one involving a clash between the parents and grandparents, it is not inevitable that the grandparents will lose out.[215] As seen using a parallel analysis, the court must consider the interference with each right individually with an 'intense focus' on the specific right claimed. Adopting such an approach in this case it is necessary to look carefully at the values underlying the rights claimed. For the grandparent seeking contact the value at stake is the relationship with her grandchildren. In a contact case the whole relationship is at stake. For parents there is the value of deciding with whom their child will have a relationship. It is not clear to me that comparing these values will necessarily lead to a preference for the parental wish, especially where the relationship with the grandparent is a good one and the inconvenience to the parent limited. It is argued that Kaganas and Piper's argument that 'grandparents' rights are inferior to those of parents' is too much of a generalisation. That may be true generally but it is not correct to suggest that any parental right will always trump a grandparental right.

Wilson J in *Re W (Contact Application: Procedure)*[216] held: 'I anticipate that, when the Human Rights Act 1998 comes into force, it will be argued that a child's respect for his or her family life under Article 8 of the Convention requires the absence of such a presumption in the case of a grandparent to be revisited.' That may be putting it too strongly. First, grandparents do not automatically have a right to respect for their family life. It will only be where there is a strong relationship between the grandparents and the child that there needs to be good reason for not ordering contact. Second, simply because a grandparent has a right does not mean that having that contact promotes the welfare of the child.

---

[212] Eg *Nielsen v Denmark* (1989) 11 EHRR 175.
[213] D Harris, M O'Boyle, and C Warbrick, *Law of the European Convention on Human Rights* (London, Butterworths, 1995) 317.
[214] *L v Finland* [2000] 2 FLR 118.
[215] *Re S (A Child) (Identification: Restrictions on Publication)* [2004] UKHL 47; *Campbell v MGN Ltd* [2004] UKHL 22.
[216] [2000] 1 FCR 185.

If the courts were to create such a presumption, that would need to come from the empirical data and that is unclear.[217]

In conclusion, an approach under the ECHR would recognise that grandparents with a close relationship with their grandchildren would be able to rely on their right to respect for their family life under Article 8. This right could be interfered with if necessary in the interests of others. It is unlikely that the courts will place much weight on the rights of parents to determine how their children will be raised; rather the focus will be on the harm to the children of court-ordered contact. If that was real harm an interference in the rights of grandparents would be justified.

Religious Issues

Next, the potential relevance of the HRA to family law cases involving religious issues will be considered.[218] Article 9 of the ECHR states that:

1. Everyone has the right to freedom of thought, conscience and religion;
   this right includes freedom to change his religion or belief and freedom, either alone or in community with others and in public or private, to manifest his religion or belief, in worship, teaching, practice and observance.
2. Freedom to manifest one's religion or beliefs shall be subject only to such limitations as are prescribed by law and are necessary in a democratic society in the interests of public safety, for the protection of public order, health or morals, or for the protection of the rights and freedoms of others.

Article 9 protects religious beliefs. In *Kalaç v Turkey*[219] the ECtHR held that not every religiously inspired belief was protected under Article 9:

Article 9 does not protect every act motivated or inspired by a religion or belief. Moreover, in exercising his freedom to manifest his religion, an individual may need to take his specific situation into account.

The line between a religious belief and a belief which is motivated by a religion is a complex one and raises complex issues which are beyond the scope of this book. However, the Court will generally accept a person's profession of belief and will not consider in detail whether a person's beliefs are genuinely held or not. As the ECtHR in *Metropolitan Church of Bessarabia v Moldova*[220] stated:

In principle, the right to freedom of religion as understood in the Convention rules out any appreciation by the state of the legitimacy of religious beliefs or of the manner in which these are expressed.

---

[217] See further J Herring, *Older People in Law and Society* (Oxford, Oxford University Press, 2009) ch 8.
[218] For discussion see R Taylor, 'Parental Responsibility and Religion' in R Probert, S Gilmore and J Herring (eds), *Responsible Parents and Parental Responsibility* (Oxford, Hart, 2009); C Hamilton, *Family Law and Religion* (London, Sweet & Maxwell, 1995) 144; J Fortin, *Children's Rights and the Developing Law* 2nd edn (Cambridge, Cambridge University Press, 2005) 42–3; SE Mumford, 'The Judicial Resolution of Disputes Involving Children and Religion' (1998) 47 *ICLQ* 117 and S Langlaude, *The Right of the Child to Religious Freedom in International Law* (Leiden, Nijhoff, 2007) ch 4.
[219] (1997) 27 EHRR 552, para 27.
[220] (2002) 35 EHRR 306, 335, para 117.

Notably, the right to hold a protected belief is absolute, while the right to manifest the belief is qualified.

The freedom to manifest religion in Article 9(2) is not as expansive as may at first appear. It does not give a person the right to manifest religion at any time and in any place.[221] Hence in *Karaduman v Turkey*[222] a student could not rely on her religious beliefs to refuse to remove a headscarf for the purposes of an identification photograph. Generally the ECtHR takes the view that where a person has a choice of whether to use a particular service he cannot complain if he chooses to use a service which has a rule to which he objects on religious grounds. To be protected by Article 9 the practice must be 'intimately linked'[223] with the religious belief.

The question of what constitutes an interference in an Article 9 right is also complex. In *X v Denmark*[224] there was a conflict between a clergyman and his church over a matter of belief. It was held that the church's regulation of its clergy's beliefs was not an interference in his manifestation of his belief. Indeed he always had the choice to leave his job. In *Kjeldsen, Busk Madsen and Pedersen v Denmark*[225] parents' religious objections to sex education in state schools was rejected on the ground that they could send their children to state schools or educate them at home. Similarly in *Stedman v United Kingdom*[226] an applicant who objected to working on Sundays was told she could resign her post and find a job where she did not need to work on Sundays.

If an interference in the Article 9 right to manifest religion is demonstrated, the final question is whether the interference can be justified. Under Article 9(2) a limitation or interference must be prescribed by law and necessary in a democratic society for one of the permissible purposes. It must also be shown that the intervention is proportionate.

There are two main kinds of family case where religious issues can become relevant.[227] First, there are those where the dispute is between the two parents. In *Hoffmann v Austria*[228] there was a residence dispute over a child. This centred on the fact that although the child had been raised a Roman Catholic the mother had recently become a Jehovah's Witness. It was held that the Supreme Court in Austria had allowed the religious beliefs of the parents to dominate the issue of residence. That meant that the mother had been discriminated against on the basis of her religious beliefs and with Articles 8, 9 and 14. The ECtHR added that it would be permissible to rely on the impact of the religious practices, but not on the faith itself. Andrew Bainham,[229] with much justification, complains about this line of reasoning. Where the practice is an inevitable part of the religious belief, discriminating on the basis of the practice is in effect discriminating on the basis of the belief. It would not be accepted that an employer who objected to employees wearing turbans was not, in fact, discriminating against Sikhs. Indeed in *R (Begum) v Denbigh High School Governors* the House of Lords had little difficulty in determining that a school uniform policy

[221] *Kalaç v Turkey* (1997) 27 EHRR 552, para 27; *Ahmad v United Kingdom* (1981) 4 EHRR 126, para 11.
[222] (1993) 74 DR 93.
[223] *Hasan and Chaush v Bulgaria* (Application No 30985/96) [2002] 34 EHRR 1339, 1358, para 60.
[224] (1976) 5 DR 157.
[225] (1976) 1 EHRR 711, paras 54 and 57.
[226] (1997) 23 EHRR CD 168.
[227] For an excellent discussion of this article see C Evans, *Freedom of Religion under the European Convention on Human Rights* (Oxford, Oxford University Press, 2001).
[228] (1993) 17 EHRR 293.
[229] A Bainham, 'Religion, Human Rights and the Fitness of Parents' (1995) *CLJ* 48.

discriminated against those with religious beliefs which dictated that they wear something prohibited by the policy. It is suggested that the correct approach is that the court should take harmful religious practices into account when making decisions about children. Doing so will constitute discrimination on the grounds of religious belief,[230] but that can be justified if it can be shown that the practice causes clear harm to the child.

While it is improper to discriminate against a parent simply on the basis of their religious beliefs that does not mean that a child must suffer serious harm due to the beliefs of the parents. In *Re P (Section 91(14) Guidelines) (Residence and Religious Heritage)*[231] Orthodox Jewish parents had placed their Down's syndrome child into care. They objected to her placement with Catholic foster parents and sought her return. While the Court of Appeal accepted that a child's religious heritage carried some weight, that did not justify the removal of the child from the foster parents, an arrangement which was working well.

English family law has traditionally seen the right of the parent to determine their child's religious upbringing as an aspect of parental responsibility.[232] Indeed a failure to raise a child within a religion could be seen as indicating a person was an inappropriate parent: the poet Shelley was deprived of custody of his children as it was said he lived his life without religious or moral principles.[233] The current position has been summarised by Wall J in *Re J* in this way:

> The Children Act 1989 does not impose any obligation on parents in respect of religious upbringing or instruction. Section 3, which defines parental responsibility, describes it as 'all the rights, duties, powers, responsibilities and authority which by law a parent of a child has in relation to the child and his property'. Parental responsibility thus clearly includes the right to bring up children in a particular religious faith, or in none.[234]

So the current position taken by the courts, and reinforced by the HRA, is that the particular religion or lack of religion of a parent should not be a factor in residence or contact disputes, unless there are particular religious practices which harm the child.

Where a religious practice is harmful, a parent could rely on the right under Article 9 which protects freedom of thought, conscience and religion. However, manifestation of belief can be limited under Article 9(2). Instructive in this regard is *Williamson*.[235] There, applicants sent their children to a private religious school and wanted the teachers to be permitted to use corporal punishment. However, the law does not permit corporal punishment in schools.[236] The parents' claim that this interfered with the manifestation of their religious beliefs failed. Rather surprisingly their Lordships found that the law did interfere with the manifestation of the parents' religious beliefs, although they found such interference justified. The House of Lords noted that the parents regarded themselves under a Biblical obligation to use corporal punishment as part of the education of children. It was found that the parents' beliefs were coherent; met an 'adequate degree of seriousness and

---

[230] At least where that religious practice is an aspect of the religion: see *Williamson v Secretary of State for Education and Employment* [2005] UKHL 15.

[231] [1999] 2 FLR 573. See also *Palau-Martinez v France* [2004] 2 FLR 810.

[232] *Re Agar-Ellis* (1878–79) L R 10 Ch. D. 49; (1883) L R 24 Ch. D. 317.

[233] *Shelley v Westbrooke* (1817) Jac 266.

[234] *Re J (Specific Issue Orders: Muslim Upbringing and Circumcision)* [1999] 2 FLR 678, 685.

[235] *Williamson v Secretary of State for Education and Employment* [2005] UKHL 15. See the discussion of this case with respect to corporal punishment in ch 6 at pp 237–9.

[236] Education Act 1998 s548.

importance'; and were 'consistent with basic standards of human dignity and integrity'.[237] There was no need to show, according to Lord Nicholls, that the belief was capable of rational justification or of precise explanation. As to whether it was a manifestation of religion, the approach of the Court of Appeal that corporal punishment was not a 'clear, uniform and agreed' requirement of Christianity and so not a manifestation of religion failed.[238] The House of Lords instead considered whether the applicants perceived themselves to be under a religious obligation.[239] They did in this case. The approach of their Lordships is understandable. The approach of the Court of Appeal could lead the courts into tricky issues about what were or were not fundamental tenets of particular faiths. Their Lordships went on to find that the interference in the manifestation of parents' religious beliefs was justified. It pursued the legitimate aim of protecting all schoolchildren from corporal punishment. The issue had been carefully considered by Parliament and could not be said by the courts to be an improper interference in the rights of parents. Baroness Hale added:

> This is, and has always been, a case about children, their rights and the rights of their parents and teachers. Yet there has been no one here or in the courts below to speak on behalf of the children. No litigation friend has been appointed to consider the rights of the pupils involved separately from those of the adults. No non-governmental organization, such as the Children's Rights Alliance, has intervened to argue a case on behalf of children as a whole. The battle has been fought on ground selected by the adults. This has clouded and over-complicated what should have been a simple issue.[240]

What is noticeable about their Lordships' judgments is that some respect was shown to the fact the harm to the children was sought in the name of manifestation of religion. In other words the courts require a stronger justification to interfere in harmful parental upbringing when the parents are manifesting their religion than in other cases.

Of course, generally parents are given a broad discretion to raise their children as they wish.[241] In this sense the freedom of parents to raise their children in religious matters does not differ from other matters. Indeed, there are relatively few rights which may be classified as specifically religious rights.[242] As already mentioned, it seems where religious issues are involved that the courts may need slightly more evidence of harm to the child to justify intervention in family life than they would do otherwise. Also, parents are permitted to remove their children from religious education and collective worship at schools.[243] Oddly it seems that until the child is a sixth-former she does not have the right to remove herself from religious education.[244] Arguably another issue where there is special protection for religious decisions is male[245] circumcision.[246] This seems to be

[237] *Williamson* (n 235), para 23.
[238] *Williamson v Secretary of State for Education* [2002] EWCA Civ 1926, para 35.
[239] *Williamson* (n 235), paras 32 and 65.
[240] *Ibid*, para 71.
[241] See S Gilmore, J Herring and R Probert, 'Parental Responsibility—Law, Issues and Themes' in R Probert, S Gilmore and J Herring (eds), *Responsible Parents and Parental Responsibility* (Oxford, Hart, 2009).
[242] Taylor, 'Parental Responsibility and Religion' (n 218).
[243] This right is currently contained in the School Standards and Framework Act 1998, s71.
[244] Education and Inspections Act 2006, s55.
[245] Female circumcision is prohibited under the Female Genital Mutilation Act 2003.
[246] *Re J (Specific Issue Orders: Child's Religious Upbringing and Circumcision)* [1999] 2 FLR 678; [2000] 1 FLR 571. For criticism see H Gilbert, 'Time to Reconsider the Lawfulness of Ritual Male Circumcision' [2007] *European Human Rights Law Review* 279.

accepted as lawful even where the procedure is not medically in the best interests of the child. It is unlikely that a parent could consent to other procedures which were not medically indicated which would have an impact on the body of the child.[247] As Rachel Taylor argues, circumcision can be regarded as an aspect of fulfilment of the parents' religious obligations: 'It allows parents to fulfil their own religious obligations by permanently marking the child with the symbol of their religion at an age where he is not capable of accepting that religion for himself.'[248] However, it does so at the expense of that being a 'mark' which is indelible.

The Religion of a Child

Generally the courts have avoided determining what religion a child has.[249] In fact there is no real need to do so.[250] In *Re J (Specific Issue Orders: Child's Religious Upbringing and Circumcision)*,[251] a father argued that his son was a Muslim and should be circumcised in accordance with Islamic practice. The mother, a Christian, objected to the circumcision. Thorpe LJ held:

> Some faiths recognize their religion as a birthright derived from either the child's mother or the child's father. Some recognize religion by some ceremony of induction or initiation, but the newborn does not share the perception of his parents or of the religious community to which the parents belong. A child's perception of his or her religion generally depends on involvement in worship and teaching within the family. From this develops the emotional, intellectual, psychological and spiritual sense of belonging to a religious faith. So far, for all practical purposes, the courts have been right to focus upon religious upbringing and it is no surprise to me that there is no reported case focusing on a child's religion.[252]

As children grow up, courts have been willing to accept that children can form their own religious beliefs.[253] In *Re R (A Minor)(Residence: Religion)*[254] the ability of the child with strong religious views to continue living within his religious tradition was seen as an important factor in a dispute over residence.

Another case involving the religious rights of children was Shabina Begum, who wanted to wear a jilbab to school. This was not permitted by her school's uniform policy. The school allowed girls to wear a shalwar kameez, which was satisfactory dress for many Muslim girls, but was not regarded as appropriate by Shabina. She refused to attend school unless she was permitted to wear the jilbab and the school refused to allow her to attend unless she complied with their dress code. She applied for a judicial review of the school's decision, arguing that her rights to manifest her religion under Article 9 of the ECHR had been infringed. The school appealed.

---

[247] M Fox and M Thomson, 'Short Changed? The Law and Ethics of Male Circumcision' (2005) 12 *International Journal of Children's Rights* 161.

[248] Taylor, 'Parental Responsibility and Religion' (n 218).

[249] N Lowe and G Douglas, *Bromley's Family Law* 10th edn (Oxford, Oxford University Press, 2007) 377 refers to a parent's rights to determine the religion of a child, but seems doubtful: see Taylor, *ibid.*

[250] *Re J (Specific Issue Orders: Child's Religious Upbringing and Circumcision)* [2000] 1 FLR 571, 575.

[251] *Ibid.*

[252] *Re J (Specific Issue Orders: Child's Religious Upbringing and Circumcision)* [2000] 1 FLR 571, 575.

[253] CRC, Art 14.

[254] [1993] 2 FCR 525.

The Court of Appeal found for the applicant (*R (on the application of Begum) v Headteacher and Governors of Denbigh High School.*[255] At the heart of their judgment was the decision that the school had approached the question in the wrong way. The school had focused on whether the dress code had been appropriate, rather than starting with the fact that the pupil had a right to wear religious clothing and then considering whether there was a sufficiently good reason to justify an interference with her right. The school appealed to the House of Lords.[256]

The House of Lords disagreed with the Court of Appeal's criticism about the way the school had approached the question. The majority of their Lordships held that the dress code at the school did not interfere with Shabina's rights under Article 9 to freedom of religion. This right did not entitle one to manifest one's religion at any time and place. Shabina's right here was not interfered with because there was nothing to stop her going to another school where she was allowed to wear a jilbab. Her family had chosen the school with knowledge of its uniform requirements. With respect, this is a surprising conclusion. A public house which barred people of a certain race could not claim it was not discriminating on the grounds of race based on the fact that other pubs welcomed people of all races.

Their Lordships unanimously agreed that even if Shabina's Article 9 rights were infringed, there was a sound justification for doing so. Lord Bingham felt respect had to be owed to the head, teachers, staff and governors in making the delicate decision about their school. Baroness Hale provides the clearest explanation for the justification of the school policy:

> The school's task is also to promote the ability of people of diverse races, religions and cultures to live together in harmony. Fostering a sense of community and cohesion within the school is an important part of that. A uniform dress code can play its role in smoothing over ethnic, religious and social divisions ... Social cohesion is promoted by the uniform elements of shirt, tie and jumper, and the requirement that all outer garments be in the school colour. But cultural and religious diversity is respected by allowing girls to wear either a skirt, trousers, or the shalwar kameez, and by allowing those who wished to do so to wear the hijab. This was indeed a thoughtful and proportionate response to reconciling the complexities of the situation.[257]

There are two points of particular interest for family lawyers in this case. First, the case is an interesting example of how one child's rights may clash with the rights of other children. Here it was argued by the school that respecting Shabina's right to wear what she wished might interfere with the rights of other children to wear what they wanted to by creating pressure to wear the most conservative style of dress permitted. A second point of interest lies in the lack of emphasis placed by most of their Lordships on the fact that Shabina was a teenager. An argument could be made that, during teenage years, while one is formulating and developing one's own ideas of the world, rights of freedom of thought and religion should be protected particularly strongly. This argument would mean that an interference with a right of a teenager to religious freedom might require an even stronger justification than a similar interference with the rights of an adult. This point was taken up by Baroness Hale, but is not touched upon in the other speeches.

In *R (Playfoot) v Governing Body of Millais School*[258] Lydia Playfoot complained about the fact that she was not able to wear a 'purity' ring. This was said to be a symbol of her

[255] [2005] EWCA Civ 199.
[256] [2006] UKHL 15.
[257] Paras 97–8.
[258] [2007] ELR 484.

belief that she should abstain from sexual intercourse prior to marriage. It was held that the wearing of the ring was not 'intimately linked' to her religious belief. She was not obliged by her belief to wear the ring.[259] This meant that Article 9 was not engaged. Further, she had voluntarily chosen to go to the school which had publicised its uniform policy and there were other ways she could demonstrate her belief (for example by a keychain). This case also raised an Article 14 claim. This was rejected on the basis that the school had considered possible exceptions to the policy and followed government guidance on school policy decisions. There was no evidence that she was discriminated against on the basis of her religion.

That case can be contrasted with *R (Watkins Singh) v Governing Body of Aberdare Girls' High School*[260] where a school barred the claimant, a 14-year-old Sikh pupil, from wearing a Kara (a bangle worn by Sikhs). Notably in this case the claim was based on the Race Relations Act 1976 (as amended) and the Equality Act 2006. Such a claim could not have been made in the earlier cases because the amended Acts were not yet in force. Her applicant under the new legislation was successful. The court made little reference to the HRA principles and focused on the provision of the 1976 Act.

These decisions raise some complex issues about the nature of religious rights under the ECHR and the appropriate weight to be attached to them. There is not space to consider all the issues raised by this important case and in any event the arguments have been well rehearsed elsewhere.[261]

Relocation

The area of relocation provides another useful example within which to consider how a human rights approach would differ from a welfare approach. The courts tend to deal with an application by a parent to relocate under the welfare principle.[262]

In the current leading case of *Payne v Payne*,[263] Thorpe LJ conducted a detailed consideration of the case law, summarising it in two propositions:

    (a) the welfare of the child is the paramount consideration; and
    (b) refusing the primary carer's reasonable proposals for the relocation of her family life is likely to impact detrimentally on the welfare of her dependent children. Therefore her application to relocate will be granted unless the court concludes that it is incompatible with the welfare of the children.[264]

---

[259] Reference was made to made to *X v United Kingdom* (Application No 5442/72) (1975) 1 DR 41 where contributions to a religious magazine were not a necessary part of the applicant's religion and so not covered by Art 9. Although in *Sahin v Turkey* (Application No 44774/98) [2004] ELR 520, para 66 it was emphasised that Art 9 could protect a religious practice even if it was not an essential part of a person's religion.

[260] [2008] EWHC 1865 (Admin).

[261] See, eg, S Edwards, 'Imagining Islam … of Meaning and Metaphor Symbolising the Jilbab' [2007] *Child and Family Law Quarterly* 247; M Malik, 'Religious Freedom and Multiculturalism: *R (Shabina Begum) v Denbigh High School*' (2008) 19 *Kings Law Journal* 2.

[262] M Hayes, 'Relocation Cases: Is the Court of Appeal Applying the Correct Principles?' [2006] *Child and Family Law Quarterly* 351.

[263] [2001] 1 FLR 1052. The case is discussed in A Perry, '*Payne v Payne*: Leave to remove children from the jurisdiction' [2001] *Child and Family Law Quarterly* 455.

[264] [2001] 1 FLR 1052, at para 26.

Building on these propositions, Thorpe LJ suggested that trial judges should follow the following discipline:

(a) Pose the question: is the mother's application genuine in the sense that it is not motivated by some selfish desire to exclude the father from the child's life? Then ask, is the mother's application realistic, by which I mean founded on practical proposals both well researched and investigated? If the application fails either of these tests, refusal will inevitably follow.
(b) If, however, the application passes these tests then there must be a careful appraisal of the father's opposition: is it motivated by genuine concern for the future of the child's welfare or is it driven by some ulterior motive? What would be the extent of the detriment to him and his future relationship with the child were the application granted? To what extent would that be offset by extension of the child's relationships with the maternal family and homeland?
(c) What would be the impact on the mother, either as the single parent or as a new wife, of a refusal of her realistic proposal?
(d) The outcome of the second and third appraisals must then be brought into an overriding review of the child's welfare as the paramount consideration, directed by the statutory checklist in so far as appropriate.[265]

Although Thorpe LJ was keen to emphasise that there was no presumption in favour of allowing relocation, as Mary Hayes has shown, the effect of this discipline and the previous case law has been to tilt the scales heavily in favour of the relocating parent.[266] This additional weight can particularly be seen in the paragraph immediately following the discipline set out above, where Thorpe LJ emphasised that:

In suggesting such a discipline I would not wish to be thought to have diminished the importance that this court has consistently attached to the emotional and psychological well-being of the primary carer. In any evaluation of the welfare of the child as the paramount consideration great weight must be given to this factor.[267]

Indeed, in later cases Thorpe LJ has stated that this paragraph is to be read as part of the discipline itself.[268] Recently he has held:

The bar as to practicalities that must be jumped by the relocation applicant is set at a wide variety of heights depending on the facts and circumstances of the case. In this commonplace category of cross-border family creation, where the primary carer is returning to a completely familiar environment, the bar is obviously set considerably lower than in the case of an applicant who, in pursuit of some dream or ambition, is proposing to take the children to an unknown and untried environment. The bar is set particularly low where the primary carer is returning to the completely familiar home life after such a brief absence. In this instance the mother had only been in this country for six years in total.[269]

The impact of this is that although the court purports to be applying the welfare test, in these cases, the reality is that many of the important issues are disguised. Indeed John Eekelaar has pointed to the law on relocation as an example of a the 'lack of transparency' objection to the welfare principle—namely that although the court purports to consider only the welfare of the child, in fact a broader range of considerations are taken into account.

[265] [2001] 1 FLR 1052, at para 40.
[266] M Hayes, 'Relocation Cases' (n 262).
[267] [2001] 1 FLR 1052, at para 41.
[268] *Re B (Leave to Remove: Impact of Refusal)* [2004] EWCA 956, para 14.
[269] *Re F and H (Children: Relocation)* [2008] 2 FLR 1667, para 9.

Use of human rights in this context would ensure that a clearer presentation of the issues would be made. Using the kind of parallel analysis explained above, there will need to be a consideration of each party's rights. We need not go into the issue in as much detail as we did with contact, but the court will need to consider the resident parent's Article 8 right to freedom of movement and the non-resident parent's Article 8 right to maintain and develop a relationship with his child, the child's right in stability in her residential family life, and the child's right to maintain contact. Where the child is old enough to form and express her own views, she may have a right under Article 8 for those views to be considered.[270]

In relocation cases it is quite likely that the rights will not readily be resolved in the parallel analysis. It will therefore be necessary to undertaking the 'ultimate balancing exercise': if the rights are simply incommensurable, the rights-based approach will not be capable of producing a principled resolution to the clash of rights. As suggested above, that will involve a consideration of the underlying values in relation to the rights in question.[271]

In relocation cases one value will be personal autonomy.[272] At the heart of the right to autonomy is the right to be able to develop one's vision of the good life free from improper interference from either the state or other people.[273] This means that in a relocation case where there are clashing rights one question to ask is the extent to which the proposed order will blight the plans for the life of the individuals concerned. The court will give strong protection to a claim where an order will prevent a party pursuing a major aspect of their life plans, and less weight where the order will affect a more marginal aspect of a person's life. This acknowledges that not all interferences in a person's autonomy are equal. Some are major setbacks in a life plan, others are minor interruptions.[274] Not all interferences with your autonomy are equal. Some are major setbacks in your plan for your life; others are minor interruptions.

How such considerations may play out in a relocation case may vary. Herring and Taylor have argued:

> Therefore, when dealing with a clash between the rights of the mother and father in a relocation case the court should consider which interference will constitute a greater blight on the vision of the good life that each had. In developing a vision of the good life, it is likely that most parents would place great value both on their freedom of movement and consequent freedom to develop new relationships and opportunities, and on their relationship with their children. In most relocation cases the question will be how far the court's decision will *interfere* with that vision. For example, to deny relocation to enable a mother to pursue a new relationship is likely to have a more serious impact on her ability to live her chosen vision of the 'good life' than a father having substantial but less frequent contact with his child. Where the mother has no particular reason to relocate and the relocation will effectively bring to an end a strong father–child relationship it would, no doubt, be found that permitting the relocation would be greater interference with the father's autonomy than denying it would be for the mother.[275]

---

[270] *Sahin v Germany* [2003] 2 FLR 671 at para 73 (Grand Chamber), *Sommerfeld v Germany* [2003] 2 FLR 671 (Grand Chamber), although in these cases the Court appeared to treat the question as an aspect of the fathers' right.

[271] *Campbell v MGN* [2004] UKHL 22, paras 55–6.

[272] *Pretty v UK* [2002] 2 FLR 45, para 61.

[273] J Raz, *The Morality of Freedom* (Oxford, Oxford University Press, 1986).

[274] J Herring and R Taylor, 'Relocating Relocation' (n 139) (on which the above material has relied).

[275] *Ibid.*

They go on to argue that the rights of children will need to be considered too, although given their emphasis on autonomy they struggle to find a role for children who have not developed a vision of the good life. They suggest building on John Eekelaar's writings[276] that the question to ask is: 'Which interference in a child's rights will constitute a greater hindrance in the goal of providing the child with the opportunity of developing her own vision of the "good life"?'[277]

This causes them to conclude:

> Where relocation would not cause detriment to the child and would enable reasonable contact between father and child, it is likely that a mother with carefully considered plans would be permitted to relocate. This is because refusal to allow relocation would negate the mother's freedom to live an autonomous life, whereas permitting relocation would change, but not destroy, the father's enjoyment of a relationship with his child. This is not to deny that the lessening of contact will be a serious interference with the father's rights and that usually his relationship with his child will play an important part in his life; however, denying freedom of movement to the mother is likely to be a greater blight on her vision of the good life.

Not everyone will agree with that balancing. Indeed, as they accept, reasonable people using their approach could reach a rather different conclusion.

Conclusion

This Chapter has considered the way that human rights analysis can assist in dealing with disputes over children. Particular focus has been on the use of children's rights in the context of contact disputes. Many general themes emerge, but the following are of particular significance. First, a human rights analysis improves the quality of reasoning in these cases. It requires a consideration of the rights of each individual, rather squeezing all the relevant issues into the prism of child welfare. Second, it enables the analysis of issues which do not fit into a welfare model, such as intrinsic values. Third, it has been shown how a human rights analysis need not be (although it can so easily be) inimical to a feminist approach. Indeed we have argued that a human rights analysis can require a proper consideration of the interests of mothers in their own rights, rather than simply conduits of child welfare. Finally we have sought to clarify the way that a human rights analysis can be used to deal with more complex cases concerning child welfare.

---

[276] J Eekelaar, 'The Interests of the Child and the Child's Wishes: The Role of Dynamic Self-Determinism' (1994) 8 *International Journal of Law, Policy and the Family* 42, 53.
[277] Herring and Taylor, 'Relocating Relocation' (n 139).

8

Human Rights and
Child Protection

Introduction

The law on child protection is one area of English family law where the HRA has been particularly significant.[1] At first, this might seem surprising. The area of child protection might be thought to be one where the welfare of the child would outweigh other considerations and where the flexibility and discretion inherent in the welfare principle would be preferred over claims of substantive and procedural justice that underpin a rights-based approach. However, the fact that rights have gained significance in this area should not, on reflection, be surprising. Issues surrounding child protection, quite rightly, lead to powerful emotions and strong desires to protect children from harm. But it is precisely the strength of the emotions that can justify an emphasis on rights. The emotional pull of welfarism in this area is such that all other values and interests are too easily set aside. Indeed, the history of child protection is replete with examples of cases where social workers, motivated by the desire to protect children, have inappropriately removed children from their homes, causing them significant harm.[2] A rights-based approach can provide a counterbalance to the paternalist tendency which would otherwise dominate.[3]

There is another important benefit that flows from a rights-based approach. That is that emphasising children's rights to protection means that duties to protect can be imposed upon the state. Seeing the issue of protection from abuse as part of an obligation to protect children's fundamental human rights, rather than the general social services offered to promote the welfare of children, puts greater emphasis on the responsibilities of the state. Too many tragedies can be found within the history of English child protection law where children have been left to suffer at the hands of abusers, due to the state's failure to protect them.[4]

A central starting point for a consideration of the ECtHR's application in cases of child protection is *W v UK*.[5] W was removed under a parental rights resolution by the local authority (a procedure no longer available[6]). The parents were told this was to be a temporary

---

[1] Although see F Kaganas, 'Child Protection, Gender and Rights' in J Wallbank, S Choudhry and J Herring (eds), *Rights, Gender and Family Law* (London, Routledge, 2009) who sees the impact of the Act to be very limited.

[2] Eg Lord Clyde, *The Orkney Inquiry* (London, Department of Health, 1992). Of course there are also plenty of examples where the state has inappropriately not intervened.

[3] Although see *S (A Child Acting by the Official Solicitor) v Rochdale Metropolitan Borough Council and the Independent Reviewing Officer* [2009] 1 FLR 1090 for a case where the Official Solicitor brought a claim on behalf of a child, complaining that a local authority had failed to take care proceedings to protect her.

[4] A very recent example is the Baby P tragedy: Home Office, *Keeping Children Safe, Issue 6* (London, Home Office, 2009).

[5] *W v UK* (1987) 10 EHRR 29.

[6] The case was heard prior to the coming into force of the CA.

measure, but the local authority, without warning, arranged long-term fostering with a view to adoption and restricted, and then terminated, the parents' contact with W. The parents took the case to the ECtHR. At the heart of the argument of the UK government was that in this context parents had no rights, only responsibilities. As long as it could be shown that what was done was in the best interests of the child, no complaint could be made. This was strongly rejected by the Court. The ECtHR made it clear that parents did have rights, as did children. Even more significantly they emphasised that simply because a child is taken into care does not mean that parents lose their rights. Even though a child was in care, parents had a right to be consulted and involved in the decision-making process to an extent sufficient to protect their interests. As will become clear, this is a not uncontroversial approach; nevertheless, it has come to dominate the approach of the ECtHR ever since.

It is tempting to see child protection cases simply in terms of a clash between the interests of parents and children. Yet there are important social interests too. Baroness Hale has written of the way that the law on child protection tells us something about our society:

> Taking a child away from her family is a momentous step, not only for her, but for her whole family, and for the local authority which does so. In a totalitarian society, uniformity and conformity are valued. Hence the totalitarian state tries to separate the child from her family and mould her to its own design. Families in all their subversive variety are the breeding ground of diversity and individuality. In a free and democratic society we value diversity and individuality. Hence the family is given special protection in all the modern human rights instruments including the European Convention on Human Rights (Art 8), the International Covenant on Civil and Political Rights (Art 23) and throughout the United Nations Convention on the Rights of the Child. As Justice McReynolds famously said in *Pierce v Society of Sisters* 268 US 510 (1925) at 535, 'The child is not the mere creature of the State'.[7]

It is clear, too, from guidance issued by the government on the CA that the law's approach to child protection is based on a strong presumption that it is best for children to be raised by their families:

> [t]he Act is based on the belief that children are generally best looked after within the family with their parents playing a full part in their lives and with least recourse to legal proceedings.[8]

Children's Rights to Protection from Abuse

The ECHR recognises that children have a right to be protected from abuse.[9] Depending on the severity of the abuse it could amount to an interference with the child's rights under Article 3 or Article 8. Where the child has been killed, Article 2 becomes engaged.[10]

---

[7] *Re B (Children)* [2008] UKHL 35, para 20.
[8] Department for Children, Schools and Families, *The Children Act 1989 Guidance and Regulations, Volume 1, Court Orders* (London, TSO, 2008), para 1.8.
[9] Article 19 of the CRC also provides rights to protection from abuse. It provides that:

'(1) State Parties shall take all appropriate legislative, administrative, social and educational measures to protect the child from all forms of physical or mental violence, injury or abuse, neglect or negligent treatment, maltreatment or exploitation, including sexual abuse, while in the care of parent(s), legal guardian(s) or any other person who has the care of the child.
(2) Such protective measures should, as appropriate, include effective procedures for the establishment of social programmes to provide necessary support for the child and for those who have the care of the child, as well as for other forms of prevention and for identification, reporting, referral, investigation, treatment and follow-up of instances of child maltreatment described heretofore, and, as appropriate, for judicial involvement.'

[10] J Cooper, *Cruelty—An Analysis of Article 3* (London, Sweet & Maxwell, 2003).

The harms in Article 3 have been broadly enough defined to cover most forms of child abuse. They are not limited to physical injuries and so sexual abuse and the causing of mental suffering are included.[11] Further, the age and degree of vulnerability of the victim are relevant in assessing whether the conduct falls within Article 3.[12] This means that it is particularly likely that abuse of a child will infringe Article 3. Conduct which breaches Article 3 is not restricted to positive acts. Neglecting a child to such an extent that she suffers serious mental abuse could be included.[13] Also, it is important to emphasise that Article 3 is an absolute right. Nothing can justify its contravention.[14] Therefore the fact that the child may be an illegal immigrant,[15] or has committed a crime, does not diminish her entitlement to protection under Article 3.

There is one ambiguity concerning the remit of Article 3 which is particularly relevant here, and that is whether the intention of a person treating a child in a humiliating or degrading way affects whether or not the conduct breaches Article 3.[16] This is most clearly relevant in cases of child neglect, or cases of abuse which are said to reflect culturally accepted practices. In both such cases it may be claimed that there was no intention to harm the child and so Article 3 is irrelevant.

The correct view, it is submitted, is that intention should be regarded as an aggravating feature. In *V and T v United Kingdom*[17] where the case concerned whether criminal proceedings brought against an 11 year old breached Article 3, the fact that the proceedings were not intended to humiliate or harm the child were said to be relevant in concluding that there was no breach of Article 3.[18] Acts done with the purpose of humiliating or harming the individual are particularly degrading. However, lack of intention should not be seen as offering mitigation. In support of this claim it should be emphasised that we are talking about the right of a person not to be treated in a particular way, not the blameworthiness of the person doing the act. If a person is not intending to degrade another, that may be an argument for saying that they are not fully to blame for behaving as they did; it is not an argument for saying the victim's rights were not infringed.

The Obligation of State Protection: Article 3

Article 3 can be infringed by the state either directly or indirectly. A direct intervention would arise where the state's officers engaged in acts which infringed Article 3.[19] It could include acts of officers expressly authorised by the state or officers of the state acting in excess of their orders.[20] The indirect infringement arises where the state is under an

---

[11] *Price v the United Kingdom*, No 33394/96, paras 24–30 and *Valašinas v Lithuania* [2001] ECHR 479. For a broader discussion of sexual abuse issues see S Ashenden, *Governing Child Sexual Abuse* (Aldershot, Ashgate, 2004).

[12] *Mubilanzila Mayeka and another v Belgium* [2006] 3 FCR 637.

[13] [2000] 2 FCR 245, para 98.

[14] Eg *Mubilanzila Mayeka and another v Belgium* [2006] 3 FCR 637; *Chahal v United Kingdom* (1997) 23 EHRR 413, paras 79–80. Although if the treatment is justified this may mean that it does not amount to torture or inhuman or degrading treatment: *Herczegfalvy v Austria* (1992) 15 EHRR 437, para 82.

[15] *Mubilanzila Mayeka and another v Belgium* [2006] 3 FCR 637.

[16] *Savenkovas v Lithuania* [2008] ECHR 871/02.

[17] *V and T v United Kingdom* (2000) 30 EHRR 121.

[18] *Labita v Italy*, ECtHR, Application No 26772/95, para 120.

[19] *Cyprus v Turkey* (1980) 2 EHRR 25, para 159. See for further discussion M Burton, 'Failing to Protect: Victims' Rights and Police Liability' (2009) 72 *MLR* 272.

[20] *Gezer v Secretary of State for the Home Department* [2004] EWCA Civ 1730.

obligation to protect individuals from such treatment given by others but fails to do so.[21] This obligation can require positive acts from the state, including the following:

— an obligation not to place an individual in a position where they can be abused;[22]
— an obligation to pass criminal laws prohibiting conduct which breaches Article 3;[23]
— an obligation to protect individuals from anyone's conduct which breaches Article 3;[24]
— an obligation to investigate arguable breaches of Article 3.[25]

These will now be considered in the context of child abuse.

An Obligation not to Place an Individual in a Position where they can be Abused

Where a state places an individual in a position where they are at risk of torture or inhuman or degrading treatment at the hand of another, there will be a breach of Article 3.[26] The Court of Appeal has held that it matters not whether this is seen as a direct or an indirect breach of Article 3:

> The State's duty to protect individuals from Article 3 ill-treatment will, depending on the circumstances, sometimes involve refraining from action, and sometimes involve taking action. In the context of the duty to protect, the difference is serendipitous.[27]

In *Gezer v Secretary of State for the Home Department*[28] a family of homeless asylum seekers were housed on the Toryglen estate in Glasgow. It was claimed that the estate was infamous for its racist attacks and intimidation. Soon after the family arrived they were assaulted, abused and harassed. The Court of Appeal accepted that they had suffered conduct which interfered with Article 3 rights. There was also no dispute that the state owed an obligation to protect people from abuse and this included not putting people in a place where they were liable to be abused. The issue concerned the degree of risk that needed to be proved before the state was found to have breached its obligations. Laws LJ referred to:

> a sliding scale of instances in which Article 3 might be engaged: from those where the State enjoyed no power of discretion or judgment but was simply forbidden to cause or perpetrate the act which would violate Article 3, to those where the State might enjoy a considerable margin of discretion as to the adoption and exercise of policy notwithstanding that the action taken might be sufficiently grave to meet the Article 3 standard.[29]

As this quote suggests, the court did not produce a clear definition of what degree of risk of harm would generate indirect liability. Rather, a consideration is required of severity of the harm caused; who is perpetrating the harm; and the government's reasons for acting or not acting as it did. A crucial factor for the Court of Appeal in this case was that the state had not compelled the family to move to the estate, but had offered them the option

---

[21] *A v UK* [1998] 2 FLR 959.
[22] *Gezer v Secretary of State for the Home Department* [2004] EWCA Civ 1730.
[23] *A v UK* [1998] 2 FLR 959.
[24] *Assenov v Bulgaria* (1999) 28 EHRR 652.
[25] *Indelicato v Italy* (2002) 35 EHRR 1330; *Assenov v Bulgaria* (1998) 28 EHRR 652, para 102.
[26] *Gezer v Secretary of State for the Home Department* [2004] EWCA Civ 1730, para 28.
[27] *Ibid.*
[28] *Ibid.*
[29] *Ibid*, para 33.

of moving to the estate.[30] The applicants had decided to take up the option, but that was their decision. It is submitted that while this argument may have carried some weight in relation to the adults,[31] in relation to the children it should not. They can hardly be said to have chosen to move to the dangerous area.[32]

What, of course, is really behind the decision in *Gezer* is a concern with the courts intervening in relation to decisions which are, in effect, resource-driven. Given the limited housing stock and range of competing claims upon it, imposing individual obligations on a local authority can be problematic. Requiring a local authority to house an asylum-seeking family in an area with no history of racist attacks may be to require the impossible. Although there is a well-established tradition of courts backing away from interfering in resource-based decisions,[33] this is less well established in ECHR jurisprudence. For example, in *Olsson v Sweden*[34] the administrative difficulties that caused the separate placement of siblings a substantial distance from each other could play only a 'secondary role' in justifying the infringement of their Article 8 rights. In that case it was concluded that the infringement was unjustified.

Nuala Mole[35] has argued that as Article 3 is an absolute obligation, resources could never justify an interference. This is not convincing in the context of failure to protect from abuse because the state is only required under Article 3 to take reasonable steps to protect a person from abuse. Resources can therefore be relevant in determining what is reasonable.[36] So while Mole is correct to argue that resource limitations cannot justify a positive interference in Article 3 rights, they can affect the extent of the state's obligations under Article 3.[37] Joanna Miles's consideration of this issue concludes:

> Accordingly, provided proper consideration has been given in forming resource allocation policy to the various obligations of the authority to protect the rights of its various clients, and provided the authority's priorities can be shown to have a rational basis, given the relative importance of the rights to be protected, it might be expected that the limitations that finite resources then impose on operational measures will rarely, if ever, give rise to liability under the Convention.[38]

This is, perhaps unfortunately, likely to be the approach adopted by the courts.[39] Nevertheless it should be extremely rare that it would be thought reasonable to allocate resources in a way which left children suffering torture or inhuman or degrading treatment.

---

[30] Although Moses J at first instance emphasised that the family had nowhere else to live. The Court of Appeal took the view that there was a choice, albeit a bleak one, at para 37.

[31] Although, of course, to argue one has a choice worthy of its name when the alternative is homelessness is debatable. Further, whether the choice was an informed one is doubtful too.

[32] For a discussion of this case see S Palmer, 'A Wrong Turning: Article 3 ECHR and Proportionality' (2006) 65 *CLJ* 438.

[33] Eg *R v Cambridgeshire Area Health Authority ex parte B* [1995] 2 All ER 129. See further D O'Sullivan, 'The Allocation of Scarce Resources and the Right to Life under the ECHR' [1998] *PL* 389.

[34] (1989) 11 EHRR 259.

[35] N Mole, 'Local Authorities and the European Court' [2001] *Family Law* 667.

[36] *Z v United Kingdom* [2001] 2 FCR 246.

[37] See further the discussion in ch 2. For further discussion see S Palmer, 'A Wrong Turning' (n 32); J Miles, 'Human Rights and Child Protection' [2001] *Child and Family Law Quarterly* 431.

[38] J Miles, 'Human Rights and Child Protection' (n 37) 441.

[39] Although see ch 2 for a discussion of the proper scope of judicial deference.

Obligation to Pass Laws to Prohibit Conduct which Breaches Article 3

A state is required to ensure that there is protection in the law from conduct which breaches Article 3. It appears that such legal protection should include both criminal sanctions and civil remedies to enable a person to seek official protection from potential breaches. In *A v United Kingdom*[40] a boy was caned by his step-father. When the man was prosecuted for assault he successfully relied on the defence of 'reasonable chastisement'. The boy took the case to the ECHR where it was held that the state had failed to provide him with protection through the criminal law from acts which amounted to torture or inhuman or degrading treatment. Following this decision, section 58 of the Children Act 2004 has been passed meaning that the defence of reasonable chastisement is only a defence to assault or battery. Whether that is sufficient to render the law compliant with ECHR obligations is open to question.[41]

Apart from this provision, children and vulnerable adults are protected by the same criminal laws as any other person. But this many not be sufficient to ensure protection for children on these issues. A good case can be made for saying that to ensure there is effective protection from breaches of Article 3, more is required than the standard laws against assault, battery, theft and so forth. Indeed in the current criminal law in England and Wales there are specific provisions designed to protect children or vulnerable adults. These include:

— the offence of cruelty, neglect, ill-treatment and exposure of a child under 16;[42]
— a raft of sexual offences protecting children in the Sexual Offences Act 2003;[43]
— prohibitions restricting doing certain activities to children, including tattooing, or employment;[44]
— prohibitions on the sale of substances to children, including alcohol and tobacco;[45]
— failing to protect a child or vulnerable adult from being killed.[46]

Is this raft of criminal law measures sufficient to ensure that a child's rights are protected? It is difficult to think of conduct which might amount to torture and inhuman or degrading treatment which is not covered by the current criminal provision, outside the context of corporal punishment. Perhaps the largest gap is the lack of a general criminal liability to fail to rescue a child in peril. Criminal lawyers point out that a person can walk past a child drowning in a pond, without fear of liability, unless they owe the child a particular duty of care (for example, because they are the child's parent, or are employed as a lifeguard).[47] If it could be shown that the creation of such a liability would increase the number of children rescued from death or serious injury then it may be that the absence

---

[40] *A v UK* [1998] 2 FLR 959.

[41] We discuss this issue further at 208–20. For a detailed discussion of this see S Choudhry, 'Parental Responsibility and Corporal Punishment' in R Probert, S Gilmore and J Herring, *Responsible Parents and Parental Responsibility* (Oxford, Hart, 2009).

[42] Children and Young Persons Act 1933.

[43] Eg Sexual Offences Act 2003, ss9–24.

[44] Eg Tattooing of Minors Act 1969.

[45] Eg Licensing Act 1969 and Children and Young Persons (Protection from Tobacco) Act 1991.

[46] Domestic Violence Crimes and Victims Act 2004 s5. The offence is discussed in detail in J Herring, 'Mum's not the Word: an Analysis of Section 5, Domestic Violence Crimes And Victims Act 2005' in S Cunningham and C Clarkson, *Criminal Liability for Non-Aggressive Death* (London, Ashgate, 2008).

[47] See J Herring, *Criminal Law* 6th edn (Basingstoke, Palgrave, 2009) ch 3.

of a general 'easy rescue' statute could be said to infringe the state's obligations. However, there is little evidence that that such a statute affects how people behave when coming across others in peril.[48] It is, therefore, unlikely that the failure to have a general liability for omissions in criminal law infringes children's rights.

As regards civil remedies that are available to protect children, the courts are entitled to make a care or supervision order on the application of a local authority if the threshold criteria in section 31(2) of the Children Act 1989 are met. These provide:

> A court may only make a care order or a supervision order if it is satisfied—
>
>> (a) that the child concerned is suffering, or is likely to suffer, significant harm; and
>> (b) that the harm, or likelihood of harm, is attributable to—
>>> (i) the care given to the child, or likely to be given to him if the order were not made, not being what it would be reasonable to expect a parent to give to him; or
>>> (ii) the child's being beyond parental control.

The phrase 'significant harm' is sufficiently broad to mean that it is extremely unlikely that conduct which will constitute a breach of a child's Article 3 or Article 8 rights will fail to meet this hurdle. Harm is defined in section 31(9) of the Children Act 1989 as 'ill-treatment or the impairment of health or development, including, for example, impairment suffered from seeing or hearing the ill-treatment of another'. This last clause covers, for example, the harm a child may suffer while witnessing the domestic violence of her mother.[49] 'Ill-treatment' includes 'sexual abuse and forms of ill-treatment which are not physical, including, for example, impairment suffered from seeing or hearing the ill-treatment of another'; 'development' is defined as 'physical, intellectual, emotional, social or behavioural development'; and 'health' means 'physical or mental health'.[50] The civil law legislative provisions appear to be in place to ensure there is adequate protection of children's rights in this context, with one caveat. That is over the extent to which the concept of significant harm should vary given the circumstances of the parents, or their cultural background.

Two recent cases discuss the issues. In *Re L (Children)*[51] the local authority was concerned about parents with learning difficulties who were raising a girl aged 10 and a boy aged 7.[52] In particular in the past the father had allowed a paedophile to visit the home where he had abused the girl. There were also unproven allegations that the father had whipped the children with belts and proven allegations of domestic violence. The most interesting part of the Court of Appeal's judgment, which revoked the care orders and ordered that the case be re-heard, were the comments that:

> family courts do not remove children from their parents into care because the parents in question are not intelligent enough to care for them or have low intelligence quotas. Children are only removed into care (1) if they are suffering or likely to suffer significant harm in the care of their

---

[48] J Dressler, 'Some Brief Thoughts (Mostly Negative) About "Bad Samaritan" Laws' (2000) 40 *Santa Clara Law Review* 971.

[49] *Re R (Care: Rehabilitation in Context of Domestic Violence)* [2006] EWCA Civ 1638.

[50] CA, s31(9).

[51] *Re L (Children)* [2006] 3 FCR 301.

[52] See the discussion of parents with learning difficulties in T Booth, W Booth and D Mcconnell, 'Parents With Learning Difficulties, Care Proceedings and the Family Courts: Threshold Decisions and the Moral Matrix' [2004] *Child and Family Law Quarterly* 409; and A Dimopoulos, 'Intellectually disabled parents before the European Court of Human Rights and English Courts' (2009) 1 *European Human Rights Law Review* 70.

parents; and (2) if it is in their interests that a care order is made. Anything else is social engineering and wholly impermissible.[53]

At the re-hearing Hedley J made this point:

> Society must be willing to tolerate very diverse standards of parenting, including the eccentric, the barely adequate and the inconsistent. It follows too that children will inevitably have both very different experiences of parenting and very unequal consequences flowing from it. It means that some children will experience disadvantage and harm, while others flourish in atmospheres of loving security and emotional stability. These are the consequences of our fallible humanity and it is not the provenance of the state to spare children all the consequences of defective parenting. In any event, it simply could not be done.[54]

He went on to state that 'the threshold may be comparatively low. However, it is clear that it must be something unusual; at least something more than the commonplace human failure or inadequacy'.[55] Hedley J's comments that simply because parents have a low IQ does not automatically render them unfit should be welcomed. There is much more to parenthood than having a high IQ. Each parent will have different aspects of their character and background which affect their parenting ability. No two parents will be same and that should be a cause of celebration rather than concern.

In *Re K; A Local Authority v N and Others*[56] a local authority sought an emergency protection order to protect a young woman from a forced marriage. The court declined to make an order, in the face of the young woman's opposition to it, but held the following:

> The task of the court considering threshold for the purposes of s 31 of the 1989 Act may be to evaluate parental performance by reference to the objective standard of the hypothetical 'reasonable' parent, but this does not mean that the court can simply ignore the underlying cultural, social or religious realities. On the contrary, the court must always be sensitive to the cultural, social and religious circumstances of the particular child and family. And the court should, I think, be slow to find that parents only recently or comparatively recently arrived from a foreign country— particularly a country where standards and expectations may be more or less different, sometimes very different indeed, from those with which they are familiar—have fallen short of an acceptable standard of parenting if in truth they have done nothing wrong by the standards of their own community.[57]

There are concerns that these cases may be seen as raising the bar as to what counts as 'significant harm'. Children's rights to protection from having their human rights interfered with exist whatever the personal characteristics of their parents. There is a danger in some of these comments that threshold criteria are in place as a way of judging or blaming parents. If children are suffering harm which interferes with their Article 3 rights then their human rights deserve protecting whatever the cultural background or religious beliefs of their parents. However, when deciding how the children should be protected then the cultural background and reasons for the behaviour should be given due weight.[58]

---

[53] *Re L (Children)* [2006] 3 FCR 301, para 49.
[54] *Ibid*, para 50.
[55] *Ibid*, para 56.
[56] [2007] 1 FLR 399.
[57] *Ibid*, para 26.
[58] For further discussion of human rights and issues of cultural relativism see, eg, X Li, *Ethics, Human Rights and Culture: Universalism and Cultural Relativism in Ethics* (Basingstoke, Palgrave, 2006).

Despite the points made in this section, empirical studies suggest that it is rare for the threshold criteria not to be established, at least for emergency protection orders.[59] Indeed, the researchers found that it was almost unknown for magistrates to refuse an order.[60] Even for care orders it seems that in reality these are rarely refused;[61] although that might indicate that care orders are only applied for in the most extreme cases, which, arguably, may not be often enough.

Obligation to Intervene to Protect

Where the state is aware that a person is suffering or is about to suffer torture or inhuman or degrading treatment, it is under a duty to intervene to protect them. There is a particularly strong obligation where that individual is a child or a vulnerable adult.[62] That much is very clear from the authorities. What is less clear is precisely when this duty arises and precisely what is required of the authority to meet its obligations.

A leading case in this area is *Z v UK*.[63] Four siblings suffered abuse and neglect at the hands of their parents. The local authority was aware of their treatment but had failed to intervene. The ECtHR had no difficulty in finding that the treatment that the children suffered amounted to inhuman and degrading treatment and interfered with their Article 3 rights. The family had been referred by a health visitor to the social services in October 1987. Over the course of the next four years neighbours, family members, GPs, teachers, social workers and police all made further reports to social services. The concerns raised included that the children were stealing food; they were locked out of the house; screaming was heard; the children were bruised; the children were dirty; and they were having social and psychological problems. Between the first notification in October 1987 and June 1992 no steps were taken to remove the children, although there were 11 different professionals' meetings. In December 1992 an interim care order was made, with a consultant child psychologist stating that it was one of the worst cases of neglect and emotional abuse she had seen.

The ECtHR stated:

> The Court re-iterates that Art 3 enshrines one of the most fundamental values of democratic society. It prohibits in absolute terms torture or inhuman or degrading treatment or punishment. The obligation on high contracting parties under Art 1 of the Convention to secure to everyone within their jurisdiction the rights and freedoms defined in the Convention, taken together with Art 3, requires states to take measures designed to ensure that individuals within their jurisdiction are not subjected to torture or inhuman or degrading treatment, including such ill-treatment administered by private individuals (see *A v UK* (1998) 5 BHRC 137 at 141 (para 22)). These measures should provide effective protection, in particular, of children and other vulnerable persons and include reasonable steps to prevent ill-treatment of which the authorities had or ought to have

---

[59] J Masson, 'Research—Emergency Intervention to Protect Children: Using and Avoiding Legal Controls' [2005] *Child and Family Law Quarterly* 75.

[60] J Masson, D McGovern, K Pick and M Winn Oakley, *Protecting Powers. Emergency Intervention for Children's Protection* (Chichester, NSPCC, 2007), report that approximately 90 per cent of applications are granted and, in their study, no application was refused. A small number of applications were withdrawn following agreements (177).

[61] Masson *et al*, *Protecting Powers* (n 60) report that in the 'overwhelming' majority of cases, an emergency order is followed by a change of carer or a long-term protective order (207). See also DfES and DCA, *Review of the Child Care Proceedings System in England and Wales*, 2006, para 4.7.

[62] *Mubilanzila Mayeka and another v Belgium* [2006] 3 FCR 637.

[63] *Z v UK* [2001] 2 FCR 246.

had knowledge (mutatis mutandis, *Osman v UK* (1998) 5 BHRC 293 at 321, [1999] 1 FLR 193 at 223 (para 116)).[64]

The ECtHR was not saying that in every case where there was abuse the state would have interfered with an individual's Article 3 rights. The potential liability is limited.

First, it must be shown that the local authority knew, or ought to have known, about the abuse. In *E v UK*[65] it was found that even though the social services did not know of the abuse, they ought to have known.

> Even if the social services were not aware he was inflicting abuse at this time, they should have been aware that the children remained at potential risk. The fact that at the relevant time there was not the knowledge of the prevalence of, and persistence of, sexual offenders victimising children within a family that there exists now, is not significant in this case where, as the applicants emphasise, the social services knew that there had been incidences of sexual abuse resulting in criminal offences and were under an obligation to monitor the offender's conduct in the aftermath of the conviction.

By contrast in *DP v UK*[66] the ECtHR found that it could not be said that the authority had known or ought to have known about the abuse the children were suffering from their mother's partner (NC):

> The Court is not persuaded therefore that there were any particular aspects of the turbulent and volatile family situation which should have led the social services to suspect a deeper, more insidious problem in a family which was experiencing financial hardship, occasional criminal proceedings and with a mother observed to be 'less caring' than she should be. Far from NC being perceived as a risk element in this scenario, the social services considered that there were grounds for believing, at least in the early years, that he was a positive influence, providing a father figure for the growing number of children, support for the mother and some added wage-earning capacity. In view of the apparent assistance of the mother in covering for NC and the silence of all the children notwithstanding their numerous contacts with various professionals over the years, the Court does not consider that the social services can be criticised for failing to instigate an investigation into the possibility of some additional underlying problem.[67]

The courts are yet to provide a clear direction on what degree of risk must be foreseen before liability might arise. The best approach, it is submitted, is that any real risk that a child is suffering or will suffer torture or inhuman or degrading treatment should generate an obligation. The House of Lords in *Chief Constable of Hertfordshire v Van Colle*[68] held that for the purposes of Article 2 there needs to be 'a real and immediate risk to the life' of an identified individual from the criminal acts of a third party before the police could be found to have breached an individual's rights under Article 2. That might be followed as a suitable test to be used in cases of child abuse.

Second, it must be shown that the local authority failed to take steps reasonably open to it to intervene to protect the child.[69] In *Z v UK* it was accepted that cases where there were suspicions about child abuse were not straightforward: 'The Court acknowledges the

---

[64] *Ibid*, para 73.
[65] *E v UK* [2002] 3 FCR 700.
[66] *DP v UK* [2002] 3 FCR 385.
[67] *Ibid*, para 112.
[68] [2008] UKHL 50.
[69] *E v UK* [2002] 3 FCR 700, para 92.

difficult and sensitive decisions facing social services and the important countervailing principle of respecting and preserving family life.' In *Z* itself it was held that the evidence clearly established that the intervention was required. At one time it was suggested that a breach of Article 2 or 3 would only arise if there was a systemic failure by the local authority, but later cases have established that a single failure to intervene can infringe Article 3.[70]

In *DP v UK*[71] concerns that things were not right in the family were insufficient to provide a reason to intervene:

> While there were times when both applicants showed significant distress in the family environment, both also showed strong ties to the family. After the first applicant was placed in temporary foster care in May 1980, she returned home at her own request. The second applicant was placed in a Children's Home from 1982 to 1984, with alternate weekends at home, and though on some occasions he showed reluctance to go home, on other occasions he appeared to enjoy the visits. For the social services to be justified in taking the draconian step of cutting permanently both applicants' links with their family would have required convincing reasons, which were not apparent at that time.[72]

In *DP and JC v United Kingdom (Application No 38719/97)*[73] the child welfare authorities were aware of multiple—especially financial—problems in the family and also truanting and some incidental violence; but they were not aware of any sexual abuse. The ECtHR noted:

> Social service records refer to the second applicant's problem of soiling which led to involvement by medics and a period as an inpatient ... concerns about truanting by a number of children ... Incidents of [sporadic] violence.

It concluded:

> These cannot be regarded as revealing a clear pattern of victimization or abuse. The Court is not persuaded therefore that there were any particular aspects of the turbulent and volatile family situation which should have led the social services to suspect a deeper, more insidious problem in a family which was experiencing financial hardship, occasional criminal proceedings and with a mother observed to be 'less caring' than she should be.[74]

As this decision makes clear, to render a public authority liable for infringing a child's right to protection from abuse under Article 3 or 8 it must be shown not only that the authority was aware or ought to have been aware of the abuse, but also that given that knowledge, they should have intervened.

It does not need to be shown that if the local authority had intervened the abuse would not have occurred. As was explained in *E v UK*:

> The test under Art 3, however, does not require it to be shown that 'but for' the failing or omission of the public authority ill-treatment would not have happened. A failure to take reasonably available measures which could have had a real prospect of altering the outcome or mitigating the harm is sufficient to engage the responsibility of the state.[75]

---

[70] *Kontrová v Slovakia* (Application No 7510/04).
[71] [2002] 3 FCR 385.
[72] Para 113.
[73] [2003] 1 FLR 50, at paras 109–12.
[74] Para 112.
[75] [2002] 3 FCR 700, para 99.

The Court went on to find that the UK government had infringed the children's rights, saying:

> The Court is satisfied that the pattern of lack of investigation, communication and co-operation by the relevant authorities disclosed in this case must be regarded as having had a significant influence on the course of events and that proper and effective management of their responsibilities might, judged reasonably, have been expected to avoid, or at least minimise, the risk or the damage suffered.[76]

Third, a local authority is not required to act on the basis of unproven suspicions. In *Re B (Care Proceedings: Standard of Proof)*[77] Baroness Hale, having reviewed the ECtHR case law, concluded:

> But there is nothing in those cases to suggest that the authorities are failing in their duty to protect children from inhuman or degrading treatment because they are unable permanently to remove children from their families on the basis of unproven allegations.[78]

Finally, under Article 3 the obligation is absolute. So once the state is aware of the abuse and that it would be reasonable to intervene, there are no reasons which can justify not intervening. Notably in *Re B (Care Proceedings: Diplomatic Immunity)*[79] diplomatic immunity was insufficient as a reason for preventing intervention. In that case it was held that the positive obligations on the state to protect children from abuse could justify reading the Diplomatic Privileges Act 1964 so as to enable care proceedings to be taken in respect of a child of a person covered by diplomatic immunity.[80]

The significance of this discussion for English law is as follows. First, once a court has determined that a child is facing a risk of conduct that would infringe Article 3, the court must protect the child. The threshold criteria should be interpreted in such a way as to ensure an order can be made. Once the level of abuse has reached the Article 3 level, the interests of parents cannot justify not protecting the child. Second, where the court is aware that a child needs protection it must take steps to protect the child. Although the court is prevented from making a care order without the application of the local authority, it must use any powers it has to ensure that the child is protected. This may require the use of wardship or the inherent jurisdiction.

The above analysis means that where a local authority fails to meet its obligations under Article 3 a child could sue the local authority under sections 6 and 7 of the HRA.[81] The remedies under that Act could include ordering the local authority to act to protect the child or if it is too late to do that, to award damages.

Article 8 and the Obligation to Protect from Abuse

Article 8 protects the right of the child to respect for his or her family and private life. Within the right to respect for private life is the right to bodily integrity. But there is more

---

[76] Para 100.

[77] [2008] 2 FLR 141.

[78] Para 77.

[79] *Re B (Care Proceedings Diplomatic Immunity)* [2002] EWHC 1751.

[80] Para 40, although the court felt able to interpret the 1964 Act in that way, even without needing recourse to the HRA.

[81] *S (A Child Acting by the Official Solicitor) v Rochdale Metropolitan Borough Council and the Independent Reviewing Officer* [2009] 1 FLR 1090.

to it than this. The right to private life includes the right to 'psychological integrity ... a right to personal development, and the right to establish and develop relationships with other human beings and the outside world'.[82] So not only does the Article require protection of individuals from physical violence, it also protects them from conduct which attacks their emotional well-being to such an extent that their personal development is hindered. This can include physical, psychological and emotional abuse or neglect. Article 8 will be relied upon in the child abuse context where the abuse is not severe enough to infringe Article 3. However, there have been few cases in the context of child protection where the ECtHR has found Article 8, but not Article 3, engaged.[83]

As with Article 3 there is an obligation on the state under Article 8 to protect individuals from interferences with Article 8 rights by others. However, unlike Article 3, the Article 8 right is not absolute. It can be interfered with if the requirements of Article 8(2) are met. Therefore, if the case involves only Article 8 level abuse, then, even though the local authority could intervene to protect the child, there may be reasons justifying non-intervention.

A good example of a case where Article 8 rights arose in this context is *R (on the application of G) v Barnet London Borough Council; R (on the application of W) v Lambeth London Borough Council; R (on the application of A) v Lambeth London Borough Council*,[84] a decision by the House of Lords concerning the duties owed by local authorities to children in need under section 17 of the CA. This states:

> It shall be the general duty of every local authority (in addition to the other duties imposed on them by this Part)—(a) to safeguard and promote the welfare of children within their area who are in need; and (b) so far as is consistent with that duty, to promote the upbringing of such children by their families, by providing a range and level of services appropriate to those children's needs.

Their Lordships heard several appeals together. The cases all involved children in need claiming that they were entitled to particular resources under section 17. For example, one involved a sibling who suffered autism and who had been assessed as requiring re-housing as a result. The local authority felt unable to provide alternative accommodation to that currently offered, given the other claims on their housing stock. The argument of the applicants which was of most interest in this context is that under Article 8 the local authority was obliged to protect the children from harms which would result from not being provided with the resources. It was notable that for the minority, the obligation under Article 8 led to an interpretation of section 17 which required the duty to promote the welfare of children in need to be enforceable. However, the majority found the duty in section 17 to be unenforceable at law. Notably, in reaching that conclusion the majority made no mention of the child's rights.

In fact the majority need not have feared rights-based arguments. The issue which really lay behind the surface of this case was the potential impact of the decision on the housing policies of the boroughs. Accepting the arguments of the claimants, it was feared, would have the impact of driving a coach and horses through the housing policies. Lord Scott explained:

> If a parent or parents have become intentionally homeless or for any other reason are not entitled to look to the local authority for housing accommodation, the local authority is entitled, in my

---

[82] *Pretty v UK* [2002] 2 FCR 97, para 61.
[83] U Kilkelly, *The Child and the European Convention on Human Rights* (London, Ashgate, 1999) 174–7.
[84] [2004] 1 All ER 97.

opinion, to adopt a general policy under which it is made clear that it will make accommodation available to the children of the family in order to prevent the children becoming homeless, but will not permit the parents to use the children as stepping stones by means of which to obtain a greater priority to be re-housed than that to which they would otherwise be entitled.[85]

This could, then, provide a reason under Article 8(2) to justify any interference with the rights of the child or parents. What was happening in this case was that parents who were intentionally homeless, and hence unable to making a housing claim in their names, were making the application through the children. There is a real dilemma here. Protecting the children's rights means allowing parents to find ways of jumping the housing queue; while punishing the parents for their bad housing choices ends up punishing the children. While in this case the broader housing policy issues justified not protecting the child's Article 8 rights, in cases of abuse a failure to intervene and offer protection would be harder to justify.

When a Local Authority May Take a Child into Care

As is well known, section 31 of the CA sets down the threshold criteria which must be satisfied before the court can grant a supervision or care order. In addition to satisfying the criteria the court must be satisfied that making the order will promote the welfare of the child and that it is better to make an order than no order at all.[86]

From the point of view of the ECHR, any intervention by means of a care or supervision order will amount to an interference with a family's rights under Article 8(1); but that interference can be justified if it can be shown that making the order was necessary in the interests of the child[87] under Article 8(2). Clearly, therefore, under neither the ECHR nor the CA can a child be removed from parents merely after proof that it would be in the child's interests to be removed.[88] That is clear from Article 8 and is reflected in the existence of the threshold criteria in section 31.

Indeed, at first sight the approach advocated within the ECHR and the CA are readily compatible. Only if the child has faced or is facing significant harm will the threshold criteria be met; and also only then will the interests of the child be sufficient to justify an interference in the family life. The threshold criteria therefore, usefully, ensure that interventionist orders are only made when there is sufficient justification for ECHR purposes.

When May a Child be Taken into Care?

The ECtHR has accepted that whether the intervention in family life involved in removing a child from the care of her parents is justified is a matter over which contracting states may differ and so there is a margin of appreciation. In fact it is rare for the ECtHR to find a removal itself to infringe the Convention. However, the ECtHR has explained that 'a stricter scrutiny is called for both of any further limitations, such as restrictions placed

---

[85] Para 141.
[86] CA, s1(1) and (5).
[87] Or for the protection of public health or morals.
[88] *L v Sweden* (1984) 40 DR 140, 151.

by those authorities on parental rights and access, and of any legal safeguards designed to secure an effective protection of the right of parents and children to respect for their family life'.[89] As this quotation indicates, most of the European judicial attention has been on issues relating to parental access to children in care and procedural issues concerning care proceedings, rather than on the legitimacy of the removal of the child itself. Nevertheless, some guidance has been offered on when intervention is justified.

First, the intervention must be in accordance with the law. In other words the intervention must be justified by specific provision in the law and the law must be sufficiently accessible. This appears to rarely be an issue.[90] In *R (G) v Nottingham CC*[91] social workers were very concerned about a young woman who was pregnant. They removed the baby shortly after birth, without obtaining a court order. While it was accepted that they were acting in what they regarded as the best interests of the baby, they were acting without any formal court order or legal authorisation. The taking was, therefore, illegal.[92] That, of course, is an unusual case. But it emphasises that even if the state interference is necessary to protect a child, if it lacks legal foundation it will infringe Article 8.

Second, the intervention must be for one of the legitimate aims set out in Article 8(2): the 'protection of the rights and freedoms of others' or the 'protection of health or morals'. This must be the aim of the state throughout the time of interference.[93] In this context it is unlikely that anything apart from the interests of the child will justify removal of a child from her parents.[94]

Third, the intervention must be found to be necessary and it is this requirement which tends to generate the greatest debate.[95] The following statement in *Kutzner v Germany*[96] is significant:

> The fact that a child could be placed in a more beneficial environment for his or her upbringing will not on its own justify a compulsory measure of removal from the care of the biological parents; there must exist other circumstances pointing to the 'necessity' for such an interference with the parents' right under Article 8 of the Convention to enjoy a family life with their child.[97]

Removing a child from parents must be regarded as an 'interference of a very serious order'. Only 'sufficiently sound and weighty considerations in the interests of the child' will justify it.[98] In determining whether or not the removal of the child is necessary, the interests of the child will be crucial.[99] Of course, where there has been a serious harm to the child or the child is at risk of serious harm there will be no difficulty in finding an interference with the right to respect for family life necessary and justified. Hence in *Gnahore v France*,[100] where a father had been charged with wounding his son, it was obvious that the intervention was

---

[89] *Johansen v Norway* (1996) 23 EHRR 33, para 64; *HK v Finland* (Application No 36065/97), para 109.
[90] See, eg, *Berecova v Slovakia* (Application No 74400/01).
[91] *R (G) v Nottingham CC* [2008] EWHC 152 (Admin).
[92] BBC News Online, 'Girl wins damages over taken baby', 18 February 2008.
[93] Hale LJ in *Re C and B (Care Order: Future Harm)* [2001] 1 FLR 611, para 31.
[94] *Olsson v Sweden* (1989) 11 EHRR 259, 272; *KA v Finland* [2003] 1 FCR 201, para 138.
[95] Wall LJ in *Re S (Adoption Order or Special Guardianship Order)* [2007] 1 FLR 819, para 49.
[96] *Kutzner v Germany* [2003] 1 FCR 249.
[97] Para 60.
[98] *Olsson v Sweden* (1989) 11 EHRR 259, 272; *KA v Finland* [2003] 1 FCR 201, para 138.
[99] *Görgülü v Germany* [2004] 1 FCR 410, para 41; although para 43 suggests that particular importance should be attached to the interests of the child.
[100] (2002) 34 EHRR 38, para 56.

justified. But it need not be anything as extreme as that. In that same case when the renewal of the care order was sought, the primary emphasis was on the domineering personality of the father and the limits that were placed on the child to develop socially and educationally as a result. These were found to justify the continuation of the child's removal.

In *RK v UK*[101] a couple had a child taken into a care following a facture of her femur which was diagnosed by a paediatrician to be non-accidental. However, the child was later found to suffer from brittle bone disease. Before the ECtHR it was accepted that the removal of the child was an infringement of the parents' Article 8(1) rights, but what was disputed was whether the interference had been 'necessary in a democratic society'. The ECtHR held that this required a consideration of whether the reasons given were 'relevant and sufficient' and whether the decision-making process had been fair and ensured protection of the Article 8 rights.[102] It was held in this case that the reasons for interfering were relevant and sufficient and aimed at protecting M. It was emphasised that the mere fact that professionals made mistaken judgments or assessments did not per se render child-care measures incompatible.[103] Notably the Court emphasised that as soon as there were questions about the original diagnosis, further tests were quickly pursued and when the truth was revealed, M was returned home quickly.

Some particular aspects of the ECtHR's approach to justifying state intervention in cases of child protection will now be discussed in more detail.

Proportionality

Under the Convention jurisprudence it must be shown that the interference is a proportionate response to the risks facing the child. This requires that there is no less interventionist way of protecting the child. So, if the court is choosing between making a supervision or a care order and is satisfied that either will adequately protect the child, the less interventionist supervision order should be preferred.[104] Similarly, before removal a court should be satisfied that it is not possible with appropriate support for the parents to enable the child to remain with them.[105] So in *Kutzner v Germany*[106] while the ECtHR accepted that it had been shown that it would be beneficial for the children to be removed from their parents and placed with alternative carers, that was insufficient to justify the children's removal. It had not been shown that if the parents were given help and advice (they suffered from learning difficulties) the children could not safely remain with them.

Applying this principle, in *Re C and B*[107] Hale LJ was critical of any suggestion that once the threshold criteria had been met, a judge was automatically justified in making a care order. She said that this ignored the principle of proportionality:

> Nevertheless one comes back to the principle of proportionality. The principle has to be that the local authority works to support, and eventually to reunite, the family, unless the risks are so high

---

[101] [2008] ECHR 38000/05.
[102] Para 34.
[103] Para 36.
[104] *Re C and B (Care Order: Future Harm)* [2001] 1 FLR 611 (CA); *Re O (A Child) (Supervision Order: Future Harm)*, [2001] 1 FCR 289 (CA).
[105] *Kutzner v Germany* [2003] 1 FCR 249, para 75.
[106] *Re G (a child)* [2003] 1 FCR 249 (CA).
[107] *Re C and B (Care Order: Future Harm)* [2001] 1 FLR 611 (CA).

that the child's welfare requires alternative family care. I cannot accept Mr Dugdale's submission that this was a case for a care order with a care plan of adoption or nothing. There could have been other options. There could have been time taken to explore those other options. Even as between those two, it is not necessarily the case that the care order was the better option than nothing. All of this needed serious consideration and dealing with in the judgment.

This reasoning has been adopted in later cases. In *Re G (a child)*[108] Thorpe LJ was critical of the trial judge for failing to address the proportionality issue with sufficient care, stating:

> Because the judge did not in his judgment evaluate the various strands in the risk analysis which was presented to him, it follows that he did not in his judgment adequately articulate his analysis of the balancing exercise; his balancing on the one hand the fact that the parents are currently providing an adequate level of parenting against, on the other hand, the risk that in future something might go wrong. Thus he failed properly to address the crucial question as to whether what was being proposed by the local authority, namely a final care order and adoption, was a proportionate response to what was feared in this case. The ultimate question for the learned judge was to reach a conclusion as to whether, to adopt Hale LJ's language, the risks were so high that H's welfare required alternative family care.

More succinctly in another case he stated:

> Accordingly he must not sanction such an interference with family life unless he is satisfied that that is both necessary and proportionate and that no other less radical form of order would achieve the essential end of promoting the welfare of the children.[109]

The importance of proportionality has also recently been emphasised by the Court of Appeal in *Re T (A Child)(Care Order)*.[110] There Sir Mark Potter held:

> Since the advent of the Human Rights Act 1998 it is necessary also to emphasise and have regard to the issue of proportionality when contemplating the removal of parental responsibility from, or its enforced sharing by, those otherwise entitled to exercise it exclusively.

The notion of proportionality is not simply a matter of assessing whether the severity of the risk justifies the degree of intervention. The issue of timing may be relevant too. Intervention to the extent required may be justified, but not now. This issue has been raised especially in issues relating to the removal of children at birth. In *K and T v Finland*[111] it was held:

> There must be extraordinarily compelling reasons before a baby can be removed from the care of its mother, against her will, immediately after birth as a consequence of a procedure in which neither she nor her partner has been involved. The court is not satisfied that such reasons have been shown to exist … The authorities had known about the forthcoming birth for months in advance and were well aware of K's mental problems, so that the situation was not an emergency … The Government have not suggested that other possible ways of protecting the new-born baby J from the risk of physical harm from the mother were even considered.

---

[108] [2007] EWCA 395, para 13.
[109] *Re B (Children) (Care: Interference with Family Life)* [2004] 1 FCR 463 (CA), para 34.
[110] [2009] EWCA Civ 121.
[111] [2001] 2 FCR 673.

The timing issue is also relevant in cases where the facts are uncertain. In such a case it may be regarded as disproportionate to make a final order now, rather than wait until the future when the facts may be clearer. As Thorpe LJ in *Re H (a child) (interim care order)* stated:

> In my judgment, the Arts 6 and 8 rights of the parents required the judge to abstain from premature determination of their case for the future beyond the final fixture, unless the welfare of the child demanded it. In effect, since removal from these lifelong parents to foster parents would be deeply traumatic for the child, and of course open to further upset should the parents' case ultimately succeed, that separation was only to be contemplated if B's safety demanded immediate separation.[112]

If the court decides that a supervision order is the proportionate response then it is the responsibility of everyone involved, the court, local authority and parents, to ensure it works.[113]

A Duty to Perfect Parents?

One particular aspect of the proportionality doctrine needs to be considered further. If there are good grounds to justify the removal of the children from the parents, but the parents argue that with extensive assistance and support they could adequately care for the child, to what extent does the doctrine of proportionality require that such assistance be offered?

As mentioned earlier, in the ECtHR decision of *Kutzner v Germany*[114] an interference of the parents' Article 8 rights was demonstrated because the option of giving adequate support to the parents so that they could care for their child had not been examined. The English courts have been more hesitant about this. In *Re G (Interim Care Order: Residential Assessment)*[115] the House of Lords stated 'there is no Article 8 right to be made a better parent at public expense'.[116] As is clear from this quotation the argument had been considered on the parent's behalf. The question is less obvious from the child's perspective. Is it justifiable to mount a major interference in the child's right of family life with her parents, if expenditure in improving the abilities of the parents could remove the need for removal? A parent may not have a right to be made a better parent, but that does not mean a child does not have the right not to be removed from her parents without the state being convinced it is necessary to do so.

Certainly the English courts have accepted that the option of leaving children with their parents must be considered and a proper assessment of the parent's abilities may be required before a removal is justified.[117] The difference in approach arises where the conclusion of the assessment is that with further assistance and support the parents could safely care for the child. It is suggested that such a conclusion would render removal of the

---

[112] *Re H (A Child) (Interim Care Order)* [2003] 1 FCR 350 (CA), para 39.
[113] *Re O (a child) (supervision order: future harm)* [2001] 1 FCR 289 (CA). See also *Re C (Care Order or Supervision Order)* [2001] 2 FLR 466 (CA).
[114] [2003] 1 FCR 249.
[115] *Re G (Interim Care Order: Residential Assessment)* [2005] UKHL 68, para 24.
[116] Hence they argued that while a residential assessment can be used to assess parents it can be used to assess a child: *Re L and H (Residential Assessment)* [2007] EWCA Civ 213.
[117] *Re L and H (Residential Assessment)* [2007] EWCA Civ 213; *L (Children) (Care Proceedings: Significant Harm)* [2006] EWCA Civ 1282, paras 34 to 35.

child unjustifiably disproportionate, unless there were good reasons why the local authority could not reasonably be expected to offer those services. This would take us back to the resources issue discussed above.

A rather different issue is the efforts the government has been making to 'catch early' 'problem families' and provide them with services and help. Felicity Kaganas[118] has written:

> While family privacy is protected by law and while it appears to be accorded considerable respect within family policy, there is a potentially contradictory, or at least divergent, strand of family policy that is gaining increasing prominence in government programmes. This aspect of family policy could lead to greater intrusion in the family. It is aimed at breaching the ramparts of the private family to inculcate in parents 'better' attitudes to their children and to promote 'better' child care practices. Of course, in a society that assumes that children can and should be protected, it is well established that family privacy must yield to the demands of child protection. But it seems that it is now also considered acceptable to seek to intervene in families other than those posing an immediate risk to children. It seems that whereas previously family policy was concerned primarily with ensuring that parents did no harm to their children, the state is now demanding more: parents are expected to do good.

She goes on to argue that these burdens are particularly bourn by mothers:

> While intervention can save children and can help parents, it can also be coercive and oppressive. The introduction of advice and education for parents may mean that parents are faced with even more potential sources of pressure or reasons for coercion; if they do not accept the advice and attend the parenting classes as instructed, for example, they face the risk of being adjudged irresponsible. And since it is overwhelmingly mothers who are, and who are expected to be, responsible for children's safety and well-being, it is they who must co-operate and conform to the professionals' norms of good mothering. It is mothers who are examined, it is mothers who might be found wanting and it is mothers who must change so as to fit the mould of the 'good' mother. Engaging in the new programme for supporting families carries risks for mothers and the offer of support has, paradoxically, the potential to burden them.[119]

Suspicion of Harm

Where it is found that there is simply a suspicion of harm, is this sufficient to remove a child? It certainly is under English law where all that is required is that there is a real risk of significant harm—although that finding of a real risk must be based on facts proved on the balance of probability.[120] The ECtHR has not considered the issue in detail, although in *L v Finland*[121] it was confirmed that suspicion was sufficient to take a child into care and a finding of fact about the abuse was not required. However, there was little analysis of precisely what level of risk was required.

In *HK v Finland*[122] the fact that the applicant was suspected of sexual abuse was sufficient to justify removal. Again, there was no discussion over the degree of suspicion or

---

[118] F Kaganas, 'Child Protection, Gender and Rights' (n 1). See also H Ferguson, *Protecting Children in Time. Child Abuse, Child Protection and the Consequences of Modernity* (Basingstoke, Palgrave Macmillan, 2004) 3.
[119] F Kaganas, 'Child Protection, Gender and Rights' (n 1).
[120] *Re H (Minors) (Sexual Abuse: Standard of Proof)* [1996] AC 563 (HL).
[121] [2000] 3 FCR 219.
[122] *HK v Finland* (Application No 36065/97).

risk required, although the Court noted that there was 'good cause' for the suspicions.[123] It is also important to emphasise that in these cases at least some contact between the parents and children was retained. Suspicions were not used to completely terminate family life. Indeed had they been, that might well have constituted a breach. The House of Lords in *Re H and R*[124] has held that children should not be removed merely on the basis of suspicions. Only facts proved on the balance of probabilities can be relied upon to establish the threshold criteria. Lord Nicholls explained this, partly in terms of parents' rights: 'They are not to be at risk of having their child taken from them and removed into the care of the local authority on the basis only of suspicions, whether of the judge or of the local authority or anyone else.'[125] Baroness Hale, when considering the issue in *Re B (Children)*,[126] confirmed that unproven allegations should not be relied upon to take a child into care.

Removal of Newborns

There have been quite a number of cases before the ECtHR concerning the removal of newborn children.[127] The Court appears particularly reluctant to find that such removals are justified under the ECHR. Hence it has been said that removal of a newborn is 'extremely harsh'[128] and the reasons justifying an application need to be 'extraordinarily compelling', detailed and precise.[129] The reasons for this strict approach appear to be a combination of points. First, it is hard to believe that the mother will pose a direct risk to the baby in the hours, and maybe days, following the birth, especially where the baby is in a hospital. Therefore, even if the baby will need to be removed at some point it is not clear it needs to be immediately following the birth. Second, there is the view that the hours following birth are a time of huge personal significance to the mother and perhaps to the baby. The ECtHR has referred to the 'shock and distress' that removal would cause.[130] Denial of this time between the two requires especially strong justification. Third, the courts have found removal of newborn babies where there has been no involvement in the decision making with the family hard to justify.[131] The Court may take some convincing that a less interventionist route was not possible.[132] Munby J has held that if removal of a newborn is required, then lengthy periods of contact, most days of the week, are required and if the mother wishes breastfeeding facilities should be made available,[133] although Bodey J in another decision held that each case had to be resolved on its own merits and there was no hard and fast rule about breastfeeding.[134] Munby J

---

[123] At para 106.
[124] *Re H and R* [1996] 1 All ER 1.
[125] *Ibid*, 23.
[126] *Re B (Children)* [2008] UKHL 35.
[127] *K and T v Finland* [2000] 3 FCR 248. See also *P, C and S v United Kingdom* [2002] 3 FCR 1; *Haase v Germany* [2004] 2 FCR 1; *Venema v Netherlands* [2003] 1 FCR 153.
[128] *P, C, and S v UK* [2002] 3 FCR 1.
[129] *Ibid*.
[130] *K and T v Finland* [2000] 3 FCR 248, para 168.
[131] *Ibid*.
[132] *Haase v Germany* [2004] 2 FCR 1.
[133] *Re M (Care Proceedings: Judicial Review)* [2003] EWHC 850 (Admin), para 44.
[134] *Kirklees Metropolitan District Council v S (Contact to Newborn Babies)* [2006] 1 FLR 333.

has held that not permitting any contact between a recently born baby and mother is a 'something which lies at the very extremities of the court's powers. Extraordinarily compelling reasons must be shown to justify an order under section 34(4) at this early stage in the proceedings.'[135]

In *Re D (unborn baby)(emergency protection order: future harm)*[136] the proposed removal of a newborn was approved. On an earlier occasion during supervised contact the mother had blindfolded her child, pinned her to the floor and threatened her with a knife. She had repeatedly said that her children would be better off dead than being in the care of the local authority. A consultant psychologist reported that if she was informed of the plan to remove her child at birth there was a high probability that she would harm herself, her child or others. While accepting that the summary removal of a child from her parents was 'draconian' and 'extremely harsh', and accepting that normally a parent needed to be fully involved in the decision-making process concerning her child, the decision was approved. Further it was held that the child could be removed immediately following the birth, given the 'highly unusual' facts of the case.

Care Plans

When a local authority applies for a care order it must prepare a care plan, outlining what it would like to do with the child during the care order.[137] The court will consider the care plan carefully when determining whether to make the order. The care plan becomes key when the court is considering whether making a care order is a proportionate interference with the Article 8 rights. It is key because a care order can lead to vastly differing consequences for a child. At one extreme a child can be removed from her parents; at the other the child could remain with her family, although under the close watch of the local authority.

There are two particular difficulties which can arise in relation to care plans. The first is a case where the court is satisfied that a care order is appropriate, but believes that the plans the local authority have are unduly interventionist. In such a case the court can refuse to make the order.[138] Commonly the judge will make an interim care order, asking the local authority to reconsider the care plan. In *Re S and W (children) (care proceedings: care plan)*[139] the Court of Appeal summarised the key propositions following the House of Lords decision in *Re S (children: care plan), Re W (children: care plan)*:[140]

> What appears not to be understood, however, and thus needs to be clearly repeated, is that not only does the court have the duty rigorously to scrutinise the care plan and to refuse to make a care order if it does not think the plan in the child's best interests; the court also has the right to invite the local authority to reconsider the care plan if the court comes to the conclusion that the plan—or any change in the plan—involves a course of action which the court believes is contrary

---

[135] *Re K (Contact)* [2008] 2 FLR 581, para 25.
[136] [2009] All ER (D) 266 (Mar).
[137] CA, s31A.
[138] *Re S (Children) and W (A Child)* [2007] EWCA Civ 232 paras 30, 35, 48 and 96. See also *Re X, Barnet London BC v Y and Z* [2006] 2 FLR 998.
[139] [2007] 1 FCR 721 (CA).
[140] [2000] UKHL 10.

to the interests of the child, and which would be likely to lead the court to refuse to make a care order if the local authority were to adhere to the care plan it has proposed.[141]

A second problem concerns cases where a court has made a care order on the basis of a particular care plan, but then the local authority embarks on a different plan.[142] Baroness Hale has stated that these departures from care plans are commonly caused by a lack of resources.[143] The question then arises as to what extent the court can control how a local authority looks after a child in care. The House of Lords considered the question in *Re S (children: care plan), Re W (children: care plan)*.[144] There it was held that once a care order was made, the court had no control over how a local authority implemented the care plan. Their Lordships specifically rejected the suggestion of the Court of Appeal[145] that when making a care order a court could star items on a care plan, meaning that if the local authority wished to depart from those items, court authorisation would be required first. The Court of Appeal had justified this proposal by relying on the HRA. Hale LJ explained that the starred items would be those where departure from the care plan would risk infringing the rights of the child or parents. The Court of Appeal's starring procedure was necessary to provide effective protection of these rights.

The House of Lords soundly rejected the Court of Appeal's approach as contrary to the principles underlying the CA. Lord Nicholls of Birkenhead referred to the following 'cardinal principle':[146]

> The court operates as the gateway into care, and makes the necessary care order when the threshold conditions are satisfied and the court considers a care order would be in the best interests of the child. That is the responsibility of the court. Thereafter the court has no continuing role in relation to the care order. Then it is the responsibility of the local authority to decide how the child should be cared for.[147]

It is interesting that the House of Lords did not reject this human rights argument out of hand. Indeed, they seem to have accepted it. Where they disagreed with the Court of Appeal was over the use of the HRA to change the law. There was nothing in the CA to support their starred items suggestion and the HRA could only be used to interpret legislation and not to amend it.

The House of Lords recognised that there was a potential gap in the protection available to family and children. An application under section 7 of the HRA offers the best route to pursue a claim that human rights have been interfered with in the way a care plan has been

---

[141] Para 30.

[142] *K and T v Finland* [2000] 3 FCR 248 makes it clear that Art 8 breaches can occur in the way the care plan is implemented.

[143] [2001] 2 FCR 450, at para 60.

[144] *Re S (children: care plan), Re W (children: care plan)* [2000] UKHL 10. This case is discussed in N Mole, 'Case Commentary: A Note on the Judgment from the Perspective of the European Convention for the Protection of Human Rights and Fundamental Freedoms 1950—*Re W and B*; *Re W (Care Plan)* and *Re S (Minors) (Care Order: Implementation of Care Plan)*; *Re W (Minors) (Care Order: Adequacy of Care Plan*' [2002] *Child and Family Law Quarterly* 447; C Smith, 'Case Commentary: Human rights and the Children Act 1989—*Re W and B*; *Re W (Care Plan)* and *Re S (Minors) (Care Order: Implementation of Care Plan)*; *Re W (Minors) (Care Order: Adequacy of Care Plan)*' [2002] *Child and Family Law Quarterly* 427.

[145] [2001] EWCA Civ 757.

[146] For an argument that this principle is not as cardinal as suggested see J Herring, 'The Human Rights of Children in Care' (2002) 118 *LQR* 534.

[147] *Re S (children: care plan), Re W (children: care plan)* [2000] UKHL 10, para 28.

departed from. Such a claim could either be a substantive claim, for example that the way the care plan has been implemented has been unjustifiably interventionist in family life, or a procedural claim that the family has not been adequately involved in decisions over how the care plan will operate.[148]

This, however, leaves a concern about the rights of children in care. The protection of their rights rests on assuming that parents bring the matter to court, which they may be unwilling or unable to do. Lord Mackay of Clashfern, in a concurring speech, astutely commented:

> As a practical matter I do not see how a child who has no person to raise the matter on his behalf can be protected from violation of his or her human rights or the rights conferred on him or her by our domestic law, other than by reliance on an effective means by which others bring the violation to notice.[149]

One response to these concerns is to say that this is often the case with children's rights. They are often relying on others to bring claims on their behalf. The position we have here is no different from any other walk of life where there may be concerns that a child's rights are being interfered with. So, as Lord Nicholls saw it in *Re S; Re W*,[150] although the CA enabled the local authority to act in a way which interfered with human rights (by inappropriately departing from a care plan), the Act itself was not incompatible with the ECHR and so a declaration of incompatibility under the HRA was inappropriate. This is true, but it overlooks three important points. First, as already mentioned, there are positive obligations on the state to protect individuals' rights. It might be thought that giving local authorities the discretion to decide how to implement a care plan satisfies this obligation. However, the cases before their Lordships demonstrate that local authorities (often through no fault of their own) can be unable to protect the human rights of children in care. Second, this is a case where the state has chosen to intervene in a way that endangers children's rights to respect for their family life. In such a case it is arguable that there needs to be a secure mechanism of ensuring that that intervention is compatible with human rights. Third, children who have been taken into care are extremely vulnerable and so the state should have especial obligations to ensure that their rights are protected. Lord Nicholls held that the failure to provide a remedy for infringement of rights might infringe Article 6. However, the HRA did not assist because the lack of remedy for children was a 'statutory lacuna, not a statutory incompatibility'.[151] This is a surprising statement. Is Lord Nicholls really suggesting that Article 6's right of access to a court is only relevant under the HRA if there is a positive statutory prohibition on access? If so, Article 6's protection under the HRA is very limited and is of no use for young children.[152]

---

[148] *Re G (care: challenge to local authority's decision)* [2003] EWHC 551 (Fam).
[149] *Re S (children: care plan), Re W (children: care plan)* [2000] UKHL 10, para 113.
[150] [2000] UKHL 10.
[151] Para 86.
[152] J Miles, 'Human Rights and Child Protection' [2001] *Child and Family Law Quarterly* 431 argues that this reveals the shortcomings due to the failure to incorporate Art 13 of the ECHR into the HRA. Since *Re S (children: care plan), Re W (children: care plan)* [2000] UKHL 10 s31A was inserted into the CA by s121(2) of the Adoption and Children Act 2002, which makes it mandatory for a local authority to keep the care plan under review.

Procedural Rights in Child Protection Law

Parents of children in care can make essentially two kinds of HRA complaint about the care of children. First, that the local authority infringed the Article 8 rights of the child, parents or family by separating the child and parents, or otherwise interfering in family life. That is what we have just been discussing. Second, that the procedures used in reaching the decision about the child failed to adequately involve the child or her parents. It is perfectly possible that the procedures used by a local authority will interfere with the parents' rights, even though the actual decision reached is compatible with the rights of the family.

Some general observations will be made about the involvement of families before a more detailed examination will be undertaken. First, as has already been emphasised, simply because a child has been taken into care does not mean that a parent's rights come to an end. Indeed, even though it may be inappropriate for a child and parent to have contact, that does not mean that there is no right to family life. So even the most vile abuser of children still has a right to respect to respect for family life, and restriction in the way his child is cared for must be justified under Article 8.[153] Second, the European Court has been at pains to stress that it recognises that this is a sensitive area and so it is not appropriate to impose inflexible requirements. Rather the court will consider whether 'the parents have been involved in the decision-making process, seen as a whole, to a degree sufficient to provide them with the requisite protection of their interests'.[154] As indicated in that quote, and this is a point that has been emphasised repeatedly by the UK courts, although there may have been a particular time when the parents were not adequately involved, if during the process, seen as a whole, they were sufficiently involved then there would be no breach of their rights. Hence it has been suggested that a single failure in terms of procedural fairness is unlikely to render the process as a whole procedurally unfair.[155] In *Re J*, although Wilson LJ held that the ECHR requirements on procedural fairness[156]

> must not be used as a bandwagon, to be drawn across the tracks of the case and to de-rail the proceedings from their prompt travel towards the necessary conclusions referable to, and in the interests of the child … [W]e will support those who deal robustly with suggestions of such minor non-compliance … as could never sensibly be translated into an infringement of human rights.[157]

A third point to emphasise is that when considering procedural fairness, fault of the parent may be a relevant factor. So in *Re P (Care Proceedings: Father's Application)*[158] a father who was informed that his child was the subject of care proceedings and encouraged to seek legal advice took 18 months to apply to be joined as a party. To grant him leave would cause further delay which the court held would harm the child. He had brought the situation upon himself by his delay. So, the court will not assume that the lack of parental involvement in decision making about children in care is necessarily the fault of the local authority.

Finally, Munby J in *Re C (Care Proceedings: Disclosure of Local Authority's Decision-Making Process)*[159] explained that the requirements of procedural fairness apply to all

---

[153] Although for a challenge to that view see J Herring, 'Respecting Family Life' (2008) 75 *Amicus Curiae* 21.
[154] *W v UK* (1988) 10 EHRR 29.
[155] *Re V (A Child) (Care: Pre-Birth Actions)* [2006] 2 FCR 121 (CA).
[156] Set out in *Re L* [2002] EWHC 1379 (Fam).
[157] *Re J (A Child) (Care Proceedings: Fair Trial)* [2006] EWCA Civ 545, para 30.
[158] *Re P (Care Proceedings: Father's Application)* [2001] 2 FCR 279 (FD).
[159] *Re C (Care Proceedings: Disclosure of Local Authority's Decision-Making Process)* [2002] EWHC 1379 (Fam), para 90.

bodies that are involved in child protection proceedings. However, if a claim is to be brought directly under section 7 of the HRA it can only be brought against a public authority. An individual doctor or social worker, for example, could not be sued under section 7.

The General Principles of Procedural Fairness

In *Re G (care: challenge to local authority's decision)*[160] Munby J set out the general principles concerning the protection of the procedural rights of parents of children in care.

[43] The fact that a local authority has parental responsibility for children pursuant to s 33(3)(a) of the Children Act 1989 does not entitle it to take decisions about those children without reference to, or over the heads of, the children's parents. A local authority, even if clothed with the authority of a care order, is not entitled to make significant changes in the care plan, or to change the arrangements under which the children are living, let alone to remove the children from home if they are living with their parents, without properly involving the parents in the decision-making process and without giving the parents a proper opportunity to make their case before a decision is made. After all, the fact that the local authority also has parental responsibility does not deprive the parents of their parental responsibility.

[44] A local authority can lawfully exercise parental responsibility for a child only in a manner consistent with the substantive and procedural requirements of Art 8. There is nothing in s 33(3)(b) of the Children Act 1989 that entitles a local authority to act in breach of Art 8. On the contrary, s 6(1) of the Human Rights Act 1998 requires a local authority to exercise its powers under both s 33(3)(a) and s 33(3)(b) of the Children Act 1989 in a manner consistent with both the substantive and the procedural requirements of Art 8.

[45] In a case such as this, a local authority, before it can properly arrive at a decision to remove children from their parents, must tell the parents (preferably in writing) precisely what it is proposing to do. It must spell out (again in writing) the reasons why it is proposing to do so. It must spell out precisely (in writing) the factual matters it is relying on. It must give the parents a proper opportunity to answer (either orally and/or in writing as the parents wish) the allegations being made against them. And it must give the parents a proper opportunity (orally and/or in writing as they wish) to make representations as to why the local authority should not take the threatened steps. In short, the local authority must involve the parents properly in the decision-making process. In particular, the parents (together with their representatives if they wish to be assisted) should normally be given the opportunity to attend at, and address, any critical meeting at which crucial decisions are to be made.

Later in his judgment he acknowledged that in emergencies it may not be possible to involve the parents to as great an extent as might normally be appropriate.[161]

In a more recent judgment the notion of fairness in the proceedings was put in these terms by the Court of Appeal:[162]

Professionals, and in particular local authorities, engaged in care proceedings will infringe the rights of parents and other individual parties to them under both Art 6 and Art 8 of the European

---

[160] *Re G (care: challenge to local authority's decision)* [2003] EWHC 551 (Fam).
[161] *Ibid*, para 30. See also *Venema v The Netherlands* [2003] 1 FLR 551.
[162] Summarising the judgments of Holman J in *Re M (care: challenging decisions by local authority)* [2001] 2 FLR 1300 and of Munby J in *Re L (care proceedings: disclosure of local authority's decision-making process)* [2002] 2 FCR 673 (FD).

Convention for the Protection of Human Rights and Fundamental Freedoms 1950 unless overall they conduct themselves with such integrity, transparency and inclusiveness as to satisfy their rights, necessarily to be construed in a wide sense, to a fair hearing and to respect for their private and family life.[163]

The references here to integrity and transparency suggest that the issue is not simply one of ensuring that the parents as individuals are treated fairly but that the procedures are conducted openly. In other words, not only must justice be done, it must be seen to be done. However, a departure from good practice will not automatically lead to a finding that there has been a breach of human rights. The departures need to be 'sufficiently substantial to infect the fairness of the proceedings'.[164]

Of course, the remedies in relation to a procedural breach are problematic. In many cases the court may conclude that despite the procedural breaches, the case for making the order requested by the local authority was overwhelming. Or that so much time has passed since the making of the order that it would cause too much harm to the child to re-open it. In such cases only financial orders may be available and even then they may be very modest. Where, however, there is still time, the court may require proper procedural requirements to be complied with before a care order is made.[165]

Procedural Rights under Articles 6 and 8

Complaints about procedural unfairness within public law proceedings relating to children can raise issues relating to both Article 6 and Article 8.[166] Although on its face Article 8 does not appear to involve questions of procedure, the courts have read requirements of procedure into it. In *McMichael v UK*[167] it was held:

> Whilst Article 8 contains no explicit procedural requirements, the decision-making process leading to measures of interference must be fair and such as to afford due respect to the interests safeguarded by Article 8.

The differences between the procedural protections in Article 6 and 8 are as follows. First, Article 6 concerns fairness in the trial procedure. This is not limited to the judicial process itself, but includes procedures connected to litigation.[168] It includes the way evidence for a hearing was taken;[169] a requirement for expert evidence to be used in child protection cases;[170] 'the opportunity for the parties to have knowledge of and comment on the observations filed or evidence adduced by the other party'.[171] By contrast Article 8 covers any decision concerning the child. Munby J in *Re C* explained: 'Art 8 guarantees fairness in the

---

[163] *Re J (A Child) (Care Proceedings: Fair Trial)* [2006] 2 FCR 107 (CA), para 3.
[164] *Ibid*, para 26.
[165] *Re M (Care: Challenging Decisions by a Local Authority* [2001] 2 FLR 1300 (FD).
[166] *Re C (Care Proceedings: Disclosure of Local Authority's Decision-Making Process)* [2002] EWHC 1379 (Fam).
[167] (1995) 20 EHRR 205, 239, para 87.
[168] *Golder v UK* (1979–80) 1 EHRR 524; *Ruiz-Mateos v Spain* (1993) 16 EHRR 505; *Dombo Beheer BV v Netherlands* (1993) 18 EHRR 213; *McMichael v UK* (1995) 20 EHRR 205; and *McGinley and Egan v UK* (1998) 4 BHRC 42.
[169] *Mantovanelli v France* (1997) 24 EHRR 370.
[170] *Elsholz v Germany* [2000] 3 FCR 385.
[171] *Ruiz-Mateos v Spain* (1993) 16 EHRR 505 at 542 (para 63): *Buchberger v Austria* [2001] ECHR 32899/96, para 50.

decision-making process at *all* stages of child protection.'[172] The rights extend during the whole time the child is in care and include implementation of the care plan.[173] Therefore a decision to move a child from one foster carer to another, for example, would fall within Article 8, but not Article 6.

Second, the protection for Article 6 rights is absolute, while under Article 8 interference with those rights can be justified, under paragraph 2. Therefore, if the procedural failings are a breach of both Article 6 and Article 8 rights, it is preferable for the claimant to rely on an Article 6 claim. That said, conduct which falls short of the highest standard of procedural fairness might not lead to an interference with a fair trial under Article 6, but still amount to an infringement of Article 8.

Specific Requirements of Procedural Fairness

This Chapter will now consider more precisely what is required by procedural fairness in child protection litigation under Articles 6 and 8. This is not intended to be a complete list, but rather an indication of the kind of issues which have been considered by the courts.

Notice

Where the local authority has concerns about the parenting being offered to children it should, where possible, warn parents of their concerns.[174] In *Re C (care proceedings: disclosure of local authority's decision-making process)*[175] it was held:

> Social workers should, as soon as ever practicable: (a) notify parents of material criticisms of and deficits in their parenting or behaviour and of the expectations of them; and (b) advise them how they may remedy or improve their parenting or behaviour.[176]

If the local authority plans to remove children, the local authority should give notice to parents.[177] Of course these points will not apply in an emergency. Where children are facing an immediate and serious threat, children can be removed without notice, and there is nothing in the Convention to challenge that.[178] However, it will require an *immediate* need to remove the child. In *Haase v Germany*[179] children were removed from the family under an ex parte application after the local authority saw a report prepared by a psychological expert for the purposes of assessing an application for financial assistance from the state. The report expressed concerns at deficiencies in the parenting which were jeopardising the children's well-being. The ECtHR held that removal under an ex parte application was only appropriate where there was imminent danger. In this case, although there were

---

[172] *Re C (Care Proceedings: Disclosure of Local Authority's Decision-Making Process)* [2002] EWHC 1379 (Fam), para 88.

[173] *Re G (Care: Challenge to Local Authority's Decision)* [2003] 2 FLR 42 (FD).

[174] *G v N County Council* [2009] 1 FLR 774.

[175] *Re C (Care Proceedings: Disclosure of Local Authority's Decision-Making Process)* [2002] 2 FCR 673 (FD).

[176] *Ibid*, para 154.

[177] *K and T v Finland* [2000] 3 FCR 248; *P, C and S v United Kingdom* [2002] 3 FCR 1.

[178] *Re X (Emergency Protection Orders)* [2006] EWHC 510 (FD); *K and T v Finland* [2000] 3 FCR 248; *P, C and S v UK, Venema v Netherlands* [2003] 1 FCR 153; *Covezzi and Morselli v Italy* (2003) 38 EHRR 28; and *Haase v Germany* [2004] 2 FCR 1; *HK v Finland* (Application No 36065/97), para 106.

[179] [2004] 1 FCR 1.

legitimate concerns about the child, the imminence of danger had not been adequately demonstrated. A contrasting case is *Venema v The Netherlands*,[180] where the child was removed in emergency proceedings from the parent, as the mother was suspected of suffering from Münchhausen syndrome by proxy. She had not been involved in the decision-making process. In this case it was held that it had not been shown why the doctors and authorities could not have discussed their concerns with the mother. There was no evidence that doing so would have posed a risk to her.

In *X Council v B and others (emergency protection orders)*,[181] it was emphasised that the use of an emergency protection order removing a child without notice to the parents was a 'terrible and drastic remedy'. Indeed Munby J questioned whether the law on EPOs was compliant with the ECHR, in particular the lack of appeal for 15 days and the fact that if the order was made ex parte, reasons did not have to be given for two days and that there was no way of challenging an ex parte EPO for three days.[182] In his judgment he urged courts to ensure that the EPO was only used if it was proportionate and to only be as long as necessary. McFarlane J[183] subsequently held that a copy of Munby J's judgment should be available whenever an emergency protection order was sought.

There is some research evidence which suggests that local authorities are reluctant to use police powers or EPOs.[184] Rather, agreements between the parties are preferred. It may be thought that this is a convenient way of by-passing human rights concerns. If the parents have agreed to a programme of intervention, it can hardly be said that their right to respect for their private life has been interfered with. Or can it? Although it may be thought that parents entered these agreements freely, there was of course the ever-present threat of court proceedings if they did not, with the application being even stronger because the local authority could say that the parents had refused to co-operate with the local authority, even where the agreements were entered into voluntarily, because any request by a parent for return of the child would be met with a threat to apply for an EPO.[185] In fact Article 8 is broad enough to include cases where intervention in family life is done by agreement. The consent of the parent to the intervention will not necessarily justify an interference in the child's right to family life.

Preparation and Disclosure of Expert Reports and Other Evidence

Parents should be provided with full disclosure of the relevant materials that the local authority have in relation to their case. Munby J in *Re C (care proceedings: disclosure of local authority's decision-making process)*[186] stated:

> The local authority should at an early stage of the proceedings make full and frank disclosure to the other parties of all key documents in its possession or available to it, including in particular contact recordings, attendance notes of meetings and conversations and minutes of case conferences, core group meetings and similar meetings. Early provision should then be afforded for inspection of

---

[180] [2003] 1 FLR 552.
[181] [2007] 1 FCR 512.
[182] *Re X (Emergency Protection Orders)* [2006] EWHC 510 (Fam), para 38.
[183] *Ibid.*
[184] J Masson, 'Emergency Intervention to Protect Children: Using and Avoiding Legal Controls' [2005] *Child and Family Law Quarterly* 75.
[185] *Ibid.*
[186] *Re C (care proceedings: disclosure of local authority's decision-making process)* [2002] 2 FCR 673 (FD).

any of these documents. Any objection to the disclosure or inspection of any document should be notified to the parties at the earliest possible stage in the proceedings and raised with the court by the local authority without delay.

Hence in *McMichael v UK*[187] it was held that failure to disclose a report from a social worker which was being relied upon in care proceedings amounted to a violation of the parents' Article 8 rights. Such a right, however, can be interfered with if necessary in the interests of others.[188] So, where a father who had previously been violent to the mother sought disclosure of documents which might have disclosed her whereabouts, the court agreed that there was no need to make the disclosure.[189] The reasons for non-discourse need to be compelling.[190] Court approval of non-disclosure should be sought, especially where the document is an important part of the authority's case.[191] In *Venema v The Netherlands* the obligation was expressed in this way:

> It is essential that a parent be placed in a position where he or she may obtain access to information which is relied on by the authorities in taking measures of protective care or in taking decisions relevant to the care and custody of a child. Otherwise, the parent will be unable to participate effectively in the decision-making process or put forward in a fair or adequate manner those matters militating in favour of his or her ability to provide the child with proper care and protection.[192]

Not only is there to be disclosure of expert reports and evidence, but where an expert is to be instructed, parents should be involved in preparing the brief for the expert.[193]

Access to Legal Advice

An important part of the right to a fair trial under Article 6 is the right to confidential legal advice.[194] This is necessary to ensure that the parents are not at a disadvantage in presenting their case and their evidence at the hearing.[195] In *P, C, S v UK*[196] the European Court held that there was no right to legal aid or to legal representation. However, the circumstances of a case may mean that the right to a fair trial required such representation:

> The complexity of the case, along with the importance of what was at stake and the highly emotive nature of the subject matter, lead this Court to conclude that the principles of effective access to court and fairness required that P receive the assistance of a lawyer. Even if P was acquainted with the vast documentation in the case, the Court is not persuaded that she should have been expected to take up the burden of conducting her own case. It notes that at one point in the proceedings, which were conducted at the same time as she was coping with the distress of the removal of S at birth, P broke down in the court room and the judge, counsel for the guardian ad litem and a social worker, had to encourage her to continue.

---

[187] (1995) 20 EHRR 205.
[188] *L v UK* [2000] 2 FLR 225.
[189] *Re B (Disclosure to other Parties)* [2002] 2 FCR 32.
[190] *Re W (Care Proceedings: Disclosure)* [2003] 2 FLR 1023.
[191] *TP and KM v UK* [2001] 2 FCR 289.
[192] Para 92.
[193] *Re C (Care Proceedings: Disclosure of Local Authority's Decision-Making Process)* [2002] 2 FCR 673 (FD).
[194] *Re L (Investigation: Privilege)* [1996] 1 FLR 731 (FD).
[195] *Dombo Beheer v The Netherlands* (1993) 18 EHRR 213.
[196] [2002] 3 FCR 1; discussed in N Mole, 'Adoption, Article 8 and the European Court—*P, C and S v United Kingdom*' (2002) *International Family Law Journal* 114.

Involvement of Parents at Planning Meetings

Article 8 normally requires that parents be permitted to attend planning meetings in respect of their child. Hence in *Re M (Care: Challenging Decisions by Local Authority)*[197] the exclusion of the parents from a crucial 'decisive' permanency planning meeting concerning the long-term future care of the child constituted an infringement of her Article 8 rights. However, in this area, as always, it is important to remember that the courts will consider the issue looking at the overall fairness of the process. So, if a parent is not permitted to attend one meeting, but is allowed to attend subsequent ones, and is informed of what happened at the meeting she did not attend and is given an opportunity to express her views on what had happened, this may well mean that overall Article 6 or 8 rights are not infringed.[198]

It is not just planning meetings which a parent may have a right to attend, but also other meetings which play a central role in the decision-making process involving the child may be involved. In *Re L (Care: Assessment: Fair Trials)*[199] it was held that where a report was likely to have preponderant influence on the assessment of facts concerning a child in care proceedings then the parents should have been invited to attend a meeting between the psychiatrist, the local authority and the guardian. In this case there were particular concerns because the primary recommendation of the psychiatrist in his draft report prepared for the meeting was very different from that in the final report after the meeting.[200] The fact that the mother had not been informed about the meeting was not consistent with the local authority's duty to use transparent and fair procedures.

Means of Challenging Local Authority Decisions

Articles 6 and 8 require there to be a means of challenging local authority decisions. However, this does not mean that in every case where someone wishes to challenge a local authority decision they have a right to a public court hearing.[201] This is of most relevance in issues concerning the care of a child after a care order has been made. The appeals process will require an oral hearing if there are important issues that cannot be resolved on the written materials.[202]

Keeping Parents Informed

If children have been taken into care, there is a duty on the state under Article 8 to keep parents informed about their children. This would include basic information about where the children are and important issues that might arise in their upbringing. In *S and G v Italy*[203] this included the fact that the leaders of a children's home had criminal antecedents.

Regular Review

The local authority must keep the care of a child under review and reconsider 'from time to time' the family's present circumstances and the possibility of reunification.[204] The

---

[197] *Re M (Care: Challenging Decisions by Local Authority)* [2001] 2 FLR 1300 (FD).

[198] *Scott v UK* [2000] 1 FLR 938; *Re C (Care Proceedings: Disclosure of Local Authority's Decision-Making Process)* [2002] 2 FCR 673 (CA).

[199] [2002] EWHC 1379 (Fam).

[200] Although in this case it was held that subsequent involvement of the mother meant that this earlier fairness was 'remedied'.

[201] *Elsholz v Germany* [2000] 2 FLR 486.

[202] *Ibid.*

[203] [2000] 2 FLR 771.

[204] *Johansen v Norway* (1996) 23 EHRR 33.

European Court in *R v Finland* found a breach of Article 8 due to the lack of a 'serious and sustained' effort to achieve reconciliation.[205] The details of that obligation will be discussed further shortly.

Delay

Articles 6 and 8 require courts and local authorities to deal with cases within a reasonable length of time.[206] In deciding whether the delay is reasonable, account will be taken of the complexity of the case and the conduct of the complaint.[207] However, the court will be particularly concerned where the delay in bringing the case to court is likely to affect the outcome of the case.[208] Of course this is not news to family lawyers. The CA prominently places in section 1(2) the 'no delay' principle.

Contact with Children in Care

As emphasised several times in this Chapter, even though a child is taken into care this does not mean that the family life between the child and parent comes to an end.[209] One of the consequences of this is that the right of contact between a child and parent may remain even after a care order has been made.[210] Stopping contact between the child and her parents is likely to be an interference in both the parents' and the child's rights under Article 8.[211] As was stated in *Johansen v Norway*:[212]

> [T]aking a child into care should normally be regarded as a temporary measure to be discontinued as soon as circumstances permit and any measures of implementation of temporary care should be consistent with the ultimate aim of reuniting the natural parent and child. In this regard a fair balance has to be struck between the interests of the child in remaining in public care and those of the parents in being reunited with the child. In carrying out this balancing exercise, the Court will attach particular importance to the best interests of the child, which depending upon their nature and seriousness may override those of the parent. In particular … the parent cannot be entitled under Article 8 of the Convention to have such measures taken as would harm the child's health and development.

Where all forms of contact between parents and children (for example, telephone and letter) are stopped, this will be particularly hard to justify.[213]

The particular emphasis placed on the retention of contact in the ECHR is reflected in section 34 of the CA. This requires a local authority to obtain the leave of the court before terminating the contact between a child in care and a parent. The significance the CA attaches to contact is revealed by the fact that this is one of the few decisions about

---

[205]   *R v Finland* [2006] 2 FCR 264.
[206]   *Erkner and Hofauer v Austria* (1987) 9 EHRR 464.
[207]   *Vallée v France* (1994) 18 EHRR 549.
[208]   *H v United Kingdom* (1987) 10 EHRR 95; *Re C (Care Proceedings: Disclosure of Local Authority's Decision Making Process)* [2002] 2 FCR 673, para 249.
[209]   *Olsson* judgment of 24 March 1988, Series A No 130, p 29, para 59.
[210]   *Eriksson v Sweden* (1990) 12 EHRR 183.
[211]   *Kuimov v Russia* [2009] ECHR 32147/04.
[212]   *Johansen v Norway* (1997) 23 EHRR 33.
[213]   *Andersson v Sweden* (1992) 14 EHRR 615.

children in care which is not left to the discretion of the local authority. When the courts are considering granting leave to a local authority to cease contact they will now consider the human rights of the parents and the child.[214] Even before the HRA the courts had accepted that there was a presumption in favour of allowing contact.[215] The HRA has reinforced that presumption. The court will consider the extent to which allowing contact to continue might disrupt the plans the local authority have for the long-term care of the child. But the local authority will need to persuade the court that the benefit of its long-term plan justifies the cessation of contact.[216] That is likely to be only where there is no hope of rehabilitation of the child with the birth family.[217]

It should be emphasised that obligations in relation to contact under the ECHR are positive. So it may not be sufficient for the local authority to passively allow contact; they may be required to act positively to enable that to happen.[218] The efforts to secure contact must be 'effective and coherent'.[219] In *Olsson v Sweden*[220] the placing of siblings with separate foster parents a long distance from each other and their parents could not be justified by 'administrative difficulties'.

Where a person other than a parent of the child wishes to have a contact order in respect of a child in care they will need the leave of the court under section 34(3) of the CA 1989.[221] The courts have held that in considering applications for leave they will take into account the factors listed in section 10(9) of the CA. In particular the court will consider the applicant's relationship with the child, the likelihood of success of an application[222] and the wishes of the parents. In recent years the courts have accepted the relevance of arguments under Article 6, which means that there will need to be a full inquiry before refusing leave is justified.[223]

Continuing Duty to Reunite

As already mentioned, in *Johansen v Norway*[224] the ECtHR has held that taking a child into care should be regarded as a temporary measure. The aim of intervention should be to reunite the family, but as the following paragraph from the judgment of *R v Finland*[225] summarises, this is not an absolute duty:

> The positive duty to take measures to facilitate family reunification as soon as reasonably feasible will begin to weigh on the competent authorities with progressively increasing force as from the commencement of the period of care, subject always to its being balanced against the duty to consider the best interests of the child (see *K and T v Finland*). After a considerable period of time

---

[214] In *Re F (Care: Termination of Contact)* [2000] 2 FCR 481 it was held that s34 and its interpretation by the courts were compliant with the ECHR.

[215] *Re B (Children in Care: Contact)* [1993] 1 FCR 363; *Re E (Children in Care: Contact)* [1994] 1 FCR 584.

[216] *Re E (Children in Care: Contact)* [1994] 1 FCR 584.

[217] *Re L (Minors) (Care Proceedings: Appeal)* [1996] 2 FCR 352 (CA).

[218] *Scozzari and Giunta v Italy* (Applications Nos 39221/98 and 41963/98).

[219] *Ibid.*

[220] (1989) 11 EHRR 259.

[221] *Re W (Care Proceedings: Leave to Apply)* [2005] 2 FLR 468; *Re M (Care: Contact: Grandmother's Application for Leave)* [1995] 2 FLR 86.

[222] Only if the application is 'obviously unsustainable' should leave not be granted.

[223] *Re J (Leave to Issue Application for Residence Order)* [2002] EWCA Civ 1346.

[224] (1997) 23 EHRR 33.

[225] [2006] 2 FCR 264 (CA), para 89.

has passed since the child was originally taken into public care, the interest of a child not to have his or her *de facto* family situation changed again may override the interests of the parents to have their family reunited (see *KA v Finland*).

As the court went on to emphasise, the minimum expected of the state is to examine the case anew from time to time. It added this warning:

> The possibilities of reunification will be progressively diminished and eventually destroyed if the biological parent and the child are not allowed to meet each other at all, or only so rarely that no natural bonding between them is likely to occur.[226]

Although the 'ultimate aim' of state intervention should be the reunion of the child with her family, it must be emphasised that a parent is not entitled to measures which would harm a child.[227]

A dramatic example of the practical significance of this duty to reunite was *Re B*.[228] There a child had been removed from the father, but the care plan had completely failed. The child pleaded to be reunited with the father. The father was willing to improve on his parenting ability. The court approved the return of the child to the father.

Liability of the Local Authority where it wrongly Intervenes

The courts have held that if parents believe that an application to take a child into care is an improper interference with their right to respect for their family life, the correct way to use these arguments is simply to use them to defend the care proceedings, rather than instituting separate human rights arguments.[229] Where, however, there were no other proceedings in which the arguments could be made (for example, the complaint was over the way a care plan was being implemented), an application under section 7 or 8 of the HRA could be made.[230]

If, however, there are no ongoing proceedings to deal with the claim, the parents or child could seek to bring proceedings against the local authority. There are two main causes of action a claimant is likely to use. The first is tort and the second is through the HRA.

Liability in Tort Law

Looking first at liability in tort, such a claim in unlikely to succeed. In a series of decisions the courts have established the following:

— doctors, social workers or police investigating suspicions of child abuse do not owe the children's parents a duty of care.[231] So even if it is shown that the professionals act negligently in their investigations, no action in tort can be brought. No distinction will be made between evaluations, judgments or operational matters;[232]

---

[226] *Ibid*, para 90.
[227] *KA v Finland* [2003] 1 FCR 201 and 230.
[228] *Re B (Children)* [2008] EWCA Civ 131.
[229] *Re V (Care Proceedings: Human Rights Claims)* [2004] 1 FLR 944.
[230] *Re L (Care Proceedings: Human Rights Claims)* [2004] 1 FCR 289.
[231] *JD v East Berkshire Community Health NHS Trust* [2005] UKHL 23.
[232] *L v Reading BC* [2007] EWCA Civ 1313.

— a local authority in deciding whether to place a child on the child protection register does not owe a duty of care to the parents.[233]

The policy behind these rulings was explained by the House of Lords in *JD v East Berkshire Community Health NHS Trust & Ors*.[234] That is based on a concern that fear of liability in tort could mean that a professional will be diverted from considering what is best for a child. Lord Nicholls explained:

> A doctor is obliged to act in the best interests of his patient. In these cases the child is his patient. The doctor is charged with the protection of the child, not with the protection of the parent. The best interests of a child and his parent normally march hand-in-hand. But when considering whether something does not feel 'quite right', a doctor must be able to act single-mindedly in the interests of the child. He ought not to have at the back of his mind an awareness that if his doubts about intentional injury or sexual abuse prove unfounded he may be exposed to claims by a distressed parent.[235]

In *Z v UK*[236] the ECtHR, hearing an appeal from the HL decision in *X v Bedfordshire*, held that the failure to provide a remedy in tort amounted to a breach of Article 13. There was no breach of Article 6 because that Article is concerned with procedural fairness rather than the fairness of the substantive law.[237] However, it should be noted that Article 13 has not been implemented in the HRA, so a challenge on the tort law could not rely on that Article. However, a claim under sections 7 and 8 of the Act could succeed.

In *Lawrence v Pembrokeshire*[238] it was held that the HRA did not require a change in the law in relation to tort. In relation to Article 6 the courts have consistently held that the right to a fair trial cannot be used to challenge the substantive law. Article 6 does not guarantee any particular rights or obligations under the law, but rather guarantees access to the courts to give effect to any rights that the law provides.[239] In other words the mere fact that the law does not permit you to succeed in a claim does not mean you have not had a fair trial. So it is Article 8 which provided the primary route of challenging the law of tort remedy. However, the Court of Appeal saw Article 8 issues and duty of care issues as separate. Article 8, they explained, is about considering the justification for an interference in family life, while a breach of a duty of care concerns who is liable to pay damages. There was, therefore, no interference with an Article 8 right by the lack of a tort remedy. This argument overlooks the positive duties that the state has preventing breaches of Article 8 rights. If it could be shown (which is probably unlikely) that imposing a tort law duty of care would make it less likely that there would be interference in Article 8 rights, then the absence of that law could be said to mean the state had failed to comply with its obligations under Article 8.

The issue of tort liability arose in a different context in *Lambert v Cardiff CC*.[240] Mr and Mrs Lambert were approved as foster carers for a teenage girl. Although the council was aware that she had made allegations of sexual abuse against men in the past, only one

---

[233] *Lawrence v Pembrokeshire CC* [2007] EWCA Civ 446.
[234] [2005] 2 AC 373.
[235] *Ibid*, para 85.
[236] J Miles, 'Human Rights and Child Protection' (n 152).
[237] See also *TP and KM v UK* [2001] 2 FCR 289.
[238] [2007] EWCA Civ 446.
[239] J Miles, 'Human Rights and Child Protection' (n 152).
[240] [2007] EWHC 869 (QBD).

incident was passed on to the Lamberts. Similarly they did not inform the Lamberts of her history of violence towards children. Towards the end of the placement A made a false allegation of abuse against Mr Lambert and started a campaign of harassment, which caused the claimant psychiatric injury. The claimants sought damages from the council. The court found that the relationship between foster parents and councils was regulated by the statutory scheme for fostering and it was not possible to find a contract between the parties. It was accepted by the judge that there was a breach of a duty in passing on the important information concerning one allegation of abuse and the history of violence. However, he found that even if disclosure had been made, the Lamberts would have taken her on, and so the breach did not cause any loss.

Sections 7 and 8 of the Human Rights Act

Under sections 7 and 8 of the HRA a complainant can seek a remedy if their rights have been infringed.[241] In *Re S (Minors) (Care Order: Implementation of Care Plan); Re W (Minors) (Care Order: Adequacy of Care Plan)* Lord Nicholls of Birkenhead appeared to suggest that the section 7 remedy will be used 'as a long stop' and only after other remedies have been explored. In particular it should not be used where the issues can be raised as a defence to an application for a care order or supervision order. Any section 7 claim should be brought against the local authority rather than the court which made the order.[242]

It is easy to exaggerate the potential scope of the section 7 remedy. There are two important limitations to emphasise. First, a breach of one of the relevant Articles in the ECHR must be established. In determining that, it must be recalled that local authorities have a margin of appreciation to make sensitive decisions concerning child protection. Quite how this will work in this context is as yet unclear, but it is not impossible that something akin to the *Bolam* test will be relied upon, whereby a breach will only be found if no reasonable local authority would have reacted in that way. Second, section 7 does not lead to an automatic right to a reedy. The court has discretion as to what remedy, if any, should be granted. It is perfectly feasible that a court would decide not to award any damages at all. The court must consider if it is 'just and appropriate' to award damages. In making that decision it could take into account public policy factors.[243] The ECtHR in deciding whether to award damages requires the breach to be 'manifest and grave'.[244] It remains to be seen whether blameworthiness will be a relevant factor.[245] It may, for example, not even be necessary that the infringement of the right was negligent. The court will be guided by the level of damages that the ECtHR awards and should be 'no less liberal'.[246]

---

[241] Law Commission Report on 'Damages under the Human Rights Act 1998' (Law Com 266: *Report on a Reference under s 3(1)(e) of the Law Commission Act 1965*).

[242] *Hinds v Liverpool County Court, Liverpool City Council* [2008] 2 FLR 63. That case also confirms that a claim cannot be brought against an individual expert witness based on the HRA.

[243] R Bailey-Harris and M Harris, 'Local Authorities and Child Protection—The Mosaic of Accountability' [2002] *Child and Family Law Quarterly* 117.

[244] *Francovich and Bonifaci v Italy* [1991] ECR I-5357.

[245] R Bailey-Harris and M Harris, 'Local Authorities and Child Protection—The Mosaic of Accountability' (n 243).

[246] *Anufrijeva v Southwark London BC; R (on the application of N) v Secretary of State for the Home Dept; R (on the application of M) v Secretary of State for the Home Dept* [2003] 3 FCR 673, para 57.

In one of the few decisions considering the issues of damage, *Re C (breach of human rights: damages)*,[247] following lengthy negotiations it was agreed that the claimant should be allowed six months to show she had the ability to parent her son, M, in the long term. After a short time, the local authority decided to terminate the plan at a meeting to which the claimant was not invited. While the judge concluded that there was no procedural breach in excluding the claimant from the meeting to decide to remove her child, there was a procedural breach in not including her in the decision-making process to abandon the original care plan. In considering a claim for damages for the breach of her Article 8 rights the judge concluded that it was not necessary to award damages. Indeed, he added, 'I do not think that the concept of damages sits easily with the welfare jurisdiction of family law'. Such a comment was held on appeal by Wilson LJ to be misplaced.

On appeal the Court of Appeal agreed that there had been insufficient involvement of the mother in the decision-making process. However, the court emphasised that this was a procedural breach only. The decision to move to adoption could not be criticised. Therefore seeking to award damages for 'compensation for loss of opportunity' to prove that she was a fit parent, as had been argued on the mother's behalf, was inappropriate. In fact the court held although she should have been invited to attend the meeting, the evidence suggested she would not have been able to participate at the relevant time. This led Wilson LJ to conclude that although 'things had not been done according to the book', the procedural breach was not significant.[248] Further, the breach could not be said to have caused any independent or additional injury to the claimant, extra to the adoption. He added that 'satisfaction to the person whose right has been infringed must be "just" and that, but only if such be "necessary" in order to afford just satisfaction, an award of damages should be made'.[249] He concluded: 'On the spectrum of seriousness the infringement of human rights perpetrated by the local authority in the present case must, on any objective view, be seen to rank near to the low end.'[250] It was explained that damages are favoured where the wrong done by the intervention cannot be corrected and a mere statement that the local authority had acted improperly is insufficient.

Damages are not the only remedy available under section 7. A court can order the local authority to return the child. In *G v N County Council*[251] MacFarlane J found a series of procedural flaws in the way the local authority had removed a child. These amounted to a breach of the mother's Article 8 rights. She sought the return of the child under an application brought under the HRA. MacFarlane J approached the issue in this way:

> A's circumstances and his welfare are undoubtedly an important part of the considerations that the court has, but they are not the only consideration or the overriding or paramount consideration. A question which it seems to me is helpful to ask is to consider what the situation would be if the local authority had acted properly and had given the mother due notice of what it was proposing and she had applied to the court under the Human Rights Act to prevent the removal taking place before the local authority took action. What would the result have been on the basis of the

information that the local authority put forward to this court which mother's counsel accepts is the basis upon which the matter has to be determined at this stage?[252]

He determined that even if the procedures had been correctly followed, a care order would still have been made. More controversially he added that the fact that the removal had already taken place was a factor to consider:

> A, of course, has now been out of his mother's care for 3 weeks. It is in a way wrong and unfair for the court to put any substantial weight on that factor, because that state of affairs has been achieved, as I have found, by the unlawful actions of the local authority, and I bear that thought in mind. But I also have in mind the observations that I have already read out from Thorpe LJ in *Re W (Children) (Care: Interference With Family Life)* at para [27] to the effect that once a child has been removed it is harder to mount and succeed in an application for his return, given that the child will have suffered the experience of removal and will have been placed in a neutral setting.[253]

While much attention has been paid to the new cause of action provided in section 7 of the HRA, as this discussion shows the remedies available may, in fact, be limited. Damages will rarely be available and, where they are, they will not be able to compensate for loss of a child. As *G v N County Council* shows,[254] where the child has been removed from the family a court will take some convincing that returning the child will benefit the child.

Liability of Individuals Making Allegations of Child Abuse

There may be circumstances in which a parent who is wrongly investigated for suspected child abuse may wish to bring proceedings against the individuals involved. In *Juppala v Finland*[255] a grandmother of a child suspected his father had abused him after finding a bruise on his back. She reported her concerns to a doctor who then notified the relevant authorities. The father successfully sued the mother in defamation. The mother's application to the ECtHR succeeded. She claimed that allowing the defamation action interfered with her rights under Articles 8 and 10. It was held that the importance of protection for children from abuse meant that a state could not allow defamation to be used in cases of allegations of abuse:

> If the source of the abuse is the parent, the child is at risk from his primary and natural protector within the privacy of his home. Child abuse is indeed a hard form of criminal conduct to combat, because its existence is difficult to uncover. Babies and young children are unable to tell, older children are often too frightened. The question raised by this application is how to strike a proper balance when a parent is wrongly suspected of having abused his or her child, while protecting children at risk of significant harm. In considering these questions, the starting point is to note that the applicant acted properly in considering whether the bruise on the boy's back had been deliberately inflicted. Having become suspicious, she consulted a medical doctor who rightly decided to communicate to the child welfare authorities the suspicion which he personally formed having examined and interviewed the boy. That is the essential next step in child protection. The seriousness of child abuse as a social problem requires that persons who act in good faith (see, *mutatis mutandis, Guja v Moldova (Application No 14277/04)* (unreported) 12 February 2008),

---

[252] Para 47.
[253] Para 51.
[254] [2009] 1 FLR 774.
[255] *Juppala v Finland* (Application No 18620/03) [2009] 1 FLR 617.

in what they believe are the best interests of the child, should not be influenced by fear of being prosecuted or sued when deciding whether and when their doubts should be communicated to health care professionals or social services. There is a delicate and difficult line to tread between taking action too soon and not taking it soon enough. The duty to the child in making these decisions should not be clouded by a risk of exposure to claims by a distressed parent if the suspicion of abuse proves unfounded.[256]

This seems an entirely correct way of dealing with the issue. Child abuse is so difficult to detect that people must be free to voice suspicions without fear of legal action.

Secure Accommodation Orders

The leading case on secure accommodation orders and human rights is *Re K (a child) (secure accommodation order)*.[257] The case involved a 15-year-old boy who had learning difficulties and had displayed for some time abusive behaviour to others. A series of secure accommodation orders were made against him. He appealed against them, arguing that they were contrary to Article 5 ECHR. It was argued that K's right to liberty under Article 5 had been interfered with, and that none of the exceptions in Article 5(1) applied. Factor (d) allows for the detention of a minor following a lawful order for the purposes of educational supervision. However, it was argued that section 25 of the CA did not include educational supervision as a justification for a secure accommodation order. The majority of the Court of Appeal[258] agreed that the secure accommodation order deprived liberty under Article 5 of the ECHR and so had to be justified by reference to one of the exemptions. The court held that the order could be justified under (d). Although section 25 did not refer to education, all children under 16 had to be educated and therefore the secure unit housing K would have to educate. Anyway the phrase educational supervision should be understood to include education in a broad sense. The order could therefore be justified under Article 5(1)(d).[259]

Adoption and the Human Rights Act

The Right of the Unmarried Father to be involved in the Making of the Order

One important aspect of the ECtHR's interventions in the law on adoption has been to emphasise the right of anyone with Article 8 rights in respect of the child to be involved in proceedings relating to adoption. Hence in *Keegan v Ireland*[260] an unmarried father

---

[256] Para 42.
[257] [2001] 1 FCR 249.
[258] Dame Elizabeth Butler-Sloss P and Judge LJ; Thorpe LJ dissenting.
[259] M Parry, 'Secure Accommodation—The Cinderella Of Family Law' [2000] *Child and Family Law Quarterly* 101.
[260] [1994] 3 FCR 165.

was found to have had his Article 8 rights infringed when he was denied any role in the decision-making and judicial process concerning his child's adoption.

It would be quite wrong to assume that every father, therefore, has the right to be involved in adoption proceedings. First, the father must establish that he has family life with the child.[261] If the pregnancy resulted from a casual liaison with the mother and the father has not been involved with the raising of the child, establishing family life with the child will be problematic.[262] Second, Article 8 rights are not absolute rights and therefore there may be circumstances which justify not involving a father with family life in decisions concerning adoption. Hedley J has referred to the need for compelling reasons to justify not informing a father of the adoption proceedings.[263] It would, therefore, be justifiable not to inform the father about the adoption proceedings if doing so would place the child or mother at risk of violence.[264]

More controversial will be cases where the argument for not informing the father of the adoption is to protect the privacy of the mother.[265] In *Z CC v R*[266] the mother of a newborn baby did not want her family to know of the pregnancy and birth. The guardian sought the guidance of the court over whether the baby's wider family members should be informed so that they could be assessed as suitable carers for the child. The wider family were found to have family life with the baby, but their rights could be interfered with in order to protect the mother's rights of privacy.[267] Generally in such cases the rights of the mother to anonymity have been seen to trump any rights of the grandparents to be considered as carers of the child. This was explained by Holman J in *Re R (a child) (adoption: disclosure)*:[268]

> There is, in my judgment, a strong social need, if it is lawful, to continue to enable some mothers, such as this mother, to make discreet, dignified and humane arrangements for the birth and subsequent adoption of their babies, without their families knowing anything about it, if the mother, for good reason, so wishes.[269]

However, it would be wrong to think that the privacy rights of the parents will always win out in such cases. In *Birmingham CC v S, R and A*[270] an unmarried couple's relationship had ended before the birth of the child. There were serious concerns over the mother's ability to care for the child, especially given her previous history of parenting. It was likely that the child would be removed from the parents before birth and the local authority was considering assessing both sets of grandparents as alternative carers. However, the father strongly objected, having initially agreed. He did not want his parents to know he had fathered a child. He was living with devout Muslim parents who did not know about his relationship with the mother or the birth of the child. He argued that his parents would not

---

[261] *Re H Re G (A Child) (Adoption Disclosure)* [2001] 1 FCR 726.

[262] *Re J (Adoption: Contacting Father)* [2003] 1 FLR 933.

[263] *Re C (Adoption: Disclosure to Father)* [2005] EWHC 3385.

[264] *Re H Re G (A Child) (Adoption Disclosure)* [2001] 1 FCR 726; *Re M (Adoption: Rights of Natural Father)* [2001] 1 FLR 745.

[265] *Re R (A Child) (Adoption: Disclosure)* [2001] 1 FCR 238.

[266] [2001] FL 8.

[267] In *Re J (Adoption: Contacting Father)* [2003] 1 FLR 933, Bennett J declared that it was lawful for the local authority not to inform a father or his family of the existence of a child or its impending adoption their relationship was causal and he had not seen the mother for some time.

[268] [2001] 1 FCR 238.

[269] [2001] 1 FCR 238, 241.

[270] [2006] EWHC 3065 (Fam).

accept the child even if they were told about him. However, the Court of Appeal held that the father's objections were not a proper assessment of whether his mother might wish to care for the child. They explained:

> Adoption is a last resort for any child. It is only to be considered when neither of the parents nor the wider family and friends can reasonably be considered as potential carers for the child. To deprive a significant member of the wider family of the information that the child exists who might otherwise be adopted, is a fundamental step that can only be justified on cogent and compelling grounds.[271]

Such grounds were not found in that case.

A rather different attitude can be detected in *Re C (A Child) (Adoption: Duty of Local Authority)*[272] where the Court of Appeal confirmed that there was nothing in the Adoption and Children Act 2002 which compelled a local authority to disclose the identity of a child to the extended family against the mother's wishes. Under the Act the question of whether the wider family should be informed was simply one of statutory interpretation and required an assessment of what is in the best interests of the child. One factor in that assessment is the child's interest in retaining her identity within the birth family. However, that is only one factor and indeed the Court of Appeal thought that section 1 did not privilege the birth family over adoptive parents, 'simply because they are the birth family', although placing a child with a birth family will 'often be in the best interests of the child'.[273]

What is striking about this approach is that it regards the informing of the wider family as an aspect of the question with whom a child be placed. In other words it does not regard the informing of the wider family as protecting the family's right to know; or indeed of their entitlement to be involved in the proceedings, even if their contribution is unlikely to influence the court's decision. As to any HRA claims it was held that the father had no family right with the child and so he could not claim a right to be informed of the birth. Interestingly it was held that the grandparents did have a right, but their interference with their rights was justified. Brief mention was made of the argument that the child may have a right to family life, but any interference in that could be justified if the adoption was approved under Article 8(2). Andrew Bainham has, with some justification, described the case as 'glaringly mother focused', adding: 'The decisive criterion governing involvement of the father or wider birth family on either side is effectively the mother's own decision.'[274] However, even if the court had considered the separate rights of the child, the father and the wider family members in a thorough human rights analysis, it may well have decided that the right of the mother to keep the pregnancy a private matter was of sufficient weight to outweigh the interests of the other parties.

The contrast between the two cases is striking and it is clear that there are a number of issues at play. First, there is the argument in *Birmingham CC v S, R and A*[275] that care within the family is less interventionist in family life than arranging care outside the family and so that possibility should be investigated properly to ensure that extra-familial

---

[271] Para 75.
[272] [2007] EWCA Civ 1206. For further discussion of this case see B Sloan, 'Adoption, Welfare and the Procreative One-Night Stand' [2008] *CLJ* 33.
[273] Para 18.
[274] A Bainham, 'Arguments About Parentage' (2008) 67 *CLJ* 322, 350.
[275] [2006] EWHC 3065 (Fam).

care is proportionate. Second, there is the argument in *Re C (A Child) (Adoption: Duty of Local Authority)*[276] over whether the father and wider family life had Article 8 rights in relation to the child, with the rather surprising conclusion that the father did not, but the grandparents did.[277] Both these arguments reflect an interesting issue about the definition of family life and whose family life we are talking about. If the focus is on the right of the child to family life and this is taken to include a right to be raised by her family, it could be argued that a court should be satisfied that wider family members are not appropriate as carers of a child. However, if a child's primary right to family life is to be cared for by her parents, or at least have contact with them, it is not hard to imagine cases where contact is more likely to flourish where the child is cared for outside the family. That might be so where, for example, the relationship between the child's grandparents and parents is bad. A third issue is that there may be practical limits on what a local authority can do if a mother puts a child up for adoption and refuses to give information about a father. In such a case the court should not seek to compel the mother to reveal information about the father.[278] Munby J has held that trying to do so would be 'deeply unattractive and unsettling'.[279]

The Grounds for Making an Adoption Order

In line with principles already established in this Chapter it is clear that an adoption order, with its termination of formal legal ties between the parents and the child, is a significant interference in their right to respect for family life. To justify such an order it is necessary to show that the order is proportionate and necessary. It is, therefore, much harder to justify an adoption order than to justify a supervision order or care order. In deciding whether or not an adoption order is in the welfare of the child, the court must consider the checklist in section 1(4) of the Adoption and Children Act 2002. This is as follows:

(a) the child's ascertainable wishes and feelings regarding the decisions (considered in the light of the child's age and understanding);
(b) the child's particular needs;
(c) the likely effect on the child (throughout his life) of having ceased to be a member of the original family and become an adopted person;
(d) the child's age, sex, background and any of the child's characteristics which the court or agency considers relevant;
(e) any harm (within the meaning of the Children Act 1989) which the child has suffered or is at risk of suffering;
(f) the relationship which the child has with relatives, and with any other person in relation to whom the court or agency considers the relationship to be relevant, including —
  (i) the likelihood of any such relationship continuing and the value to the child of its doing so;
  (ii) the ability and willingness of any of the child's relatives, or of any such person, to provide the child with a secure environment in which the child can develop, and otherwise to meet the child's needs;
  (iii) the wishes and feelings of the child's relatives, or of any such person, regarding the child.

---

[276] [2007] EWCA Civ 1206.
[277] In *Re L (Adoption: Contacting Natural Father)* [2008] 1 FLR 1079 it was held that if it was not known who the father was it should not be assumed that he did not have family life with the child.
[278] *Re L (Adoption: Contacting Natural Father)* [2008] 1 FLR 1079.
[279] Para 38.

In addition, to have been satisfied that the adoption order will promote the welfare of the child, the child's parents must consent to the adoption or their consent must be dispensed with. The court can dispense with the consent of a parent whose consent is required in two circumstances:

1. 'The parent or guardian cannot be found or is incapable of giving consent.'[280] This provision will be used in cases where the parent or guardian has disappeared or is unknown (for example if the baby was found abandoned outside a hospital and the mother has never been identified). It is also used if the parent is suffering a mental disability which means she lacks capacity to consent.
2. 'The welfare of the child requires the consent to be dispensed with.'[281]

The grounds for an adoption order raise a number of human rights issues.[282]

The Views of the Child

The child's own views about the proposed adoption are likely to be very important, if not crucial, to a determination of the child's welfare. At one time it was proposed that an adoption order could not be made in respect of a child over the age of 12 without his or her consent. This did not appear in the final Act. However, it is hard to imagine a case where a court will decide that an adoption, against the wishes of a teenager, will promote his or her welfare.[283] Nevertheless the fact that in theory a mature child could be adopted against their wishes indicates a potential lack of adequate respect for the child's autonomy rights, protected by Article 8. These are discussed further in chapter 6.

In *Re M (Adoption or Residence Order)*[284] the views of a 12 year old that she no longer wanted to be regarded as the sister of her siblings were decisive in ordering a residence order in favour of the applicants, rather than an adoption. The Court of Appeal was brave in doing this because the applicants had stated that they would not be able to care for the child if only granted a residence order and threatened that if they were denied an adoption order they would return the child to the local authority. In the face of strong evidence that it was in the interests of the child to live with the applicants, the Court of Appeal trusted that the applicants would not carry through with their threats. In addition to a residence order, it also made an order under section 91(14) of the CA preventing the birth mother making an application for an order under that Act without the leave of the court. This would provide some limited protection to the applicants from concerns that the birth mother would be constantly seeking to interfere with the way they were raising the child.

Proportionality

As we have seen, a state interference in the right to respect for private and family life is only justified if it is a proportionate response to the risks facing the child. A key human rights

---

[280] ACA 2002, s52(1)(a). See *Haringey v Mr and Mrs E* [2006] EWHC 1620 (Fam) for such a case.
[281] ACA 2002, s52(1)(b).
[282] S Choudhry, 'The Adoption and Children Act 2002, the Welfare Principle and the Human Rights Act 1998: A Missed Opportunity [2003] *Child and Family Law Quarterly* 119.
[283] The Adoption Agencies Regulations 2005 require the agency to counsel the child and ascertain his or her wishes and feelings and report on these to the adoption panel, if appropriate.
[284] [1998] 1 FLR 570.

issue in adoption law is whether the law is sufficient to ensure that an adoption order is only made where it is a proportionate response to a danger facing the child.

The ECtHR case law in this area is difficult to interpret. There is one line of cases which appears to suggest that only in the most exceptional cases will adoption be regarded as a necessary and proportionate response to the situation the child is facing. In *Johansen v Norway*,[285] considering the adoption of a child in care, it was held that

> the applicant [the mother] had been deprived of her parental rights and access in the context of a permanent placement of her daughter in a foster home with a view to adoption by the foster parents. These measures were particularly far-reaching in that they totally deprived the applicant of her family life with the child and were inconsistent with the aim of reuniting them. Such measures should only be applied in exceptional circumstances and could only be justified if they were motivated by an overriding requirement pertaining to the child's best interests.

To similar effect is *Görgülü v Germany*.[286] There a child had been placed for adoption just four days after his birth. The father was unaware of what had happened. When he did, he sought custody of his 18-month-old child who by this time was being cared for with foster carers. This was rejected by the German Court of Appeal on the basis that the child would suffer psychological damage if moved. The ECtHR found this to be a breach of Article 8.[287] Proportionality was key. Even accepting the concerns of psychological damage an intermediate position should have been considered of introducing the child to the father and gradually increasing the levels of contact.[288]

A reading of these cases might suggest that an ECHR perspective would regard adoption as a proportionate response only in the most extreme of cases. However, a far more pro-adoption approach can be found in *Söderbäck v Sweden*.[289] The child had been living perfectly happily with her mother and step-father for several years. The adoption was sought to 'regularise' the relationship between the step-father and child. It might be thought that this case could hardly be one where adoption was a last resort. The distinction with the approach in *Johansen* was justified in *Söderbäck* in this way:

> While it is true that the adoption in the present case, like the contested measures in the Johansen case, had the legal effect of totally depriving the applicant of family life with his daughter, the context differs significantly. It does not concern the severance of links between a mother and a child taken into public care but, rather, of links between a natural father and a child who had been in the care of her mother since she was born. Nor does it concern a parent who had had custody of the child or who in any other capacity had assumed the care of the child. Accordingly, in the Court's view, it is inappropriate in the present case to apply the approach employed in the Johansen judgment.[290]

Given the limited nature of the contact between the father and the child and the fact the adoption reflected the de facto situation, the court held that the adoption was within the margin of appreciation.

---

[285] (1997) 23 EHRR 33.
[286] [2004] 1 FCR 410.
[287] The Court seemed to assume the father had family life with the child. Presumably this was on the basis that he was in a committed relationship with the mother at the time of the conception.
[288] [2004] 1 FCR 410.
[289] [1999] 1 FLR 250.
[290] Para 31.

It seems what is crucial for the case is that the father had only a very limited relationship with his daughter. Although the adoption might affect his formal legal status it was not going to affect the day-to-day relationship he had with her. By contrast in cases where a child is to be removed from parents and placed for adoption that will clearly impact on the practical nature of their relationship.

Perhaps the most useful case is the following. In *Eski v Austria*[291] it was stressed that where an adoption takes place against the wishes of the father, if he has family life it will interfere in that right.[292] The ECtHR accepted that in two recent cases (*Söderbäck v Sweden*[293] and *Kuijper v the Netherlands*[294]) the adoption against the wishes of the father had been found not to have improperly infringed his rights. In those cases it was explained that the father had not had custody of the child and had only had limited contact. Further, the adoptions formalised and consolidated the de facto ties that existed.[295] An additional factor in *Kuijper* was that the teenage child supported the application. Adoption was said in *Eski* to be a 'far-reaching' measure.[296] The arguments in favour of the adoption in favour of the mother and her current partner were that the child had lived with the mother since the age of two and the father had not assisted in the upbringing of the child. His contacts with the child were said to be infrequent and limited. Indeed there had been no contact in recent years. Meanwhile the child had been living with the partner since the age of six. This was a case where the adoption was not going to set in motion the bonding of the adopter and child (as had been the case in *Keegan v Ireland*[297]) but rather was formalising ties that already existed (like *Söderbäck*[298]); also in *Eski* the nine year old supported the adoption. All these factors led the court to find that the adoption was compatible with the ECHR.

In the context of English law when considering an application for an adoption order the court must recall the alternative orders that it can make.[299] These include: (i) a residence order in favour of the applicants;[300] (ii) a special guardianship; (iii) no order. The key issue in many contested adoptions is whether adoption is a preferable alternative to a residence order in favour of the would-be adopters, or a special guardianship in their favour. All these options would lead to the child living with the applicants, but, unlike adoption, the birth parents would not lose their parental status. Also, significantly, the formal links between the child and his or her wider family (for example siblings, grandparents) would remain. The court will have to weigh up the benefits of retaining the broad links with the birth family with the benefits of security offered by an adoption. Masson has argued that it will be particularly difficult to justify making an adoption order, rather than a residence order, if a relative is seeking to adopt the child.[301] Holman J in *Re H (Adoption Non-Patrial)*[302]

---

[291] *Eski v Austria* [2007] ECHR 80, para 34.
[292] *Ibid.*
[293] [1999] 1 FLR 250.
[294] *Kuijper v the Netherlands* (Application No 64848/01).
[295] *Eski v Austria* [2007] ECHR 80, para 36.
[296] *Ibid*, para 38.
[297] (1994) 18 EHRR 342.
[298] Para 39.
[299] *Re P (Children)(Adoption: Parental Consent)* [2008] 2 FCR 185.
[300] The ACA 2002 has amended s12 of the CA so that a residence order can last until the child's 18th birthday.
[301] J Masson, 'Paternalism, Participation and Placation: Young People's Experiences of Representation in Child Protection Proceedings in England and Wales' in J Dewar and S Parker (eds), *Family Law: Processes, Practices, Pressures* (Oxford, Hart, 2003) 32.
[302] [1996] 1 FLR 717, 726.

summarised the benefits of an adoption order over a residence order in favour of the would-be adopters:

> It is well recognised that adoption confers an extra and psychologically and emotionally important sense of 'belonging'. There is real benefit to the parent/child relationship in knowing that each is legally bound to the other and in knowing that the relationship thus created is as secure and free from interference by outsiders as the relationship between natural parents and their child.

In *Re B (A Child) (Sole Adoption by Unmarried Father)*[303] the Court of Appeal declined to make an adoption on the basis that the present fostering arrangements were working well and there was no particular benefit to be gained by an adoption.

The English courts have used the language of proportionality when considering adoption orders. A good example *is Re B (Adoption Order)*,[304] which involved an application by the local authority for an adoption order despite the agreement of all the other parties involved that a fostering arrangement would be appropriate. Thorpe LJ stated:

> It does not seem that the judge considered whether the interference with the father's right to family life which would result from the making of an adoption order was necessary and proportionate in accordance with Art 8(2) of the Convention. It seems to me in this case that it is very hard indeed to demonstrate the necessary proportionality given the completely satisfactory arrangement that was open for judicial approval in the confirmation of the status quo for J, just as it had been confirmed for the older children of the family.[305]

By contrast, controversially, the House of Lords approved of an adoption by a father of his child, with the mother's consent. The sole purpose of the adoption was to terminate the mother's legal status. She wished to have nothing to do with the child and the father felt insecure while the mother retained parental responsibility. Hale LJ (as she then was) in the Court of Appeal held:

> [I]t is difficult indeed to argue that there is a pressing social need to deprive A of all legal relationship with one half of her family of birth … she already has a full and secure legal and factual relationship with her father. If there is any need to give her more, it can be provided for in a package of orders along the lines discussed. In my view, it would be a disproportionate response to her current needs to turn her from the child of two legal parents, with two legal families, into the child of only one parent, with only one legal family. Section 15(3) has to be given effect in such a way as to avoid that result.[306]

The House of Lords disagreed. Interestingly Lord Nicholls thought that only the child's rights needed to be considered as given that the mother had consented to the adoption, the issue of her rights did not fall for consideration.

> The court considers the advantages and disadvantages adoption would have for the child. The court decides that an adoption order is best for the child in all the circumstances. I do not see how an adoption order made in this way can infringe the child's rights under Article 8. Under Article 8 the adoption order must meet a pressing social need and be a proportionate response to that need: see, for example, *Silver v United Kingdom* (1983) 5 EHRR 347, 376–377, paragraph 97(c). Inherent in both these Convention concepts is a balancing exercise, weighing the advantages

---

[303] [2002] 1 FCR 150 (CA).
[304] [2001] 2 FLR 26 (CA).
[305] Para 20.
[306] Para 40.

and the disadvantages. But this balancing exercise, required by Article 8, does not differ in substance from the like balancing exercise undertaken by a court when deciding whether, in the conventional phraseology of English law, adoption would be in the best interests of the child. The like considerations fall to be taken into account. Although the phraseology is different, the criteria to be applied in deciding whether an adoption order is justified under Article 8(2) lead to the same result as the conventional tests applied by English law. Thus, unless the court misdirected itself in some material respect when balancing the competing factors, its conclusion that an adoption order is in the best interests of the child, even though this would exclude the mother from the child's life, identifies the pressing social need for adoption (the need to safeguard and promote the child's welfare) and represents the court's considered view on proportionality. That is the effect of the judge's decision in the present case. Article 8(2) does not call for more.[307]

This equating of the human rights approach and the welfare approach has been discussed in chapter 3. It is notable here that even a small amount of welfare renders the intervention in family life necessary and proportionate. That, with respect, is a very weak reading of these concepts.

Proportionality is an important issue when the court is having to choose between an adoption order and a special guardianship order.[308] In *Re S (Adoption Order or Special Guardianship*[309] it was held:

> The court will need to bear Article 8 of ECHR in mind, and to be satisfied that its order is a proportionate response to the problem, having regard to the interference with family life which is involved. In choosing between adoption and special guardianship, in most cases Article 8 is unlikely to add anything to the considerations contained in the respective welfare checklists. Under both statutes the welfare of the child is the court's paramount consideration, and the balancing exercise required by the statutes will be no different to that required by Article 8. However, in some cases, the fact that the welfare objective can be achieved with less disruption of existing family relationships can properly be regarded as helping to tip the balance.[310]

In *Re S (Adoption Order or Special Guardianship Order)*[311] Wall LJ in the Court of Appeal emphasised that once it is decided whether a child should be removed from parents and placed with alternative carers the courts must consider whether an adoption order or a special guardianship order is appropriate. In making that decision the human rights issues were significant. The court must ensure the order made was proportionate. As special guardianship was a less fundamental interference with the birth family's life, this would be preferred if there was nothing to choose between the two orders in terms of the child's welfare. Wall LJ did add that this Article 8 reasoning in most cases was unlikely to add anything to the factors a court would take into account when considering the welfare checklist. This is probably correct. Where the Article 8 reasoning will be particularly relevant is in cases which are finely balanced. If it has not been shown that the adoption order will promote the child's welfare to a noticeably greater extent than a special guardianship

---

[307] Para 31.
[308] A Hall, 'Special Guardianship and Permanency Planning: Unforeseen Consequences and Missed Opportunities' [2008] *Child and Family Law Quarterly* 359.
[309] [2007] EWCA Civ 54.
[310] Para 49.
[311] *Re S (Adoption Order or Special Guardianship Order)* [2007] EWCA Civ 54.

order would, then the proportionality arguments will tip the balance in favour of special guardianship.

These cases suggest that the courts are at least taking seriously the fact that the greater interference in family life constituted by an adoption order than other orders, means that more is required to justify an adoption order. There is, therefore, a need to show why a less interventionist order will not adequately protect the rights of all involved.

Dispensing with Consent

As already noted, the requirement of the consent of the parents to adoption can be dispensed with if that is required by the welfare of the child.[312] Prior to the 2002 Act, under the Adoption Act 1976 parents' objections to adoption could only be overridden if they were unreasonably withholding their consent to the adoption. One way of reading section 1 of the 2002 Act is that for adoption the welfare of the child is in effect the sole criterion and the new law offers no independent protection of the rights of the parents.[313] This has led to heavy criticism by some who fear that to permit the adoption of children against the wishes of parents simply on the basis that it would be better for the child rides roughshod over the importance attached to parental rights. Can any parent be particularly confident that it is impossible to find someone else who would be better at raising his or her child?[314] More significantly for the purposes of this book it can be claimed that an adoption law which was based solely on the welfare of the child is in danger of inadequately protecting the Article 8 rights of parents.

However, there are a number of ways in which, despite the wording of section 52(1)(b), the rights of parents could be taken into account. It should be noted that the section states that only if the welfare of the child requires dispensing with the consent of the parent can the court do that. This might suggest that, if it is shown that adoption is only slightly in the interests of the child, this will be insufficient to *require* the consent to be dispensed with. In *Re P (Placement Orders: Parental Consent)*[315] the Court of Appeal held that the word 'requires' carries a connotation of being imperative—that dispensing with the consent is not just reasonable or desirable but required in the interests of the child. A strong reading of the word 'requires' can also be justified by reference to the HRA. Given the emphasis in the ECtHR jurisprudence on the strong reasons required to make an adoption order, at least where the parents are currently in a relationship with the child, the court should give a strong interpretation. It should be added that if the child has lived with the would-be adopters and has developed a close relationship with them it is arguable that the would-be adopters and child have developed family life which is also protected under Article 8. Such an argument is likely to be strongest where the child has lived with the applicants for a considerable period of time.[316] In *Re P (Placement Orders: Parental Consent)*[317] the Court of

---

[312]   ACA, s52(1)(b).

[313]   Although at the adoption order stage the welfare test applies, at the placement stage the s31 threshold criteria will have to be satisfied. Therefore it will have to have been shown that the parenting of the child caused or risked the child significant harm before a child can be adopted against the parent's wishes.

[314]   C Barton, 'Adoption and Children Bill 2001' (2001) 30 *Family Law* 731.

[315]   [2008] EWCA Civ 535.

[316]   *Re B (A Child) (Adoption Order)* [2001] 2 FCR 89.

[317]   [2008] EWCA Civ 535.

Appeal emphasised that proportionality played a role in determining whether dispensing with parental consent was required:

> In assessing what is proportionate, the court has, of course, always to bear in mind that adoption without parental consent is an extreme—indeed the most extreme—interference with family life. Cogent justification must therefore exist if parental consent is to be dispensed with in accordance with s 52(1)(b) ... Section 52(1) is concerned with adoption—the making of either a placement order or an adoption order—and what therefore has to be shown is that the child's welfare 'requires' *adoption* as opposed to something short of adoption. A child's circumstances may 'require' statutory intervention, perhaps may even 'require' the indefinite or long-term removal of the child from the family and his or her placement with strangers, but that is not to say that the same circumstances will necessarily 'require' that the child be adopted.[318]

What, however, this approach does not directly reveal is whether the objections of the parents to adoption carry any weight which is independent of a welfare assessment. The issue is revealed in *Re R (Placement Order)*[319] where Sumner J dispensed with the consent of Muslim parents to adoption. They opposed adoption as being contrary to Muslim practice. The judge held that the children's welfare required adoption despite the objections of the parents. He explained:

> I have also considered whether the children's welfare requires such a drastic step as adoption for Muslim children of Muslim parents. The history I find demands nothing less if their essential needs are to be met.[320]

Although he does not say so explicitly it seems, therefore, that the religious objections of the parents did carry some weight, even though not enough to justify not making the adoption order.

The rights of the birth parent were discussed in *Kearns v France*[321] where a woman gave birth in France, wishing to do so anonymously. She had an interview for half a day and signed a document, indicating that she wished the child go into state care and requesting secrecy. She also consented to adoption. Six months later, after the child had been placed with prospective adopters, she sought to withdraw her consent to the adoption and sought the return of the child. It was held by the ECHR that there was no consensus among Member States over the period of reflection required or whether and when consent to adoption can be withdrawn. Given the competing interests and the diversity in practice, the French system was held to be compatible with the ECHR. The Court accepted that the relationship between the mother and child was within family life.[322] France had a two-month time limit for withdrawing consent. The welfare of the child was said to be paramount.[323] The Court accepted the government's arguments that child-welfare professionals believed that placing the child with a new family quickly was beneficial. Factors also relied upon were the woman's age (36);[324] the fact her mother accompanied her; and the lengthy

---

[318] Paras 124, 126.
[319] [2007] EWHC 3031 (Fam).
[320] Para 118.
[321] [2008] ECHR 35991/04.
[322] Para 72.
[323] Para 79.
[324] Although in *VS v Germany* No 4261/02, 22 May 2007 the consent of a minor was taken as valid by the German courts and this was upheld by the ECtHR.

interviews with social services.[325] This case suggests that a mother who is seeking to revoke consent to adoption several months after it has been given will struggle to prove that the ECHR requires that she be permitted to revoke her consent.

Open Adoption

Another aspect here is the issue of open adoption, that is adoption supported with a contact order. Where an open adoption is thought appropriate it is nevertheless permissible to make an adoption where there is no contact. In *Clark v UK*[326] a child was placed with adopters who were opposed to contact with the birth family, despite the professional opinion that open adoption would be desirable. The birth family made an application to the ECtHR. The case settled before hearing, suggesting that the government thought it likely they would lose.

In many cases where it is thought appropriate for there to be continuing contact between the parent and child, adoption will not be a proportionate response to the situation. However, even where an adoption order has been made, that will not necessarily end the child's right to family life with his or her birth family and so any termination of contact will need to be justified.

Interestingly, the courts have been reluctant to make a court order requiring contact between the child and the birth family.[327] The argument the courts have accepted is that if the adopters are happy for there to be contact there is no need for the court to make an order requiring it;[328] and if the adopters do not want there to be contact, it would be wrong to force them to do so.[329] This means that trust between the birth families and adopters is key. Section 46(6) of the 2002 Act now requires the court to consider, when making an adoption order, whether to make a contact order in respect of the child. It remains to be seen whether this will be interpreted as encouraging the courts to make contact orders. Under the old law what tended to happen was that agencies produced written agreements which clearly set out the kind of contact between the child and the birth family that was expected. These agreements are not, however, enforceable. If the adopted parents refuse to permit contact as expected it would be possible for the birth parents to apply for an Article 8 contact order. However, they will need the leave of the court before the court will hear their application. The court is likely to grant leave only where the maintenance of contact with the birth family is of such benefit to the child as to justify overriding the privacy of the adoptive family. Forcing contact against the wishes of the adopters is unlikely to benefit the child in the long run.[330] One of the few cases where the Court of Appeal held that leave should be granted was *Re T Minors (Adopted Children: Contact)*[331] where the adopters had failed to provide an annual report to the adopted children's adult half-sister. Notably this case, it was held, did not greatly interfere

---

[325]   Para 81.
[326]   *Clark v UK* Application No 23387/94.
[327]   *Re R (Adoption: Contact)* [2005] EWCA Civ 1128.
[328]   *Re T (Adoption: Contact)* [1995] 2 FLR 251.
[329]   *Ibid.*
[330]   *Down Lisburn Health and Social Services Trust v H* [2006] UKHL 36.
[331]   [1995] 2 FLR 792.

in the private and family life of the adoptive parents.[332] In *Re P (Children) (Adoption: Parental Consent)*[333] it was held to be of fundamental importance that two siblings keep in contact.[334] The Court of Appeal held that in such a case the court should order contact, rather than leaving it to be dealt with informally by the local authorities and adopters. But such a case is still rare. Contact orders made in favour of birth family members against adoptive parents will be 'extremely unusual'.[335]

The Position of Would-be Adopters

The ECtHR has consistently held that there is no 'right to adopt' a child.[336] However, in rejecting such a claim it is not clear what such a claimed right might look like. If the suggestion is that the state has an obligation to supply a child for adoption to any person who wishes to adopt, it is so preposterous that it is surprising that the court has taken the time to reject it. The claim may be that if it is in a child's best interests to be adopted by a person then a person has the right to adopt the child. Or perhaps that in selecting adopters the state must not improperly discriminate between applicants. These more realistic claims require more attention.

In *Fretté v France*[337] the ECtHR accepted that the allegation that the state had rejected an applicant for adoption based on his sexual orientation could amount to a claim that Article 8 in conjunction with Article 14 was involved. The Court did not explain why. It said that 'the right to respect for family life presupposes the existence of a family and does not safeguard the mere desire to found a family'.[338] Whether, therefore, the Court regarded this as a case which although not directly involving Article 8 involves issues close to Article 8, thereby rendering Article 8 relevant, or whether it was seen as a matter of private life is uncertain.[339] In that case, controversially, the Court held that the decision not to allow a gay or lesbian person to adopt was justifiable discrimination:

> The total lack of consensus as to the advisability of allowing a single homosexual to adopt a child means that States should be afforded a wide margin of appreciation and, according to the Court's case-law, it was not for the Court to take the place of the national authorities and take a categorical decision on such a delicate issue by ordaining a single solution.[340]

This is particularly controversial, given that Article 14 discrimination requires objective and reasonable justification.

What about the position of a person who has been selected as an adopter, but no adoption order has formally been made? In *Pini and Bertani v Romania*[341] couples had adoption

---

[332] Contrast *Re S (Contact: Application by Sibling)* [1998] 2 FLR 897.
[333] [2008] 2 FCR 185.
[334] See also *Re H (Leave to Apply for Residence Order)* [2008] EWCA Civ 503.
[335] *Re R (A Child) (Adoption: Contact)* [2007] 1 FCR 149.
[336] *Fretté v France* [2003] 2 FCR 39; *X v Belgium and the Netherlands*, No 6482/74.
[337] [2003] 2 FCR 39.
[338] *Fretté v France* [2003] 2 FCR 39, para 32.
[339] The partly dissenting judgments of Judges Bratza, Fuhrmann and Tulk saw the issue as clearly one of private life.
[340] *Fretté v France* [2003] 2 FCR 39, para 41.
[341] [2005] 2 FLR 596.

orders made by the Romanian courts, but these were later revoked. The would-be adopters were held to have Article 8 rights. The court explained:

> Admittedly, by guaranteeing the right to respect for family life, Article 8 presupposes the exis-
> tence of a family (see *Marckx* and *Abdulaziz, Cabales and Balkandali*), a requirement which does
> not seem to have been met in the instant case as the applicants did not live with their respective
> adopted daughters or have sufficiently close *de facto* ties with them, either before or after the adop-
> tion orders were made. However, this does not mean, in the Court's opinion, that all intended fam-
> ily life falls entirely outside the ambit of Article 8. In this connection, the Court has previously held
> that Article 8 may also extend to the potential relationship between a child born out of wedlock
> and his or her natural father (see *Nylund v Finland*), or apply to the relationship that arises from
> a lawful and genuine marriage, even if family life has not yet been fully established (see *Abdulaziz,
> Cabales and Balkandali*).[342]

Notably it would be too much to read into this that merely a person selected for adoption automatically has family life with the child. However, it is clear from Article 8 jurisprudence that family life may be established in two ways either by de facto family ties or formal legal ones. So a would-be adopter who had had a child placed with him or her for a notable length of time may be able to establish a close enough relationship to amount to family life. Of course it is a matter of debate how long that time would need to be. An alternative claim would be to argue that the status granted by a placement order in English law is sufficient to amount to a family tie.

Adoption and Discovering Biological Parenthood

Given the emphasis that the ECHR has placed on discovering genetic parenthood[343] one might have suspected that a strong right would be recognised for an adopted child to discover the circumstances of her birth. However, the ECtHR has not taken a strong line on this. The leading case is *Odievre v France*.[344] The Court found no difficulty in accepting that:

> Birth, and in particular the circumstances in which a child is born, forms part of a child's, and
> subsequently the adult's, private life guaranteed by Article 8 of the Convention.[345]

The Court went on to note that the claim here that an adopted person be allowed to find out information about their birth was a claim to a positive behaviour by the state, but that that could be required under Article 8. The Court regarded the case as involving a clash between the Article 8 rights of the parties:

> The expression 'everyone' in Article 8 of the Convention applies to both the child and the mother.
> On the one hand, people have a right to know their origins, that right being derived from a wide
> interpretation of the scope of the notion of private life. The child's vital interest in its personal
> development is also widely recognised in the general scheme of the Convention (see, among
> many other authorities, *Johansen v Norway*; *Mikulić*; and *Kutzner v Germany*). On the other hand,
> a woman's interest in remaining anonymous in order to protect her health by giving birth in

---

[342] *Ibid*, para 143.
[343] *Mikulić v Croatia*, No 53176/99, paras 54 and 64.
[344] [2003] 1 FCR 621.
[345] *Ibid*, para 29.

appropriate medical conditions cannot be denied. In the present case, the applicant's mother never went to see the baby at the clinic and appears to have greeted their separation with total indifference (see paragraph 12 above). Nor is it alleged that she subsequently expressed the least desire to meet her daughter. The Court's task is not to judge that conduct, but merely to take note of it. The two private interests with which the Court is confronted in the present case are not easily reconciled; moreover, they do not concern an adult and a child, but two adults, each endowed with her own free will.

In addition to that conflict of interest, the problem of anonymous births cannot be dealt with in isolation from the issue of the protection of third parties, essentially the adoptive parents, the father and the other members of the natural family. The Court notes in that connection that the applicant is now 38 years old, having been adopted at the age of four, and that non-consensual disclosure could entail substantial risks, not only for the mother herself, but also for the adoptive family which brought up the applicant, and her natural father and siblings, each of whom also has a right to respect for his or her private and family life.[346]

The Court found a degree of diversity in practice over disclosure of birth records in adoption cases and felt this was an area in which the states should have a margin of appreciation.

Perhaps the most interesting part of the Court's decision is its attempts to distinguish *Gaskin* and *Mikulic*. It explained:

The issue of access to information about one's origins and the identity of one's natural parents is not of the same nature as that of access to a case record concerning a child in care or to evidence of alleged paternity. The applicant in the present case is an adopted child who is trying to trace another person, her natural mother, by whom she was abandoned at birth and who has expressly requested that information about the birth remain confidential.[347]

It is not quite clear what point of difference the Court is seeking to draw here. Is it that the kind of information being sought is different? That seems unlikely. Evidence of one's paternity is no different from evidence of the identity of one's natural parents. So it must be the competing rights of the other party that are in issue. So in adoption where the birth mother has requested the information be kept secret there is a clash with her rights; that is not the same as where a child is seeking to establish paternity. As the court later emphasises, in this case there is the conflict between the interests of the mother and the applicant. Also there are the interests of the adoptive family and the wider interest claimed by the French government in avoiding abortions by allowing a child to be placed for adoption at birth and guaranteeing anonymity. Despite the fact that the Court did not find any other countries which had the same policy in this area as France, it held that the matter fell into the margin of appreciation.

An adopted person in England and Wales seeking to discover information about his or her birth family could seek access to the following:[348]

1. *Birth certificates.* The Registrar-General is required under section 79 of the Adoption and Children Act 2002 to keep records to enable adopted people to trace their original

---

[346] *Ibid*, para 44.
[347] Para 43.
[348] Disclosure of Adoption Information (Post Commencement Adoptions) Regulations 2005, SI 2005/888.

birth registration. This would enable a person to discover the details of their birth, including the name of their mother. There is no absolute right to obtain a copy of the birth certificate. This is demonstrated by *R v Registrar-General, ex p Smith*,[349] where the Court of Appeal held that the Registrar-General was entitled to restrict the access of Smith to his birth records. Smith was in prison in Broadmoor, having killed his cell-mate in the belief that he was killing his mother. It was held that he might use the knowledge of his birth mother to harm her and the court held that it was therefore proper for the registrar to deny him access.

2. *Information from adoption agencies.* When the Adoption and Children Bill was first introduced it sought to restrict access of adopted children to information about their birth. This was justified on the basis of data protection concerns and a need to protect the human rights of the birth parents. However, these proposals were highly controversial and it was felt by many groups involved that they paid insufficient attention to the rights of adopted people to know their genetic identity. As a result the government amended the Bill and the Act requires adoption agencies to provide details which would enable an adopted person to obtain their birth certificate. They will also be able to obtain information from the court which made the adoption order.[350] If the agency does not wish to disclose the information it can obtain a court order permitting non-disclosure.[351] If it is 'protected information', in that it concerns private information about other people, then the agency can fail to disclose it although they should also take reasonable steps to ascertain the views of the people involved.

3. *The Adoption Contact Register.* If birth families wish to contact adopted children, they can use the Adoption Contact Register. This is provided by the National Organisation for Counselling Adoptees and Parents (NORCAP); it facilitates contact between adopters and birth families. At 30 June 2001 just under 20,000 adoptees and 8,500 relatives had placed names on the register; 539 pairs of records were linked.[352]

These measures go some way towards recognising a person's rights to know about their genetic origins,[353] which has been held to be an important aspect of a person's right to private life, protected by Article 8 of the ECHR.[354] It should be noted that in fact adopted children who do seek information about their birth parents are particularly interested in finding out about their mothers.[355] It is also important to appreciate that even where contact is made, this does not usually lead to an ongoing relationship.[356]

---

[349] [1991] FCR 403.

[350] ACA 2002, s60(4).

[351] ACA 2002, s60(3).

[352] J Eekelaar, 'Contact and the Adoption Reform' in A Bainham, B Lindley, M Richards and L Trinder, *Children and Their Families* (Oxford, Hart, 2003) 255.

[353] Howe and Feast (2000).

[354] *MG v UK* [2002] 3 FCR 289.

[355] P Sachdev, *Adoption, Reunion and After* (Washington, Child Welfare, 1992), found that only 20 % of adopted children said they ever thought about their birth father.

[356] D Howe and J Feast, *Adoption, Search and Reunion* (London, The Children's Society, 2000), report a study that only 51 per cent of adopted children who had found their birth mother had continued the contact. However, 97 per cent of adopted people who had located their birth parents had no regrets about doing so.

Revocation of Adoption

The Court of Appeal has recently considered the issue of revocation of adoption in *W v Norfolk County Council*,[357] where several years after four children had been removed from the Websters it was discovered that the removal had probably been based on a misdiagnosis and had therefore been wrongful. The difficulty was that the children had now been placed with adopters and, it was presumed, had settled with them. The Court of Appeal followed an established line of authority that only in exceptional cases could an adoption be revoked. There was no fundamental flaw in the procedure in this case and, on the basis of the evidence presented, the court order or process could not be flawed. The court did consider whether the HRA required a re-examination of the issues, but Wall LJ concluded: 'In my judgment, the European authorities do not assist Mr and Mrs Webster.' Unfortunately, no explanation is offered for his conclusion. No attempt was made to ascertain whether or not Mr and Mrs Webster had any human rights in this case and whether or not there was a justification for their interference. Worse was the failure to consider the position of the children in this case. Did the children have Article 8 rights in relation to their birth family? If so, was there a sufficient justification to interference in their rights? In this case there is an argument that the children had rights under Article 8 in relation to Mr and Mrs Webster which had been established through the years they had lived together as a family. Once family life under Article 8 is established it seems that the right to respect for it is never lost (see, for example, *Johansen v Norway*). The children's rights had to be respected unless an interference could be justified in the name of either the adopter's rights or the children's own interests. It is submitted that at most this might justify not changing the residence of the child, but it does not justify there being no contact between the children and birth parents. Certainly it does not justify a failure to consider fully the children's current rights and welfare.[358]

Conclusion

The following observations are offered by way of conclusion. First, it is noticeable that the greatest impact of the HRA in the area of child protection has been in relation to procedural matters. Sonia Harris-Short argues:

> It is therefore evident that the courts are taking the 1998 Act extremely seriously in public law cases and, in particular, are imposing increasingly high standards on local authorities in terms of their decision-making processes. The substantive changes they are demanding in local authority practices are again to be welcomed—they can only work to the advantage of both the parent and the child.[359]

Indeed, the effect of the HRA on procedural issues is greater than it has been in relation to substantive issues. However, the question must be asked whether such procedural changes are of any benefit. Is the involvement of parents in decision making likely to improve the

---

[357] [2009] EWCA 59.
[358] J Herring, 'Revoking Adoptions' (2009) 159 *New Law Journal* 377.
[359] S Harris Short, 'Family law and the Human Rights Act 1998: Judicial Restraint or Revolution?' [2005] *Child and Family Law Quarterly* 329.

quality of the decisions or is it likely simply to increase the levels of bureaucracy and red tape? Perhaps these questions are impossible to answer. Or more importantly they do not really matter. The involvement of parents and wider family members in decision making is not necessarily a matter of improvement of the quality of decision making, but a recognition of the importance of the interests at stake and the requirements of justice. Even then, it must be accepted that it is easy to exaggerate the significance of human rights in this context.[360] As Masson *et al* observe:

> The introduction of human rights law has brought further scrutiny to child protection practices but has not resulted in a clear basis for balancing the rights of children to physical safety and of parents to respect for family life, interpreted in this context as involvement in all decisions about their children and the limitation of intervention to cases where it is essential. Human rights judges, recognising the vulnerability of children, especially babies, the huge responsibility child protection laws place on social workers and the wide variety of circumstances where protection may be required, have found it difficult to identify either minimum procedural standards or substantive tests which can distinguish legitimate and illegitimate intervention.[361]

Second, there has been a concern that the use of rights in the area of child protection will only weaken the protection provided for children. Such suggestions should be firmly rejected. As seen earlier the human rights analysis has placed upon local authorities the duty to protect children from harm. This can only improve protection. While the rights of parents in this area are protected, the ECtHR has persistently stated that the interests of the parents can justify an interference in the rights of the adult. Indeed the ECtHR has made it clear that the human rights of parents in this context should not be used in a way which harms children.[362]

Third, there is a concern that a focus on rights overlooks the fact that financial constraints play a major role in a local authority's decision making. The particular concern is that a focus on the rights of the individuals in the particular case may fail to adequately take into account the need for the local authority to use their finite resources for all those children who need local authority intervention. Indeed there are several cases where that is clearly a major issue for the courts. For example the interpretation of section 17 in *R (G) v Barnet London Borough Council,* [363] that the court could not compel a local authority to offer treatment services, but rather only assessment, reveals the reluctance of the courts to control how a care plan is implemented. Indeed in *R (G) v Barnet London Borough Council* the House of Lords said:[364]

> The financial resources of local authorities are finite. The scope for local authorities to increase the amount of their revenue is strictly limited. So, year by year they must decide what priority to give to the multifarious competing demands on their limited resources. They have to decide which needs are the most urgent and pressing. The more money they allocate for one purpose, the less they have to spend on another. In principle, this decision on priorities is entrusted to the local authorities themselves. In respect of decisions such as these council members are accountable to the local electorate.[365]

---

[360] F Kaganas, 'Child Protection, Gender and Rights' (n 1).
[361] J Masson, D McGovern, K Pick and M Winn Oakley, *Protecting Powers* (n 60) 54.
[362] *Johansen v Norway* (1997) 23 EHRR 33.
[363] [2003] UKHL 57.
[364] [2003] UKHL 57.
[365] At para 11.

It should not, however, be thought that this issue is in any sense unique to child protection. There are many areas of law where there is a tension between budgetary concerns and human rights issues. Yet it seems that the area of child protection is one where the lack of resources plays a major role in the ineffectiveness of child protection and can restrict the effectiveness of human rights arguments.[366] Earlier we discussed the extent to which resources may be relevant in determining whether in the context of Article 3 a local authority acted in a reasonable way when aware of a risk that a child was being abused. Lurking behind the issue of the extent to which care plans should be enforceable by courts is the issue of resources.[367] Recently increases in the fees for local authorities seeking to bring care proceedings have led to claims that local authorities are being deterred from issuing child protection litigation.[368] Further restrictions on the availability of legal aid for parents of children being taken into care has led to concerns about the quality and availability of legal advice for families in care proceedings.[369] That so often budgetary concerns are used to justify a failure to ensure adequate protection of some of our society's most vulnerable members should be a source of great shame.

---

[366] B Wilkinson, 'Child Protection: The Statutory Failure' [2009] *Family Law* 420.

[367] J Herring, 'The Human Rights of Children in Care' (n 146).

[368] F Kaganas, 'Child Protection, Gender and Rights. A judicial review challenge to the increase in fees failed: *R (Hillingdon London Borough Council) and Others v Lord Chancellor and Secretary of State for Communities and Local Government*' [2009] 1 FLR 39.

[369] J Mason, 'Controlling costs and maintaining services—the Reform of Legal Aid for Care Proceedings' [2008] *Child and Family Law Quarterly* 425; P Welbourne, 'Safeguarding children on the edge of care: policy for keeping children safe after the *Review of the Child Care Proceedings System, Care Matters* and the *Carter Review of Legal Aid*' [2008] *Child and Family Law Quarterly* 335.

9

Domestic Violence

The Extent of the Problem and the Recognition and Use of a Human Rights Discourse

The current definition of domestic violence used by the British government is:

> [A]ny incident of threatening behaviour, violence or abuse (psychological, physical, sexual, financial or emotional) between adults who are or have been intimate partners or family members, regardless of gender or sexuality.[1]

Violence directed against women by their intimate partners is, however, an epidemic of global proportions that has devastating physical, emotional, financial and social effects on women, children, families and communities around the world.[2] The World Health Organization's multi-country study on domestic violence[3] found that the lifetime prevalence of physical violence by an intimate partner ranged between 13 per cent and 61 per cent. At its most severe, intimate partner violence leads to death; studies of femicide from Australia, Canada, Israel, South Africa, and the United States of America reveal that their husbands or boyfriends killed 40 to 70 per cent of female murder victims.[4] In Europe, a recent report[5] funded by the European Commission revealed that across the 13 countries that had conducted national prevalence studies on violence against women, one-fifth to one-quarter of all women have experienced physical violence at least once during their adult lives, and more than one-tenth have suffered sexual violence involving the use of force. Figures for all forms of violence, including stalking, were as high as 45 per cent and secondary data analyses also supported an estimate that about 12 to 15 per cent of all women have been in a relationship of domestic abuse after the age of 16.

A great deal of research concerning the incidence of domestic violence in the UK has also been conducted which has, in turn, led to a significant governmental commitment to

---

[1] www.crimereduction.homeoffice.gov.uk/dv/dv01.htm. An adult is defined as any person aged 18 years or over. Family members are defined as mother, father, son, daughter, brother, sister, and grandparents, whether directly related, in-laws or step-family. This also includes issues of concern to black and minority ethnic (BME) communities such as so-called 'honour-based violence', female genital mutilation (FGM) and forced marriage.

[2] Population-based studies to document the scope and prevalence of intimate partner violence have been conducted in 71 countries around the world. See the UN Secretary General's in-depth study of all forms of violence against women, July 2006 at www.un.org/womenwatch/daw/vaw/SGstudyvaw.htm#more.

[3] www.who.int/gender/violence/who_multicountry_study/en/, which was implemented in Bangladesh, Brazil, Ethiopia, Japan, Namibia, Peru, Samoa, the former Serbia and Montenegro, Thailand and the United Republic of Tanzania.

[4] M Harway and J O'Neil (eds), *What Causes Men's Violence Against Women* (Thousand Oaks, Sage Publications, 1999) 93.

[5] M Martinez and M Schrottle, *Report on the State of European Research on the Prevalence of Interpersonal Violence and its Impact on Health and Human Rights*, Feb 2006 www.cahrv.uni-osnabrueck.de/reddot/Executive_summary_of_State_of_European_research.pdf.

the formulation of specific laws and policies to tackle the issue.[6] However, it is clear that domestic violence continues to be a problem within British society. Although domestic violence is chronically under-reported, research[7] estimates that it accounts for 16 per cent of all violent crime and that it will affect one in four women and one in six men in their lifetime. Further, 77 per cent of victims of domestic violence are women and domestic violence has more repeat victims than any other crime (on average there will have been 35 assaults before a victim calls the police). Other research has found that one incident of domestic violence is reported to the police every minute[8] and that on average, two women a week are killed by a current or former male partner and nearly half of all female murder victims are killed by a partner or ex-partner.[9] It is also apparent that the problem is not confined to adult women. Another recent survey found that 16 per cent of the teenage girls that were questioned (whose average age was 15) had been hit by their boyfriends. A further 15 per cent had been pushed and 6 per cent forced to have sex by their boyfriends.[10] Domestic violence can also be measured in terms of its costs to wider society. A recent Home Office study[11] estimated that the total annual costs of domestic violence to the criminal justice system, health services, social services, housing and civil legal aid amounted to £3.1 billion each year. The cost to the economy was found to be a further £2.7 billion.

The gathering of such evidence is still, however, a relatively recent phenomenon due to the fact that international recognition of the problem was only brought about due to the intensive grass-roots work and lobbying by the international women's movement. Integral to the recognition was therefore an acceptance of the fact that violence against women was global, systematic and rooted in power imbalances and structural inequalities between men and women. Furthermore, the identification of the link between violence against women and discrimination was key to the recognition that the issue was one of human rights. Thus, as the UN Secretary General has noted,[12] categorising domestic violence against women as a violation of human rights has a number of important consequences. It clarifies the binding obligations on states to prevent, eradicate and punish such violence and to be held accountable to them. Claims on the state in this respect thus 'move from the realm of discretion and become legal entitlements'[13]—addressing the issue as one of human rights therefore empowers women, 'positioning them not as passive recipients of discretionary benefits but as active rights holders'.[14] Human rights also provide a unifying set of norms that can be used to hold states accountable for compliance with their obligations, to monitor progress and to promote a consistent understanding of the issue. It can also facilitate the development of a more inclusive and integrated human rights discourse by taking into account gender perspectives and the wide variety of factors that shape and reinforce

---

[6] www.equalities.gov.uk/domestic_violence/archive_sept2004.htm#govt_actions.

[7] Crime in England and Wales 2006/2007 report, www.homeoffice.gov.uk/rds/crimeew0607.html.

[8] E Stanko, 'The Day to Count: A Snapshot of the Impact of Domestic Violence in the UK' (2000) 1 (2) *Criminal Justice*, available at www.domesticviolencedata.org/5_research/count/count.htm#police.

[9] C Flood-Page and J Taylor (eds), *Crime in England and Wales 2001/2002: Supplementary Volume* (London, Home Office, 2003) 12.

[10] NSPCC *Teen Abuse Survey of Great Britain* (NSPCC, London, 2005).

[11] S Walby, *The Cost of Domestic Violence* (Women and Equality Unit, London, 2004). See also S Brand and R Price, *The Economic and Social Costs of Crime*, Research Study 217 (Home Office, London, 2000).

[12] UN Secretary General, *In Depth Study of all Forms of Violence Against Women* July 2006 at www.un.org/womenwatch/daw/vaw/SGstudyvaw.htm#more 17-18.

[13] *Ibid*, 18, para 39.

[14] *Ibid*, 18, para 40.

experiences of discrimination and violence. The result is that a number of international[15] and regional[16] human rights instruments now exist which can be used to assert the rights of battered women against their home countries on the basis that they articulate a state's duty to protect fundamental human rights that are commonly violated in domestic violence cases. Those rights include the right to life, the right to physical and mental integrity, the right to equal protection of the laws and the right to be free from discrimination. It has been argued,[17] therefore, that there are three ways in which domestic violence can be understood as a human rights violation. First, as articulated by a number of international human rights instruments,[18] states are not only obligated to refrain from committing violations themselves, but are also responsible for otherwise 'private' acts if they fail to fulfil their duty to prevent and punish such acts. Consequently, when the state fails to ensure that its criminal and civil laws adequately protect the victims of domestic violence and consistently hold abusers accountable, or that its agents (such as police and prosecutors) implement the laws that protect victims of domestic violence, it has not acted with due diligence to prevent, investigate and punish violations of women's rights. This failure could also be seen as a form of sexual discrimination.[19]

Second, states are required under international law to provide all citizens with equal protection of the law. If a state fails to provide individuals who are harmed by an intimate partner with the same protections it provides to those harmed by strangers, it has failed in respect of this obligation. Thus, when law enforcement officers respond quickly to reports of stranger violence but fail to respond to reports of domestic violence and when judges impose lower sentences on those who assault strangers than those who assault their intimate partners, the victims of domestic violence have been denied equal protection.

Third, advocates and scholars increasingly recognise that domestic violence is a form of torture. Under international human rights law, torture is severe mental or physical pain or suffering that is intentionally inflicted either by a state actor or with the consent or acquiescence of a state actor for an unlawful purpose. As Coomaraswamy argues,[20] the dynamics of domestic violence closely resemble the defining elements of torture: '(a) it causes severe physical and or mental pain, it is (b) intentionally inflicted, (c) for specified purposes and (d) with some form of official involvement, whether active or passive'. The similarities between these violations are striking particularly because domestic violence and torture are

---

[15] The International Bill of Human Rights, comprising the Universal Declaration of Human Rights 1948, the International Covenant on Civil and Political Rights 1966 and the International Covenant on Economic, Social and Cultural Rights 1966, sets forth general human rights standards that victims of domestic violence may invoke against their state of citizenship if that state is a party to the above instruments. The same can be done under the Convention on the Elimination of All Forms of Discrimination Against Women 1979, together with its Optional Protocol of 2000, and under the Convention Against Torture and Other Cruel, Inhuman, or Degrading Treatment or Punishment 1984.

[16] The European Convention for the Protection of Human Rights and Fundamental Freedoms 1950, the American Convention on Human Rights 1969, together with the Inter-American Convention on the Prevention, Punishment and Eradication of Violence Against Women 1994 and the African Charter on Human and Peoples' Rights 1981 are the major regional human rights documents that may be invoked by victims of domestic violence.

[17] R Coomaraswamy, 'Combating Domestic Violence: Obligations of the State' (2000) 6 *Innocenti Digest* 11.

[18] The Committee on the Elimination of Discrimination Against Women in General Recommendation 19. This responsibility is reflected, as well, in the Declaration on the Elimination of Violence against Women and the Vienna Declaration and Programme of Action from the 1993 World Conference on Human Rights.

[19] M Dempsey, 'Toward a Feminist State: What Does "Effective" Prosecution of Domestic Violence Mean?' (2007) 70(6) *MLR* 908–35.

[20] R Coomaraswamy, 'Combating Violence' (n 17).

often perpetrated for the same unlawful purpose, namely, to establish and maintain power and control over another.

Unfortunately, the articulation and development of domestic violence as a human rights issue at the international level has not been replicated within the domestic legal system despite the existence of the ECHR and its incorporation via the HRA. As the authors have noted elsewhere,[21] what is particularly striking is the total lack of reference to human rights when discussing the issue by both the executive and the judiciary. For example, the National Action Plan on Domestic Violence[22] published by the Home Office and the most recent guidelines on sentencing in domestic violence cases[23] make no reference to human rights at all. Similarly, court decisions on domestic violence have paid little or no attention as to how the HRA affects the issues raised.[24] The reluctance to use rights in working against domestic violence is, perhaps, understandable. Traditionally, rights have been used to restrict legal intervention in the area of domestic violence. The right of privacy has been interpreted to mean the law should be reluctant to intervene in a 'domestic dispute'; the right of autonomy has been used to justify the view that if a victim does not want a prosecution then her wishes should be respected; and the importance of property rights means that only in the most exceptional of cases is it said to be justifiable to remove an abuser from his home. Further, a report into prosecution of domestic violence has stated that in court cases human rights arguments are usually made by respondents or defendants.[25] However, it is clear that not only can this use of the human rights discourse, in most cases, be challenged by the structure of the provisions of the human rights instruments,[26] it can also be used as a powerful legal tool to combat domestic violence and ensure that national states are complying with their obligations towards the victims of domestic violence. In addition, it is now widely accepted by scholars, advocates and practitioners that human rights law does, in fact, apply to 'private' conduct such as domestic violence. It should also be added that viewing the issue as one of human rights does not preclude other approaches to preventing and understanding the nature of domestic violence such as those found in the spheres of education, health, and criminal justice. Rather the use of human rights should be viewed as one of the many important tools that can be used towards its elimination.

There are three ways in which this is possible at the domestic level. First, under the HRA public authorities are required to protect victims of violence.[27] This means that the government, police, prosecution authorities and courts are required to take positive

---

[21] S Choudhry and J Herring, 'Righting Domestic Violence' (2006) 20 (1) *International Journal of Law, Policy and the Family* 95 and S Choudhry and J Herring, 'Domestic Violence and the Human Rights Act 1998' [2006] 4 *PL* 752.

[22] www.crimereduction.homeoffice.gov.uk/domesticviolence/domesticviolence51.htm (Home Office, March 2005).

[23] www.sentencing-guidelines.gov.uk/docs/domestic_violence.pdf (Sentencing Guidelines Council, December 2006).

[24] Only in relation to the committal proceedings that will concern Art 6 rights of the defendant. See *Practice Direction: Committal Applications*, which is intended to ensure that committal proceedings are conducted in a manner that is compliant with Convention rights, *Mubarak v Mubarak* [2001] 1 FCR 193 at 203 and 207 (CA); *DPP v Tweddell* [2001] EWCA 188 (Admin) and *Clibbery v Allan* [2002] EWCA 45 (Civ).

[25] Her Majesty's Inspectorate of Constabulary and Crown Prosecution Service Inspectorate (HMIC/CPS) *A Joint Inspection of the Investigation and Prosecution of Cases Involving Domestic Violence* (London, 2004) para 7.20.

[26] In the sense that Art 3 is an absolute right and Art 8, although qualified, allows for the rights of the victim to take priority: S Choudhry and J Herring, 'Righting Domestic Violence' and 'Domestic Violence and the HRA' (n 21).

[27] *Islam (AP) v Secretary of State for the Home Department* [1999] 2 All ER 545.

steps to protect victims of violence. Rights in the domestic violence context should not be seen as restraining government activity, but rather compelling it. Second, that where the court must balance the property and privacy interests of the abuser and the right to protection of the victim, the HRA should be used to require the courts to place most weight on the interests of the victim. Third, the HRA requires particular attention to be paid to the interests of children. Growing evidence of the harmful impact of domestic violence on children's welfare can be used to necessitate state intervention in order to protect children.

Current Responses and Issues Concerning Domestic Violence in the UK

The current way of ensuring that victims of domestic violence are adequately protected at the domestic level is via the availability of criminal proceedings brought by the state[28] or civil proceedings brought by the victim. However, despite the fact that under UK criminal law there are a variety of offences that exist to cover domestic violence, at least where it results in physical injury, research has demonstrated that the criminal justice system is not complying with its obligations towards the victims of domestic violence. The difficulty lies, in particular, with the police and prosecution response to such cases. A recent report by Her Majesty's Inspectorate of Constabulary and the Crown Prosecution Service Inspectorate admitted:[29]

> Until relatively recently, for example, dominant police culture depicted violence in the home as 'just another domestic'—a nuisance call to familiar addresses that rarely resulted in a satisfactory policing outcome. To the service's credit, tremendous efforts have been made in the last five years or so to overturn this stereotype and ensure that domestic violence is treated as a serious incident, requiring a high standard of professional investigation. The CPS too has raised the profile of domestic violence, issuing revised policy and guidance and setting up a network of Area domestic violence coordinators. But all too often, policies and rhetoric are not matched on the ground by effective responses and solid investigative practice.

Further, although the figure for successful prosecutions has risen from 46 per cent in 2003 to 67 per cent overall (of charges resulting in convictions), and 70 per cent in some areas with specialist domestic violence courts[30] the increase in successful prosecutions represents only an increase in the percentage of charges resulting in convictions. Thus, as the Home Office Select Committee notes, 'without linking this to data on incidence, arrests, charges or cautions, which are an integral part of the picture, the increase in successful prosecutions does not tell us much about the criminal justice response to domestic violence.'[31] What we do know, however, is that in areas in which the attrition process has been tracked, the overall conviction

---

[28]   Under the Offences Against the Persons Act 1861 and the Protection from Harassment Act 1997.

[29]   HMIC/CPSI, *A Joint Inspection* (n 25) 6.

[30]   House of Commons, 'Domestic Violence, Forced Marriage and "Honour" Based Violence', Sixth Report of Session 2007–08 (1) HC 263-I (House of Commons, London, 13 June 2008) para 265 (presentation by J Dunworth of the Home Office Domestic Violence Unit, 15 January 2008, to the Home Affairs Committee). These specialist courts were first established in 2005 and are intended to enable domestic violence cases to be fast-tracked, and to be heard by specially trained magistrates, with support for victims from specialist staff, including Independent Domestic Violence Advisers and Multi-Agency Risk Assessment Conferences.

[31]   House of Commons, 'Domestic Violence, Forced Marriage and "Honour" Based Violence' (n 30) para 266.

rate for domestic violence, the percentage of incidents reported to police which result in a "conviction, is extremely low at around 5 per cent and is comparable to the conviction rate for rape, which is around 5.7 per cent.[32] There is also evidence that prosecution authorities are reluctant to take such cases to court unless there is a very high chance of success[33] and that similar attitudes exist within the police force. Research[34] across three police districts in the UK found that of the 869 domestic violence incidents recorded by the police only a third were deemed to have a power of arrest attached. Of the incidents with a power of arrest 76 per cent led to arrest and 27 per cent of these incidents led to prosecution; 14 per cent were convicted and of these only four men were given custodial sentences. A number of other issues were identified: the police and criminal justice agencies underestimated their role in increasing attrition and overestimated the withdrawal from the criminal justice system of those who were victimised; the criminal justice agencies did not always pursue cases and did not provide those who were victimised with the support they needed to proceed. At court, contact between children and alleged offenders was likely to lead to more lenient outcomes and further, court outcomes did not stop chronic offenders from continuing their violence and harassment.

A victim of domestic violence may also choose to bring civil proceedings under the Family Law Act 1996 (FLA 1996) or the Protection from Harassment Act 1997. However, the FLA 1996 provides a complex set of provisions which mean that the criteria for granting orders, and the range of orders available, depend upon whether the applicant is married to the respondent, or whether the applicant and/or respondent has a property interest in the home in question. It is not possible here to provide a complete analysis of the FLA 1996 and its interpretation,[35] but it is notable that the courts have described the making of an occupation order, removing the respondent from his home, as 'draconian' and requiring 'exceptional circumstances' in order to justify it.[36]

Finally, the impact of domestic violence on any children of the family has become an issue of serious concern. Research has demonstrated that children can experience domestic violence not only as direct victims but also as witnesses. Thirty per cent of domestic violence starts in pregnancy[37] and between four and nine women in every hundred are abused during their pregnancy and/or after the birth.[38] At least 750,000 children a year witness

---

[32] In areas in which the attrition process has been tracked, eg in the Northumbria Police Force area, where, out of a total of 2,402 domestic violence incidents, perpetrators were arrested, charged and convicted in only 120 incidents (5 per cent). M Hester and N Westmarland, 'Domestic Violence Perpetrators' (2007) 66 *Criminal Justice Matters* 34–6.

[33] N Cahn, 'Innovative Approaches to the Prosecution of Domestic Violence Crimes: An Overview' in E Buzawa and C Buzawa (eds), *Domestic Violence: The Changing Criminal Justice Response* (Westport, CT, Auburn House, 1992).

[34] M Hester, J Hanmer, S Coulson, M Morahan and A Razak, *Domestic Violence: Making it Through the Criminal Justice System* (University of Sunderland and Northern Rock Foundation, 2003). Available at www.nr-foundation.org.uk; M Hester 'Making it Through the Criminal Justice System and Domestic Violence' (2006) 5(1) *Social Policy and Society* 79–90.

[35] However, see also S Choudhry and J Herring, 'Domestic Violence and the HRA' (n 21).

[36] Eg *Chalmers v Johns* [1999] 2 FCR 110.

[37] G Lewis, J Drife *et al*, *Why Mothers Die: Report From the Confidential Enquiries into Maternal Deaths in the UK 1997–99* (2001) commissioned by the Department of Health from RCOG and NICE (London, RCOG Press, 2001); G Lewis and J Drife, *Why Mothers Die 2000–2002: Report on confidential enquiries into maternal deaths in the United Kingdom* (CEMACH, 2005); M McWilliams and J McKiernan, *Bringing It Out into the Open: Domestic Violence in Northern Ireland* (London, HMSO, 1993).

[38] A Taft, 'Violence Against Women in Pregnancy and After Childbirth: Current Knowledge and Issues in Healthcare Responses' (2002) *Australian Domestic and Family Violence Clearinghouse*, Issues Paper 6. Available from: www.austdvclearinghouse.unsw.edu.au/PDF per cent20files/Issuespaper6.pdf.

domestic violence[39] and in London 30 per cent of domestic violence murders are witnessed by children.[40] The effects are serious; children who live with domestic violence are at increased risk of behavioural problems, emotional trauma, and mental health difficulties in adult life.[41] Nearly three quarters of children deemed to be 'at risk' live in households where domestic violence occurs and 52 per cent of child protection cases involve domestic violence.[42] However, despite this, as the Home Office Select Committee[43] noted in its recent report on the issue, under-18s are still excluded from the government's definition of domestic violence, which refers to 'any incident of threatening behaviour, violence or abuse (psychological, physical, sexual, financial or emotional) between adults, *aged 18 and over*'. Furthermore, post-separation contact between children and the abusive parent has also become a crucial area in the campaign to eradicate further violence. A study by Women's Aid in 2004 found that 29 children in 13 families were killed between 1994 and 2004 as a result of contact arrangements in England and Wales.[44] Moreover, despite evidence from court files, which indicates that nearly 25 per cent of private law contact cases involve allegations of domestic violence,[45] of 28,641 applications for contact in the Family Courts, only 58 resulted in a non-contact order, and more recent figures show a further decrease.[46] This Chapter will therefore provide a detailed analysis of the impact of the ECHR and the HRA on these issues and the domestic provisions that will be most affected.

The Impact of the European Convention on Human Rights and the Human Rights Act 1998—the Right to Protection from Violence

Article 2

Article 2 of the ECHR provides that:

> Everyone's right to life shall be protected by law. No one shall be deprived of his life intentionally save in the execution of a sentence of a court following his conviction of a crime for which this penalty is provided by law.

---

[39] Department of Health, *Secure Futures for Women: Making a Difference* (London, Department of Health, 2002)

[40] *Findings from the Multi-Agency Domestic Violence Murder Reviews in London* (London, Metropolitan Police, 2003) 10.

[41] J Kolbo, EH Blakely and D Engleman, 'Children Who Witness Domestic Violence: A Review of Empirical Literature' (1996) 11 (2) *Journal of Interpersonal Violence* 281–93; R Morley and A Mullender, '*Domestic Violence and Children: What We Know From Research*' in A Mullender and R Morley, *Children Living With Domestic Violence: Putting Men's Abuse of Women on the Childcare Agenda* (London, Whiting and Birch, 1994); M Hester, C Pearson and N Harwin, *Making an Impact: Children and Domestic Violence: A Reader* (London, Jessica Kingsley, 2000, new edn 2007).

[42] DOH, *Secure Futures for Women* (n 39); E Farmer and M Owen, *Child Protection Practice: Private Risks and Public Remedies* (London, HMSO, 1995).

[43] House of Commons, 'Domestic Violence, Forced Marriage and "Honour" Based Violence' (n 30) para 51.

[44] H Saunders, *Twenty-Nine Child Homicides: Lessons Still to be Learnt on Domestic Violence and Child Protection* (Bristol, Women's Aid Federation of England, 2004).

[45] C Smart *et al*, *Residence and Contact Dispute in Court* (University of Leeds, Centre for Research on Family, Kinship and Childhood, 2003).

[46] House of Commons, 'Domestic Violence, Forced Marriage and "Honour" Based Violence' (n 30) para 288, citing a 2005 report by the Judicial Statistics Department quoted in evidence from the Men's Advice Line.

Deprivation of life shall not be regarded as inflicted in contravention of this Article when it results from the use of force which is no more than absolutely necessary:

(a) in defence of any person from unlawful violence;
(b) in order to effect a lawful arrest or to prevent escape of a person lawfully detained;
(c) in action lawfully taken for the purpose of quelling a riot or insurrection.

Article 2 is therefore a 'non-derogable' right: it may not be denied even in time of war or other public emergency threatening the life of the nation.[47] However, it is not entirely absolute, as its terms not only preserve the death penalty[48] but also permit the use of force. It is therefore regarded as one of the most important rights in the Convention:

> Article 2 ranks as one of the most fundamental provisions in the Convention—indeed one which, in peacetime, admits of non-derogation under Article 15. Together with Article 3 of the Convention [the prohibition of torture], it also enshrines one of the basic values of the democratic societies making up the Council of Europe.[49]

As a result of this the ECtHR has said that its provisions must be strictly construed.[50] Article 2 contains two fundamental elements which are reflected in its two paragraphs: a general obligation to protect the right to life 'by law', and a prohibition of deprivation of life, delimited by a list of exceptions. Although this is similar to the structure of Articles 8 to 11 of the Convention there are some differences.[51] First, additional weight is given to the right by virtue of the fact that the right itself must be 'protected by law' as opposed to being merely 'provided for'. Second, while states are not generally required to incorporate the Convention into their domestic law, as far as the right to life is concerned, they must still at the very minimum have laws in place which protect that right to an extent and in a manner that substantively reflect the Convention standards of Article 2.[52] The concept of 'law' as required by the Convention in turn means that the relevant rules must be accessible, and reasonably precise and foreseeable in their application.[53] Third, as far as the second paragraph is concerned, Article 2 allows for exceptions to the right to life only when this is 'absolutely necessary' for one of the aims set out in sub-paragraphs (2) (a)–(c) as opposed to, under Articles 8–11, being simply 'necessary in a democratic society' for the 'legitimate aims' listed in them. Finally, the Court has held that Article 2 imposes a 'positive obligation' on states to investigate deaths that may have occurred in violation of this Article.[54]

The Duty to Investigate Deaths

Article 2 imposes on the state both negative obligations not to take life intentionally, and positive obligations to protect life. The way in which the negative duty is to be fulfilled is not specified but it is presumed that, at the very minimum, the intentional killing of

---

[47] Although 'deaths resulting from lawful acts of war' do not constitute violations of the right to life, see Art 15(2).

[48] Despite this the HRA has given effect to Arts 1 and 2 of Protocol No 6 to the Convention which provide for the complete abolition of the death penalty except in respect of acts committed in time of war or 'imminent threat of war'.

[49] *McCann and others v the United Kingdom* [1995] ECHR 31 para 147, with reference to *Soering v the United Kingdom* (1989) 98 ILR 270 para 88.

[50] *McCann* (n 49) para 147.

[51] D Korff, 'The Right to Life—A Guide to the Implementation of Article 2 of the ECHR', *Human Rights Handbook No 8* (Strasbourg, Council of Europe, 2006), at 7.

[52] Cf the discussion of domestic law in the *McCann* (n 49) paras 151–5.

[53] *Sunday Times v the United Kingdom (I)* (1979) 2 EHRR 245 para 49.

[54] *McCann* (n 49) para 161.

another ought to be criminalised.[55] The positive duty to protect life has also been interpreted to include a duty to investigate unnatural deaths, including but not confined to deaths in which state agents may be implicated.[56] The duty to institute an effective, independent investigation into a death which engages Article 2 may be discharged through a number of forms of inquiry[57] and the criteria for an Article 2-compliant inquiry have been set out by the ECtHR in *Jordan v UK*.[58] They require that:

— the inquiry must be on the initiative of the state;
— it must be independent;[59]
— it must be capable of leading to a determination of whether any force used was justified, and to the identification and punishment of those responsible for the death;
— it must be prompt and proceed with reasonable expedition;
— it must be open to public scrutiny to a degree sufficient to ensure accountability;
— the next-of-kin of the deceased must be involved in the inquiry to the extent necessary to safeguard their legitimate interests.

These criteria have been adopted and applied at the domestic level. In *R (on the application of Amin (Imtiaz)) v Secretary of State for the Home Department*[60] where the deceased had been beaten to death by his cell mate in a young offender institution, the House of Lords made it clear that these criteria must be applied in all cases where the right to life was engaged, including cases where a death was alleged to have resulted from negligence on the part of agents of the state, as well as cases where a death had resulted from the use of force. Thus, wherever either individual or systemic failings of public bodies may have resulted in loss of life, the Article 2 duty to investigate the death, in accordance with the criteria set out in *Jordan*,[61] has been held to apply.[62] Further, the duty to ensure that an effective investigation has taken place will also apply to intentional or non-intentional killing by a non-state agent. In *R (on the application of Challender) v Legal Services Commission*[63] the court relied on comments made by the ECtHR in *Menson v the United Kingdom*[64] regarding the need to carry out an effective investigation in cases where there had been no state involvement, to hold that the obligation would be engaged with regard to the unlawful killing of the deceased who had been found dead in a

---

[55] D Feldman, *Civil Liberties and Human Rights* 2nd edn (Oxford, Oxford University Press, 2002) 181.

[56] *McCann v UK* (n 49); *Ergi v Turkey* (2001) 32 EHRR 18; *Yasa v Turkey* (1999) 28 EHRR 408.

[57] In the UK, it may be discharged through the inquest, through investigations by bodies such as the Independent Police Complaints Commission (IPCC), as well as through prosecutions which may follow from such inquiries.

[58] *Jordan v UK* (2003) 37 EHRR 2 paras 105–9.

[59] Both *Gulec v Turkey* (1999) 28 EHRR 121 and *Ogur v Turkey* (2001) 31 EHRR 40 show that Art 2 requires an investigation that is independent of those implicated in the events under scrutiny. *Ergi* (n 56) states that the investigation must be independent, both institutionally and in practice.

[60] *R (on the application of Amin (Imtiaz)) v Secretary of State for the Home Department* [2003] UKHL 51.

[61] *Jordan* (n 58).

[62] See *R (on the application of Middleton) v HM Coroner for Western Somerset* [2004] UKHL 10; *R (Khan) v Secretary of State for Health* [2003] EWCA 1129 (Civ); *The Commissioner of Police for the Metropolis v Hurst* [2005] EWCA 890 (Civ).

[63] *R (on the application of Challender) v Legal Services Commission* [2004] EWHC 925 (Admin).

[64] *Menson v the United Kingdom* Application No 47916/99 (2003) 37 EHRR 220 para 50: the Court stated that the duty may arise 'even where the state is not directly involved in the death (whether through the acts of agents of the state or because the deceased was in the care of the state) … the state's obligation to ensure the effective implementation of domestic laws protecting the right to life can be a sufficient basis for the need to carry out an effective investigation even in cases with no state involvement in the death'.

friend's flat. This duty has been further strengthened,[65] in the context of victims of domestic violence, by statutory provision for the establishment of 'domestic homicide reviews'[66] in relation to the death of a person aged 16 or over which may have resulted from violence, abuse or neglect by a person to whom he was related or with whom he was or had been in an intimate personal relationship[67] with a view to identifying the lessons to be learnt from the death. The decision to reject the inclusion of child deaths[68] and suicides within the context of domestic violence from the ambit of the provisions, however, is unclear, particularly as this omission may only serve to potentially strengthen a claim under this limb of Article 2.

A Positive Obligation to Protect Individuals from Violence by Others

There have been a number of cases in which relatives of people killed by other private persons, and people nearly killed by other private persons themselves, claimed that the state ought to have protected the victims, but failed to do so. The ECtHR first recognised this aspect of Article 2 in *LCB v United Kingdom*[69] and significantly extended the principle in the subsequent case of *Osman v the United Kingdom*,[70] which concerned the obsessive former teacher of a 15-year-old boy, who ultimately wounded his pupil and killed the boy's father. The teacher had a history of such infatuations and there had been a series of increasingly serious incidents involving the teacher, who was then suspended following a psychiatric evaluation. The applicants demonstrated that in the months before the fatal attack the police had been given information that should have made clear the extent of the danger of assault. Despite such information being made available to the police, the suspect's home had not been searched, nor had any special measures been put in place to protect the Osman family. The case therefore concerned the question of whether the authorities could and should have done more to protect the victims and following the dismissal of civil proceedings for negligence against the police on public policy grounds.[71] In confirming the Commission's earlier opinion that a breach of Article 2 had not occurred, the ECtHR (in a Grand Chamber judgment) found that the applicants had failed to show that the authorities knew or ought to have known that the lives of the Osman family were at real and immediate risk from the teacher, or had enough evidence to either charge him or have him committed to a psychiatric hospital. They could therefore not be criticised for relying on the presumption of innocence, or for failing to use powers of arrest and detention where there was such insufficient evidence. The Court also stressed:

> the difficulties involved in policing modern societies, the unpredictability of human conduct and the operational choices which must be made in terms of priorities and resources and the need to ensure that the police exercise their powers to control and prevent crime in a manner which fully

---

[65] These reviews have recently been held to fulfil the UK's obligations with regard to the duty to effective investigation under Art 2: *R (on the application of Mullane) v West Berkshire Safer Communities Partnership* [2006] EWHC 2499 (Admin).

[66] Domestic Violence, Crime and Victims Act 2004, s9. Relevant authorities (chief constables for England and Wales, local authorities, local probation boards, health authorities and primary care trusts) will have a duty to have regard to Secretary of State Guidance (yet to be published) which will provide details as to leadership, format, timing and participants to take part in the reviews.

[67] See also s9(1)(b), which adds 'or a member of the same household as himself'.

[68] Despite the fact that the Domestic Violence, Crime and Victims Act 2004 creates a new offence in s5 of causing or allowing the death of a child.

[69] *LCB v United Kingdom* [1998] 27 EHRR 212.

[70] *Osman v the United Kingdom* [1998] 29 EHRR 245.

[71] *Hill v Chief Constable of West Yorkshire Police* [1989] AC 53.

respects the due process and other guarantees which legitimately place restraints on the scope of their action to investigate crime and bring offenders to justice, including the guarantees contained in Articles 5 and 8 of the Convention.[72]

Thus the positive obligations flowing from Article 2 of the Convention should, in a policing context, be 'interpreted in a way which does not impose an impossible or disproportionate burden on the authorities'.[73] Nonetheless, the case is significant for the comments made in respect of what *would* be sufficient to establish a breach of Article 2 in such circumstances:

> [I]t must be established ... that the authorities knew or ought to have known at the time of the existence of a real and immediate risk to the life of an identified individual or individuals from the criminal acts of a third party and that they failed to take measures within the scope of their powers which, judged reasonably, might have been expected to avoid that risk. The Court does not accept the Government's view that the failure to perceive the risk to life in the circumstances known at the time or to take preventive measures to avoid that risk must be tantamount to gross negligence or wilful disregard of the duty to protect life ... Such a rigid standard must be considered to be incompatible with the requirements of Article 1 of the Convention and the obligations of Contracting States under that Article to secure the practical and effective protection of the rights and freedoms laid down therein, including Article 2.[74]

In two recent and highly significant decisions, the ECtHR has demonstrated its willingness to extend the positive obligations inherent in Article 2 to the victims of violence within the domestic context. In the case of *Kontrova v Slovakia*[75] the applicant first made contact with her local police station when she filed a criminal complaint against the husband in which she alleged that he had beaten her with an electric cable the previous day, and submitted a medical report which confirmed that her injuries would incapacitate her from work for up to seven days. She also alleged that there was a long history of physical and psychological abuse by her husband. Some two weeks later she attended the same police station with her husband to withdraw the complaint and they were both advised that in order to avoid a prosecution they would have to provide another medical report confirming that she had not been incapacitated from work for more than six days. The report was produced and a few days later the same police officer decided to take no further action. In the early hours of the following morning, the police were contacted to report that the husband had a shotgun and was threatening to kill him and the two children. The applicant herself made a similar phone call later that night. The police eventually came, but by that time, the husband had gone. The wife was taken by the police to her parents' home and invited to the police station to make a formal record of the incident. Although that was done, no criminal complaint was registered. Five days later, the applicant visited the police station again to inquire after her first complaint, which she had withdrawn, and the latest incident with the shotgun. Later that night the husband shot and killed both him and the two children.

Despite the fact that three of the police officers involved in the case were found guilty of dereliction of duty, the applicant was unsuccessful in her attempts to receive compensation from the Police Department in the Constitutional Court. As a result, she sought relief from the ECtHR based upon alleged breaches of her Article 2, 6, 8, and 13 rights. However, it was

---

[72] *Osman* (n 70) para 116.
[73] *Osman* (n 70) para 116.
[74] *Osman* (n 70) paras 115–16.
[75] *Kontrova v Slovakia* Application No 7510/04 [2007] ECHR 31 May 2007.

under Article 2 that the Court found her rights had been breached by the failures of the police to act. The ECtHR reiterated the general principles of Article 2 set out in *LCB*[76] and *Osman*[77] above and, in particular, the duty, in appropriate circumstances, to a positive obligation on the authorities to take preventive operational measures to protect an individual whose life is at risk from the criminal acts of another individual. Noting that the domestic law of Slovakia established that the police had an array of specific obligations in response to the applicant's situation which

> included, inter alia, accepting and duly registering the applicant's criminal complaint; launching a criminal investigation and commencing criminal proceedings against the applicant's husband immediately; keeping a proper record of the emergency calls and advising the next shift of the situation; and taking action in respect of the allegation that the applicant's husband had a shotgun and had made violent threats with it.[78]

Owing to the fact that the police had, as established by the domestic courts, failed to ensure that these obligations were complied with and the direct consequence of these failures was the death of the applicant's children, a violation of Article 2 had thus occurred. Further, noting that in the event of a breach of Articles 2 and 3 of the Convention, which rank as the most fundamental provisions of the Convention, compensation for the non-pecuniary damage flowing from the breach should in principle be available as part of the range of possible remedies.[79] The inability of the applicant to obtain compensation for the non-pecuniary damage that had occurred constituted a violation of Article 13.[80]

The applicability of the Convention to the victims of domestic violence has recently been further developed in another case, the facts of which are worth setting out in some detail. In *Opuz v Turkey*[81] the applicant was married and had three children. Between April 1995 and March 1998 there were four incidents of extremely violent and threatening behaviour towards her and her mother from her husband which came to the notice of the authorities. In the fourth assault the applicant's husband ran a car into her and her mother which resulted in both women being medically certified as having sustained life-threatening injuries. Criminal proceedings were brought against the husband on three of those occasions and he was twice remanded in custody and released pending trial. However, the complaints were withdrawn by the women, following pressure and death threats from the husband. The legal proceedings were therefore stopped despite the fact that the authorities were aware of the reason for their withdrawal. The husband was eventually convicted for just one count and sentenced to three months' imprisonment which was later commuted to a fine. The threats and violence, however, continued. In October 2001 the applicant was stabbed seven times and taken to hospital. Her husband was charged with knife assault and given another fine. In April 1998, October and November 2001 and February 2002 the applicant and her mother filed complaints with the prosecution authorities about his threats and harassment, claiming that their lives were in immediate danger and requesting that the authorities take immediate action such as his detention. In response to those requests for protection, the

---

[76] *LCB* (n 69).
[77] *Osman* (n 70).
[78] *Kontrova* (n 75) para 54.
[79] *Keenan v the United Kingdom*, Application No 27229/95 [2001] 33 EHRR 913 para 130.
[80] The Court did not feel it was necessary to examine the Art 8 and Art 6 claims made.
[81] *Opuz v Turkey* Application No 33401/02 9 June 2009.

husband was questioned and his statements taken down; he was then released. Finally, during an attempt to move to another town with her daughter, the applicant's mother-in-law was shot and killed by her husband in March 2002. It took until March 2008 for him to be convicted for murder and illegal possession of a firearm and to be sentenced to life imprisonment. However, the original sentence was mitigated and changed by the court to 15 years and 10 months' imprisonment and a fine because it regarded the accused as having committed the offence as a result of provocation by the deceased and took into account his good conduct during the trial. The court also ordered his release pending his appeal in view of the time he had spent in pre-trial detention.[82] In April 2008 the applicant filed another criminal complaint with the prosecution authorities in which she requested the authorities to take measures to protect her due to the fact that since his release her now ex-husband had started threatening to kill her and her new boyfriend. It was only after intervention from the Director of the International Law and Relations Department which was initiated by notice of the application to the ECtHR that the government finally informed the Court in November 2008 that the police authorities had taken specific measures to protect the applicant from her former husband. These included distributing the photograph and fingerprints of the applicant's husband to police stations in the region so that they could arrest him if he appeared near the applicant's place of residence.

The applicant brought her complaints under Articles 2, 3 and 14, all of which were successful. In relation to Article 2 specifically, she complained that the authorities had failed to safeguard the right to life of her mother. In dealing with this aspect of the case the Court first confirmed the *Osman*[83] test with regard to the expectations imposed upon national authorities when complying with positive obligations to protect the right to life.[84] It then went on to review the history of violence in the case in order to ascertain whether the national authorities had fulfilled their positive obligation to take preventive operational measures to protect the applicant's mother's right to life and concluded that they had not. This was for a number of reasons. First, it was clear that there was escalating violence against the applicant and her mother by her husband. Second, the crimes committed by him were sufficiently serious to warrant preventive measures and there was a continuing threat to the health and safety of the victims. Third, when examining the history of the relationship, it was obvious that the perpetrator had a record of domestic violence and there was therefore a significant risk of further violence. Finally, the victims' situations were also known to the authorities with the mother herself having submitted a petition to the Public Prosecutor's Office stating that her life was in immediate danger. As a result the Court found that the local authorities could have foreseen a lethal attack by the defendant. The Court then turned to the question of whether the authorities displayed due diligence to prevent the killing of the applicant's mother. Bearing in mind the regularity of the assaults and threats and their seriousness, by often involving knives and guns, the Court considered that it did not appear that:

> [T]he local authorities sufficiently considered the above factors when repeatedly deciding to discontinue the criminal proceedings against the defendant. Instead, they seem to have given

---

[82] The appeal proceedings are still pending before the Court of Cassation.

[83] *Osman* (n 70).

[84] *Opuz* (n 81) para 129: Thus: 'For a positive obligation to arise, it must be established that the authorities knew or ought to have known at the time of the existence of a real and immediate risk to the life of an identified individual from the criminal acts of a third party and that they failed to take measures within the scope of their powers which, judged reasonably, might have been expected to avoid that risk.'

exclusive weight to the need to refrain from interfering in what they perceived to be a 'family matter'. Moreover, there is no indication that the authorities considered the motives behind the withdrawal of the complaints. This is despite the applicant's mother's indication to the Diyarbakır Public Prosecutor that she and her daughter had withdrawn their complaints because of the death threats issued and pressure exerted on them by HO.[85]

The Court then went on to review the prosecutorial policy in Turkey which was dependent upon a complaint being brought by a victim of domestic violence which was, in turn, based on the argument that to intervene in a 'private' matter such as this may have led to a breach of the applicant's and her mother's right to private life under Article 8 of the Convention.[86] This issue is an important one not least because a number of jurisdictions take a similar view which is based upon a legitimate concern that to 'force' a prosecution against the wishes of a victim does not respect victim autonomy in choosing to withdraw her statement.[87] After reviewing the practice in a number of jurisdictions,[88] the ECtHR noted that there seemed to be no general consensus among states parties regarding the pursuance of the criminal prosecution against perpetrators of domestic violence when the victim withdraws her complaints. However, in what appears to be a green light to 'soft no-drop' prosecution policies[89] as a means of complying with their due diligence duties under Article 2, the Court observed that a number of factors[90] could be taken into account when deciding whether to pursue the prosecution. The point being that authorities must undertake some sort of assessment of the seriousness of the case when considering whether to continue a prosecution where the victim has withdrawn her co-operation. Victim privacy and autonomy cannot, as the authors have previously argued,[91] therefore be used as a means to sidestep a state's positive obligations under the ECHR to protect a victim of domestic violence where that violence is serious and involves children.

> It can be inferred from this practice that the more serious the offence or the greater the risk of further offences, the more likely that the prosecution should continue in the public interest, even if victims withdraw their complaints.[92]

The Court therefore concluded that in requiring a complaint from the victim in order for an investigation and prosecution to take place, in addition to a minimum sickness period

---

[85] *Ibid*, para 143.

[86] *Ibid*, para 137.

[87] S Choudhry, 'Mandatory Prosecution and Arrest as a Form of Compliance with Due Diligence Duties in Domestic Violence: the Gender Implications' in S Choudhry, J Herring and J Wallbank, *Rights, Gender and Family Law* (London, Routledge-Cavendish, 2009); M Dempsey, 'Toward a Feminist State' (n 19).

[88] *Opuz* (n 81) paras 87–8.

[89] The CPS policy in the UK is a good example of this: 'Generally, the more serious the offence because of, for example, the presence of children, or the level of violence used or the real and continuing threat to the victim or others, the more likely the CPS are to prosecute in the public interest, even if the victims do not wish the same.' See also S Choudhry, 'Mandatory Prosecution' (n 87).

[90] These were: the seriousness of the offence; whether the victim's injuries are physical or psychological; if the defendant used a weapon; if the defendant has made any threats since the attack; if the defendant planned the attack; the effect (including psychological) on any children living in the household; the chances of the defendant offending again; the continuing threat to the health and safety of the victim or anyone else who was, or could become, involved; the current state of the victim's relationship with the defendant; the effect on that relationship of continuing with the prosecution against the victim's wishes; the history of the relationship, particularly if there had been any other violence in the past; and the defendant's criminal history, particularly any previous violence.

[91] S Choudhry and J Herring, 'Righting Domestic Violence' and 'Domestic Violence and the HRA' (n 21) and S Choudhry, 'Mandatory Prosecution' (n 87).

[92] *Opuz* (n 81) para 139.

of 10 days the legislative framework in Turkey at the time thus 'fell short of the requirements inherent in the State's positive obligations to establish and apply effectively a system
punishing all forms of domestic violence and providing sufficient safeguards for the victims'.[93] Further, in failing completely to assess the threat posed by the applicant's husband
the government could not argue that he failed to pose an imminent threat to her and her
mother.[94] Moreover, failing to detain him or take any preventative operational measures to
protect the applicant and her mother thus constituted a failure to display due diligence.[95]
A breach of Article 2 had thus occurred.

The implications of this judgment for the victims of domestic violence are significant.
Authorities can no longer rely on the victim to make a complaint in order for an arrest
or prosecution to take place and although the Court fell short of *requiring* a prosecution
where the victim has withdrawn her complaint it would seem that the decision not to prosecute must be made by reference to the factors set out. In addition, although the *Osman*[96]
test was confirmed it would seem from both *Kontrova*[97] and *Opuz*[98] that the victims of
domestic violence are to be regarded as especially vulnerable and deserving of a thought-
out risk assessment. This is no doubt due to the raft of international and regional instruments that were referred to in detail at the beginning of the Court's judgment in *Opuz*.[99] In
addition, it appears from *Kontrova*[100] that the likelihood of a breach of a requirement will
almost certainly be found where the authorities have failed to satisfy, in particular, their
own domestic obligations towards such victims, particularly where Articles 2 and 3 are
engaged. If this is the case, it is also clear that civil liability for damages ought to be made
available under Article 13.

Article 2 in the Domestic Courts

The general question of what will constitute a 'risk to life' has been held to be a question
of commonsense application to individual circumstances.[101] However, the question of
how much deference will be paid to the primary decision maker (in this case the law-
enforcement agencies) is an interesting one and will enter into the process, in the
Osman[102] and *Kontrova*[103] sense, when the court is assessing both whether there was a risk
to life and whether the failure to take measures within the scope of the authority's powers
was unreasonable given the operational choices that were faced by it. In *Bloggs 61R (on
the application of Bloggs 61) v Secretary of State for the Home Department*,[104] which concerned the Prison Service's decision to move a prisoner from a protected witness unit to a
mainstream prison regime, the Court of Appeal gave contradictory messages with regard
to the degree of deference to be given in such cases. Although they held that, in examining the risk assessment that had been carried out by the Prison Service, any potential

---

[93] *Ibid*, para 145.
[94] *Ibid*, para 147.
[95] *Ibid*, para 148.
[96] *Osman* (n 70).
[97] *Kontrova* (n 75).
[98] *Opuz* (n 81).
[99] *Ibid*, paras 72–90.
[100] *Kontrova* (n 75).
[101] *R (on the application of Bloggs 61) v Secretary of State for the Home Department* [2003] EWCA 686 (Civ).
[102] *Osman* (n 70).
[103] *Kontrova* (n 75).
[104] *Bloggs 61* (n 101).

interference with the right to life required the most anxious scrutiny stopping short of merits review,[105] the court also remarked that it was 'still appropriate' to show some deference to the special competence of the Prison Service with regard to the safety of an inmate. What was made clear in the case, however, was that the degree of deference given to the primary decision maker with regard to a case involving Article 2 ought to be less than that given to the qualified Convention rights. However, as Amos notes, this is not an approach that has been taken in any other case where the positive duty under Article 2 has been raised. Thus, in *R (on the application of H) v Ashworth Hospital* Authority,[106] the Administrative Court stated that, given the fundamental nature of the right to life, it had to examine the factual evidence for itself to determine whether or not there was a risk to life. It would appear that the approach in *H*[107] was the correct one given that this was the one followed by the House of Lords in its recent decision in *Van Colle and another v Chief Constable of Hertfordshire*,[108] discussed below.

In terms of what action is taken to avoid a risk of life where that has been found to exist, it is fair to say that the English judiciary has generally accepted and applied the *Osman*[109] principles in relation to the steps that are required to be taken by public authorities when safeguarding lives,[110] and moreover, has been recently reaffirmed by the House of Lords in *Van Colle*:[111]

> [T]he court must be satisfied that the authorities knew or ought to have known 'at the time' of the existence of 'a real and immediate risk to the life' of an identified individual from the criminal acts of a third party. If they failed to take measures within the scope of their powers which, judged reasonably, might have been expected to avoid that risk, the positive obligation will have been violated.[112]

The case concerned the alleged negligent failure of the police to protect a witness in a theft case from his death by the hands of the accused, who had previously threatened him. The family of the deceased based their claim on section 6 of the HRA, arguing that the police, as a public authority, had acted in a way which was incompatible with the deceased's Article 2 rights by failing to do what was reasonable to expect of them to avoid the risk to his life to which he had alerted them and on section 8, which empowers the courts to award damages against them if this was found. The Court of Appeal had upheld the first instance decision which reversed the long line of authority, first established in *Hill v Chief Constable of West Yorkshire*[113] and more recently confirmed by the House of Lords in *Brooks v Commissioner of Police of the Metropolis*,[114] that had held that, on grounds of public policy and in the absence of special circumstances, the police could not be held liable in tort for failing to

---

[105] M Amos, 'Separating Human Rights Adjudication From Judicial Review—*Huang v Secretary of State for the Home Department* and *Kashmiri v Secretary of State for the Home Department*' (2007) *European Human Rights Law Review* 679, para 185.
[106] *R (on the application of H) v Ashworth Hospital Authority* [2001] EWHC 872 (Admin) at 86.
[107] *H* (n 106).
[108] *Chief Constable of Hertfordshire v Van Colle and another* [2008] UKHL 50.
[109] *Osman* (n 70).
[110] See *Venables v News Group Newspapers* [2001] 2 WLR 1038; *R (on the application of H) v Ashworth Hospital Authority* [2001] EWHC (Admin) 872 and *Bloggs 61* (n 101).
[111] *Van Colle* (n 108).
[112] *Ibid* (Lord Hope) para 66.
[113] *Hill* (n 71).
[114] *Brooks v Commissioner of Police of the Metropolis* [2005] UKHL 24.

protect individuals against harm caused by criminals—referred to as the 'core principle' by Lord Steyn in the latter case.[115] However, this decision was shortly to be unanimously reversed by the House of Lords on the basis that the *Osman*[116] test had not been satisfied. In order to reach this conclusion their Lordships first took the opportunity to resound-ingly reject the argument[117] that a lower threshold to that set out in *Osman*[118] should apply where it was the conduct of the state authorities that exposed an individual to the risk of his life (such as in the case of a prosecution witness).[119] Having done so their Lordships went on to conclude that, despite the fact that the detective involved in the case had been disci-plined for his failure to perform his duties conscientiously and diligently, it could not be said that he should have apprehended such violence on the facts and circumstances which were or should have been known to him at the time. In reaching this conclusion much was made of the fact that as the deceased was to be a witness to the relatively minor offence of theft, the most the detective ought to have apprehended was a risk of witness intimidation and certainly not a risk of murder.[120]

The appeal in *Van Colle*[121] was heard with that of *Smith (FC) (Respondent) v Chief Constable of Sussex Police (Appellant)*,[122] which was a common law claim of negligence which had previously been struck out at first instance as showing no cause for action[123] but had then later been restored and remitted for trial on Mr Smith's successful appeal to the Court of Appeal. A claim had not been made under the HRA due to the fact that it had been brought outside the one-year limitation period for an action. Smith therefore had to establish that the police owed him a duty of care—and therefore reverse the 'core principle' of police immunity set out in *Brooks*. Of the two cases it is, however, *Smith*[124] that is of particular relevance due to the fact that the case involved domestic violence between a gay couple. The facts were as follows.[125] Smith and Jeffrey lived together as partners. However, in December 2000 Jeffrey assaulted Smith because he had asked for a few days' break from their relationship. The assault was reported to the police, who arrested Jeffrey and detained him overnight. No prosecution followed. After a time apart, during which Smith moved to Brighton, Jeffrey renewed contact and wanted to resume their relationship; Smith did not. From January 2003 onwards Jeffrey sent Smith a stream of violent, abusive and threatening telephone, text and internet messages, including death threats. On 24 February 2003 Smith contacted Brighton police by dialling 999. He reported his earlier relationship with Jeffrey, the previous history of violence and Jeffrey's recent threats to kill him. Two officers were assigned to the case and they visited Smith that afternoon. He again reported his previous relationship with Jeffrey (including the earlier violence) and the threats. The officers declined to look at the messages, made no

---

[115]   *Brooks* (n 114) para 30.
[116]   *Osman* (n 70).
[117]   Made in *R (A and others) v Lord Saville of Newdigate and others* [2002] 1 WLR 1249 para 28.
[118]   *Osman* (n 70).
[119]   *Van Colle* (n 108) para 70 (Lord Hope); para 34 (Lord Bingham), para 87 (Lord Phillips).
[120]   *Ibid*, paras 67–8 (Lord Hope); 37–9 (Lord Bingham).
[121]   *Ibid*.
[122]   *Smith (FC) (Respondent) v Chief Constable of Sussex Police (Appellant)* [2008] UKHL 50.
[123]   Based on the general immunity against negligence principle which had been established in *Hill* (n 71) and *Brooks* (n 114) on public policy grounds.
[124]   *Smith* (n 122).
[125]   *Smith* (n 122) (Lord Bingham's summary).

entry in their notebooks, took no statement from Smith and completed no crime form. They told Smith that it would be necessary to trace the calls and that he should attend at Brighton Police Station to fill in the appropriate forms. Later that evening Smith received several more messages from Jeffrey threatening to kill him. Smith filled in the forms the next day. The information he provided to the police included Jeffrey's home address and reference to the death threats he had received. Smith then went to London, since Jeffrey had said he was coming to Brighton. He contacted the Brighton Police from London to check on progress, but was told it would take four weeks for the calls to be traced. The messages continued. One read: 'I'm close to u now and I am gonna track u down and I'm not gonna stop until I've driven this knife into u repeatedly.' Smith went to Saville Row Police Station to report his concern. An officer there contacted the Brighton Police and advised Smith that the case was being dealt with from Brighton and he should speak to an inspector there when he returned home. On return to Brighton on 2 March 2003 Smith told an inspector that he thought his life was in danger and asked about the progress of the investigation. He offered to show the inspector the threatening messages he had received, but the inspector declined to look at them and made no note of the meeting. He told Smith the investigation was progressing well, and he should call 999 if he was concerned about his safety in the interim. On 10 March 2003 Smith replied to a communication he had received from the police that day, giving the telephone numbers from which Jeffrey had been sending the text messages. He received a further text message from Jeffrey saying 'Revenge will be mine'. On 10 March Jeffrey attacked Smith at his home address with a claw hammer. He suffered three fractures of the skull and associated brain damage, and has suffered continuing injury, both physical and psychological. Jeffrey was arrested at his home address (provided by Smith to the police) on 10 March. He was charged and in March 2004 he was convicted of making threats to kill and causing grievous bodily harm with intent. He was sentenced to 10 years' imprisonment with an extended period on licence.

Their Lordships' judgments with respect to *Smith*[126] were much more detailed on account of the potential impact the case may have had upon the well-established common law principles discussed above. Suffice to say, the Court of Appeal's attempt to generate a common law duty of care by the existence of a parallel ECHR duty was rejected on the basis of the same policy reasons espoused in *Hill*[127] and *Brooks*,[128] that being that the imposition of liability might have an adverse impact on the way the police carry out their functions by encouraging defensive policing which, rather than being concerned with fighting crime, would become more concerned with fighting negligence claims. This, it was argued, would not be in the interests of the whole community. Lord Bingham's proposal in his dissenting judgment to replace the 'core' principle with a legal principle (which he termed the 'immunity principle') that would apply on the individual facts of the case was forcefully rejected on the basis that it would not provide enough protection against these risks to policing. For Lord Hope a retreat from the 'core' principle could not be justified even where there were 'shortcomings of the police in some cases'.[129] In doing so he displayed not only a striking

---

[126] *Smith* (n 122).
[127] *Hill* (n 71).
[128] *Brooks* (n 114).
[129] *Smith* (n 122) para 75 (Lord Hope).

lack of understanding of the complex issues involved in cases of domestic violence, but also on the basis of the evidence discussed above, a somewhat overoptimistic vision of the police's response to it:

> It is an unfortunate feature of the human experience that the breakdown of a close relationship leads to bitterness, and that this in its turn may lead to threats and acts of violence. So-called domestic cases that are brought to the attention of the police all too frequently are a product of that phenomenon. One party tells the police that he or she is being threatened. The other party may say, when challenged, that his or her actions have been wrongly reported or misinterpreted … A robust approach is needed, bearing in mind the interests of both parties and of the whole community. Not every complaint of this kind is genuine, and those that are genuine must be sorted out from those that are not … Some cases will require more immediate action than others. The judgment as to whether any given case is of that character must be left to the police.[130]

Although the judgment in *Smith*[131] is somewhat depressing from the development of the law of negligence, in such cases the prospects of a future claim against the police under the HRA are not, however, necessarily doomed. First, the reluctance to allow the claim to proceed does not necessarily translate into a conclusion that it would have failed had the claim been brought under the HRA. What is clear from some of the majority judgments is that a major motivation behind the need to preserve the 'core' principle was also the desire to preserve the distinct character of the common law of negligence as against a claim brought under the HRA.[132] There were also some indications in the judgments that had the case been brought under the HRA the outcome would not necessarily have been failure. Lord Bingham, when referring to the necessary test to be satisfied under Article 2, in relation to *Van Colle*,[133] specifically referred to the development of the *Osman*[134] test by the ECtHR in *Kontrova*:[135]

> It is plain from *Osman*[136] and later cases that Article 2 may be invoked where there has been a systemic failure by member states to enact laws or provide procedures reasonably needed to protect the right to life. But the Article may also be invoked where, although there has been no systemic failure of that kind, a real and immediate risk to life is demonstrated and individual agents of the state have reprehensibly failed to exercise the powers available to them for the purpose of protecting life. *Kontrova*[137] is such a case.[138]

And:

> Thus stupidity, lack of imagination and inertia do not afford an excuse to a national authority which reasonably ought, in the light of what it knew or was told, to make further enquiries or investigations: it is then to be treated as knowing what such further enquiries or investigations would have elicited.[139]

---

[130] *Smith* (n 122) para 76 (Lord Hope).
[131] *Ibid.*
[132] *Ibid*, para 82 (Lord Hope); paras 136–9 (Lord Phillips).
[133] *Van Colle* (n 108).
[134] *Osman* (n 70).
[135] *Kontrova* (n 75).
[136] *Osman* (n 70).
[137] *Kontrova* (n 75).
[138] *Smith* (n 122), para 31 (Lord Bingham).
[139] *Ibid*, para 32 (Lord Bingham).

Both Lord Bingham[140] and Lord Hope[141] in distinguishing *Van Colle*[142] from *Osman*[143] relied heavily on the particular facts of the case which he felt did not demonstrate that an imminent risk to the deceased's life was, in effect, reasonably foreseeable. These included nothing in the defendant's record that indicated he had a propensity to commit violence, no indication that the threats to kill were meant seriously or imminent given the relatively minor charge of theft that was at stake and the fact that the disciplinary panel found that although there was sufficient evidence to justify the arrest of Brougham for attempting to pervert the course of justice and that he should have been arrested they did not find that the detective involved should have apprehended any imminent threat to the life or safety of the deceased.[144] It is certainly arguable that the facts of *Smith*[145] in comparison were more persuasive than that of *Van Colle*[146] as at the very minimum he had furnished the police 'with apparently credible evidence that Jeffrey, whom he identified and whose whereabouts were known, presented a specific and imminent threat to his life or safety'.[147] Further, systemic failures by the police of the kind that were referred to by Lord Bridge are arguably, on the basis of much empirical study, much more likely with regard to cases involving repeated domestic violence. The perpetrators themselves are also much more likely to 'fit' into the category of person who could reasonably be assumed to present a risk of imminent danger to the victim than the perpetrator in *Van Colle*.[148] Article 2 claims against the authorities such as that of Sabina Akhtar,[149] who was stabbed to death by her husband a few days after the CPS had decided that there was insufficient evidence to proceed with a prosecution despite the fact that she had reported to the police that he had been violent to her 25 times and had threatened to kill her, could hold a good chance of success if it could be shown that they did indeed have or ought to have had knowledge that the victim's life was at imminent risk.

In summary, although there will be a high level of scrutiny of the way that the risk of life was assessed, the question of whether the *action* taken by the police to avoid it was reasonable may be harder to satisfy if the courts continue to adopt a restrictive interpretation of *Osman*.[150] That is not to say, however, that were a more persuasive Article 2 claim, similar in facts to *Kontrova*,[151] to come before a differently constituted House of Lords that this interpretation would remain the same. It is certainly possible that the court may be persuaded by the application of the *Osman*[152] principles by the ECtHR in that case. What can be said for certain after *Smith*[153] is that it is highly unlikely that any retreat on the 'core' principle of immunity within the common law of negligence will occur before this happens, if at all.

---

[140] *Ibid*, paras 36–40 (Lord Bingham—with whose assessment all the other Lords agreed).
[141] *Ibid*, paras 67–8 (Lord Hope).
[142] *Van Colle* (n 108).
[143] *Osman* (n 70).
[144] *Smith* (n 122), paras 67–8 (Lord Hope).
[145] *Ibid*.
[146] *Van Colle* (n 108).
[147] *Smith* (n 122), para 60 (Lord Bingham).
[148] *Van Colle* (n 108).
[149] 'Charity to Sue Over Domestic Violence Victim Sabina Akhtar', 14 May 2009, www.timesonline.co.uk/tol/news/uk/Article6287902.ece#cid=OTC-RSS&attr=989864.
[150] See JR Spencer, 'Suing the Police for Negligence: Orthodoxy Restored' 68(1) *CLJ* 25–7.
[151] *Kontrova* (n 75).
[152] *Osman* (n 70).
[153] *Smith* (n 122).

This is undoubtedly due to the continuing pull of the resource-driven policy reasons set out in *Hill*[154] and *Brook*.[155] Indeed, Lord Phillips[156] went so far as to say that he thought that any dilution of the 'core' principle of immunity in such cases was an area where the law would better be determined by Parliament, observing that the Law Commission had just published a consultation paper on administrative redress and public bodies. It may be that legislative reform is what is needed to break the hold of *Hill*[157] upon the courts.

Article 3

Article 3 of the ECHR provides that:

'No one shall be subject to torture or to inhuman or degrading treatment or punishment.'

Article 3 thus prohibits, in absolute terms, torture or inhuman or degrading treatment or punishment. No provision is made for exceptions and no derogation from it is permissible, even in time of war or other national emergency.[158]

The Meaning of Inhuman and Degrading Treatment[159]

The development of a number of general principles can be discerned from an examination of the reasoning of the ECtHR on Article 3.[160] The Court has referred to the need for the alleged 'ill-treatment' to attain a minimum level of severity[161] if it is to fall within the scope of Article 3. Treatment involving actual bodily injury or intense physical or mental suffering will generally qualify as 'ill treatment'.[162] Treatment which humiliates or debases an individual; shows a lack of respect for, or diminishing human dignity; or arouses feelings of fear, anguish or inferiority capable of breaking an individual's moral and physical resistance, may also be characterised as degrading and fall within the prohibition of Article 3.[163] In considering whether treatment is 'degrading', the Court will have regard to whether its object was to humiliate and debase the person concerned and whether, as far

---

[154] *Hill* (n 71).

[155] J Morgan, 'Policy Reasoning in Tort Law: the Courts, the Law Commission and the Critics' (2009) 125 *LQR* 215.

[156] *Van Colle* (n 108), para 102 (Lord Phillips).

[157] *Hill* (n 71).

[158] *Chahal v the United Kingdom* (1997) 23 EHRR 413, para 79.

[159] The Court has stated in *Ilaşcu And Others v Moldova And Russia* (Application No 48787/99) (2004) 40 EHRR 1030, para 426, that 'it was the intention that the Convention should, by means of this distinction, attach a special stigma to torture, which requires deliberate inhuman treatment causing very serious and cruel suffering'. See also Y Arai-Yokoi, 'Grading Scale of Degradation: Identifying the Threshold of Degrading Treatment or Punishment Under Article 3 ECHR' (2003) 21 (3) *Netherlands Quarterly of Human Rights* 385, who argues that, despite its absolute nature, the Strasbourg organs have introduced an element of gradation or relativity into Art 3 by setting the threshold of gravity at the lowest level for degrading treatment or punishment. Thus, in practice, a finding of torture may require a much higher level of severity of mistreatment.

[160] For a comprehensive analysis of these principles see D Feldman, *Civil Liberties* (n 55) ch 5.

[161] *Ireland v United Kingdom* [1979] 2 EHRR 25, para 162; *Tyrer v the United Kingdom* (1979–80) 2 EHRR 1, para 30, and *A v United Kingdom* (1999) 27 EHRR 61, para 20.

[162] See *Ireland* (n 161), para 167; *Pretty v UK* (2002) 35 EHRR 1, para 52.

[163] See, amongst recent authorities, *Price v the United Kingdom* (2002) 34 EHRR 53, paras 24–30 and *Valašinas v Lithuania* Application No 44558/98 (2001) 12 BHRC 266, para 117.

as the consequences are concerned, it adversely affected his or her personality in a manner incompatible with Article 3.[164]

The Court has also made it clear that the assessment of treatment is relative and will depend upon all the circumstances of the case. Factors that have been taken into account by the Court have included the nature and context of the treatment; its duration; its physical and mental effects; and, in some cases, the sex, age and state of health of the victim.[165] Thus, just because a form of conduct is not degrading treatment for one person does not mean that it cannot be so for another.

The Court, which views the ECHR as a living instrument,[166] has also stated that it will be possible to reclassify its definition of ill-treatment in light of developments in policy of the Member States.[167]

The Positive Duty of the State Under Article 3

Article 3 imposes primarily a negative obligation on states to refrain from inflicting serious harm on persons within their jurisdiction. Most cases involving Article 3 have involved state agents or public authorities inflicting treatment on individuals.[168] These cases will also be discussed in Chapter 8, but are summarised here. However, the Court has been developing a certain level of flexibility in addressing the application of Article 3 within the 'private context'.[169] The Court has, for example, recognised that the state can be under positive obligations to protect one individual from having their rights under Article 3 infringed by another individual.[170] In *E and Others v United Kingdom*[171] the Court held:

> Article 3 enshrines one of the most fundamental values of a democratic society ... The obligation on all contracting parties under Article 1 of the ECHR ... taken in conjunction with Article 3, requires States to take measures designed to ensure that individuals within their jurisdiction are not subjected to torture or inhuman or degrading treatment, *including such ill-treatment administered by private individuals* [emphasis added].

A positive obligation on the state to provide protection against inhuman or degrading treatment from another individual has thus been found to arise in a number of cases. In *A v the United Kingdom*[172] a child applicant successfully complained that the government had failed to protect him from degrading treatment carried out towards him by his stepfather.

---

[164] Even the absence of such a purpose cannot conclusively rule out a finding of a violation of Art 3: *Valašinas* (n 172) 101.

[165] See among other authorities *Costello-Roberts v United Kingdom* (1995) 19 EHRR 112.

[166] *Tyrer* (n 161).

[167] In *Selmouni v France* [2000] 29 EHRR 403, for example, the Court stated that it had 'previously examined cases in which it concluded that there had been treatment which could only be described as torture ... However, having regard to the fact that the Convention is a "living instrument which must be interpreted in the light of present-day conditions" ... the Court considers that certain acts which were classified in the past as "inhuman and degrading treatment" as opposed to "torture" could be classified differently in future. It takes the view that the increasingly high standard being required in the area of the protection of human rights and fundamental liberties correspondingly and inevitably requires greater firmness in assessing breaches of the fundamental values of democratic societies.'

[168] Cases have ranged from prison and detention: *Ireland* (n 161) to corporal punishment: *Tyrer* (n 161), para 31.

[169] *D v the United Kingdom* [1997] 24 EHRR 423, para 49.

[170] For a useful analysis of the positive obligation on states under the ECHR see A Mowbray, *The Development of Positive Obligations under the European Convention on Human Rights by the European Court of Human Rights* (Oxford, Hart Publishing, 2003).

[171] *E and Others v United Kingdom* [2003] 36 EHRR 31.

[172] *A* (n 161).

The stepfather had caned him on a number of occasions causing him significant bruising but had not, however, been held criminally liable for his actions[173] due to his successful use of the defence of reasonable parental chastisement. The Court reasoned that Article 3 required states not only to protect individuals from treatment administered by private individuals which breached Article 3, but also that:

> Children and other vulnerable individuals, in particular, are entitled to State protection, in the form of effective deterrence, against such serious breaches of personal integrity.[174]

The Court thus concluded that, by allowing a defence of reasonable parental chastisement to a charge of assault on a child, English criminal law did not provide adequate protection to the applicant against treatment or punishment contrary to Article 3. A violation of Article 3 had therefore occurred.[175]

However, it was not until the decision in *Z and Others v the United Kingdom*[176] that the nature and extent of positive obligations under Article 3 arising within English civil law came before the Court. The case concerned four sibling child applicants who alleged that the local authority had failed to take adequate protective measures in respect of the severe neglect and abuse which they were suffering at the hands of their parents, contrary to Articles 3 and 8. Moreover, they had no access to a court, contrary to Article 6, or to an effective remedy, contrary to Article 13, in respect of this failure. These alleged breaches, it was argued, were due to the House of Lords having held that,[177] as a matter of principle, local authorities could not be sued for negligence or for breach of statutory duty in respect of the discharge of their functions concerning the welfare of children. Their action for damages for negligence and/or breach of statutory duty had, therefore, been struck out as revealing no cause of action.[178]

In respect of Article 3 the Court found that there had been a violation, as it was clear that the neglect and abuse suffered by the children reached the threshold of inhuman and degrading treatment. This treatment was brought to the attention of the local authority in October 1987 and despite its statutory duty to protect the children they were only taken into emergency care, at the insistence of their mother, on 30 April 1992. Over that period of four and a half years they had been subjected

> in their home to what the consultant child psychiatrist who examined them referred as horrific experiences ... The Criminal Injuries and Compensation Board had also found that the children had

---

[173] Of assault occasioning actual bodily harm pursuant to OAPA s47.

[174] *A* (n 161), para 22. Reference was also made to the CRC, Arts 19 and 37.

[175] The Court did not think it was necessary to examine the applicant's claim that he had also suffered a breach of his right to respect for private life under Art 8 having found a violation of Art 3.

[176] *Z and Others v the United Kingdom* [2002] 34 EHRR 3.

[177] Reported as *X and Others v Bedfordshire County Council* [1995] 3 All ER 352.

[178] This decision became the leading authority in the UK in this area; however, it was distinguished by the House of Lords in two significant judgments concerning the extent of liability of local authorities in child care matters. In *W and Others v Essex County Council* [1998] 3 All ER 111, foster parents who brought a claim for damages for negligence against a local authority who placed a known suspected sexual abuser within their home had their appeal against the striking out of their action upheld by the House of Lords in relation to the sexual abuse and psychiatric illness suffered by their three children and inflicted by the foster child. In *Barrett v London Borough of Enfield* [1999] 3 WLR 79, the plaintiff, who had been in care most of his life, claimed that the local authority had negligently failed to safeguard his welfare causing deep-seated psychiatric problems. Here, the House of Lords held that the judgment in *X and Others* (n 187) did not, in this case, prevent a claim of negligence being brought against a local authority by a child formerly in its care.

been subject to appalling neglect over an extended period and suffered physical and psychological injury directly attributable to a crime of violence.[179]

In addition, the Court reiterated that Article 3 imposed an obligation on states to take measures designed to ensure that individuals within their jurisdiction were not subjected to such treatment, including that administered by private individuals.[180] These measures, the Court stated, should provide effective protection

> in particular, of children and other vulnerable persons and include reasonable steps to prevent ill-treatment *of which the authorities had or ought to have had knowledge* [emphasis added][181]

The issue came before the European Court again, in 2002, in *E v United Kingdom*,[182] concerning four sibling applicants who had been sexually abused by their stepfather over a long period of time. Despite being convicted of indecently assaulting two of them in 1977, and being placed on probation, the stepfather was permitted continuing close contact with the family. In 1989, he was convicted of further serious acts of indecency against three of them after they reported the abuse to the police. The applicants submitted that there were material faults in the handling of the situation by the social services and that they sustained loss and damage as a result. Further, the local authority was aware of proven sexual abuse in January 1977 and that this had been ongoing for some time before January 1977. They therefore, it was argued, knew of the risk of future ill-treatment to the children and ought to have been aware of the continuation of actual abuse. An application for compensation to the Criminal Injuries Compensation Board was successful. However, the Local Government Ombudsman, who concluded that he had no jurisdiction to investigate their allegations, rejected their application for an investigation into the alleged negligence and misadministration of the local authority.[183]

In its judgment the Court reiterated the principle that states should provide effective protection in relation to children and vulnerable adults, particularly where the authorities had or ought to have had knowledge of abuse.[184] Thus, in this case, the Court was satisfied, on the evidence, that the social services should have been aware that the family's situation disclosed a history of past sexual and physical abuse from the stepfather. Of particular note is the Court's response to the government's argument that, notwithstanding any acknowledged shortcomings, it had not been shown that matters would have turned out any differently:

> The test under Article 3 however does not require it to be shown that 'but for' the failing or omission of the public authority ill-treatment would not have happened. *A failure to take reasonably available measures which could have had a real prospect of altering the outcome or mitigating the harm* is sufficient to engage the responsibility of the State [emphasis added].[185]

As a result, the Court was satisfied that the pattern of lack of investigation, communication and co-operation by the relevant authorities amounted to a breach of Article 3.

---

[179] *Z and Others* (n 176) para 74.

[180] *A* (n 161), para 22.

[181] *Z and Others* (n 176) para 73.

[182] *E v United Kingdom* (n 171).

[183] This was due to the fact that he was precluded from doing so by the Local Government (Scotland) Act 1975 s24(4). The applicants argued that they were, in turn, precluded from suing the local authority for damages in negligence due to the effect of *X v Bedfordshire County Council* (n 177).

[184] *E* (n 171) para 88. *Z and Others* (n 176) applied. See also *Stubbings v UK* [1997] 23 EHRR 213, para 64.

[185] *E* (n 171) para 99.

In summary, therefore, the Court has established that particular regard will be given to children and vulnerable adults when considering the extent of the positive obligations that are to be imposed on Member States towards them, notwithstanding that the 'treatment' at issue is being meted out by private individuals. Liability under Article 3 will thus be incurred if the following criteria are met:

— the treatment concerned comes within the definition established under Article 3;
— the state ought to have or had knowledge that such treatment was occurring;
— the state failed to take reasonably available measures that could have mitigated the resulting harm.[186]

Is Domestic Violence Torture, Inhuman and Degrading Treatment?

Domestic violence should often be sufficiently intense to engage Article 3. This will be clearly so where the victim is suffering serious injuries. Nevertheless, even domestic abuse, which is non-physical, can come within this prohibition when it is recalled that creating feelings of inferiority or lack of respect of dignity can be included. The following points should also be emphasised. First, it has been suggested that domestic violence is in part caused by a desire to exercise control over a female partner.[187] Second, when domestic violence is viewed within the wider context of violence of oppression against women, as a number of feminist commentators have argued, it may be seen to be of a particularly degrading nature.[188] Under this analysis the lack of legal protection, at least historically, that women have been offered, has, in effect, acted as a warrant for this abuse. Third, conduct which amounts to severe emotional abuse (and not physical violence alone) which leads to an overbearing of an individual's personality can constitute domestic violence and may also, in turn, amount to degradation. Finally, psychological research into victims of domestic violence and the controversial 'battered women's syndrome' reveals the clear and highly significant psychological impact that it can have on women, even where each individual incident may appear relatively minor when seen in isolation.[189]

The question of whether domestic violence can fall within the definition of Article 3 treatment has now been settled. The question was directly addressed by the ECtHR for the first time in its highly significant decision in *Opuz v Turkey*,[190] the facts of which are set out above. The applicant, a victim of domestic violence, also alleged that the injuries

---

[186] J Rogers, 'Applying the Doctrine of Positive Obligations in the European Convention on Human Rights to Domestic Substantive Criminal Law in Domestic Proceedings' [2003] *Crim LR* 690 emphasises that it will need to be shown that the criminal law provides an effective deterrent.

[187] E Schneider, *Battered Women and Feminist Lawmaking* (Virginia, Yale University, 2000) 5–6. It is noteworthy that the two most common triggers of domestic violence are pregnancy and actual or suspected infidelity—see Home Office, *Safety and Justice* Cm 5847 HMSO 18 (Home Office, London, 2003). Although it is not possible to prove why these events should be linked with domestic violence, it is suggested that both situations may produce a feeling within the abuser of a loss of control over his partner.

[188] E Schneider, *Battered Women* (n 196) and L Smith, 'Domestic Violence: An Overview of the Literature' [1989] HO Research Study 107; MDA Freeman, 'Legal Ideologies: Patriarchal Precedents and Domestic Violence' in MDA Freeman (ed), *The State, the Law and the Family: Critical Perspectives* (London and New York, Sweet & Maxwell, 1984).

[189] L Walker, *The Battered Woman Syndrome* (New York, Springer, 1984); L Walker, 'Post-Traumatic Stress Disorder in Women: Diagnosis and Treatment of Battered Woman Syndrome' (1991) 28 (1) *Psychotherapy* 21; GT Hotaling and DB Sugarman, 'A Risk Marker Analysis of Assaulted Wives' (1990) 5 (1) *Journal of Family Violence* 1, at 7.

[190] *Opuz* (n 81).

and anguish she had suffered as a result of the violence inflicted upon her by her husband had amounted to torture within the meaning of Article 3 of the Convention. Furthermore, by consistently failing to take any action to protect her from his violence in response to her repeated requests for help, the state had made her feel debased, hopeless and vulnerable. The ECtHR agreed, coming to this conclusion by a straightforward application of the principles that it had developed in relation to Article 3 discussed above. Of particular relevance was the principle that children and other vulnerable individuals, in particular, are entitled to state protection, in the form of effective deterrence, against serious breaches of personal integrity. The Court thus considered, as the authors had earlier predicted,[191] that the applicant and therefore other victims of domestic violence could fall within the group of 'vulnerable individuals' entitled to state protection that were referred to in *A v the United Kingdom*.[192] Relevant factors in coming to this conclusion that were cited by the Court were the violence suffered by the applicant in the past, the threats issued by her husband following his release from prison, and her fear of further violence. Significantly, the Court also took into account independent evidence that had been produced by a number of advocacy groups and Amnesty International of the particular situation of domestic violence victims in Turkey.[193] Reference was thus made to the applicant's social background, 'namely the vulnerable situation of women in south-east Turkey'[194] as a further relevant factor. Importantly, the Court also acknowledged that domestic abuse which is non-physical can also come within Article 3:

> The Court observes also that the violence suffered by the applicant, in the form of physical injuries *and psychological pressure*, were sufficiently serious to amount to ill-treatment within the meaning of Article 3 of the Convention [emphasis added].[195]

The Court then turned to the question of whether the national authorities had taken all reasonable measures to prevent the recurrence of violent attacks against the applicant's physical integrity. After reviewing the response of the authorities in some detail, the Court considered that it had not. Although the authorities had responded each time a complaint had been made, the reliance upon the applicant's continued involvement for further action and the general inadequacy of the measures taken against her husband meant that the local authorities had failed to demonstrate the required diligence to prevent the recurrence of violent attacks against the applicant.[196] The Court thus concluded that there had been a violation of Article 3 of the Convention 'as a result of the State authorities' failure to take protective measures in the form of effective deterrence against serious breaches of the applicant's personal integrity by her husband'.[197]

Mention should also be made of the applicant's complaint under Article 14. The right under Article 14 is not, however, a freestanding one; the ECtHR has held that it has effect solely in relation to the 'rights and freedoms' safeguarded by those provisions. Thus, Article 14 will only be engaged if the facts of the case fall within the ambit of one or more of

---

[191] S Choudhry and J Herring, 'Righting Domestic Violence' and 'Domestic Violence and the HRA' (n 21).
[192] *A* (n 161).
[193] *Opuz* (n 81) paras 91–106.
[194] *Ibid*, para 160.
[195] *Ibid*, para 161.
[196] *Ibid*, para 166–75.
[197] *Ibid*, para 176.

the other Convention rights.[198] A difference in treatment will only be held to be discriminatory if it does not have an objective and reasonable justification, that is, if it does not pursue a legitimate aim or if there is no reasonable relationship of proportionality between the means employed and the aim sought to be realised.[199] The applicant therefore complained, in conjunction with Articles 2 and 3, that she and her mother had been discriminated against on the basis of their gender. Her claim was essentially that the domestic law of Turkey was discriminatory and insufficient to protect women and that despite a number of reforms, domestic violence is still tolerated and impunity is granted to perpetrators by the judicial and administrative bodies.[200] Interights,[201] which had been given leave by the President to intervene in the case, submitted that the failure of the state to protect against domestic violence meant that it had also failed in its obligation to provide equal protection of the law based on sex. They also made the further argument which was being increasingly recognised internationally that violence against women was a form of unlawful discrimination. In terms of the meaning of discrimination, the Court set out that it had to take into account the international-law background to the legal question before it.[202] In this context, this meant having regard to the provisions of more specialised legal instruments and the decisions of international legal bodies, such as on the question of violence against women. After reviewing the relevant provision of CEDAW, the United Nations Commission on Human Rights, the Belém do Pará Convention and the Inter-American Commission, the Court concluded that:

> [T]he State's failure to protect women against domestic violence breaches their right to equal protection of the law and that this failure does not need to be intentional.[203]

The Court then went on to consider the approach to domestic violence in Turkey. Although there had been significant legislative reform in the provision of protection for victims it was, after reviewing the reports of two NGOs,[204] 'the general attitude of the local authorities, such as the manner in which the women were treated at police stations when they reported domestic violence and judicial passivity in providing effective protection to victims'[205] that was the problem. The Court also took into account similar findings by the CEDAW Committee on Turkey.[206] As a result, the Court found that the domestic violence affected mainly women and that the general and discriminatory judicial passivity in Turkey created a climate that was conducive to domestic violence. Furthermore, due to the fact that the Court had established that the criminal law system did not have an adequate

---

[198] *Petrovic v Austria* (2001) 33 EHRR 307, para 22.

[199] *Ibid*, para 30 and WK Wright, 'The Tide in Favour of Equality: Same-Sex Marriage in Canada and England and Wales' (2006) 20 (3) *International Journal of Law, Policy and the Family* 249 for a detailed application of Art 14 to this issue.

[200] *Opuz* (n 81) paras 178–9.

[201] The International Centre for the Legal Protection of Human Rights. Interights holds consultative status with the United Nations Economic and Social Council, the Council of Europe and the African Commission on Human and Peoples' Rights. It is accredited with the Commonwealth Secretariat and is authorised to present collective complaints under the European Social Charter.

[202] *Opuz* (n 81) para 184.

[203] *Ibid*, para 191.

[204] The Diyarbakır Bar Association and Amnesty International—the findings of these reports were unchallenged by the government.

[205] *Opuz* (n 81) para 192.

[206] *Ibid*, para 197.

deterrent effect capable of ensuring effective protection of the Articles 2 and 3 rights of the applicant and her mother the Court considered that the violence suffered by them both may be regarded as gender-based violence which is a form of discrimination against women. There had therefore been a violation of Article 14, in conjunction with Articles 2 and 3.

The significance of this element of the decision is threefold. First, it demonstrates the acceptance and application by the ECtHR of a number of international instruments and decisions in relation to domestic violence. Second, it demonstrates that a state's obligation under Article 14 cannot simply be satisfied by the passing of appropriate legislation alone. What is also required to be demonstrated is that the legislation is reasonably *effective*. The decision thus underlines the need to fully implement and carefully monitor the effectiveness of domestic violence policy and legislation. Finally, although uncontested in *Opuz*,[207] it is nevertheless clear that the Court's willingness to refer to the reports provided by NGOs and advocacy groups means that such evidence will be of considerable importance when it comes to any future assessment by the Court of a state's obligation in this regard.

Occupation Orders under the FLA 1996 and Article 3

The civil law relating to domestic violence in England and Wales is primarily[208] contained in Part IV of the FLA 1996.[209] The Act enables victims of domestic violence to apply for orders to protect them from further violence. Two main orders can be made under the Act: the non-molestation order and the occupation order. The interpretation of the FLA by the courts is, as the authors have discussed elsewhere,[210] marked by a reluctance to make occupation orders. This is due in part to recognition of the severity of interference in a person's rights, which is caused by an order removing him from his house.

Only an 'associated person'[211] is able to apply for an occupation order or a non-molestation order, but the availability of the occupation order is also dependent upon whether the applicant is 'entitled' or 'non-entitled'. An entitled applicant is defined by section 33 as one who holds a property right or matrimonial home right in relation to the home in respect of which he or she is seeking an occupation order. If the applicant is not entitled to occupy the property, the availability of the occupation order will turn upon the status of the applicant.[212] Further, it is obvious from the provisions of the Act that the availability of an occupation order is much more limited for cohabitants who do not hold any property rights than for those who do.[213] The starting point for an application for an occupation order by an entitled applicant is section 33(7), which sets out the 'significant harm' test. This subsection was introduced specifically to encourage courts to make occupation orders in cases where without court intervention the applicant would be likely to suffer significant harm due to the respondent's action. The section is in mandatory terms:

---

[207] *Ibid.*

[208] Civil remedies may be available in some domestic violence cases under the Protection from Harassment Act 1997: Parliamentary Assembly, Council of Europe, Committee on Equal Opportunities for Women and Men, *Domestic Violence* (2002), para 12.

[209] J Herring, *Family Law* (Harlow, Longman, 2009) ch 6 and M Burton, *Legal Responses to Domestic Violence* (Routledge-Cavendish, 2008) for a comprehensive summary of the law in this area.

[210] S Choudhry and J Herring, 'Domestic Violence and the HRA' (n 21).

[211] As defined in s62(3).

[212] However, in the unlikely event that neither the applicant or the respondent is entitled to occupy, s37 or s38 must be used.

[213] S Choudhry and J Herring, 'Domestic Violence and the HRA' (n 21) outlines the difference in treatment.

if the judge is satisfied that the applicant will suffer significant harm at the hands of the respondent, he or she must make an order unless satisfied that the harm the respondent will suffer if an order is made is equal or greater. If the significant harm test is not satisfied, the court must still go on to consider the general factors under section 33(6)[214] to decide whether on the basis of them an order should be made. Otton LJ in *Chalmers v Johns*[215] suggested that the phrase 'significant harm' in the balance of harm test had to be harm that was 'considerable, or noteworthy or important'.[216] However, the finding that significant harm has to be 'considerable' harm may, as the authors have argued elsewhere,[217] give too wide an interpretation to the word 'significant'. Several cases have been before the Court of Appeal concerning situations where, although there is much unpleasantness, there is no 'violence'. *Re Y*[218] involved a family described as 'at war … with itself'. On one side was a father and son and on the other the mother and pregnant daughter. The relationship between the daughter and father was described by the Court of Appeal as 'pretty appalling', involving 'frequent rows and fights'. As the trial judge put it: 'There is hatred in the house; there is dislike; there is constant fighting.'[219] No occupation order was granted on the basis that the case was not sufficiently serious to justify making the draconian order. Similarly in *G v G*,[220] where the couple had two children living with them (aged 15 and 12), the Court of Appeal held that 'the friction between the parties was only the product of their incompatible personalities and the heightened tensions that any family has to live with whilst the process of divorce and separation is current'.[221] In both cases the courts regarded the intolerable atmosphere as part of the ordinary tension of divorce and therefore not sufficiently serious to make as draconian an order as ordering the removal of one of the adults from the house. However, in doing so, it is argued that the courts are failing to appreciate the impact not only on the adults but also the children in these kinds of case.[222] Whenever a child is living in a household in which there is domestic violence there is, as demonstrated above, a real risk that the child's Article 3 rights are being infringed. The definition of the term 'significant harm' is thus inextricably linked to the nature of the order being sought: an order interfering with property rights. In addition there is an obvious reluctance to make an occupation order unless the conduct is regarded as severe enough to justify the infringement of property rights. However, where the conduct concerned falls within the definition of Article 3 this reasoning process has to be incompatible with Article 3. The duties imposed by Article 3 would mean that *any* interference with property rights that would occur in making the occupation order would be justifiable regardless of the Article 8 rights of the respondent. Further, given that at least the more serious forms of domestic violence would fall within the definition of Article 3, it is suggested that this be used as

---

[214]   *Chalmers v Johns* [1999] 1 FLR 392; *Mabey v UK* (1996) 22 EHRR 123; *Khatun v UK* (1998) 26 EHRR 212; *Chapman v UK* (2001) 33 EHRR 399 and *O'Rourke v UK* Application No 39022/97 ECHR 26 June 2001.

[215]   *Chalmers* (n 214).

[216]   *Ibid*, 398.

[217]   S Choudhry and J Herring, 'Domestic Violence and the HRA' (n 21) 2. The danger is revealed in *Re Y* [2000] 2 FCR 470 where, remarkably, Ward LJ had doubts whether a pregnant 16 year old who was involved in 'frequent rows and fights' including one 'fairly ferocious fight' with her father could not be said to be suffering 'significant harm'.

[218]   *Re Y* (n 217).

[219]   *Ibid*, para 10 (Mr Recorder Marsh).

[220]   *G v G* [2000] 2 FLR 36.

[221]   *Ibid*, 39.

[222]   S Choudhry and J Herring, 'Domestic Violence and the HRA' (n 21) 3.

a guide by the court when deciding whether significant harm has occurred. This would ensure that any remaining element of discretion in granting occupation orders is removed and that the court's obligations under Article 3 are being fully served.

Where the issue of whether significant harm has occurred is *not in dispute* it is clear that the existing domestic legislation goes some way towards directing a court's hand towards making an occupation order. Where the application for an occupation order is brought under section 33(7) of the FLA, if an applicant is likely to suffer significant harm without a court order then the court *must* make an order, unless it is persuaded that the significant harm suffered by the respondent if an order is made will be equal or greater. Further, as the Court of Appeal in *Chalmers v Johns*[223] emphasised, even where the applicant's predicted harm is less than the respondent's it is still open to the court to make an occupation order, considering the general factors in section 33(6).

Similarly if the applicant is non-entitled and the application is brought under one of the other sections, the court has a discretion to decide whether or not to grant an occupation order. However, although unlikely, the discretionary element of the decision-making process in relation to 'non-entitled' applicants does, nevertheless, *allow* for an occupation order to be refused. This would be the case even where the conduct complained of fell within the definition of Article 3. Thus, if the courts are to comply with their section 6 obligations fully, a correct application of the Strasbourg interpretation of the positive obligations in this context would require the discretionary element relating to the non-entitled applicant being removed.[224] This would be the case even where other rights and interests are claimed due to the nature and context of the conduct complained of. Although the issue of whether certain protection for domestic violence victims should be dependent upon their individual property rights has not directly been raised at Strasbourg it is difficult to imagine that this difference in treatment towards victims could, after the *Opuz*[225] decision, be said to be compatible with Article 14. Such a change, although mainly symbolic (in that in practice it rarely makes a difference), would nevertheless ensure that all victims of this type of conduct are treated equally under Article 3 and Article 14 from the outset.

Article 3 Claims under the Human Rights Act

The effect of an Article 3 claim under the HRA within the domestic violence context is, as yet, untested, given that the majority of such claims have arisen in cases concerning the application of the *Soering*[226] principle[227] to the proposed deportation of failed asylum seekers or illegal immigrants who may be at risk of Article 3 type treatment in the destination

---

[223] This was due to the fact that he was precluded from doing so by the Local Government (Scotland) Act 1975 s24(4). The applicants argued that they were, in turn, precluded from suing the local authority for damages in negligence due to the effect of *X v Bedfordshire CC* (n 177).

[224] The authors have argued elsewhere that such a removal would constitute a radical reform of the statute and one which, arguably, goes beyond the type of reform that can be achieved by judicial rectification via a s3 interpretation. As a result, realistically, change can only occur via a declaration of incompatibility under s4: S Choudhry and J Herring, 'Domestic Violence and the HRA' (n 21) 16.

[225] *Opuz* (n 81).

[226] *Soering* (n 49).

[227] *Ibid*. The expulsion of an alien by a contracting state may give rise to an issue under Art 3, and hence engage the responsibility of that state under the Convention, where substantial grounds have been shown for believing that the person in question, if expelled, would face a real risk of being subjected to treatment contrary to Art 3 in the receiving country. In these circumstances, Art 3 implies the obligation not to expel the person in question to that country.

state. Other claims have arisen in cases involving the medical treatment of incapacitated[228] and detained patients,[229] the provision of treatment under the NHS[230] and the provision of a subsistence level of support to those claiming asylum.[231] Nevertheless, it is possible to discern a similar pattern of principles to that found at the ECtHR. In *R (on the application of Bagdanavicius) v Secretary of State for the Home Department*,[232] a deportation case where the risk of harm emanated from non-state actors, the House of Lords confirmed that a breach of the state's positive obligations towards the potential victim would only occur if it had failed to provide reasonable protection.[233] In terms of the risk of treatment, Lord Brown[234] considered that the risk had to be one of the 'proscribed treatments'[235] rather than merely a risk of harm. The subsequent case of *R (on the application of Gezer) v Secretary of State for the Home Department*[236] was noteworthy for the attempt to introduce an element of deference into the question of whether the state has fulfilled the positive obligations under Article 3. Here, G appealed against a decision refusing his application for judicial review of a decision of the National Asylum Support Service (NASS) to disperse him and his family to a council estate in Glasgow and a later decision to return them to Glasgow. G and his family had claimed asylum in the United Kingdom. G was also diagnosed with psychotic depression and NASS was notified of that fact. It subsequently offered G and his family accommodation on a council estate in Glasgow pursuant to its dispersal programme and indicated that, if the offer was declined, it would withdraw all financial support. Accordingly, the family moved to the estate; however, the family was subjected to racial abuse and harassment, culminating in an attack at their flat. They subsequently returned to London. G argued that, where danger flowed from a proposed action by the state itself, the state's duty was to provide protection where the individual faced a risk of ill-treatment contrary to Article 3 of the ECHR. Further, G argued that NASS should have appreciated that, because of his fragile psychological state, he was especially vulnerable, and should therefore have made enquiries so as to ensure that he was not exposed to the treatment that he and his family suffered at the estate.

Although the Court of Appeal was in agreement with the lower court's assessment that the treatment the family had suffered had crossed the Article 3 threshold, the question of whether the action taken by the NASS was sufficient to discharge the positive obligations owed to the applicant and his family was, according to the court, one which could be subject to a degree of deference to the decision-making body. The degree of deference to be given was, in turn, according to Laws LJ, dependent upon the application of the 'sliding

---

[228] *R (on the application of Burke) v General Medical Council* [2005] EWCA 1003 (Civ).

[229] See *R (on the application of B) v S (Responsible Medical Officer, Broadmoor Hospital)* [2005] EWHC 1936 (Admin).

[230] *R (on the application of Watts) v Bedford Primary Care Trust* [2003] EWHC 2228 (Admin).

[231] *R (on the application of Limbuela) v Secretary of State for the Home Department* [2005] UKHL 66.

[232] *R (on the application of Bagdanavicius) v Secretary of State for the Home Department* [2005] UKHL 38.

[233] *Ibid*, para 24.

[234] His judgment is also notable for its failure to grasp that the question of whether the threshold of treatment for Art 3 has been crossed by a non-state actor (or the state) is entirely separate from the question of whether the state had fulfilled its positive obligations towards the victim: 'Non-state agents do not subject people to torture or the other proscribed forms of ill-treatment, however violently they treat them: what, however, would transform such violent treatment into Article 3 ill-treatment would be the state's failure to provide reasonable protection against it': *Bagdanavicius* (n 232) para 24.

[235] Treatment that crosses the Art 3 threshold.

[236] *R (on the application of Gezer) v Secretary of State for the Home Department* [2003] EWHC 860 (Admin).

scale' which he had first referred to in *R (on the application of Limbuela) v Secretary of State for the Home Department*:[237]

> This figure of a spectrum seems to imply the existence of a point upon the spectrum which marks the dividing line, in terms of State acts or omissions, between what violates Article 3 and what does not. There *is* such a point, but it does not, I fear, provide a bright line rule by which the court may readily determine whether any particular set of facts falls on this or that side of the line. The point is at the place between cases where government action is justified notwithstanding the individual's suffering, and cases where it is not. Various factors will determine where this place is to be found. They will include the severity of the threatened suffering, its origin in violence or otherwise, and the nature of the government's reasons or purpose in acting as it does.[238]

In *Gezer*,[239] Laws LJ considered that the scale would be applicable to a range of instances in which Article 3 might be engaged:

> From where the State enjoyed no power of discretion or judgment but was simply forbidden to cause or perpetrate the act which would violate Article 3, to those where the State might enjoy a considerable margin of discretion as to the adoption and exercise of policy notwithstanding that the action taken might be sufficiently grave to meet the Article 3 standard.[240]

Thus, as G and his family had a choice as to whether to accept the offer of housing at the estate (despite the fact that financial support would have been withdrawn if they had declined)[241] it was clear that the state, through NASS, had not imposed a compulsory result on the individual. That fact meant that the case fell at the less serious end of the spectrum of cases that engaged Article 3 and thus did not impose a requirement on NASS to enquire into the conditions at the estate to ensure that G would be saved from harm. It was further held that the Secretary of State, through NASS, enjoyed a wide power of discretion as to the administration of any scheme of support to be administered under section 95 of the Immigration and Asylum Act 1999. As the facts showed, once NASS had become aware of the problems at the estate and had investigated them, it had withdrawn any requirement that the family return to the same address as a condition of its support pursuant to section 95. In those circumstances, the court held that the Secretary of State had fulfilled his duty to protect G from Article 3 ill-treatment and, accordingly, there had been no violation of Article 3.

   The introduction of a degree of deference to the state in cases where the treatment had crossed the Article 3 threshold by Laws LJ in *Limbuela*[242] and *Gezer*[243] clearly did not have any basis in Strasbourg jurisprudence. More importantly, it had the worrying effect of watering down the absolute nature of the Article by implying that there were degrees of ill-treatment that might be capable of justification if they arose in the administration or execution of government policy. This was quite different from what was actually required by the ECtHR: to consider whether the state had taken reasonably available measures

---

[237] *R (on the application of Limbuela) v Secretary of State for the Home Department* [2004] EWCA 540 (Civ).
[238] *Limbuela* (n 237), para 68 (Laws LJ).
[239] *Gezer* (n 236).
[240] *Ibid*, para 33 (Laws LJ).
[241] Elias J, however, disagreed with this as a means of affecting the Art 3 duty: *ibid*, para 57.
[242] *Limbuela* (n 237).
[243] *Gezer* (n 236).

to mitigate the harm when assessing its culpability under Article 2. As a result, when *Limbuela*[244] came before the House of Lords on appeal, the House took the opportunity to address the inappropriateness of the application of the 'spectrum analysis' to Article 3 cases:[245]

> The exercise of judgment is required in order to determine whether in any given case the treatment or punishment has attained the necessary degree of severity. It is here that it is open to the court to consider whether, taking all the facts into account, this test has been satisfied. But it would be wrong to lend any encouragement to the idea that the test is more exacting where the treatment or punishment which would otherwise be found to be inhuman or degrading is the result of what Laws LJ refers to as legitimate government policy. That would be to introduce into the absolute prohibition, by the back door, considerations of proportionality. They are relevant when an obligation to do something is implied into the Convention. In that case the obligation of the state is not absolute and unqualified. But proportionality, which gives a margin of appreciation to states, has no part to play when conduct for which it is directly responsible results in inhuman or degrading treatment or punishment. The obligation to refrain from such conduct is absolute.[246]

For the moment, therefore, it is reasonably clear that where the Article 3 threshold has been crossed it is inappropriate for the courts to defer to government policy or introduce an element of proportionality into the assessment of state liability.

Conclusions on Article 3 and Domestic Violence

In summary, although Article 3 is drafted in absolute terms, the *duties* imposed by it are not. The police, local authorities and courts are only under a duty to intervene in *so far as is reasonable* to protect a victim of domestic violence, including children affected by domestic violence, where the violence amounts to torture, inhuman or degrading treatment. The government has certainly demonstrated some effort towards complying with this duty, in terms of both prevention and response. In relation to adult victims there has been a significant amount of policy and resource commitment. CPS, ACPO, local authority and judicial guidance are regularly updated and take into account the substantial amount of research in the area. Further, in compliance with Recommendation Rec(2002)5 of the Council of Europe[247] the government has published and updated its National Domestic Violence Delivery Plan[248] on how it intends to achieve the goal of the protection of women against violence. In addition, the definition of harm was amended by the Adoption and Children Act 2002[249] to make clear that when a court is considering whether a child has suffered, or is likely to suffer harm, it must consider harm that a child may suffer not just from domestic

---

[244] *Limbuela* (n 237).

[245] *Ibid*.

[246] *Ibid*, para 55 (Lord Hope).

[247] Committee of Ministers of the Council of Europe, 'Recommendation on the Protection of Women Against Violence' Rec(2002)5. The Recommendation specifically asks that Member States 'consider establishing a national plan of action for combating violence against women' as a means towards 'ensuring that all measures are co-ordinated nation-wide and focused on the needs of the victims and that relevant state institutions as well as non-governmental organisations (NGOs) be associated with the elaboration and the implementation of the necessary measures'.

[248] The plan and the updated progress reports can be found on the Home Office website at www.crimereduction.homeoffice.gov.uk/dv/dv017.htm.

[249] Implemented in January 2005.

violence, but also from witnessing it. Section 7 of the Children and Adoption Act 2006[250] also extends the duty to private law Children Act proceedings in requiring officers from the Children and Family Court Advisory and Support Service (CAFCASS) to carry out risk assessments in such proceedings where they consider that there is cause to suspect that a child is at risk of harm. The officers are then required to inform the court of their findings in respect of the risk of the child who is suffering harm, so that the court can consider what action should be taken. Notwithstanding such efforts, it must be remembered that when an assessment is undertaken of the conduct of the state in relation to Article 3 cases the real issue is whether the state was properly to be regarded as responsible for the conduct that was prohibited by Article 3 rather than whether this was as a result of legitimate government policy. Thus, the actual implementation of such policies must be closely monitored in order to ensure that state obligations are really being fulfilled. In practical terms, this could mean that a failure by law-enforcement agencies and local authorities to answer effectively a call for help from a victim of domestic violence, or, having attended the scene, to provide effective protection from domestic violence or, indeed, to fail to prosecute or otherwise offer protection could violate the victim's rights under Article 3. Finally, it must also be noted that because of the absolute nature of the Article, it is certainly arguable that Article 3 rights should be viewed as being particularly weighty when the court conducts the balancing exercise between any competing rights such as Articles 6 or 8.

Article 13 and the Right to a Remedy

Article 13 of the ECHR may also impose additional duties on Member States. If an 'arguable complaint' can be established to the effect that another substantive Convention right has been breached this may, in turn, also establish a right under Article 13,[251] which provides:

> Everyone whose rights and freedoms as set forth in this Convention are violated shall have an effective remedy before a national authority notwithstanding that the violation has been committed by persons acting in an official capacity.

Although section 1 of the HRA 1998 has not incorporated Article 13, it is clear that the HRA 1998 does go some way towards providing for an effective remedy for a breach of Convention rights.[252] In addition, should the matter be brought before the ECtHR it is also clear that Article 13 can be read into the requirements of Article 3.[253]

Here, Feldman's[254] argument that Article 3 will also impose a duty to investigate alleged violations and a duty to make provision for securing the legal accountability of people who inflict torture or inhuman or degrading treatment or punishment on others is particularly relevant. He notes that in *Aydin v Turkey*[255] it was held that Article 13 would be violated

---

[250] Section 7 of the Act came into force on 1 October 2007. However, revised forms (commonly known as 'Gateway' forms), for applications for child contact and residence were introduced on 31 January 2005. Courts are now required to consider whether an incident of domestic violence—not just from direct violence but also from witnessing violence towards another—has had an adverse impact on the child, or might affect the child in the future.

[251] Amongst others: *Z and Others* (n 176), para 108 and *DP and JC v UK* [2003] 36 EHRR 14, para 134.

[252] By virtue of HRA ss2(1), 3(1), 6(1), 7, and 8.

[253] *Z and Others* (n 176) and *E v UK* [2003] 36 EHRR 31.

[254] D Feldman, *Civil Liberties* (n 55) ch 5.

[255] *Aydin v Turkey* 25 EHRR 251, paras 1103–9.

where state authorities fail to conduct an adequate investigation of an allegation that someone has been a victim of inhuman or degrading treatment. Factors taken into account by the Court when assessing the adequacy of the investigation were: the speed of its instigation, the independence of the investigator, the vigour and efficiency of the investigation and the thoroughness of the report of the findings.

However, Feldman goes on to assert that despite the existence of these duties the current approach in the UK towards the duty on the police and other agencies to investigate allegations of behaviour amounting to torture and inhuman or degrading treatment is a restrictive one.[256] He concludes that the existence of these limitations means that it is unclear as to whether this current restrictive approach will, in fact, meet the requirements of both Articles 3 and 13 of the ECHR. The decision in *Aydin v Turkey*,[257] however, concerned alleged infliction of treatment contrary to Article 3 involving potential criminal responsibility on the part of security forces officials. The Court has recently clarified the obligations imposed on states concerning the relationship between Article 13 and Article 3 within the 'private context'. In *Z and Others v the United Kingdom*[258] (considered above) the Court held that the outcome of the domestic proceedings brought by the applicants meant that they, and any children with complaints such as theirs, could not sue the local authority in negligence however foreseeable and severe the harm suffered and however unreasonable the conduct of the local authority in failing to take steps to prevent that harm.[259]

The Court stated that:

> Where alleged failure by the authorities to protect persons from the acts of others is concerned, Article 13 may not always require that the authorities undertake the responsibility for investigating the allegations. There should however be available to the victim or the victim's family a mechanism for establishing any liability of State officials or bodies for acts or omissions involving the breach of their rights under the Convention. Furthermore, in the case of a breach of Articles 2 and 3 of the Convention, which rank as the most fundamental provisions of the Convention, compensation for the non-pecuniary damage flowing from the breach should in principle be available as part of the range of redress.[260]

Thus the Court found that, because the applicants did not have available to them an appropriate means of obtaining a determination of their allegations, the local authority had failed to protect them from inhuman and degrading treatment and prevented the possibility of obtaining an enforceable award of compensation for the damage suffered. They were, consequently, not afforded an effective remedy in respect of the breach of Article 3 and accordingly, there had also been a violation of Article 13.

---

[256] This, he argues, is because of three limitations of English law, two of which are particularly relevant to domestic violence. First, the courts would not ordinarily intervene on public law grounds to require the police to investigate a particular offence or to oversee how such investigations are carried out. Second, a failure to investigate would not usually give rise to liability in negligence in private law because it has been held by the House of Lords that a private law duty towards the public at large could not be imposed in respect of the investigation of a crime, or towards a person identified as a likely victim of an assailant. See *Hill* (n 111), *Osman v Ferguson* [1993] 4 All ER 344, CA, *Costello-Roberts* (n 165) and *Cowan v Chief Constable for Avon and Somerset Constabulary* [2001] EWCA 1699 (Civ). D Feldman, *Civil Liberties* (n 55) at 260.

[257] *Aydin* (n 255).

[258] *Z and Others* (n 176).

[259] However, the gap they identified in domestic law was one that gave rise to an issue under Art 13 and not Art 6(1) of the Convention: CA Gearty, 'Unravelling Osman' (2001) 54 (2) *MLR* 159, CA Gearty, 'Osman Unravels' (2002) 65 (1) *MLR* 87 for a comprehensive account of this particular line of reasoning.

[260] *Z and Others* (n 176) para 109.

These same principles were reiterated by the Court as part of its reasoning in two judgments following *Z and Others*.[261] In both *DP and JC v United Kingdom*[262] and *E v United Kingdom*[263] (discussed above) the Court found that a violation of both Article 3 and Article 13 had occurred. Both cases involved local authorities failing to protect the applicants from a breach of their Article 3 rights.

Thus Feldman's point is well taken:[264] the absence from national law of a right to an effective remedy under Article 13 for violations of Article 3 constitutes particularly strong reasons for national courts to adopt the ECtHR's extended interpretation of Article 3 as including a right to an effective investigation. In terms of providing a remedy, the Court has set out[265] that what is required within the 'private context' is simply a mechanism for establishing any liability of state officials or bodies for acts or omissions involving the breach of their rights under the Convention. The use of sections 6, 7 and 8 by the courts, acting as public authorities within the HRA 1998, should, as has been argued,[266] provide a remedy for violations of substantive Convention rights that is effective within the meaning of Article 13 without the need to develop the law of negligence. This interpretation of the duties imposed by both Articles 3 and 13 towards the victims of domestic violence could result in the provision of legal accountability for a failure by the public authorities including the police or local authorities to protect them. Whether the UK courts are minded to adopt such an interpretation, however, is a moot point, given the House of Lords' rather restrictive view of the development of the law in this area.[267]

Article 8

Article 8 provides:

1. Everyone has the right to respect for his private and family life, his home and his correspondence.
2. There shall be no interference by a public authority with the exercise of this right except such as is in accordance with the law and is necessary in a democratic society in the interests of national security, public safety or the economic well-being of the country, for the prevention of disorder or crime, for the protection of health or morals, or for the protection of the rights and freedoms of others.

The ECtHR has held that although Article 8 is primarily concerned with protecting individuals and families from unwanted state intrusion, it also imposes positive obligations upon the state. It is necessary to consider this issue in relation to all aspects of Article 8.

Balancing Article 8 Rights in Civil Cases and the Process of Qualification

When considering an application that an abusive partner be removed from a home, or have their contact restricted with their child or children, the court will have to

---

[261] *Ibid.*
[262] *DP and JC* (n 251) para 135.
[263] *E* (n 253) paras 109–10.
[264] D Feldman, *Civil Liberties* (n 55) 261.
[265] *Z and Others* (n 176), para 109.
[266] See A Lidbetter and J George, 'Negligent Public Authorities and Convention Rights—The Legacy of Osman' (2001) 6 *European Human Rights Law Review* 599.
[267] *Van Colle* (n 108).

undertake a balancing exercise between the competing individual Article 8 rights of the parties. The respondent can, for example, make a claim concerning his own rights to respect for private and family life and the right to respect for the home. As Article 8 is a 'qualified' right, once the Court has decided that Article 8(1) is 'engaged' by an alleged interference with the right it will then turn to a detailed consideration of whether the qualifications contained in Article 8(2) have been established. As is well known, this will require an assessment of whether the interference was prescribed by the law, whether the interference was necessary in the interests of one of the listed, legitimate aims and, finally, whether the interference was necessary in a democratic society in pursuance of the legitimate aim.

Thus, any interference with a right must be shown to have been in response to a pressing social need to act for that purpose and to be a proportionate response to that purpose.[268] Proportionality thus becomes a 'vehicle for conducting a balancing exercise' by requiring a balance between the nature and extent of the interference against the reasons for interfering.[269] In general, in determining the issue of proportionality whether the measures taken are 'necessary in a democratic society', the Court will consider whether, in the light of the case as a whole, the reasons adduced to justify them were relevant and sufficient for the purpose of paragraph 2 of Article 8[270] and in making this assessment, the Court will afford the national authorities a margin of appreciation, in recognition of the fact that they are better placed to the primary judgment as to the needs of the parties involved and the appropriate balance to be struck between them. The extent of the margin of appreciation to be accorded to states in such circumstances will, however, vary in the light of the nature and seriousness of the interests at stake.[271] The margin also varies according to the context of the individual facts of a case.[272]

Balancing Cases Involving Children

When approaching any question concerning Article 8, the ECtHR starts from the stance that wherever family life is found to be in existence, each of the family members will be entitled independently to respect for their family life. It does not regard the child's interests in this respect as paramount, that is, as displacing considerations of other members' rights.[273] Each family member's right to respect for family life (private life is not usually considered separately, although in some circumstances this might be a significant possibility) is accorded equal weight before a decision is made as to what extent, if at all, the rights of all the family members are in conflict. The Court will then consider whether any interference with the rights of family members is justified as 'necessary' under Article 8(2); it is

---

[268] *Silver v United Kingdom* 5 EHRR 347, para 97.

[269] D Feldman, *Civil Liberties* (n 55) 57.

[270] *Olsson v Sweden (No 2)* (1992) 17 EHRR 134, para 68.

[271] *K and T v Finland* Application No 25702/94 (2000) 31 EHRR 18, para 166 and *Kitzner v Germany* [2002] 35 EHRR 25, para 67.

[272] *Johansen v Norway* (1997) 23 EHRR 33, para 64 and *K v Finland* (2003) 36 EHRR 18, para 168.

[273] For a recent example where paramountcy was not applied see *Hansen v Turkey* [2004] 1 FLR 142, para 98. The Court has, however, recently used the word 'paramount' in relation to children's interests in *Zawadka v Poland* Application No 48542/99, para 67 but diluted this term by referring again, in the same paragraph, to the need to take into account 'more particularly' the best interests of the child. It does not seem, therefore, that the Court used 'paramount' in the same sense as the CA.

only at this point that the welfare of the child becomes relevant[274] and will not inevitably result in the child's interests prevailing.[275]

It is also clear that although the Court is prepared to concede a margin of appreciation to the national authorities in private family law cases where clashes between the Article 8 rights of the child and the parent occur, it is not as wide as in certain 'clash of rights' instances in other contexts:[276] the Court is prepared to be fairly interventionist where the right of one party to family life would be almost entirely abrogated by the restriction in question.[277] However, Strasbourg clearly accords special importance to the best interests of the child: where a significant conflict between the claims of another party and those interests arises, it will tend to allow the child's interests to determine the outcome. This Court has also demonstrated a greater willingness to give special consideration to children's rights,[278] which in turn has been attributed to the growing influence upon the Strasbourg jurisprudence[279] of the CRC.[280] Both the Commission and the Court have referred to the provisions of the CRC in children's cases since it came into force in 1990, and this development in approach is evidenced by a number of recent cases.[281] More significantly, in succeeding judgments, the Court has reaffirmed the established position whereby the varying Convention rights of the parties concerned are considered by starting from a basis of presumptive equality.[282] In other words, within the margin of appreciation of the Member State, a fair balance must be struck between the Article 8 rights of the child and those of the parent, albeit attaching particular importance to the former, thereby ruling out the use of a presumption that precludes that balancing exercise.

---

[274] Although the welfare of the child will, to some extent, be relevant when the Court considers its right to family life at the first stage under Art 8(1) it will not be considered in relation to the Art 8(1) rights of the other parties.

[275] This is contrary to the current domestic judicial interpretation of Art 8. See S Choudhry and H Fenwick 'Taking Fathers' Rights Seriously' (2005) 25 (3) *OJLS* 453; H Fenwick, 'Clashing Rights, the Welfare of the Child and the HRA' (2004) 67 *MLR* 889, which attacks the effect of the principle in the case of clashes between media freedom and the privacy of the child; S Choudhry, 'The Adoption and Children Act 2002, the Welfare Principle and the HRA 1998—a Missed Opportunity' (2003) 15 (2) *Child and Family Law Quarterly* 119; H Fenwick, D Bonner and S Harris-Short, 'Judicial Approaches to the HRA' [2003] 52 *International and Comparative Law Quarterly* 549 at 572–84 esp. at 582–4.

[276] *Otto-Preminger Institut v Austria* (1994) 19 EHRR 34; *Tammer v Estonia* (2003) 37 EHRR. 43.

[277] *Johansen v Norway* (n 272).

[278] The ECHR itself contains few explicit references to children and their rights, which is generally believed to be due to the era of its inception.

[279] U Kilkelly, 'The Best of Both Worlds for Children's Rights? Interpreting the European Convention on Human Rights in light of the UN Convention on the Rights of the Child' (2001) 23 *Human Rights Quarterly* 308 and M Woolf, 'Coming of Age? The Principle of the Best Interests of the Child' (2003) (2) *European Human Rights Law Review* 205 for an overview of how the principle has been interpreted by the European Court of Human Rights and the UK courts within the context of the CRC.

[280] Article 3 of the CRC states: 'in all actions concerning children, whether undertaken by public or private courts of law, administrative authorities or legislative bodies, the best interests of the child shall be a *primary* consideration'. The UK has ratified the CRC and is therefore bound under international law to comply with its requirements. It is still, however, not part of UK law.

[281] *L v Finland* [2001] 31 EHRR 30 at para 118; *Elsholz v Germany* [2000] 2 FLR 486.

[282] Thus, in *Hansen v Turkey* [2004] 1 FLR 142 the Court found, 'the rights and freedoms of all concerned must be taken into account, and more particularly the best interests of the child and his or her rights under Article 8 of the Convention. Where contact with the parent might appear to threaten those interests or interfere with those rights, it is for the national authorities to strike a *fair balance* between them' (emphasis added). See also *Görgülü v Germany* Application No 74969/01 (2004), para 43 and *Hoppe v Germany* (2004) 38 EHRR 15, para 44 for evidence of this approach.

The 'Parallel Analysis' Approach

It is thus apparent from the Strasbourg jurisprudence just discussed that an individual right cannot figure merely as an exception to another individual right and, in addition, that it cannot be entirely abrogated without an application of the paragraph 2 tests. Instead, the 'parallel analysis' approach must be utilised: both rights must be considered as exceptions to the other, by applying all the tests within paragraph 2 of Article 8.[283] Unlike Strasbourg the Family Division court will have all the parties as family members before it and all will claim that their rights are equally at issue. As a result the domestic courts will need to deal explicitly with the question of clashing rights. Of significant note is the requirement to attach particular importance to the best interests of the child when carrying out the balancing exercise concerning Article 8. This should provide a powerful justification to reinterpret any existing domestic requirements to hold such interests as paramount[284] but will also, if necessary, introduce a relatively higher consideration towards the interests of children where no such requirement currently exists. The practical application of this 'parallel analysis' with regard to the clear clash of rights that would occur in a case concerning domestic violence will be considered below.

The Right to Respect for 'Private and Family Life'

The right to private life is a wide-ranging right. Of particular relevance to the domestic violence context are two points. First, 'the concept of private life covers the physical and moral integrity of the person'.[285] In *X and Y v The Netherlands*[286] the lack of effective protection under the criminal law against sexual assault for a mentally ill woman was said to amount to an infringement of her right to private life. The state, it was said, is required under Article 8 to protect one person's right to private life against unwanted contact or infringements to moral integrity. The state may thus be required to protect a citizen from serious violence under Article 3, and less serious incidents under Article 8.[287] Mental health and stability is said to be part of a person's moral integrity.[288]

Second, the ECtHR has stated that Article 8 is concerned with protecting a person's physical and psychological integrity[289] and their right to identity and personal development.[290] Once this is identified as at the heart of Article 8, domestic violence can readily be seen as involving an interference with the parties' right to develop their personality. Clear links have been established between being a victim of domestic violence and a variety of emotional and psychological problems.[291]

---

[283] S Choudhry and H Fenwick, 'Clashing rights, the Welfare of the Child and the Human Rights Act 1998' (2005) 25 *OJLS* 453 and G Phillipson, 'Transforming Breach of Confidence? Towards a Common Law Right to Privacy Under the HRA' (2003) 66 (5) *MLR* 726. For recent examples of judicial application of the parallel analysis see *Campbell v MGM* [2004] 2 AC 457 and *Re S* [2005] 1 AC 593.

[284] In proceedings brought under the CA by virtue of s1 and the so called 'paramountcy principle'.

[285] *X and Y v the Netherlands* (1986) 8 EHRR 235.

[286] *Ibid* (n 285).

[287] *Costello-Roberts* (n 165).

[288] *Bensaid v The United Kingdom* [2001] 33 EHRR 10.

[289] *Pretty v UK* (2002) 35 EHRR 1, para 61.

[290] *Bensaid v the United Kingdom* (n 288) para 45.

[291] Parliamentary Assembly, *Domestic Violence* (n 219), para 12.

A consideration of 'family life' for the purposes of Article 8 necessitates, at first, a definition of what actually constitutes a 'family'. An examination of the Strasbourg jurisprudence on this point reveals that the Court has included a husband and wife and children (whether adopted or illegitimate) in its definition; however, it has not confined itself to marriage-based relationships alone. An unmarried couple can constitute a family.[292] A child will automatically have family life with his/her mother and married father. However, in *Lebbink v The Netherlands*[293] the Court stated that a child born out of other de facto 'family' ties such as the 'parties living together out of wedlock' was *ipso iure* part of that 'family' unit from the moment and by the very fact of its birth and, therefore, a relationship amounting to family life will exist between them.[294] As a rule, however, cohabitation may be a requirement for such a relationship although, exceptionally, other factors may also serve to demonstrate that a relationship has sufficient constancy to create de facto 'family ties'.[295] The existence or non-existence of 'family life' for the purposes of Article 8 is, thus, essentially, a question of fact depending upon the real existence, in practice, of close personal ties.[296]

Article 8 imposes positive obligations on the state. Most of the case law has concerned the positive obligations imposed on a state to protect the family life between a parent and child. It is well established in the Court's case law that the mutual enjoyment by parent and child of each other's company constitutes a fundamental element of family life, and domestic measures hindering such enjoyment can amount to an interference with the right protected by Article 8 of the Convention.[297] Thus, there may be, in addition, positive obligations inherent in effective 'respect' for private or family life.[298] These obligations may involve the adoption of measures designed to secure respect for family life in relations between private individuals, including both the provision of a regulatory framework of adjudication and enforcement to protect individual rights.[299] Thus, where the existence of a family tie has been established, the state must, in principle, act in a manner calculated to enable that tie to be developed and take measures that will enable a parent and child to be reunited.[300] This applies not only to cases dealing with the compulsory taking of children into public care and the implementation of care measures, but also to cases where contact and residence disputes concerning children arise between parents and/or other members of the children's family.[301]

However, the Court has also made it clear that the state's positive obligations concerning the reunification of a parent and a child on the breakdown of the parental relationship

---

[292] In deciding whether they do, the court will consider 'whether the couple live together, the length of their relationship and whether they have demonstrated their commitment to each other by having children together or by any other means': *X, Y and Z v the United Kingdom* Application No 21830/93 (1997) 24 EHRR 143.

[293] *Lebbink v the Netherlands* Application No 45582/99 (2005) 40 EHRR 18, para 35.

[294] Amongst others *Elsholz* (n 281), para 43, and *Yousef v the Netherlands* Application No 33711/96 [2002] 3 FCR 577.

[295] *Kroon v the Netherlands* Series A No 297 (1995) 19 EHRR 263, para 30. Here the birth of four children between the applicant and her partner had occurred despite a lack of cohabitation.

[296] *K and T* (n 271) para 150.

[297] Amongst others, *Johansen* (n 271) para 52.

[298] *X and Y* (n 285).

[299] *Glaser v the United Kingdom* Application No 32346/96 (2001) 33 EHRR 119, para 63.

[300] See, amongst others, *Eriksson v Sweden* [1990] 12 EHRR 183, para 71 and *Gnahoré v France* Application No 40031/98 (2002) 34 EHRR 38, para 51, *Zawadka* (n 284), *Bajrami v Albania* Application No 35853/04 (2008) 47 EHRR 22 and *Sobota-Gajic v Bosnia and Herzegovina* Application No 27966/06 [2007] ECHR 896.

[301] *Hokkanen v Finland* [1994] 19 EHRR 159, para 55.

are not absolute. In *Kosmopoulou v Greece*[302] it was held that whilst national authorities must do their utmost to facilitate such a reunion, any obligation to apply coercion in this area must be limited. This is due to the need to take into account the interests as well as the rights and freedoms of all concerned and, more particularly, the best interests of the child and his or her rights under Article 8 of the Convention. Where contact with the parent might appear to threaten those interests or interfere with those rights, it is for the national authorities to strike a fair balance between them.[303] The key consideration is, therefore, whether the state has taken all such steps to facilitate contact as can reasonably be demanded in the particular circumstances of each case.[304]

Regard must also be had to the fair balance that has to be struck between the competing interests of the individual and the community as a whole, including other concerned third parties. In both cases, the state enjoys a certain margin of appreciation.[305]

Thus, it can be seen that within the context of domestic violence the state may be required to intervene in order to protect the family lives of the abused parent and any children under its Article 8 obligations.[306] If the relationship between the child and parents is being severely disrupted by any violence (even if it is not being directed at the child), there is a strong case for claiming that both the child's and the abused parent's right to family life are being interfered with. This may then, in turn, create a positive obligation upon the state to intervene to protect their rights of family life. The ECtHR has recently considered this very issue in *Bevacqua and another v Bulgaria*[307] in which, following the parents' separation and during extended custody proceedings in Bulgaria, the applicant mother agreed to the father having contact with the three-year-old child. However, the father subsequently refused to return the child to the mother's care, and thereafter refused the applicant contact. After recovering the child from kindergarten, the applicant was threatened by the father, who eventually entered her home to recover the child and used violence against her. The applicant then moved to a hostel for victims of domestic violence in another town, but the authorities threatened to prosecute her for abduction of the child. To make matters worse, the Bulgarian courts then failed to make an interim order concerning the custody of the child despite the applicant's request for such an order. In order to avoid prosecution, the applicant then agreed that she and the father would care for the child in alternate months. However, while the child was living with the father there was further violence by the father against the applicant and after a series of further proceedings, the applicant was eventually granted custody of the child, the domestic courts having accepted that witnessing such behaviour from the father was a bad example for the child. Crucially, however, the father was not prosecuted for any of the violence used against the applicant both before and subsequent to this decision. As a result the applicants (mother and child) complained that the authorities had failed to take the necessary measures to secure respect for their family life and failed to protect the first applicant against the violent behaviour of her

---

[302] *Kosmopoulou v Greece* [2004] 1 FLR 800, para 45.

[303] *Ignacollo-Zenide v Romania* Application No 31679/96 25 January 2000, para 94.

[304] *Hokkanen v Finland* (n 312), para 58. See also *Chepelev v Russia* Application No 58077/00 26 July 2007.

[305] *Z and Others* (n 176) para 41.

[306] Where a child is being affected by the violence herself or himself the case is likely to fall within Art 3. It may even be argued that if the family life is characterised by abuse the family life ceases to be entitled to respect and so is no longer protected by Art 8: J Herring, 'Respecting Family Life' [2008] 75 *Amicus Curiae* 21.

[307] *Bevacqua and another v Bulgaria* Application No 71127/01 ECHR 12 June 2008.

former husband relying on Articles 3, 8, 13 and 14 of the Convention. However, the ECtHR considered that, in this case, the complaints fell to be considered under Article 8 alone although it was also emphasised that a state's positive obligations in this context could arise in some cases under Articles 2 or 3 and in other instances under Article 8 taken alone or in combination with Article 3 of the Convention.[308] After a detailed examination of the facts the Court went on to hold that the authorities' duty under Article 8 towards both applicants (parent and child) had required the examination of the interim measures application with due diligence and without delay and to secure the enjoyment of both applicants' right to normal contacts between them; however, this had not occurred:

> The cumulative effects of the District Court's failure to adopt interim custody measures without delay in a situation which affected adversely the applicants and, above all, the well-being of the second applicant and the lack of sufficient measures by the authorities during the same period in reaction to Mr N's behaviour amounted to a failure to assist the applicants contrary to the State's positive obligations under Article 8 of the Convention to secure respect for their private and family life.[309]

There are a number of significant aspects to this decision. First, the judgment reiterates the development of a positive obligation to include, in certain circumstances, a duty to maintain and apply in practice an adequate legal framework affording protection against acts of violence by private individuals.[310] Second, there is the reliance by the Court on a number of international instruments to emphasise the particular vulnerability of the victims of domestic violence and the need for active state involvement in their protection. The terms of the Recommendation Rec(2002)5 of the Committee of Ministers of the Council of Europe on the protection of women against violence[311] and Article 4(c) of the United Nations General Assembly Declaration on the Elimination of Violence against Women[312] were quoted in detail, as were comments by the Special Rapporteur on violence against women and the case law of a number of international bodies concerning the issue of domestic violence.[313] Thus, although the Court reiterated that the sphere of the relations of individuals between themselves was in principle a matter that fell within the domestic authorities' margin of appreciation, it was also able to rely on the absence of compliance with the aforementioned provisions as a means of emphasising the failure to respect the Article 8 rights of the victims in this case notwithstanding the application of this margin.[314] Finally, and of most significance, was the articulation by the Court of the second applicant's (the child's) right to respect for family life and the ability to effectively exercise his right to regular contact with his mother. Of particular note was the clear recognition by the Court of the adverse affects upon him of having to witness the violence between his parents.[315]

---

[308] *Ibid*, para 65.

[309] *Ibid*, para 84.

[310] *Ibid*, para 65.

[311] Recommendation of the Committee of Ministers of the Council of Europe on the Protection of Women Against Violence, Rec(2002)5, adopted 30 April 2002, states that Member States should introduce, develop and/or improve where necessary national policies against violence based on maximum safety and protection of victims, support and assistance, adjustment of the criminal and civil law, raising of public awareness, training for professionals confronted with violence against women and prevention.

[312] Which urges states to 'exercise due diligence to prevent, investigate and, in accordance with national legislation, punish acts of violence against women, whether those acts are perpetrated by the State or private persons'.

[313] *Bevacqua* (n 307) para 53.

[314] *Ibid*, paras 82–3.

[315] *Ibid*, para 79.

Contact, Domestic Violence and Article 8

Contact disputes in general have been discussed further in Chapter 7. However, in this section the relevance of domestic violence in contact disputes will be considered. Although not discussed in *Bevacqua*,[316] the fact remains that the father in such cases is also entitled to claim his right to exercise family life with his child under Article 8. Moreover, a domestic court, unlike the ECtHR, will be required to consider *all* the Article 8 claims of those involved even though this will inevitably result in a clash of rights between those family members. The issue is not just one of ensuring that family members are protected from violence under Article 8, but also that doing so does not disproportionately interfere with the right to mutual enjoyment of family life in terms of contact between the non-resident parent and the child and the effect this may have on the family life of the resident parent who has experienced violence from the other. It is at this juncture, however, that the debate concerning the appropriate balancing of the individual Article 8 rights of all the parties involved intersects with the domestic debate concerning the appropriateness of allowing contact between a child and a formerly violent parent. Indeed, the effects of witnessing or experiencing violence on children are such that there have been a number of calls for a legal presumption against contact in such cases.[317]

However, although the domestic family law courts have shown an increasing awareness of the potential effects of domestic violence on children it is fair to say that there has been a reluctance to implement such a presumption largely due to the existence and operation of the paramountcy principle.[318] That is to say that even where domestic violence is a factor, it must, like all other factors, if necessary, be overridden by what is in the best interests of the child. The leading authority in this area is the conjoined appeals of *Re L; Re V; Re M; Re H (Contact: DV)*[319] in which the Court of Appeal stressed that there was no presumption against contact in cases involving domestic violence and that it was one important factor in the overall balancing exercise of section 1(3) of the Children Act. The decision was particularly significant for the fact that the court commissioned and took into account expert evidence on the effects of domestic violence from academic psychologists, which concluded that domestic violence in itself was not a reason to refuse contact. As a result, the court set out a two-stage approach that should be taken in cases involving allegations of domestic violence. First, the court should decide whether the allegations concerning domestic violence are made out or not. Second, if they are made out the court should weigh up the risks involved and the impact of contact on the child against the positive benefits (if any) of contact. Any risk of harm to the resident parent should also be considered. A number of other more detailed guidelines were referred to, the aim being that, although there was no presumption against contact in such cases, they would at least ensure that the courts would take the matter seriously and allow the courts to refuse contact if necessary. In addition to this decision there was a general consensus by judges that fears concerning the

---

[316] *Ibid.*

[317] M Kaye, 'Domestic Violence, Residence and Contact' (1996) 8 *Child and Family Law Quarterly* 285; M Hester and C Pearson, 'Domestic Violence and Children—the Practice of Family Court Welfare Officers' (1997) 9 *Child and Family Law Quarterly* 281 and A Perry, 'Safety first? Contact and Family Violence in New Zealand' (2006) 18 (1) *Child and Family Law Quarterly* 1.

[318] *Re H (Minors) (Access)* [1992] 1 FLR 148 as an example of the application of the test to contact cases and *Re H (Contact: Domestic Violence)* [1998] 2 FLR 42 at 56, paras A to D.

[319] *Re L; Re V; Re M; Re H (Contact: DV)* [2000] 2 FLR 334.

commitment of the father and the security of the mother where contact was granted could be alleviated by allowing either indirect[320] or supervised contact only either at a relative's home or at a contact centre as a prerequisite to unsupervised contact in the future.[321]

However, it quickly became apparent that the decision had little effect on the refusal of contact in such cases. Thus, despite the fact that violence is raised as a reason for restricting contact in 22 per cent of disputes reaching the courts[322] and is established/admitted in over a third of cases requiring welfare reports,[323] the statistics (discussed above) demonstrate that contact is refused in a comparatively small number of cases.

There were also examples of court decisions in favour of contact that could be doubted even on the grounds of child welfare.[324] A series of high-profile campaigns by a number of organisations thus continued to highlight the potentially serious consequences of the courts getting the decision on contact wrong. One piece of research, which surveyed a number of cases where contact had been ordered despite the presence of domestic violence as a factor, suggested that 25 per cent of children were abused as a result of the contact.[325] There was also concern that allowing contact would enable the violent former partner to continue to dominate and exercise power over the resident parent and, more worryingly, use such arrangements to discover her whereabouts.[326] A study by Women's Aid[327] in particular highlighted 29 cases where children had been killed during or in connection with contact meetings. The findings were so disturbing that they prompted a report into the cases by Nicholas Wall LJ[328] to the President of the Family Division. However, his report concluded that eight of the 11 children who had died in these cases did so as a result of parental actions which could not reasonably have been foreseen or anticipated by the court on the material available before it. The remaining three children were the subjects of two cases, in both of which the judge was presented with consent orders agreed between the representatives of the parties. It was not clear, however, whether the court should have been more proactive in investigating the circumstances and refusing contact despite such agreement. In addition, there were arguments in both cases for the order being made in what were genuinely believed to be the best interests of the child despite earlier indications of violence between the parents. A further report[329] by the Family Justice Council was subsequently commissioned to consider,

---

[320]   *Re L; Re V; Re M; Re H* (n 319).

[321]   *Re O* (Contact: Imposition of Conditions) [1995] 2 FLR 124, 128.

[322]   C Smart, V May, A Wade and C Furniss (2003) 1, 'Residence and Contact Disputes in Court' (London, Department for Constitutional Affairs).

[323]   'Contact, Separation and the Work of Family Court Staff' (2002) 8 Napo.

[324]   See *Re J-S (A Child) (Contact: Parental Responsibility)* [2002] 3 FCR 433.

[325]   M Hester, 'One Step Forward and Three Steps Back? Children, Abuse and Parental Contact in Denmark', (2002) 14 (3) *Child and Family Law Quarterly* 267.

[326]   M Kaye, J Stubbs and J Tolmie, 'Domestic Violence and Child Contact Arrangements' (2003) 17 (1) *Australian Journal of Family Law*; J Masson and C Humphreys, 'Facilitating and Enforcing Contact: The Bill and the Ten Per Cent' (2005) 35 *Family Law* 548; and JL Hardesty and CH Chung, 'Intimate Partner Violence, Parental Divorce and Child Custody: Directions for Intervention and Future Research' (2006) 55 *Family Relations* 200.

[327]   H Saunders, *Twenty Nine Child Homicides* (Bristol, Women's Aid 2004).

[328]   N Wall, Lord Justice of Appeal, 'A Report to the President of the Family Division on the Publication by the Women's Aid Federation of England Entitled *Twenty Nine Child Homicides: Lessons Still to be Learnt on Domestic Violence and Child Protection* with Particular Reference to the Five Cases in which there was Judicial Involvement' (Royal Courts of Justice, March 2006). Can be found at www.judiciary.gov.uk/docs/report_childhomicides.pdf.

[329]   The Family Justice Council's Report and Recommendations to the President of the Family Division, '"Everybody's Business"—How Applications for Contact Orders by Consent Should be Approached by the Court in Cases Involving Domestic Violence', February 2007. Can be found at www.family-justice-council.org.uk/docs/contactsummary.pdf.

and make recommendations about, what approach should be adopted by the court when asked to make a contact order by consent, in cases where domestic violence was present. In evidence to the Home Affairs Select Committee, the Council stated: 'A cultural change is required, with a move away from "contact is always the appropriate way forward" to "contact that is safe and positive for the child is always the appropriate way forward".'[330] In pursuance of this aim the Council has recently issued a new practice direction[331] for the courts along these lines, which is accompanied by very strict guidelines. Of particular note is the requirement for the court to consider whether, subject to the seriousness of the allegations made and the difficulty of the case, it is appropriate for the child who is the subject of the application to be made a party to the proceedings and be separately represented.[332]

How do these domestic developments fit in with the requirements of Article 8 in relation to the divergent claims to family life that could be raised by the family members involved? The answer is that it is clear, as indicated in the detailed discussion above, that the ECHR does allow for a proportionate interference of an Article 8 right to family life as long as the interference satisfies the process of qualification within Article 8(2). Further, owing to the number of Article 8 claims at play in a contact dispute that involves domestic violence, the parallel analysis will also need to be employed, that is, all three Article 8 rights must be considered as exceptions to the other, by applying all the tests within paragraph 2 of Article 8. The court should also acknowledge that, although not paramount, the interests of any children involved should be of particular importance. The key consideration in such a case will therefore be whether the state has taken all the necessary steps to facilitate contact between the violent parent and the children as can reasonably be demanded in the special circumstances of the case. It may be that in the striking of a fair balance between the differing rights of the family members involved, the nature and extent of the violence is considered too great to grant a request for any form of contact where such contact could threaten the interests or interfere with other family members' rights. However, it may also be the case that allowing supervised or unsupervised contact may, according to the individual facts of a case, be the more proportionate response bearing in mind the positive obligations that are owed to parents, under Article 8, to facilitate contact between a parent and child, if possible. What is also important to bear in mind is the recent acknowledgement by the ECtHR of the detrimental effects that witnessing domestic violence may have on a child and therefore *their* right to family life. It may follow, therefore, that a cautious approach to contact in such cases would not be regarded as disproportionate.

Despite the fact that there is no explicit reference to it either in the case law or relevant reports, the current state of domestic law on contact in such cases would appear to comply with the requirements of Article 8. The practice direction in particular allows for a detailed consideration of exactly the kind of issues that would be relevant to the proportionality exercise and a separate consideration of the child's interests. However, the continued application of the paramountcy principle would appear to be incompatible with the requirement for an equal consideration of the differing rights involved, most particularly, the right to family life

---

[330] 'Domestic Violence, Forced Marriage and "Honour" Based Violence' (n 30), para 287.

[331] Family Justice Council, 'Practice Direction: Residence and Contact Orders: Domestic Violence and Harm'. The Practice Direction can be accessed on the Family Justice Council's website at www.family-justice-council.org.uk/docs/Domestic_Violence_PD.pdf.

[332] Practice Direction (Residence and Contact Orders: Domestic Violence and Harm) [2009], 1 FCR 233 (n 342) para 17.

of the parent who has experienced the violence. Its presence is thus able to actively hinder the proper application of the parallel analysis and may potentially facilitate the inappropriate granting of contact under the guise of what is in the best interests of the child.

The Right to Respect for the 'Home'

Establishing a 'Home' for the Purposes of Article 8

The definition given to a 'home' by Strasbourg has been a wide one, though it should be noted that this aspect of Article 8 is not dependent upon, nor directed to the protection of, property interests or contractual rights. In *Gillow v United Kingdom*[333] the Court referred to the establishment of 'sufficient and continuing links' to a property as a highly relevant factor when considering whether it was a home for the purposes of Article 8(1). The test used to establish a 'home' was further expanded by the Commission in *Buckley v United Kingdom*[334] when the Court described the 'home' as:

> An autonomous concept, which does not depend on classification under domestic law. Whether or not a particular habitation constitutes a 'home', which attracts the protection of Article 8(1), will depend on the factual circumstances, namely, the existence of sufficient and continuous links.

This definition of the home has been repeatedly referred to by the ECtHR[335] and has been expressly approved of by the House of Lords in a number of subsequent judgments.[336] The development of positive obligations binding on Member States in this area has, however, not been as extensive as in the case of the right to respect for family life. The imposition of positive obligations by the ECtHR has, it would seem, tended to centre on the ability to enjoy a home and, therefore, upon the issue of respect rather than the provision of a home per se.[337]

The Court has also made it abundantly clear that any attempt to interpret this aspect of Article 8(1) in order to impose an obligation to provide a home will be resoundingly rejected. Thus in *Chapman v United Kingdom*, the Court stated:[338]

> It is important to recall that Article 8 does not in terms give a right to be provided with a home. Nor does any of the jurisprudence of the Court acknowledge such a right ... Whether the State provides funds to enable everyone to have a home is a matter for political not judicial decision.

---

[333] *Gillow v United Kingdom* [1986] 11 EHRR 335, para 46.

[334] *Buckley v United Kingdom* [1996] 23 EHRR 191, para 63.

[335] *Mabey v United Kingdom* [1996] 22 EHRR 123 (CD); *Khatun v United Kingdom* [1998] 26 EHRR 212 (CD); *Chapman v United Kingdom* [2001] 33 EHRR 399 and *O'Rourke* (n 214).

[336] *London Borough of Harrow v Qazi* [2003] UKHL 43.

[337] For a general summary of the positive obligations imposed by the Court in this area see AR Mowbray, *The Development of Positive Obligations under the ECHR by the European Court of Human Rights* (Hart Publishing 2004) ch 6, 181–6. This aspect of Art 8(1) has, thus, been interpreted to impose an obligation upon Member States not to cause, or allow others to create, environmental pollution of such an extent that it may interfere with the right to respect for the home: *Powell and Rayner v UK* [1990] 12 EHRR 355; *Lopez Ostra v Spain* [1994] 20 EHRR 277; *Hatton v United Kingdom* [2003] 37 EHRR 28; *Fadeyeva v Russia* [2005] ECHR 55723/00; *Guerra v Italy* [1998] 26 EHRR 357 and AR Mowbray, '*Guerra and Others v Italy*: the Right to Environmental Information under the European Convention on Human Rights' (1998) 6 (3) *Environmental Liability* 81; and to ensure that the right to respect for the home is not applied in a discriminatory manner: *Larkos v Cyprus* [1999] 30 EHRR 597.

[338] *Chapman v United Kingdom* [2001] 33 EHRR 399 at 427–8, para 99 and *O'Rourke* (n 214) at 5. Unless the failure to provide assistance would raise an issue in relation to the private life of an individual: see *Marzari v Italy* [1999] 28 EHRR CD 175 at 179–80 where, despite being recognised as severely disabled, the applicant had been allocated an apartment which he considered to be inadequate for his needs. He refused to pay rent for it and was subsequently evicted. The Court found that his eviction from his apartment interfered with his rights under Art 8(1).

This analysis was subsequently relied upon by the House of Lords in *Qazi v London Borough of Harrow*[339] when it held that a defendant tenant who had lived in a house as his only home throughout the tenancy, and had remained there after his right to do so had ceased, had established sufficient and continuous links for the house to constitute his home for the purposes of Article 8(1). However, in terms of Article 8(2) and the question of whether possession proceedings taken against a defendant could be defended on the ground that they infringed the right to respect for the home, the House was divided. By a three to two majority the House held that 'an Article 8 defence can never prevail against an owner entitled under the ordinary law to possession'.[340] In doing so the majority sought to rely on a number of ECtHR decisions[341] to rule that Article 8 could not be relied upon to defeat proprietary or contractual obligations to possession by the local authority.[342] This interpretation of Article 8(2), unsurprisingly, attracted significant criticism not only for revealing a selective reading of ECHR jurisprudence but also for containing assertions that were not securely rooted in Strasbourg precedent.[343] The House of Lords clearly viewed Article 8 as being more pertinent to the need to protect an individual against arbitrary interferences by public authorities and the right to respect for privacy and security with the home[344] rather than the development of positive obligations upon Member States in relation to the provision of a home, particularly where this would result in the interference of contractual or property rights.[345] A subsequent ECtHR decision provided further impetus for a review of the decision. *Connors v United Kingdom*[346] concerned a successful application for eviction by Leeds City Council of Mr Connors and his family from two plots that they occupied on a gypsy site run by the council in pursuance of their unconditional right to terminate a licence.[347] The parties agreed that the applicant's eviction resulted in his Article 8 rights being engaged and the issue before the Court was, therefore, whether the interference with those rights was justified under Article 8(2). The Court held that owing to the fact that the eviction of the applicant and his family did not conform to the procedural

---

[339] *Qazi v London Borough of Harrow* [2003] UKHL 43. For a comprehensive summary of the Court of Appeal judgment in this case and a review of the European Court's jurisprudence on this point see I Loveland, 'When is a House not a Home under Article 8 ECHR' [2002] (2) *PL* 221. See also SJ Bright, 'Ending Tenancies by Notice to Quit: The Human Rights Challenge' (2004) 120 *LQR* 398.

[340] *Qazi* (n 339), para 152 (Lord Scott of Foscote).

[341] *S v United Kingdom* [1986] 47 DR 274, *Ure v United Kingdom* Application No 28027/95 27 November 1996, *Wood v United Kingdom* [1997] 24 EHRR CD 69, *Di Palma v United Kingdom* [1986] 10 EHRR 149 and *Marzari v Italy* [1999] 28 EHRR CD 175.

[342] *Qazi* (n 339), para 78 (Lord Hope): 'My understanding of the European jurisprudence leads me to the conclusion that Article 8(2) is met where the law affords an unqualified right to possession on proof that the tenancy has been terminated'.

[343] I Loveland, 'The Impact of the HRA on Security of Tenure in Public Housing' [2004] (3) *PL* 594.

[344] Such as the deliberate destruction of homes by the security forces as in *Selcuk and Asker v Turkey* [1998] 26 EHRR 477, *Akdivar v Turkey* [1996] 1 BHRC 137 and *Mentes v Turkey* [1997] 26 EHRR 59.

[345] This point was clearly illustrated by Lord Millet in *Qazi* (n 339), para 101: 'Article 8(2) stipulates that interference with the right must not be arbitrary; it must be in accordance with the law … The interference must also be justified. In most cases Article 8(2) calls for a balance to be struck between the applicant's right to "respect" for his home and some competing public interest, such as national security, public safety, the prevention of disorder or crime, the protection of health or morals, and so on. But Article 8(2) also permits interference with the right where it is necessary "for the protection of the rights and freedoms of others". Those others include but are not limited to private citizens. They include landowners whether they are private citizens or public authorities.'

[346] *Connors v United Kingdom* [2005] 40 EHRR 9.

[347] Under the Caravan Sites Act 1968 a local authority is given an unconditional right to terminate a licence on 28 days' notice (by court order only) and without any need to demonstrate cause.

safeguards, there had been a violation of Article 8 of the Convention.[348] The particularly vulnerable position of gypsies and the perceived need to facilitate the gypsy way of life was referred to extensively by the Court in its reasoning.[349] However, the *general* principles that would be applied within this context were also emphasised:

> The Court has also stated that in spheres such as housing, which play a central role in the welfare and economic policies of modern societies, it will respect the legislature's judgment as to what is the general interest unless that judgment is manifestly without reasonable foundation … Where general social and economic policy considerations have arisen in the context of Article 8 itself, *the scope of the margin of appreciation depends upon the context of the case, with particular significance attaching to the extent of the intrusion into the personal sphere of the applicant* [emphasis added].[350]

These passages were thus referred to in the subsequent Court of Appeal decision of *Leeds City Council v Price*[351] in its review of the earlier House of Lords decision in *Qazi*.[352] *Leeds* concerned an appeal relating to a successful claim for possession of land by the council against a gypsy family, the lower court having applied the *Qazi*[353] decision. The council's title to the land was not disputed and it was accepted by the family that their only defence to the claim for possession was that this would infringe their rights under Article 8 and that, in the light of the *Connors*[354] decision, the decision by the House of Lords in *Qazi*[355] could be wrong. After a considered review of both *Qazi*[356] and *Connors*[357] the court stated:[358]

> The decision in *Connors's* case … is unquestionably incompatible with the proposition that the exercise by a public authority of an unqualified proprietary right under domestic law to repossess its land will never constitute an interference with the occupier's right to respect for his home, or will always be justified under Article 8(2). To that extent *Connors's* case is incompatible with *Qazi's* case.

Further:[359]

> [W]e do not consider that the reasoning of the court in *Connors's* case … can be confined to the treatment of gypsies … The decision in *Connors's* case does not exclude the possibility that a particular statutory regime may itself achieve the balance required by Article 8(2), so that, if the judge complies with it, the requirements of Article 8(2) will be satisfied. Equally, however, the decision in *Connors's* case does not exclude the possibility that, if a statutory regime is to comply with the Convention, it must require a public authority to weigh in the balance the impact of its actions on the individual affected and permit the individual affected to challenge in the courts the conclusion reached by the public authority.

However, since the court was bound to follow the *Qazi*[360] decision the appeal was dismissed. Permission was granted, however, to appeal to the House of Lords and the case was

---

[348] *Connors* (n 346), para 94.
[349] *Ibid*, paras 84–95.
[350] *Ibid*, para 82.
[351] *Leeds City Council v Price* [2005] 1 WLR 1825.
[352] *Qazi* (n 339).
[353] *Ibid*.
[354] *Connors* (n 346).
[355] *Qazi* (n 339).
[356] *Ibid*.
[357] *Connors* (n 346).
[358] *Ibid*, para 26 (Lord Phillips).
[359] *Ibid*, para 29 (Lord Phillips).
[360] *Qazi* (n 339).

later joined with *R (on the application of Kay) v Lambeth*[361] in which the applicants, who were not gypsies, had become tenants following the granting, by Barnet local authority, of a lease of their dwellings to a housing trust. Barnet, which sought repossession of its homes because the claimants were trespassers, subsequently lawfully terminated the leases. The House of Lords constituted itself as a seven-judge Committee in order to revisit its decision in *Qazi*[362] in the light of the court's judgments in *Connors*.[363] Although the judgments from the House are difficult to draw together as they vary in points of agreement throughout, the majority (Lords Hope, Scott, Brown and Baroness Hale) held that the judgment in *Connors*[364] was not incompatible with the view of the majority in *Qazi*[365] that there was no need for a review of the issues raised by Article 8(2) to be conducted by the County Court if the case was of a type where the law itself provided the answer, as in that situation a merits review would be a pointless exercise. In such a case an Article 8 defence, if raised, should simply be struck out. To do otherwise would, the court felt, upset the balance that housing legislation had achieved between 'the competing claims to which scarcity gives rise'[366] and would produce the undesirable effect of increasing the already high administrative burden upon local authorities and the courts. The court considered that in this context Parliament was the 'person with responsibility for a given subject matter and access to special sources of knowledge and advice'.[367] Even though the legislation had been passed prior to the HRA the clear implication was that the relevant issues of proportionality with Convention rights had effectively been considered during the parliamentary debates prior to its passage.[368] As such, Parliament's judgment in this respect ought to be given a high degree of deference. It was not necessary, therefore, the court held, for a local authority to plead or prove in every case that domestic law complies with Article 8. Courts should proceed on the assumption that domestic law strikes a fair balance and is compatible with Article 8 without the need of recourse to Article 8(2). However, in the light of the judgments in *Connors*[369] and *Blečić*[370] the court felt it necessary to emphasise that a person evicted might, however, have a defence to possession proceedings in exceptional cases,[371] namely (1) where he challenged the domestic law as itself being incompatible with Article 8 (as in *Connors*) or (2) he challenged the action of the public authority landlord on public law grounds, on the basis that the authority's actions constituted an abuse of power. The minority (Lords Bingham, Nicholls and Walker), however, held that a defendant to possession proceedings brought by public authorities should be permitted in principle to raise an Article 8 defence during the County Court possession proceedings. Lord Bingham expressed it as follows:

> I do not accept, as the appellants argued, that the public authority must from the outset plead and prove that the possession order sought is justified. That would, in the overwhelming majority of

---

[361] *R (on the application of Kay) v Lambeth* [2004] EWCA Civ 289 (Civ).
[362] *Qazi* (n 339).
[363] *Connors* (n 346).
[364] *Ibid.*
[365] *Qazi* (n 339).
[366] *Kay* (n 361), para 33 (Lord Bingham).
[367] *Ibid.*
[368] M Amos, 'Separating Human Rights Adjudication From Judicial Review' (n 105).
[369] *Connors* (n 346).
[370] *Blečić v Croatia* (2004) 41 EHRR 185.
[371] *Kay* (n 361), para 38 (Lord Bingham). Accordingly, neither applicant satisfied these requirements and thus the appeals were dismissed.

cases, be burdensome and futile. It is enough for the public authority to assert its claim in accordance with domestic property law. If the occupier wishes to raise an Article 8 defence to prevent or defer the making of a possession order, it is for him to do so and the public authority must rebut the claim if, and to the extent that, it is called upon to do so. In the overwhelming majority of cases, this will be in no way burdensome. In rare and exceptional cases it will not be futile.

Although *Qazi*[372] had been brought before the ECtHR, the complaint had been dismissed as being manifestly ill founded and inadmissible and, furthermore, the decision of the House of Lords in *Qazi* was not cited in *Connors*.[373] These two facts clearly appealed to the majority of the House in *Price*[374] and Lord Scott in particular certainly felt they vindicated the House's earlier decision in *Qazi*.[375] However, not all agreed on this point. Lord Bingham considered that 'the refusal of leave does not necessarily import approval of the reasoning of the judgment which is it sought to challenge'[376] and that the lack of citation of *Qazi*[377] in *Connors*[378] may have been because the majority reasoning was inconsistent with the basis upon which the United Kingdom's case was put and had been put on earlier occasions.[379]

In any event, the issue was to come before the ECtHR again and, this time, the Court was able to fully review the English judgments within the context of domestic violence. In *McCann v United Kingdom*[380] the applicant and wife were joint secure tenants. However, his wife and children moved out of the home after allegations of domestic violence. Both occupation and non-molestation orders were obtained, allowing her to return. However, owing to another incident involving the applicant, she was re-housed to another property under the local authority's domestic violence policy and the applicant moved back into their former home. Their relationship subsequently improved and the applicant's estranged wife supported his application for a transfer to a smaller home where contact with children could be maintained. Despite this, on the same day the application was made, the housing authority visited the wife and asked her to sign a notice to quit without explaining the effect of doing so for the applicant, which was to extinguish his right to live in the house or exchange it for another local authority property. On realising the effect she sought to withdraw the notice; however, it was by then effective and the housing proceedings for possession were issued. In the meantime the housing authority, in accordance with its domestic violence policy,[381] had refused the applicant's application to accede to the former tenancy of the house and decided that, in any event, because he had no dependants living with him, he would not qualify for a dwelling originally allocated to a qualifying family that had been re-housed.

---

[372] *Qazi* (n 339).
[373] *Connors* (n 346).
[374] *LCC v Price* (n 351).
[375] *Ibid*, para 154 (Lord Scott).
[376] *Ibid* (n 351), para 23 (Lord Bingham).
[377] *Qazi* (n 339).
[378] *Connors* (n 346).
[379] *LCC v Price* (n 351), para 23 (Lord Bingham).
[380] *McCann* (n 49).
[381] Birmingham City Council's Allocations Policy provides (3.7.1): 'Domestic violence is included in the Department's revised Conditions of Tenancy as a breach of the Tenancy agreement. Action will be taken [against those] who have been found to have subjected another person to domestic violence. This could include perpetrators losing their home or being classed as intentionally homeless.' It would, however, be open to a person who has been made homeless following an allegation of domestic violence to challenge the truth of the allegation and claim that he has been made unintentionally homeless and that the local authority have a statutory duty to re-house him.

At the possession hearing the applicant argued that the claim for possession breached Article 8(2) and particularly because of the manner in which the notice to quit had been obtained. At first instance the County Court judge agreed and dismissed the claim for possession on the basis that had the notice to quit not been obtained the local authority would have had to apply for a possession order under section 84 of the Housing Act 1985, which would have given the applicant the opportunity to persuade the court that it would not be reasonable to grant the order. The authority appealed to the Court of Appeal, who allowed the appeal on the basis of *Qazi*.[382] The applicant then sought permission to judicially review the authority's procurement of the notice to quit, but the application was dismissed. A further request to appeal to the Court of Appeal was refused and the applicant was thus evicted from property.

The ECtHR took the opportunity to review the House of Lords judgments in *Qazi*[383] and *Price*, noting both the views of the majority and minority in each case. Starting with a reiteration of the general principle that whether a property is to be classified as a 'home' is a question of fact and is not dependent upon the lawfulness of the occupation under domestic law[384] they agreed that the dwelling house was the applicant's home for the purposes of Article 8(1) despite the fact that following the service of the notice to quit by the wife he had no right under domestic law to occupy it. It was further agreed that the effect of the notice to quit was to interfere with the applicant's right to respect for his home. This interference was, however, held to be in accordance with the law and pursued the legitimate aim of protecting the rights and freedoms of others in two respects: the right to regain possession against an individual who had no contractual or other right to be there and to ensure that the statutory scheme for housing provision was properly applied. The central question was, therefore, under Article 8(2) whether the interference was proportionate with the aim pursued and thus 'necessary in a democratic society'. However, it was held that this was a question of procedure as well as substance. The relevant principles for assessing the necessity of an interference with the right to 'home' by the application of summary possession proceedings that had been set out in *Connors*[385] still applied. However, in direct disagreement with the majority of the House of Lords in *Price*[386] it was held that *Connors*[387] was not confined to cases involving eviction of gypsies or cases where the applicant sought to challenge the law itself rather than its application in a particular case.

> The loss of one's home is a most extreme form of interference with the right to respect for the home. Any person at risk of an interference of this magnitude should in principle be able to have the proportionality of the measure determined by an independent tribunal in light of the relevant principles under Article 8 of the Convention, notwithstanding that, under domestic law, his right of occupation has come to an end.[388]

By bypassing the statutory scheme contained in section 84 of the Housing Act 1985 and seeking to obtain a notice to quit from the wife, the local authority had therefore failed to give any consideration to the applicant's right to respect for his home. This was exacerbated

[382] *Qazi* (n 339).
[383] *Ibid.*
[384] *McCann* (n 49), para 46. See also *Buckley v UK* (1996) 23 EHRR 101.
[385] *Connors* (n 346).
[386] *LCC v Price* (n 351).
[387] *Connors* (n 346).
[388] *McCann* (n 49), para 50.

by the fact that, under domestic law, it was not open to the County Court in summary proceedings to consider any issue concerning the proportionality of the possession order, save
in exceptional cases.[389] Of particular significance was the ECtHR's willingness to scrutinise
the professed aims of this particular legislative housing scheme and policy. Thus, the Court
did not agree with the House of Lords' contention that the grant of the right to the occupier to raise an issue under Article 8 would have serious consequences for the functioning
of the system or for the domestic law of landlord and tenant. Rather, in agreeing with the
minority in *Price*,[390] the Court considered that it would be only in very exceptional cases
that an applicant would succeed in raising an arguable case, which would require a court
to examine the issue; in the great majority of cases, an order for possession could continue
to be made in summary proceedings. As a result, it was immaterial whether Mrs McCann
understood or intended the effects of the notice to quit; what mattered was whether the
procedural safeguards required by Article 8 for the assessment of the proportionality of
the interference were not met. Owing to the fact that the summary procedure enabled the
applicant to be dispossessed of his home without any possibility to have the proportionality of the measure determined by an independent tribunal, it followed that there has been
a violation of Article 8 of the Convention in the instant case.

The significance of the decision for the victims of domestic violence is twofold. First, it
appears to confirm that the approach of the House of Lords in *Qazi*[391] and *Price*[392] that
Article 8(2) was largely irrelevant to any claim concerning the occupation of a 'home' by an
individual who does not hold a contractual or proprietorial interest in it was wrong. This
should mean that the holder of an occupation order must be given an opportunity by the
courts to defend a claim for possession against either a public[393] or private landlord/owner
under Article 8(2). Thus, a proprietary or contractual interest in the family home cannot
automatically trump her Article 8 right to respect for the home. It would certainly be hard
to believe that a court would not regard the particular context of domestic violence and
the resultant intrusion into the personal sphere of the victim as qualifying any such claims
for possession. Second, local authorities would presumably have to amend their housing policies and procedures with respect to those accused of domestic violence in order
to ensure that they too are given an opportunity to defend a claim for possession with
respect to their Article 8 rights. Rather fortunately for local authorities and the courts,
the issue came before the House of Lords again in *Doherty v Birmingham City Council*.[394]
Doherty, like *Connors*,[395] involved a notice of termination served upon a gypsy who was
entitled to just four weeks' notice of the termination of his residence in his home which

---

[389] *McCann* (n 49), para 52: where, as the Court of Appeal put it in the present case, 'something has happened
since the service of the notice to quit, which has fundamentally altered the rights and wrongs of the proposed
eviction'. Further, the availability of judicial review did not resolve the matter as it did not provide any opportunity
for an independent tribunal to examine whether the applicant's loss of his home was proportionate under Art 8
to the legitimate aims pursued because it is not well adapted for the resolution of sensitive factual questions and
did not provide any greater opportunity than the county court for an independent tribunal to examine proportionality under Art 8(2).

[390] *LCC v Price* (n 351).

[391] *Qazi* (n 339).

[392] *LCC v Price* (n 351).

[393] Although the majority of the House of Lords limited the application of *Price* to public landlords, *McCann*
could be of equal application to private landlords/owners by virtue of the horizontal effect of the HRA.

[394] *Doherty v Birmingham City Council* [2008] UKHL 57.

[395] *Connors* (n 346).

was a caravan on a local authority site. The House had already heard argument but not given judgment in the case when *McCann*[396] was decided and so the parties were invited to give written submissions on the case before judgment was handed down. Unfortunately, as Loveland notes,[397] the House did not heed the Court of Appeal's earlier request for 'clear and straightforward guidance' after they had had the unenviable task of trying to untangle the ratio of the House's earlier judgment in *Kay*[398] in order to apply it to *Doherty*. Instead, an equally divergent set of judgments are evident; we see Lord Scott and Lord Hope responding to the ECtHR's assessment of their understanding of the requirements of Article 8 with some degree of contempt with both judges deciding that the ECtHR had failed to properly understand the domestic law: Lord Hope thus referred to the *McCann*[399] judgment as 'almost useless',[400] Lord Scott similarly felt 'it demonstrated an imperfect understanding of domestic law or procedure'.[401] By doing so both judges were also able to bring the *Connors*[402] decision within the 'special circumstances' exception of the mirror principle under section 2 of the HRA and thus justifying their decision not to take it into account under domestic law.[403] For Lord Walker and Lord Mance their views on the matter were more ambiguous; in both opinions there was some evidence to suggest that although they considered *Kay*[404] inconsistent with *McCann*[405] they felt bound to follow *Kay*[406] because that was heard by a seven-member panel as opposed to the five that were sitting in *Doherty*.[407] In sum, *Doherty*[408] has not fully answered the question of how Article 8 should be applied in such cases, which, as Loveland concludes, leaves us with some question marks over the compatibility of Article 8 to our residential possession laws. At the time of writing there is already one case[409] on this area making its way through the appeal process and thus it would seem that this debate within housing law will roll on until a definitive judgment is delivered by the House.

Conclusions on the Right to Protection from Violence

The discussion in this Chapter has demonstrated that a number of Convention rights can and should be utilised on behalf of the victims of domestic violence. Two of those Articles, Articles 2 and 3, are absolute, and as has been shown impose obligations upon the state to take reasonable steps to protect victims of domestic violence from a risk to their lives or

---

[396] *McCann* (n 49).
[397] I Loveland, 'A Tale of Two Trespassers: Reconsidering the Impact of the Hunan Rights Act on Rights of Residence in Rented Housing: Part Two' (2009) *European Human Rights Law Review* 495.
[398] *Kay* (n 361).
[399] *McCann* (n 49).
[400] *Doherty* (n 394), para 20.
[401] *Ibid*, para 88.
[402] *Connors* (n 346).
[403] See the discussion on s2 in ch 8.
[404] *Kay* (n 361).
[405] *McCann* (n 49).
[406] *Kay* (n 361).
[407] I Loveland, 'A Tale of Two Trespassers: Part Two' (n 410).
[408] *Doherty* (n 394).
[409] *R (on the application of Weaver) v London and Quadrant Housing Trust* [2008] EWHC 1377 (Admin)—for a discussion of this see I Loveland, 'A Tale of Two Trespassers: Part Two' (n 410).

of degrading treatment. Although the *Osman*[410] test may be a difficult test to satisfy due to the resource implications a successful claim may have upon law enforcement agencies, it has been suggested that it is not impossible. The application of the test within the particular context of domestic violence has much potential for a claim under Article 2. It is clear, however, that any reliance upon the development of the law of negligence in this area in favour of victims is unlikely to occur since the House of Lords judgment in *Smith*.[411] In terms of Article 3, state obligations will arise where the victim is suffering torture, inhuman or degrading treatment, which has been defined as including behaviour that degrades, humiliates, or shows a lack of respect for another. It is suggested that most physical violence in the context of domestic violence and other forms of abuse could be caught by this categorisation. Where children are affected by domestic violence the obligation under Article 3 to intervene to protect the child, in particular, is likely to arise. Although the duties imposed upon the state by Article 3, within the private context, are not absolute it may, however, still be difficult for the state to justify non-intervention by reference to the rights of others within the context of domestic violence. Where the domestic abuse falls below the level required by Article 3 the state may still be under an obligation to protect victims of domestic violence under the right to respect for family life and the right to moral and physical integrity as aspects of Article 8, which is a qualified right. Any interference between the family life of a child and its parent must, therefore, be minimal and proportionate. This may have some impact upon the decision to grant an occupation order where it would inevitably result in the immediate separation of a parent and child. In addition, the right to respect for the home may, accordingly allow a victim of domestic violence in possession of an occupation order to defend a claim for possession of private property on the basis of her Article 8 rights; however, this has not yet been made explicit by the English courts. The current interpretation by the UK courts of a perpetrator's right to defend possession proceedings by a local authority, however, is relatively unclear and would not appear to be in line with Strasbourg. Finally, what this Chapter has sought to demonstrate above all is that should the relevant authorities fail to provide victims of domestic violence with the appropriate protection and/or intervention, all the above-mentioned Convention rights should, in conjunction with the HRA, have the ability to provide for an effective remedy for their breach despite the fact that Article 13 was not incorporated.

[410] *Osman* (n 70).
[411] *Smith* (n 122).

10

Financial Disputes and Human Rights

Relatively little attention has been paid by family lawyers to the potential impact of the HRA on financial disputes and obligations between family members.[1] This is, perhaps, not surprising. The area of ancillary relief is one that is notoriously based on judicial discretion. At first sight rights have little role to play in an area of the law which is dominated by a desire to ensure the financial needs of the parties, especially the children, are met. Nevertheless, as will be seen, there is a role for human rights to play in this area. Indeed it is noticeable that in recent years 'rights talk' has been used in judicial decisions on financial orders on divorce with the concepts of fairness and discrimination playing a major role.[2]

This Chapter will first consider the law on ancillary relief as it relates to spouses and civil partners. It will then consider the issues relating to cohabitants and those surrounding inheritance.[3]

Ancillary Relief

On divorce or dissolution of a civil partnership the court has the power to make wide-ranging financial orders under the MCA or the CPA. The court is required to take into account the factors listed in section 25 of the MCA,[4] with the first consideration being given to the interests of any children. For the vast majority of cases it is the needs of the parties and children which dominate the exercise of the discretion.[5] For very wealthy couples there is greater room for manoeuvre and in recent years the law has been developing, with the House of Lords decisions in *White v White*[6] and *Miller v Miller; McFarlane v McFarlane*[7] leading the way. These have emphasised the principles of needs, equality and compensation.[8]

Much has been written on this case law and this Chapter will not seek to provide a summary of the current position. Instead our focus will be on what, if anything, can be added by a human rights analysis.

---

[1] M Perry, 'British Property Law and Human Rights' (2007) 5 *Santa Clara Law Review* 2.
[2] A Diduck, 'Public Norms and Private Lives: Rights, Fairness and Family Law' in J Wallbank, S Choudhry and J Herring (eds), *Rights, Gender and Family Law* (London, Routledge, 2009).
[3] We shall not consider the potential impact of the HRA on the law surrounding bankruptcy.
[4] See also CPA, Sch 5, in similar terms.
[5] R Bailey-Harris, 'The Paradoxes of Principle and Pragmatism: Ancillary Relief in England and Wales' (2005) 19 *International Journal of Family Law and Policy* 229; J Miles, 'Property law v family law: resolving the problems of family property' (2003) 23 *Legal Studies* 624.
[6] [2000] UKHL 54.
[7] [2006] UKHL 24.
[8] For a detailed discussion of the law see J Herring, *Family Law* 4th edn (Harlow, Pearson, 2009) ch 5.

Article 1 of Protocol 1

Article 1 protects the right of peaceful enjoyment of possessions:

> This Convention right provides that every natural or legal person is entitled to the peaceful enjoy-
> ment of his possessions. No one shall be deprived of his possessions except in the public interest and
> subject to the conditions provided for by law and by the general principles of international law.
>
> The preceding provisions shall not, however, in any way impair the right of a State to enforce such
> laws as it deems necessary to control the use of property in accordance with the general interest or
> to secure the payment of taxes or other contributions or penalties.

This Article is designed to protect the right to property.[9] Its primary role is to protect
individuals from the expropriation of their property or the interference in their property
interests by the state or public bodies.[10] Article 1 of Protocol 1 protects 'possessions'. These
include existing possessions or assets, but also include a 'legitimate expectation' of obtaining a property right.[11] However, it does not extend to the right to acquire property.[12]

The Grand Chamber in *Pye v UK*[13] set out its three main elements:

> Article 1 of Protocol No 1, which guarantees the right to the protection of property, contains three
> distinct rules: 'the first rule, set out in the first sentence of the first paragraph, is of a general nature
> and enunciates the principle of the peaceful enjoyment of property; the second rule, contained
> in the second sentence of the first paragraph, covers deprivation of possessions and subjects it to
> certain conditions; the third rule, stated in the second paragraph, recognises that the Contracting
> States are entitled, amongst other things, to control the use of property in accordance with the
> general interest ... The three rules are not, however, 'distinct' in the sense of being unconnected.
> The second and third rules are concerned with particular instances of interference with the right
> to peaceful enjoyment of property and should therefore be construed in the light of the general
> principle enunciated in the first rule' (see, as a recent authority with further references, *Anheuser-
> Busch Inc v Portugal* [2007] ECHR 73049/01, para 62).

In order for an interference in property rights to be justified there must be a fair balance
struck between the general interest of the community and the weight to be attached to the
individual's rights.[14] Where the state seeks to rely on the second paragraph of the Article
then it must be shown that there is a 'reasonable relationship of proportionality between
the means employed and the aim sought to be realised'.[15]

The protocol appears, at first, to be a very relevant Article for the law on ancillary relief.
It might be thought that any order of the court redistributing property would interfere
with a spouse's or civil partner's rights. But such a claim has been strongly rejected by
Coleridge J in *Charman v Charman (No 2)*, who stated:

> the suggestion that a lump sum order made pursuant to s 23 and s 25 of the Matrimonial Causes
> Act 1973 (as expounded upon by the House of Lords) and following a nine day hearing with the

---

[9] *Marckx v Belgium* (1979) 2 EHRR 330, para 63.
[10] *NG v KR (pre-nuptial contract)* [2009] 1 FCR 35, para 103.
[11] *Kopecký v Slovakia* Application No 44912/98.
[12] *Ibid.*
[13] [2007] ECHR 44302/02, para 52.
[14] *Beyeler v Italy* Application No 33202/96.
[15] *Pye v UK* (n 13) para 55, citing *AGOSI v the United Kingdom*, judgment of 24 October 1986, Series A
No 108, para 52.

fullest and most skilful representation, in some way breaches the husband's right to 'peaceful enjoyment of his possessions' (per Art 1 of the First Protocol) is, in my judgment, frankly absurd. I entirely agree with Mr Pointer's exposition in this regard. These 'human rights' arguments have never yet been successfully deployed in these applications. I hope this is the last we shall see of them.[16]

It is a shame that Coleridge J did not explain further why he thought such arguments were 'absurd'. It seems hard to deny that there has been an interference with the husband's enjoyment of his possessions when he is required to transfer some of his property to the wife. It should be emphasised that English family law does not recognise any form of community of property regime, where property on marriage becomes jointly owned.[17] So there is a genuine change of legal ownership when a court makes, for example, a lump-sum order. This must surely involve an interference with property interests. It may, therefore, be that Coleridge J believes that the interference in an ancillary relief case will be always justified as being 'in the public interest and subject to the conditions provided for by law'. This seems to be the interpretation given to his comments by Moylan J in *C v C*:[18]

> Further, the husband has relied upon the right to the peaceful enjoyment of possessions provided by Art 1, Protocol 1 of the European Convention for the Protection of Human Rights and Fundamental Freedoms 1950. In *Charman v Charman* Coleridge J was met with similar arguments which he despatched simply and with an expression of hope that 'This is the last time we shall hear of or see them'. I agree. It is not clear to me that this Article applies at all to the exercise by the court of its powers under the Matrimonial Causes Act 1973. However, even if it does, the power given to the court under that Act is clearly proportionate and strikes a fair balance.

Most significantly Lord Nicholls, albeit in an obiter dictum, indicated in *Wilson v First County Trust Ltd*[19] that Article 1 did apply to ancillary relief orders:

> Article 1 of the First Protocol has a similar character. It does not confer a right of property as such nor does it guarantee the content of any rights in property. What it does instead is to guarantee the peaceful enjoyment of the possessions that a person already owns, of which a person cannot be deprived except in the public interest and subject to the conditions provided for by law: *Marckx v Belgium* (1979) 2 EHRR 330 at para 50. Here too it is a matter for domestic law to define the nature and extent of any rights which a party acquires from time to time as a result of the transactions which he or she enters into. One must, of course, distinguish carefully between cases where the effect of the relevant law is to deprive a person of something that he already owns and those where its effect is to subject his right from the outset to the reservation or qualification which is now being enforced against him. The making of a compulsory order or of an order for the division of property on divorce are examples of the former category. In those cases it is the making of the order, not the existence of the law under which the order is made, that interrupts the peaceful enjoyment by the owner of his property. The fact that the relevant law was already in force when the right of property was acquired is immaterial, if it did not have the effect of qualifying the right from the moment when it was acquired.

The most detailed discussion of the issue can be found in Baron J's judgment in *NG v KR (pre-nuptial contract)*.[20] There he confirmed that a transfer of property order or a

---

[16] [2006] EWHCA 1879, para 126.
[17] E Cooke, A Barlow and T Callus, *Community of Property. A Regime for England and Wales* (London, Nuffield Foundation, 2006).
[18] [2009] 1 FLR 8, para 96.
[19] [2003] UKHL 40, para 106.
[20] [2009] 1 FCR 35

lump sum order amounted to an interference in a person's peaceful enjoyment of their possessions and therefore Article 1 of the First Protocol was engaged. However, he accepted that normally a maintenance support payment would involve a breach of Article 1.[21] The husband, who was seeking financial support on divorce, had sought to argue that because his claim for maintenance was based on need, the Article was not engaged. However, in this case the lump sum payment, although in effect capitalised maintenance, amounted to an interference in property right because a substantial sum was involved.[22] Baron J rejected an argument that the law on ancillary relief in section 25 of the MCA operated in an arbitrary way and so infringed Article 1. He explained:

> The 1973 Act provides a bespoke remedy in each case because its terms enable the judge to take into account all the circumstances of the case. Section 25 only highlights a number of specific factors. Miss Booth [counsel for the wife] argues that this results in an element of uncertainty so that parties can never be sure what the result will be after the application of the statutory criteria. It is this uncertainty that may lead to arbitrary results with the consequence that A1P1 [Article 1 of the First Protocol] is breached. I do not accept that argument. The court is enjoined to apply the 1973 Act fairly. The House of Lords in *White*; *Miller and McFarlane* and the Court of Appeal in *Charman v Charman* [2007] EWCA Civ 503 set down clear guidance and principles which judges must apply. Some professionals took time to assimilate their Lordships' speeches but to my knowledge most cases continue to settle before trial. To enable this to occur the perceived outcome must be within sufficiently settled parameters of an expected award. By its nature, every piece of litigation involves a degree of uncertainty because no one can ever predict how a tribunal will decide the facts or interpret the law. But there is nothing arbitrary in the application of the 1973 Act in financial proceedings. I accept Mr Mostyn's formulation that s 25 of the 1973 Act strikes a fair balance between existing property rights and the entitlement of the claiming party to share, to receive compensation or have his needs met. This fair balance is well within the margin of appreciation afforded to this country.[23]

Consequently, he found that Article 1 of the First Protocol was not breached as a result of the method by which the English courts resolved financial applications on divorce pursuant to the Act.

So it seems the current judicial approach, based on admittedly limited authority, is that although the Article 1 right is infringed in an ancillary relief case, it is invariably a justifiable breach. If that is the correct interpretation of his view, it raises a number of questions.

First, if a district judge has made an utterly flawed order requiring the husband to pay the wife a lump sum, based on some fundamental error of law, would that not be an unjustified interference with the First Protocol? It would seem that it would. The interference needs to be justified by law, and misapplication of the law may infringe the rights under Article 1. While this would be true, it is unlikely it would apply to any case, except one where the judge clearly misapplied the law.

Second, if the Article does apply to ancillary relief proceedings this would appear to create a slight presumption in favour of not making any capital order, because any order interfering with the Article 1 property rights of the parties would have to be justified. This is of limited practical significance. While there is no direct equivalent in the MCA to the

---

[21] Para 104, citing *M v Secretary of State for Work and Pensions* [2006] UKHL 11.
[22] Para 104.
[23] Para 135.

'no order principle' found in the CA,[24] a judge will not make a financial order unless there is a good reason for doing so.

Third, and most interestingly, it raises the basis of the question of the justification for ancillary relief law. The current law is largely justified on the principle of fairness between the parties, with the well-known enunciation of this by Lord Nicholls in *White v White*:

> Divorce creates many problems. One question always arises. It concerns how the property of the husband and wife should be divided and whether one of them should continue to support the other. Stated in the most general terms, the answer is obvious. Everyone would accept that the outcome on these matters, whether by agreement or court order, should be fair. More realistically, the outcome ought to be as fair as is possible in all the circumstances. But everyone's life is different. Features which are important when assessing fairness differ in each case. And, sometimes, different minds can reach different conclusions on what fairness requires. Then fairness, like beauty, lies in the eye of the beholder.[25]

In *Miller v Miller; McFarlane v McFarlane*[26] the House of Lords have explained that the principles of meeting needs, equality and compensation can be used in determining what will be a fair result. So, the justifications currently used by the courts for the development of the law on ancillary relief have focused on fairness to the individuals rather than the wider interests of society.[27] However, under Article 1 of the First Protocol, any justification must be in terms of the interests of wider society.

One of the authors[28] has claimed that the current law improperly focuses on the interests of the individuals, ignoring the issues relevant to the wider society. These included the avoidance of costs on the public purse; the encouragement or discouragement of child care and care of dependants; promoting the stability of marriage; promoting gender equality; combating individualist norms. The Article concludes:

> This Article has sought to set out briefly eight interests which the state or wider community has in financial orders made on divorce. No doubt many more could be found. What they demonstrate is that these orders are not simply an attempt to weigh up the interests or competing claims of the spouses to the assets in question. The matter is not simply a 'private' one, analogous to a contractual dispute, where the courts should seek to achieve a result which is fair as between the parties. In pursuing one of these broader community goals the state may seek to impose an order which is not fair to the parties.[29]

What is significant for our purposes it that the justification for an interference in Article 1 of the First Protocol must be a public interest. This might mean that more weight should be attached to the kind of public interests mentioned in this paragraph.[30]

A rather different question is whether a person seeking to make a financial claim on divorce or dissolution can rely on Article 1 of the First Protocol. A useful discussion is found

---

[24] CA, s1(5).

[25] *White v White* [2000] UKHL 54, para 1.

[26] [2006] UKHL 24.

[27] J Herring, 'Why Financial Orders on Divorce Should be Unfair' (2005) 19 *International Journal of Law, Policy and the Family* 218.

[28] *Ibid.*

[29] *Ibid*, 228.

[30] For an excellent discussion of which obligations in this context should be regarded as interpersonal and which owed by the state see L Ferguson, 'Family, Social Inequalities, and the Persuasive Force of Interpersonal Obligation' (2008) 22 *International Journal of Law, Policy and the Family* 22.

in *Ram v Ram*.[31] That case concerned some rather complex provisions of section 423 of the Insolvency Act 1986. In brief the wife sought an order transferring property back to her husband, which he had earlier transferred to his father and brothers. She sought this order so that she could make a claim against him under the MCA. There was no doubt that the transaction should be set aside, the question was whether the money be transferred back to the bankrupt husband (so the wife could claim it under ancillary relief proceedings) or back to the trustee in bankruptcy (which would then, in effect, be beyond the wife's claim). One of the wife's arguments involved Article 1 of the First Protocol. The Court of Appeal stated that Article 1 did not protect the wife's expectation that in family proceedings she would receive 'a defined share in the matrimonial pot'. This confirms the orthodox understanding of English matrimonial property law, that the parties retain ownership in their own property until the court makes an order redistributing the property. She had no entitlement or right in her husband's property; at most it was an expectation that a court would make her an award.[32] The court added that once an order was made, she would have rights that could involve Article 1.[33]

In any event, the court held that the second paragraph of Article 1 allowed the individual states a wide margin of appreciation to implement social policies. The Court of Appeal noted that the ECtHR had said only if the state's assessment was 'manifestly without reasonable foundation' would the European Court intervene.[34] The judge's order in this case could not be said to be so.

The wife also sought to rely on Article 14. She could only rely on that provision if her contingent interests fell within Article 1 or sufficiently within its ambit to engage Article 14. The court was willing to assume that it did.[35] On the assumption that it did, it was found that the judge did not discriminate against her as the effect of the order was to return her to the position she would have been in if the transaction had not taken place. More significantly her gender did not affect her disadvantage.

Ram v Ram therefore indicates that a spouse or civil partner wishing to rely on Article 1 of the First Protocol to boost a claim for ancillary relief is unlikely to meet with any success. However, the Article could be used in two ways. First, as a 'piggyback' right for a claim under Article 14. In other words if the law on ancillary relief operates in a way which discriminates against the claimant, Article 1 of the First Protocol can be used in conjunction with Article 14 as the basis for the discrimination claim. Second, it may be argued that procedural and enforcement mechanisms in connection with ancillary relief claims may also raise issues in connection with Article 1.

Article 5 of the Seventh Protocol

Article 5 of the Seventh Protocol states as follows:

> Spouses shall enjoy equality of rights and responsibilities of a private law character between them, and in their relations with their children, as to marriage, during marriage and in the event of its dissolution. This Article shall not prevent States from taking such measures as are necessary in the interests of the children.

[31] [2005] 2 BCLC 476.
[32] *Marckx v Belgium* (1979) 2 EHRR 330 and *Inze v Austria* (1987) 10 EHRR 394.
[33] [2005] 2 BCLC 476, para 32.
[34] *James v United Kingdom* (1986) 8 EHRR 123.
[35] Para 35.

The Seventh Protocol has not been ratified by the UK government. However, in the White Paper, 'Rights Brought Home: The Human Rights Bill' the government set out a commitment to ratifying and incorporating the Seventh Protocol. In it the government accepted that:

> there is, however, a difficulty with this [incorporation] because a few provisions of our domestic law, for example in relation to the property rights of spouses, could not be interpreted in a way which is compatible with Protocol 7. The government intends to legislate to remove these inconsistencies when a suitable opportunity occurs and then to sign and ratify the Protocol.[36]

The government has said that it will sign it when a suitable opportunity occurs.[37] That was back in 1997! The Protocol, more importantly, is not included within the HRA. The government's explanation is that there might be a conflict between family law principles and the Article. Presumably the concern is that the Protocol could create some form of presumption of equal sharing of property on divorce, which would conflict with the broad discretion given to the courts in the MCA.

That concern is ill-founded. The explanatory memorandum to the Protocol says that Article 5 'should not be understood as preventing the national authorities from taking due account of all relevant factors when reaching decisions with regard to the division of property in the event of the dissolution of marriage'.[38] Heather Swindles *et al* argue:

> It is, therefore, arguable that Art 5 should simply be interpreted as treating parties on the basis of an equal footing in the application before the court rather than imposing a requirement of 'equal division' in every case. The latter approach could be seen as a blunt instrument in such circumstances as a very short childless marriage or where most of the wealth is inherited from one party or in the context of pension sharing.[39]

So, even if in the future the Article does become protected through the HRA, it is unlikely to have any significant impact. Indeed the House of Lords in *White*[40] and *Miller; McFarlane*[41] referred to the principle of non-discrimination as a key one in this area of the law. In the former case Lord Nicholls stated:

> In seeking to achieve a fair outcome, there is no place for discrimination between husband and wife and their respective roles.

In *S v S*[42] Singer J referred explicitly to the court's desire to ensure there was no gender discrimination in the law on ancillary relief. Although none of these developments has been based explicitly on Article 5 of the Seventh Protocol, they are clearly consistent with it.

Article 8

Article 8 may also be used in relation to an ancillary relief claim. It is unlikely that an order which simply impacted on the standard of living of the parties or a child would be

---

[36] Para 4.15.
[37] Home Office, *Rights Brought Home* (London, HMSO, 1997) paras 4.15 and 4.16.
[38] Para 38.
[39] H Swindell, C Gargan and A Neaves, *Family Law and the Human Rights Act 1988* (Bristol, Jordans, 1989) para 12.9.
[40] [2000] UKHL 54.
[41] [2006] UKHL 24.
[42] [2006] EWHC 2339 (Fam), para 100.

sufficient to engage Article 8. However, it may be argued that the right to a home in Article 8 is relevant. A detailed discussion of the right to a home is given in Chapter 9 and so only provide a brief summary will be given here. The definition given to a 'home' by Strasbourg has been a wide one, though it should be noted that this aspect of Article 8 is not dependent upon, or directed to the protection of, property interests or contractual rights. The test used to establish a 'home' was further expanded by the Commission in *Buckley v UK*[43] when the court described the 'home' as:

> [A]n autonomous concept which does not depend on classification under domestic law. Whether or not a particular habitation constitutes a 'home' which attracts the protection of Article 8(1) will depend on the factual circumstances, namely, the existence of sufficient and continuous links.[44]

The Article does not give a right to a home.[45] However, once a right to the home has been established, any interference in the rights must be established.

This may be relevant in two ways for an ancillary relief claim. First, if the order affected the housing arrangements for the parties or the children. In *M v B (ancillary proceedings: lump sum)*,[46] Thorpe LJ stated that:

> In all these cases it is one of the paramount considerations, in applying the s 25 criteria, to endeavour to stretch what is available to cover the need of each for a home, particularly where there are young children involved. Obviously the primary carer needs whatever is available to make the main home for the children, but it is of importance, albeit it is of lesser importance, that the other parent should have a home of his own where the children can enjoy their contact time with him. Of course there are cases where there is not enough to provide a home for either. Of course there are cases where there is only enough to provide one. But in any case where there is, by stretch and a degree of risk-taking, the possibility of a division to enable both to rehouse themselves, that is an exceptionally important consideration and one which will almost invariably have a decisive impact on the outcome.[47]

As the quote from Thorpe LJ indicates, and as is required by section 25(1) of the MCA, meeting the needs, and particularly the housing needs of any children, is the court's first consideration. But meeting the housing needs of both parties where that is possible is properly a goal under Article 8 too. While Article 8 does not create a right to a home, merely a right to respect for a person's home,[48] an order which required a spouse to sell their home and left them without sufficient money to find another would appear to breach Article 8 and require justification. No doubt such justification could be found within the second paragraph of Article 8, particularly in terms of the welfare of any child.[49]

Second, if a party, as a result of an ancillary relief order, was unable to afford to maintain contact with his or her children this could involve a claim under Article 8. The argument would be that, as discussed in Chapter 6, a parent has a right of contact with a child under Article 8. Where a court order has in effect made contact impossible, there is an interference in their rights. There has been no reported case where such an argument has been

---

[43] (1996) 23 EHRR 191.
[44] Para 52.
[45] *Chapman v UK* Application No 27238/95; *Harrow LBC v Qazi* [2004] 1 AC 983.
[46] [1998] 1 FLR 53.
[47] At 54.
[48] *Qazi v London Borough of Harrow* [2003] UKHL 43.
[49] L Fox, 'The Meaning of Home: A Chimerical Concept or a Legal Challenge' (2002) 29 *Law and Society* 580.

made,[50] and it would require unusual circumstances before a court would be persuaded that the parent was indeed so badly off as a result of a court order that he was unable to fund contact.

Article 6: Procedural Issues in Ancillary Relief Cases

Ancillary relief cases, like all other civil litigation, must comply with the requirements of a fair trial as found in Article 6. This includes, in particular, a requirement of 'equality of arms'.[51] A number of aspects of this are relevant to ancillary relief.

First, Article 6 includes a right to equal access to relevant documentation.[52] In particular the ECtHR has explained that 'it also implies, in principle, the opportunity for the parties to have knowledge of and discuss all evidence adduced or observations filed with a view to influencing the Court's decision'.[53] This is done in English law through the obligations on parties to make disclosure of all relevant materials, and responses to questions raised as a result of that disclosure.[54] While most lawyers will admit that a failure to make full disclosure within an ancillary relief case is rampant,[55] it is unlikely that the law could do much more than it could to enforce the obligation, at least in a way which is proportionate to the costs that would be involved in disclosure.[56] It may be claimed that because the Family Proceedings Rules do not apply to applications under Schedule 1 of the CA the obligations of disclosure in such applications are inadequate. That said, there is nothing to stop a party applying for further disclosure in such cases if that is needed.

Second, equality of arms also involves an equal access to effective legal representation.[57] Where one party is much wealthier than the other and is therefore able to obtain more expert or more extensive legal advice, the courts have been willing to make maintenance pending suit orders to fund representation.[58] Otherwise a spouse would need to rely on legal aid, if they were to claim it. Were a party able to show that they were at a significant disadvantage due to the lack of appropriate legal advice then an Article 6 claim may arise. Indeed a party could use Article 6 to bolster their application for maintenance pending suit to cover legal costs.

Third, Articles 6 and 8 can clash where a party in a divorce seeks a financial order against a third party. In *M v M (Third Party Subpoena: Financial Conduct)*[59] Peter Hughes QC held that an order for disclosure against a third party was an intrusion into that person's privacy interfering with their Article 8 rights. Such an interference was oppressive and unwarranted

---

[50] Although see below where such claims have been made in relation to the child support legislation.
[51] *A v A (Maintenance Pending Suit)* [2001] 1 FLR 377.
[52] *McMichael v United Kingdom* [1995] 2 FCR 718.
[53] *Švenšionienė v Lithuania* [2009] 1 FLR 509, para 23.
[54] The detailed requirements of disclosure are found in the Family Proceedings Rules (Statutory Instrument 1991 No 1247).
[55] See *Mahon v Mahon* [2008] EWCA Civ 901.
[56] Although see *Behzadi v Behzadi* [2008] EWCA Civ 1070 and *Mahon v Mahon* [2008] EWCA Civ 901 for an indication that the courts are trying to be tough on non-disclosure, at least in big money cases.
[57] *Ankerl v Switzerland* Application No 17748/91.
[58] *G v G (Maintenance Pending Suit: Costs)* [2002] EWHC 306 (Fam), [2003] 2 FLR 71. In *A v A (Maintenance Pending Suit)* [2001] 1 FLR 377 a wife was able to get maintenance pending suit to cover her legal fees after her legal aid certificate had been discharged.
[59] [2006] 2 FLR 1253 (FD). The case was heard on other grounds in the Court of Appeal, *sub nom Morgan v Morgan* [2006] EWCA 1852.

unless shown to be necessary and proportionate to the issues in the case. In that case the interference was justified given the relationship between the third party and the husband (they were lovers) and the inability of the court to deal with the application by other means, such as drawing adverse inferences.

Fourth, Article 6 claims were raised in *Mubarak v Mubarak (Contempt in Failure to Pay Lump Sum: Standard of Proof)*.[60] There Bodey J, in a judgment upheld by the Court of Appeal, refused to hear a father's application to reduce the periodic payments while he was still in contempt for failing to pay the lump sum order. This was held to be a justifiable interference in any Article 6 rights the father had. It was important to note that the court referred to the appellant's 'grossly contumacious refusal to pay'. Had his refusal been a result of an inability to pay, no doubt any interference in Article 6 rights would be harder to justify.

Discrimination and Article 14

Article 14 of the ECHR states:

> The enjoyment of the rights and freedoms set forth in this convention shall be secured without discrimination on any ground such as sex, race, colour, language, religion, political or other opinion, national or social origin, association with a national minority, property, birth or other status.

Article 14 is not a freestanding right and can only be claimed in conjunction with another right in the Convention.[61] Strictly speaking it is not necessary to find an actual breach of another Article as long as it falls within the ambit of a Convention right.[62]

Having established that the claim falls within the ambit of a Convention right it must be shown that there is a difference in treatment between the complainant and a person in the same position as the complainant, but without the characteristic which is said to mark the discrimination. So in a case of alleged sex discrimination the court would compare how a female complainant was treated as compared with a similarly placed male.

The list of prohibited grounds of discrimination are not closed. This is revealed by use of the words 'such as' in Article 14. So, in *Salgueiro da Silva Mouta v Portugal*[63] the ECtHR held that sexual orientation would be included within the list of prohibited grounds of discrimination. Even if discrimination is shown, it is open to the discriminating party to show that the discrimination was justified on the basis of an objective and reasonable reason.[64]

As already indicated, it is likely that the strongest ECHR arguments to be made in the area of ancillary relief are to be made on the basis of discrimination. In this context this will involve using Article 14 in combination with a claim under Article 8 or Article 1 of the First Protocol. The following are some of the grounds of discrimination that may be relied upon.

---

[60] *Mubarak v Mubarak* [2007] EWCA Civ 879.

[61] For a general discussion of Art 14 see D Feldman, *Civil Liberties and Human Rights in England and Wales* (Oxford, Oxford University Press, 2002), 142–8 and W Wright, 'The Tide in Favour of Equality' (2006) 20 *International Journal of Law, Policy and the Family* 249; A Baker, 'Article 14 ECHR: a Protector, Not a Prosecutor' in H Fenwick, G Phillipson and R Masterman, *Judicial Reasoning and the Human Rights Act 1998* (Cambridge, Cambridge University Press, 2008).

[62] R Wintemute, 'Within the ambit': How big is the "gap" in Article 14 of the European Convention on Human Rights?: Part 1' (2004) *European Human Rights Law Review* 4.

[63] Application No 33290/96.

[64] *A v Secretary of State for the Home Department* [2004] UKHL 56 para 54.

Non-financial Contributions

In several of the recent leading cases discrimination has been cited as a major reason for changing the courts' approach to ancillary relief cases. Lord Nicholls in *Miller v Miller; McFarlane v McFarlane*[65] opened his speech with these words:

> These two appeals concern that most intractable of problems: how to achieve fairness in the division of property following a divorce. In *White v White* [2001] 1 AC 596 your Lordships' House sought to assist judges who have the difficult task of exercising the wide discretionary powers conferred on the court by Part II of the Matrimonial Causes Act 1973. In particular the House emphasised that in seeking a fair outcome there is no place for discrimination between a husband and wife and their respective roles. Discrimination is the antithesis of fairness. In assessing the parties' contributions to the family there should be no bias in favour of the money-earner and against the home-maker and the child-carer. This is a principle of universal application. It is applicable to all marriages.[66]

Baroness Hale explained:

> In these non-business-partnership, non-family asset cases, the bulk of the property has been generated by one party. Does this provide a reason for departing from the yardstick of equality? On the one hand is the view, already expressed, that commercial and domestic contributions are intrinsically incommensurable. It is easy to count the money or property which one has acquired. It is impossible to count the value which the other has added to their lives together. One is counted in money or money's worth. The other is counted in domestic comfort and happiness. If the law is to avoid discrimination between the gender roles, it should regard all the assets generated in either way during the marriage as family assets to be divided equally between them unless some other good reason is shown to do otherwise.[67]

Baroness Hale is explicit that the reason that financial and domestic contributions in a marriage should be treated equally is in order to avoid gender discrimination.[68] Recently Charles J also made this most explicit: 'In determining what is a fair distribution of financial resources following the breakdown of a marriage there is to be no gender discrimination.'[69] Although no explicit reference in making these points is made to the HRA, it is likely without these developments an Article 14 claim could be made in a case where there was unjustified discrimination between a child carer and a money-maker. But it may still be argued that discrimination between financial and non-financial contributions remains, and that this constitutes indirect gender discrimination.

In *Charman v Charman*[70] it was acknowledged that in rare cases an exceptional contribution through money terms could justify the court departing from the 'principle of equal division' that would otherwise normally apply in big money cases involving a lengthy marriage. However, the court was at pains to point out that the special contribution argument could be used by both money earners and non-earners:

> The notion of a special contribution to the welfare of the family will not successfully have been purged of inherent gender discrimination unless it is accepted that such a contribution can, in principle, take a number of forms; that it can be non-financial as well as financial; and that it can

---

[65] [2006] UKHL 24.
[66] Para 1.
[67] Para 150.
[68] See also *Charman v Charman* [2007] EWCA 503 Civ, para 80.
[69] [2007] EWHC 459 (Fam).
[70] [2007] EWCA 503 Civ.

thus be made by a party whose role has been exclusively that of a home-maker. Nevertheless in practice, and for self-evident reasons, the claim to have made a special contribution seems so far to have arisen only in cases of substantial wealth generated by a party's success in business during the marriage. The self-evident reason is that in such cases there is substantial property over the distribution of which it is worthwhile to argue.[71]

This approach may enable the courts to claim there is no discrimination on the grounds of gender in these cases. Nevertheless, as the court acknowledged, child care and home making are in their nature hard to value and it is difficult to see how a court would determine that an exceptional contribution had been made. Would care of a seriously disabled child be an exceptional contribution? Notably although there have been several cases where a money earner's contribution has been exceptional, there has not been one where it has been argued that a home maker's contribution is.[72] If, as the court indicates, the reality is that the claim of special contribution can be made by a money earner, but not a child carer, that may amount to gender discrimination.

Matrimonial Assets

In *White*[73] and *Miller; McFarlane*,[74] it was suggested that generally in a big money case involving a short marriage there should be a division of 'matrimonial property'. In short, those are the assets that the couple generated during the marriage and would not include assets that a partner had acquired prior to the marriage, or indeed after it.[75] However, there is a difference in view between Lord Nicholls and Baroness Hale in *Miller; McFarlane* over how 'matrimonial property' is to be understood. Lord Nicholls treated any property acquired during the marriage, except gifts and inheritances, as matrimonial property. Baroness Hale used a narrower understanding of the term and restricted it to assets generated by the efforts of both parties. It would not include assets which were produced by the efforts of one party alone. She explained that in relation to non-family assets 'it simply cannot be demonstrated that the domestic contribution, important though it has been to the welfare of the family as a whole, has contributed to their acquisition'.[76] The difference between the views would be revealed in a case involving a business project in which the wife was not involved in any way (perhaps she did not even know about it). This could be a matrimonial asset subject to the yardstick of equality for Lord Nicholls because it was an asset acquired during the course of the marriage. But it would not be a family asset under Baroness Hale's test if the wife could not be said to have contributed to its acquisition. It seems that of the two views it was Baroness Hale's which attracted the most support of the other members of the House of Lords and has been supported in subsequent cases.[77]

There are concerns over the uncertainty that Baroness Hale's approach develops. More significantly for the purposes of this book, it appears to perpetuate the kind of discrimination between the money-earner and the homemaker that *White* was seeking to remove. Do we ask of the child carer or homemaker whether their contributions were family assets

---

[71] [2007] EWCA 503 Civ, para 80.
[72] Eg *Sorrell v Sorrell* [2005] EWHC 1717 (Fam).
[73] [2000] UKHL 54.
[74] [2006] UKHL 24.
[75] Although the matrimonial home is generally treated as matrimonial property, even if acquired by one of the parties prior to the marriage.
[76] Para 151.
[77] Most notably in *Charman v Charman* [2007] EWCA 503 Civ.

or not? Is it possible to disaggregate those aspects of a money earner's activities which are referable to assistance from a spouse and those which are not? It seems to introduce a discrimination between the home maker who also helps in business matters and the home maker who does not. Is it right that a wife who has a severely disabled child to care for and so does nothing to help in her husband's business should be disadvantaged as compared with a spouse who has time to spare to do so? There are certainly dangers that Baroness Hale's approach could work to the disadvantage of those engaging in extensive child care and that could create discrimination and a claim relying on Article 14.[78] There would appear to be two primary issues. The first is whether a distinction between the significance attached to money earning and child caring/home making was, in effect, gender discrimination. Given the empirical evidence[79] that women still undertake more child care and home making than men there should be little difficulty in establishing that attaching legal significance to these different forms of labour is discriminatory. Much harder will be the question of whether any such discrimination is justifiable. The argument that is likely to be relied upon is that money making is readily measurable while child care is so difficult to value.[80] This argument could, however, be used to claim that as care cannot be valued, no distinction should be drawn. It may be that any perceived unfairness to multi-millionaire spouses of not considering their contribution is insufficient to justify discrimination on the basis of sex.

Future Income

The jurisprudence of the courts in the area of ancillary relief has now acknowledged that during a marriage one party may lose out financially as a result of their family obligations, typically child care. As the burden of child care falls primarily on women it is often wives who lose out as a result of a marriage. In *McFarlane*[81] the House of Lords specifically acknowledged the need to ensure that, where it would be fair to do so, a spouse who had suffered an economic disadvantage during the marriage be compensated for her loss. In that case this required the ordering of periodic payments to ensure that Mrs McFarlane, who had given up her career to look after the children, was compensated for the resulting negative impact on her ability to produce income for herself. This to some extent protects women whose careers suffer as a result of the marriage. However, it only does so to a limited extent. First, it offers no protection for a woman whose career has suffered, but the husband's income is insufficient to enable an effective periodic payments order to be compensation. Second, the courts' desire to produce a clean break may mean that full compensation may not be made.[82] In *VB v JP*,[83] the President of the Family Division stated:

> On the exit from the marriage, the partnership ends and in ordinary circumstances a wife has no right or expectation of continuing economic parity ('sharing') unless and to the extent that consideration of her needs, or compensation for relationship-generated disadvantage so require. A clean break is to be encouraged wherever possible.[84]

---

[78] L Glennon, 'The Limitations of Equality Discourses on the Contours of Intimate Obligations' in J Wallbank, S Choudhry and J Herring (eds), *Rights, Gender and Family Law* (n 2).
[79] Discussed in detail in J Herring, 'Why Financial Orders on Divorce Should be Unfair' (n 27).
[80] *Charman v Charman* [2007] EWCA 503 Civ, para 80.
[81] [2006] UKHL 24.
[82] Although in *McFarlane* [2006] UKHL 24 the House of Lords was clear that a preference for a clean break should not prevent the court making a periodical payments order where that was required in the name of fairness.
[83] [2008] EWHC 112 (Fam).
[84] At para 59.

As that approach indicates, the desire for a clean break may mean that full compensation may not be available. An Article 14 claim may arise if the law fails to ensure effective compensation for those whose child-care activities harm their income generation. As already discussed, the success of this would depend on whether it could be shown that this amounted to sex discrimination and if so whether there was justification for the discrimination.

A slightly different argument relates to a claim that one spouse may have contributed to the other spouse's earning potential. This, though uncontroversial now, will generate a share in the wealth created during the marriage, but what of the wealth they may earn after the divorce? Could a wife claim that she contributed to putting the husband in a position where he was capable of earning the sums he did and that she should, therefore, be entitled to a share in his future earnings? In *H v H*[85] such an argument was accepted by Charles J, but in restrictive terms. First, a wife would need to show that 'but for' her contribution the husband would not have been earning at the level he was. In many cases this will be hard to do. Second, even where the wife can demonstrate this she will not be entitled to substantial sums because the balance of his income will be earned by his work and endeavours after the marriage, rather than relating back to the help the wife offered during the marriage. In that case the wife was awarded one-third, one-sixth and one-twelfth of his income for the three years after the marriage. It is unclear yet whether such orders will become common. A failure to recognise the full value of a non-financial contribution may be said to raise Article 14 issues. If it was accepted that this was sex discrimination (the failure being one that worked generally against the interests of women) it would be necessary to consider the issue of justification. John Eekelaar[86] has argued that it is important that the clean break principle is upheld and that claims against future income can undermine that. Further there are doubts over the extent to which a person's earning potential can be regarded as a result of their spouse's efforts. Or at least whether it is possible to accurately calculate the extent to which it is. These difficulties may be seen as justifying the rejection of the 'earning potential as marital property' argument. However, in response it may be said that a failure to accept the argument means that the full value of the child care or home making is not being recognised in big money cases.

Domestic Violence

Generally speaking, domestic violence plays little role in financial orders on divorce.[87] The courts have been very strict in their interpretation of section 25(2)(g) of the MCA, which permits them to consider the conduct of the parties during the marriage when assessing the level of financial award.[88] Domestic violence is unlikely to affect the level of the award, unless the behaviour can be said to affect the earning capacity of the parties.[89]

Does this failure to take a broader account of domestic violence constitute improper discrimination? The first point may be made that rates of domestic violence are higher against women than against men and the impact of domestic violence is more serious.[90]

---

[85] [2008] 2 FCR 714.

[86] J Eekelaar, 'Property and Financial Settlement on Divorce—Sharing and Compensating' [2006] *Family Law* 754.

[87] D Hodson, 'Spare the Child and Hit the Pocket: Toward a Jurisprudence on Domestic Abuse as a Quantum Factor in Financial Outcomes on Relationship Breakdown' (2005, paper presented at the World Congress on Family Law).

[88] *S v S* [2007] Fam 106.

[89] See, eg, *Jones v Jones* [1975] 2 WLR 606.

[90] See J Herring, *Family Law* (n 8) ch 6 for a detailed discussion of the statistics.

Any disadvantageous treatment for victims of domestic violence can thereby be seen to discriminate against women and amount to gender discrimination. But is the failure of the law on ancillary relief to take into account domestic violence except in the most serious of cases, discriminatory?

It is argued that it is. Generally the courts are reluctant to take into account domestic violence in ancillary relief cases. Cases where domestic violence (or child abuse) has been taken into account include a wife shooting a husband with intent to endanger life;[91] a husband attacks a wife with a razor inflicting serious injuries;[92] husband sexually abuses the children;[93] the wife incites others to kill the husband;[94] husband assaults the wife with a knife;[95] husband attempts to rape the wife and serious assault;[96] husband abducts the children;[97] and husband attempts to murder wife.[98] However, when a husband smashed his wife's head against a shower pole and hit her several times while she was lying on the floor, it was insufficient to amount to conduct.[99] It was memorably held that it created a 'gulp factor' but not a 'gasp factor'. This indicates that only in the most serious kinds of case is domestic violence taken into account. However, the approach of the courts can be said to be discriminatory in two ways.

First, the courts may be said, at least in some cases, to overemphasise the significance of some kinds of behaviour. Consider, for example, *Clarke v Clarke*,[100] where a wife left her older wealthy husband following their reception. Subsequently she engaged in a range of conduct including having affairs, and forcing the man into a caravan in his garden. Thorpe LJ said of her behaviour: 'It would be hard to consider graver financial misconduct.'[101] However, the wife was not violent to the husband. At worst she had been unfaithful to him and sought to get as much money from him as she could. But to classify that as a case which is clearly worse than a case of domestic violence involves a failure to appreciate the significance of domestic violence.[102]

Second, the courts have failed to recognise the economic impact of domestic violence. As well as the more important psychological and physical significance of domestic violence, it can impact on a woman's self-esteem and potential to develop a career.[103] This is rarely considered or discussed in an ancillary relief case.

If the argument that the economic impact of domestic violence is not taken sufficiently into account is accepted, it could lead to a claim that the law on ancillary relief is discriminating against women, who make up the bulk of domestic violence victims.[104] This could be used to form the basis of a claim under Article 14, combined with Articles 8 or Article 1 of the First Protocol.

---

[91] *Armstrong v Armstrong* [1974] SJ 579.
[92] *Jones v Jones* [1976] Fam 8.
[93] *S v S* [1982] Fam 183.
[94] *Evans v Evans* [1989] 1 FLR 351.
[95] *A v A* [1995] 1 FLR 345.
[96] *H v H* [1994] 2 FLR 801.
[97] *Al-Khatib v Masry* [2002] 1 FLR 1053.
[98] *H v H* [2006] 1 FLR 990.
[99] *S v S* [2007] Fam 106 para 57.
[100] [1999] 2 FLR 498.
[101] At 509.
[102] On which see, further, M Madden Dempsey, *Prosecuting Domestic Violence: A Philosophical Analysis* (Oxford, Oxford University Press, 2009).
[103] *Ibid*, ch 2.
[104] See further the discussion in ch 9.

Enforcement

There has been some discussion over enforcement of financial decisions and Convention rights.[105] There is no doubt that Article 6 applies to debtors whose debts are being enforced. For example, they are entitled to the presumption of innocence and the right to time to prepare for a defence. In *Mubarak v Mubarak*[106] the Court of Appeal concluded that the procedure for judgment summons breached Article 6 rights by reversing the onus of proof from the creditor to the debtor. This defect in the procedures surrounding judgment summonses were remedied so that now the procedure should be compliant with the rights of the debtor.[107] In particular they clearly place the burden of proof on the creditor and there is protection of the debtor's right to silence.

Child Support Issues

In a series of cases the courts have stated that the use of the Child Support Act 1991 and the lack of effective challenge to actions or inactions of the agency did not interfere with the rights of children and parents.

In *R (on the application of Denson) v Child Support Agency*[108] the focus had been on Article 8 and Article 1 of the First Protocol. The claim was that the operation of the child support system interfered with a non-resident parent's property and their right to respect for their private life. Munby J found, in a judicial review application, that the Child Support Act 1991 was compliant with both Articles. There was a proportionality between the aims of the legislation: to increase parental responsibility and reduce taxation; and the means employed to do so: a formula used to ascertain the amount paid. Predictably the Court of Appeal in *Rowley v Secretary of State for the Department of Work and Pensions*[109] found that the Secretary of State did not owe a duty of care to qualifying children or their parents in exercising their function under the Child Support Act and so an action in tort could not be brought by a parent or child unhappy with the way their case was being dealt with by the Child Support Agency (CSA).

The most significant challenge to the child support legislation came in *R (on the application of Kehoe) v Secretary of State for Work and Pensions*,[110] which provided an opportunity for the courts to consider whether a child or a child's resident parent's ECHR rights were interfered with by the lack of means of challenging a failure by the CSA. The claims were based on Article 6 and an argument that the lack of an effective legal remedy to the non-action of the CSA constituted a denial of her right to a fair hearing. Ms Kehoe applied to the CSA under section 4 of the Child Support Act 1991 for a maintenance assessment to

---

[105] Z Pabani, 'Enforcement of Ancillary Relief Orders' [2008] *Family Law* 355; P Rutter, 'Judgment Summonses: the Final Nail in the Coffin' [2008] *Family Law* 433; J Southgate, 'Judgment Summonses: Still Scope for a Comeback' [2003] *Family Law* 436.

[106] [2001] 1 FCR 193. See also *Corbett v Corbett* [2003] EWCA Civ 559.

[107] Family Proceedings (Amendment) Rules 2003, SI 2003 No 184, which amended Family Proceedings Rules 1991, rr 7.4–7.6.

[108] [2002] EWHC (Admin) 154, [2002] 1 FCR 460.

[109] [2007] 3 FCR 431.

[110] [2005] UKHL 48, discussed in N Wikeley, 'A Duty but not a Right: Child Support after *R (Kehoe) v Secretary of State for Work and Pensions*' [2006] *Child and Family Law Quarterly* 287.

be made against her former husband in connection with her four children. Her application was made in 1993, but the assessment was not made until 1995. The difficulties continued, with arrears accumulating following unsuccessful attempts at enforcement by the agency. By 2003 the amount owing was £17,000. The applicant left England for Spain and the CSA closed its file. Ms Kehoe instituted proceedings against the Secretary of State for Work and Pensions. She claimed, first, that the CSA delays in assessing and enforcing the payments infringed her rights under Articles 6 and 7 of the ECHR, as protected by the HRA. Secondly, that section 8 of the Child Support Act (which prevented the court making orders in connection with child maintenance when the CSA was dealing with the children) infringed her rights under Article 6 to a fair trial. This was because it denied a resident parent access to courts in connection with problems in receiving financial support from the non-resident parent.

The majority of their Lordships held that the Child Support Act 1991 deliberately gave a parent with care no right to recover or enforce maintenance, subject to certain exceptions in section 8 which did not apply here. Article 6 of the Convention was not engaged because that concerned safeguarding legal rights which existed under national law. As the applicant had no rights under national law to enforce child support payments, she could not complain about the inability to enforce those payments relying on Article 6.

A key element in their Lordships' reasoning was that Mrs Kehoe had no legal right to child maintenance. Lord Bingham held that this lack of legal right for caring parents to enforce maintenance payments was an 'essential' aspect of the Child Support Scheme set out in the 1991 Act.[111] Lord Hope put it this way:

> The Act uses the word 'duty' in s 1(3), where it refers to the duty of the absent parent with respect to whom the assessment was made to make the payments, and the word 'obligation' in s 4(2)(b), where it refers to the enforcement of the obligation to pay child support maintenance in accordance with the assessment. But nowhere in the Act is it said that the absent parent owes a duty, or is under an obligation, to pay that amount to the person with care. Nor is it said anywhere that the person with care has a right which she can enforce against the absent parent.[112]

Lord Bingham made it clear that it was not for the House of Lords to decide whether this policy was a sensible one for the legislature to adopt. This is largely a reflection of the courts' defence to the legislature, as discussed in Chapter 1. But it was not simply a matter of deference. As Lord Walker pointed out, a caring parent had some rights in law.[113] If the CSA was to illegally use or fail to use its powers, an action for judicial review could be brought.

The majority rejected the relevance of Article 6. They emphasise that Article 6 could not be used to complain about the fact that one did not have a particular legal right, but could only be used where one had a legal right but was being prevented from enforcing it. Lord Hope argued that the CSA scheme simply did not give Mrs Kehoe a legal right and so Article 6 was not engaged:

> It is not enough to bring Art 6(1) into play to assert that, as the whole object of the scheme is that the person with care is the person who will ultimately benefit from the enforcement process, Mrs Kehoe should be allowed at least some say in how that process is conducted. I respectfully

---

[111] Para 5.
[112] Para 33.
[113] Para 45.

agree with Latham LJ that it seems unsatisfactory that she should not have that right, as the agency's priorities are inevitably different from those of the person with care of the child, who may disagree profoundly with the agency as to how the proceedings in which she has such an obvious interest should be conducted (see [2004] 1 FCR 511 at [102]). But the fact is that the 1991 Act itself, which is the only source from which it could be derived, does not give her that right. The scheme of the 1991 Act is not designed to allow the person with care to play any part in the enforcement process at all. It is not possible to envisage how that might be done without rewriting the scheme which the Act has laid down. In my opinion this is not even a case where it can be said that the existence of a right to participate in this process is arguable.[114]

In a powerful dissenting speech Baroness Hale laid her cards on the table with her opening sentence: 'My Lords, this is another case which has been presented to us largely as a case about adults' rights when in reality it is a case about children's rights.'[115] She emphasised that it has long been accepted that children who are too young to fend for themselves have to be provided for by their parents. She was adamant that the Child Support Act 1991 does not represent the totality of parents' obligations to support their children. As she pointed out, section 78(6) of the Social Security Administration Act 1992 still retains an obligation on parents to maintain their child. Indeed, section 8 of the Child Support Act itself does not prevent the courts making further orders in respect of children outside the aegis of the Child Support Act, for example, where the child is disabled (section 8(8)); or to make property adjustment or lump sum orders under, for example, Schedule 1 of the CA. She argued that the 1991 Act represents the minimum a child should receive but is not the limit of the rights available.[116] This enabled her to hold that a child has a right to be maintained by its parents which exists independently of the 1991 Act. Such a right therefore engages with Article 6. Article 6 therefore required an effective way for the enforcement of the child's right. The Child Support Act 1991, in not providing an effective mechanism of enforcing adequate support, failed to adequately protect the child's right under Article 6. Although there was the option (which Lord Walker had mentioned) of judicial review, this was an inadequate protection of a child's rights.

Baroness Hale argued:

it is difficult to think of anything more important for the present and future good of society than that our children should be properly cared for and brought up. We who are nearing the end of our productive lives will depend more than most upon the health, strength and productivity of the following generations. The human infant has a long period of dependency in any event. But we have added to that by our requirements that they be educated up to the age of 16 and disabled from earning their own living until then. Someone must therefore provide for them.[117]

She also held:

The 1991 Act contemplates that, as a minimum, children should have the benefit of the maintenance obligation as defined under the formula; but it does not contemplate that children should be limited to their rights under that Act; in appropriate circumstances, they may be supplemented or replaced in all the ways recounted earlier.[118]

---

[114] Para 42.
[115] Para 49.
[116] Para 70.
[117] Para 49.
[118] Para 70.

This, she held, generated rights under Article 6. She was not convinced that a judicial review provided protection for the rights of children:

> The problem is that this is exactly what the system is trying to do. It is trying to enforce the children's rights. It is sometimes, as this case shows, lamentably inefficient in so doing. It is safe to assume that there are cases, of which this may be one, where the children's carer would be much more efficient in enforcing the children's rights. The children's carer has a direct and personal interest in enforcement which the Agency, however good its intentions, does not. Even in benefit cases, where the state does have a direct interest in enforcement, it is not the sort of interest which stems from needing enough money to feed, clothe and house the children on a day to day basis. Only a parent who is worrying about where the money is to be found for the school dinners, the school trips, the school uniform, sports gear or musical instruments, or to visit the 'absent' parent, not only this week but the next and the next for many years to come, has that sort of interest. A promise that the Agency is doing its best is not enough. Nor is the threat or reality of judicial review. Most people simply do not have access to the Administrative Court in the way that they used to have access to their local magistrates' court. Judicial review may produce some action from the Agency, but what is needed is money from the absent parent. Action from the Agency will not replace the money which has been irretrievably lost as a result of its failure to act in time.[119]

The difference between the majority and minority approaches is striking. Most notable is the emphasis on the rights of the child which is at the heart of Baroness Hale's judgment. For the majority the focus is on the right of the caring parent. Indeed the majority approach is notable for its absence of a detailed examination of the issue from the point of view of the child's rights. This point is particularly important given the reforms to the law on child support in the Child Maintenance and Other Payments Act 2008.[120] What if a proposed agreement is reached between parents which sets the level of child support at a very low amount? If children have an independent right to an appropriate level of child support then the state must ensure a degree of protection of their rights. If, however, this is essentially seen as a private matter for the parents, which is how it is regarded in the 2008 Act, then there is a danger that children's rights will be inadequately protected.

As Nick Wikeley[121] points out, one of the odd things is that a civil court can make a consent order embodying the terms of the agreement of a couple over child maintenance which would certainly generate a civil right to child maintenance. It seems odd that, where the parent is on benefits and so the Agency applies, it does not. Particularly odd that a non-resident parent can therefore in effect determine whether or not the resident parent and child have Article 6 rights by deciding not to reach an agreement and so involve the Agency.

Ms Kehoe's case was heard by the ECHR.[122] In short, they found the remedy of judicial review was sufficiently effective to protect any Article 6 rights she had. Although the remedies available may be limited, it was adequate to protect her rights. This is by contrast with the approach of the ECtHR, which has consistently found that judicial review is not

---

[119] Para 72.
[120] N Wikeley, 'Child Support Reform—Throwing the Baby out with the Bathwater' [2007] *Child and Family Law Quarterly* 434.
[121] *Ibid.*
[122] Application No 2010/06.

an effective remedy to deal with the breaches of an individual's Convention rights.[123] The Court added:

> Furthermore, in assessing whether the possibility of applying to the courts for judicial review provided the applicant with effective access to court, the Court must also give due weight to the Government's arguments as to the purpose and context of the child support system within England and Wales. The provision of a state enforcement scheme for maintenance payments *inter alia* benefits the many parents with care of children who do not have the time, energy, resources or inclination to be embroiled in ongoing litigation with the absent parent and allows the State to pursue those absent parents who default on their obligations leaving their families in the charge of the social security system and the taxpayer. The mere fact that it is possible to envisage a different scheme which might also allow individual enforcement action by parents in the particular situation of the applicant is not sufficient to disclose a failure by the State in its obligations under Article 6.[124]

It seems, therefore, that challenges to the child support legislation are unlikely to succeed. Especially once the 2008 Act scheme comes into operation, it is difficult to imagine a court accepting that the HRA rights of the parties come into play. The most likely route of challenge would come if an application is brought by a child claiming that the level of financial support agreed between her or his parents is inadequate to such an extent that her or his Article 8 rights are interfered with. That would very rarely be the case.

Complaints by Payers of Child Support

Payers of child support have also sought to use the ECHR to challenge the child support system. In *Logan v UK*[125] a father complained that the child support maintenance had been set at such a high level that he could only afford to see his child once a month, even though he was entitled to see him once a fortnight. This, he argued, interfered with his Article 8 rights, in that it failed to show respect for his right to family life with his child. The Commission rejected his complaint, holding:

> The Commission notes that the relevant legislation, insofar as it seeks to regulate the assessment of maintenance payments from absent parents, does not by its very nature affect family life. Nor, in the light of the factual information supplied by the applicant regarding his income and expenses, including the cost of visiting his children every fortnight, does the commission consider that the applicant has shown that the effect of the operation of the legislation in his case is of such a nature and degree as to disclose any lack of respect for his rights under Article 8. In the circumstances, the commission does not therefore find it necessary to go on to consider whether, had there been an interference, it would have been justified within the meaning of Article 8(2) of the Convention.[126]

Similarly in *Burrows v UK*[127] a complaint by a father that having to pay 20 per cent of his gross income in child support affected his family life with his new family was also rejected. His claim relying on Article 1 of the First Protocol failed:

> In that regard, the commission recalls that the legislation about which the applicant complains is a practical expression of a policy relating to the economic responsibilities of parents who do

---

[123] *Z v UK* (2002) 34 EHRR 3.
[124] Para 49.
[125] (Application No 24875/94) (1996) 22 EHRR CD 178.
[126] (1996) 22 EHRR CD 178 at 181.
[127] Application No 27558/95.

not have custody of their children. Essentially it relates to the payment by an absent parent to the parent with care of the child[ren] for the purposes of their maintenance. The relevant legislation compels an absent parent to pay money to the parent with custody of the child. The commission observes that in all contracting states to the Convention, the legislation governing private law relations between individuals includes rules which determine the effects of these legal relations with respect to property, and in some cases, compel a person to surrender a possession to another. Examples include the division of inherited property, the division of matrimonial estates, and in particular the seizure and sale of property in the course of execution. This type of rule, which is essential in any liberal society, cannot in principle be considered contrary to Art 1 of Protocol No 1. However, the commission must nevertheless make sure, that in determining the effect on property of legal relations between individuals, the law does not create such inequality that one person could be arbitrarily deprived of property in favour of another.[128]

The Commission also found:

As regards whether the relevant measures are in the public interest, the commission notes that while one specific aim of the measures is to make absent parents, who are able to do so, pay for the maintenance requirements of their children, the measures are not intended solely for the benefit of the children but for the benefit of the tax-payer in general who bears the burden of paying for single parents who claim social welfare benefits. In many cases therefore, while the children are no better off since social welfare benefits are removed and replaced with payments by the absent parent, the burden on the tax-payer in general is reduced. The commission considers that the aims of reducing taxation and increasing parental responsibility must be considered as in the public interest for the purposes of Art 1 of Protocol No 1. The commission further recalls that, while a contracting state enjoys a certain margin of appreciation as regards interference with the peaceful enjoyment of possession in the public interest, it must respect a reasonable relationship of proportionality between the means employed and the legitimate aim. In view of the fact that the applicant is not required to pay a disproportionate percentage of his gross income in maintenance payments, approximately 20 per cent, and taking into account the disposable income that he is left with, the commission considers that the United Kingdom has not acted disproportionately in pursuing the legitimate aims referred to above. In the circumstances the commission does not consider the relevant measures to be disproportionate to the legitimate aim they pursue and considers that a fair balance has been struck between the interests of the community as a whole and those of the individual.[129]

In *Stacy v UK*[130] a complaint that the obligation to supply information to the CSA infringed Article 8 rights also failed. The Court found that the law stuck a fair balance between the competing interests:

... satisfied that a fair balance has been struck between the interests of individuals, namely, provision of a mechanism to avoid harmful disclosures, and the interests of the general community that the state recover child support maintenance from absent parents to reduce the burden on the taxpayer of single parent families. It finds accordingly that the requirement imposed on the applicant to provide information relevant to the enforcement of the financial obligations of absent parents arising in connection with their children is not disproportionate and may be regarded as necessary in a democratic society for the legitimate aims referred to above.[131]

---

[128]   Para 31.
[129]   Para 40.
[130]   19 January 1999.
[131]   Para 20.

As these cases indicate, challenges from payers of child support are unlikely to find much ammunition in relying on the ECHR. The approach of the courts is well summarised in *R (on the application of Denson) v Child Support Agency*[132] by Munby J:

> There is, in my judgment, a pressing social need to ensure that parents fulfil their responsibilities to their children. The statutory scheme, and the CSA's administration of it, strike a fair and reasonable balance between, on the one hand, the absent parent's responsibilities for his or her children and, on the other hand, the need for a system that (i) produces fair and consistent results, (ii) preserves the parents' incentive to work, (iii) reduces the dependency of parents with care on income support and (iv) provides consequent savings to tax-payers. In other words the statutory scheme achieves a reasonable relationship of proportionality between the legitimate aims of the legislation and the means employed.[133]

In *Treharne v Secretary of State for Work and Pensions*[134] the CSA had failed to collect a maintenance assessment made against a father in respect of several children. The mother requested enforcement but the Agency failed to do so until it was too late to make effective enforcement. The children, when they became adults, claimed that the failures of the Agency interfered with their Article 8 rights to respect for their private and family life. They sought an award for damages under the HRA. The claim failed. Cranston J found that the regime was a 'discreet and comprehensive' regime that attempted to reconcile competing interests. The scheme, seen as a whole, satisfied the state's Article 8 obligations. The fact that the scheme did not work well in a particular case did not cast doubt on the overall fairness of the scheme.

Perhaps more significantly it was found that Article 8 only generated a claim against the state for a minimal level of financial support in relation to a child. In this case the children were no worse off than many other children whose families were dependent on benefits. Cranstone J explained:

> As a matter of principle family life in Art 8 is constituted by the love, trust, confidence, mutual dependence and unconstrained social intercourse which exists within the family and private life by the sphere of personal and sexual autonomy. The same conclusion must surely apply in the converse situation where persons have less money as a result of the CSA failing to collect arrears of maintenance. That may make family life and private life tougher and perhaps more stressful than it would be, but it cannot be said to affect the core values attached to these concepts.[135]

This approach, if supported at appellate level, as well it might, would drive the last nail into any potential HRA claim in relation to child support.

Property Rights and Unmarried Couples

As is well known, there is a marked difference in the legal treatment of the financial consequences of divorce and relationship breakdown where the couple are unmarried and where the couple are civil partners or spouses. For an unmarried couple the court only has the power to declare who is the owner of property, while for a married couple

[132] [2002] 1 FCR 460.
[133] Para 32.
[134] [2008] EWHC 3222 (QB).
[135] Para 31.

and civil partners the court has wide ranging powers to redistribute property and require ongoing support payments. From a human rights point of view of number of issues can be raised.[136]

Any claim by a cohabitant who is seeking to use the HRA to challenge the application of the law to her case will need to point to a Convention right that is affected.[137] We have already seen that the claims that are likely to be affected are Article 8 and Article 1 of the First Protocol. This is likely to be combined in the case of a cohabitant that there has been discrimination on the basis of sex or marital status, relying on Article 14.

Relying on these Articles for a cohabitant can be problematic. As seen in Chapter 1, Article 8's primary purpose is to protect individuals from arbitrary interference by public authorities in family and private life, in home and correspondence. However, the Article has been interpreted to include both positive and negative obligations on the state. The right to respect for the home appears particularly relevant for the cohabitant, who is seeking a share in a partner's home. The first point to emphasise is that the right to respect for a home is not restricted to where a person has a property right in the home.[138] It is the living in the place as a home, rather than legal ownership, which generates the coverage of the Article 8 right. Similarly Protocol 1, Article 1 can cover claims against possession in which a person has a genuine interest, even if the applicant has no formal ownership rights.[139] However, an interference of Protocol 1, Article 1 rights will normally involve a person being deprived of their ownership rights, or a restriction on these rights.[140] As Lord Hope stated in *Wilson v First County Trust Ltd*[141] Article 1 neither confers a right of property nor guarantees the content of any rights in property.[142] The Article merely guarantees the peaceful enjoyment of property which an individual already owns.[143] It seems, therefore, if the applicant has no property right in their home, they cannot utilise Article 1 of the First Protocol or Article 8 to found a right to have a share in the home they have lived in. Simone Wong argues:

> it is unlikely that the right to respect for the home will extend to include a property-conferring right, i.e. to grant proprietary rights where none previously existed. Family property disputes are often fuelled by the need to establish such rights, e.g. through a constructive trust. Any extension of the material scope of Article 8 to a property-conferring right would be controversial per se since the existence of such a right is not reflected in the jurisprudence of the European Court. Hence, the right to respect for the home under Article 8 cannot be interpreted as comprising an obligation to confer or to secure proprietary rights to an individual.[144]

---

[136] S Wong, 'Constructive Trusts over the Family Home: Lessons to be Learned from Other Commonwealth Jurisdictions?' (1998) 18 *Legal Studies* 369; S Wong, 'Re-thinking *Rosset* from a Human Rights Perspective' in A Hudson (ed), *New Perspectives on Property Law, Human Rights and the Home* (London. Cavendish, 2003).

[137] S Caballero, 'Unmarried Cohabiting Couples before the European Court of Human Rights: Parity within Marriage' (2005) 11 *Columbia Journal of European Law* 151.

[138] *Harrow London Borough Council v Qazi* [2003] 4 All ER 461; *Gillow v UK* (1986) 11 EHRR 335. See also D Rook, *Property Law and Human Rights* (London, Blackstone Press, 2001), 105–6.

[139] *Sporrong v Sweden* (1982) 5 EHRR 35; *Lithgow v UK* (1986) 8 EHRR 329.

[140] *Marckx v Belgium* (1979) EHRR 330 para 50; *Inze v Austria* (1987) 10 EHRR 394.

[141] [2003] 4 All ER 97 para 106.

[142] D Rook, *Property Law and Human Rights*, 105–6; and J Howell, 'Land and Human Rights' (1999) 63 *Conveyancer* 287.

[143] *Iatridis v Greece* (2000) 30 EHRR 97. See further T Allen, *Property and the Human Rights Act 1998* (Oxford, Hart, 2005), ch 1 and A Coban, *Protection of Property Rights within the European Convention on Human Rights* (Aldershot, Ashgate, 2004).

[144] S Wong, 'Trusting in Trust(s): The Family Home and Human Rights' (2003) 11 *Feminist Legal Studies* 119. For similar views see Howell, 'Land and Human Rights' (n 142).

It is submitted that we do not need to be as pessimistic as Wong is about the potential claim for two reasons. The first is that if an individual has a legitimate interest in their home which is protected by Article 8 (even if not a legal right of ownership as such), that interest must be protected, unless there is a good enough reason to justify an interference. In the case of a dispute between two cohabitants over the ownership of a home after break-up it is hard to see what order could be made which would protect the interests of the non-owning cohabitant in the property, save granting a formal interest in the property. Possibly an occupation order could be made protecting her interest in occupation, but that may still not fully protect her interest in the home. In response it might be said that the interest that is being protected is the right to respect for a home and not her right to a share in a home. This is correct and so our argument could operate where granting a proprietal interest was the only effective way of protecting her human right to respect for her home. It may be that that would very rarely be found to be so.

Second, it might be argued that the resolution of a property dispute between cohabitants over ownership of a home falls within the ambit of Article 1 of the First Protocol or Article 8 to a sufficient extent to bring in Article 14. So, the strongest basis for a human rights claim for a cohabitant who is unable to establish a property interest in the home she has shared with her partner is not to argue that the law is failing to protect her Article 8 or Article 1 rights, but rather that the denial of her claim is discriminatory. There are two ways such a claim may be made.

Discrimination on the Basis of Marital Status

It is clear that there is a difference in legal treatment based on marital status as between married and cohabiting couples in the way their financial issues are dealt with at the end of their relationship. It is not controversial to suggest that this could amount to discrimination under Article 14. However, two major hurdles would face a cohabitant arguing that the unavailability of the financial orders on divorce discriminated against her.

First would be a difficulty in finding what right could be relied upon in conjunction with Article 14, remembering that Article 14 is not a free-standing claim. What human right is lost if a cohabitant is not able to claim a portion of their partner's wealth? As just argued, a strong case can be made for arguing that the dispute over financial orders on separation can fall within the scope of rights under Article 8 or Article 1 of the First Protocol.

Second, there would be the question of whether the discrimination in treatment can be justified. The European Court has been consistent in finding that differences between married and unmarried couples can be justified if there is a rational basis for doing so.[145] In *Saucedo Gomez v Spain*[146] the applicant had cohabited with her partner for 18 years. On separation she sought the use of their home and financial relief. Her claim was dismissed in Spain as she was unmarried. The Commission declared her complaint inadmissible: differences in treatment between the married and the unmarried had a legitimate aim and were objectively and reasonably justified as being for the protection of the traditional family. The discrimination was not disproportionate, particularly in view of the fact that she herself

---

[145] *McMichael v United Kingdom* [1995] 2 FCR 718.
[146] Application No 37784/97.

had chosen not to marry. It must be remembered that Strasbourg leaves the contents of legislation to individual states. The Court stated:

> Social reality shows the existence of stable unions between men and women [outside marriage] … It is not however for the Court to dictate, nor even to indicate, the measures to be taken in relation to such unions, the question being one within the margin of appreciation of the respondent government, which has the free choice of the means to be employed, as long as they are consistent with the obligation to respect family life protected by the Convention.

It is submitted that it is unlikely that the ECtHR will find that the failure to provide equivalent financial orders for married and unmarried parties is unjustified discrimination. It is true that in *Re P*[147] the House of Lords found that a Northern Ireland order which prohibited unmarried couples from adopting was discriminatory on the basis of Article 14. However, in part, that was because there was a complete bar on unmarried couples adopting and their Lordships held that it could not logically be said that an unmarried couple would never be the best people to adopt a child. It would be a very different argument to say that all unmarried couples should have the same property rights as married couples. Nevertheless what *Re P*[148] does show is that the English courts can choose to go further than the Strasbourg courts because they do not need to take account of the margin of appreciation doctrine.[149] In *Miron v Trudel*[150] the Supreme Court of Canada held that marital status is an analogous ground of discrimination and that excluding a cohabiting couple from services available to a married couple is potentially discriminatory. However, the courts have been reluctant to go so far as to allow unmarried couples to have access to ancillary relief proceedings.[151] This is likely to be the same approach that the ECtHR would take.

The strongest argument that the current law is discriminatory would build on the work of Lisa Glennon. She argues that some of the reasons which the courts have applied in relation to married couples apply equally to cohabitants and there is no reason why the law should distinguish between them on the application of those principles, but that on other bases there are. She holds that needs and compensation relate to relationship characteristics, especially the relationship-induced economic detriment of the primary caregiver. But equal sharing is different. That she sees as based on the 'assumed structural organisation of the relationship'.[152]

> Bearing this in mind when reflecting on current legal ideology, it seems that, at a conceptual level, parallels can be seen in how caregiving, by itself, creates *inter partes* obligations in both the post-divorce and the unmarried context. In relation to both, caregiving labour creates remedial obligations based upon the negative economic position of the primary caregiver. For divorcing spouses this is, of course, coupled with the equal sharing principle. However, as we have seen this is based, not on caregiving functions *per se,* but on the *status* of the relationship, the scope of which is integrally bound to the duration of the marriage and not the duration of the contributions of the primary carer. The potential transposition of this particular distributive model to non-marital

---

[147]   [2008] UKHL 38.
[148]   [2008] UKHL 38.
[149]   See further ch 1.
[150]   [1995] 2 SCR 418.
[151]   *Nova Scotia v Walsh* (2002) 119 ACWS (3d) 42.
[152]   L Glennon, 'Obligations Between Adult Partners: Moving from Form to Function?' (2008) 22 *International Journal of Law, Policy and the Family* 22.

relationships is problematic as it involves searching for a substitute for marriage as a signal of commitment to the co-operative endeavour of the relationship.[146] Indeed, the Law Commission does not attempt to replicate this principle, or a variant of such, for separating cohabitants, even those who are parents to a common child(ren), and sought to distance its proposals from the ancillary relief regime. Thus, this confirmation of marriage as a rights-bearing status has reinforced the regulatory gap between married and unmarried relationships, while the value placed on the contributions of the primary caregiver vis-à-vis the other parent in both systems appears to be relegated to an economic accounting exercise designed to mitigate the loss to the disadvantaged caregiver. Thus, contrary to twentieth-century predictions that *parenthood* would become the primary basis to substantiate obligations between adult partners, legal policy has not yet engaged in an 'overt' debate about such obligations without distortions being presented by overreliance on whether the parenting is taking place *within* or *outside* marriage.[153]

Glennon's argument would require a careful examination of the reasons why financial orders are made on divorce or dissolution. If, as she suggests, at least some of those reasons apply with equal validity to unmarried couples, then they should at least have access to financial orders which would reflect the application of those principles. That might not necessarily mean that the position for unmarried couples and married couples or civil partners would be identical, but there would need to be a clear justification for any differences.

Gender Discrimination

A rather different argument would be to claim that the current law on constructive and resulting trusts and proprietary estoppel[154] which is used to deal with property disputes between cohabitants discriminates against women in a number of ways.[155] It will be assumed that readers are familiar with the current law.[156]

The Emphasis on Conversations

The Law Commission has commented:

> The primary emphasis accorded by the law in cases of this kind to express discussions between the parties ('however imperfectly remembered and however imprecise their terms') means that the tenderest exchanges of a common law courtship may assume an unforeseen significance many years later when they are brought under equity's microscope and subjected to an analysis under which many thousands of pounds of value may be liable to turn on fine questions as to whether the relevant words were spoken in earnest or in dalliance and with or without representational intent.[157]

As the Law Commission acknowledges, many of the cases involving constructive claims involve disputes over whether or not the parties reached an agreement over the ownership of property. Some claim that women are less likely than men to bring up financial issues

---

[153] *Ibid.*
[154] *Q v Q* [2009] 1 FLR 935.
[155] R Bailey-Harris, 'Law and the Unmarried Couple-Oppression or Liberation?' [1996] *Child and Family Law Quarterly* 137; A Barlow and C Lind, 'A Matter of Trust: the Allocation of Rights in the Family Home' (1996) 19 *Legal Studies* 468.
[156] See Herring, *Family Law* (n 8) ch 4.
[157] Law Commission, *Cohabitation: The Financial Consequences of Relationship Breakdown, Report 307* (London, Law Commission, 2007) para 192.

and be sufficiently assertive to obtain a clear statement from their partner about property interests of the kind that will generate a claim under a constructive trust.[158] Whether this is true or not it is not the kind of claim which is amenable to empirical proof and the court is unlikely to rely on a vague generalisation about men and women to find the law on constructive trusts constitutes sex discrimination. Even if empirical proof were available, it may still be argued that the law understandably will want to focus on the agreements of the parties and so a focus on conversations is justified.

The Emphasis on Financial Contributions

As is well documented, the law on constructive trusts places much weight on financial contributions, with little or no weight placed on non-financial contributions.[159] Most notoriously in *Burns v Burns*[160] Mrs Burns lived in a house with her partner, to whom she was not married but took his name, for over 20 years. The house they lived in was in his name alone. Although she had contributed significantly as a mother and 'housewife' and had even paid some bills, she was not entitled to a share in the property. This case has faced continued criticism most recently from Douglas, Pearce and Woodward who complain: 'The continuing criticism of this case lies in the failure of the law to call her partner to account for the benefits he had enjoyed during their relationship, simply because these were not valued in financial terms.'[161]

It is true that some of the most recent cases may indicate a loosening of the courts' approach but even if the courts are moving towards the position where a non-financial contribution can be used to infer a common intention to share,[162] it is still likely to be true that a financial contribution will be in a privileged position when finding a constructive trust, with it being harder to prove.[163]

The Law Commission[164] has recognised that the current system discriminates against claimants who have not made a direct financial contribution to the general household expenses. These are likely to be people who have undertaken care work in respect of children or other relatives. They are likely to be women. Even if it is accepted that the focus on financial contributions involves indirect discrimination on the basis of sex, it may still be claimed that financial contributions provide the strongest evidence of the parties' intentions as to legal ownership.[165] This, however, is not convincing. It assumes that individuals value their money more than their domestic labour and indeed that money is more valuable than child care or other household tasks. Indeed housework may be more directly linked to the house itself than the payment of a mortgage contribution. It is suspected that an approach to constructive trusts which did not attach significance to housework and care responsibilities within a relationship could form the basis for a claim under Article 14.

---

[158] Law Commission, *Sharing Homes: A Discussion Paper* (London, Law Commission, 2002) para 2.107.

[159] For criticisms of the law see C Rotherham, 'The Property Rights of Unmarried Cohabitees: The Case for Reform' [2004] *Conveyancer* 268; The Law Society, *Cohabitation: The Case for Clear Law: Proposals for Reform* (London: Law Society, 2002).

[160] [1984] Ch 317.

[161] G Douglas, J Pearce and H Woodward, 'Cohabitants, Property and the Law: A Study of Injustice' (2009) 72 *MLR* 24.

[162] [2007] UKPC 53.

[163] A Barlow, 'Cohabitation Law Reform—Messages from Research' (2006) 14 *Feminist Legal Studies* 167.

[164] Law Commission, *Sharing Homes* (n 158) paras 2.107 and 2.112.

[165] *Stack v Dowden* [2007] UKHL 17.

Lack of Legal Basis

There could be a claim that the current law lacks a sufficiently clear basis to amount to law and thereby cannot justify any interference in a party's Article 8 rights to respect for their home. That is because any interference must be justified under Article 8(2) and therefore be 'in accordance with the law'.[166] This is a claim that is more likely to be made by the holder of legal title who is found to hold their property on constructive trust. The Law Commission has had this to say about the notion of common intention, which is key to claims about a constructive trust:

> 'Common intention' has been described as a 'myth'.[167] It is certainly difficult to explain every decided case on the basis of the parties' intention being 'express' or 'implied', and there is ample evidence of courts taking an inventive approach to the facts and discovering a common intention where none in truth exists. The parties may never have discussed the matter save in the most general terms, and they may well have been under some misconception as to the rights conferred on them by virtue of their status (married or otherwise) pursuant to the general law.[168]

In relation to at least some of the cases, the astute comment of one critic is certainly justified:

> The necessary common intention can be either express or implied, but it is supposed to be real, and not invented by the judge. However, it seems clear that this rule has little connection with judicial practice. Agreements are in reality found or denied in a manner quite unconnected with their actual presence or absence.[169]

Despite these points the courts are generally very reluctant to find that a law is too vague to constitute law for the purposes of the ECHR.[170] It is therefore unlikely, despite the law in this area being so uncertain, that it amounts to 'law' for the purposes of the ECHR.

In conclusion there is some scope for HRA claims in this area. The most promising line of challenge is that there is insufficient reason why unmarried couples do not have access to ancillary relief claims, based on at least some of the arguments used in favour of a married couple or civil partner. Second, that the current trusts law used to deal with claims between cohabitants may constitute sex discrimination on the lack of weight attached to non-financial contributions to a household.

Inheritance

Human rights claims could also be made in relation to inheritance. The ECtHR has found breaches of the ECHR, especially where discrimination is found. It is clear that there is no automatic right to succession, but the law on succession does fall within the ambit of Article 9. Hence in *Camp and Bourimi v Netherlands*[171] the Dutch law which stated that an illegitimate child could not inherit from his father's estate unless the father had recognised

[166] *Silver v UK* (1983) 5 EHRR 347.
[167] N Glover and P Todd, 'The Myth of Common Intention' (1996) 16 *Legal Studies* 325.
[168] Law Commission, *Sharing Homes* (n 158) para 2.106.
[169] S Gardner, 'Rethinking Family Property' (1993) 109 *LQR* 263, 264.
[170] See eg [2004] EWCA Crim 2375.
[171] [2000] 3 FCR 307.

the child was found to infringe Article 8 rights in a discriminatory child.[172] Similarly it has been found that laws of inheritance which drew a distinction between adopted children and biological children of the deceased,[173] and between a mother's children from her husband and from a lover,[174] were found to breach Article 8 combined with Article 14. It seems unlikely that an HRA claim could be made for a person who did not succeed under succession unless the argument was made in terms of discrimination. Article 8 does not itself give a right to inheritance.

In English law the area most susceptible to challenge might be the law on same-sex relationships. The categories of persons who are entitled to make a claim under the Inheritance (Provision for Family and Dependants) Act 1975 are specified in section 1. They include:

[a person who] during the whole of the period of two years ending immediately before the date when the deceased died, … was living—

(a) in the same household as the deceased, and
(b) as the husband or wife of the deceased [section 1(1A)]

a person if for the whole of the period of two years ending immediately before the date when the deceased died the person was living—

(a) in the same household as the deceased, and
(b) as the civil partner of the deceased [section 1(1B)]

any person … who immediately before the death of the deceased was being maintained, either wholly or partly, by the deceased [section 1(1)(e)].

That provision on the face of it does not discriminate on the grounds of marital status or on the grounds of sexual orientation. However in *Haynes v Bedger*[175] an applicant was not found to be living as the civil partner of the deceased because the couple's relationship was clandestine and they went to great lengths to keep it secret. The court added that a civil partnership in its nature involved public acknowledgement of the relationship.[176] However, that argument fails to place sufficient weight on the fact that many same-sex couples will not be open about their relationship because of the negative attitudes still held by many within our society against same-sex couples. It is not an essential element of a civil partnership that the partners let their friends and family know that they have entered a partnership. A restrictive interpretation of living together as civil partners may mean that a challenge relying on Article 8 and 14 could be made.

Tax Exemptions

It has been held that inheritance tax exemptions available on inheritance come within the scope of Article 1 of the First Protocol: *Burden v United Kingdom*.[177] In that case two elderly sisters claimed that their inability to claim the exemptions or to be able to enter into a

---

[172] See also *Marckx v Belgium* (1979) 2 EHRR 330; *Inze v Austria* (1987) 10 EHRR 394.
[173] *Mazurek v France* [2000] 5 *International Family Law* 78.
[174] *Pla and Puncernau v Andorra* (Application No 69498/01) [2004] 2 FCR 630.
[175] [2008] EWHC 1587 (Fam).
[176] Para 125.
[177] Application No 13378/05 [2007] 1 FCR 69.

status which would enable them to claim them meant that they were discriminated against. The Grand Chamber of the ECHR rejected their complaint:

> The Grand Chamber commences by remarking that the relationship between siblings is quali-tatively of a different nature to that between married couples and homosexual civil partners under the United Kingdom's CPA 2004. The very essence of the connection between siblings is consanguinity, whereas one of the defining characteristics of a marriage or CPA 2004 union is that it is forbidden to close family members (see para 17, above, and, generally, *B and L v UK* (App no 36536/02) (admissibility decision, 29 June 2004)). The fact that the applicants have chosen to live together all their adult lives, as do many married and CPA 2004 couples, does not alter this essential difference between the two types of relationship.
>
> Moreover, the Grand Chamber notes that it has already held that marriage confers a special status on those who enter into it. The exercise of the right to marry is protected by Art 12 of the conven-tion and gives rise to social, personal and legal consequences (*B and L v UK* (App no 36536/02) (admissibility decision, 29 June 2004) at para 34). In *Shackell v UK* (App no 45851/99) (admis-sibility decision, 27 April 2000), the court found that the situations of married and unmarried heterosexual cohabiting couples were not analogous for the purposes of survivors' benefits, since 'marriage remains an institution which is widely accepted as conferring a particular status on those who enter it'. The Grand Chamber considers that this view still holds true.[178]

The ECtHR went on to explain why it felt that the CPA had provided an effective protection for the rights of same-sex couples:

> 65. As with marriage, the Grand Chamber considers that the legal consequences of civil partner-ship under the CPA 2004, which couples expressly and deliberately decide to incur, set these types of relationship apart from other forms of cohabitation. Rather than the length or the supportive nature of the relationship, what is determinative is the existence of a public undertaking, carrying with it a body of rights and obligations of a contractual nature. Just as there can be no analogy between married and CPA 2004 couples, on one hand, and heterosexual or homosexual couples who choose to live together but not to become husband and wife or civil partners, on the other hand (see *Shackell v UK* (App no 45851/99) (admissibility decision, 27 April 2000)), the absence of such a legally binding agreement between the applicants renders their relationship of cohabitation, despite its long duration, fundamentally different to that of a married or civil partnership couple. This view is unaffected by the fact that, as noted in para 26, above, member states have adopted a variety of different rules of succession as between survivors of a marriage, civil partnership and those in a close family relationship and have similarly adopted different policies as regards the grant of inheritance tax exemptions to the various categories of survivor; states, in principle, remaining free to devise different rules in the field of taxation policy.[179]

Judges Zupan and Borrego provided powerful dissenting judgments. They were not con-vinced that the majority had explained why consanguinity meant that the relationship was different from other couples. Indeed, Judge Zupan suggested that one could argue that the congruity means that the blood tie makes the relationship closer. Judge Borrego felt that the argument of the majority was a statement of fact and not an explanation.

Although there is much force in the minority judgments, it seems that this case has settled the question of the compatibility of the current UK tax exemptions with the ECHR. The broader issue raised by the case which the majority avoided was the question of what

---

[178] Paras 62 and 63.
[179] Para 65.

kinds of relationship between adults should be regulated or privileged. Currently, civil partnership and marriage are. But what is it that makes these relationships suitable for state intervention and protection? After all, two people living together in a sexual relationship are not providing any particular benefit to the rest of society. An alternative vision for family law would focus on relationships of care for dependants, rather than sexual relationships.[180] This would make the carer-dependant the paradigm relationship for family law, rather than marriage. That would produce a very different kind of family law.

Conclusion

This Chapter has considered some of the issues which are raised in connection with ancillary relief cases from an HRA perspective. Two major themes emerge. The first is, as the courts have recently acknowledged, the law has been riddled with aspects which constitute indirect sex discrimination. In particular this has occurred through a failure to attach due weight to child care and housework. The law has favoured those during a marriage who have generated wealth, over those who have contributed to a marriage through child care or other household activities. That has generally favoured men over women. While the courts in dealing with ancillary relief claims have been beginning to combat these discriminatory aspects of the law, it seems there is still some way to go before ensuring there is full equal value attached to both financial and non-financial contributions. Certainly in relation to the trust law which is used to deal with disputes between cohabitants it seems that the courts have some way to go to ensure that the focus on financial contributes is not such as to constitute sex discrimination.

The second issue is the distinction that is drawn between civil partners and married and unmarried couples. The issues raised by the distinction are complex and it is unlikely that a court would rule that the ECHR requires that cohabitants should be treated in the same way as married couples or civil partners. However, it does seem now that the distinctions that the law draws must be justified in some way. Given, as argued above, that some of the principles which underpin the law on ancillary relief apply equally to cohabitants, it seems that the HRA requires there to be some form of redistributive regime for unmarried couples, even if it is not the same as that available for married couples and civil partners.[181]

There is a third issue here. That is, how we are to understand the ideas of equality and fairness in this context. In particular whether we are seeking to achieve fairness as between the parties or whether fairness involves a consideration of the wider social inequalities that women in particular face. If fairness does involve a consideration of these, is it appropriate to use financial orders on divorce to seek to resolve them?[182]

---

[180] M Fineman, *The Autonomy Myth* (New York, New Press, 2004).

[181] Law Commission, *Cohabitation* (n 157) is an obvious starting point for developing one.

[182] Diduck, 'Public Norms And Private Lives: Rights, Fairness and Family Law' (n 2).

11

Concluding Thoughts

In this Chapter we seek to draw out some of the primary themes from our analysis of the relevance of the ECHR to English family law. We have not sought to consider every possible scenario in which a rights-based analysis could be used nor explored every permutation of thinking that such an analysis could provide. What we have tried to do is to examine some of the potentials offered by the ECHR to family law. The following are some of the key points we have sought to convey.

The Importance of Recognising Rights in Family Law

The primary reason for doing so is contained in the HRA and the clear duty imposed upon the courts in (a) section 3(1) to ensure that in so far as it is possible, legislation is read in a way which is compatible with the rights protected by the ECHR; and (b) in section 2 to take into account the judgments of the ECtHR.[1] It is clear that these duties are not being fully complied with as a matter of course. We have highlighted many instances in this book where human rights analysis has either simply not been undertaken in the English Family courts, despite the clear injunction to do so in the HRA; it has been undertaken at a superficial level.[2] The most obvious example of this has been the ready assumption that the welfare principle in section 1 of the CA is compatible with the ECHR. While we agree that the outcomes in the large majority of cases would be the same as those reached by using the welfare approach, we have argued throughout this book that there could be a difference in the borderline cases.

Second, we have argued that even if this analysis is incorrect, there are still major benefits in using an HRA analysis in terms of the reasoning that is employed. It ensures that each party involved will know that their particular interests are being considered. By requiring the judge to ensure that the rights of each party are taken into account and that any breach in a party's rights is justified, the ECHR approach contains several benefits. First, each party can leave the decision feeling that the issue has been looked at from their perspective. The existence of their rights has been acknowledged and a justification for any breach provided. While it would be naive to believe this will mean that parties will not be aggrieved at decisions which go against them, there will, at the very minimum, be an acknowledgement of the impact of the decision upon them. Second, it will aid clarity in decision making. John Eekelaar has complained that the welfare test suffers from a

---

[1] See ch 1.
[2] Although see *Re P* [2008] UKHL 38, which demonstrates the potential of the HRA.

'transparency objection' in that basing an approach solely on the welfare of the child leads to judges smuggling in the interests of adults under the guise of being the interests of children.[3] We find this a convincing criticism of the welfare principle, but, like Eekelaar, we do not argue that judges are wrong in considering the interests of adults. The problem is that the welfare principle prevents them doing so overtly. A rights analysis enables them to openly consider the interests of adults, while at the same time still giving special protection to the interests of children.

Third, a major benefit with a rights-based approach is its focus on the positive obligations that the ECHR places on the state.[4] Traditionally rights have been seen as useful to restrict government action, but as we have seen the ECHR jurisprudence has developed positive obligations on the state. In particular, the state is required to ensure protection from torture or inhuman or degrading treatment, and act positively as an aspect of the right to respect for family life. In family law, these themes have particular significance in the areas of child protection and domestic violence.

Fourth, the notion of proportionality which plays a major part in the reasoning of the ECtHR has been adopted as a sophisticated tool of legal analysis and serves as a check upon the level of intervention into family life that is being proposed by the court. It has been readily adapted into the jurisprudence of the English courts on the law on child protection.[5] Importantly it restricts state intervention not only to circumstances in which it is necessary, but also restricts it to the extent it is necessary.

Summary of the Chapters

In Chapter 1 we provided an introduction to the ECHR. We briefly introduced the Articles of the Convention that are of most relevance to family lawyers. The Chapter focused on three themes within the jurisprudence of the ECtHR which are of particular relevance to the subject of this book. First, it highlighted that the ECHR, while primarily limiting state action in a way which infringes individuals' rights, also imposes positive obligations on the state to act in a way which ensures protection of rights. In the family law context this is particularly relevant in that it requires the state to act positively to protect the rights of children and victims of domestic violence. It also requires the state to intervene to ensure proper respect is shown for family life under Article 8.

Second, the Chapter considered the 'margin of appreciation' through which the ECtHR recognises that individual states have a discretion when balancing competing rights of individuals or balancing the rights of individuals and the interests of the state. It demonstrated that the use of the margin of appreciation has not always been consistent; however, we have identified some general principles which are followed by the ECtHR in utilising it. Family law is an area of law where the margin of appreciation is particularly significant. The issues raised in family law are likely to involve issues of public policy and morality and therefore are apt to be left to the discretion of individual states. However, family law issues

---

[3] J Eekelaar, 'Beyond the Welfare Principle' [2002] *Child and Family Law Quarterly* 237.
[4] See the discussion on child protection in ch 8 and domestic violence in ch 9.
[5] Chapter 8.

are also likely to be ones of particularly intimate nature and therefore involve especially important rights.

Third, the Chapter analyses the notion of proportionality and illustrates that the ECtHR has generally utilised a 'fair balance' test when determining whether an intervention in rights is proportionate. In part this is due to the relationship between the margin of appreciation doctrine and the notion of proportionality. It is also due in part to the type of issues that Article 8 will raise, and often involving clashes of rights between individuals.

In Chapter 2, we examined the HRA. The Chapter summarises the primary provisions of the Act. It notes that the impact of the HRA on family law has been, to date, less than might be expected. There have been only two declarations of incompatibility in family law cases and there has been a tendency for the court to argue that the there is no incompatibility between the law in the CA and the ECHR. That is an argument we reject later in the book. The Chapter examines some of the themes that emerge in the interpretation of the HRA. One is the extent to which the HRA can operate horizontally (that is, it creates claims between individuals). While it is clear that the Act can have horizontal effect, this will only be of use where there is a presently existing common law claim that can be adapted to give effect to the Convention claim or where proceedings are brought against a public authority. As the Chapter discusses, the term public authority for the purposes of the HRA has been interpreted in a narrow way and, particularly, in the area of contracted-out services. That limits the usefulness of the HRA claim. The Chapter also undertakes an assessment of the use and appropriateness of 'deference' shown by domestic courts to the state's or public authority's assessment of the competing rights and interests involved in an HRA claim. In family law, as at Strasbourg, it is clear that what is key to the amount of deference shown is the subject matter and the context. However, the courts have also shown a willingness to go further than Strasbourg on some matters where it has accorded a wide margin of appreciation and this has been because they have deemed them to be of fundamental or constitutional importance.

Chapter 3 considers the theoretical issues raised by using human rights in the context of family law. It discusses the nature of rights and their relationship with duties. There is also a consideration of some of the theoretical approaches to rights. The Chapter then focuses on the controversy surrounding rights and their use in a family law setting. In particular the Chapter considers complaints that rights can promote individualistic values and can work against the interests of women. We recognise that there are some strong concerns with the use of rights reasoning, particularly in the context of family law. However, we believe that these concerns are not an inevitable aspect of rights reasoning and that it is possible to avoid the pitfalls. For example, we accept that rights-based reasoning can be and has been used to promote an individualistic way of imagining human beings and their legal position.[6] However, there is scope within rights reasoning to develop approaches which recognise and give value to relationships and our mutually independent nature. The writings on relational autonomy, for example, provide a basis for doing that.[7] Indeed the recognition of a right to respect for family life involves an acknowledgement of the

---

[6] See S Choudhry, J Herring and J Wallbank, 'Welfare, Rights, Care and Gender in Family Law' in J Wallbank, S Choudhry and J Herring (eds), *Rights, Gender and Family Law* (London, Routledge, 2009).

[7] J Herring, 'Relational Autonomy and Family Law' in J Wallbank, S Choudhry and J Herring (eds) *Rights, Gender and Family Law* (n 6).

significance of relationships. We see great value in approaches based on, for example, an ethic of care, but do not see rights as necessarily being inconsistent with these. It is true that rights can operate in an isolating way which valorises individualistic values, but they need not. We have sought in this book to promote a system of rights which recognises the importance of rights and as providing a bedrock against which relationships of care can be supported and recognised. Indeed, we suggest that given the status that rights talk has in our legal and political system those sympathetic to approaches based on, for example, an ethic of care may more effectively promote such an approach by finding ways in which rights-based approaches can do this, than seeking to have talk of rights removed from the legal agenda. That is something which is not going to happen any time soon.

Chapter 4 considered the issue of marriage. The ECHR has had a marked impact on this area in relation to transgender persons. The GRA was passed as a direct result of decisions of the ECtHR and the House of Lords, which had found English law incompatible with the ECHR. As a result of that legislation transgender people can have legal recognition of their 'acquired gender' through a gender recognition certificate. The ECHR has also been a powerful vehicle to advance the rights of same-sex couples. As the Chapter highlights, without the CPA it is likely that the English law would fail to comply with the requirements of the ECHR. To date it seems that the courts have not been willing to accept human rights arguments that same-sex couples should be allowed to marry. In the Chapter we discuss the arguments that can be made to advance that claim. The Chapter also considers the rights to marry of prisoners and immigrants and highlights the need for strong justification before any interference in the right to marry can take place.

Chapter 5 considers the relevance of the HRA in issues of parenthood and parental rights. It demonstrates that, as with domestic law, the ECtHR has battled with the competing understanding of parenthood based on genetic or social factors. To some extent this debate has been evaded by the ECtHR as the Convention focuses on the right to respect for family life, rather than requiring a definition of who is a parent. However, we argue that Article 8 provides a way of recognising that respect for family life opens a route to recognition of the relationship between children and a range of adults with whom they are in a close relationship. While this does not resolve the question of whether greater weight should be attached to social or biological parenthood, it does provide a better method of examining the claims of different adult–child relationships. The Chapter also considers the question of parental responsibilities, through an examination of the law on corporal punishment. While Article 8 recognises the rights of parents to raise their children, this is subject to protection of the rights of the child. The balancing exercise provided by Article 8 provides a powerful means of recognising both the legal protection for the decision making of a parent, but also the state's obligation to protect children from harm.

Chapter 6 considers children's rights. While the ECtHR has been keen to emphasise the rights a child has to protection, especially in the areas of child abuse and corporal punishment, the Court has rarely considered the extent to which a child might have autonomy rights. However, the language of Article 8, and particularly the right to respect for private life, would seem to create room for a development of a child's rights jurisprudence within the ECHR. The Chapter also considers how the correct balance should be struck between the interests of children and parents. While the CA has generally been interpreted to mean that the interests of children are paramount and therefore will always trump the interests of adults, the ECtHR appears to take a less robust approach. While recognising that children's interests deserve special protection the ECtHR appears to have accepted that this means that there may be occasions on which the interests of adults will trump the interests of children. Despite this, the UK courts have claimed that there is no conflict between an approach based on the CA and the ECHR. This Chapter disputes that claim. The Chapter also claims that the UK's law on representation of children in family cases and on access to courts is open to challenge as a breach of Article 6 or 8 rights.

Chapter 7 discuses the use of human rights analysis in cases involving disputes over children. Contact disputes, in particular, have generated considerable debate over the correct role that rights should play. It was argued in this chapter that a human rights analysis improves the reasoning used by the courts. In particular it means that the interests of each party can be considered and be weighed up. By contrast, an approach based on the welfare principle has the danger that the claims of parents must be forced artificially into claims about the welfare of the child. In particular it enables the human rights of women to be considered in their own rights, rather than mothers being regarded as simply conduits of child welfare.

One of the areas of family law which has been particularly affected by the HRA is that of child protection, which is discussed in Chapter 8. There are two areas in particular where the ECtHR has contributed significantly to the law in this area. First, there is the clear obligation on the state and public authorities to protect children from abuse. We argue that where the abuse is such that it interferes with the child's Article 3 rights, there is an absolute duty on the state to intervene to protect the child. However, that is only an obligation to take reasonable steps and only arises when the state knows or ought to know of the abuse. Even where the level of harm does not reach Article 3, it will engage Article 8, then this too will create a duty to intervene, but non-intervention may be justified under the terms of Article 8(2). This opens up the possibility of public authorities being the subject of claims under the HRA where they have failed to protect victims of child abuse. Second, the ECtHR has developed a set of procedural rights that deserve protection in child protection matters. However, these requirements are slightly watered down by the fact that a single breach will not necessarily constitute an interference in the human rights of the parents, if the procedure seen as a whole provides adequate protection of their rights. The Chapter also emphasises the difficulties facing local authorities given funding shortages for child protection work. Many of the failures to respect rights in this area can be traced back to resource issues. This highlights the need for adequate funding if human rights are to be respected in this sensitive area.

Chapter 9 considers the issue of domestic violence. The Chapter demonstrates the way that the ECHR can be used to protect victims of domestic violence and impose obligations on the state to ensure that reasonable steps are taken to protect victims. Where the risk to a victim of domestic violence is death or torture or inhuman or degrading treatment then the obligations (under Articles 2 or 3) is absolute. Even where the harm risked is less and only involves an interference with Article 8 rights, there is still an obligation to protect on the state, but it is not an absolute one. Whichever right is invoked, the state is only required to take reasonable steps to protect a victim from violence. That is likely to be the focus in any complaint that a public authority's failure to protect led to an interference in a person's rights. Where the risk is clear and serious and a way of protecting the victim could easily be taken, it is hard to imagine a court will not find an interference in rights. Where children are suffering the consequences of domestic violence the obligations on the state may be particularly heavy. This obligation on the state is particularly relevant when the CPS or the police are making arrest or prosecution decisions. A failure to adequately protect victims of domestic violence could open the police up to an HRA claim. The rights are also significant in relation to civil claims. Where a party is seeking an occupation order in order to achieve protection from violence we argue that where Article 2 or 3 rights are engaged, the court may be required to make the order. In cases where Article 8 is involved there needs to be a balance between the protection rights of the victim and the property rights of the respondent. It will be rare where such a balance will not find in the applicant's favour.

Chapter 10 considers the relevance of the ECHR to family property disputes. This has been an area where human rights have been given little academic or judicial attention. The Chapter illustrates a number of ways in which the ECHR could, in fact, be used to challenge the existing law—in particular through claims that the law constitutes gender discrimination in failing to attach equal weight to money-earning and child-caring or home-making contributions. In the application of the trusts law in this area the law appears particularly open to complaints that it operates in a discriminatory way. There are also issues which arise in the differences in treatment of married couples and civil partners, and other cohabitants. To date the ECtHR has found differences in the treatment between these groups justifiable on the basis that the state is entitled to treat formalised relationships differently from informal ones. However, that may be subject to further human-rights challenges in years to come.

Issues Outstanding

We have sought in this book to describe how an approach based on the ECHR would deal with some of the cases that trouble family courts. As far as possible we have relied upon ECtHR case law and the decisions of the English courts in dealing with them. However, there are still a number of issues where the ECHR jurisprudence is not yet fully developed.

First, as discussed in chapter 6, the case law on children's autonomy rights is at a very early stage of development. There is little indication yet from the ECtHR on how much weight should be attached to the autonomy rights of children and in particular how they are to be balanced against their rights to protection and the rights of other people.

Second, we have acknowledged the difficulties that arise in assessing the strength of various rights and in particular how much harm is necessary to justify an interference in that right. We have suggested that too often the ECtHR has failed to explain why it is that a particular right is important and this creates difficulties in determining when its breach can be justified. For example in Chapter 6 we highlighted how, although it is accepted that a right of contact is generally regarded as included within the right to respect for family life, it has not really been explained what it *is* about contact that generates this right. In particular what is still unclear is whether there is an intrinsic value in contact which is not dependent on an assessment that contact is beneficial to a child. These questions are highly controversial but will require a response as the ECHR jurisprudence is developed.

Third, we acknowledge that our support for the 'parallel analysis' as being the correct approach to deal with cases of clashing rights is yet to be fully implemented across the board and that it will require much more 'work' from the courts in terms of justification. In doing so, we have relied upon academic discussion which has built on some judicial dicta. It remains to be seen whether the courts will follow the route predicted and outlined by academic commentators.

Fourth, as discussed in Chapter 2 the notion of 'margin of appreciation' has played a major role in the reasoning of the ECtHR. Through it the ECtHR is able to recognise that on controversial issues surrounding ECHR rights individual states may take different approaches. However, as explained in that Chapter, when a national court comes to apply the ECHR the question arises as to how the courts are to respond to issues which the ECtHR has decided fall within a state's 'margin of appreciation'. Is that to be left to the legislature of particular countries or can the English courts decide for themselves what approach English law will take in interpreting such rights? The law on this issue is still developing, but it is clear that there are some issues where the English courts will be willing to set out how they understand the interpretation of a right.

Fifth, the courts are still struggling with the correct remedies to use when it is found that rights have been interfered with. This is particularly relevant in the case law on procedural rights in child protection cases. Where it is found that there has been a breach in the procedures leading to the removal of a child who has settled into alternative care it is difficult to determine what remedy to order, especially where the judge believes that even if the correct procedures were followed the child would still have been removed. In such a case, ordering the return of the child is unlikely to be in the child's interests; while ordering financial compensation from cash-strapped local-authority child services departments has obvious disadvantages.

Sixth, the courts are still working through the use of human rights in a culturally diverse society—in particular, the issue of whether membership of a particular ethnic or religious community might mean that one's human rights reflect the standards expected within that community. In addition, there is the question of whether people's rights are the same regardless of membership of that community. If one takes the latter view, one may still hold that cultural differences are relevant in the issue of justification.[8] This is an issue which will attract considerable attention in the years to come.

Looking Backwards and Forwards

Looking back at the highlights of the impact of the HRA there are some clear and undeniable changes that have been brought about as a result of that legislation: the GRA; improved legal recognition of same-sex partners, leading to the CPA; and increased procedural rights for parents in child protection cases are all direct responses to the legislation. But the impact may be greater than that. It has introduced a new way of examining family law cases. While the willingness of the judiciary to articulate their reasoning in terms of human rights has been generally limited, there are notable exceptions to this. Munby J and Baroness Hale, for example, have been particularly notable in their willingness to utilise HRA reasoning. Further, it has been adopted extensively by academics and in family law textbooks. These may permeate the attitude of the law in more subtle ways than the direct changes to the law mentioned above. Indeed it is notable that many campaign groups use the language of rights to make their case, be that fathers, grandparents, or those seeking

---

[8] See ch 9 for a discussion of these issues in relation to the question of polygamous marriage. See also M Freeman, *Human Rights* (Cambridge, Polity Press, 2002) ch 2.

more open courts. In this book we have outlined a wide range of areas where we believe the opportunities offered by the HRA could be used to develop a more sophisticated way of analysing complex family law cases.

What must be acknowledged, however, is the uncertainty about the future of the HRA. The Conservative party has indicated a desire to replace the HRA with a Bill of Rights.[9] The precise policy has not been articulated in detail and it is still unclear whether the new Bill of Rights would include the ECHR, but have added responsibilities or rights or explanatory provisions; or whether the new Bill of Rights would bear no relation to the ECHR. Nor is it clear the extent to which opting out of the ECHR is a feasible or politically realistic option. The Labour government, meanwhile, has indicated that it supports the ECHR, although it is considering whether some kind of Bill of Rights is required which it will add on to the ECHR. The government document, *Rights and Responsibilities: Developing our Constitutional Framework*[10] sees a new Bill of Rights as necessary not to alter the ECHR, but to add to it. The government states:

> Responsibilities have not been given the same prominence as rights in our constitutional architecture. This is despite the fact that many duties and responsibilities already exist in statute, common law and our ethical framework, and despite the fact that the text and case law of the European Convention on Human Rights, given recognition in our law through the Human Rights Act 1998, require a balance to be struck between the two.[11]

The document lacks many concrete proposals. However, one theme is particularly apparent from the passage just quoted, and that is the emphasis upon responsibilities, although the document seems more interested in the responsibilities of citizens than the responsibilities of government. Consider, for example, this comment on the position of children's rights and responsibilities:

> Children and young people can help themselves to achieve wellbeing, though their right to do so does not depend on them fulfilling these responsibilities. A Bill of Rights and Responsibilities might set out expectations, for example, that children and young people should respect the rights of others, use opportunities to make a positive contribution to society, and take full advantage of the opportunities offered to them including the chance to express their own views.[12]

What has not been clarified is to what extent the expectations and rights referred to in this paragraph will be legally enforceable or what their content will be. If, as the JCHR recommends,[13] a Bill of Rights were to include detailed rights for children and socioeconomic rights such as a right to education, health, housing and an adequate standard of living, this would be an obvious improvement upon not only the HRA but also the ECHR.

It is thus difficult to assess either the government's or the Conservative Party's plans to repeal the HRA and replace it with a 'British Bill of Rights' without knowing its content. Nonetheless, as far as this book is concerned, we have sought to demonstrate how the jurisprudence of the ECtHR has provided English family law with useful and sophisticated tools of analysis that can be employed in family law cases. If the HRA were to be repealed, these may or may not be lost. What is clear is that a new Bill of Rights would provide an exciting

---

[9] R Taylor, 'Cameron calls for repeal of Human Rights Act', *The Guardian* 12 May 2006.
[10] Ministry of Justice, *Rights and Responsibilities: Developing our Constitutional Framework* (TSO, 2009).
[11] Page 8.
[12] Page 21.
[13] JCHR report 'A Bill of Rights for the UK?' Twenty-ninth Report of Session 2007–08, p 5.

opportunity to add to the existing human rights protection provided for by the HRA. It is even more important, therefore, that the UK judiciary is adequately prepared for the task.

Conclusion

We believe that the HRA has opened up exciting new ways of looking at family law. What might previously have been regarded as solely empirical questions of what is in a child's interests can be revealed to involve a complex weighing up of the rights and interests of the parties involved. The use of rights emphasises the obligations that the state owes to children and vulnerable adults. Further, rights can be used to emphasise the responsibilities and obligations that people have towards each other. We do not suggest for a moment that a rights-based approach provides all the answers to the difficult issues of family law. What it does do is to clarify thinking about what those issues are and provide some intellectual tools to begin to resolve them.

INDEX